THE BURNS MANTLE BEST PLAYS
OF 1947-48

SEVERAL YEARS ago, when Burns Mantle completed his long and brilliant career as drama critic of the New York *Daily News*, he was succeeded by John Chapman, who had been his associate on the paper and in several of the earlier volumes of the Burns Mantle *Best Plays*. It was altogether appropriate, therefore, that Mr. Chapman should be selected to carry on the tradition of the famous Burns Mantle *Best Plays* and this he has ably done in the current volume.

This is the thirty-first volume in the *Best Plays* series which, with its annuals and its two decade volumes, reaches back to the turn of the century and is without equal in its recording of American life in one of its most colorful and sensitive aspects. Certainly no more dependable and profitable sequence of volumes has been found in American bookstores and libraries during our lifetime.

The ten best plays are included, as usual, by excerpt and summary, and the yearbook material contains invaluable data for theatergoers and lovers of the drama.

The ten *Best Plays* are: *A Streetcar Named Desire, The Heiress, Command Decision, Mister Roberts, The Winslow Boy, Allegro, Me and Molly, Eastward in Eden, Skipper Next to God, An Inspector Calls.*

THE BURNS MANTLE
BEST PLAYS OF 1947-48

AND THE
YEAR BOOK OF THE DRAMA
IN AMERICA

EDITED BY
JOHN CHAPMAN

With Illustrations

DODD, MEAD AND COMPANY
NEW YORK   -   -   -   1948

"A Streetcar Named Desire," copyright, 1947, by Tennessee Williams
Revised version copyright, 1948, by Tennessee Williams
Copyright and published, 1948, by New Directions, New York

"Mister Roberts," copyright, 1947, by Thomas Heggen and Joshua Logan
Copyright in Canada, 1948, by the authors
Copyright and published, 1948, by Random House, New York

"Command Decision," copyright, 1946, 1947 and 1948 by William Wister Haines
Copyright and published, 1948, by Random House, New York

"The Winslow Boy," copyright, 1946, by Terence Rattigan

"The Heiress," copyright, 1948, by Ruth Goodman Goetz and Augustus Goetz.
Dramatic composition copyright, 1945, under the title, "The Doctor's Daughter,"
and, 1946, under the title, "Washington Square," by Ruth Goodman and Augustus
Goetz. Published by Dramatists' Play Service, New York.

"Allegro," copyright, 1947, by Richard Rodgers and Oscar Hammerstein II
Copyright and published, 1947, by Alfred A. Knopf, New York
Music and lyrics copyright and published, 1947, by Williamson Music Inc., New York

"Eastward in Eden," copyright, 1947, by Dorothy Gardner
Copyright and published, 1948, by Longmans Green & Co., New York
Revised version copyright, 1948, by Dorothy Gardner

"Skipper Next to God," copyright, 1945, by Jan de Hartog

"An Inspector Calls," copyright, 1945, by J. B. Priestley

"Me and Molly," copyright, 1947 and 1948, by Gertrude Berg

COPYRIGHT, 1948,
By DODD, MEAD AND COMPANY, INC.

INTRODUCTION

DURING the season of 1919-20, Burns Mantle, drama critic of the New York *Evening Mail* and New York theatre correspondent of the Chicago *Tribune,* chose ten good plays, compiled the statistical record of the season and thus produced a volume entitled "The Best Plays of 1919-20, and the Year Book of the Drama in America." Its reception was sufficient to encourage him to do it again the following year. And all of the years to come until February 9, 1948, when he died in the Forest Hills, N. Y., home from whose compact and orderly study had come the volumes which have recorded the modern history of American drama.

And an exciting history it has been—the record of a period in which American dramatists and American players, managers and methods have influenced the stages of the rest of the world. To carry his history back to the beginning of the Twentieth Century, Mantle and Garrison P. Sherwood compiled two more volumes covering the drama events between 1899 and the year in which Mantle began his own task.

In the foreword of his first volume, dated June 15, 1920, at Forest Hills, Mantle wrote: "For the selection of these particular plays no more is claimed than that they represent the best judgment of the editor, variously confirmed by the public's endorsement. The intention frankly has been to compromise between the popular success, as representing the choice of the people who support the theatre, and the success with sufficient claim to literary distinction of text or theme to justify its publication."

The "best judgment of the editor" was that the best plays of 1919-20 were John Drinkwater's "Abraham Lincoln," Eugene O'Neill's "Beyond the Horizon," James Forbes' "The Famous Mrs. Fair," Zoe Akins' "Déclassée," St. John Ervine's "Jane Clegg," Sem Benelli's "The Jest" (as adapted by Edward Sheldon), Salisbury Field's "Wedding Bells," Rachel Barton Butler's "Mamma's Affair," Guy Bolton's and George Middleton's 'Adam and Eva" and Booth Tarkington's "Clarence."

All of these plays still live in the memories of many playgoers, but some of them were of no ultimate importance. This was always so in the seasons to follow, and is so this year, and will be so next year. But in each annual record will be found the names of dramatists who have had enduring influence. O'Neill . . . Sheldon . . . Tarkington . . . Drinkwater . . .

And the players! In that season of 1919-20 there were not alone the current favorites, the stars of the time, but also the young people who were to achieve fame. There were, in the casts of the Ten Best, John Barrymore, Lionel Barrymore, Mary Boland, Glenn Hunter, Helen Hayes, Alfred Lunt, Ethel Barrymore, Clare Eames, Wallace Eddinger, Margaret Lawrence, Frank McGlynn, Charles Gilpin, Raymond Hackett, Effie Shannon, Robert Edeson, Richard Bennett, Louise Closser Hale, Margaret Wycherly, Helen Westley, Dudley Digges, Henry Travers and many others who did so much to make the American stage vigorous, accomplished and admirable.

In this volume there are, no doubt, plays of no ultimate importance, dramatists of no lasting influence and players who may soon be forgotten; but here also are names to be remembered. Which names? Which will be familiar a generation beyond this?

Burns Mantle would have been eager to know; eager to witness and then to record their progress.

So am I eager, and so is anybody who has ever experienced the excitement and the pleasure so generously offered by the living theatre.

For nearly twenty years I was Mantle's assistant, associate, collaborator and friend. When he retired as critic for the New York *Daily News,* I became the paper's official playgoer. And now it devolves upon me to repeat: "For the selection of these particular plays no more is claimed than that they represent the best judgment of the editor . . ." And to acknowledge, as Burns Mantle so often did, the selfless and priceless help of Clara Sears Taylor in compiling the statistical record. This volume is titled "The Burns Mantle Best Plays," in memory of and gratitude toward the man who began them all.

JOHN CHAPMAN

Westport, Conn., June, 1948

CONTENTS

ILLUSTRATIONS

THE BURNS MANTLE BEST PLAYS
OF 1947-48

THE BURNS MANTLE BEST PLAYS
OF 1947-48

THE SEASON IN NEW YORK

IT is doubtful if there ever has been or ever will be a completely distinguished theatrical season; nevertheless, the New York year just closed has had its moments of distinction. Among some thirty revivals there were such happy affairs as Maurice Evans' discovery that Bernard Shaw's 1905-model comedy, "Man and Superman," remains an extremely sagacious comedy; Katharine Cornell's sumptuous mounting of "Antony and Cleopatra," with a Shakespearean actor of genuine stature, Godfrey Tearle, as Antony; the late-season discovery that the Ferenc Molnar-P. G. Wodehouse "The Play's the Thing" still is a lightly saucy bit, and a long-due visit of the D'Oyly Carte Opera Company, which convinced playgoers that neither time nor a world war had dulled the glister of a superlative comic-opera troupe.

As for new dramas, one of them bowled over both the Critics' Circle and the Pulitzer Prize Committee; yet three or four others had quality sufficient to merit an award without one's having to apologize for overgenerosity. There were individual acting performances which won great public approval, like Paul Kelly's in "Command Decision," Judith Anderson's in "Medea," Beatrice Lillie's in "Inside U.S.A." and Wendy Hiller's in "The Heiress." There also were comforting instances in which entire companies, carefully chosen and inspired by able directors, maintained an excitingly high level of performance—such as, for example, the casts of "A Streetcar Named Desire," "The Winslow Boy" and "Mister Roberts."

To this editor, the happiest detail of the season was the strength shown by the off-Broadway theatre. As yet no neighborhood playhouse has spawned a new Theatre Guild or found a new O'Neill; but last season the will to do so was apparent, and the ability to do so was not inconsiderable.

The Experimental Theatre, with the official blessing and backing of all branches of the commercial theatre, improved the quality of its offerings in this, its second, season. In some quarters it was chided for leaning upon such names as Charles Laughton and John Garfield, who certainly are not young hopefuls deserving of a break; but to my mind an experimental theatre has as much right as a commercial theatre to engage any player who strikes its fancy and whom it can persuade to come along for the ride. One of the Experimental Theatre's one-week offerings, "Skipper Next to God," became one of the ten best plays of the season and had a commercial success, thereby regaining for the ET some of the money it had, from highest purpose, lost. Another ET offering which moved uptown for a Broadway run was the ingenious and enjoyable series of "Ballet Ballads," in which song, story and dance were combined in novel and pleasant fashion.

Another group of hopefuls, New Stages, Inc., operating in small quarters below Washington Square without benefit of subsidy or official blessing, turned up Jean-Paul Sartre's melodramatic account of Southern prejudice, "The Respectful Prostitute." I happened to be one who failed to sense a necessary quality of genuineness in this *guignol,* but the public, which likes its little shocks, became very fond of the play and made it into an uptown success. Subsequently, the hopefuls of New Stages, Inc., began quarreling among themselves.

Before getting too far away from the Experimental Theatre and into the chronology of the season, one should mention as a memorable event the American National Theatre Album at the Ziegfeld Theatre. This was a $100-a-ticket Sunday Night benefit for the American National Theatre and Academy, which is the official patron of the ET. No such glittering, successful, enthusiastic and enjoyable benefit had been seen in this city in years and years. The stage, from top to bottom, back to front and pit to grid, paid itself a glowing, pulse-quickening and prideful tribute.

The season beginning June 1, 1947, has been subjected to the usual number of analyses, which have some variations in detail. According to the New York *Times,* there were forty-three new plays, nine musicals, three revues, thirty revivals and four "miscellaneous." Not counting such miscellania as Edith Piaf, a sad French singer, and Maurice Chevalier, a gay one, this makes eighty-five productions, or two fewer than were listed in the previous year's Mantle book. According to the New York *Herald Tribune,* the count was eighty productions, of which ten were hits. The United Press counted up to a total of eighty-seven, including fifteen musicals, six of which made money, and fifty-two comedies and dramas, of which sixteen were profitable. The variation in statistics depended on how the individual compiler regarded off-Broadway productions which subsequently were given Broadway showings.

The season began June 2 on a rather harsh note, when a musical entitled "Louisiana Lady" opened, only to close two nights later. The following night Mary Boland arrived from Hollywood and managed to stay until June 7 in a comedy undeserving of her talents and unattractive to her following, titled "Open House." A dramatization of Vera Caspary's "Laura" stuck it out from late June to early August, but obviously was no competitor of the excellent film version of the book.

The New York City Theatre Company hopefully—too hopefully —began a summer stand with a version of "Rip Van Winkle," which many observers found not quaint enough to be interesting.

With September came the real launching of the season with two unhappy and short-lived comedies titled "The Magic Touch" and "I Gotta Get Out"; the latter got out in 4 performances. The first of the invasions of Broadway by off-Broadway productions was Theodore Ward's dignified and fitfully impressing drama of Negroes just after the Civil War, "Our Lan'."

Sooner or later a hit would come, and it did on the night of September 29 when Wendy Hiller and Basil Rathbone were revealed in the Ruth and Augustus Goetz dramatization of Henry James' "Washington Square," which the authors had titled "The Heiress." A period piece of quiet intensity, it was admirably staged by Jed Harris.

Within a week came another stalwart of the season, William Wister Haines' "Command Decision," in which Paul Kelly made an impressive return to the stage. Mr. Kelly won *Variety's* "Best Actor" poll of the drama critics. But, three nights before the arrival of this solid drama of the Air Forces, a great deal of pleasant anticipation had been dashed when a new play by Donald Ogden Stewart, "How I Wonder," was presented. Mr. Stewart, long-time scenario writer and one-time author of amusing plays and essays, had involved Raymond Massey and a young ex-model named Meg Mundy in a confused consideration of life, political thought, astronomy and the atom bomb. Hardly anybody shared, Mr. Stewart's wonderment, and Miss Mundy later redeemed herself by giving a highly effective performance as "The Respectful Prostitute."

A formula musical biography of P. I. Tschaikowsky, "Music in My Heart," succeeded in making even the composer's melodies sound commonplace. Not even the attractive ebullience of Brit-

ain's Cicely Courtneidge could make a go of a musical play
about the English black market, "Under the Counter." I found
this item quite charming, but others thought it slight. This sus-
ceptibility of mine to charming but slight British offerings was to
be evidenced more than once during the season.

An old dramatic poem by Robinson Jeffers, "Dear Judas," was
given a solemn and thorough production by that individualist
among theatrical managers, Michael Myerberg, but its consideration of the story of Jesus and Judas failed to move enough of its
few auditors. Jeffers later got on the hit list when Judith Anderson arrived in a new treatment of "Medea" which he had written
for her a year or so before.

Anticipation was followed by disillusion once again when, on
October 7, Joyce Redman and Francis L. Sullivan appeared in a
quaint and laughable thriller, "Duet for Two Hands." One's
hopes had been high, for Miss Redman had won her New York
audience the year before with her performance of Doll Tearsheat
in the Old Vic Company's rollicking performance of "Henry IV,
Part 2"; and Mr. Sullivan had deliciously chilled the American
population in a fine British movie, "Great Expectations."

The enduring wit and wisdom of Bernard Shaw and the theatrical sagacity of Maurice Evans added luster to the playbill the
evening after the Sullivan-Redman fiasco, when a revival of "Man
and Superman" was offered. Most people had forgotten how
funny this play was, and Mr. Evans had given it a handsome
production in which the even more handsome Frances Rowe revealed herself as a comedienne of high style.

Twenty-four hours after "Superman" came "High Button
Shoes," and twenty-four hours after that there arrived the immensely ballyhooed "Allegro." The first of these musicals was an
unpretentious, loose-leaf version of Stephen Longstreet's auto-
biographical novel, "Some Liked Them Handsome," about dear
old Rutgers in 1913. Its attractions included an engaging performance by Nanette Fabray, a pretty miss who had been in
any number of musicals and now found herself a star; an in-
sanely delightful ballet staged by Jerome Robbins in the manner
of a Mack Sennett Keystone Komedy chase, and a song, "Papa,
Won't You Dance with Me."

The Rodgers-Hammerstein "Allegro" was something else again
—no less than the biography of one Joseph Taylor, Jr., from the
day of his birth to his middle thirties, when he finally got some
sense in his head . . . all carefully set to illustrative music by
Mr. Rodgers. This Theatre Guild production was the leading

money-grosser throughout the season.

Euripides' "Medea" was given a vigorous and colorful treatment by the poetic Mr. Jeffers, and the almost superhuman Miss
Anderson gave it an even more vigorous and colorful performance.
There were some, including this observer, who felt that, on the
first night at least, the actress had started off on so high an emotional pitch that she could not keep building tension and horror
clear to the end of the drama. She had, I felt, overtrained a bit.
But her performance was sufficiently remarkable to win her a
"best performance" citation and to bring great crowds to see one
of the two most relentlessly tragic works in all drama—the other
being "Oedipus." Indeed, Miss Anderson exhausted herself and
had to suspend performances for a spell. A falling-out between
star and management shortened the run of the play.

Some of the colleagues whom I most respect would have included "Medea" among the best plays of this volume. I did, indeed, give it thorough consideration before regretfully excluding
it. For one thing, it was another of countless treatments of one
of the most ancient of dramas. For another, Mr. Jeffers' prose-
poetry does not easily lend itself to condensation and selection.
For a third, a proper treatment of the work in such a book as
this must, I felt, have included a suitably profound and decently
exhaustive analysis of Mr. Jeffers' approach to the classic, and a
recounting of how this version may have differed from other
texts of the past. It would have been presumptuous of me to
pose as a Greek scholar with a specialized knowledge of "Medea"
—and, supposing I had carried it off, it would have been interesting mainly to other Greek scholars. Furthermore, who knows
that Miss Anderson would not have been just as electrically effective in, say, the Gilbert Murray version?

The first of J. B. Priestley's two plays of the season, "An Inspector Calls," was a pleasant contrast to the previous night's im-
mersion in the purest of tragedy. In a quiet and easy fashion
it toyed with death, social responsibility and the indefinability
of time. Very deftly the author maneuvered an eerie ending for
an enjoyably absorbing exercise in suspense, and among those who
gave good performances were Thomas Mitchell and George Melville Cooper.

The last three October dramas all were British. After "An
Inspector Calls" came John van Druten's "The Druid Circle."
(Mr. van Druten has been an American citizen for some time,
but he can, when he wants, still be British in approach, style and
subject-matter.) In the vein of his earlier and better "Young

Woodley," the author was contemplating the miseries of love and education in an impoverished university. One fine moment of comedy provided by Ethel Griffies was insufficient relief, and "The Druid Circle" had a struggle of it for about five weeks.

A better fate was in store for Terence Rattigan's "The Winslow Boy," and the drama, with an uncommonly smooth imported cast, duplicated its London success. On first viewing I found it less absorbing than did most, but on subsequent readings I discovered its sound workmanship. If I can find an alibi for an initial slight lack of cordiality, it must be that I had a slight touch of indigestion from too much British-style drama during that week, and that I should have seen something like "High Button Shoes" between the main courses.

The first of the November offerings, Jan de Hartog's "This Time Tomorrow," gave no promise of a "Skipper Next to God" to come. It was portentous and dull, and the Theatre Guild was rather badly stuck with it. Nobody, though, could have been worse stuck than was Harry Rosen, who chose to offer "Trial Honeymoon" next.

The visit of Edith Piaf, a professional waif from France who sang typically French recitatives about the little prostitute down at the corner over there, threw many auditors into transports of appreciation, but not this one. I got much, much more fun out of Les Compagnons de la Chanson, a group of nine young singing comedians who came over with her.

The "Daddy Long Legs" plot has always been a good one. Newest example was F. Hugh Herbert's "For Love or Money," an amiable and unoffending bit of fluff about an ageing matinee idol and an innocent but healthy young girl. The daughter of the movies' Gene Lockhart, June, won plaudits as the girl.

It had not been a mistake to revive "Man and Superman," but it definitely was an error on the part of the always-luminous Jane Cowl to appear in a revival of St. John Ervine's "The First Mrs. Fraser." Shaw had much the more authoritative grasp of the relationship and antagonism between males and females.

In every season there are dramas which deserved better than what they got—which was quick withdrawal. Notable among these was "Eastward in Eden," by Dorothy Gardner, which appeared at the Royale November 19 and disappeared 15 performances later, insufficiently aided by the high regard which some of the reviewers had for it. The *Times'* Brooks Atkinson, for instance, concurred in this editor's judgment in naming "Eden" among the best ten.

From the sparse facts about the life of Emily Dickinson, the Amherst poet, and from Dickinson verse and prose, Mrs. Gardner imagined a haunting and affecting romance. I think she had a little trouble with one scene of fantasy, but in the main she wrote a tender, loving costume play, and in the leading role, Beatrice Straight gave a luminous performance.

Late in November Katharine Cornell and her director husband, Guthrie McClintic, lavished their talents and resources upon a production of "Antony and Cleopatra," which won popular approval, and the first of the December offerings was "A Streetcar Named Desire." This completely successful drama won praise for everybody, starting with the author and including all members of an uncommonly well-selected cast and their director Elia Kazan. The producer was a newcomer, Irene Selznick, who up to the moment had been known chiefly as the daughter of Hollywood's Louis B. Mayer and as the former wife of Hollywood's David O. Selznick.

Emmet Lavery, author of a previous season's "The Magnificent Yankee" and a screenwriter of prominence, was represented by "The Gentleman from Athens," a comedy about Washington and politics which seemed to be more a statement about Mr. Lavery's belief in the democratic process than it was a play. Two long-known vaudeville and night club performers, Paul and Grace Hartman, had a surprise hit in an unpretentious but affable revue, "Angel in the Wings." This show, with hardly any scenery and no chorus, was a personal triumph for the stars and their master of ceremonies, Hank Ladd.

One of the curious things about theatre folk is their unquenchable ambition to invade other mediums and see what they can turn up or turn out. Every so often, a dramatist attempts a stage version of Dostoievsky's "Crime and Punishment" and a manager puts it on. Just before Christmas an adaptation by Rodney Ackland arrived, with John Gielgud in the role of Rodion. It was stunning, visually, and overwhelming to a very large cast. Two-pound Russian novels don't often make serviceable eight-ounce dramas, and once again Dostoievsky proved too much for everybody to handle.

Marc Blitzstein's angry theatrical prank, "The Cradle Will Rock," had a short end-of-the-year revival, and so did Marcel Pagnol's "Topaze," which seemed much less witty than when it was first produced. The real year-end gift to playgoers was the return of the D'Oyly Carte Opera Company in a repertoire of eight Gilbert and Sullivan bills. The Savoyards were headed, as usual, by Darrell Fancourt and Martyn Green, and as usual, they were a complete delight. The Company seemed at least as good as the one which, some years before the war, took New York by storm.

A new group, the New York City Center Theatre Company, began the first of two short seasons at the City Center on January 8 with a reasonably lively production of Ben Jonson's bawdy romp, "Volpone," and in the ensuing month also offered a revival of "Angel Street" and an evening of one-act plays by Chekhov. The Chekhov sketches may have made fine exercises in acting for Richard Whorf and José Ferrer, but they were anything but great as theatre.

"Harvest of Years," a drama about a California Scandinavian family, was complicated and uninteresting, and an English importation, "Power Without Glory," failed to move fast enough to move its audiences.

Florence Ryerson and her husband, Colin Clements, had written hundreds of plays for the amateur theatrical market—a very solid and steady market, by the way—with only an occasional glance toward Broadway. A California couple, they could always write and frequently did write movies if they needed extra money. Only one of their dramas, "Harriet," had been a Broadway success—largely because Helen Hayes played Harriet Beecher Stowe. In mid-January Miss Ryerson and Mr. Clements were represented by a quite successful comedy, "Strange Bedfellows," which concerned itself with the woman's suffrage movement in San Francisco before the Fire. During the tryout in Philadelphia, Mr. Clements became ill, and he died shortly after the New York premiere.

"Angel in the Wings" had proved that audiences still would go to something simple, if it were amusing enough, and further proof came with the arrival of another revue, "Make Mine Manhattan." The success of "Manhattan" was heartening to lovers of the revue form of entertainment.

The first mistake of 1948 was a comedy, "The Men We Marry." With nothing in its favor, it eked out 3 performances. Another mistake was Peter Viertel's and Irwin Shaw's drama, "The Survivors"—but this one was worth making. The authors had sought to state their philosophy—which was that war never settles anything and therefore there should be no war—in the terms of a tale about a frontier feud in the 1860s. Their minds and hearts were in the right places, but their judgment was faulty in letting most of their characters talk too much.

In Sweden and Germany, Strindberg's "Dodsdancen" is regarded as a comedy—a very bitter one, of course, but funny enough to be presented with liveliness rather than with the solemnity which usually is accorded a pioneer among modern dramatists. In Germany some years ago Oscar Homolka made a great success with "Dodsdancen," and a young man named Peter Goldbaum saw him. One day, Goldbaum promised himself, he would adapt the Strindberg drama and get Homolka to play it in English in New York. And he did, with Robin Short as co-adapter. Homolka, one of the most gifted of character players—as those who saw either the stage or screen versions of "I Remember Mama" will recall—gave a thorough and resourceful performance as Edgar, the scheming tyrant, but New Yorkers would not accept the play. This, I felt, was a pity.

The end of January brought an acceptable musical comedy about the ballet business, "Look, Ma, I'm Dancin'," and the Experimental Theatre's production of "Skipper Next to God." For no more than taxi fare in lieu of wages, the movies' John Garfield gave a dynamic performance as the Skipper. Jan de Hartog, whose first production of the season was windy and muddled, proved with "Skipper Next to God" that he is a dramatist of pith and purpose. The play ran for two months and could have lasted to the season's end, if Mr. Garfield hadn't been forced to return to Hollywood at the end of February.

A curiously unsatisfying comedy was "Kathleen," by an Irish dramatist and critic, Michael Sayers. Mr. Sayers' play, about a girl who pretends to be pregnant, was supposed to have philosophic and nationalistic overtones, but these overtones escaped any possible auditors and "Kathleen" endured only 3 performances.

I think we all expected too much from Dublin's Gate Theatre Players, who arrived February 10. The Gate company came over here, honestly and unpretentiously, as a stock company hoping to show us the kind of theatre Dubliners were interested in. Their first offering was Shaw's "John Bull's Other Island"—a comedy almost contemporary with "Man and Superman" but not nearly as durable. Their next was Denis Johnston's "The Old Lady Says 'No'!" and the third was "Where Stars Walk," a fantasy by one of their members, Micheal MacLiammoir. Mr. MacLiammoir's last name caused New York typesetters no end of trouble, but they mastered it; his first name, however, threw them. No printer would believe that an Irishman named Mike would spell his name Micheal instead of the regular way.

Hilton Edwards, manager and a star of the Gate Theatre players, was surprised and hurt at the failure of the New York engagement. In a newspaper interview he made the profound and discouragingly true observation that New York audiences do not have the patience to listen as do the audiences of Dublin and London. We all grew impatient with the talkative Shaw and were puzzled by the involvements of Johnston's impressionistic methods. Not many seemed to care much, either, about a king and a princess of ancient times returning to modern Ireland as a pair of house servants, which was the burden of Mr. MacLiammoir's rather charming little play.

If ever a success was assured in advance, "Mister Roberts" was it. By the time this comedy about Navy life arrived at the Alvin Theatre and got its scenery set up for a February 18 opening, tickets were gone for weeks ahead. Word of tryout successes had beaten the play to town—and for once, New Yorkers agreed with out-of-town opinions; predisposed, too, were the many who had read the best-selling Thomas Heggen novel from which the play was made. Although it was by no means profound, "Mister Roberts" was show business at its best. A few bone-pickers argued that the comedy was a "cartoon" or that it took a Rover Boys attitude toward the war. Granting a certain truth in these accusations, I find them pleasant nevertheless—for most certainly there is no law against show business being show business.

The perennially eager Eva Le Gallienne, hoping to retrieve some lost glory and cash for the American Repertory Theatre, offered short and unimpressive engagements of "Hedda Gabler" and "Ghosts." The most devoted of Ibsenites appeared to have gone a bit stale. Not a bit stale was a plump, dark-eyed woman, Gertrude Berg, who came to the Belasco late in February in her own comedy, "Me and Molly." And she could have been, for she had written a radio serial about the Goldbergs of the Bronx for something like sixteen years, and had now made a play about the tribe. The play was slight in structure, but it was affectionate, human and funny. In addition to making her debut as a playwright, Mrs. Berg made her debut as an actress, playing the Molly who good-humoredly and wisely managed a temperamental husband and a highly active collection of children, relatives and neighbors.

The Experimental Theatre had been scolded so much in letters-to-the-editor departments for offering so many foreign scripts that it abandoned plans to present Jean-Paul Sartre's "The Respectful Prostitute," and a young co-operative group calling themselves

New Stages took it up and made a success of it.

The story went that Sartre, the French existentialist, had knocked off this play in a couple of weeks, his admittedly slight knowledge of the American South having been bolstered by information from two American friends. The result was a technically slick little melodrama of almost Grand Guignol speed and force. It found such great favor on Bleecker Street that it was moved uptown to the Cort, where it continued to gather satisfying crowds. The play brought considerable renown to Meg Mundy for her portrayal of the title character. Your editor was one who felt that "The Respectful Prostitute" was at base insincere and opportunistic, and he further believed that insincerity and opportunism were not desirable qualities in a drama dealing with race prejudice. Here was a play that was indeed a cartoon, and one or two of its characters were downright caricatures. A short play, "Prostitute" was slightly bolstered by a Thornton Wilder sketch, "The Happy Journey," which is familiar to devotees of amateur theatricals.

In "The Art of Murder," an admirable essay on the detective story, Raymond Chandler wrote that the English may not be the best writers in the world, but they are the best dull writers. J. B. Priestley, who had opened his season with the quietly suspenseful and ingenious "An Inspector Calls," now came forth with a drama titled "The Linden Tree," which seemed to illustrate Mr. Chandler's point. "The Linden Tree" was a thoughtful drama about postwar England, whose burden was that too many Britons in middle life were disillusioned and ready to call it quits. The hope of England, said Mr. Priestley, lay in the wisdom of the very old and the enthusiasm of the very young. His spokesman at the Music Box was Boris Karloff, playing a 65-year-old Professor. The drama was a fine success in England and won the Ellen Terry award there, but it lasted only 7 performances here. American audiences did not have the patience to listen, and therefore they missed a drama of considerable skill and profundity.

Rose Franken Meloney had a hit some years ago in a family comedy drama, "Another Language." Returning to the same family—some years older now—she essayed another piece, "The Hallams." Something was missing; the tribe now had become a houseful of bores.

Another Shaw comedy, "You Never Can Tell," proved an unsuccessful Theatre Guild attraction. "Joy to the World," a mid-March arrival, continued into the Summer. This was a comedy about Hollywood in the accepted "Once in a Lifetime" manner, but with a serious point. Allan Scott, the author, is a screen-writer, and in his play he expressed the belief that films should not merely purvey joy to the world but should also take part in the world and be serious about it once in a while. Mr. Scott's hero got into farcical studio messes because he wanted to film the life of Samuel Gompers and was told by his bosses that he couldn't make a picture about Labor.

Michael Redgrave's and Flora Robson's "Macbeth" split play-goers into two camps, the stronger of which was the one which didn't like what it saw. "Macbeth" has never been one of Shake-speare's box-office hits—in our time, anyway—nor was it now. Some of those who sat in judgment at it failed to be moved by the principals' performances as Mr. and Mrs.; others, including this viewer, felt that here was an admirable production which made a fast, taut melodrama of an ancient thriller.

One of the mysteries of many seasons turned out to be Keith Winter's "The Rats of Norway," a one-time London success which, every season, one American manager or another would an-nounce as impending on Broadway. After a record number of false starts, "The Rats" finally arrived under the aegis of young James S. Elliott, and the mystery was, how had the drama in-trigued so many would-be sponsors? It was a turgid affair con-cerning repressed and misdirected sex impulses in an English school.

Elisabeth Bergner has proved more than once that she has a loyal personal following, and she almost proved it again in "The Cup of Trembling," in which she appeared late in April. She gave one of her amazingly detailed performances as a lady alco-holic who finally is cured with the help of psychiatry, a beating from her husband and the spiritual ministrations of Alcoholics Anonymous. This drama, based by Louis Paul on a novel by Mr. Paul, was a wordy affair in spite of desperate last-minute trim-ming, and its professional viewers did not take it very seriously. But Miss Bergner's audience did take her seriously, as usual. When business was insufficient to keep "The Cup of Trembling" at the Music Box, an attempt was made to reopen it at another playhouse, so that all the Bergner fans might see it; but negotia-tions ultimately collapsed.

One of the happy surprises of the waning season was a revival of Ferenc Molnar's "The Play's the Thing," in an adaptation by P. G. Wodehouse. This airy little exercise in sophistication as it is practiced in castles on the Riviera proved to be as gay as ever, thanks to expert staging by Gilbert Miller and the assured, easy playing of Louis Calhern and Arthur Margetson.

A not entirely happy event was the last-of-April arrival of the revue, "Inside U.S.A." Perhaps too much had been expected of it, even though its stars were Beatrice Lillie and Jack Haley and its authors included Arnold Auerbach, Moss Hart, Arnold B. Horwitt, Arthur Schwartz and Howard Dietz. It was a very handsome revue, quite lavish considering the impossibly high costs these days, and in it Miss Lillie was supremely funny. Without her, "Inside U.S.A." would not have been funny enough of the time to make it a first class revue. The unpretentious "Make Mine Manhattan" was, in these eyes, better.

José Ferrer, Richard Whorf and the New York City Theatre Company returned to the City Center for three Spring fortnights of revivals—Ben Jonson's "The Alchemist," Eugene O'Neill's four "S.S. Glencairn" one-acters and the Capek brothers' "The Insect Comedy"—all reasonably well done for the popular trade.

Another off-Broadway *succès d'estime*, Richard Harrity's rueful one-act comedy about some bums in Central Park titled "Hope Is the Thing with Feathers," was brought to Broadway by Eddie Dowling. Two more Harrity playlets, "Home Life of a Buffalo" and "Gone Tomorrow," were added, but the only notable thing about them was the reuniting of Mr. Dowling and his wife, Ray Dooley, as a vaudeville team. Seven performances were enough.

Still other off-Broadway ventures got their commercial hearings. The Experimental Theatre's "Ballet Ballads," in which such talented creators as composer Jerome Moross, lyrist John Latouche and choreographers Katherine Litz, Hanya Holm and Paul Godkin merged their arts, was given commercial sponsorship at the Music Box. These three offerings, each consisting of song, story and dance, were a pleasant and effective novelty.

For late May consumption Ladislas Fodor wrote a pointless and quite tasteless drama, "The Vigil," in which Biblical characters appeared in a modern American courtroom for an investigation of the events from Christ's death to His resurrection. Such people as Mary Magdalene, Simon Called Peter and Pontius Pilate did not seem very interesting in modern clothes.

From the Lenox Hill Playhouse came, to no avail, Arthur Goodman's "Seeds in the Wind," in which some child survivors of Lidice banded together in the mountains to wrest the world from grown-ups in the correct belief that grown-ups have managed the world very badly so far. Once he had stated his idea, Mr. Goodman couldn't develop it satisfactorily, and his drama had a brief and profitless career. Unsuccessful, too, was a revival of Jerome Kern's "Sally," in spite of the amusing presence of Willie Howard.

The most notable closing of the season was that of "Oklahoma!" on May 29 after 2,248 performances at the St. James Theatre. When it announced the closing date, the Theatre Guild tallied up 2,202 performances and regretfully pointed out that this phenomenal attraction had failed to reach or pass the world record for a long run set in 1916 in London by the musical "Chu Chin Chow." This statistically minded observer called the Guild to check its figures, and found that the management had failed to count 46 performances. Two of these were Stage Relief Fund and Actors' Fund benefits; the others were special, cut-rate Tuesday matinees for men and women in uniform in 1944.

Burns Mantle always figured, and I agree, that a performance is a performance as long as somebody sees it and has paid to get in. The day after the closing the Theatre Guild officially reconsidered and pridefully admitted that "Oklahoma!" was indeed the new world champion, musical division, and it may be that its record will be unchallenged during the next thirty-two years.

There could have been more plays last season, and there should have been more playhouses; but, all in all, things weren't so bad.

THE SEASON IN CHICAGO

By Claudia Cassidy

Drama Editor of the *Chicago Tribune*

THE Chicago drama critic should be careful about looking back over his shoulder, even for statistical purposes. The cumulative evidence of a full season's horrors is what drives him to doubling in such brass as writing a column, invading the brokerage business, or pretending to be a music critic in his all too spare time. A year ago the town showed signs of lapsing into pre-boom theatrical torpor, and in 1947-48, it lapsed. This was the season of revivals, of return engagements, and of return engagements of revivals. Inexplicably, unless the booking office has plans for better things, it was also the season in which the Great Northern was sumptuously restored, the Erlanger launched on a six-figure operation in air conditioning, and the Studebaker promised the same refreshment.

It was the season when no manager looked dourly at a morning paper critic rushing to his deadline, missing, to be sure, the best part of the show. As of mid-November, 1947, Chicago printers abandoned the linotype for the picket line, and reviews came out a day late in varitype. According to the theory that the future of the theatre depends on less hurried reviews by less harried reviewers, all this leisure should have produced some profoundly significant result. Unfortunately, all that happened was the barrage of telephone calls the morning after each opening, in which indignant customers stated their opinion of a reviewer too dilatory to deliver an opinion with the breakfast coffee.

For queasy digestions, the gesture was all too often thumbs down. An inclusive count adds up to 40 shows in 1947-48, three more than in the previous season, but because of the high percentage of disaster it also adds up to 265 weeks of playgoing as against 280 a year ago. From the first of June, 1947, to the end of May, 1948, Chicago had 21 plays, of which 11 were new, 9 were return engagements or revivals, and 1 was held over from the previous season. There were 19 musicals, 7 of them new, 9 return engagements or revivals, and 3 held over. Of these 38 productions, 17 lasted 3 weeks or less. Barring holdovers (in the two-season lap "Born Yesterday" ran 33 weeks, "Call Me Mister" 20, "Carousel" 23 and "The Red Mill" 9) the long run record went to the 26 weeks of Tallulah Bankhead's highly public "Private Lives," which caused Noel Coward to burst into tears when he saw it, though whether from gratification or exasperation no other man can say.

There was less room for doubt in the reaction of the Bankhead audience. Opening night was a shambles of the delighted and the dismayed. Even the latter succumbed to the spirit of the evening when Miss Bankhead saluted her cheering fans with a throaty "God bless you," only to have a hoarser voice from the balcony reply, "God bless you, too." One critic's reaction caused the resourceful Miss Bankhead to address her as follows: "When you wrote about 'The Little Foxes' I said O God, I wish she was on that big paper, but when I saw what you said about 'Private Lives' I said O God, I wish she was back on that little one." P.S. "Private Lives" ran four times as long.

If Tallulah was the season's volcano, Katharine Cornell was its glowing climax, and the night of November 3 its gayest, as you could choose between the return after seven seasons of the Lunts, in "O Mistress Mine," and the arrival of Mary Martin, who played hob with the widespread conviction that only Ethel Merman could score a bull's-eye with "Annie Get Your Gun."

It was typical of Cornell that she brought "Antony and Cleopatra" even though it meant building a new platform stage for an already costly production limited to four Chicago weeks by Godfrey Tearle's English bookings. The gesture paid royal dividends. It would not surprise me if on our opening night she gave her finest performance. At any rate, a revival I had seen in Detroit tryout and reluctantly considered a respectable failure suddenly took on the stature, the fusion and the focus of triumph.

One look at the incomparable Lunts and playgoing was fun again. One look at delectable Mary Martin and Chicago wanted to know why the Shubert marquee blazoned such nonsense as Limited Engagement. It was simple, if not sensible. Miss Martin knew she had the show of a lifetime in "Annie" and she wanted to spread the news over the land. She stipulated not more than 8 weeks in any city. Richard Rodgers and Oscar Hammerstein II talked her into 12 for Chicago. Irving Berlin and a reported slice of the profits tilted it to 17. "Annie" set a number of records, not the least of them the number of smoldering would-be customers who couldn't get in to see it.

"Show Boat" was a consolation prize from the same producers.

With Billy House as Cap'n Andy it tied up at the Shubert with such success there was no immediate mooring for the Chicago company of "High Button Shoes," affectionately anticipated because it held Eddie Foy, Jr., who took the curse off a return engagement of "The Red Mill" when he substituted for the injured Buster West. Where in the first edition you couldn't see the tulips for the corn, this time you couldn't see the corn for Mr. Foy.

You will get some idea of the caliber of the season's plays when you hear that the town fell with cries of joy on "John Loves Mary," sleekly staged with Jan ("good as gold") Sterling replacing Nina Foch as a highly successful heroine. "Lady Windermere's Fan" came without Penelope Ward or a reasonable facsimile. The Theatre Guild opened its season with the hocus-pocus of "This Time Tomorrow." The prize winning "All My Sons" veiled its presumable virtues in a blur of inferior performance. That psychoanalytical study of "The Little Foxes" known as "Another Part of the Forest" had its undeniable points, but they, too, were dulled by cast changes involving the loss of Percy Waram, and by a cut down production which banished the illusion of time and place established by the Hubbards' deep south portico.

Bert Lahr was admired in the burlesque sequences that gave his revival its name, but wistful memories clung to the late Hal Skelly for a dancing exit. Maurice Chevalier hadn't changed at all, which was as it should be. "All Gaul Is Divided," a farce about soldiers in the French black market, was good enough to deserve to be better, and a revival of "The Chocolate Soldier" with Billy Gilbert was gay enough to be welcomed in a town beaten about the ears with unconscionable revivals of "The Swing Mikado," "The Student Prince" and "The Firefly." Bobby Clark came back with "Sweethearts," but it didn't go the second time. He had to do the impossible—live up to the memory of himself.

The turkeys were always with us. "Laura" came back with K. T. Stevens and Hugh Marlowe, and "The Voice of the Turtle" came back without them. Billie Burke and Grant Mitchell looked in with "Accidentally Yours," in which Mr. Mitchell was required to confuse a Jeanie from a masquerade with a genie from a bottle. Bert Wheeler was one Roger Podger in a maudlin misadventure called "Benchwarmer," which had at its big moment the performance of the Bach-Gounod "Ave Maria" on the xylophone. "Sleep It Off" was believed to have set a new low as Jackie Cooper hypnotized Ann Corio in a fraternity house (Paula

Stone was the unbilled director of this one) but the authors were vindicated on the arrival of "Mary Had a Little," an excavation in theatrical sewage best described by the customer who walked out in act two, remarking, "Filthy little stinker, isn't it?"

There are times, of course, when audiences are in there pitching for a hit, and that was true the night "My Romance" opened the Great Northern. The Shuberts had restored the historic house (it opened in 1896 with Henry Miller in "Heartsease") at a cost of something like half a million dollars. They left the charm but took out the posts, put in a new floor, new foyers, air conditioning and all the trimmings. It's a beguiling sight in pale French blue and faded Pompeian red. Even the governor was there to wish it well. •

The theatre was fine, the show not so happy. It lasted three weeks, giving way to "High Button Shoes." "My Romance" had a beautiful heroine in Anne Jeffreys, but to do a Doris Keane she needed a better book and some music. The music, by the way, was credited to Denes Agay, with an assist from Philip Redowski. Redowski, rumor reports, is J. J. Shubert. Rumor further reports that, smitten by the muse, he hums. It is taken down for posterity.

This was the season the Civic Theatre decided to test the rule about hiring eight musicians it didn't need. It just meant they took four days off with pay. This was the season Spike Jones put music in its place beneath glowering portraits of Beethoven and Bach, the season Michael Myerberg astounded his "Lute Song" admirers with a cornfed revival (Zasu Pitts and Guy Kibbee) of "The Late Christopher Bean." More happily, this was the season William Leonard, drama critic of the Chicago *Journal of Commerce*, collaborated with the Chicago *Stagebill* in a theatre year-book making theatrical commentators infallible for the last 25 seasons.

For this yearbook, herewith the record of the 1947-48 season:

Shubert Theatre (52 weeks): "Carousel," 22 weeks' holdover, a total of 23; "Annie Get Your Gun," 17; "Show Boat," 13 to date.

Blackstone Theatre (47 weeks): "Call Me Mister," 17 weeks' holdover, a total of 20; "The Chocolate Soldier," 11; "The Firefly," 4½; return engagement of "The Red Mill," 6; "Sleep It Off," 2; "The Student Prince," 2½ weeks; "Antony and Cleopatra," 4.

Harris Theatre (45 weeks): "Laura," 3; "Private Lives," 26; "John Loves Mary," 16 to date.

Erlanger Theatre (37 weeks): "Born Yesterday," 19 weeks' holdover, a total of 33; "Another Part of the Forest," 2; Maurice Chevalier, 1; "All My Sons," 3; "The Voice of the Turtle," 3; "Lady Windermere's Fan," 6; "Sweethearts," 3.

Selwyn Theatre (34 weeks): "Accidentally Yours," 2; "Benchwarmer," 1; "This Time Tomorrow," 3; "O Mistress Mine," 17; "Burlesque," 8; "The First Mrs. Fraser" (Jane Cowl), 3 to date.

Studebaker Theatre (24½ weeks): "Toplitzky of Notre Dame," 1; "Musical Depreciation Revue," 10; "The Medium" and "The Telephone," 4; "Tropical Revue," 4½; "Mary Had a Little," 2; "Shylock and His Daughter," 2; "Blossom Time," 1 to date.

Civic Opera House (11 weeks): "The Red Mill," 8 weeks' holdover, a total of 9; "The Swing Mikado," 3.

Civic Theatre (9½ weeks): "The Late Christopher Bean," 3; "All Gaul Is Divided," 3; "Anna Lucasta," 3½.

Great Northern Theatre (5 weeks): "My Romance," 3; "High Button Shoes," 2 to date.

THE SEASON IN SAN FRANCISCO

By Fred Johnson

Drama Editor of the San Francisco *Call-Bulletin*

SAN FRANCISCO'S theatrical year-end—apart from Broadway's seasonal reckoning—found playgoers in rueful retrospect of their twelve months' entertainment and in not too optimistic peering toward the future.

If they were not to be served with more frequent attractions from the East, what might be done at this west shore outpost for betterment of its legitimate theatre? The discriminating cash supporters could do little else than hope, along with an organization or two of the same mood, but also of a mind to do something about it.

Out of the combined aspirations, at this writing, had come a municipal theatre of more than a little promise and the plans of a Civic Theatre Association with the aim of a permanent and professional group.

These hopeful trail-blazers had been spurred by a year of almost unprecedented dearth in top-grade entertainment, which indicated a field well worth the tilling.

In what had been playfully called the legitimate theatre—in adjacent houses under a single management—had appeared such stop-gap bookings as Spike Jones' Musical Depreciation Revue (a hit of the year, incidentally), a Magic on Ice divertissement, a sepia dance extravaganza, a vaudeville show, the Ballet Theatre and, in utter extremity, the film version of "Mourning Becomes Electra."

There had been nine touring attractions, all of which won the eager appreciation of hungering patrons. Of the five play productions originating in Los Angeles or Hollywood, all had soon expired save one.

These were apart from two of the San Francisco and Los Angeles Civic Light Opera Association's attractions which came at the theatrical year's beginning. These were "The Three Musketeers" and "Louisiana Purchase," starring William Gaxton, Victor Moore and Vera Zorina, the original trio. The 1947 season of General Director Edwin Lester's musicals had begun with a

22

revival of "Rosalinda" and a return engagement of "Song of Norway," playing to capacity for five weeks—one more than "Louisiana Purchase." The prolonged season, ending late in August, was one of the Association's most brilliantly successful.

Of the West Coast play offerings confined to local touring, a revival of "Angel Street" alone made its mark, playing to full houses for one month—a run credited to the co-starring of Gregory Peck and Laraine Day.

Clarence Kolb and Max Dill, a popular comedy team for many years after the century's turn, ventured a revival of their antiquated comedy success, "The High Cost of Loving." A sentimental brand of support which spelled capacity business for one week failed them for the remainder of a month's forced run.

Another coast casualty was "Girl of the Golden West," which the long quiescent Louis O. Macloon revived, with Hollywood's Victor Jory, Catherine Craig and James Ellison heading the cast. And one week exhausted the appeal of two other productions from Southern California. "The Master's Chair," a new psychological drama by Rand Elliott and Albert Dickason, was presented by Lawrence Stanhope, featuring film players Ona Munson, Richard Ney and Jorja Curtwright. On the sadder side was Guy Bates Post's reappearance in his old success, Edward J. Locke's "The Climax."

In contrast was the welcome given Charlotte Greenwood in a national touring company of "I Remember Mama," with Kurt Katch featured as Uncle Chris. Its run of six weeks was second only to that of "Oklahoma!" in its return engagement of two months.

Another of the city's favorites—a permanent resident—was Ina Claire in George Kelly's "The Fatal Weakness," with Kathryn Givney and Howard St. John. Her local stage reign, linked to social festivity as Mrs. William R. Wallace, Jr., was for a full and profitable month.

Accorded the same term was Gertrude Lawrence in six playlets of Noel Coward's revived "Tonight at 8:30" series, with the British Graham Payn in the old Coward roles except for one performance when, due to illness, he was replaced by the actor-author in "Hands Across the Sea."

Film actress Lucille Ball, making her stage debut in Elmer Rice's "Dream Girl," with Scott McKay and Hayden Rorke, could have prolonged her stay for more than a fortnight under different booking arrangements.

The phenomenal "Mary Had a Little" comedy, which had far

outdone in favor such attractions as "The Magnificent Yankee" in the previous year, returned for a healthy two weeks, exceeding in profit the lean three chalked up by "Call Me Mister." The latter revue offered an example of the hazards in bringing large musical companies this far West. But even so, its failure in a three weeks' run indicated a loss in topical interest.

There may have been the same attitude toward "The Voice of the Turtle" on its second visit, with Haila Stoddard, Sheila Bromley and Philip Faversham as its comedy trio. The patronage was accounted fair—for eleven days.

Taking over the long-idle Tivoli Theatre for five weeks, Ray Spencer presented "Deep Are the Roots," with Hollywood's Robert Warwick and Rose Hobart among its principals. The controversial drama failed in awaking the expected interest. As the season closed, Joe E. Brown returned in the touring company of "Harvey," nearing the close of his third season, for a scheduled month's run.

The San Francisco and Los Angeles Light Opera Association opened its ninth (1948) season in May with Victor Herbert's "Naughty Marietta," featuring moviedom's Susanna Foster, Wilbur Evans and Edward Everett Horton. It was to be followed by "Annie Get Your Gun," starring Mary Martin; "Sweethearts," with Bobby Clark, and the premiere of "Magdalena," the Association's second original production, starring Irra Petina, John Raitt and Dorothy Sarnoff.

The municipally operated Bay Theatre made advancement during the year, ending its season with a near-professional production of "Mary of Scotland"; the Theatre Arts Colony also progressed as one of the more important little theatres, and the Straw Hat Theatre, a revue company originating in the suburbs, won its first metropolitan recognition in theatre and hotel engagements before a trek to Honolulu.

The San Francisco Theatre Association, after more than two years of preparation, announced its plans for a permanent, professional theatre, dependent upon the success of a fund-raising campaign scheduled for early fall.

THE SEASON IN SOUTHERN CALIFORNIA

By Edwin Schallert

Drama Editor of the *Los Angeles Times*

AN improved approach manifested itself in stage activities during the season of 1947-48 in Southern California. While there was a lack of brilliant highlighting events, there was more theatre than usual, and much of it was consistently better than in the past.

Enterprises of West Coast origin particularly showed development. Summer play-giving caught on, and evidently is becoming a stimulus to ambitions and plans that center in Los Angeles and Hollywood. While certain organizations that started early in the fiscal year—ranging from July 1, 1947, to May 1, 1947, as covered in this report—were not able to fulfill their dreams, they at least helped the general trend toward integration of show-staging. There was consequently progress, in spite of setbacks.

Outstanding still as a handicap in the sprawling community of Los Angeles and its environs is the absence of theatres strategically located. One senses that these will eventually be built on the West Side adjacent to Beverly Hills and West Los Angeles, or along Wilshire Blvd., but so far little or nothing has really happened to bring such construction to realization.

Rumored is a theatre to be built by the Shuberts, and another as a component of a large building project on West Wilshire. A certain need has been supplied, of course, by houses like Las Palmas adjacent to Hollywood Blvd., the Coronet on La Cienega Blvd., not far from the Turnabout, and El Patio, but none of these is ideal from commercial standpoints, or in all respects, artistic.

Downtown the Biltmore Theatre remains dominant as the home of road attractions, and a few emanating from the Coast. The Belasco serves mostly for West Coast productions. The Mayan during the year passed over to burlesque and movies. Philharmonic Auditorium is used for light opera.

Apart from El Capitan, home of Ken Murray's "Blackouts," which rounded out its fifth season; Theatre Mart, with "The Drunkard" that was finishing its 15th year, Beaux Arts and Musart, there are comparatively few other locations where plays may be presented in the city, and even the established centers are not all entirely suitable environments. Nor do the popular summer theatres qualify in the best sense either, but that is less important in such situations.

New York Theatre Guild through the American Theatre Society sponsored some of the year's best entertainment. Besieged by the public was the all too short visit of Alfred Lunt and Lynn Fontanne in "O Mistress Mine," which stayed at the Biltmore for only two weeks, and probably could easily have drawn packed houses for four or five. Lunt himself said he had not realized the possibilities since the couple's last visit seven years ago. The potential audience has greatly increased for such events as this. Proof enough was the enormous revenue exceeding $300,000 derived by the Metropolitan Opera during its less than two weeks sojourn at Shrine Auditorium.

Gertrude Lawrence made her stay brief and effective in "Tonight at 8:30." Noel Coward, who directed the revival, was present, and the company of players included Graham Payn, Norah Howard, Philip Tonge, Valerie Cossart and Sarah Burton. Homer Curran, Russell Lewis and Howard Young joined with the Theatre Guild as producers, and they, too, were associated with "I Remember Mama," starring Charlotte Greenwood, with Kurt Katch as Uncle Chris, and Jean Ruth from Paramount as the eldest daughter and narrator. Lewis and Young, with Curran, are accomplishing much for class in Coast presentations.

"The Fatal Weakness" with Ina Claire was still another American Theatre Society offering that found responsive audiences. Appearing with the star in principal roles were Howard St. John and Kathryn Givney. Miss Claire had been missed as a personality of the stage for all the war years, in spite of her adjacent residence in San Francisco.

A surprisingly popular feature of the season was the appearance of Gregory Peck and Laraine Day in a revival of "Angel Street" that stemmed from La Jolla's Summer theatre. They climaxed a Coast tour with a well-attended engagement at the Biltmore. While the critical estimates of the splendidly mounted production were variable, there was no question of the lure of the film names. Ernest Cossart, Elizabeth Patterson and Elizabeth Fraser acted the other parts, and Shepard Traube staged the play.

Out of La Jolla, too, came Eve Arden with "Biography" to play at Las Palmas early in the season. Barry Sullivan was her leading man, with other principals including Sig Rumann, John Hoyt and Russell Hicks. It was an enjoyable revival.

Again a motion picture celebrity advantaged a stage show when

Lucille Ball arrived in "Dream Girl" at the Biltmore. That show had misfortunes during its run, for Miss Ball lost her voice completely, due to a strep throat, at one stage, and her first replacement, June Havoc, was also taken ill. Finally Haila Stoddard was flown out to the Coast to carry on for a few days until Miss Ball was able to resume. All this hurt the overall attendance. But Miss Ball was rated superior in the interpretation by all who saw her, while Scott McKay was very well liked. Hayden Rorke and Lela Bliss were featured in the company.

Miss Stoddard, who helped save the day for "Dream Girl," figured in the 1947-48 annals as the star of "Voice of the Turtle" early in the season, with Philip Faversham and Sheila Bromley as her aides. Like "Voice of the Turtle" the redoubtable "Harvey" returned during the season with Joe E. Brown also repeating as star. Maurice Chevalier was a luminous Christmas holiday influence in his one-man show, demonstrating in his public reception that there was no diminution of his fame since his American screen days.

Few productions of Coast origin exceeded in significance "Deep Are the Roots," which ran for 10 weeks at the Belasco, and was excellently enacted in the Ray Spencer production under the direction of John Berry by a cast including Robert Warwick, Rose Hobart, Curt Conway, Don Beddoe, James Edwards, Betsy Blair (Mrs. Gene Kelly), Jessie Grayson and Frank Lynn. Were all Coast enterprises as well organized there would be no debate as to their value or appeal. Miss Blair was a surprise hit in the Arnaud d'Usseau-James Gow play, but no less impressive was the work of practically all others in the competent group.

High level in bringing things up to date in the theatre was also attained by Nancy Coleman, John Emery and Tamara Geva early in the season when they appeared in "No Exit," by Jean-Paul Sartre, at the Coronet. Toward the end of the fiscal year came "All My Sons" at Las Palmas as proffered by the Actors' Lab with Lloyd Bridges, Roman Bohnen, Georgia Backus, Arthur O'Connell and Mary Davenport, with Phil Brown directing.

"Dark of the Moon," some seasons old in New York, fared well at Coronet with Carol Stone and Hurd Hatfield as its main principals, and Emory Parnell, Jane Darwell, Henry Brandon and Leona Roberts in the support. Pete Seeger interluded with folk singing. As a Pelican production this was one of the best.

That organization, incidentally, had its difficulties during the season after a brave beginning. "Skin of Our Teeth" inaugurated its regime, followed by "Galileo" with Charles Laughton, and later

"The House of Bernarda Alba" by Garcia Lorca was on the agenda. "House of Bernarda Alba" was presented as an American premiere, apart from a Pasadena Playhouse production at the Playbox, and the cast included Ona Munson, Helen Freeman, Mary Servoss, Gertrude Hoffman, Ruth Sanderson, Marjorie Nelson, Frances Rey, Anne Muir. Translation of this all-women tragedy was made by Richard O'Connell and James Graham Lujan, and there was a musical score by Darius Milhaud. Play did not start off too well during the engagement, though it accumulated interest. The general sentiment was that it was too depressing.

The new was tried in earnest at the Coronet with "The Vigil" by Ladislas Fodor, a play which deserved much better recognition than it got. The public rushed to the theatre the closing nights, but in the earlier stages "The Vigil" drew badly. Heading the cast were Henry Wilcoxon, Ruth Matteson and Ian MacDonald, but there were many superior efforts on the part of such people as Nana Bryant, King Donovan, Tom Fadden, Aubrey Mather, Paul Newlan, Wilton Graff, C. S. Ramsayhill, Maurice Cass, Milton Parsons, Edward Van Sloan, Joan Woodbury and Eve McVeagh. Alexander Markey produced the play.

"Declaration" by Janet and Philip Stevenson was brought to the stage by Actors Lab as a study of Jefferson and his times, with Lloyd Gough, Ian MacDonald, Mervyn Williams, Paul McVey, Stanley Waxman, Roman Bohnen, Jeff Corey and Bert Conway in the initial cast. First presented at the Actors Lab, it was later transferred to the Musart.

More intriguing was the debut of "Sam Ego's House," by William Saroyan, as offered with central staging by the Circle Players, with principal parts played by H. George Stern, Ken Harvey, George Englund, William Schallert, Terry Kilburn, Sydney Chaplin, Larry Salters, Julian Ludwig, Naomi Stevens and Kathleen Freeman. The play was no better than most that Saroyan has contributed since "The Time of Your Life," but it ran for more than two months. Mabel Albertson directed.

A strange mixture of "Dead End," "Wisdom Tooth" and various other ingredients was made visible in "The Stone Jungle" by Paul Peters, tried out first experimentally at the Coronet and later staged commercially with Shepperd Strudwick dreaming back to his boyhood. Richard (Dickie) Moore as a leading juvenile, Ralph Hodges, Noel Rayburn, Rusty Tamblyn, Marvin Davis, John Bennes, Jimmy Ogg and Ian MacDonald gained attention, but the play did not look like New York.

More effective was the Coast production of "Brooklyn U.S.A.," briefly essayed in New York about Pearl Harbor time. By John Bright and Asa Bordages, this was produced by Lionel Stander first at the Hollytown, with a strong cast headed by Richard Benedict, Jody S. Gilbert, Olive Deering, Benny Baker, Edmund Mac-Donald, Shimen Ruskin, Rick Vallin, Richard Irving and others, and then was moved to El Patio. As a commercial venture it fell short, and ended in disagreements.

Robert Milton tried "Sunrise in My Pocket" by Edwin Justus Mayer at the Ben Bard Theatre, which seemed much overwritten even for a historical subject. "Angel Face," by Steve Fisher and Sloan Nibley, with John Howard starred, "Dipper Over Gimbels'," by Helen Sloan Stetson, and "Thieves' Paradise," by Myron C. Fagan, were brought to the stage, the last named twice in controversial fashion because of its attack on Communism. Irene Corlett, Sean McGlory, Joyce Arling and George Meader were in "Dipper Over Gimbels' " and Michael Whalen, Dian Fauntelle, Martha Mayo, Marshall Bradford, Ruth Brady, Noel Cravat and Helen Wallace were in the Fagan offering with Balkan setting at El Patio Theatre.

There were many other experimentations mainly in little theatres, but to be classed with the major ones, of course, was "Galileo," starring Charles Laughton, which has already been mentioned. His supporting cast included Frances Heflin and Hugo Haas, while Joseph Losey staged the play.

Pasadena Playhouse retained its place as the locale for better efforts with, first, its Summer festival drawn from notable events in the past repertoire including "Mrs. Wiggs of the Cabbage Patch," "Midsummer Night's Dream," "Melloney Holtspur," "School for Scandal," "Arms and the Man," "Alice Sit-by-the-Fire," "The Great God Brown" and "Girl of the Golden West."

During the regular season the following were given: "Joan of Lorraine," "The Bees and the Flowers," "Our Hearts Were Young and Gay," "Years Ago," "The Magic Rowan," by James Shaw Grant—an American premiere; "Barretts of Wimpole Street," "Apple of His Eye," "Made in Heaven," "Another Part of the Forest"—first time on West Coast; "Woman Bites Dog"—Coast first; "Love from a Stranger," "Russet Mantle," "King Richard III" and "The Millionairess." Impending at time of closing this account was the world premiere of "This Young World," besides "The Circle," "Craig's Wife" and "Angel Street." The 14th Annual Midsummer Festival was to be dedicated to the California Centennial—favorite plays of Gold Coast days.

Seen in Glasgow by Gilmor Brown, "The Magic Rowan" was brought to this country by the producer as a quaint study of life in the Hebrides. It is based on the superstition that whoever eats the fruit of the Rowan tree is cleansed of malice, hate and envy, and this has an effect through a mystically inclined young couple upon the narrow-minded people with whom they are associated.

In the professional sphere William Eythe made a contribution in bringing "The Glass Menagerie" back to the stage with Joan Lorring as the young crippled girl, and Leif Erickson in a very brilliant portrayal of the gentleman caller. Mary Perry appeared as the mother.

Remote from such idealism was the pruriently popular "Mary Had a Little"—with John Hubbard, Claire Carleton, Mary Ellen Popel, Mary Roche, Fred Sherman and Gerald Oliver Smith, which had a run.

"Of Mice and Men" was revived with Forrest Tucker, Douglas Fowley, Wallace Ford and Shelley Winters, but was poorly presented. "Love on the Dole," "The Skin Game," "Time of Your Life" and "The Adding Machine" were produced by the Circle Players. Call Board continued its interesting history with a varied repertoire. Showcases and little theatres, headed by the Geller and Bliss Hayden, proceeded on their way, added to by interesting new groups like Century Theatre, Horseshoe Theatre, etc. "Emperor Jones" was staged at Las Palmas with Morris Buchanan.

The Padua Hills Theatre, the Turnabout, with Elsa Lanchester still starred, and the Puppeteers; "Gaslights" at the Daly Opera House in its fourth year, pursued their way, while "The Pilgrimage Play," "The Mission Play" and outdoor pageant of "Ramona" inscribed further history.

Stars who joined the Summer theatre parade in 1947 included Diana Lynn, Guy Madison, Ruth Hussey, Kent Smith, Richard Basehart, Beatrice Pearson, Richard Haydn, Una O'Connor, Janis Paige, Charles Korvin, Benay Venuta, Peggy Knudsen, Dane Clark, Lon Chaney, Jr., Geraldine Brooks, Constance Bennett, William Henry, Leslie Brooks, and Don De Fore, which was the best showing yet from Hollywood. These appeared at Laguna Beach and La Jolla, besides Peck, Miss Day, Sullivan and Miss Arden, already referred to.

On the Holiday Stage at Tustin such players as Rhonda Fleming and James Ellison in the new play, "Time 'n' Todd," Mabel Albertson, Oliver Cliff, Sterling Holloway, Adeline De Walt Reynolds, Vera Marshe and George Reeves were seen. The Tent

Theatre offered "Three's a Family" and "The Play's the Thing" before folding. Sam Levene, who directed "Time 'n' Todd" at Tustin, appeared in a revival of "Three Men on a Horse" in town.

The Los Angeles Civil Light Opera closed its season in 1947 with a triumphant revival of "Louisiana Purchase," featuring traditional stars, William Gaxton, Victor Moore, Irene Bordoni and Vera Zorina, and opened its 1948 season dazzlingly with Mary Martin in "Annie Get Your Gun." The Greek Theatre open-air operetta season was enormously successful, repertoire including "Rose Marie," "Blossom Time," "Bitter Sweet," "Desert Song" and "The Great Waltz." Spotlighted were Jan Clayton, John Howard, Pinky Lee, Collette Lyons, Brian Sullivan, Miliza Korjus, John Shafer, Andzia Kuzak, Paul Keast, Frank Hornaday, Anne Jeffreys, Robert Shafer, Gabrielle, the chanteuse.

Only visiting musical worthy of comment was "Call Me Mister" early in season, for the return of "Oklahoma!" lies beyond this review. Earl Carroll's, Florentine Gardens and Slapsie Maxie's as theatre restaurants continued their revues and vaudeville. At the Coronet Theatre a holiday revue was essayed but not too successfully. But the general spread in theatricals was notable.

A STREETCAR NAMED DESIRE

A Play in Eleven Scenes

By Tennessee Williams

THE production of "The Glass Menagerie," with the late Laurette Taylor and Eddie Dowling, made a success out of a struggling young dramatist named Tennessee Williams. It brought him money, fame and the Critics' Circle prize. It also, according to Mr. Williams, came near halting his career.

He told the story in an unusually self-revealing piece in the drama section of the New York *Times* in November, 1947, just before the opening of his newest play, "A Streetcar Named Desire." The success of "The Glass Menagerie," he related, snatched him out of virtual oblivion and from the precarious tenancy of furnished rooms to a suite in a first-class Manhattan hotel.

"The sort of life which I had had previous to this popular success was one that required endurance, a life of clawing and scratching along a sheer surface and holding on tight with raw fingers to every inch of rock higher than the one caught hold of before," he wrote. "But it was a good life because it was the sort of life for which the human organism is created."

In his hotel suite Williams had the luxury of room service and the flattery of many admirers. But he became depressed. He got sick of hearing people say, "I loved your play." He began to realize that he was walking around dead in his shoes. He underwent another of a series of eye operations for a cataract, and during this period of treatment and recovery he turned his sight inward upon himself.

"When the gauze mask was removed," he reported, "I found myself in a readjusted world." He checked out of his handsome suite, packed some papers and belongings and went to Mexico. Here, at Chapala, he went to work again—on a play called "The Poker Night," which later was retitled, "A Streetcar Named Desire." Williams had fought off success—temporarily; for when "A Streetcar" was produced it brought him more renown, more royalties and another Critics' Circle prize.

It brought success, too, to a new theatrical producer—Irene Mayer Selznick, daughter of Hollywood's Louis B. Mayer and

32

former wife of Hollywood's David O. Selznick. To direct the play Mrs. Selznick engaged Elia Kazan, and Jo Mielziner was enlisted to design the setting, which, by an ingenious use of gauze, depicts both the exterior and the interior of a two-story corner building on a New Orleans street which is named Elysian Fields, between the L & N tracks and the river.

"The section is poor, but, unlike corresponding sections in other American cities, it has a raffish charm. The houses are mostly white frame, weathered gray, with rickety outside stairs and galleries and quaintly ornamented gables. This building contains two flats, upstairs and down. Faded white stairs ascend to the entrances of both."

It has just turned dark of an evening early in May. In a barroom somewhere around the corner a Negro is playing a "blue piano." Eunice, who occupies the upstairs flat, is sitting on the steps of the building chatting with a Negro woman neighbor—"for New Orleans is a cosmopolitan city where there is a relatively warm and easy intermingling of races in the old part of town." Around the corner come Stanley Kowalski, who lives in the ground-floor flat, and his friend Mitch. Both are 28 or 30, roughly dressed in blue denim work clothes. Stanley is carrying a bowling jacket and a red-stained package of meat, and they have been talking about a bowling match. When Stanley reaches the foot of the steps he bellows, "Hey, there! Stella, baby!"

Stella, his wife, comes out on the first-floor landing and mildly admonishes, "Don't holler at me like that." She is a gentle young woman, about 25, of a background obviously different from her husband's. Stanley tosses the package of meat to her and with Mitch starts back around the corner—going bowling.

"Can I come watch?" asks Stella.

"Come on."

Stanley and Mitch disappear around the corner and in a moment Stella starts after them, leaving Eunice and the Negro woman still taking the air.

There now appears a daintily dressed woman of 30 or so, whose delicate beauty must avoid a strong light. There is something about her uncertain manner, as well as her white clothes, that suggests a moth. She is carrying a suitcase. She looks at a slip of paper, then at the building, then at the paper again, with an expression of shocked disbelief.

"What's the matter, honey?" asks Eunice. "Are you lost?"

With faintly hysterical humor the newcomer explains, "They told me to take a streetcar named Desire, and then transfer to one called Cemeteries and ride six blocks and get off at—Elysian Fields!"

That's just where she is now, Eunice assures her.

"I'm looking for my sister, Stella DuBois. I mean—Mrs. Stanley Kowalski. This—can this be—her home?"

It is, Eunice assures her—but Stella is out watching her husband bowl. The Negro woman offers to go tell Stella her sister has come, and Eunice offers to let the visitor in. Blanche, the sister, is dismayed as she is led into the apartment. The first room is primarily a kitchen, but it also contains a folding bed; beyond it is the bedroom, and here there is a narrow door to the bathroom.

Eunice wants to talk. "So you're Stella's sister! . . . I think she said you taught school. . . . And you're from Mississippi, huh? . . . She showed me a picture of your home-place, the plantation. . . . A place like that must be awfully hard to keep up. . . ."

Blanche, who is about ready to drop, finally makes the friendly Eunice realize she wants to be alone. When Eunice has gone Blanche sits in a chair, hunched stiffly, as if she were cold. A cat screeches and she catches her breath with a startled gesture. Suddenly she notices a whiskey bottle in a half-opened closet, pours herself half a tumbler, tosses it down, replaces the bottle, washes the tumbler and resumes her seat. "I've got to keep hold of myself," she says faintly.

Stella comes quickly around the corner to the door of her flat. Bursting in, she calls joyfully, "Blanche!"

BLANCHE—Stella, oh, Stella, Stella! Stella for Star! (*She begins to speak with feverish vivacity as if she feared for either of them to stop and think. They catch each other in a spasmodic embrace.*) Now, then, let me look at you. But don't you look at me, Stella, no, no, no, not till later, not till I've bathed and rested! And turn that over-light off! Turn that off! I won't be looked at in this merciless glare! (STELLA *laughs and complies.*) Come back here now! Oh, my baby! Stella! Stella for Star! (*She embraces her again.*) I thought you would never come back to this horrible place! What am I saying? I didn't mean to say that. I meant to be nice about it and say—Oh, what a convenient location and such— Ha-a-ha! Precious lamb! You haven't said a *word* to me.

STELLA—You haven't given me a chance to, honey! (*She laughs but her glance at* BLANCHE *is a little anxious.*)

BLANCHE—Well, now you talk. Open your pretty mouth and talk while I look around for some liquor! I know you must have some liquor on the place! Where could it be, I wonder? Oh, I spy, I spy! (*She rushes to the closet and removes the bottle; she is shaking all over and panting for breath as she tries to laugh. The bottle nearly slips from her grasp.*)

STELLA (*noticing*)—Blanche, you sit down and let me pour the drinks. I don't know what we've got to mix with. Maybe a coke's in the icebox. Look 'n' see, honey, while I'm—

BLANCHE—No coke, honey, not with my nerves tonight! Where—where—where is—?

STELLA—Stanley? Bowling! He loves it. They're having a—found some soda!—tournament. . . .

BLANCHE—Just water, baby, to chase it! Now don't get worried; your sister hasn't turned into a drunkard; she's just all shaken up and hot and tired and dirty! You sit down, now, and explain this place to me! What are you doing in a place like this?

STELLA—Now, Blanche—

BLANCHE—Oh, I'm not going to be hypocritical, I'm going to be honestly critical about it! Never, never, never in my worst dreams could I picture— Only Poe!—only Mr. Edgar Allan Poe!—could do it justice! Out there I suppose is the ghoul-haunted woodland of Weir! (*She laughs.*)

STELLA—No, honey, those are the L & N tracks.

BLANCHE—No, now seriously, putting joking aside. Why didn't you tell me, why didn't you write me, honey, why didn't you let me know?

STELLA (*carefully, pouring herself a drink*)—Tell you what, Blanche?

BLANCHE—Why, that you had to live in these conditions!

STELLA—Aren't you being a little intense about it? It's not that bad at all! New Orleans isn't like other cities.

BLANCHE—This has got nothing to do with New Orleans. You might as well say—forgive me, blessed baby! (*She suddenly stops short.*) The subject is closed!

STELLA (*a little dryly*)—Thanks! (*During the pause, BLANCHE stares at her. She smiles at BLANCHE.*)

BLANCHE (*looking down at her glass, which shakes in her hand*)—You're all I've got in the world, and you're not glad to see me!

STELLA (*sincerely*)—Why, Blanche, you know that's not true.

BLANCHE—No?—I'd forgotten how quiet you were.

STELLA—You never did give me a chance to say much, Blanche.

So I just got into the habit of being quiet around you.

BLANCHE (*vaguely*)—A good habit to get into. . . . (*Then, abruptly.*) You haven't asked me how I happened to get away from the school before the Spring term ended.

STELLA—Well, I thought you'd volunteer that information—if you wanted to tell me.

BLANCHE—You thought I'd been fired?

STELLA—No, I—thought you might have—resigned. . . .

BLANCHE—I was so exhausted by all I'd been through my— nerves broke. (*Nervously tamping cigarette.*) I was on the verge of—lunacy, almost! So Mr. Graves—Mr. Graves is the high school superintendent—he suggested I take a leave of absence. I couldn't put all those details into the wire. . . . (*She drinks quickly.*) Oh, this buzzes right through me and feels so *good!*

STELLA—Won't you have another?

BLANCHE—No, one's my limit.

STELLA—Sure?

BLANCHE—You haven't said a word about my appearance.

STELLA—You look just fine.

BLANCHE—God love you for a liar! Daylight never exposed so total a ruin! But you—you've put on some weight. Yes, you're just as plump as a little partridge! And it's so becoming to you!

Blanche chatters feverishly on, fishing for compliments about her looks and only momentarily taken aback at learning that there are just two rooms and she'll be sleeping on the folding bed. "But there's no door between the rooms, and Stanley—will it be decent?" she falters.

"Stanley is Polish, you know," offers Stella by way of explanation.

"I brought some nice clothes to meet all your lovely friends in."

Stella fears Blanche won't think they are very lovely; they're Stanley's friends—a mixed lot. She thinks Stanley and Blanche will get along all right "if you'll just try not to—well—compare him with men that we went out with at home."

In an uneasy rush Blanche takes up a new topic: "You're going to reproach me—but before you do—take into consideration— you left! I stayed and struggled! You came to New Orleans and looked out for yourself! I stayed at Belle Reve and tried to hold it together!" She is becoming increasingly hysterical as Stella strives to learn what she is driving at.

"The loss—the loss . . ."

"Belle Reve?" asks the unbelieving Stella. "Lost, is it? No!"
Blanche nods.

"But how did it go? What happened?"

Losing all control, Blanche self-pityingly launches upon a recital of all the deaths there had been in the family. "And now
you sit there telling me with your eyes that I let the place go!
How in hell do you think all that sickness and dying was paid
for? . . . And I with my pitiful salary at the school. Yes, ac-
cuse me! Sit there and stare at me, thinking I let the place go! *I*
let the place go? Where were *you!* In bed with your—Polack!"

Stella, who has begun to weep, has had enough. She flings into
the bathroom to wash her face as Stanley, Mitch and Eunice's
husband, Steve, come around the corner talking about a date for
poker tomorrow night. Mitch says it can't be at his place because his mother is still sick. "All right, we'll play at my place,"
decides Stanley. "But you bring the beer."

Mitch goes on, Steve goes upstairs to Eunice, and Stanley, entering his home, is confronted by Blanche. Now one can get a
longer, closer look at him: he is strongly, compactly built, and all
his movements and attitudes bespeak the animal joy he has in his
own being. He sizes up women at a glance, with sexual classifi-
cations, and he now sizes up this stranger in his home.

Drawing involuntarily back from his stare, she guesses, "You
must be Stanley. I'm Blanche."

"Stella's sister?"

"Yes."

"H'lo," is his matter-of-fact greeting. Informed that Stella is
in the bathroom, he quizzes his sister-in-law directly, and with
perfect unconcern begins removing his sweaty shirt. He learns
that she lives in Laurel and that she teaches English.

"You going to shack up here?"

Blanche thinks she will, if it isn't inconvenient.

"Good."

A cat screeches again, and Blanche springs up. "What's that?"

"Cats," says Stanley. "Hey, Stella! Haven't fallen in, have
you?" He grins at Blanche. "I'm afraid I'll strike you as being the unrefined type. Stella's spoke of you a good deal. You
were married once, weren't you?"

The music of a polka rises up, faint in the distance, as Blanche
replies, "Yes. When I was quite young."

"What happened?"

"The boy—the boy died." Sinking down in a chair she falters, "I'm afraid I'm going to be sick!" Her head falls on her arms. . . .

SCENE II

It is six o'clock the following evening; Stanley comes in from outside, leaving the door open to the sound of the barroom piano. Stella is finishing dressing and Blanche is in the bath. It is Stanley's poker night, and Stella is going to take Blanche to dinner and keep her out until the party breaks up. Blanche is soaking in the tub, Stella explains, to quiet her nerves.

"Stan, we've—lost Belle Reve!"

She pleads with her husband to be nice to Blanche—to say something nice about her appearance—and not to mention the baby. "I haven't said anything yet; I'm waiting until she gets in a quieter condition."

Stanley doggedly goes back to the news about Belle Reve. He wants to know just how it happened—but Stella can't tell, exactly. While Blanche sings blissfully in the bath, Stanley maintains his pursuit of details, but elicits none. His wife doesn't know about any papers or anything.

STANLEY—In the state of Louisiana we have the Napoleonic code, according to which what belongs to the wife belongs to the husband and vice versa. For instance, if I had a piece of property, or you had a piece of property—

STELLA—My head is swimming!

STANLEY—All right. I'll wait till she gets through soaking in a hot tub and then I'll inquire if *she* is acquainted with the Napoleonic code. It looks to me like you have been swindled, baby, and when you're swindled under the Napoleonic code I'm swindled *too*. And I don't like to be *swindled*.

STELLA—There's plenty of time to ask her questions later, but if you do now she'll go to pieces again. I don't understand what happened to Belle Reve, but you don't know how ridiculous you are being when you suggest that my sister or I or any one of our family could have perpetrated a swindle on anyone else.

STANLEY—Then where's the money if the place was sold?

STELLA—Not sold—*lost, lost!* (*He stalks into the bedroom, and she follows him.*) Stanley! (*He pulls open the wardrobe trunk standing in the middle of the room and jerks out an armful of dresses.*)

STANLEY—Open your eyes to this stuff! You think she got

them out of a teacher's pay?

STELLA—Hush!

STANLEY—Look at these feathers and furs that she come here to preen herself in! What's this here? A solid gold dress, I believe! And this one! What is these here? Fox-pieces! (*He blows on them.*) Genuine fox fur-pieces a half a mile long! Where are your fox-pieces, Stella? Bushy snow-white ones, no less! Where are your white fox-pieces?

STELLA—Those are inexpensive Summer furs that Blanche has had a long time.

STANLEY—I got an acquaintance who deals in this sort of merchandise. I'll have him in here to appraise it. I'm willing to bet you there's thousands of dollars invested in this stuff here!

STELLA—Don't be such an idiot, Stanley! (*He hurls the furs to the daybed. Then he jerks open a small drawer in the trunk and pulls up a fistful of costume jewelry.*)

STANLEY—And what have we here? The treasure chest of a pirate!

STELLA—Oh, Stanley!

STANLEY—Pearls! Ropes of them! What is this sister of yours, a deep-sea diver who brings up sunken treasures? Or is she the champion safe-cracker of all time! Bracelets of solid gold, too! Where are your pearls and gold bracelets?

STELLA—Shhh! Be still, Stanley!

STANLEY—And diamonds! A crown for an empress!

STELLA—A rhinestone tiara she wore to a costume ball.

STANLEY—What's rhinestone?

STELLA—Next door to glass.

STANLEY—Are you kidding? I have an acquaintance that works in a jewelry store. I'll have him in here to make an appraisal of this. Here's your plantation, or what was left of it, here!

STELLA—You have no idea how stupid and horrid you're being! Now close that trunk before she comes out of the bathroom!

STANLEY (*kicking the trunk partly closed and sitting on the kitchen table*)—The Kowalskis and the DuBois have different notions.

STELLA (*angrily*)—Indeed they have, thank heavens! *I'm* going outside.

Snatching hat and gloves, Stella goes out on the porch to wait for her sister. Blanche finally emerges from the bathroom in a red satin robe and airily greets Stanley with "Here I am, all freshly bathed and scented, and feeling like a brand-new human being!" Stanley is ominously unimpressed. Drawing the curtain between the rooms, Blanche slips into a flowered print dress, then coyly asks her brother-in-law to come in and help with some buttons. He comes in, but refuses to do any buttoning.

"It looks like my trunk has exploded," she observes.

"Me an' Stella were helping you unpack."

Airily Blanche fishes for a compliment on her appearance, but Stanley doesn't go for that stuff. He never met a woman that didn't know if she was good-looking or not without being told. He is equally stolid when Blanche tries to fetch him with a compliment: "When you walked in here last night I said to myself— 'My sister has married a man!'" He still has the Napoleonic code on his mind, and he wants to talk about it. When Stella calls for Blanche to come along, Blanche asks her to run to the drug store and get her a coke—and the quizzing about the house continues.

Still in a gay mood, Blanche sprays herself with her atomizer, then playfully sprays Stanley, who growls, "If I didn't know that you was my wife's sister I'd get ideas about you!"

"Such as what?"

"Don't play so dumb. You know what! Where's the papers?"

There *were* some papers, somewhere, she admits. Stanley roughly shoves her trunk open and begins a search. Blanche interferes, extracting a tin box and opening it. Stanley notices a sheaf of papers beneath the box and snatches them. They are love letters, Blanche protests, and when he starts to examine them she loses her airy manner in a burst of ferocity. "Now that you've touched them I'll burn them," she cries.

After a moment she recovers, begins going through the tin box and finally hands it over to Stanley, who begins grubbing through it. Taking a large envelope, she pours the papers it contains on the table. "Here all of them are, all papers! Take them, peruse them—commit them to memory, even! I think it's wonderfully fitting that Belle Reve should finally be this bunch of old papers in your big, capable hands! . . . I wonder if Stella's come back with my lemon-coke. . . ."

For once Stanley is a bit sheepish. "You see," he explains, "under the Napoleonic code—a man has to take an interest in his wife's affairs—especially now that she's going to have a baby."

Blanche accepts this news dreamily and goes to the outside door just as her sister comes back from the drug store. "Stella, Stella

for Star! How lovely to have a baby!" As Steve and Pablo
arrive, carrying a case of beer, the two women depart around
the corner, with Blanche's desperate laughter ringing out and
the blue piano and a hot trumpet sounding louder. . . .

SCENE III

The poker game has been going on a long time. The players
are Stanley, Steve, Mitch and Pablo. There are slices of water-
melon on the table, and bottles and glasses. Stanley lurches up,
tosses some melon rinds on the floor and announces, "Nothing
belongs on a poker table but cards, chips and whiskey."

The game proceeds, but Mitch would like to go home to his
sick mother. "Aw, for the sake of Jesus, go home then!" growls
Stanley—but instead Mitch goes to the bathroom.

Stella and Blanche appear outside; Blanche hastily powders her
face and they both enter. Stella introduces Steve and Pablo to
her sister, then inquires how much longer the game is going on.
"Till we get ready to quit," announces Stanley brusquely.

The women go into the bedroom. "I think I will bathe," announces Blanche.

"Again?"

"My nerves are in knots. Is the bathroom occupied?" She
knocks, and Mitch emerges. "Blanche," says Stella, "this is Harold Mitchell. My sister, Blanche DuBois." Mitch awkwardly acknowledges the introduction, then returns to the game—with a
backward look at Blanche.

Blanche wants to know all about him, for he "seems superior
to the others," and Stella provides the information. Mitch works
at the plant Stanley travels for; his mother is sick; he is un-
married. Blanche removes her blouse and stands in the light
through the portieres in her pink silk brassière and white skirt;
Stella changes to a kimono.

"You hens cut out that conversation in there!" yells Stanley.

"This is my house," retorts Stella, "and I'll talk as much as I
want to!" To Blanche she comments, "He's half drunk," and
repairs to the bathroom. Blanche goes leisurely to a small radio,
turns it on, moves back into the streak of light in the doorway,
raises her arms and stretches, then indolently occupies a chair.
The radio gives out rumba music, to the annoyance of Stanley,
who commands that it be turned off. Steve and Pablo are all
for letting the music continue, but Stanley charges into the bedroom, switches off the radio—stops short at the sight of Blanche

in the chair. She returns his look without flinching, and he returns to the game, roughly closing the portieres.

Mitch again has himself dealt out and heads for the bathroom. "Hello," Blanche greets him softly. "The little boys' room is busy right now." "We've been drinking beer," Mitch awkwardly explains.

Blanche dons her red satin wrapper and asks Mitch for a cigarette. He offers one in a silver case, which she admires. "Read the inscription," he urges, striking a match and moving closer. She reads with feigned difficulty:

> "And if God choose,
> I shall but love thee better—after—death.

"Why, that's from my favorite sonnet by Mrs. Browning!"

Mitch explains there is a story connected with the inscription: the case was given to him by a girl who is dead now, and she knew she was dying when she gave it. He ignores Stanley's command to return to the game and continues his tête-à-tête. Blanche craves a favor. She has bought a Chinese lantern and asks Mitch to put it over the light bulb. "I can't stand a naked light bulb," she announces, "any more than I can a rude remark or a vulgar action." The impressed Mitch adjusts the lantern on the bulb and asks her more about herself.

"Mitch!" bellows Stanley.

Mitch—*Coming!*

Blanche—Gracious, what lung-power! . . . I teach high school. In Laurel.

Mitch—What do you teach? What subject?

Blanche—Guess!

Mitch—I bet you teach art or music? (Blanche *laughs delicately*.) Of course I could be wrong. You might teach arithmetic.

Blanche—Never arithmetic, sir; never arithmetic! (*With a laugh*.) I don't even know my multiplication tables! No, I have the misfortune of being an English instructor. I attempt to instill a bunch of bobby-soxers and drug-store Romeos with reverence for Hawthorne and Whitman and Poe!

Mitch—I guess that some of them are more interested in other things.

Blanche—How very right you are! Their literary heritage is not what most of them treasure above all else! But they're sweet things! And in the Spring, it's touching to notice them making their first discovery of love! As if nobody had ever known it before! (*The bathroom door opens and* STELLA *comes out.* BLANCHE *continues talking to* MITCH.) Oh! Have you finished? Wait—I'll turn on the radio. (*She turns the knobs on the radio and it begins to play "Wien, Wien, nur du allein."* BLANCHE *waltzes to the music with romantic gestures.* MITCH *is delighted and moves in awkward imitation like a dancing bear.* STANLEY *stalks fiercely through the portieres into the bedroom. He crosses to the small white radio and snatches it off the table. With a shouted oath, he tosses the instrument out the window.*)

STELLA—*Drunk—drunk—animal thing, you!* (*She rushes through to the poker table.*) All of you—please go home! If any of you have one spark of decency in you—

BLANCHE (*wildly*)—Stella, watch out, he's— (STANLEY *charges after* STELLA.)

MEN (*feebly*)—Take it easy, Stanley. Easy, fellow. Let's all—

STELLA—You lay your hands on me and I'll— (*She backs out of sight.* STANLEY *advances and disappears. There is the sound of a blow.* STELLA *cries out.* BLANCHE *screams and runs into the kitchen. The men rush forward and there is grappling and cursing. Something is overturned with a crash.*)

BLANCHE (*shrilly*)—My sister is going to have a baby!

MITCH—This is terrible.

BLANCHE—Lunacy, absolute lunacy!

MITCH—Get him in here, men. (STANLEY *is forced, pinioned by the two men, into the bedroom. He nearly throws them off. Then all at once he subsides and is limp in their grasp. They speak quietly and lovingly to him and he leans his face on one of their shoulders.*)

STELLA (*in a high, unnatural voice, out of sight*)—I want to go away! I want to go away!

MITCH—Poker shouldn't be played in a house with women.

BLANCHE (*rushing into the bedroom*)—I want my sister's clothes! We'll go to that woman's upstairs!

MITCH—Where is the clothes?

BLANCHE (*opening the closet*)—I've got them! (*She rushes through to* STELLA.) Stella, Stella, precious! Dear, dear little sister, don't be afraid! (*With her arms around* STELLA, BLANCHE *guides her to the outside door and upstairs.*)

Stanley, recovering, inquires dully what has happened. "You just blew your top," Mitch informs him. There are various suggestions about wet towels, black coffee and cold showers, but Stanley shakes off his would-be helpers and heads for the bathroom. The guests rush to the poker table, sweep up their money and hasten out . . . and in the bar around the corner somebody is playing "Paper Doll" slow and blue.

After a moment Stanley emerges, dripping water, and still in his clinging wet polka dot drawers. "Stella!". he sobs. "My baby doll's left me!" Still crying, he dials the telephone. "Eunice?" he asks. "I want my baby." He waits a moment, hangs up and dials again. "I'll keep right on ringin' until I talk with my baby," he threatens. An indistinguishable shrill voice is heard from the instrument and he hurls it to the floor. The rooms grow dark, the blue music rises, and the outer walls of the building appear in the night light.

Stanley stumbles, half dressed, to the porch, throws back his head like a baying hound and repeatedly bellows his wife's name. Eunice calls down from her apartment door that Stella isn't coming down, and Stanley continues his bellowing. He even becomes humble, pleading, "Eunice, I want my girl to come down with me"—but Eunice merely slams her door.

He bawls his wife's name again. Somewhere a clarinet moans a low tone. The upstairs door opens again, and Stella slips down the rickety stairs in her robe. They come together with low animal moans; he falls to his knees and presses his face to her belly. Her eyes go blind with tenderness as she catches his head and raises him level with her. He snatches the screen door open, lifts her off her feet and carries her into the dark flat as Blanche slips fearfully down from above, calling, "Where is my little sister?"

She stops before the dark entrance of Stella's home, then, catching her breath as if struck, rushes down to the sidewalk and looks right and left as if for a sanctuary. Mitch appears. "She ran downstairs and went back in there with him," exclaims Blanche.

"Sure she did. . . . They're crazy about each other." Comfortingly, Mitch invites her to sit on the steps and have a cigarette. "Thank you for being so kind! I need kindness now. . . ."

SCENE IV

After a sleepless night at Eunice's, Blanche comes down to find her sister stirring lazily in bed; the table is sloppy with the remains of breakfast and the debris of the poker night, and Stanley's gaudy pajamas lie across the threshold of the bathroom. Stella can't understand Blanche's hysterically tender greeting.

"How could you come back in this place last night?" asks Blanche. "Why, you must have slept with him!"

Stella, getting up in a calm, leisurely way, remarks, "Blanche, I'd forgotten how excitable you are. You're making much too much fuss about this."

It was too bad it happened, she continues—but he was as good as a lamb when she came back. He has always smashed things; on their wedding night here he snatched off one of her slippers and broke all the light bulbs with it—which sort of thrilled her. Now he has taken the radio to be fixed.

In Blanche's opinion, Stella is married to a madman. "Your fix is worse than mine is! . . . I'm going to *do* something. Get hold of myself and make myself a new life!"

She cannot understand that her sister doesn't *want* a new life. "We've got to get hold of some money; that's the way out!" She plans feverishly. There is Shep Huntleigh. . . . She ran into him in Miami last Winter. . . . He had a Cadillac convertible—and oil wells all over Texas. He could do it; he could certainly do it."

"Do what?" queries Stella.

"Why—set us up—in a shop."

She springs to the telephone to call Western Union, then changes her mind and begins writing a message on a piece of Kleenex with an eyebrow pencil: "Darling Shep. Sister and I in desperate situation . . ."

Laughingly, Stella tells her to stop being ridiculous, but Blanche's air of panic becomes more intense. She must find a way out for them, and she cannot understand Stella's calm acceptance of life with Stanley.

"What you are talking about is brutal desire—just—Desire!— the name of that rattletrap streetcar that bangs through the Quarter. . . ."

Stella is unmoved. "I have told you I love him," she asserts.

BLANCHE—Then I *tremble* for you! I just—*tremble*—for you. . . .

STELLA—I can't help your trembling if you insist on trembling! (*There is a pause.*)

BLANCHE—May I—speak—*plainly?*

STELLA—Yes, do. Go ahead. As plainly as you want to. (*Outside, a train approaches. They are silent till the noise subsides. They are both in the bedroom. Under cover of the train's noise* STANLEY *enters from outside. He stands unseen by the women, holding some packages in his arms, and overhears their following conversation.   He wears an undershirt and grease-stained seersucker pants.*)

BLANCHE—Well—if you'll forgive me—he's *common!*

STELLA—Why, yes, I suppose he is.

BLANCHE—Suppose!   You can't have forgotten that much of our bringing up, Stella, that you just *suppose* that any part of a gentleman's in his nature!   *Not one particle, no!*   Oh, if he was just—*ordinary!*   Just *plain*—but good and wholesome, but—*no.* There's something downright—*bestial*—about him!   You're hating me saying this, aren't you?

STELLA (*coldly*)—Go on and say it all, Blanche.

BLANCHE—He acts like an animal, has an animal's habits! Eats like one, moves like one, talks like one!   There's even something—subhuman—something not quite to the stage of humanity yet!   Yes, something—apelike about him, like one of those pictures I've seen in—anthropological studies!   Thousands and thousands of years have passed him right by, and there he is—Stanley Kowalski—survivor of the Stone Age!   Bearing the raw meat home from the kill in the jungle!   And you—*you* here—*waiting* for him!   Maybe he'll strike you or maybe grunt and kiss you! That is, if kisses have been discovered yet!   Night falls and the other apes gather!   There in the front of the cave, all grunting like him, and swilling and gnawing and hulking!   His poker night! —you call it—this party of apes!   Somebody growls—some creature snatches at something—the fight is on!   *God!*   Maybe we are a long way from being made in God's image, but, Stella—my sister—there has been *some* progress since then!   Such things as art—as poetry and music—such kinds of new light have come into the world since then!   In some kinds of people some tenderer feelings have had some little beginning!   That we have got to make *grow!*   And *cling* to, and hold as our flag!   In this dark march toward whatever it is we're approaching . . . *Don't— don't hang back with the brutes!*   (*Another train passes outside.* STANLEY *hesitates, licking his lips.   Then suddenly he turns stealthily about and withdraws through the front door.   The women are still unaware of his presence.   When the train has passed he calls through the closed front door.*)

STANLEY—Hey!   Hey, Stella!

She goes to him at the door, embraces him fiercely.   Over her head he grins through the curtains at Blanche . . . as a piano, trumpet and drums are heard. . . .

SCENE V

Stella is dressing and Blanche, reading a letter she has written, is laughing at herself for being such a liar. "Darling Shep," she quotes, "I am spending the Summer on the wing, making flying visits here and there. And who knows, perhaps I shall take a sudden notion to *swoop* down on *Dallas!* . . . Most of my sister's friends go North in the Summer but some have homes on the Gulf and there has been a continued round of entertainments, teas, cocktails and luncheons—"

There is a racket above—Eunice shouting an accusation at Steve about a blonde, and Steve denying it. There is a clatter of aluminum striking a wall and an angry roar from Steve; there is a crash, then a relative hush. Brightly, Blanche queries, "Did he kill her?"

But Eunice hasn't been killed. She comes down the stairs, announces she is going to call the police, and vanishes around the corner. Blandly, Stella comments, "Some of your sister's friends have stayed in the city."

Stanley, in a green and scarlet silk bowling shirt, trots up the steps and bangs into the kitchen. He reports that Eunice hasn't gone for the police—she's getting a drink at the Four Deuces. When Steve comes down, nursing a bruised forehead and looking for his wife, Stanley informs him of her whereabouts.

"That rutting hunk!" exclaims Steve, as he affects boldness in heading for the saloon.

"I must jot that down in my notebook," says Blanche. "Haha! I'm compiling a notebook of quaint little words and phrases I've picked up here."

"You won't pick up nothing here you ain't heard before," Stanley observes meaningfully. He bangs around the flat, slamming a bureau drawer and throwing shoes in a corner, and Stella goes in and out of the closet. Blanche brightly guesses that her brother-in-law, who is so forceful and dynamic, was born under the sign of Aries, but she's wrong—from the closet Stella informs her Stanley was born the day after Christmas.

"Capricorn—the Goat!"

Blanche informs them *her* birthday is the fifteenth of next month; her sign is Virgo, the Virgin. Stanley accepts this information contemptuously; advancing on Blanche a little, he asks, "Say, do you happen to know somebody named Shaw?"

The effect upon her is one of faint shock. She dampens a handkerchief from a cologne bottle and answers carefully that everybody knows somebody named Shaw.

"Well, this somebody named Shaw is under the impression he met you in Laurel, but I figure he must have got you mixed up with some other party because this other party is someone he met at a hotel called the Flamingo."

Blanche, laughing breathlessly, agrees that this Shaw must have been mistaken, for the Flamingo is not the sort of establishment she'd dare to be seen in. Well, says the thoroughgoing Stanley, Shaw goes in and out of Laurel all the time and can check on it and clear up any mistake. Blanche closes her eyes as if faint.

Everything has been fixed up between Steve and Eunice, for they come home from the Four Deuces arm-in-arm just as Stanley departs for there, telling his wife to come when she's ready. There is a murmur of thunder in the air.

BLANCHE—Stella! What have you heard about me?

STELLA—Huh?

BLANCHE—What have people been telling you about me?

STELLA—Telling?

BLANCHE—You haven't heard any—unkind—gossip about me?

STELLA—Why, no, Blanche, of course not!

BLANCHE—Honey, there was—a good deal of talk in Laurel.

STELLA—About *you,* Blanche?

BLANCHE—I wasn't so good the last two years or so, after Belle Reve had started to slip through my fingers.

STELLA—All of us do things we—

BLANCHE—I never was hard or self-sufficient enough. When people are soft—soft people have got to court the favor of hard ones, Stella. Have got to be seductive—put on soft colors, the colors of butterfly wings, and glow—make a little—temporary magic just in order to pay for—one night's shelter! That's why I've been—not so awf'ly good lately. I've run for protection, Stella, from under one leaky roof to another leaky roof—because it was storm—all storm, and I was—caught in the center. . . . People don't see you—*men* don't—don't even admit your existence unless they are making love to you. And you've got to have your existence admitted by someone, if you're going to have someone's protection. And so the soft people have got to—shimmer and glow—put a—paper lantern over the light. . . . But I'm scared now—awf'ly scared. I don't know how much longer I can turn the trick. It isn't enough to be soft. You've got to be soft *and attractive.* And I—I'm fading now! (*The afternoon has faded to dusk.* STELLA *goes into the bedroom and turns on the light under the paper lantern. She holds a bottled soft drink in her hand.*) Have you been listening to me?

STELLA—I don't listen to you when you are being morbid! (*She advances with the bottled coke.*)

BLANCHE (*with abrupt change to gaiety*)—Is that coke for me?

STELLA—Not for anyone else!

BLANCHE—Why, you precious thing,'you! Is it just coke?

STELLA (*turning*)—You mean you want a shot in it!

BLANCHE—Well, honey, a shot never does a coke any harm! Let me! You mustn't wait on me!

STELLA—I like to wait on you, Blanche. It makes it seem more like home. (*She goes into the kitchen, finds a glass and pours a shot of whiskey into it.*)

BLANCHE—I have to admit I love to be waited on. . . . (*She rushes into the bedroom.* STELLA *goes to her with the glass.* BLANCHE *suddenly clutches* STELLA's *free hand with a moaning sound and presses the hand to her lips.* STELLA *is embarrassed by her show of emotion.* BLANCHE *speaks in a choked voice.*) You're—you're—so *good* to me! And I—

STELLA—Blanche.

BLANCHE—I know, I won't! You hate me to talk sentimental! But, honey, *believe* I feel things more than I *tell* you! I *won't* stay long! I won't, I *promise* I—

STELLA—Blanche!

BLANCHE (*hysterically*)—I won't, I promise. I'll go! Go *soon!* I will *really!* I *won't* hang around until he—throws me out. . . .

STELLA—Now will you stop talking foolish?

With shaking hand Blanche holds a glass while Stella pours the fizzing drink; it spills a bit on her dress and Blanche screams piercingly. Mitch is coming at seven, she explains: "I guess I'm feeling nervous about our relations."

She hasn't told Mitch her age, she goes on, and has given him only one good-night kiss. "I want to *deceive* him enough to make him want me—"

"Do you want *him?*" asks the practical Stella.

"I want to *rest!* I want to breathe quietly again! Yes—I *want* Mitch . . . *very badly!*"

The impatient Stanley returns, a drink under his belt, and hollers outside for his wife and Steve and Eunice. The quartet sets off happily, and Blanche is alone. Dark settles deeper, and the music from the Four Deuces is slow and blue. . . .

There is a knock at the door, Blanche calls "Come in," and a young man does. He is collecting for the paper. No, thanks, he won't take a drink on the job, and if the lady of the house is out he'll come back later.

Coquettishly Blanche delays him, asking for a light, then asking about him. He's going to college—pre-medical. He yearns for the door as Blanche goes on: "Don't you love these long, rainy afternoons in New Orleans when an hour isn't just an hour but a little piece of eternity dropped in our hands?—And who knows what to do with it!"

The piano blues comes up in the background. "Young man! Young, young man! Has anyone ever told you that you look like a young prince out of 'The Arabian Nights'?" He laughs bashfully. "Well, you do, honey lamb! Come here. I want to kiss you just once, softly and sweetly on your mouth." She presses her lips to his lingeringly. "Now run along, now, quickly! It would be nice to keep you, but I've got to be good—and keep my hands off children."

The student stares a moment, then makes his escape just as Mitch comes round the corner with a bunch of roses.

"My Rosenkavalier!" Blanche greets him gaily. "Bow to me first . . . now present them! *Ahhhh—merciiii!*"

Mitch beams at her self-consciously and they depart.

SCENE VI

They come back about 2 A.M. Blanche is exhausted, Mitch stolid but depressed. Evidently they've been to an amusement park, for he is carrying a plaster statuette of Mae West. He is ready to say good night and catch an owl-car over on Bourbon.

"Is that streetcar named Desire still grinding along the tracks at this hour?" asks Blanche.

He asks haltingly for a kiss.

"Why do you always ask me if you may?"

"I don't know whether you want me to or not."

Blanche explains that she's flattered—but a girl alone in the world has to keep a firm hold on her emotions or she'll be lost. "I guess you are used to girls that like to be lost."

"I like you," declares Mitch, "to be exactly the way you are, because in all my—experience—I have never known anyone like you."

She invites him in for a nightcap; they'll not turn on the lights.

and will pretend they are in a little artists' café in Paris. Sending Mitch into the bedroom, she clatters around the kitchen, finding a candle and a bottle with two drinks left, and joins him.

"Je suis la Dame aux Camellias! Vous etes—Armand! Understand French?" Mitch doesn't. *"Voulez-vous coucher avec moi ce soir? Vous ne comprenez pas? Ah, quelle dommage!"*

She takes the reluctant Mitch's alpaca coat, urges him to loosen his collar, skillfully admires his physique and gets him to boasting about his gym prowess at the Athletic Club. Before long she is guessing his weight—wrong—and he tests hers by lifting her at the waist. He fumblingly embraces her, but she is gently reproving; she is playing her cards very carefully.

They talk some about Stanley: Mitch and he were together in the Two Forty-first. No . . . Stanley hasn't talked much about Blanche. He is surprised to be told that Stanley has been very rude to her, and if Stella weren't about to have a baby she couldn't endure things here. Stanley is common—stalks through the rooms in his underwear and has to be told to close the bathroom door. He hates her.

Mitch switches the subject. "How old are you?" he asks. Blanche dissimulates nervously. His mother wanted to know, he explains. "I told my mother how nice you were, and I liked you. . . . She wants me to settle down before she—" He clears his throat and shuffles nervously.

"You will be lonely when she passes on, won't you?" asks Blanche softly. "I understand what that is. I loved someone too, and the person I loved I lost."

He was a boy, she recalls, and she was sixteen, and she discovered love. There was something different about him, a nervousness, a softness and tenderness about him that wasn't like a man's. He had come to her for help, but she didn't know it then —didn't know it until after they had run away and married.

"I didn't know anything except I loved him unendurably but without being able to help him or help myself. Then I found out . . . By coming suddenly into a room that I thought was empty—which wasn't empty, but had two people in it . . . the boy I had married and an older man who had been his friend for years. . . ."

An L & N locomotive is heard approaching and Blanche claps her hands to her ears and crouches. The headlight glares into the room as the engine thunders past. When it has gone Blanche straightens up and resumes her story—and faint in the distance is heard the music of the polka. . . .

"Afterwards we pretended that nothing had been discovered. Yes, the three of us drove out to Moon Lake Casino, very drunk and laughing all the way. We danced the varsoviana.

"Suddenly the boy I had married broke away from me and ran out of the casino. A few moments later—a shot!" The music stops abruptly; then, as Blanche continues her narrative, resumes again, in a major key now.

"I ran out. . . . Then I heard voices say—Allan! Allan! The Grey boy! He'd stuck the revolver into his mouth. . . ." Swaying, and with her face covered, she goes on: "It was because —on the dance floor—unable to stop myself—I'd suddenly said— 'I saw! I know! You disgust me. . . .' And then the search-light which had been turned on the world was turned off again and never for one moment since has there been any light that's stronger than this—kitchen—candle. . . ."

Mitch moves awkwardly toward her, and the volume of the polka increases. "You need somebody," he says tenderly, draw-ing her into his arms. "And I need somebody too. Could it be— you and me, Blanche?"

She stares at him vacantly for a moment, then with a soft cry huddles in his embrace. "Sometimes," she breathes, "there's God —so quickly!"

SCENE VII

It is Blanche's birthday—the 15th of September, and the table has cake and flowers and Stella is finishing up the decorations when Stanley comes home and wants to know what it's all for. Stella tells him about the birthday and Blanche now being in the tub.

"Temperature 100 on the nose and she soaks herself in a hot tub," he snorts. "Set down! I've got the dope on your big sister, Stella."

While Blanche carols a popular tune in the bath, Stanley gets down to what he has learned from reliable sources. "Lie Number One: All this squeamishness she puts on! You should just know the line she's been feeding to Mitch! He thought she had never been more than kissed by a fellow! But Sister Blanche is no lily! Ha-ha!"

The supply man down at the plant, he explains to his disbeliev-ing wife, has been going through Laurel for years and knows all about Blanche.

"She is as famous in Laurel as if she was President of the United States, only she is not respected by any party!" The supply man stops at the Flamingo—and that is where Blanche stayed after Belle Reve slipped through her fingers. "But even the management of the Flamingo was impressed by Dame Blanche! In fact, they was so impressed by Dame Blanche that they requested her to turn in her room key—for permanently!"

Blanche continues her song in the bath; her sister refuses to believe Stanley, but he insists he has made a thorough check. "And as time went by," he goes on, "she became a town character. Regarded as not just different but downright loco—nuts. . . . That's why she's here this Summer, visiting royalty, putting on all this act—because she's practically told by the mayor to get out of town.

"Yes, did you know there was an army camp near Laurel and your sister's was one of the places called 'Out of Bounds'?"

Stella doesn't want to hear any more—but she does. Lie Number Two: Blanche hasn't resigned from school; she has been kicked out before the end of the term. "A seventeen-year-old boy she'd gotten mixed up with!"

Stella is almost ill now. Her sister opens the bathroom door and asks for a towel to dry her hair; Stella dazedly gets one. Then, not yet believing all she has heard, she tells Stanley about Blanche's early marriage and the tragedy which followed it. Rather gently he takes his wife by the shoulders, but she pulls away and continues putting candles on the cake.

"Company expected?" he asks.

"We asked Mitch to come over for cake and ice cream."

"I wouldn't be expecting Mitch over tonight."

It dawns on Stella that Stanley has told Mitch what he just told her; after all, they were buddies in the war. "Is Mitch through with her?" she asks.

"No, I don't think he's necessarily through with her—just wised up! He's not going to marry her. Maybe he *was*, but he's not going to jump into a tank with a school of sharks." He hollers for Blanche to leave the bathroom.

"She's not stayin' here after Tuesday," he continues. "Just to make sure I bought her ticket myself. A bus ticket!"

Blanche finally emerges with a gay peal of laughter, but as Stanley passes her a frightened look appears in her face. She begins brushing her hair, exclaiming that she feels so good after her long, hot bath. Stella, in the kitchen, answers sadly and doubtfully, "Do you, Blanche?"

Slowly the hair-brushing stops. "Something has happened! What is it?"

"Why, nothing has happened, Blanche."

"You're lying! Something has!" She stares fearfully at her sister, who pretends to be busy at the table. At the Four Deuces the piano goes into a hectic breakdown. . . .

SCENE VIII

Three-quarters of an hour later, with a golden dusk falling, Stanley, Stella and Blanche are completing a dismal birthday supper. The fourth place at the table is vacant and Blanche has a tight, artificial smile on her drawn face. Forcedly, to liven things up, she attempts to tell a funny story—an old one to Stanley, and badly told.

"Apparently Mr. Kowalski was not amused," admits Blanche.

"Mr. Kowalski," replies his wife, "is too busy making a pig of himself to think of anything else! . . . Your face and fingers are disgustingly greasy. Go and wash up and help me clear the table."

Stanley begins to clear the table by hurling a plate to the floor. His fury rising, he throws more dishes. "Don't ever talk that way to me! 'Pig—Polack—disgusting—vulgar—greasy!'—them kind of words have been on your tongue and your sister's too much around here!" Stella begins to weep and her husband stalks out on the porch.

Blanche suspects that Stanley has told something about her to Mitch, and goes to the bedroom to phone Mitch while Stella goes out on the porch and stares reproachfully at her husband. Somebody at Mitch's number says he isn't in, and Blanche leaves a message for him to call—it's very important. She remains by the phone with a lost, frightened look as Stanley clumsily takes his wife in his arms. "Stell, it's gonna be all right after she goes and after you've had the baby." They go back in and Stella lights the candles on the cake as Blanche returns from the bedroom.

The telephone rings—but Stanley takes it and it isn't for Blanche. It's Mac, about a bowling date. When he has this fixed up he comes back and announces, "Sister Blanche, I've got a little birthday remembrance for you. . . . Ticket! Back to Laurel! On the Greyhound! Tuesday!"

The music of the varsoviana steals in softly and continues playing. Blanche tries to smile, then tries to laugh, finally runs to the bathroom where coughing, gagging sounds are heard.

"You needn't have been so cruel to someone alone as she is,' reproaches Stella. Stanley, unmoved, changes into his bowling shirt.

"When we first met, me and you," he declares, "you thought I was common. How right you was, baby. I was common as dirt. You showed me the snapshot of the place with the columns. I pulled you down off them columns and how you loved it, having them colored lights going! And wasn't we happy together, wasn't it all okay till she showed here?"

An odd look which Stanley doesn't notice comes over Stella's face. She begins a slow, shuffling progress from the bedroom to the kitchen, leaning and resting on whatever she can touch. Quietly she tells him, "Take me to the hospital."

Supporting her, murmuring indistinguishably, he leads her outside. The varsoviana is heard, rising with sinister rapidity, as Blanche comes out of the bath twisting a washcloth and whispering the words of the song: *"El pan de mais, el pan de mais . . ."* The light fades. . . .

SCENE IX

Some time has passed. Blanche is hunched in a bedroom chair in her scarlet satin robe. There is a bottle of liquor near her, and the tune of the rapid, feverish polka still is heard. The music is in her mind. There is a ring at the door: "Me. Mitch."

Frantically, Blanche hides the bottle, dabs her face with cologne and powder, then lets him in. "Hello, beautiful!" She offers him her lips, but he pushes past her. He rejects her forced coquettishness, declines a drink.

"Something's the matter tonight," says Blanche. "But never mind. I won't cross-examine the witness. I'll just—"

She touches her forehead vaguely. The polka starts up again.

"—pretend I don't notice anything different about you! That —music again. . . ."

"What music?" asks Mitch.

"The varsoviana. The polka tune they were playing when Allan —wait!"

A distant revolver shot is heard.

"There now, the shot! It always stops after that. . . . Yes, now it's stopped."

"Are you boxed out of your mind?" inquires Mitch.

Blanche retrieves the liquor from the closet, saying, "We've had so much excitement around here this evening that I *am* boxed out of my mind!" Mitch warns her to lay off Stan's liquor. "He says you been lapping it up all Summer like a wildcat!" He now observes that it is dark in here. "I don't think I ever seen you in the light. That's a fact!" Over Blanche's frightened protests he snatches the Chinese lantern off the light bulb, turns the switch and stares at her as she cries and covers her face. Slowly and bitterly he declares:

"I don't mind you being older than what I thought. But all the rest of it—Christ! That pitch about your ideals being so old-fashioned and all that malarkey that you've dished out all Summer."

He didn't want to believe Stanley, he goes on, but he checked with the traveling man at the plant and with a merchant in Laurel on the phone. "Didn't you," he pursues, "stay at a hotel called the Flamingo?"

Blanche cries, "I stayed at a hotel called the Tarantula Arms. . . . Yes, a big spider. That's where I brought my victims." She pours herself a drink. "Yes, I had many intimacies with strangers. After the death of Allan—intimacies with strangers was all I seemed able to fill my empty heart with. . . ."

Laughing and sobbing convulsively, she tells Mitch everything —about the seventeen-year-old boy in school, and about her hope in Mitch. "You said you needed somebody. Well, I needed somebody too. I thanked God for you, because you seemed to be gentle—a cleft in the rock of the world that I could hide in!"

Dumbly staring, Mitch accuses, "You lied to me, Blanche."

BLANCHE—Never inside, I didn't lie in my heart. . . . (*A* VENDOR *comes around the corner. She is a blind Mexican woman in a dark shawl, carrying bunches of those gaudy tin flowers that lower-class Mexicans display at funerals and other festive occasions. She is calling barely audibly. Her figure is only faintly visible outside the building.*)

MEXICAN WOMAN—*Flores. Flores. Flores para los muertos. Flores. Flores.*

BLANCHE—What? Oh! Somebody outside . . . I—I lived in a house where dying old women remembered their dead men. . . .

MEXICAN WOMAN—*Flores. Flores para los muertos. . . .* (*The polka tune fades in.*)

BLANCHE (*as if to herself*)—Crumble and fade and—regrets— recriminations. . . . "If you'd done this, it wouldn't've cost me that!"

MEXICAN WOMAN—*Corones para los muertos. Corones . .*

BLANCHE—Legacies! Huh. . . . And other things such as bloodstained pillow-slips—"Her linen needs changing"—"Yes, Mother. But couldn't we get a colored girl to do it?" No, we couldn't, of course. Everything gone but the—

MEXICAN WOMAN—*Flores.*

BLANCHE—Death—I used to sit here and she used to sit over there and death was as close as you are. . . . We didn't dare even admit we had ever heard of it!

MEXICAN WOMAN—*Flores para los muertos, flores—flores.* . . .

BLANCHE—The opposite is desire. So do you wonder? How could you possibly wonder! Not far from Belle Reve, before we had lost Belle Reve, was a camp where they trained young soldiers. On Saturday nights they would go in town to get drunk—

MEXICAN WOMAN (*softly*)—*Corones* . . .

BLANCHE—And on the way back they would stagger onto my lawn and call—"Blanche! Blanche!"—The deaf old lady remaining suspected nothing. But sometimes I slipped outside to answer their calls. . . . Later the paddy-wagon would gather them up like daisies . . . the long way home. . . . (*The* MEXICAN WOMAN *turns slowly and drifts back off with her soft mournful cries.* BLANCHE *goes to the dresser and leans forward on it. After a moment,* MITCH *rises and follows her purposefully. The polka music fades away. He places his hands on her waist and tries to turn her about.*)

BLANCHE—What do you want?

MITCH (*fumbling to embrace her*)—What I been missing all Summer.

BLANCHE—Then marry me, Mitch!

MITCH—I don't think I want to marry you any more.

BLANCHE—No?

MITCH (*dropping his hands from her waist*)—You're not clean enough to bring in the house with my mother.

BLANCHE—Go away, then. (*He stares at her.*) Get out of here quick before I start screaming fire! (*Her throat is tightening with hysteria.*) Get out of here quick before I start screaming fire! (*He still remains staring. She suddenly rushes to the big window with its pale blue square of the soft Summer light and cries wildly.*) Fire! Fire! Fire! (*With a startled gasp,* MITCH *turns and goes out the outer door, clatters awkwardly down the steps and around the corner of the building.* BLANCHE *staggers back from the window and falls to her knees. The distant piano is slow and blue.*)

SCENE X

After a few hours of fairly steady drinking since Mitch left, Blanche has reached a mood of hysterical exhilaration. She has dragged her wardrobe trunk to the center of the bedroom, strewn flowery dresses over it, and has decked herself out in a somewhat soiled and crumpled white satin evening gown. Now she is placing the rhinestone tiara on her head before the mirror and is murmuring excitedly as if to a group of spectral admirers:

"How about taking a swim, a moonlight swim at the old rock quarry? If anyone's sober enough to drive a car . . ."

Tremblingly she lifts a hand mirror for a closer inspection, catches her breath and slams down the mirror so violently it cracks. There is honky-tonk music from the Four Deuces, and Stanley comes home from the hospital, still in his bowling shirt. He informs Blanche that Stella is doing okay; the baby won't arrive before morning and they've told him to go home and get a little shut-eye.

"Does that mean we are to be alone in here?"

"Yep. Just me and you, Blanche. Unless you got somebody hid under the bed. What've you got on those fine feathers for?"

Oh, Blanche explains, after he left she got a wire. A telegram from an old admirer inviting her for a Caribbean cruise on a yacht. Shep Huntleigh.

Stanley removes his shirt, rips the sack from a quart beer bottle, can't find an opener, pounds the cap on the corner of the table. A geyser of foam shoots up and Stanley, laughing happily, exclaims, "Ha-ha! Rain from heaven! Shall we bury the hatchet and make it a loving-cup, huh?" After all, it's a red-letter night for them both—Blanche having an oil millionaire and him having a baby.

She draws back, declining the beer, and Stanley roots in the bottom drawer of the dresser until he finds a brilliant pair of silk pajamas—the ones he wore on his wedding night. "Here's something I always break out on special occasions. . . . When the telephone rings and they say 'You've got a son,' I'll tear this off and wave it like a flag!"

Blanche babbles on about her own good fortune—how divine it will be to have privacy once more. Her man from Dallas is a gentleman and respects her, and a cultivated woman, a woman of intelligence and breeding, can enrich his life immeasurably. She has been foolish, casting her pearls before swine—meaning Stanley and his friend Mr. Mitchell.

"He came to see me tonight," she relates. "He dared to come here in his work clothes! And to repeat slander to me, vicious stories that he had gotten from you! I gave him his walking papers. . . ."

But he came back, she goes on, with a box of roses. He implored forgiveness, but she spurned him.

Stanley gets curious about when all this happened; was it before or after the telegram came? As a matter of fact, he decides, there wasn't no wire at all, and there isn't no millionaire, and Mitch didn't come back. "There isn't a goddamn thing but imagination!"

Warmed up now, Stanley pours it into Blanche. Look at her in her worn-out Mardi-Gras outfit, rented from some ragpicker! "I've been on to you from the start!" He goes into the bathroom.

Lurid reflections appear on the walls around Blanche. Catching her breath, she jiggles the hook of the telephone. Operator, operator, operator! Mr. Shep Huntleigh of Dallas. He's so well known he doesn't require any address. No, she can't find it right now. Hold on, please. . . .

Warily Blanche crosses into the kitchen. The night is filled with inhuman voices, like cries in a jungle. The back walls of the room have become transparent and the sidewalk outside can be seen. A prostitute has just rolled a drunkard, and he pursues her. A policeman's whistle sounds and the figures disappear. Some moments later the Negro woman whom Blanche saw when she first arrived rounds the corner, rooting excitedly in the sequined bag the prostitute has dropped. Blanche, pressing knuckles to lips, returns to the phone.

Now she gets Western Union. "Take down this message! 'In desperate, desperate circumstances! Help me! Caught in a trap. Caught in—' Oh!"

Stanley has come out of the bathroom in his silk pajamas. Deliberately he puts the phone back on the hook and stands between her and the outer door. "Let me get by!" she gasps. "I've got to get out somehow!"

Stanley laughs. "You think I'll interfere with you?" He has stood aside a bit; the blue piano goes softly, and the inhuman jungle voices rise up. Stanley is struck by a new idea. Softly, as he steps toward her, he says:

"Come to think of it, maybe you wouldn't be bad to—interfere with. . . ."

Blanche moves backward through the door to the bedroom,

smashes a bottle on the table and faces him, clutching the broken top.

"Oh, so you want some rough-house!" growls Stanley. "All right, let's have some rough-house!" He springs toward her, over-turning the table and catching her wrist as she strikes at him with the bottle top. "Tiger—tiger! Drop that bottle top! Drop it! We've had this date with each other from the beginning!"

Blanche, moaning, sinks to her knees. Stanley carries her to the bed as the trumpet and hot drums in the Four Deuces sound loudly. . . .

SCENE XI

It is some weeks later, and another of Stanley's poker nights, just like the last fateful one—Stanley, Pablo, Mitch and Steve playing, and Stanley boasting about his luck. In the bedroom, Stella is packing Blanche's trunk as Eunice comes through, bring-ing some grapes and reporting that the baby is sleeping like a little angel upstairs.

Blanche is bathing. "What did you tell her?" asks Eunice.

"I—just told her that—we'd made arrangements for her to rest in the country," replies Stella. "She's got it mixed in her mind with Shep Huntleigh."

From the bathroom Blanche calls that if there's a phone call for her she will call right back . . . and she'd like the yellow silk dress, and the turquoise pin, and a bunch of artificial violets.

"I don't know if I did the right thing," Stella continues to her friend. "I couldn't believe her story and go on living with Stanley."

Blanche appears. She has a tragic radiance in her red satin robe. The varsoviana rises audibly as she enters the bedroom. Did she get a call from Shep Huntleigh? Not yet.

In the kitchen the poker game continues, but at the sound of Blanche's voice Mitch drops an arm and his gaze dissolves into space. "Hey, Mitch, come to!" Stanley commands.

At the sound of his voice, Blanche is shocked. With sudden hysteria she demands what is going on; Stanley pushes back his chair to rise, but Steve places a restraining hand on his arm. Stella and Eunice try to quiet Blanche who cries, "Why are you looking at me like that? Is something wrong with me?" They assure her she looks wonderful.

"I understand you are going on a trip," prompts Eunice.

"Yes, Blanche *is*," replies Stella. "She's going on a vacation."

Feverishly Blanche dresses, then announces, "Well, I'm ready to go."

"She's going to walk out before they get here," Eunice warns in a whisper. Stella persuades her sister to wait until the game breaks up in the other room, and she lets them push her into a chair. "I can smell the sea air," she exclaims. "The rest of my time I'm going to spend on the sea. . . ."

As she contemplates this pleasant future, a doctor and a matron climb the porch steps and the doctor rings. Eunice goes casually to see who it is, and Blanche wonders if it is for her. It *is* someone for her, Eunice announces on returning. Faintly the varsoviana is heard again. "Is it the gentleman I was expecting from Dallas?"

Eunice thinks it is. They're waiting in front of the house.

"They! Who's 'they'?"

There's a lady with him, Eunice explains. A lady in a sort of a plain tailored outfit.

"Shall we go, Blanche?" urges Stella. "I will go with you."

Blanche moves fearfully to the portieres and Eunice draws them open. To the card players Blanche says, "Please don't get up. I'm only passing through." She steps onto the porch and catches her breath as she encounters the doctor.

"You are not the gentleman I was expecting." She starts back up the steps, whispering to Stella, "That man isn't Shep Huntleigh." The polka music continues in the distance. She slips back into the flat with a peculiar smile and wide and brilliant eyes. The doctor and matron follow her in; outside, Stella closes her eyes and clenches her hands, and Eunice gives her a comforting embrace.

Blanche rushes into the bedroom, shrilly explaining to Stanley that she forgot something. Again those reflections appear on the walls, and the music and the jungle cries are weirdly distorted. The matron advances on one side, Stanley on the other. "Now, Blanche, now, Blanche," soothes the matron—but Blanche screams and tries to break past her.

The men in the kitchen spring to their feet as Stella flees again to the porch, with Eunice following. "Oh, my God, Eunice; help me!" she begs. "Don't let them do that to her; don't let them hurt her. . . ." Gently Eunice holds her, tells her she has done the right thing—the only thing she could do. Inside, Stanley tells the doctor he'd better go into the bedroom.

Mitch has started there too, but Stanley blocks him. "You!" cries Mitch wildly. "You done this; all o' your goddamn rutting with things you— I'll kill you!" He lunges to strike at Stanley, but Steve restrains him and Mitch collapses at the table, sobbing.

In the bedroom, the matron has caught Blanche's arm and prevented flight. Blanche scratches wildly, and the matron pins her arms. Blanche slips to her knees.

"Jacket, doctor?" asks the matron.

"Not unless necessary." He takes off his hat; his voice is gentle and reassuring as he crouches in front of Blanche and addresses her, "Miss DuBois."

Her terror subsides a little and the lurid reflections fade from the walls. She stares at him with desperate pleading, and he smiles. "Ask her to let go of me," begs Blanche.

"Let go," orders the doctor. He draws her up gently, supports her with his arm and leads her through the portieres. Blanche, holding tight to his arm, says, "Whoever you are—I have always depended on the kindness of strangers."

As they leave the house, Stella, a few steps up toward Eunice's flat, sobs her sister's name. Blanche walks on without turning, followed by the doctor and the matron. Eunice comes down from above and gives Stella her baby. In the kitchen, the men return silently to their places about the table—except Stanley.

Stanley goes to the porch, looks up at his wife. "Stella?" he asks uncertainly. She sobs with inhuman abandon. "Now, honey. Now, love. Now, now, love," he soothes. He kneels beside her and his fingers find the opening of her blouse. Her sobs and his murmurs fade, and the music of the blue piano and the trumpet comes up as Steve, at the table, announces: "This game is seven-card stud."

THE CURTAIN FALLS

MISTER ROBERTS

A Play in Two Acts

By Thomas Heggen and Joshua Logan

IT is likely that a great many people were struck with the theatrical possibilities of Thomas Heggen's novel about war in the Pacific, "Mister Roberts." One of them was Leland Hayward, Hollywood literary agent who has become a stage producer, and Mr. Hayward acquired the dramatic rights. Another was Joshua Logan, a top-ranking director, who read the book on a vacation in Cuba and was enchanted by it.

Logan wanted to make "Mister Roberts" into a play as well as direct it. After a talk with the willing Hayward, it was decided that Heggen, too, have a hand in the dramatization. After all, the book was his; it was he who had spent three of his four years in the Navy on sea duty, and knew whereof he had written. Logan's war service was of a different variety—as a captain in the Air Forces Combat Intelligence.

Of all the season's successes, none was as completely assured beforehand as "Mister Roberts," unless it was "Allegro," which had had quantities of pre-opening publicity and an immense advance sale. The Logan-Heggen play was a hit long before it opened, and after the premiere the critics were unanimous and enthusiastic in their approval of the play itself and of the skill with which it was staged and acted.

The main setting is the amidships section of a Navy cargo ship, the *AK 601*. Dominating center stage is a covered hatch, and rising behind it is the house; one is looking aft, and at the sides of the house are passageways leading to the after part of the ship. Over the passageways are 20 mm. gun tubs, with ladders leading to them. There is an opening in the hatch cover leading to the crew's compartment below. In the center of the house is the crew's compartment below. In the center of the house is the door to the Captain's cabin, and the pilothouse and flying bridge are indicated above.

The only object which differentiates this ship from any other Navy cargo vessel is a small, scrawny palm tree, potted in a five-gallon can, beside the Captain's door. Painted in large white letters on the can is the legend, "PROP.T OF CAPTAIN, KEEP AWAY." It is dawn and most of the men are sleeping when Chief Johnson, about 40, clad in dungaree shirt and pants and a chief petty officer's cap, comes forward along a passageway and starts below. He is obviously chewing tobacco. He notices the palm tree, cautiously crosses to the Captain's door, peers into the porthole to see that he is not being watched, then deliberately spits tobacco into the tree container. Then he goes below, whistles shrilly and chants, "Reveille. . . . Hit the deck. . . . Greet the new day. . . . Reveille. . . ."

"Okay, Chief, you done your duty," someone calls. "Now get your big fat can out of here!" Someone else says, "Thanks, Chief. Now go back to bed and stop bothering us." Duty done, Johnson shuffles up to the deck and disappears aft; there is a sound of snoring below. After a moment Lieutenant (junior grade) Roberts comes along a passageway wearing khaki and an officer's cap. He carries a rumpled piece of writing paper on which much work has been done and a good bit scratched out. Getting a new idea, he sits on the hatch cover and begins writing as Doc joins him.

Doc is 35 or 40, also in khaki; he is a lieutenant (senior grade). A stethoscope sticks out of his hip pocket. Wiping sweat off his neck with a handkerchief, he greets Roberts with "That you, Doug?"

"Hello, Doc," is the weary reply. "What are you doing up?"

"I heard you were working cargo today so I thought I'd get ready. On days when there's any work to be done I can always count on a big turnout at sick call. . . . I attract some very rare diseases on cargo days. That day they knew you were going to load five ships I was greeted by six more cases of beriberi—double beriberi this time. So help me, I'm going down to the ship's library and throw that old copy of *Moby Dick* overboard!"

Doc senses there is something wrong with the preoccupied Roberts, but the young man denies it. Doc is skeptical of the denial and Roberts at length confesses, "I've been up all night, Doc. I saw something last night when I was on watch that just about knocked me out."

Doc voices alarm.

"I was up on the bridge," Roberts continues. "I was just standing there looking out to sea. I couldn't bear to look at that island any more. All of a sudden I noticed something. Little black

specks crawling over the horizon. I looked through the glasses
and it was a formation of our ships that stretched out for miles!
Carriers and battleships and cans—a whole task force, Doc!"

Doc protests that Roberts should have broken him out—he's
never seen a battleship. Dreamily but urgently, his companion
declares, "I thought I was on those bridges—I thought I was
riding West across the Pacific. . . . And then I looked down
from our bridge and saw our Captain's palm tree! . . . The Admiral John J. Finchley award for delivering more toothpaste and
toilet paper than any other Navy cargo ship in the safe area of
the Pacific. Read this, Doc—see how it sounds."

It is another application for a transfer—a stronger wording
this time, telling the Bureau of Naval Personnel that the appli-
cant, having served two years and four months aboard this vessel as cargo officer, feels that his continued service aboard will
only reduce his usefulness and increase disharmony. Duty aboard
a destroyer is preferred.

It's an old story to Doc. There has been one of these letters
a week, and the Captain always disapproves of them before for-
warding them. Doug might as well face the fact that he is stuck
on this old bucket, thinks the medical officer—but Roberts won't
give up hope.

Dowdy, 35 or 40, in dungarees, hard-bitten, comes up from the
hatchway and informs Roberts the men are getting up. "The
poor punch-drunk bastards! Mister Roberts, when are you going to the Captain again and ask him to give this crew a liberty?
These guys ain't been off the ship for over a year except on duty."

Roberts *did* ask the Captain, last night—and the Captain said
"No." He hands Dowdy his letter, orders him to have Dolan
type it up and then bring a couple of men aft. He goes aft himself.

The door to the cabin opens and the Captain, in pajamas,
bathrobe and officer's cap, waters his palm tree from an oil can,
looks at it tenderly and goes back in.

Dowdy has got men moving below. Yawning, buttoning pants,
tucking in shirts and all comatose, Schlemmer, Insigna, Stefanowski, Mannion, Wiley, Reber and Lindstrom hit the deck.
Dowdy gives some of them scrapers and wire brushes, orders them
to attack a rust patch. Insigna is detailed to cleaning four pairs
of binoculars and a spy glass. The work is only a little more
desultory than the conversation.

Insigna notices a new building on the island. Taking the spy glass, he calls, "Hey, Stefanowski!   Which end of this do you look through?"

"It's optional, Sam," is the reply.   "Depends on what size eyeball you got."

Insigna trains the spy glass on the island and exclaims that the Japs must have taken it, for there's a red and white flag on the new building.   "Japs!" snorts Mannion.   "We never been within five thousand miles of a Jap!"   Mannion informs Insigna that it's a hospital flag.

Insigna, who has kept on looking, suddenly rises, gasping.   "Oh, my God!   She's bare-assed!" he exclaims.   A *she* taking a shower. Instantly the others grab binoculars and focus on the hospital. Stefanowski discovers another one by the washbasin taking a shampoo.   "Yeah," says Insigna indignantly, "but why the hell don't she take her bathrobe off?   That's a stupid goddamn way to take a shampoo!"

"What's the red mark she's got . . . there?" asks Mannion about the one in the shower.   A birthmark, he is informed.   He won't believe it.   She just sat in some red paint.

The men agree that the girls are beautiful—twins, maybe; but when the girls vacate the shower the men find holding the glasses wearying.   Stefanowski suggests that they take turns watching, with Mannion on the first watch.

Insigna doesn't like Mannion and now states that he doesn't trust him.   There is a noise from the cabin and Stefanowski cries, "Flash Red!"   The men immediately begin working in earnest as the Captain, now in khaki, enters and satisfies himself that they are working.   All but Mannion, who, intent with his glasses, hasn't noticed the Captain.   The officer watches him suspiciously for a moment, then takes the ladder to the bridge.   "Flash White!" is the call.

"Hey, Mannion.   Anyone in there yet?"

MANNION (*watching something happily through glasses*)—No, not yet!

INSIGNA (*picks up spy glass and looks, and rises quickly*)— Why, you dirty, miserable cheat!   (*Instantly all the men are at the glasses.*)

LINDSTROM—There's one in there again!

STEFANOWSKI—The hell with her—she's already got her clothes on!

INSIGNA—And there she goes! (*Slowly lowers his glass, turning to* MANNION *threateningly.*) Why, you lousy, cheating crud!

MANNION (*idly swinging his glasses*)—That ain't all. I seen three!

STEFANOWSKI—You lowdown Peeping Tom!

LINDSTROM (*hurt*)—Mannion, that's a real dirty trick.

INSIGNA—What's the big idea?

MANNION—Who wants to know?

INSIGNA—*I* want to know! And you're damn well going to tell me!

MANNION—You loud-mouthed little bastard! Why don't you make me?

INSIGNA—You're damn right I will. Right now! (*He swings on* MANNION *as* LINDSTROM *steps clumsily between them.*)

LINDSTROM—Hey, fellows! Fellows!

INSIGNA—No wonder you ain't got a friend on this ship . . . except this crud, Wiley. (*He jerks his head in direction of* WILEY, *who stands behind him on hatch cover.* WILEY *takes him by shoulder and whirls him around.*)

WILEY—What'd you say?

STEFANOWSKI (*shoving* WILEY)—You heard him! (MANNION *jumps on the hatch cover to protect* WILEY *from* STEFANOWSKI. INSIGNA *rushes at* MANNION *and for a moment they are all in a clinch.* LINDSTROM *plows up on the hatch and breaks them apart. The men have suddenly formed into two camps—*MANNION *and* WILEY *on one side,* INSIGNA *and* STEFANOWSKI *facing them.* LINDSTROM *is just an accessory, but stands prepared to intervene if necessary.*)

MANNION (*to* WILEY)—Look at them two! Everybody on the ship hates their guts. The two moochingest, no-good loud-mouths on the ship! (STEFANOWSKI *starts for* MANNION *but* INSIGNA *pulls him back and steps menacingly toward* MANNION.)

INSIGNA—Why, you slimy, lying son-of-a-bitch! (*Suddenly* MANNION *hits* INSIGNA, *knocking him down. He jumps on* INSIGNA *who catches* MANNION *in the chest with his feet and hurls him back.* WILEY *and* STEFANOWSKI *start fighting with* LINDSTROM, *attempting to break them apart.* MANNION *rushes back at* INSIGNA. INSIGNA *sidesteps* MANNION'S *lunge and knocks him to the deck.* INSIGNA *falls on him. They wrestle to their feet and stand slugging. At this point* ROBERTS *and* DOWDY *run on from the passageway.* ROBERTS *flings* INSIGNA *and* MANNION *apart.* DOWDY *separates the others.*)

ROBERTS—Break it up! Break it up, I tell you! (INSIGNA *and* MANNION *rush at each other.* ROBERTS *and* DOWDY *stop them.*)

DOWDY—Goddamn you guys, break it up!

Insigna and Mannion continue to curse and snarl at each other, until Roberts sends Mannion with a detail to work on the Number Two hatch and Insigna up to the bow to clean the glasses.

Dowdy confides that he had to stop three fights down in the compartment last night. "They've got to have a liberty, Mister Roberts," he pleads.

"They sure do," agrees the lieutenant. "Call a boat for me, will you? I'm going ashore."

"Are you going over the Captain's head?"

"No, I'm going around his end—I hope."

Fade Out

During the darkness voices can be heard over the squawk box issuing orders with a "Now hear this . . . now hear this." Then a voice informs, "Because in violation of the Captain's orders a man has appeared on deck without a shirt on, there will be no movies again tonight—by order of the Captain."

When the lights come up they reveal the stateroom shared by Ensign Pulver and Roberts. There are a double bunk, two lockers, a desk, a washbasin and a medicine chest. An officer has his head inside Roberts' locker and is throwing shirts over his shoulder as he looks for something. Dolan, entering, thinks it is Roberts, and says, "Here's your letter, Mister Roberts."

But the man in the locker is Pulver. He explains he is looking for a shoe box and somebody must have stolen it. No, Mister Roberts hasn't come back from the island yet.

Dolan gives Pulver the letter and the ensign begins reading it as Dolan vanishes. Obviously the letter has dismayed the ensign, and when he hears Roberts and Doc talking outside he hides it under a blanket in his bunk.

"Hey, Frank," says the incoming Roberts, "has Dolan been in here yet with my letter?"

Innocently Pulver replies, "I don't know, Doug boy. I just came in here myself."

Doc wants to know what Roberts has been up to on the island, and the young lieutenant elucidates. The Port Director—the guy who decides where to send the ship next—used to drink a quart

of whiskey every day, so Roberts thought it would be nice to
give the Port Director a bottle of Scotch—"compliments of the
Captain." It was the quart he had been saving in the shoe box.

"Oh, my God! It's really gone!" mourns Pulver, sinking to a
bunk.

Furthermore, it hasn't done any good. The Port Director took
it from Roberts and then said, "Don't bother me, I'm busy."

Pulver's dejection increases; he hints that he was planning to
give the liquor to a woman. Doc and Roberts notice the bunk
has been decorated with two fancy souvenir pillows. They worm
out of him the news that eighteen nurses flew in last night to the
hospital—all brunettes except two beautiful blonde twins, on one
of whom Pulver is now working. He has asked her out to the
ship for lunch, offering as bait a good stiff drink of Scotch.

"Doc, let's *make* some Scotch," suggests Roberts.

Doc—Huh?

Roberts—As naval officers we're supposed to be resourceful.
Frank here's got a great opportunity and I've let him down. Let's
fix him up!

Doc—Right! (*He goes to desk.* Roberts *begins removing
bottles from medicine chest.*) Frank, where's the rest of that alcohol we were drinking last night?

Pulver (*pulling a large vinegar bottle half filled with colorless
liquid from the wastebasket and handing it to* Doc)—Hell, that
ain't even the right color.

Doc (*taking the bottle*)—Quiet! (*Thinks deeply.*) Color
. . . (*With sudden decision.*) Coca-Cola! Have you got any?

Roberts—I haven't seen a Coke in four months—no, by God
it's five months!

Pulver—Oh, what the hell! (*He rises, crosses to bunk,
reaches under the mattress of the top bunk and produces a bottle
of Coca-Cola. The others watch him.* Doc *snatches the bottle.*
Pulver *says apologetically:*) I forgot I had it.

Doc (*opening the bottle and about to pour the Coca-Cola into
the vinegar bottle when he stops*)—Oh—what shade would you
like? Cutty Sark . . . Haig and Haig . . . Vat 69 . . .

Pulver (*interested*)—I told her Johnny Walker.

Doc—Johnny Walker it is! (*He pours some of the Coke into
the bottle.*)

Roberts (*looking at the color of the mixture*)—Johnny Walker
Red Label!

Doc—Red Label!

PULVER—It may look like it—but it won't taste like it!

ROBERTS—Doc, what does Scotch taste like?

DOC—Well, it's a little like . . . uh . . . it tastes like . . .

ROBERTS—Do you know what it's always tasted a little like to me? Iodine.

DOC (*shrugs as if to say "Of course" and rises. He takes a dropper from a small bottle of iodine and flicks a drop into the bottle*)—One drop of iodine—for taste. (*Shakes the bottle and pours some in glass.*)

PULVER—Lemme taste her, Doc!

DOC (*stops him with a gesture*)—No. This calls for a medical opinion. (*Takes a ceremonial taste while the others wait for his verdict.*)

PULVER—How about it?

DOC—We're on the right track! (*Sets glass down. Rubs hands professionally.*) Now we need a little something extra—for age! What've you got there, Doug?

ROBERTS (*reading labels of bottles on desk*)—Bromo-Seltzer . . . Wildroot Wave Set . . . Eno Fruit Salts . . . Kreml Hair Tonic . . .

DOC—Kreml! It has a coal-tar base! And it'll age the hell out of it! (*Pours a bit of Kreml into the mixture. Shakes the bottle solemnly.*) One drop Kreml for age. (*Sets bottle on desk and looks at wrist watch for a fraction of a second.*) That's it! (DOC *pours drink into glass.* PULVER *reaches for it.* ROBERTS *pushes his arm aside and tastes it.*)

ROBERTS—By God, it does taste a little like Scotch! (PULVER *again reaches for glass.* DOC *pushes his arm aside and takes a drink.*)

DOC—By God, it does!

PULVER (*finally getting the glass and taking a quick sip*)—It's delicious. That dumb little blonde won't know the difference.

Pulver is deeply grateful, and Roberts allows that he almost deserves such kindness—almost. He (Pulver) is the most hapless, lazy, disorganized, lecherous person Roberts has ever known. He never finishes anything he starts, sleeps sixteen hours a day, is scared of the Captain. He is always plotting against the Captain but never carries anything out.

Pulver strives to defend himself against this semi-serious tirade. He still is working on his scheme to plug up the line of the Captain's sanitary system; he thought about it for half an hour yesterday. And as for the marbles he was going to put in the Captain's overhead, so they'd roll around at night and keep him awake—well, he has been collecting marbles all the time and has five in a tin box and another in his pocket.

Having laid out the ensign to his satisfaction, Roberts wonders aloud where Dolan is with his letter, and starts to find him. Pulver gives himself away by protesting that if he were Doug he wouldn't send that letter. This isn't a bad life—with Doug, and Doc and Pulver a threesome. Roberts makes a threatening step forward and Pulver produces the letter from beneath his blanket.

"It's too strong," he protests. "Don't sign that letter, Doug; please don't! They'll transfer you and you'll get your ass shot off. You're just running a race with death, isn't he, Doc?"

Doc is on Pulver's side. "Whether you like it or not," he tells Roberts, "this sorry old bucket does a necessary job. And you're the guy who keeps her lumbering along. You keep this crew working cargo, and more than that—you keep them *alive*. It might just be that right here, on this bucket, you're deeper and more truly in this war than you ever would be anywhere else."

Roberts won't accept Doc's argument. He is sick and tired of being a lousy spectator; he believes in the war and wants to participate in it. "And I'm going to keep on sending in these letters until I do." And soon, he hopes. Patton is rolling through Germany and the last big push is shaping up in the Pacific. He signs his letter and leaves the stateroom.

Roberts' birthday is coming up and Pulver confides to Doc his plan for a fine present. From under his mattress he pulls a small cardboard roll—the center of a roll of toilet paper. "I suppose," he challenges, "it doesn't look like a firecracker."

"Not a bit like a firecracker," agrees Doc.

Pulver takes a piece of string from his bunk. "I suppose that doesn't look like a fuse."

Again Doc agrees.

"Well," announces the ensign, "just wait till old Pulver gets through with it! I'm going to get me some of that black powder from the gunner's mate. No, by God, this isn't going to be any peanut firecracker—I'm going to pack this old thing full of that stuff they use to blow up bridges, that fulminate of mercury stuff. And then on the night of Doug's birthday I'm going to throw it under the Old Man's bunk. . . ."

Fade Out

In the darkness one can hear the sound of a winch and talk of cargo loading between an LCT officer and somebody on the ship. When the lights come up Roberts is standing on the hatch cover bossing operations. A cargo net, filled with crates, is descending to the LCT. Everybody is tired, hot and sweaty. A messenger brings Roberts orders from the Captain not to give the LCT any fresh fruit. Dowdy presents a list of what the LCT wants—frozen food, toothpaste, skivvy shirts . . . which brings something to Dowdy's mind. "Can these guys take their shirts off while we're working? Corcoran just passed out from the heat."

In disregard of the Captain's order, Roberts agrees, "Hell, yes, take 'em off"—and the grateful seamen begin to do so. The LCT officer calls out a special request—for fresh fruit; they haven't had any for two months. "Dowdy," orders Roberts, "give 'em a couple of crates of oranges."

"Yes, sir."

"Compliments of the Captain."

The loading continues, and the messenger returns. "The Captain wants to see you, Mister Roberts."

"You go tell the Captain I'm busy." He continues directing the work. Payne has delivered the message, all right, for the Captain appears, followed by the messenger and Dolan. His temper is up. "Let's have this out right here and now!" he grates. "What do you mean—telling me you're busy?"

Roberts explains that a line to the LCT had parted. "You didn't want me to leave the deck with this ship coming in on us?"

"You're damn right I want you to leave the deck. When I tell you I want to see you, I mean *now*, Mister! I mean jump!"

A group of men, naked to the waist, edge in to hear the fight. The Captain points to the letter he is carrying. "By God, you think you're pretty cute with this letter, don't you? You're trying to get me in bad with the Admiral, ain't you?"

Roberts denies this.

"Then what do you mean by writing 'disharmony aboard this ship'?"

"Because it's true, Captain."

"Any disharmony on this ship is my own doing!"

"That's true too, Captain."

The skipper orders Roberts to retype the letter leaving out the "disharmony." The lieutenant protests that he is within his rights in requesting a transfer. "You ain't *never* going to leave this ship," announces the Captain. "Now get on with your work."

Suddenly he notices the shirtless men, orders them to put their shirts on in spite of Roberts' protests about the heat. To the men he shouts, "I'm giving you an order: get those shirts on!"

Nobody moves. "I'm sorry," says Roberts quietly. "Put your shirts on"—and the men do so. This increases the Captain's fury, and, speaking with quiet menace, he announces that every man who disobeyed his standing order and appeared on deck without a shirt is on report.

Again Roberts protests. "I'm responsible," he says. "I gave them permission."

So it was Roberts who disobeyed the order! From below the LCT officer calls his thanks for the oranges. Another order disobeyed. "You've just got yourself ten days in your room," pronounces the Captain. "Ten days, Mister!"

But when Roberts hands over his megaphone to the Captain and starts off, the Captain reconsiders. "Get back to that cargo! I'll let you know when you have ten days in your room and you'll damn well know it!"

Pulver, coming round the corner of the house, sees the Captain and starts back—but is too late. He has been spotted. Evidently a stranger to the Captain, who orders him to come here. The confused Pulver can think of nothing better to do than salute—which visibly startles the Captain.

"What's your name again?"

"Ensign Pulver, sir."

The Captain is glad to see one man on the ship who knows how to salute. He asks Pulver's job, learns it is officer in charge of laundry and morale; aboard ship fourteen months. Most of the time in the laundry, then, the Captain surmises—and Roberts has to hide his laughter.

The skipper asks the ensign to lunch, but Pulver protests that he can't make it today; he has to go to the hospital on the island to pick up a piece . . . of medical equipment.

"Why, I'll take care of that, Frank," volunteers Roberts. The Captain thinks this is a good idea—but the miserable Pulver wins with a further protest that this is something he has to take care of himself. "Well, some other time then," invites the Captain.

When the commander of the ship has gone, the men express their gratitude to Roberts for standing up to the Old Man. One of them asks if Roberts is going to send another letter in next week. "Are we, Dolan?" asks the lieutenant.

"You're damn right we are! And I'm the baby who's going to deliver it." Another of the men asks if he can't take the letter, but Dolan claims it's his job. "We're gonna write a really hot one next week," he proclaims.

"Got any asbestos paper?" queries Roberts. He starts off with the men happily following him.

Fade Out

Now there is excitement aboard ship. Miss Girard, a young, attractive, blonde Army nurse, arrives with Pulver. She wants to know if Pulver and the crew have seen a lot of battle action and is assured they have. They have a lot of B.F.—battle fatigue. Even Pulver has had a scratch of it.

"You should sleep more," advises the nurse.

Anxious to get the young woman to the stateroom, Pulver reminds her of that little old drink of Scotcharoo. "I just love Scotch," she confides. "My twin sister has a nickname for me that's partly because I like a particular brand and"—she giggles—"partly because of a little personal thing about me that you wouldn't understand. Do you know what she calls me? 'Red label'!"

"That's the kind I've got," announces Pulver, and is rewarded by being called God's gift to a thirsty nurstie. He begins to maneuver her toward "his" cabin—for he is, he has told her, the Executive Officer. But they encounter five of the men, Insigna, Mannion, Stefanowski, Wiley and Lindstrom, carrying the glasses, and Pulver has to introduce Mannion.

"What are you doing with those glasses?" asks the nurse.

"We're . . . cleaning them," invents Insigna, pulling out a shirt tail and beginning to polish; the others follow his example.

Before Pulver can escape with his prize, Roberts appears carrying a piece of paper and a small book, and *he* is introduced. Frank has told her all about him being Frank's roommate. She wants to know what his job is—like Frank here being Executive Officer.

"Oh, I'm just the laundry and morale officer," says Roberts dryly—and Pulver is annoyed when Miss Girard finds this is wonderful news, because she had just been made laundry and morale officer of her outfit and maybe they can compare notes.

Pulver begs to be excused, but the nurse thinks he should invite Roberts along for a drink too. Pulver urges her to come on.

"I bet you fifty bucks . . ." Insigna challenges Mannion.

"Seems to be an argument," observes the nurse.

"Yeah," says Pulver.

Well, anyhow, she tells him, the nurses are fixing up a new

dayroom and maybe they can all get together and have a party. She notices that the hospital can be seen from the ship, and points it out. Pulver takes a pair of binoculars from Wiley and looks at the island.

His voice rising, Insigna doubles his challenge to Mannion. "All right, I got a *hundred* bucks says that's the one with the birthmark on her ass."

There is a terrible silence. Miss Girard takes the glasses from Pulver and looks at the island. "Frank," she declares, "I won't be able to have lunch with you after all. Would you call the boat, please?" She bids Roberts good-by. "I promised the girls I'd help them hang some curtains," she explains, "and I think we'd better get started right away."

And, just as she leaves, she informs Mannion, "I wouldn't take that bet if I were you because you'd lose a hundred bucks."

The men are depressed at the prospect of curtains at the hospital, but Roberts picks them up by reading from the paper in his hands the best possible news—the *AK 601* is ordered to proceed to Elysium Island, arriving in seven days. "During its stay in Elysium," the order continues, "the ship will make maximum use of the recreational facilities of this port."

It means a liberty!

From the guide book he carries Roberts calls a description of the island—a Polynesian paradise . . . chief exports include rum. Since 1900, the population of its capital, Elysium City, has remained remarkably constant at approximately 30,000.

"I'll fix that!" exults Insigna.

And if the men want to know any more about the place, Dowdy can tell them, because he has been there. They run wildly off in search of Dowdy. Roberts, noticing a pair of binoculars, looks toward the island for a moment, shrugs, takes up the glasses. . . .

Fade Out

The *AK 601* has made port. The men, all in white uniforms, are in their compartment, crowded. Through a porthole can be heard Polynesian music—and through it Insigna is keeping watch and reporting what he sees . . . canoes with flowers and women in them . . . a big canoe with fat men playing guitars . . . kids diving for whatever pennies the crew will throw. The men feverishly wonder when the liberty will be announced.

Reber, a messenger, is besieged when he enters, but there is no news of a liberty—because the Captain is asleep. The only news he has is that Lindstrom can take off his whites, because he and Mister Roberts have the 12 to 4 watch tonight.

Dolan calls in the squawk box: "The Captain's messenger will report to the Captain's cabin on the double!"

Now the announcement will come, they feel. And it does—but not the one they expected. It is the Captain himself on the squawk box:

"Goddammit . . . how does this thing work? (*Sound of squawk box switch.*) This is the Captain speaking. I just woke up from a little nap and I got a surprise. I found out there were men on this ship who were expecting liberty. (*At this point the lights start dimming until the entire scene is blacked out. The speech continues throughout the darkness. Under the* CAPTAIN'S *speech the strains of Polynesian music can be heard.*) Now I don't know how such a rumor got around, but I'd like to clear it up right now. You see, it's like this. Because of cargo requirements and security conditions which has just come to my personal attention there will be no liberty as long as we're in this here port. And one other thing—as long as we're here, no man will wear white uniforms. Now I would like to repeat for the benefit of complete understanding and clearness, No LIBERTY. That is all."

Fade Out

The Captain is in his cabin, which contains a settee, a chair, a desk, a wall safe, and the ship's intercommunication board. The Captain, at his desk, has his watch in one hand and the microphone in the other. There is a knock on his door.

CAPTAIN—Come in, Mister Roberts. (*As* ROBERTS *enters, the* CAPTAIN *puts the microphone on the desk.*) Thirty-eight seconds. Pretty good time! You see, I been expectin' you ever since I made my little announcement.

ROBERTS—Well, as long as you're expecting me, what about it—when does this crew get liberty?

CAPTAIN—Well, in the first place, just kinda hold your tongue. And in the second place, sit down.

ROBERTS—There's no time to sit down. When are you going to let this crew go ashore?

CAPTAIN—I'm not. This wasn't my idea, coming to a Liberty Port. One of my officers arranged it with a certain Port Director —gave him a bottle of Scotch whiskey—compliments of the Captain. And the Port Director was kind enough to send me a little thank-you note along with our orders. Sit down, Mister Roberts. (ROBERTS *sits.*) Don't worry about it. I'm not going to make trouble about that wasted bottle of Scotch. I'll admit I was a little pre-voked about not being consulted. Then I got to thinking maybe we oughta come to this port anyway so's you and me could have a little talk.

ROBERTS—You can make all the trouble you want, Captain, but let's quit wasting time. Don't you hear that music? Don't you know it's tearing those guys apart? They're breakable, Captain! I promise you!

CAPTAIN—That's enough! I've had enough of your fancy educated talk. (*Rises, goes to* ROBERTS.) Now you listen to me. I got two things I want to show you. (*He unlocks the wall safe, opens it and takes out a commander's cap with gold braid "scrambled eggs" on the visor.*) You see that? That's the cap of a full commander. I'm gonna wear that cap some day and you're going to help me. (*Replaces cap in safe, goes back to* ROBERTS.) I guess there's no harm in telling you that you helped me get that palm tree by working cargo. Now don't let this go to your head, but when Admiral Finchley gave me that award, he said, "You got a good Cargo Officer, Morton; keep him at it, you're going places." So I went out and bought that hat. There's nothing gonna stand between me and that hat—certainly not you. Now last week you wrote a letter that said "disharmony aboard this ship." I told you there wasn't going to be any more letters. But what do I find on my desk this morning . . . (*Taking letter from desk.*) Another one. It says "friction between myself and the Commanding Officer." That ain't gonna go in, Mister.

ROBERTS—How are you going to stop it, Captain?

CAPTAIN—I ain't; you are. (*Goes to his chair and sits.*) Just how much do you want this crew to have a liberty anyhow? Enough to stop this "disharmony"? To stop this "friction"? (*Leans forward.*) Enough to get out of the habit of writing letters ever? Because that's the only way this crew is ever gonna get ashore. (*Leans back.*) Well, we've had our little talk. What do you say?

ROBERTS (*after a moment*)—How did you get in the Navy? How did you get on our side? You're what I joined to fight *against*. You ignorant, arrogant, ambitious . . . (*Rises.*) jackass! Keeping a hundred and sixty-seven men in prison because you got a palm tree for the work *they* did. I don't know which I hate worse—you or that other malignant growth that stands outside your door!

CAPTAIN—Why, you goddamn . . .

ROBERTS—How did you ever get command of a ship? I realize that in wartime they have to scrape the bottom of the barrel, but where the hell did they ever scrape you up?

CAPTAIN (*shouting*)—There's just one thing left for you, by God—a general court-martial.

ROBERTS—That suits me fine. Court-martial me!

CAPTAIN—By God, you've got it!

ROBERTS—I'm asking for it!

CAPTAIN—You don't have to ask for it, you've got it now!

ROBERTS—If I can't get transferred off here, I'll get court-martialed off! I'm fed up! But you'll need a witness. Send for your messenger. He's down below. I'll say it all again in front of him. (*Pauses.*) Go on, call in Reber! (*The* CAPTAIN *doesn't move.*) Go on, call him. (*Still the* CAPTAIN *doesn't move.*) Do you want me to call him?

CAPTAIN—No. (*He walks upstage, then turns to* ROBERTS.) I think you're a pretty smart boy. I may not talk very good, Mister, but I know how to take care of smart boys. Let me tell you something. Let me tell you a little secret. I hate your guts, you college son-of-a-bitch! You think you're better than I am! You think you're better because you've had everything handed to you! Let me tell you something, Mister—I've worked since I was ten years old, and all my life I've known you superior bastards. I knew you people when I was a kid in Boston and I worked in eating-places and you ordered me around—"Oh, busboy! My friend here seems to have thrown up on the table. Clean it up, please." I started going to sea as a steward and I worked for you then—"Steward, take my magazine out to the deck chair!"—"Steward, I don't like your looks. Please keep out of my way as much as possible!" Well, I took that crap! I took that for years from pimple-faced bastards who weren't good enough to wipe my nose! And now I don't have to take it any more! There's a war on, by God, and I'm the Captain and you can wipe my nose! The worst thing I can do to you is to keep you on this ship! And that's where you're going to stay! Now get out of here! (*He goes to his chair and sits.* ROBERTS *moves slowly toward the door. He hears the music, goes to the porthole and listens. Then he turns to the* CAPTAIN.)

ROBERTS—Can't you hear that music, Captain?

The Captain busies himself, ignoring Roberts. The lieutenant is ready to make a deal—and he knows what it will be. The

Captain announces the terms—no more letters, no more talking back, and no taking credit for getting the crew ashore.

Roberts gives his word, which the Captain accepts. Picking up the microphone, he announces a change in plan—liberty for the entire crew, commencing immediately. A song, "Roll Me Over," is started by one man and is taken up by the whole crew. Roberts is excited and happy as the singing increases in volume.

The curtain falls.

ACT II

It is 3:45 A.M.—pitch-black; but a temporary desk has been rigged at the head of the gangway and a light has been hung over it. There is a large ship's logbook on the desk; at the left of the Captain's door is a small table on which are hospital supplies. Onstage are Roberts, Doc, Lindstrom, Johnson and four seamen.

Roberts, wearing the side-arms of Officer of the Deck, holds a sheaf of yellow slips; Johnson and a seaman are holding the inert figure of another seaman, who has adhesive plaster on his face, and two more seamen are lying on the hatch cover, where Doc is bandaging one of them. All who are conscious turn to listen to the sound of a siren.

"Here's another batch, Mister Roberts," announces Lindstrom. "Another paddy wagon full. And this one's an Army paddy wagon." Johnson carries one of Doc's patients below; he's putting them on the deck because they roll out of their bunks.

A shore patrolman calls, "I got a bunch of real beauties for you this time."

"Can they walk?" calls Roberts in reply.

At the sound of a cargo winch in operation, Doc and Roberts remove two bodies from the hatch cover to make room, and soon a net is swung aboard and lowered. Its cargo is seamen—inert seamen in once-white uniforms, decorated with leis. What a liberty! exclaims Lindstrom; this is the seventh batch. At the same time, up the gangway comes a shore patrolman at the head of six men who can walk—Stefanowski, Reber, Wiley, Payne, Mannion and Insigna, all bloody, some carrying such souvenirs as Army caps and Japanese lanterns.

"They done all right," informs the shore patrolman. "Six of them busted into a formal dance and took on 128 Army bastards."

With them comes an Army M.P. who more formally confirms the report. They have made a shambles of Colonel Middleton's testimonial dinner-dance. Further testimony comes from the men themselves; they had, indeed, crashed a dance for Army personnel. The M.P. reports that thirty-eight soldiers of the U. S. Army have been hospitalized and the Colonel himself has a bruise on his shin.

"*I* did that, Mister Roberts," boasts Payne.

But this isn't all, according to the Army emissary. There were fifty young ladies present, from the finest families of Elysium, and some of them got mauled while others got their clothes torn off and went screaming into the night. The Colonel's compliments, and the Colonel wants to know what punishment will be given these men.

"Tell the Colonel I'm sure the Captain will think of something," replies Roberts, and the M.P. withdraws to do so.

With a show of severity Roberts asks the sextet what they have to say for themselves—but instead of offering any explanation Stefanowski inquires if it would be all right for them to go ashore again.

"Anybody got a fractured skull?" asks Doc. The men chorus a denial. "Okay, you pass the physical."

"Go down and take a shower first and get into some clothes," instructs Roberts, and the happy men rush to the hatchway.

From the gangway comes Dolan, leading a goat and announcing proudly that he is as drunk as one. He found this goat eating a little old palm tree and thought to himself that this ship needs a mascot. Dolan has barely gone off to bed when a shore patrolman arrives in pursuit of the goat, which, according to a tag on its collar, is the property of Rear Admiral Wentworth. Roberts relinquishes the animal to him.

Roberts is obviously in good humor, which Doc notices and inquires about when he comes up from ministering to the injured and wayward below. "Am I looking cocky?" asks Mister Roberts in response to an observation by Doc. "Maybe it's because for the first time since I've been on this ship, I'm seeing a crew."

Up to now, the lieutenant philosophizes, he has just been seeing 167 separate guys; now they are bound together. Even Insigna and Mannion are pals. He thinks the guys are strong enough now to take all the miserable, endless days ahead.

Pulver comes slowly from the gangway; at a query from Doc about how his liberty was he merely holds up seven fingers and keeps on going. He is followed by a shore patrol officer who, after calling down to two of his men, tells Roberts that the ship has been restricted for the rest of its stay in port and he has posted guards at the foot of the gangway. Furthermore, the

Captain will report to the Island Commander at 7 A.M. and he'd better be on time.

"What in particular did this?" asks Roberts.

"A little while ago six men from your ship broke into the house of the French Consul and started throwing things through the plate-glass living-room window. We found some of the things on the lawn. . . . We also found an Army private first class who was unconscious at the time. He claims they threw him too."

"Through the window?"

"That's right. It seems he took them there for a little joke. He didn't tell them it was the Consul's house; he said it was a—what we call in Alabama—a cat-house." Laughing and saluting, he adds, "If it makes you feel any better, Admiral Wentworth says this is the worst ship he's ever seen in his entire naval career."

Well, there goes the liberty. But, as Gerhart says, it was worth it.

Fade Out

It is morning and the men have been mustered in orderly formation. The Captain, followed by Roberts, comes from his cabin.

"We're being kicked out of this port," announces the Captain. "I had a feeling this liberty was a bad idea. That's why we'll never have one again. We're going to erase this blot from my record if we have to work twenty-four hours a day."

The Captain is appointing Mister Roberts to see that the men toe the line. Meaningfully, he says that Roberts is a man of his word. The men are dismissed; some leave, others gather in a group. "Roberts," orders the Captain, "take these men here back aft to handle lines. And see that they work up a sweat." He returns to his cabin.

Dolan holds Roberts and the men back with a piece of news which has just come from the Bureau of Naval Personnel: All commanding officers are directed to forward all applications for transfers from officers with 24 months' sea duty, because the heightened war offensive has created a need for experienced officers aboard combat ships.

Here, at last, is Roberts' transfer! The Captain is hanging in the ropes now, and all he needs is one more letter—which Dolan has thoughtfully typed up. All it needs is Roberts' signature.

But the lieutenant avoids signing it, making excuses that he wants to look it over and is tired now. He is snappish, and the

men can't figure out what has come over him as they follow
Roberts aft.

Fade Out

During the darkness an American radio announcer is heard giving a report, as yet unconfirmed, that the war in Europe is over.
. . . When the lights come up they reveal Roberts' and Pulver's
cabin, where Doc and Pulver are listening to the radio. Doc
turns the receiver off and the two men fall to discussing Roberts.

They, too, are puzzled. They can't believe that their friend
now is buckling for a promotion, which the Captain has hinted
is in the offing. But something is wrong. He hasn't spoken ten
words to Doc in ten days, and he won't talk to Pulver either.

Further disturbing news comes from a delegation composed of
Dowdy, Gerhart and Lindstrom: Roberts has put Dolan on report; Dolan is going up before the Captain tomorrow on account of this letter business again. "Dolan," explains Gerhart,
"was just kiddin' him about not sending in any more letters. And
all of a sudden Mister Roberts turned just white and yelled,
'Shut up, Dolan. Shut your goddamn mouth. I've had enough.'
And Dolan naturally got snotty back at him and Mister Roberts
put him right on report."

Roberts comes in and clears the cabin of all but Doc. "Doc,
transfer me, will you?" he asks emotionally. "Transfer me to
the hospital on this next island! You can do it. You don't need
the Captain's approval! Just put me ashore for examination—
say there's something wrong with my eyes, or my feet, or my
head, for Christ's sake."

Doc is not sanguine about the plan, and anyway he is interested in something else—the putting of Dolan on report. At first,
Roberts states that Dolan didn't carry out an order fast enough;
then he confesses, "It was the war. I just heard the news. The
war was ending and I couldn't get to it and there was Dolan giving me guff about something—and all of a sudden I hated him.
I hated all of them. I was sick of the sullen bastards staring
at me as though I'd sold them down the river or something. If
they think I'm bucking for a promotion—if they're stupid enough
to think I'd walk ten feet across the room to get anything from
that Captain, then I'm through with the whole damn ungrateful
mob!"

Doc—Does this crew owe you something?
Roberts—What the hell do you mean by that?

Doc—You talk as if they did.

ROBERTS (*rising and crossing to bunk, speaking quietly*)—
That's exactly how I'm talking. I didn't realize it but that's exactly the way I've been feeling. Oh, Jesus, that shows you how far gone I am, Doc. I've been taking something out on them. I've been blaming them for something that . . .

Doc—What, Doug? Something what? You've made some sort of agreement with the Captain, haven't you, Doug!

ROBERTS (*turns*)—Agreement? I don't know what you mean. Will you transfer me, Doc?

Doc—Not a chance, Doug. I could never get away with it—you know that.

ROBERTS—Oh, my God!

PULVER (*offstage*)—Doug! Doc! (*Entering.*) Listen to the radio, you uninformed bastards! Turn it up! (ROBERTS *reaches over and turns up the radio. The excited voice of an announcer can be heard.*)

ANNOUNCER—. . . this broadcast to bring you a special news flash! The war is over in Europe! THE WAR IS OVER IN EUROPE! (ROBERTS *grasps* Doc's *arm in excitement.*) Germany has surrendered unconditionally to the Allied Armies. The surrender was signed in a schoolhouse in the city of Rheims. . . . (ROBERTS *stands staring.* Doc *turns off the radio. For a moment there is silence, then:*)

Doc—I would remind you that there's still a minor skirmish here in the Pacific.

ROBERTS—I'll miss that one too. But to hell with me. This is the greatest day in the world. We're going to celebrate. How about it, Frank?

PULVER—Yeah, Doug. We've got to celebrate!

Doc (*starting to pull alcohol from the wastebasket*)—What'll it be—alcohol and orange juice or orange juice and alcohol?

ROBERTS—That's not good enough.

PULVER—Hell, no, Doc! (*He looks expectantly at* ROBERTS.)

ROBERTS—We've got to think of something that'll lift this ship right out of the water and turn it around the other way. (PULVER *suddenly rises to his feet.*)

PULVER (*shouting*)—Doug! Oh, my God, why didn't I think of this before. Doug! Doc! You're going to blow your tops when you hear the idea I got! Oh, Jesus, what a wonderful idea! It's the only thing to do. It's the only thing in the world to do! That's all! Doug, you said I never had any ideas. You said I never finished anything I started. Well, you're wrong—

tonight you're wrong! I thought of something and I finished it. I was going to save it for your birthday, but I'm going to give it to you tonight, because we gotta celebrate. . . .

ROBERTS (*waving his hands in* PULVER'S *face for attention*)—Wait a minute, Frank! What is it?

PULVER—A firecracker, by God. (*He reaches under his mattress and pulls out a large wobbly firecracker which has been painted red.*) We're gonna throw a firecracker under the Old Man's bunk. Bam-bam-bam! Wake up, you old son-of-a-bitch, IT'S V-E DAY!

ROBERTS (*rising*)—Frank!

PULVER—Look at her, Doc. Ain't it a beauty? Ain't that the greatest hand-made, hand-painted, hand-packed firecracker you ever saw?

ROBERTS (*smiling and taking the firecracker*)—Yes, Frank. That's the most beautiful firecracker I ever saw in my life. But will it work?

PULVER—Sure it'll work. At least, I think so.

ROBERTS—Haven't you tested it? It's got to work, Frank; it's just got to work!

PULVER—I'll tell you what I'll do. I'll take it down to the laundry and test it—that's my laboratory, the laundry. I got all the fixings down there—powder, fuses, everything, all hid behind the soapflakes. And if this one works, I can make another one in two minutes.

ROBERTS—Okay, Frank. Take off. We'll wait for you here. (PULVER *starts off.*) Be sure you got enough to make it loud. What'd you use for powder?

PULVER—Loud! This ain't a popgun. This is a firecracker. I used fulminate of mercury. I'll be right back. (*He runs out.*)

Doc and Roberts have a drink of alcohol and orange juice; Roberts is jubilant over Pulver's plan. They are toasting the ensign just as there is a tremendous explosion. Outside the Captain is heard bellowing, "What was that?"

Suddenly a figure hurtles into the room and stops. It looks part scarecrow, part snowman; it is Pulver, covered with soapsuds, with his uniform tattered. He is in a state of enthusiastic excitement. "Jeez," he exclaims, "that stuff's terrific!"

He is all right, he informs his friends—not burned or anything. But the laundry is kinda beat up. There's a new porthole on the starboard side where the electric iron went through "And I guess a steam-line must've busted or something—I was up to my ass in lather."

Outside, a man informs the Captain that, indeed, a steam-line must have blown up. Extent of damage not immediately discernible because the passageway is solid soapsuds. "Tell those men to be more careful," orders the Captain.

Roberts exclaims that their celebration is just getting started. He and Pulver will go down and make another firecracker and put it where it really belongs. But it can't be done, the ensign sadly declares. All the stuff he had was in the laundry and it all went up. There isn't any more.

Roberts' elation subsides and he sinks into a chair. In a moment he goes out on deck and says he is going to turn in.

"He was happy there for a minute though, wasn't he, Doc?" asks Pulver. "We gotta do something for that guy, Doc. . . . What's the matter with him, anyhow?"

"He wouldn't tell me," answers Doc. "But I know one thing he's feeling tonight and that's panic. Tonight he feels his war is dying before he can get into it."

Fade Out

During the darkness a British broadcaster is heard describing the V-E Day appearance on their balcony of the King and Queen. This broadcast continues during the ensuing scene, covering celebrations in San Francisco, New York and elsewhere. When the lights come up on the deck scene it is moonlight and the ship is under way. Insigna, Mannion, Dolan, Stefanowski and Gerhart are having a late bull session on the hatch cover.

They are talking about the steam pipe explosion, their adventures during the liberty on Elysium, food, anything. When Roberts appears one of them warns, "Flash Red!"

The men smile politely at the lieutenant; he, embarrassed, makes talk about the war in Europe being over. Finally, he manages, "Dolan, I guess I kind of blew my top tonight. I'm sorry. I'm taking you off report." Dolan ostentatiously yawns and guesses he will hit the sack. The others guess they will too, leaving Roberts alone. From the radio, he hears a patriotic speech, followed by the playing of the National Anthem.

Roberts listens for a moment, then marches to the palm tree, salutes it, rubs his hands together and, as the music reaches a climax, jerks the palm tree from its container and throws it over the side. Then, after a shrug, he walks casually off singing the tune to himself.

For a moment the stage is empty, then the Captain's lights go up and the skipper appears, in pajamas and robe and with his watering can, through his door. When he discovers the empty container he plunges back into his cabin and sounds the General Alarm. When the alarm stops he calls, almost hysterically, over the squawk box, "Every man to his battle station on the double!"

There is confusion as men in various degrees of dress, but all with helmets and life preservers, run to their posts. They wonder what it can be—an air raid, or a submarine? Some of the men don't know which gun tub to man, and Stefanowski doesn't know where his battle station is at all.

When all are distributed at their posts, Johnson, with the Captain in his cabin, calls for attention over the squawk box. The Captain comes on and demands who did it. They will stay there all night until someone confesses—or until hell freezes over. Insulting the honor of the ship by destroying the symbol of their cargo record. . . .

Stefanowski, discovering the empty container, kneels and ceremoniously bows to it.

The Captain demands a roll call by Johnson, and he can be heard commenting on each name as it is called alphabetically. "No, not Abernathy . . . Not Baker . . . No, not Pulver. He hasn't the guts. . . ."

"Roberts," calls Johnson.

"Roberts!" roars the Captain. "He's the one! Get him up here!"

Roberts appears, walking slowly, and goes into the Captain's cabin. The men move in to listen, and Lindstrom finds a position on a ladder where he can see through the cabin's porthole.

ROBERTS' VOICE—Did you want to see me, Captain?

CAPTAIN'S VOICE—You did it. You did it. Don't lie to me. Don't stand there and lie to me. Confess it!

ROBERTS' VOICE—Confess what, Captain? I don't know what you're talking about.

CAPTAIN'S VOICE—You know damn well what I'm talking about because you did it. You've doublecrossed me—you've gone back on your word!

ROBERTS' VOICE—No, I haven't, Captain.

CAPTAIN'S VOICE—Yes, by God, you have. I kept my part of the bargain! I gave this crew liberty—I gave this crew liberty, by God, but you've gone back on *your* word. (DOWD *takes off his helmet and looks at the men.*)

"A STREETCAR NAMED DESIRE"

"Jacket, Doctor?" asks the matron. "Not unless necessary," says e doctor. "Ask her to let go of me," begs Blanche.

(Richard Garrick, Jessica Tandy, Ann Dere)

Photo by John Swope.

"MISTER ROBERTS"

Lieut. Roberts (jg) issues an order aboard the AK-601, a Navy vessel which is as far away from the war as any ship can be and still stay afloat in the Pacific.

(*Henry Fonda*)

vp by Graphic House, New York.

"COMMAND DECISION"

Captain Jenks, a quitter and a coward who should be court-martialed, instead is going to be given a citation by a visiting Congressman—and General Dennis doesn't like it.

(*Paul Kelly, Arthur Franz*)

"THE WINSLOW BOY"

The Winslow boy has been sacked from the Naval Academy for forging a postal order. "Did you?" asks his father. "No," says the boy. That is all the father wants to know.

(*Michael Newell, Alan Webb*)

"THE HEIRESS"

"I have no affection for you, Father."
Dr. Sloper has told his daughter Catherine that he is ill and that
e will not recover, but he hates an ill-conducted sickroom.

(Wendy Hiller, Basil Rathbone)

"ALLEGRO"

When Joe comes back from college his first year Jennie hints that it is a long time for a girl to wait to get married, if a boy insists on going all the way through medical school.

(Roberta Jonay, John Battles)

hoto by Vandamm, New York.

"EASTWARD IN EDEN"

"Your letters have created their own image. I feel as though I now you better than I do."
Dr. Wadsworth has come to pay his first call on Emily Dickinson Amherst.

(Onslow Stevens, Beatrice Straight)

"SKIPPER NEXT TO GOD"

"If you say one word against my father . . ."

"AN INSPECTOR CALLS"

The Inspector has come to ask a few questions of the celebrants at a quiet little dinner party, and he wants to learn much from Sheila and Gerald.

(Thomas Mitchell, Rene Ray, John Buckmaster)

Photo by Vandamm, New York.

"ME AND MOLLY"

"Look, Jake, a tree!"

(*Philip Loeb, Gertrude Berg*)

ROBERTS' VOICE—I don't see how you can say that, Captain. I haven't sent in any more letters. (DOLAN, *on gun tub ladder, catches* INSIGNA's *eye.*)

CAPTAIN'S VOICE—I'm not talkin' about your goddamn sons-a-bitchin' letters. I'm talkin' about what you did tonight.

ROBERTS' VOICE—Tonight? I don't understand you, Captain. What do you think I did?

CAPTAIN'S VOICE—Quit saying that, goddammit, quit saying that. You know damn well what you did. You stabbed me in the back. You stabbed me in the back . . . aaa . . . aa . . .

JOHNSON'S VOICE—Captain! Get over to the washbasin, Captain!

CAPTAIN'S VOICE—Aaaaaaa . . .

INSIGNA—What the hell happened?

DOLAN—Quiet!

JOHNSON (*on mike*)—Will the Doctor please report to the Captain's cabin on the double? (DOC *appears from left, pushing his way through the crowd, followed by two* MEDICAL CORPSMEN *wearing Red Cross brassards and carrying first-aid kits and a stretcher.* DOC *walks slowly; he is idly attaching a brassard and smoking a cigarette. He wears his helmet sloppily.*)

DOC—Gangway . . . gangway . . .

DOWDY—Hey, Doc, tell us what's going on.

DOC—Okay. Okay. (*He enters the* CAPTAIN's *cabin followed by the* CORPSMEN, *who leave the stretcher leaning against the bulkhead. The door closes. There is a tense pause. The men gather around the cabin again.* LINDSTROM *is at the porthole.*)

REBER—Hey, Lindstrom, where's the Old Man?

LINDSTROM—He's sittin' in the chair—leaning way forward.

PAYNE—What's the Doc doin'?

LINDSTROM—He's holdin' the wastebasket.

REBER—What wastebasket?

LINDSTROM—The one the Old Man's got his head in. And he needs it too. (*Pause.*) They're helpin' him over to the couch. (*Pause.*) He's lying down there and they're takin' off his shoes. (*Pause.*) Look out, here they come. (*The men break quickly and rush back to their battle stations. The door opens and* ROBERTS, DOC *and the* CORPSMEN *come out.*)

DOC (*to* CORPSMEN)—We won't need that stretcher. Sorry. (*Calls.*) Dowdy! Come here. (DOWDY *comes down to* DOC. *He avoids* ROBERTS' *eyes.*)

ROBERTS—Dowdy, pass the word to the crew to secure from General Quarters.

DOC—And tell the men not to make any noise while they go to their bunks. The Captain's resting quietly now, and I think that's desirable.

ROBERTS—Pass the word, will you, Dowdy?

DOWDY—Yes, Mister Roberts. (*He passes the word to the crew who slowly start to leave their battle stations. They are obviously stalling.*)

DOC (*to* ROBERTS)—Got a cigarette? (ROBERTS *reaches in his pocket and offers* DOC *a cigarette. Then he lights* DOC's *cigarette.* DOC *notices the men stalling.*) Well, guess I'd better get back inside. I'll be down to see you after I get through. (*He enters cabin and stands there watching. The men move offstage, very slowly, saying, "Good night, Mister Roberts," "Good night, sir." Suddenly* ROBERTS *notices that all the men are saying good night to him.*)

DOLAN (*quietly*)—Good night, Mister Roberts. (ROBERTS *does not hear him.*) Good night, Mister Roberts.

ROBERTS—Good night, Dolan. (DOLAN *smiles and exits down hatch.* ROBERTS *steps toward hatch, removes helmet, looks puzzled as the lights fade out.*)

During the darkness the squawk box emits announcements and orders, including one for Dolan to report to the radio shack. When the lights come up they reveal the Roberts-Pulver stateroom, with Pulver reclining, Doc holding a glass and a bottle of alcohol, Roberts tying up a sea bag and Wiley waiting to take the bag down to the gangway.

Roberts is on his way—on his way so fast and unexpectedly that he will be off this bucket before he even wakes up.

"They flying you all the way to the *Livingston?*" asks Doc.

"I don't know. The radio dispatch just said I was transferred and travel by air if possible. . . . They're landing planes at Okinawa now and that's where my can is probably running around." The lieutenant can't believe his luck—he's got a destroyer, and it is one of the greatest cans out there. Pulver warns him he'd better be mighty careful around Okinawa.

Dolan appears with a file folder with copies of the radio dispatch. "You're now officially detached from this here bucket," he informs Roberts. "Let me be the first." They shake—but Roberts can't figure it out about the orders because he hasn't sent in a letter for a month. Dolan makes an unconvincing job of guessing that the Navy, needing men badly, went through some old letters.

"Listen, Mister Roberts," he urges. "We can't stand here beating our gums. . . . You seen what it said there, 'Proceed immediately.' And the Old Man says if you ain't off of here in an hour, by God, he's going to throw you off!"

Outside, the Captain can be heard giving some orders about being careful and putting it down easy. It is, explains Dolan, "a new enlarged botanical garden"—two palm trees, and a twenty-four-hour watch has already been set over them. Oh, yes —and the Captain wants to see Mister Pulver right away. He leads Pulver out.

Doc—You're a happy son-of-a-bitch, aren't you?

Roberts—Yep. You're happy about it too, aren't you, Doc?

Doc—I think it's the only thing for you. (*Casually.*) What do you think of the crew now, Doug?

Roberts—We're all right now. I think they're nice guys—all of them.

Doc—Unh-hunh. And how do you think they feel about you?

Roberts—I think they like me all right . . . till the next guy comes along.

Doc—You don't think you're necessary to them?

Roberts (*sitting on bunk*)—Hell, no. No officer's necessary to the crew, Doc.

Doc—Are you going to leave this ship believing that?

Roberts—That's nothing against them. A crew's too busy looking after themselves to care about anyone else.

Doc—Well, take a good, deep breath, Buster. (*He drinks some alcohol.*) What do you think got you your orders? Prayer and fasting? Sending in enough Wheatie box tops?

Roberts—My orders? Why, what Dolan said—one of my old letters turned up . . .

Doc—Bat crap! This crew got you transferred. They were so busy looking out for themselves that they took a chance of landing in prison for five years—any one of them. Since you couldn't send in a letter for transfer, they sent one in for you. Since they knew the Captain wouldn't sign it approved, they didn't bother him—they signed it for him.

Roberts—What do you mean? They forged the Captain's name?

Doc—That's right.

ROBERTS—Doc! Who did? Which one of them?

DOC—That would be hard to say. You see, they had a mass meeting down in the compartment. They put guards at every door. They called it the Captain's-Name-Signing contest. And every man in this crew—a hundred and sixty-seven of them— signed the Captain's name on a blank sheet of paper. And then there were judges who compared these signatures with the Captain's and selected the one to go in. At the time there was some criticism of the decision on the grounds that the judges were drunk, but apparently, from the results, they chose well.

ROBERTS—How'd you find out about this, Doc?

DOC—Well, it was a great honor. I am the only officer aboard who does know. I was a contestant. I was also a judge. This double honor was accorded me because of my character, charm, good looks and because the medical department contributed four gallons of grain alcohol to the contest. (*Pauses.*) It was quite a thing to see, Doug. A hundred and sixty-seven guys with only one idea in their heads—to do something for Mister Roberts.

ROBERTS—I wish you hadn't told me, Doc. It makes me look pretty silly after what I just said. But I didn't mean it, Doc. I was afraid to say what I really feel. I love those bastards, Doc. I think they're the greatest guys on this earth. All of a sudden I feel that there's something wrong—something terribly wrong—about leaving them. God, what can I say to them?

DOC—You won't say anything—you don't even know. When you're safely aboard your new ship I'm supposed to write and tell you about it. And at the bottom of the letter, I'm supposed to say, "Thanks for the liberty, Mister Roberts. Thanks for everything."

The downcast Pulver re-enters. "I'm the new cargo officer," he announces. "And that's not all—I got to have dinner with him tonight. He *likes* me!"

There is a polite rap on the stateroom door and Payne, Reber, Gerhart, Schlemmer, Dolan and Insigna are admitted. All carry canteen cups except Insigna, whose cup is in his belt; in his hands is a large red fire extinguisher. "Fire and rescue party. Heard you had a fire in here," he explains.

Elaborately Insigna discovers that there has been no fire. He puts the extinguisher on the desk. "In that case," he continues, "we might as well drink this stuff." Roberts, Doc and Pulver hold out glasses and Insigna fills them from his instrument—a new batch of jungle juice "in the handy new portable container."

The men already have theirs in their cups. Very clearly, it is a solemn occasion.

Hesitant and abashed, and with a good deal of prompting from his companions, Insigna explains that they couldn't let Roberts go away without a little present. In come Lindstrom, Mannion, Dowdy and Stefanowski, and Mannion is carrying a candy box which he hands to Roberts.

The lieutenant opens it amid deep silence. He holds up what he finds there. It is a brass medal shaped like a palm tree, attached to a gaudy ribbon.

LINDSTROM—It's a palm tree, see.

DOLAN—It was Dowdy's idea.

DOWDY—Mannion here made it. He cut it out of sheet brass down in the machine shop.

INSIGNA—Mannion drilled the words on it too.

MANNION—Stefanowski thought up the words.

STEFANOWSKI (*shoving* LINDSTROM *forward*)—Lindstrom gets credit for the ribbon from a box of candy that his sister-in-law sent him. Read the words, Mister Roberts.

ROBERTS (*with difficulty*)—"Order . . . order of . . ." (*He hands the medal to* DOC.)

DOC (*rises and reads solemnly*)—"Order of the palm. To Lieutenant (jg) Douglas Roberts for action against the enemy, above and beyond the call of duty on the night of 8 May 1945." (*He passes the medal back to* ROBERTS.)

ROBERTS (*after a moment—smiling*)—It's very nice but I'm afraid you've got the wrong guy. (*The men turn to* DOWDY, *grinning.*)

DOWDY—We know that, but we'd kinda like for you to have it anyway.

ROBERTS—All right, I'll keep it. (*The men beam. There is an awkward pause.*)

GERHART—Stefanowski thought up the words.

ROBERTS—They're fine words. (WILEY *enters.*)

WILEY—The boat's here, Mister Roberts. I put your gear in. They want to shove off right away.

ROBERTS (*rising*)—Thanks. We haven't had our drink yet.

REBER—No, we ain't. (*All get to their feet.* ROBERTS *picks up his glass, looks at the crew, and everyone drinks.*)

ROBERTS—Good-by, Doc.

DOC—Good-by, Doug.

ROBERTS—And thanks, Doc.

Doc—Okay.

Roberts—Good-by, Frank.

Pulver—Good-by, Doug.

Roberts—Remember, I'm counting on you. (Pulver *nods. Roberts turns to the crew and looks at them for a moment. Then he takes the medal from the box, pins it on his shirt, shows it to them, then gives a little gestured salute and exits as the lights fade out.*)

Now it is sunset, and Doc is sitting on the hatch cover reading a letter. Mannion, wearing sidearms, is on watch before the Captain's palm trees, one on each side of the door. Pulver brings in a packet of letters he has just got, and inquires what Doc's news is. The news is that Doc's wife has some new wallpaper for the living room.

Dowdy comes on, pursuing Pulver. The Captain has ordered no movies again tonight, because somebody got caught without a shirt two days ago, and Pulver has got to go in and see the Old Man.

"I did. I asked him to show a movie yesterday," says Pulver.

Pulver runs through his own envelopes. At sight of one of them he exclaims, "Doc! This is from Doug!"

He reads it. It is dated three weeks ago and must be short and sweet because they are shoving off in a couple of minutes. . . . His guess about where he was being sent was right. . . . He has met a friend of Pulver's named Fornell. . . . He has been aboard this destroyer two weeks and already there have been four air attacks. . . .

"I'm glad to be here," the letter continues. "But I'm thinking now of you, Doc, and you, Frank, and Dolan and Dowdy and Insigna and everyone else on that bucket—all the guys everywhere who sail from Taipan to Apathy and back again—with an occasional side trip to Monotony.

"But I've discovered, Doc, that the most terrible enemy of this war is the boredom that eventually becomes a faith and, therefore, a sort of suicide—and I know now that the ones who refuse to surrender to it are the strongest of all."

Right now, Roberts has written, he is looking at his brass medal, and he'd rather have it than the Congressional Medal of Honor. "It tells me what I'll always be proudest of—that at a time in the world when courage counted most, I lived among one hundred sixty-seven brave men. So, Doc, and especially you, Frank, don't let those guys down."

The letter ends abruptly because the mail orderly has arrived to pick it up. Pulver hands it to Doc and takes another envelope from his packet. "Well, for God's sake," he announces, "this is from Fornell!" He begins to read it to himself. Doc and Dowdy, who has come back, sense that something is wrong.

"Mister Roberts is dead," Pulver pronounces finally. "They took a Jap suicide plane. It killed everyone in a twin-forty battery and then it went on through and killed Doug and another officer in the wardroom. . . ."

Profoundly moved, Dowdy asks Pulver if he can please give the letter to the crew.

"No," interjects Doc, holding out the letter from Roberts. "Give them this one. It's theirs." Dowdy takes it and leaves. Doc stares straight ahead. Pulver straightens, seems to grow.

He walks casually over to Mannion, saying in a friendly voice, "Go on down and get your mail. I'll stand by for you." Mannion voices surprised thanks.

As soon as he leaves, Pulver calmly uproots the palms, one by one, and throws them over the side. Then he knocks loudly on the Captain's door and the Captain demands truculently who it is.

"Captain, this is Ensign Pulver. I just threw your palm trees overboard. Now what's all this crap about no movie tonight?"

THE CURTAIN FALLS

COMMAND DECISION

A Play in Three Acts

By William Wister Haines

THE middle of William Wister Haines' three names means that he was related on his mother's side to the late Owen Wister, whose "The Virginian" is a classic of outdoor fiction. Haines' career as a fictioneer has also been of the outdoor variety, and "Command Decision" may be classed as such even though its action is completely confined to a Nissen hut in England.

Haines, now 40, got a B.S. in economics at the University of Pennsylvania during the depression and afterward, instead of seeking a white-collar job, went where there was more money— outdoors. He had been a telephone lineman in his native Des Moines, and now he became a high tension lineman, working for seven years on power lines and the electrification of the Pennsylvania Railroad. On the side he wrote short fiction and sold it to magazines. Out of the experiences of his job he wrote two novels, "Slim" and "High Tension," which were successful.

In the Spring of 1942 he was commissioned a second lieutenant in the Air Forces; in the Fall of 1946 he emerged a lieutenant colonel. He first did intelligence work in Washington, then spent thirty-three months overseas with such outfits as the Eighth Air Force Composite Command, the Eighth Fighter Command, the Eighth Air Force and the United States Strategic Air Forces. As he had done with his high tension experience, he determined to put what he had learned in his war job into fiction.

On V-J Day he began writing "Command Decision"—not as a novel, this time, but as a play. When it was finished he sent it to his publishers, Little, Brown & Co. His editor there said it was a good job, and why not make a novel out of it? Haines dutifully did so, and the novel became a best-seller; this was a rare instance in which a book was adapted from a drama instead of the other way around.

The play went the rounds of the Broadway managers. Jed Harris had an option on it for six months, but abandoned it after a Summer tryout in Cleveland in 1946. The hit-making firm of Lindsay and Crouse took it up, hoping to get Hollywood's

Jimmy Stewart for the leading role—but nothing came of it. Most managers felt that it was too soon after the war for a war play to get over; they remembered that "What Price Glory?" and "Journey's End" came many years after World War I.

Finally Kermit Bloomgarden risked a production, with Paul Kelly in the leading part. He entrusted the staging to a newcomer among directors, John O'Shaughnessy. It became a solid hit through the 1947-48 season in New York.

The office of Brigadier General K. C. Dennis at the Headquarters of the Fifth American Bombardment Division, Heavy, in England, is the round-roofed end of a large Nissen hut. The furnishings include a couple of file cabinets, one of them straplocked and marked "Top Secret."

In an alcove at the back of the room there is a pot-bellied coal stove used for heating coffee. There are doors leading to an Operations room and to an anteroom. There are a fire extinguisher and two or three water and sand buckets. A wide-shuttered window at the side looks out upon the perimeter track and landing strips of the operating group based on Division Headquarters Airfield. A large curtain covers a Status Board on the back wall. The General's big flat-topped desk and a long map table are near the center of the room. There are switches controlling lights over the desk, table and wall-maps. There are American, British and Division flags in a rack and another rack holding three Tommy guns.

The time is about 4 o'clock of a Saturday afternoon. Presently Technical Sergeant Harold Evans appears. "He is a tough, independent graduate gunner of 25 who has finished his missions and taken a job as the General's man to improve his food, drink and amusement." Relaxed at the moment, the Sergeant pours himself a cup of coffee, selects a cigar from a box on the General's desk and is comfortably sprawled in a chair at the map table when the door opens and an accredited war correspondent, Elmer Brockhurst, lets himself in.

"Brockhurst, middle-aged, reflects the cocky, contemptuous power of the big magazine he represents."

Sergeant Evans is obviously not pleased at the appearance of Brockhurst. When the latter would indicate his right to be there by a series of impertinent questions, the Sergeant reaches calmly for one of the Tommy guns, cocks it and is prepared to order the correspondent from the room. Brockhurst produces a new pass given him by Major General R. G. Kane to replace the one that General Dennis had torn up.

Sergeant Evans doesn't think much of a pass "signed by a god-damned old Major General who can't sign his name clear enough to read," but is willing to accept it so long as Brockhurst keeps away from the wall-maps—at least until General Dennis arrives—

"Where is that Fascist megalomaniac?" demands Brockhurst.

"Who?"

"Dennis," repeats Brockhurst. "That's what he is, a Fascist megalomaniac."

"What's that?"

"A man so drunk with power he thinks he can cover anything he does with other people's blood."

"How long you been around the army?" Evans inquires.

"Long enough to know that's what Dennis is."

"That's what all generals are."

"Where is he, Sarge? Sleeping till the mission comes in?"

"You must love that guardhouse," Evans mocks, "pumping me about missions."

"Having Dennis lock me in that guardhouse taught me a lot of angles. What became of that German pilot he had there?"

"That isn't a lot of angles—that's one."

"What about that German fighter plane Dennis has under close guard in Hangar Four?—and the one he's been flying himself lately? Why did he take the worst losses of the war yesterday and then send his bombers even deeper into Germany today?"

"I thought you knew the angles."

"I know he's got one of his own Squadron Commanders under close arrest in the guardhouse right now." Evans starts and Brockhurst presses his advantage. "Why?"

"He's a bad boy—won't brush his teeth."

Suddenly Brockhurst changes the subject. "Cliff Garnett arrived in England last night by special plane."

"Who's he?"

"Brigadier General Clifton C. Garnett is Secretary to the United Chiefs of Staff in Washington."

"Oh, God! Now we'll never get the war over."

"I'll bet you Dennis' war is over this week."

"You think they'd fire Dennis for one of them pentagon bell-hops?" retorts Evans skeptically.

"Sarge, ever since General Lucas got killed and Dennis took over here the country's been shuddering at his losses—people are whispering—calling Dennis the Butcher of Bombardment."

"Oh, my aching back—"

"Wait and see!   Cliff Garnett should have had this job in the first place—he's a smart operator and the United Chiefs trust him."

"They never fired no General yet till they'd give him the Legion of Merit—and Dennis ain't got one."

"They can give 'em mighty quick. Going to miss your hero?"

"He's no hero to me," replies Evans. "I've just taken this job—after my twenty-eight missions—to chisel my way to what I really want."

Brockhurst is friendly with General Kane, he intimates. He might be willing to speak to Kane about Evans, if the Sergeant would be reasonable about explaining certain recent news angles. But the Sergeant isn't interested. All he would want anyway would be an assignment as "a bartender in a rest camp for battle-weary WACS."

General Dennis has sent for Colonel Haley. He would also have the guard bring Captain Jenks from the guardhouse. From Haley the General would like to know how many planes he can count on having for the next day's mission.

Colonel Haley believes that with the repair jobs returned to service and the thirty weatherbound planes that have just taken off from Iceland there should be about sixty in all.

"How do the boys feel, Haley?"

"They're too tired to feel, sir."

Colonel Haley continues nervously fingering a sheaf of papers he carries. General Dennis would know what is on his aid's mind.

"Another rape case, I'm afraid, sir," reports the Colonel un-happily.

"Combat crew or base personnel?"

"A navigator, sir."

"Nuts," Dennis snorts. "When's a navigator had time to get raped?"

"Complaint was he did the raping, sir. Last night."

"Between yesterday's mission and today's—?" Dennis' face registers incredulity. "Who's complaining, the girl or her mother?"

"Her mother, sir. Mrs. Daphne Magruder, Tranquillity Cottage, The High Street, Undershot-Overhill."

"I know them people, sir," speaks up Sergeant Evans.

"No doubt," is the General's ready retort. "Did our boy go there alone, Haley?"

"I'm afraid he did, sir."

"Haley! I've told you before: when these boys tomcat they're to go in pairs. How can you expect one man, flying missions, to keep the whole family happy? Have you told the Judge Advocate?"

"Not yet, sir. We're badly bottlenecked for navigators and this man has ten missions more to go on his twenty-five."

Again Sergeant Evans has a suggestion. He has a feeling that he can square the rape case if he could have a couple of gallons of ice cream from mess supply. General Dennis is very glad to accept the Evans help. Let the Sergeant collect the ice cream and get busy with the settlement.

With Evans gone, Colonel Haley has another matter to bring to his General's attention. "Grapevine says General Kane's in a huddle with the Hemisphere Commander, sir," he reports.

DENNIS—What's that got to do with us?

HALEY—Grapevine says there's a big meeting in Washington next week—and neither of them is invited.

DENNIS—That's their worry. (*Then, anxiously.*) What day next week?

HALEY—No one knows, sir.

DENNIS—Well, tomorrow's only Sunday. You're sure the weather hasn't changed?

HALEY—No, sir—last forecast is still fine.

DENNIS—Well, then we'll finish *before* the meeting.

HALEY—I hope so, sir.

DENNIS—*We* haven't had any squawk from Washington yet—?

HALEY—Not yet, sir.

DENNIS—Send Captain Jenks in here.

HALEY—Want me with you, sir?

DENNIS—No. I'll try him alone again. (*Checks* HALEY *at door.*) Has that cable come for Ted Martin yet?

HALEY—Not yet, sir. I've been checking. Mrs. Martin must be late with that baby.

DENNIS (*absently*)—She's ten years late. (*Then noticing* HALEY's *surprise:*) Keep checking; I'd like to meet Ted with good news when he lands. (HALEY *exits.* DENNIS *takes a troubled look at the sky, seats himself with a dossier of papers at his desk. A knock is heard at the door.*) Come in! (CAPTAIN LUCIUS JENKS *enters, followed by an* ARMED GUARD. JENKS *is an ordinary-looking kid in flying coveralls, momentarily sullen.* GUARD *follows him to position facing desk and salutes.*)

GUARD—Guard reporting with prisoner as ordered, sir.

DENNIS—Wait outside. (*The* GUARD *exits*.) Jenks, have you thought this over?

JENKS (*stonily*)—I thought it over this morning.

DENNIS—You've had more time.

JENKS—I don't need more time.

DENNIS—Damn it, boy, don't you realize this is serious?

JENKS—I'm not getting killed to make you a record. I'll tell the court so too, and the whole damned world.

DENNIS—What else will you tell them?

JENKS—That you lost forty bombers, four hundred men, by deliberately sending us beyond fighter cover yesterday. This morning, when we're entitled to a milk run, you order us even further into Germany.

DENNIS—Who told you you were entitled to a milk run?

JENKS—You big boys think flag-fodder like us can't even read a calendar, don't you? Where do the Air Forces get those statistical records for sorties and tonnages that General Kane announces regularly? They get 'em on milk runs over the Channel ports the last three days of every month.

DENNIS—Twelve crews took today's target for their last mission.

JENKS—They didn't have the guts to say what they thought of it. If you big shots are entitled to a record racket, so am I.

DENNIS—You were informed, at briefing, of the purpose of this mission.

JENKS—"A very significant target that can kill a lot of our people unless we knock it out." Nuts to that pep talk! Everything in Germany's made to kill people. Why can't we have targets under fighter cover, like General Kane promised?

DENNIS—He didn't promise that.

JENKS—Anyone who knows the Army knows what Kane's . . .

DENNIS—*General* Kane's—

JENKS—. . . General Kane's press interview meant. That day we lost nineteen over Bremfurt and the Air Corps turned itself inside out explaining. How do you think the public will like forty yesterday—and worse today?

DENNIS—The public isn't my business.

JENKS—How do you think it will like hearing you ordered both these attacks when Kane—General Kane—was absent?

DENNIS—And that isn't your business. You were ordered to go. After learning the target you refused.

JENKS—I've been to plenty tough targets.

DENNIS (*fingering dossier*)—You aborted from the two toughest prior to yesterday.

JENKS—For mechanical malfunctions in my plane—

DENNIS—One engineer's examination said: "Possibly justifiable." The other said: "Defect not discernible."

JENKS—It was plenty discernible to me, and my co-pilot will tell you the same thing, unless he's prejudiced—

DENNIS—He should be; he's flying your seat today, and you're a Squadron Commander. The Army had trusted you with Command. (*This bites;* JENKS *has begun to look scared.* DENNIS *resumes patiently.*) Now, if you've got any legitimate reason at all . . . (EVANS *enters.*)

EVANS (*with a note of warning*)—Major General R. G. Kane and party, sir.

General Kane, "a shrewd man of fifty-odd, tough but capable of a calculated amiability," is followed into the room by Brigadier General Clifton C. Garnett, a virile man in his late thirties, and Major Homer Prescott, "a genteel stooge."

"I'm very sorry, sir," admits Dennis, as he minds his military manners and salutes General Kane. "If I'd known you were visiting my command I should have been at the gate."

"Don't speak of it, my boy," Kane reassures him.

A moment later, Correspondent Brockhurst has crashed the conference. "I had a hunch you'd come down here today," he announces cheerily.

"General Kane, I've forbidden this man the station," interrupts General Dennis.

"Now, Casey, that's one of the things I came down about," announces General Kane.

"He was snooping in a restricted hangar and trying to worm information out of my people. I had him in the guardhouse until your counter-order."

Brockhurst addresses himself to Kane. "Kane, the American people are going to be very interested in Dennis' guardhouse."

Now General Kane has caught sight of the prisoner. "Why, Captain Jenks! Delighted to see you again, my boy!" he explodes, throwing a paternal arm around Jenks and turning to General Garnett. "Cliff, this is one of our real heroes."

"Is this the Captain Jenks who named his fortress the Urgent Virgin?" inquired Garnett.

"The best publicity we've had in this war," beams General Kane. "Three pages and ten pictures in Brockie's magazine.

What brings you to headquarters today, my boy?   Helping General Dennis?"

"A disciplinary matter, sir.   We'll attend to it later," Dennis starts to explain, motioning Jenks to the door.

"No, no!" protests General Kane, stepping in front of Jenks. "This is what you wanted to see, Cliff—real field problems.   Now, Casey, you and Captain Jenks carry on just as if we weren't here. If there's one thing I pride myself on it's not interfering with the vital work of my divisions."

DENNIS—This isn't a matter for the press, sir.

KANE (*sharply*)—Brockie is my friend, General!   (*Then, to* JENKS.)   What's the disciplinary trouble, my boy?   Some of those high-spirited young pilots of yours getting out of hand?

JENKS—Perhaps General Dennis will explain, sir.

DENNIS—Captain Jenks refused to fly today's mission as ordered, sir.   (BROCKHURST *whistles.   Others react.*)

KANE—I can't believe it.

JENKS—Do you know what today's target was, General Kane?

DENNIS (*sharply*)—Captain, you're still under Security Regulations.   There will be no mention of today's target before the press!

BROCKHURST—Security covers a lot, doesn't it, Dennis?

DENNIS—The life of every man we send across the Channel.

BROCKHURST—What about the life of this boy under you?

KANE (*to* BROCKHURST)—Brockie, there *is* a question of security, if you don't mind.

BROCKHURST—O.K., R.G.   I *was* trying to help you.   (*He exits.*)

DENNIS—The target was Schweinhafen, sir.

KANE—Schweinhafen!   You've begun Operation Stitch?

DENNIS—Began yesterday, sir, with Posenleben.

KANE—*Posenleben* . . . yesterday?   What happened?

DENNIS—Excellent results, sir.   Over three-quarters total destruction.

KANE—I mean . . . what were your losses?

DENNIS—Forty planes, sir.

KANE—*Forty!*   Good God!   Does the press know about it?

DENNIS—I put a security blackout on the whole operation as we agreed.

GARNETT (*sharply*)—Would someone mind telling a visitor the details of this Operation Stitch?

DENNIS—Kind of a three-horse parlay, Cliff; Posenleben,

Schweinhafen . . . (*Eyes* PRESCOTT *and* JENKS.) . . . and one other.

GARNETT—Well, I thought I'd written your directive myself!

DENNIS—Some things aren't in official directives, Cliff.

GARNETT—Evidently. But the United Chiefs are still running the war, Casey. Have you taken it on yourself to change their orders?

KANE—I was going to send them a provisional plan for Operation Stitch but . . . (*Lamely.*) . . . I didn't know General Dennis intended implementing it so soon. It takes a very rare weather condition.

PRESCOTT—The whole idea was General Dennis', sir.

DENNIS—And I'll explain it myself, Major! Do you wish to detain Captain Jenks any further, General Kane?

KANE (*wishing he were dead but having to deal with this*)— Did you go on the Posenleben mission yesterday, Captain?

JENKS—I did, sir. It was a bloody massacre. Today will be worse.

KANE—Any news from today's mission yet, General?

DENNIS—Colonel Martin radioed: "Primary target plastered," sir.

KANE—I mean news about losses.

DENNIS—Ted indicated fighting, sir, but no details.

For a second time General Kane brushes aside General Dennis' suggestion that there is no further need of Captain Jenks being at this conference. Kane doesn't plan to interfere, but with General Dennis' permission, he would like to have a private talk with Captain Jenks. For that purpose he steps outside, followed by the prisoner, and Major Prescott. . . .

General Garnett has a personal matter to take up with General Dennis. He (Garnett) is surprised and pained to learn that his brother-in-law (and Dennis' best friend), Tom Martin, is still flying missions despite the fact that his wife is about to have a baby. Dennis can't see that that has anything to do with the situation. When General Garnett's sister married Martin, she married the service, and naturally must abide by the consequences.

"Casey, the service needs Ted . . . for bigger jobs. And he and Helen deserve a little security now. You don't have to send him at his age."

"I don't have to send any of 'em. We could all be secure under Hitler."

Kane, Jenks and Prescott have returned to the room.

"General Dennis," announces General Kane. "Captain Jenks is obviously the victim of a shock condition induced by the strain of his nineteen missions. It's a medical problem. All he needs is a rest."

"Sir," replies Dennis, "Captain Jenks finished ten days in a rest house on Thursday and has been medically certified fit for the completion of his twenty-five missions."

General Kane's appearance has taken on a slightly apoplectic cast. He decides that the investigation should be postponed for the present. "General, this is very serious," he confesses as soon as Captain Jenks has been returned to the guardhouse.

"Every detail will be checked, sir," Dennis assures him. "It happened at five-twenty this morning. I've got the rest of the twenty-four hours to charge him."

"What charge are you considering?"

"Unless something new comes up the only possible charge is: "Desertion in the face of the enemy."

"Good God, boy!" Kane purples. "We can't shoot a national hero!"

"Do you think you'll ever have another tough mission if you don't? At Group Briefing this morning when the target was uncovered, I saw five men cross themselves. One fainted. But they went . . . and they know that Jenks didn't."

Kane understands this, but won't face the implication. Major Prescott offers a suggestion. "Couldn't a quiet transfer be arranged . . . to Transport or Training?"

"So he could go yellow there and kill passengers or students?" counters Dennis.

"Precautions could be taken," Prescott persists. "There's such a thing as the end justifying the means, sir. This case would put the honor of the Army Air Forces at stake."

"It already has," replies Dennis. "Every man in the Division knows it."

"I was thinking of the larger picture."

"You can afford to."

"Homer, go talk this over with Elmer Brockhurst," Kane breaks in. "Everything."

"Sir!" General Dennis' attitude is definitely one of protest.

"Brockie has a remarkable feel for public reaction, Casey," Kane tries to reassure him. "We've got to consider every angle on this."

General Dennis continues to explain and defend the decisions he has made. The visiting generals, and General Kane in particular, continue to seek some way to change, or at least to modify, those Dennis decisions most likely to affect the immediate future in relation to such reports as will have to be made to the United Chiefs. Finally General Garnett insists on a complete report.

"General Kane, I must insist on being briefed about this Operation Stitch. The United Chiefs will have to know."

"Haven't you told him anything about it, sir?" an incredulous Dennis demands of General Kane.

"I thought it would be fairer to let you."

"Six weeks ago a German fighter plane landed on that Number One strip," Dennis begins. "Right outside the window there."

"Shot up?" inquires Garnett.

"Not a scratch," Dennis continues. "The pilot was a Czechoslovakian engineer. He'd been forced to work for them but when they sent him up to the Baltic to test this job he flew it here to us."

"Accommodating of him," Garnett comments sarcastically.

"That cross," continues Dennis, pointing to an object nailed to the wall, "was the plane marking. I hung it there as a reminder."

"What kind of fighter was it?"

"Focke-Schmidt 1."

"Focke-Schmidt 1 . . . ?" Garnett repeats the name slowly.

Dennis pursues his story. "Remember that spy's report out of Lisbon . . . on a new jet-propelled fighter . . . Messerschmitt wing, the new Serrenbach propulsion unit . . . forty-eight thousand ceiling and six hundred at thirty thousand?"

"Our people said that was impossible," protests Garnett.

"I know. These are the tests of it."

Turning to the wall, Dennis strips a curtain mask revealing performance curves inked on graph paper. Red, blue, green and yellow curves are closely grouped, almost parallel. Above, obviously in a class by itself, is the heavy black curve of the Focke-Schmidt 1. Dennis indicates the colors as he talks.

"Lightning, Thunderbolt, Mustang, Spit Twelve and . . . Focke-Schmidt 1."

"Jesus Christ!" ejaculates Garnett. He quickly recovers. "Oh, the German job's in kilometers!"

"No, it isn't," Dennis informs him. "That's miles . . . same as the others."

GARNETT—Who made these tests?
DENNIS—Ted Martin and I.

GARNETT—Yourselves?

DENNIS—Three turns apiece.

GARNETT (*awed, tracing black curve*)—You did that . . . after what the doctors told you?

DENNIS—I wanted to be sure. It gave me a week in the hospital to think things over.

GARNETT (*ruefully, as he examines the curves*)—Of course, our new Mustangs will be a great improvement.

DENNIS—This isn't an improvement, Cliff. This is a revolution.

GARNETT—Even so, when you get enough of our new Mustangs . . .

DENNIS—Can you arrange an armistice until we get 'em?

GARNETT—Casey, I've battled the United Chiefs for every bomber you've got. I've stuck my neck out to get you Mustangs to protect them. I've fought for this Air Corps just as hard as you have. Now, when will the Germans get these jets?

DENNIS—They have three factories entering line production now . . . or, rather, they did have yesterday morning.

GARNETT—New factories?

DENNIS—No. They've converted old bomber plants. The Czech engineer thinks they've got one operating group on conversion training already.

GARNETT—Have you lost any planes to it?

DENNIS—Lost planes don't report. But last week we wrote off three reconnaissance planes for the first time in months. They were stripped to the ribs and flying at forty thousand, but something got them.

KANE—Of course, we don't *know* it was this new jet.

DENNIS—It wasn't mice. (*Moves to map and opens it.*) I've flown this plane and we've photographed the three factories.

GARNETT—Weren't they camouflaged?

DENNIS—Perfectly. We put an infra-red camera on a night fighter and caught 'em after dark with Focke-Schmidts on every apron. (*Indicates three marked spots on map.*) Posenleben, Schweinhafen and Fendelhorst. That's Operation Stitch, for Stitch in Time. . . .

GARNETT—They're deep enough in, aren't they?

DENNIS—Goering is thinking better of us these days.

GARNETT—How far beyond friendly fighter cover is that? (DENNIS *swings the conventional arc; it is woefully short of the mark.*) Casey, it's murder to send bombers that far beyond friendly fighter cover.

KANE—And I don't think it's necessary. This jet fighter may have a superior capability on paper, or even when it's flown by men like Casey and Ted Martin. But when I consider American courage and airmanship . . .

DENNIS (*indicating curves*)—Courage and airmanship don't fill gaps like this, sir.

GARNETT—Why hasn't this technical data been reported?

DENNIS—It has. Through channels. You'll hear from it next year.

GARNETT—What's your honest opinion of this, Casey?

DENNIS—This can run us out of Europe in sixty days.

KANE (*protestingly*)—That's giving them absolute perfection in production, in testing, in crew conversion, in tactics. . . .

DENNIS—That's giving them thirty days to get two groups operating and thirty more to catch one of our missions for just half an hour. I put that in my report.

GARNETT (*sharply*)—Why didn't you send this report to us? (DENNIS *is silent.* KANE *has to answer.*)

KANE—I did report to the United Chiefs that we could not exclude the possibility of encountering an unsuspected enemy capability which might compel retrospective alteration of our present estimate of the situation.

GARNETT—Did you approve this Operation Stitch, sir? (KANE *glares, but* GARNETT *is secretary to the United Chiefs.*)

KANE—I told General Dennis this constitutes a tactical emergency within the scope of a *Division* Commander's discretion.

DENNIS—It's my rap, Cliff. I consider the operation necessary.

GARNETT—Your losses are the United Chiefs' rap, Casey. Remember, half of them are Admirals. A very substantial body of opinion doesn't believe we can succeed with daylight precision bombardment over Germany.

DENNIS—A very substantial body of opinion didn't believe the Wright brothers could fly.

General Garnett would warn General Dennis that the United Chiefs are having a global reallocation meeting the following week to review the whole record. There is danger that General Dennis' course might scare the Chiefs into abandoning the whole B-29 strategy in the Pacific.

"I don't think we're justified in making a third attack tomorrow," announces General Kane.

"Sir! Concentration is the crux of this!" protests General Dennis. "You agreed to that. . . . It may be a month before we can get back to Fendelhorst. That's too long."

There is a second roar of returning bombers. These are from a group that is based ten miles north and they pass over. By count there are twelve of them. General Kane asks Dennis to find out if the twelve are the remains of a squadron or a group. He is plainly both scared and nervous. Dennis leaves the room.

A moment later, Major Prescott brings in Correspondent Brockhurst.

"What's your reaction, Brockie?" inquires General Kane. "Tell us frankly."

"You want it smooth or rough, R.G.?"

"Well, your honest reaction, Elmer."

"Your neck's out a foot."

"*My* neck . . . ?" strangles Kane.

"Unless you can pass the buck to the Hemisphere Commander. You've got a hero to court-martial . . . after record losses yesterday and probably again today. You've let security keep this so dark it stinks like Pearl Harbor. . . ."

There is the faint sound of a single bomber high overhead as Brockhurst continues. "After all, the public makes these bombers and sends you these kids. It's got a right to know."

"Go on, Elmer," prompts Kane, as Dennis comes through the door, "I want General Dennis to hear your reactions."

"He knows it," Brockhurst replies. "I've warned him that the press and public . . ."

"Press and public be goddamned!" snaps Dennis. "Your magazine would crucify us for one headline."

"When did we *ever* . . . ?"

"After Bremfurt." Dennis cuts him short. "We needed a second attack to finish there. But by the time you got done with our losses and Washington got done with your insinuations, we were told it was politically impossible to attack there again. *Politically impossible!* Today boys were killed with cannon made at Bremfurt since that attack."

"Dennis," Brockhurst shoots back, "the Air Corps spent twenty years begging us to cry Wolf at the public to get you planes. Now you've got 'em all you give us is phony official statements and alibis about security. We were asked to help Washington 'prepare the country' for the news about Bremfurt. I'm sorry the plan back-fired, but it wasn't entirely our fault."

The roar of a single plane sends them all to the window. A moment later, Garnett and Prescott hurl themselves to the floor as the approaching bomber appears to be coming directly at them.

Kane and Dennis remain erect.

"Sorry, sir," mumbles Prescott as he picks himself up from the floor. "They're not supposed to buzz the bases."

"I'll have that pilot tried!" angrily declares General Kane.

"He isn't buzzing, sir," explains Dennis. "He's in trouble. . . . Can't you see those red flares? He's got wounded aboard."

The grinding, crashing sound of a nose-in is followed by a thunderous concussion and, a moment later, the screech of a meat-wagon siren.

"Aggregate tomorrow's serviceability as soon as possible," Dennis instructs Colonel Haley, who has come in from the Operations room.

"Tomorrow! This is worse than yesterday!" storms General Kane, as Haley leaves.

"They got their target, sir," calmly answers Dennis.

Before Kane can answer that one, Sergeant Evans is in to announce the arrival of photographers from Public Relations. Who ordered them and on what authority, Major Prescott would know.

"I did, sir," blandly answers the Sergeant. "All generals have their pictures taken everywhere they go. They say it helps the boys' morale."

"Well, of course, if it helps morale," agrees General Kane, "we'll go along. . . . Casey, you will not order tomorrow's mission until I get back."

Dennis has started pacing the room distractedly. The door opens and Colonel Ted Martin enters. He is a vigorous, skeptical Air Force officer in his middle thirties—"looks exhausted, but exudes great vitality; face smoke-stained and clothes conspicuously drenched with dried blood."

The blood is that of his radio man, killed when a twenty-millimeter shell landed right on the radio panel. "Ummmm! I'm getting old," confesses Ted. "They should have had this war ten years ago."

"How do you think I feel?" Dennis inquires.

"Sorry, Grandpa!" replies Martin contritely.

"Tell me about it. Was it rough all the way?"

"No. It was a milk run for thirty-four minutes after our fighters had to turn back. Then the whole damned Luftwaffe jumped us. . . ." Martin grins. "Those boys must have a new directive too. From then back to our fighters we shot our guns hot."

"When did you get yours?"

"Just after I radioed you the strike signal. What about the rest?"

"Looks like forty-two with two down in the Channel so far."

"I was afraid of that from what I saw."

"Did you catch fire?" Dennis wants to know.

"Yes. We were having it hot and heavy so I stayed on the nose gun and Goldberg went back and put it out. He should get something for that, Casey. One of our waist gunners took one look at that fire and went right out through the bomb bay."

"Goldberg can have whatever you recommend."

"I'll think it over," Martin replies. He returns to the story of the mission. "Then after things quieted down we tried a tourniquet on the kid, but it was too late." Changing the subject, Martin asks, "Didn't I just see Old Percent and Cliff Garnett in a car?"

"Yeah. The joint's full of big wheels today." Dennis explains, "They're having a global reallocation meeting Tuesday."

"Has Cliff reallocated himself your job?" Martin inquires suspiciously.

"I think Cliff's got his eye on one of those B-29 commands in the Pacific. They start with two stars," is Dennis' reply.

A moment later, Colonel Martin's suspicions are intensified. Sergeant Evans has come in to ask where General Dennis would have General Garnett's footlocker and bedroll put.

"General Garnett's footlocker and bedroll . . . so he is moving in!" muses Martin.

"Ted, I don't envy you Cliff for a brother-in-law," chides Dennis, "but he's an able staff officer."

"Clifton has flown some of the hottest desks in Washington," admits Ted.

"We needed those guys . . . to get planes for hoodlums like you and me."

"Casey, no record after this war will be worth a damn without Command in it. Cliff knows this is still the best command in the Air Forces. Any Brigadier alive would give his next star for your job."

"When I finish Operation Stitch they can have it for Corporal's stripes. Thank God, we're two-thirds done."

"Casey, that's the hell of it; we aren't."

"You're tired. You did Posenleben yesterday and Schweinhafen today. . . ."

Martin forces his reply. "We didn't touch Schweinhafen today."

Dennis is stricken. "What? You signaled me."

"Mistake. Before I could correct it the radio man was dead. We plastered some goddamned place that looked exactly like it, forty miles from Schweinhafen. . . ." Forty-four bombers for the wrong target. Why don't you castrate me?"

"Quit hurting. You've had this coming, Ted. It's averages."

MARTIN—What will this do to Operation Stitch?

DENNIS—Set us back one day. We'll do Schweinhafen again tomorrow and Fendelhorst Monday. I'm pretty sure the weather will hold.

MARTIN—Will Kane . . . with global reallocation coming up Tuesday?

DENNIS—He'll have to.

MARTIN—Casey, he had cold feet before we started.

DENNIS—He's our Chief, Ted.

MARTIN—And a good soldier is loyal to his Chief. It says so in the book. But what kind of loyalty is that . . . to fallible men above him, half the time dopes and cowards? What about loyalty to common sense . . . and to the guys who have to do things that aren't in the book . . . like Stitch?

DENNIS—At least he didn't forbid it, Ted.

MARTIN—Did he authorize it? Did he endorse your report and go on record like a man? Not Kane. You're the goat on this one.

DENNIS—Other guys have been killed. If I get canned . . .

MARTIN—If you get canned, it's the end of honest bombardment here.

DENNIS—We've got to tell him, Ted.

MARTIN (with passion)—You can't tell him, Casey! What about the guys we've already lost? If Kane quits now, they're wasted. We either finish now or we might as well take precision bombardment back to Arizona. It's us or the Germans this week, boy, and you're the only Commander in this hemisphere with guts enough to see it through.

DENNIS—Which of us is going to tell Kane that?

MARTIN—I'll guarantee Kane won't be able to tell today's strike from Schweinhafen. Tomorrow we'll knock off Fendelhorst. Monday, when he orders his usual month-end milk run to the French channel ports, we'll go back and clean up Schweinhafen.

HALEY (entering)—Fifty-third Wing reports both of today's reconnaissance planes now two hours overdue, sir. (DENNIS *nods and* HALEY *exits.*)

MARTIN—Today it's reconnaissance planes! Six weeks from now it'll be whole divisions of bombers, unless we finish the job.

DENNIS—We'll finish, Ted. We'll make him finish!

MARTIN (*aghast*)—Casey, you and I know what Operation Stitch means. How can you tell Kane?

DENNIS—He's our Chief, Ted. He's in command.

The curtain falls.

ACT II

Sergeant Evans has returned from his mission to the home of the aggrieved complainants against the amorous navigator. The Sergeant is triumphant but wearied, which amuses Colonel Haley.

"Sir, there were two of them women, both unhappy," protests Evans.

"Only two? That wouldn't have bothered me, at your age."

"Well, sir, I hope it doesn't bother me, at your age."

Colonel Ted Martin has brought in the strike photographs covering the mistake in the intended bombing of Schweinhafen. The doctoring Lieutenant Goldberg has done on them is uncannily clever. "These pictures would fool an expert," admits Dennis.

"They'd better," insists Colonel Martin deliberately.

"Why?"

"If you report this mistake to Kane before that Tuesday meeting, you're just giving your job to Cliff."

"I'd like to think so."

"And you're giving Goering those," Martin continues, pointing to the marker of the German jet plane on the wall. "Do you like to think that?"

"No."

"These pictures," continues Martin, "will keep Kane happy for twenty-four hours. He doesn't know a strike photo from a gonorrhea smear."

When General Kane and the others return from their dinner, Ted has hidden the pictures. Now General Garnett, at Kane's suggestion, has a confession to make.

"Casey, you may think I've ratted on you but I felt our people had to know what's going on. I persuaded General Kane to let me telephone the Air Board in Washington."

"What did they say?"

"Unfortunately, most of 'em are in Florida . . . at the proving grounds."

"Testing a new typewriter?" Dennis inquires.

General Kane cannot see the joke. "Casey, I cannot tolerate this attitude. Our Public Relations Policy has put us where we are today."

"It sure has."

"Dennis, a free democracy cannot ignore public opinion," interjects Correspondent Brockhurst.

"Let's take that up when it's free again," is Dennis' rejoinder.

"What?"

"The problem now is survival, Mr. Brockhurst."

General Garnett is convinced, following his talk with Washington, that, although the Board was shocked, he can assure Dennis that he will be permitted to finish Operation Stitch—*after* Tuesday.

General Dennis does not think he can hold off that long. "I've waited five weeks for this weather," he tells General Garnett. "Twice we had one good day. This takes three in succession."

"If we ever get 'em again," Dennis continues, "the Big Wheels would be after us for headline bombing. Submarine pens! Or covering some State Department fourflush in the Balkans."

"Nobody can take the politics out of war," replies Garnett. "But I made Lester agree that since you *are* two-thirds done . . ."

This was not exactly the moment for Lieutenant Goldberg to break in with a second selection of strike photographs he had just found. But the Lieutenant is far too excited to notice. Before he knows it, General Kane has grabbed the new pictures out of his hand and is viewing them with mounting excitement—

KANE—Look, Cliff! Look! Here's the highway coming in, here's the river . . . here's the factory. . . .

GOLDBERG—You've got them upside down, sir.

DENNIS—General Kane, I'd like a minute alone with you, sir.

KANE—Of course, Casey. My God! Look at that destruction, Cliff! These will have to go to Washington by special plane.

PRESCOTT—Sir! I'd like to frame these, dramatically, on good white board with a title . . . The Doom of Schweinhafen!

KANE—Yes! The very thing, Homer!

GOLDBERG—It isn't Schweinhafen, sir.

KANE—Not Schweinhafen? What are they?

GOLDBERG—The Nautilus Torpedo Factory at Gritzenheim, sir.

GARNETT—Torpedo factory! General! This is very opportune! Half the United Chiefs are Admirals! If we get these to that meeting . . .

KANE—I'll send my own plane! (*Claps* GOLDBERG *on the*

shoulder.) You don't know what you've done for us, boy! Showing them that in the midst of the greatest air campaign in history we still think enough of the larger picture to knock out a torpedo factory too . . .

DENNIS—I'm sorry, sir. It wasn't *too*. It was instead.

KANE—Instead! You let me tell Washington that you'd destroyed Schweinhafen!

DENNIS—It was a mistake. We hit this Nautilus place.

KANE—Whose mistake?

DENNIS—Mine, sir. The briefing . . .

MARTIN—The briefing was perfect. I led the Division and I loused it up.

GOLDBERG—These gentlemen are covering for me, sir. I was well briefed and I was on the bombsight. I got mixed up in the fighting.

KANE (*his chagrin finding a focal point*)—Why did you *get* mixed up . . . were you scared?

GOLDBERG—Yes, sir. I'm always scared. But today . . .

KANE—Casey, what are you thinking of—entrusting a mission of this importance to a man who admits he's . . .

DENNIS (*furiously*)—Sir, I should like to explain to you . . .

GOLDBERG (*to* DENNIS)—It's all right, sir. General Kane doesn't understand.

KANE—Do *you* understand what I'd be justified in doing?

GOLDBERG—You ought to shoot me for wasting four hundred and forty guys this afternoon. I'd be grateful if you did. (*He turns and exits without saluting.*)

DENNIS—Sir! Lieutenant Goldberg is on the fourth mission of a *voluntary second tour of duty over German targets only.*

BROCKHURST—I think I'd take it easy on that one, R.G. (*Too late,* KANE *is stricken with contrition.* MARTIN *pours it on him with repressed fury.*)

MARTIN—Sir, that boy isn't our Division Bombardier by accident. He knows there's a German order waiting for him by name and serial number. He knew it when he volunteered for a second tour. Today he hit what we both thought was the target . . . perfectly. . . . I've just written him up for a cluster on his Silver Star.

KANE—Send the citation to me personally.

MARTIN (*sincerely*)—Thank you, sir.

It now occurs to General Kane, after a worried moment, that it might not be entirely fair to the service for him to report the

Schweinhafen mistake *immediately*. With a couple more days on Naval targets and—

"And that would be the end of Operation Stitch," muses Dennis gravely.

It is while Dennis and Kane have gone to the Operations room to talk things out that General Garnett and Colonel Martin have a chance to catch up on family affairs.

"Listen, old man. Helen is worried about your flying missions," Garnett reports.

"My insurance is paid up," snaps Ted.

"Good God, man! I don't mean that. But you know how she is."

"I should. Look, Cliff! Neither of us is going to change much. Let's drop it."

"But you've got the kid to think of now."

"That's the point. This isn't like the old barnstorming and testing. Nobody gets a kick out of this."

"Exactly."

"But if Goldberg can fly missions for my kid, so can I."

"But, Ted, you can do so much more with your experience."

"What?"

"I've been fighting for Bombardment in my own way. Now I think the United Chiefs are going to give me a B-29 command in the Pacific to make me prove what I've been saying."

"Cliff, this is not conference fighting. Can you run an operational command?"

"Joe Lucas did—until he got killed. Casey's doing it. And I'm going to have something they never had."

"What?"

"Brigadier General Ted Martin for my Chief of Staff."

"Me, a Chief of Staff . . . with all those papers?"

"Adjutants do that. But I need . . . the Air Corps needs your operating experience out there. Incidentally, I'll be able to make you a Brigadier immediately."

Martin ponders deeply while Garnett eyes him tensely. "Cliff, did Casey cook this up with you . . . to ground me gently . . . *after today?*"

"Good Lord, no! He doesn't even know this."

"Then he isn't trying to get rid of me?"

"He'd rather cut his arm off," Garnett reassures. "But he'll understand that the service needs you there . . . and it's your chance to make Brigadier. Casey isn't selfish."

"If you put it to him that way, he'd make me go."

"We'll be a perfect team," urges Garnett. "I'll fight the Navy and you can fight the Japs."

"And Helen makes the Brigadier's wife. It's very neat, Cliff."

"Damn it, Ted," replies Garnett nettled. "That war's just as much for your kid as this one. Why should you throw yourself away here when by waiting . . . ?"

"The Germans aren't waiting," Martin snaps.

"Look, if you'd rather we both ask Casey . . ."

"No, you don't. If you say a word to Casey before I think this over, the deal's off."

"All right, but think with your head. Those B-29s can save an invasion against Japan. They can save bloody beachheads and five years of guerrilla warfare. They've got to have the best we've got, Ted."

Kane and Dennis come back from their talk. Kane is still enthused. "No man alive could tell these pictures from Schweinhafen," he says. Turning to General Garnett, he asks: "Cliff—do the United Chiefs actually study strike pictures?"

"Well, sir, of course they're not trained photo interpreters themselves, but . . ."

Brockhurst and Major Prescott have joined the group. "Sir," says Prescott, addressing General Kane, "I got some draughtsmen to make three by five mountings for the panels . . . before and after pictures . . . on good white board with glossy black lettering . . . the first title will be: 'Doom of an Axis Torpedo Factory.'"

"Jesus H. Christ!" explodes General Dennis.

"General!" checks Kane.

"General, I want to get this straight," mutters Brockhurst respectfully. "Isn't a torpedo factory a worth-while target?"

"The last one would be," snaps General Dennis. "The Germans wouldn't miss the first ten."

"But you have to make a start on anything worth while."

"Fighting submarines by heavy bombardment is not worth while."

"The Navy thinks it is," Brockhurst persists. "And most people agree."

"Most people always think you can get something for nothing, Mr. Brockhurst," Dennis retorts. "We're the only force available to strike the Germans in Germany. To wipe out submarines by bombing would cost us every good weather day for a year."

"Then why don't the United Chiefs straighten this mess out?" asks Brockhurst.

"The United Chiefs," Garnett breaks in, "are half Admirals.
We have to make some concessions to interservice co-operation."

"Did you get my memorandum to the Anointed Chiefs on
that?" asks Dennis of General Kane.

"I didn't send it up, Casey," Kane confesses. "It was too provocative."

"I offered the Navy a fair trade," Dennis defends. "I wrote
them I'd bomb any Naval target in Germany . . . the day after
they took those battleships in and shelled the fighter plane factory at Bremen."

"Can I use that?" inquires Brockhurst.

"God, no!" answers General Kane with spirit. "Half the
United Chiefs are Admirals, Brockie."

"Where did I get the idea this war was against the Axis?"
Brockhurst questions sardonically.

General Dennis is again pressing his superior for a decision.
"General Kane, *may* I send tomorrow's field order?"

KANE—Casey, I can't lose another forty planes over Schweinhafen the day after I've told them I've destroyed it.

DENNIS—Sir, you can release the Division to my discretion.

KANE—Whichever of us got hung, we'd still be sabotaging the
Chief.

DENNIS—Would you rather sabotage Bombardment, sir?

KANE—Casey, I've spent twenty years working for Bombardment. The Chief's spent twenty-five. You kids don't know how
we've fought.

MARTIN—No?

KANE—*No!* You're giving your youth. We've already given
ours. I was twelve years a *Captain*, the Chief was fourteen. We
took Billy Mitchell's side when it meant Siberia. They sent us
to a Cavalry School. I was the second best pilot in America . . .
and they assigned me to keeping records of manure disposal. But
we never gave up; we never quit trying. We wrote anything we
could get printed; we got down on our knees to Hollywood char-
latans for pictures; we did those publicity stunts . . . to educate
the public and we kept our own fund for the widows. We tested
without parachutes; we flew the mail through solid glue in obso-
lete training planes. The year Hermann Goering dominated the
Munich Conference our appropriation wasn't as big as the New
York City Public Safety Budget . . . and we bought a lot of
Congressmen liquor out of our own pockets to get it.

BROCKHURST—General, why didn't you tell this story?

KANE—And spell it all out for the Germans? Not that they
didn't know and count on it . . . but you don't tell stories in
uniform. We were promised fifty thousand planes . . . and our
boys were never going to fight in foreign wars . . . so the country went back to sleep and we were called back from stables and
rifle ranges to make a modern air force . . . out of promises . . .
and what was left over after they gave our planes and instructors
to every goddamned ambassador in Washington. . . .

BROCKHURST—We were told that was to get experience.

KANE—There wasn't any experience of daylight precision bombardment. Both the Germans and British had tried it and said it
couldn't be done. The Chief said it could. . . . But we'd just
begun to get the tools to get started when we were in it ourselves
. . . with a double war . . . and a fifty thousand plane paper
air force that didn't add up to fifty serviceable bombers. . . .
(*He turns defensively to* DENNIS.)   Casey, if we'd had in 1941
the planes you've lost this week, we would have had a Munich
with the Japs that would have made Hitler's Munich look like
International Rotary!

DENNIS—Sir, we've all fought all our lives to get an air force.
Now we've got to protect our beginnings.

KANE—From what?

DENNIS (*indicating jet crosses*)—Those.

KANE—Those things? They're just our acknowledged enemies.
They fight us in the open. Do you remember the fight to get our
first experimental Fortress? Do you realize how much the Navy
wants our planes, for sub-patrol . . . and to protect the repairing
of those battleships that air power couldn't hurt? Do you know
how much the Army wants our pilots for Company Commanders?
Don't you know the British want us to switch to night area bombardment? Do you know there's a plan to fly infantry supplies
into China . . . *with bombers?* Do you know what it means that
the United Chiefs are half Admirals and the Consolidated Chiefs
half British? Don't you realize the fight it's taken for Cliff and
the others to get us any planes at all?

GARNETT—He's right, Casey. Washington's at the crossroads
on us.

KANE—On Tuesday every one of those factions will be at that
meeting with its own pet plan for winning the war by Naval
Blockade, or attrition by defensive, or a good sound saber charge.
And you want us to send the Chief in there with three days of
prohibitive losses hanging over our theory. . . .

DENNIS—Damn it, sir!   It's not a theory.   Ted demolished
Posenleben. . . .

KANE—And with time and planes and support we can do the
same to every factory in Europe. But the decision is at stake now.
It isn't just a few losses this week, or even a lot in six months.
The Germans are going to kill more of our people, of course. But
they won't be any deader than all the ones who've been killed
through the last thirty years to get us air power. You can worry
about Germany . . . and you should. But I'm fighting the
ground forces and the Navy and the Congress and the White
House and the people and the press and our Allies. You think I
don't know the boys call me Old Percent? You think I've en-
joyed spreading this mug of mine around the press like a pregnant
heiress? You think I don't know what they could do to me for
the statistics I've juggled, the strike photos I've doctored, the reports I've gilded or suppressed. I know . . . and I'd do it all
again! I've spent twenty years watching my friends killed and
broken and disgraced and discarded for one single idea . . . to
get our goddamned country Air Power!

General Dennis informs General Kane that the Intelligence
Summary is ready, and Major Lansing, the Intelligence Officer,
is sent for. He is gray-haired and self-possessed—a former insurance broker who had been an artilleryman in the last war.

"What will the Germans do tomorrow, Major?" asks Kane.

"That depends on where we go, sir."

"If we go back to Schweinhafen?"

"They'll order maximum effort as soon as we cross the 10th
meridian east, sir." The Major points out this line on the map.

Kane wants to know what the Major thinks of Operation
Stitch. "Imperative," is the reply. "We're losing forty-odd
bombers to conventional fighters for every worth-while mission
now. If they get a hundred jets we'll lose a hundred and forty
at a time."

Lansing is, as Kane puts it, a very independent Major who has
thought a lot about the Germans. He thinks the Battle of
Britain and the Battle of Malta would have been decisive if Goering had not lost his nerve over the early losses and diffused his
effort—and that they will be judging American tactics by their
own.

"What do you mean by that?" asks Kane sharply.

"The Germans never settled on one decisive target system and
paid the price for it. They know that every time we've had ba

losses we've switched to easy targets for a while."

"If we hit Schweinhafen tomorrow, will the Germans tumble?"

"I should guess that after two jet factories in quick succession they would face the truth."

"And concentrate every fighter they have in defense of Fendel-horst on Monday?"

"We'll have to expect it, sir."

Major Belding Davis, the division weather officer, has had a special flash from Iceland which he thinks General Dennis should know about. A cold mass is forming which should blanket the continent.

"When?"

"On present indications, late Monday afternoon, sir."

"I always said God must love Willi Messerschmitt!" exclaims Dennis. And to Kane: "There goes our season's weather, sir. We'll make it these next two days or bite our nails off to the elbow."

General Kane is doggedly opposed to two more days of heavy losses—just for a theory. But to Dennis it is no theory. "Cliff," he urges passionately, "we're doing what no one in this war has been able to do yet. We're making the German Air Force fight, on our *initiative* . . . over Germany, where it doesn't dare to refuse combat in order to rest and rebuild. And we're tearing it up . . . over *Germany!* The German Air Force has been the balance of power in this world ever since Munich. It took the German Army everywhere they've been. It beat the Polish Air Force in three days and the Norwegian in three hours. It forced the Maginot Line and beat the French in three weeks. . . ."

General Dennis' urgency is impressive and so is his knowledge of the war. He points out that, if the Germans had been backed up with a few more planes by their high command, they might have blockaded the North Cape and cut the Atlantic life-line to England—but now they have been forced to switch from bomber production to manufacturing jet fighters. They've had to pull whole groups off the Russians and away from Rommel to strengthen home defenses. "They know that fighters—Hurri-canes and Spits—saved England. They're developing these jets to make Europe as impregnable as the British made England."

General Kane agrees entirely, but still insists upon waiting. Dennis makes one more attempt. Wars, he points out, are lost by waiting, and there has been too much waiting at Munich, be-hind the Maginot Line and elsewhere already. If we wait again, he predicts, the Germans will put a roof on the continent and confront our armies at the Channel on D-Day with a superior air force. "I'm not trying to tell you that Operation Stitch will win the war. But no battle anywhere in this war has been won without aerial supremacy. Operation Stitch is the price of that."

General Kane orders the room cleared of all but himself and Dennis. He is going to release the Division to Dennis' discretion —let him go ahead, but on his own. "But if Washington screams for blood, I'll have to throw you to the wolves," he warns.

Dennis has won—until Sergeant Evans brings in a Top Secret Relay from Washington to General Kane, who visibly crumbles as he reads it and hands it to Dennis. "Impossible contact Air Board yet. Urgently implore low losses during critical three days next. Representatives Malcolm and Stone of House Military Affairs Committee arriving England this night. Imperative their impressions our situation favorable at any price."

A new difficulty strikes Dennis—the case of Captain Jenks, who is from Representative Malcolm's state. "An opportune time to be court-martialing a hero, isn't it?"

Looking for an out on Jenks, Kane hopes the case can be fixed medically—perhaps the Captain was insane from combat fatigue. But it won't wash with Major Rufus Dayhuff, the medical reserve officer. There was no medical excuse for Jenks' conduct; in his opinion, Jenks has been corrupted by the press and publicity policy and has got the idea that he is too valuable to continue combat.

Kane tries to dream up another angle; as Dennis points out, any simple lie will clear Jenks, but it has to be one that won't look too raw to the other crews. And he hits on it! "Jenks is from Malcolm's state. Suppose he'd had secret orders from his Commanding General—that is, me—to hold himself in readiness for special escort duty to these distinguished visitors . . ."

It sounds perfect to General Kane, and Dennis plays his trump card. "I'll fix it, sir . . . *as soon as I've ordered Schweinhafen for tomorrow.*" It is blackmail and Kane tries to argue out of it, but Dennis is immovable. The Division is left to his discretion —and at his personal risk—and he phones the guardhouse and orders the release of Jenks to the custody of General Kane, who goes to get him.

Dennis plunges into the details of ordering Operation Stitch Phase Two, for tomorrow. Edward Martin comes in, looking worried—for he has passed General Kane and the General seems to be burning like a fuse. Dennis explains the visit of the Congressmen and the deal to trade the Jenks court-martial for per mission to complete Stitch.

Colonel Martin doubts if Kane will keep his word. "I'll bet he signals me a recall in the air tomorrow," he predicts.

Martin is not going, Dennis informs him; Claude Minter, who's fresh and rested and damned good, will lead them tomorrow. "You've done two of these. I'm tired of sweating you out."

Martin won't have it. "Schweinhafen's *mine*, Casey," he insists, and Dennis gives in. "Casey," continues Martin, "Helen wants me to pick a godfather for the kid. Will you take it?"

"What are you trying to do . . . queer him for life?"

"I'm serious."

"Well, sure."

"And I want you to promise me something."

"What?"

"If he ever wants to join the Army you'll take a club and beat his brains right out through his tail."

The curtain falls.

SCENE II

It is about noon the next day and the visiting Congressmen are being given a formal presentation; Kane has been lecturing to them, using graphs and symbol exhibits—a prominent one of which is labeled "Doom of an Axis Torpedo Factory." On hand, too, are Prescott, Brockhurst and Garnett. Representative Malcolm is tagged the moment he opens his mouth:

"Gennel Kane, it's mighty inspirin' foh representatives of the American people, like me an' Misteh Stone, heah, to come oveh onto foreign soil an' fin' the American Flag flyin' an' undeh it a Fiel' Commandeh who is woythy of ouah great nation an' the boys he comman's. When we get back to ouah own post of duty in the Congress in Washin'ton, I promise you that ouah great leadehs theah, mos' of whom I am fohtunate enough to count among mah closes' frien's, are goin' to heah fum mah own lips how fohtunate this country is in some of its commandehs."

Kane makes a straightfaced reply about command being a mere trusteeship and credit belonging to "the boys." A mention he makes of shortages catches the keen ear of Representative Stone, who asks, "You mean you want more planes, General?"

KANE (*with force*)—Mr. Stone, if the nation wants aerial supremacy we must have them.

STONE (*honestly troubled*)—The nation wants aerial supremacy everywhere, General. They all tell us the same thing . . .

you people over here, the people in the Pacific, the Navy . . . you're getting most of our available replacements now. And, frankly, we're appalled at the way you're eating up our boys and bombers here. What did you tell us your loss rate is?

KANE (*indicating a discarded chart*)—Overall rate of four point eight nine since the beginning of our operations here, sir.

MALCOLM—What are losses this week, Gennel?

KANE—I'll have to tell you that tomorrow, Mr. Malcolm, when I've heard from the other Divisions. (*Trying to break it off.*) And now, gentlemen, if you'd like to inspect the station . . .

MALCOLM—Gennel Kane, the country is pretty upset about the way youah Comman' oveh heah is losin' planes an' crews. I and Misteh Stone have come oveh heah on puhpose to look into it. Now, suh, what were losses in this Division foh this week?

KANE—Have you the figures at hand, General?

DENNIS (*rising*)—Ninety-six, sir.

MALCOLM—Ninety-six . . . out of what ove'all stren'th in youah Division?

DENNIS—It varies with the replacement flow; in average it runs between one eighty and two hundred.

MALCOLM—So . . . you've lost half youah stren'th in a week?

DENNIS—Eighty-four were lost on two particularly difficult missions.

MALCOLM (*silkily*)—Well . . . ! That means neah about twenty-five per cent per mission in this Division as against Gennel Kane's ove'all average of less than five?

KANE—When these are figured into the general average, Mr. Malcolm . . .

MALCOLM—I undehstan' the gennel average, suh! Perhaps Gennel Dennis will explain the discrepancy between his Division an' that.

DENNIS—My Division has the only extension tanks for specially distant targets. Both of these operations were beyond the gasoline range of friendly fighter cover.

MALCOLM—An' the boys lost were deliberately sent beyond that range?

DENNIS—Yes.

MALCOLM—May I ask who ohdehed these operations?

DENNIS—I did.

MALCOLM—On youah own authority?

DENNIS—Yes.

KANE—General Dennis was within his technical authority.

MALCOLM (*no longer the cheerful clown. Talks now and acts the experienced prosecutor closing in for the kill*)—I undehstan' the technicalities, Gennel Kane. No one expec's a man of youah responsibilities to ohdeh every attack foh every Division every night. But the fac's appeah to be that the minute youah back was toined, Gennel Dennis took it on his own self to ohdeh these disastrous attacks.

General Dennis insists the attacks were not disastrous, but were, instead, the best bombing of the war. Malcolm is not convinced; he opines that the boys are paying a bloody price for General Dennis' record, and Dennis' anger mounts. The boys are going beyond fighter cover for the country's record, not his.

"Oh, so the *country's* responsible," pursues Malcolm. "May I ask how?"

Dennis answers this question by asking another: "How did you vote on the fortification of Guam?"

This draws a chuckle from Congressman Stone. "By God! He's got you, Arthur."

"We'll see who's got who," threatens the Southerner. He hammers away at Dennis and Dennis hammers right back. Stone breaks it up by asking Kane what is the target for today, and Dennis supplies the answer. Drawing aside the curtain covering the map, he points out three tapes leading to Cherbourg, Emden and Schweinhafen. The first two are diversionary attacks, he explains; the third is the big one.

But Malcolm has heard the Division attacked Schweinhafen yesterday. Kane interposes, explaining that the target was cloud-covered, so Colonel Martin chose to bomb the torpedo factory instead. Malcolm is still curious about fighter cover, and on the map Dennis points out where this cover ends.

"And when does Colonel Martin bomb Schweinhafen?" asks Representative Stone.

Dennis looks at his watch, replies, "In about fourteen minutes."

General Kane suggests that the visitors come have a look at the radar screen to see what kind of fighter opposition the Germans are putting up in the Cherbourg and Emden attacks; pointedly he suggests that Dennis remain behind. For a moment the two generals are alone. "Casey, for Christ's sake be careful!" Kane warns. "Malcolm's powerful!"

"Sir," counters Dennis, "are you going to let Malcolm break our bargain?"

"I'll keep it if I can."

Kane inquires about luncheon arrangements. "And plenty to drink?" Dennis hadn't thought of that. "With *Congressmen* here? Start thinking in double triples!"

Sergeant Evans informs Dennis that the officers' bar supply is exhausted, the medical officer is dry too, and the combat crews' ration stocks are low. Says Dennis, "These statesmen can go dry for one day. Maybe it will kill them."

Evans reminds Dennis of Kane's order, suggests borrowing from combat rations, and when Dennis refuses and tells him to get the hell out he sighs and says, "I knew there was a catch to this job." While Dennis watches, speechless, Evans unlocks the flag locker and produces two bottles of bourbon.

"Present from an admirer, sir," explains Evans. And, extending a bottle, continues, "It still is, sir."

Dennis, touched, wants to pay for it. "No, sir!" Evans refuses. "I'd like just one thing, sir . . . to shake your hand. . . ."

Dennis shakes, but with embarrassment. "What's this for?" he wants to know.

"Telling that servant of the people what a son of a bitch he is. . . . I'd hate breaking in a new general."

Dennis calls for Haley to tell him what fighting is being encountered on the diversions. "Not a blip, sir. General Kane is pretty scared," informs Haley.

Garnett hurries in, also with information that Kane is scared. Pityingly, Dennis muses, "A man who's broken altitude records scared of Congressmen." Then, to Garnett, "Haven't you got one of those B-29 commands sewed up for yourself?"

"Casey, the Air Corps hasn't got B-29 commands sewed up yet until the United Chiefs decide whether you've proved precision bombardment over here."

"When will it be decided?"

"Ostensibly on Tuesday. But those deals are always fixed before the meetings. They may be deciding this minute."

"No wonder you've been jittering, Cliff."

Garnett admits frankly that he's not as keen as he was now that he has seen what command is like. Now he advances a request: "I hate to ask this, but I need Ted Martin for my Chief of Staff out there in the Pacific." He explains it will mean a brigadier generalship for him—as he has already pointed out to Ted.

"So he knew about this last night?" demands Dennis. "Cliff, can't you ever do anything straight? . . . Do you think I'd have let him go today if I had known this?"

Dennis agrees to persuade Ted to take the new post as Haley and Davis bring in the weather map for tomorrow's operation. The dense mass is slowing up; the continent will be open for bombing all day, but home bases will start closing in in the middle of the afternoon.

"But our returning planes could still see the island from, say, fifteen thousand feet?" asks Dennis.

"They could see where it is, sir," replies Davis.

To Haley the General orders that every spare parachute in the Division be repacked. Realization of what this means horrifies Garnett. "Paratroops do it," says the grim Dennis. "Our crews will land on a friendly island."

"But the planes?"

"They're expendable."

A chastened war correspondent, Brockhurst, enters to proffer an apology to Dennis. "I thought you were a butcher. Compared to Kane you're a starry-eyed boy scout." Dennis brushes him off. "Kane," continues Brockhurst, "has just sent Colonel Martin a recall signal. An order to abandon primary target for a target of opportunity under fighter cover." It is Brockhurst's opinion that this order only establishes Kane's personal alibi, for the General knows that Martin is already beyond fighter cover.

Kane and his visitors return from the radar room with Malcolm full of praise for Kane's courageous order. Kane alibis to Dennis that the diversions were so obviously unsuccessful in drawing off German fighters that he felt it his duty to recall Martin. Malcolm spots the whiskey and Sergeant Evans pours for all except Dennis.

Haley brings in a message from an RAF reconnaissance plane: Large formation USAAF Fortresses . . . heading 98 . . .

"Ninety-eight . . . he's still going *into* Germany!" explodes Kane.

Haley goes on with the message: Unescorted . . . under heavy attack . . .

Malcolm again begins to splutter about slaughtering American youth, but is cut short when another message arrives addressed to Colonel Martin. "New co-pilot made first landing . . . everything fine . . . Helen."

"Ted's got a son!" exults Dennis. Shaking hands with Garnett, he offers, "Congratulations, Uncle!" Kane proposes a toast, and Dennis orders a copy to be relayed to Ted as soon as they hear his strike signal.

"You tellin' me this Cunnel out theah leadin' the attack been bohn a daddy an' you ain't even goin' to radio him?" blusters Malcolm.

"He's busy now," snaps Dennis. Kane intervenes by remind-ing the gentleman that war has its pleasant duties too, and here, now, is one of them—the decoration of Captain Jenks by Repre-sentative Malcolm.

Jenks, a citation, a medal and a photographer are brought in and as Malcolm ogles the camera the ceremony of reading the citation begins. Over the scene is heard the clattering of a tele-printer; Sergeant Evans hurries to the Ops room and returns with a strip of paper for General Dennis.

" 'No mistake this time,' " interrupts Dennis, reading. " 'Scratch Schweinhafen for me. Ted.' Jesus, Haley! He got it . . . HE GOT IT! . . . *HE GOT IT!!* Signal him about his kid."

There is a toast to Martin as the greatest combat leader in the Air Forces, which leaves Malcolm piqued and Jenks forgotten. Prescott has an idea for another picture—of General Kane "scratching" Schweinhafen on the map. Malcolm and Stone stampede to get into the picture and the photographer trains his camera on the group.

Quietly, Haley brings another message for Dennis, who reads it, puts it down quietly and steps away from it. The others watch him uneasily, and Garnett picks up the paper.

" 'Good luck, Casey,' " he reads, " 'we're on fire and go-ing. . . .' "

MALCOLM—Goin' . . . ? Finish the message, cain't you?

GARNETT—That's all there is.

MALCOLM—All . . . all . . . ? (*Steps over to* DENNIS.) Listen heah! I want to know . . .

DENNIS—Shut up!

MALCOLM (*getting it*)—You mean to tell me he's . . .

DENNIS—SHUT UP!

MALCOLM—You tellin' me to shut up afteh you've done kilt the bes' . . . (DENNIS *grabs him by the lapels and shakes him savagely.*)

KANE—Casey! (DENNIS *flings* MALCOLM *into a chair.*)

STONE—General Kane, nobody could blame General Dennis.

BROCKHURST—Let's both remember that, Mr. Stone.

GARNETT—Casey, do you realize what . . . we've done to Ted?

DENNIS—Yes.

GARNETT—But we'll have to . . . one of us will have to tell Helen.

DENNIS—I'll tell Helen . . . and then I'll tell Claude Minter's wife.

GARNETT (*eyeing him nervously*)—Claude Minter's wife?

DENNIS—Yes, I'll tell her I sent Claude to Fendelhorst tomorrow.

GARNETT—Fendelhorst! Tomorrow!

KANE—Casey, you leave me no choice. I am relieving you of your command with immediate effect. General Garnett, pending confirmation from Washington you will assume command of the Fifth Division. (*Then sincerely, to* DENNIS.) I'm sorry, my boy. I'm going to recommend you for the Legion of Merit.

The curtain falls.

ACT III

It is 8 o'clock that night, and the General's room is bare and serviceable again—bare and serviceable for a new general. Evans puts a name plate bearing Garnett's name on the desk and throws Dennis' old one in the trash box. He shakes his head disapprovingly at the singing and other noises of mild carousal he can hear outside, then puts on some coffee and gets out the cigar box. Major Dayhuff catches him red-handed with it—but it is empty.

The medical officer has had it on good authority that there won't be a mission tomorrow; Evans figures General Kane's instructions to Garnett will be "order, counter order, disorder . . . and then five feet of teleprint hot air meaning a milk run to the nearest Channel port." He figures that Kane and Washington have had it in for Dennis for a long time—"Dennis was trying to get the war over." He confides that Dennis has been ordered to return to Washington by special plane for reassignment. "Maybe they'll let him burn Top Secret waste paper."

Garnett comes in and greets the Sergeant, who informs him there's no message from General Kane. The racket outside, Evans explains, is just some of the boys. When there is the crash of a bottle outside Garnett suggests calling the guardhouse, but Evans volunteers to attend to the matter. Going to the window, he yells, "Hey, you, out there . . . shut up!"

A voice inquires who the hell is he and Evans grandiloquently introduces his unseen self as Captain George Washington Culpeper Lee. When the Sergeant declares he is speaking for Brigadier General Clifton C. Garnett there is a noise of swiftly receding feet and silence.

"I am afraid I am the real culprit, General Garnett," confesses Major Dayhuff. "I authorized a small allotment of whiskey from combat crew ration into the messes tonight."

"Is the whole base in this condition?"

"No, *sir!* It wouldn't run one percent. . . . This is a very special night, and they're veterans. They know they can fly a milk run tomorrow sound asleep."

Garnett is miffed at the assumption there is going to be a milk run. He wants to know the Major's medical estimate of the crews' condition, and is told that when Operation Stitch began Dayhuff estimated the men could stand three successive days.

Garnett excuses Dayhuff and calls Evans. Still no word from Kane—but Evans has brought coffee.

"I didn't order coffee."

"You will, sir."

"What else do I need?"

"Cigars and whiskey, sir."

"I almost never use them."

"Your visitors will, sir."

"Oh." Garnett is rather pleased. "I guess you and I will be together some time, Evans. Can you suggest anything else I need?"

"You need a new sergeant, sir."

Evans tried to get General Dennis to take him along but Dennis refused, so now the Sergeant is going to teach gunnery in Nevada.

The General sends the Sergeant for Haley, who still has no messages. Garnett is sweating; soon he is going to have to make a command decision. Kane should have held his weather conference at 1800 (6 p.m.), but maybe he is waiting for the 2000 weather. Haley reports a day's loss of thirty-nine planes. The men's morale is very good now; what the general has heard outside is a normal letdown between tough missions and easy ones. "They're pretty cheerful tonight, sir."

"Well, that's something. You always wonder if they'll be hostile to a new . . . face."

"All generals look alike to them, sir. . . . They figure a new general's always good for a couple of soft missions."

Garnett sends Haley for the latest reconnaissance pictures and resumes stewing, alone, when Captain George Washington Culpeper Lee weaves in, somewhat drunk and exaggeratedly formal.

LEE—Captain Lee reports his presence, sir.
GARNETT—Who?

LEE—Captain George Washington Culpeper Lee, sir.

GARNETT—Lee, you're drunk.

LEE—Yes, sir. I've come to report myself for that and to apologize for singing under your window and then running away.

GARNETT—Get out of here and go to bed.

LEE—I'm sorry, sir. This hasn't happened before and won't again. (*Salutes and turns to go when* GARNETT *checks him.*)

GARNETT—Lee, did you go to Schweinhafen today?

LEE (*thoughtfully, rather fuddled*)—Yes, sir. I went to Schweinhafen today and I went to Schweinhafen yesterday and I went to Posenleben Friday . . . and I've been to Hamburg . . . and Bremen . . . and Kiel . . . and Schwainfurt and Regensburg . . . (*He stops short, horrified at himself.*) Excuse me, sir. I only meant to say I'd been to twenty-four of them without taking a drink and I'm ashamed of myself for singing under your window on Easter Sunday.

GARNETT—You go to bed, Lee. It's all right . . . even if it isn't Easter Sunday.

LEE—Beg your pardon, sir. It's my Easter Sunday.

GARNETT—Yours?

LEE—Yes, sir. Resurrection, sir. Today was my twenty-fourth. All I've got to do now is knock off one more little milk run and then go home and live the rest of my life.

GARNETT—Oh. Well, don't behave like this at home.

LEE—I wouldn't think of it, sir. I'm going to get married.

GARNETT—Well, congratulations!

LEE—Yes, sir. We almost did before I came over but I thought . . . I thought she'd worry more that way.

GARNETT—I see. Now get to bed and the best of luck.

LEE—Thank you, sir. And Happy Easter to you, sir. (LEE *exits, leaving* GARNETT *to think that one over.*)

Haley brings in a message—not from Kane, but from the last Group, reporting all crews provided with freshly packed parachutes in compliance with today's order—General Dennis' last order, which has not been rescinded.

They look over the Status Board, and Haley estimates he can provide 130 bombers and 132 crews—18 crews on their last mission. "A hundred and eighty boys . . ." muses Garnett.

The General wants to be sure he understands the directive folder on his desk, which says that in the absence of explicit target designation or other order from higher headquarters, Division commanders will use their own discretion. This means, Haley assures the General, that if there's no word from Kane these instructions apply automatically.

Major Lansing brings in the pictures of Schweinhafen. They show a complete job of destruction. But there are no pictures showing parachutes, although there is some possible news on Colonel Martin. Four parachutes were seen to open after his bomber exploded, but there were no individual identifications.

Garnett asks Lansing to brief him on an easy run tomorrow, and Lansing believes the Germans will defend nothing in France because they need a rest too. On the map they look over naval objectives on the coast—minesweeper bases and such, which usually are used for "blooding" new groups.

"Major, I'd like to ask you a question," says Garnett. "If you had to decide tomorrow's mission . . . for General Kane . . . would you attack Fendelhorst?"

The Major explains a personal reason would influence him. He has a son training in a combat infantry division. "When those jets have stopped our bombardment they'll make the deadliest strafing planes ever used against ground troops. I'm afraid I couldn't help thinking of my boy going up against them."

"Yes, but what if your boy were flying a bomber tomorrow?"

"I hope I would send him to Fendelhorst, sir."

Lansing leaves Garnett to think that one over and soon Haley and Davis bring the weather report. It's Davis' own reading; General Kane's people refused either to concur or to disagree. Anyhow, the cold mass still is slowing down, and the bases will be fog-free until 1700—5 p.m.—for landings.

"Why, that's enough for . . . anything . . . isn't it?" asks Garnett. It is, even without parachutes. And if anything, the weather will improve during the night.

Haley reminds Garnett it is time to issue gas and bomb-loading orders to the Group commanders. Still unwilling to face a decision, the General expostulates that he's supposed to be getting instructions from General Kane, but Haley reminds him: "Our directive says, 'in the absence of explicit target designation or other orders . . .'"

Garnett may be saved by the bell, for Evans brings in the long-awaited message from Kane. Faintly, Garnett orders Haley to read it: "General Kane compelled proceed Hemisphere Commander's dinner for Congressmen London, consequently unable to attend weather conference here. Operating procedure will apply as per directive. General Kane desires express especial confidence General Garnett's discretion based on weather."

There is a deadly silence during which the deposed General Dennis enters in a trench coat to say good-by. His plane has landed and is being loaded with his stuff. Haley and Evans leave the two generals alone.

"Cliff," says Dennis, "I'm taking Ted's personal stuff to Helen. . . . No more news, I suppose?"

There has been more evidence of four parachutes from Ted's plane—but Dennis doesn't think Ted got away—not with an explosion where he was riding. But if he did get down and the German army caught him, he'd probably be all right; if civilians who have been bombed got him, there's no telling.

"I've been thinking all day about those six boys the Japanese captured . . . alive . . ." shudders Garnett. "I was the goy who *wanted* a B-29 command. God! When I think of ordering boys out over the Japanese . . ."

"You don't have to think about it. You've got a good job here. Good luck, Cliff."

"Good, is it? Read this." Garnett hands over the message from General Kane. "Kane," he says, "is passing the buck to me."

Garnett begs for Dennis' help, but the latter is cold. "You're going to command, Clifton . . . and you will be paid the first of every month."

Garnett tells of the visit of Captain Lee, a nice attractive kid with a lot of guts who was a little drunk.

"They're all nice attractive kids with a lot of guts," says Dennis bitterly. "The War Department has provided you with a Chaplain for that, Cliff. Tell them to do their crying to him."

GARNETT—Casey, he wasn't crying; he was happy. He told me he's going to get married.

DENNIS—And the only thing you can tell him is that you hope you won't have to kill him before he does. . . . It's your baby, Cliff, but I learned long ago to let the Chaplain handle those. He's our liaison with the Headquarters that decides that . . . if there is one.

GARNETT—Casey! What's happened to you?

DENNIS—Just what's going to happen to you . . . and the sooner I get out of here, the sooner you can get to work. (*He starts for the door and* GARNETT *checks him.*)

GARNETT—Casey! If you'll help me just this once . . .

DENNIS—It isn't just this once. It's from now on.

GARNETT—When *you* first came over here you had Ted and Joe Lucas to talk to. . . .

DENNIS—Joe never talked. He was commanding this Division then, and I was running a Group for him. That's worse. You see them at meals every day and you know a lot of them personally.

GARNETT—But at least you had Joe for a boss until he got killed in that air raid in London.

DENNIS—Did you believe that story?

GARNETT—Why . . . of course. . . .

DENNIS—Well, you're old enough to know better. Joe didn't get killed in any air raid in London. It was the night after we first sent them to Mangelburg. Joe didn't want to send them. He knew they weren't ready. Kane knew it too. But they were crowding Joe and Kane from higher up. Joe counted them in at landing that night and then he went down to London and took a hotel room and shot himself. Then I got the job. Now it's yours. Good luck, Cliff.

GARNETT—*Joe Lucas* . . . did *that* . . . How *could* he?

DENNIS—You'll see how he could. Wait till you've counted in a really bad one that you've ordered yourself. Wait till you start noticing the faces of those kids on the trucks from the replacement centers . . . the new ones coming in. Wait till you start waking up in the afternoon . . . and wondering what it is that makes *those* faces look so much like the faces of the ones you're already killing, that same afternoon. Then go out and puke up your powdered eggs and then take veronal to get back to sleep . . . and then have them wake you up and give you benzedrine to keep you awake while you count in your stragglers and plan your next mission . . . and then you'll see how Joe Lucas could have done it. . . .

GARNETT—Joe Lucas! Of all the men in the service . . .

DENNIS—Yes . . . and I've wanted to do the same thing five or six times when I've signed those field orders . . . and so will you! But that was one thing Joe did for me. He made me think that through. That only helps *one* guy.

GARNETT—But even after that . . . you had Ted. . . .

DENNIS—Yes, I had Ted. That's one thing I've done for you, Cliff. I've killed Ted. You won't have to do that.

Garnett wonders what Casey will be doing now, and Dennis guesses it probably will be a training command somewhere out West where he can have Cathy and the kids and maybe take the boys fishing now and then.

Haley appears with a statistical list Garnett has ordered—expectancy of losses over milk-run targets like Brest (4.9%), Calais (2.2%) and Dieppe (1.4%).

"Ernie," interrupts Dennis, "how did *my* good-by presents to the boys finally average out?"

"Twenty-four percent Friday, 26 percent yesterday and 29 percent today, sir. . . ."

Garnett listens, then tensely and in a low voice orders: "Haley, notify the other divisions and all our groups that tomorrow the Fifth Division will attack Fendelhorst."

Casey Dennis, half laughing, but awkward, says, "Well . . . Cliff! Good luck—General!" He starts on his way again, but the doughty Evans stops him at the door.

"Change of orders for General Dennis, sir."

"No, you don't," evades the General, but he can't escape Evans.

"From Washington, sir," insists the Sergeant.

Garnett takes the message and reads it aloud slowly:

" 'With immediate effect, General Dennis will proceed via Gibraltar, Cairo, Karachi, Calcutta and Chungking to . . .' " Horrified, realization dawns on him. "My God, Casey . . . this means a B-29 command. . . ."

Dennis instinctively and protestingly recoils. "They can't! . . . *I won't!*" Then, slowly, he asks, "Does that say 'with immediate effect'?"

"I'm afraid it does, Casey."

"Yeah," says Dennis. Then he snaps: "Evans! Get your things."

THE CURTAIN FALLS

THE WINSLOW BOY

A Drama in Two Acts

By Terence Rattigan

IN 1908 Morton Archer-Shee, a Liverpool bank manager, received from the commandant of the Royal Naval College at Osborne a letter stating that his young son George had been dismissed for forging a signature on a five-shilling money order.

George told his father he didn't do it so, with unquestioning faith in his son's word, Archer-Shee set about clearing the lad's name. He engaged one of the most famous attorneys in Britain, Sir Edward Carson, who had been a figure in the famous Oscar Wilde trial and who, later, was to become Attorney General and Solicitor General.

Rulings and decisions by the Navy could not ordinarily be protested in a civil court, but Sir Edward got George's case to trial by resorting to an ancient device known as the Petition of Right. The Archer-Shee case came to trial two years later and became an affair of profound national and political interest. George—who overslept the day the decision came in and was not in court—was exonerated. George was killed in World War I.

Terence Rattigan, a British dramatist whose greatest American success has been the Lunts' "O Mistress Mine," had come out of the Royal Air Force after World War II and had written a screenplay, "Johnny in the Clouds."

He began casting about for another idea for a picture, and in a biography of Sir Edward Carson ran across the story of the Archer-Shee trial (which also is to be found in Alexander Woollcott's collection, "Long, Long Ago"). This, he decided, would make a whale of a movie—or a whale of a play.

He made it a play, "The Winslow Boy." His only change in historical detail was to advance the time four years—a more dramatic period with World War I shaping up. "The Winslow Boy" won the Ellen Terry Award, similar to America's Pulitzer prize, in 1936, and after a run of sixteen months in London was brought to New York's Empire Theatre.

As the play opens one discovers that Ronnie Winslow should not have come home from the Osborne Naval Academy on this

134

Sunday morning of July, 1912, but here he is—a lad of 14 in a
cadet's uniform. His home is in Kensington; it is solid and comfortable, and the presence of a maid indicates an upper-middle-
class household.

Violet is surprised to see Ronnie so early, since he hadn't been
expected until Thursday; Ronnie is making an uneasy attempt at
sang-froid. When Violet tells him his parents are at church he
comments vacantly, "Oh, yes. It's Sunday, isn't it?"

"What's the matter with you?" queries the maid. "What have
they been doing to you at Osborne?"

Ronnie's preoccupation is shattered; sharply he demands,
"What do you mean?"

Violet goes upstairs to unpack the boy's luggage, which the
taxi driver has already carted up, and to make room for it in
the bedroom he shares with his brother, Dickie. Left alone,
Ronnie's air of dejection intensifies as he takes from a pocket a
sealed letter, hesitates a moment, opens and reads it. The reading increases his misery and for a moment he thinks of tearing
up the message; instead, he puts it back in his pocket.

There is a sound of voices in the hall, and with a strangled
sound Ronnie flees through the door leading from the drawing
room to the garden. Back from church, the rest of the family
comes in, chatting about the minister and the sermon. Ronnie's
father, Arthur, leans heavily on a stick; he is about 60 and pos-
sesses a rather deliberately cultured patriarchal air. Arthur's
wife, Grace, is about ten years younger and still a bit pretty.
Arthur sits heavily in his favorite chair and complains immediately of a draught—for Ronnie has left the garden door open.

Grace closes it and observes that a storm is coming. Her other
son, Dickie, a large, noisy and cheerful Oxford undergraduate,
picks up the hallway discussion of the church service. "The old
boy's so doddery now he can hardly finish the course at all. I
timed him today. It took him seventy-five seconds dead from
a flying start to reach the pulpit, and then he needed the whip
coming around the bend."

This does not strike Dickie's father as funny. "Doddery
though Mr. Jackson may seem now," he says dryly, "I very much
doubt if when he was at Oxford he failed in his pass mods."

This jab at Dickie's scholastic prowess brings a protest from
the young man. "Didn't I stay in all last night—a Saturday
night—and work?"

Both Arthur and Grace admit that Dickie stayed in, but they
have doubts about the work. The gramophone was going, for

one thing, and for another Dickie's father had observed him practicing the Bunny Hug with a girl who had dropped by.

ARTHUR—We appear to be straying from the point. Whatever animal was responsible for the posture I found you in with Edwina Gunn has little to do with the fact that to my certain knowledge you have not yet done one single stroke of work so far this vacation.

DICKIE—Oh. Well, I do work awfully fast, you know—once I get down to it.

ARTHUR—Indeed? That assumption can hardly be based on experience, I take it.

DICKIE—Dash it, Father! You are laying in to me, this morning.

ARTHUR—I think it's time you found out, Dickie, that I'm not spending two hundred pounds a year keeping you at Oxford merely that you may make a lot of useless friends and learn to dance the Bunny Hop.

DICKIE—Hug, Father.

ARTHUR—The exact description of the obscenity is immaterial.

GRACE—Father's quite right, you know, dear. You really have been going the pace a bit, this vac.

DICKIE—Yes, I know, Mother—but the season's nearly over now.

GRACE (*with a sigh*)—I wish you were as good about work as Ronnie.

DICKIE (*hotly*)—I like that. That's a bit thick, I must say. All Ronnie ever has to do with his footling little homework is to add two and two, while I—

ARTHUR—Ronnie, may I remind you, is at least proving a good deal more successful in adding two and two than you were at his age.

DICKIE (*now furious*)—Oh, yes, *I* know. *I* know. *He* got into Osborne and *I* failed. That's going to be brought up again.

GRACE—Nobody's bringing it up, dear.

DICKIE—Oh, yes, they are. It's going to be brought up against me all my life. Ronnie's the good little boy. I'm the bad little boy. You've just stuck a couple of labels on us that nothing on earth is ever going to change.

GRACE—Don't be so absurd, dear—

DICKIE—It's not absurd. It's quite true. Isn't it, Kate?

CATHERINE (*looking up from a book she has been reading in*) *the corner*)—I'm sorry, Dickie. I haven't been listening. Isn't what quite true?

DICKIE—That in the eyes of Mother and Father nothing that Ronnie does is ever wrong, and nothing that I do is ever right?

CATHERINE (*after a pause*)—If I were you, Dickie, dear, I'd go and have a nice lie-down before lunch.

DICKIE (*after a further pause*)—Perhaps you're right. (*He goes toward the hall door.*)

ARTHUR—If you're going to your room I suggest you take that object with you. (*He points to a gramophone—1912 model, with horn—lying on a table.*) It's out of place in a drawing room. (DICKIE, *with an air of hauteur, picks up the gramophone and carries it to the door.*) It might help you to concentrate on the work you're going to do this afternoon.

DICKIE (*stopping at the door, then turning slowly and speaking with dignity*)—That is out of the question, I'm afraid.

ARTHUR—Indeed? Why?

DICKIE—I have an engagement with Miss Gunn.

ARTHUR—On a Sunday afternoon? You're escorting her to the National Gallery no doubt?

DICKIE—No. The Victoria and Albert Museum.

The Winslows' third child, Catherine, has been reading a book ever since the return from church. She is about 30, and looks rather masculine. With Dickie gone, Grace bends her attention, first, to the weather, and finds that a downpour has begun; second, to her daughter.

"What are you reading, Kate?"

"Len Rogers' memoirs." Rogers, she explains, is a trades union leader.

"Does John know you're a radical?"

"Oh, yes."

"And a suffragette?"

"Certainly."

"And he still wants to marry you?"

This seems to be so, says Kate—and if the family is thinking of objecting to the marriage—which it isn't—she will elope.

Grace can't figure her daughter as being in love, because she never shows her feelings, and Arthur opines that a smitten maid would be reading Byron, not Rogers. The New Woman is definitely puzzling to the older generation—and Grace rather wishes that Catherine would consider Desmond, who is really a very good sort.

Through the garden window Grace sees a skulking figure—probably the neighboring Williamson boy; but speculation as to who he is and how wet he is getting ends when John Wetherstone —Kate's John—rings the front bell. He has come, the women hope, to ask Arthur for Kate's hand; conspiratorially, Kate and Grace make for the concealment of the dining room. "Knock on the floor with your stick—three times. Then we'll come in," suggests the young woman.

John Wetherstone is about Kate's age and is extremely well clad in morning coat and striped trousers—which he could, of course, have worn for church, but which he undoubtedly donned for the occasion in hand. He makes the proper inquiry about Mr. Winslow's health and is informed that the arthritis has been troublesome; then Arthur comes directly to cases:

"I understand you wish to marry my daughter."

"Yes, sir. That's to say, I've proposed to her and she's done me the honor of accepting me."

Arthur is keenly at work sizing John up. "I see," he says. "I trust when you corrected yourself your second statement wasn't a denial of the first? I mean, do you *really* wish to marry her?"

"Of course, sir."

So Arthur gets down to a father's cross-examination of the practical, rather than sentimental, side of the attachment—but he seems to know all the answers before John can give them. John is a subaltern in the army, and this would give him about 263 pounds a year. Then, John's father is giving him an allowance of 24 pounds a month. Total, about 500 pounds a year.

"Well, well. It all seems perfectly satisfactory. I really don't think I need delay my congratulations any longer." John gratefully takes Mr. Winslow's hand, and Arthur proceeds to outline his own financial position, just in case John might have thought he was marrying an heiress.

"The Westminster Bank pays me a small pension—350, to be precise—and my wife has about 200 a year of her own. Apart from that we have nothing, except for such savings as I've been able to make—the interest from which raises my total income to about 950 pounds per annum.

"Now, in addition to the ordinary expenses of life in Courtfield Gardens, I have to maintain two sons, one at Osborne and the other at Oxford. So, you see, I am not in a position to be very lavish as regards Catherine's dowry. I propose to settle on her

1,250 pounds, which represents precisely one-sixth of my total capital."

John calls that very generous and Arthur, with a studied air of unconcern, raps three times on the floor. Nothing happens, so Arthur struggles out of his chair, opens the dining room door and, apparently to his surprise, discovers that Catherine and Grace are there.

"Come in. John's here."

The women feign surprise and express pleasure, then Grace comes to the point. Did the talk go all right? It did, she learns, and she gives John a practically-your-mother kiss. The parents then gracefully leave the lovers alone.

"What about *your* father?" asks Catherine. "He disapproves of me, doesn't he? He has a way of looking at me through his monocle that just shrivels me up."

"He's just being a colonel, darling, that's all," comforts John.

They are interrupted by the appearance in the garden window door of the bedraggled Ronnie, who is on the verge of tears. Eyeing John, he won't talk, so John tactfully vanishes into the dining room.

"Now, darling, tell me," urges Catherine. "Have you run away?" For an answer Ronnie hands her the letter he almost tore up when he first came home, and Catherine, reading it, exclaims, "Oh, God!"

"I didn't do it," says Ronnie. "Really I didn't."

Dickie, coming in from the hall, is not surprised to see his young brother because he has seen his luggage in their room. He gives him a cheerful "Hullo."

"You stay here with him. I'll find Mother," Catherine orders.

Unlike Catherine's first thought, that Ronnie has run away from the academy, Dickie's suspicion is the correct one—that he has been sacked—for stealing, the boy admits.

"Oh, is that all? Good Lord, I didn't know they sacked chaps for *that* these days."

"I didn't do it," insists Ronnie. And, when his mother comes in, he sobs the same denial with his face buried in her dress.

"No, darling, of course you didn't," she comforts. "We'll go upstairs now and get out of those nasty wet clothes." As he goes with her the boy pleads, "Don't tell Father."

Telling Father will, indeed, be a job. "I don't want to be within a thousand miles of that explosion," says Dickie, and as if to escape the possibility he departs and Catherine calls John back in from the dining room and tells him the details.

"It's cold, calculated inhumanity," rages Catherine.

John's view is more formal. "You must remember he's not really at school. He's in the Service. They have a way of doing things in the Service which may seem to an outsider horribly brutal, but at least they're always scrupulously fair. You can take it from me, there must have been a very full inquiry before they'd take a step of this sort. . . . How will your father take it?"

"It might kill him."

In the midst of marriage arrangements and family crisis the front bell offers another interruption—the appearance on invitation of Desmond Curry for lunch. "Our family solicitor," whispers Catherine. "Be polite to him, won't you? He doesn't know about us yet. He's been in love with me for years."

Desmond has the figure of an athlete gone to seed at the age of 45 and a mildly furtive manner, rather as if he had just absconded with his firm's petty cash but hopes no one is going to be too angry about it. John finds private amusement at the thought that such a man could be in love with Catherine.

Desmond offers his congratulations immediately—for Violet has told him in the hall. He is taking it bravely as Grace comes back from putting Ronnie to bed and is followed by Arthur, bringing two bottles from the cellar.

"Hullo, Desmond," greets Arthur. "How are you? You're not looking well."

"I've strained my shoulder, you know."

Arthur opines that anybody in middle age should abandon cricket, but Desmond could never do that. Just to make conversation John inquires if Desmond is any relation to the D. W. H. Curry who used to play for Middlesex, and is truly impressed to learn that Desmond is that man.

Arthur has brought the wine bottles up for a ceremony and he rings for Violet to bring some glasses. Dickie reappears for lunch and Arthur pours some Madeira, which Violet passes.

"Catherine and John!" toasts Arthur—then, noticing Violet, asks her to join the toast and pours another glass.

"Just a sip," says Violet.

"Quite so," agrees the good-humored Arthur. "Your reluctance would be more convincing if I hadn't noticed you'd brought an extra glass—"

"Oh, I didn't bring it for myself, sir," says Violet. "I brought it for Master Ronnie."

The cat is out of the bag and the fat's in the fire. Why hasn't someone told Arthur?

"We thought it best you shouldn't know—for the time being," his wife helplessly explains.

In the face of her husband's acute concern and mounting anger there is nothing for Grace to do but offer him the letter which Catherine has turned over to her. He insists that she read it to him, even with others present.

"Confidential," it begins. "I am commanded by My Lords Commissioners of the Admiralty to inform you that they have received a communication from the Commanding Officer of the Royal Naval College at Osborne reporting the theft of a five-shilling postal order at the College on the 7th instant, which was afterward cashed at the Post Office.

"Investigation of the circumstances of the case leaves no other conclusion possible than that the postal order was taken by your son, Cadet Ronald Arthur Winslow. My Lords deeply regret that they must therefore request you to withdraw your son from the College."

There is a long pause as Grace tearfully finishes reading. Then Arthur quietly summons Violet. "Violet, ask Master Ronnie to come down and see me. . . . Perhaps the rest of you would go in to luncheon? . . . Dickie, will you decant that bottle of claret I brought up from the cellar?"

Arthur, in his chair, waits alone for his young son. ·There is a timid knock on the door.

ARTHUR—Come in. (RONNIE *appears in the doorway. He is in a dressing gown. He stands on the threshold.*) Come in and shut the door. (RONNIE *closes the door behind him.*) Come over here. (RONNIE *walks slowly up to his father.* ARTHUR *gazes at him steadily for some time without speaking.*) Why aren't you in your uniform?

RONNIE (*murmuring*)—It got wet.

ARTHUR—How did it get wet?

RONNIE—I was out in the garden in the rain.

ARTHUR—Why?

RONNIE (*reluctantly*)—I was hiding.

ARTHUR—From me? (RONNIE *nods.*) Do you remember once you promised me that if ever you were in trouble of any sort you would come to me first?

RONNIE—Yes, Father.

ARTHUR—Why didn't you come to me now? Why did you have to go and hide in the garden?

RONNIE—I don't know, Father.

ARTHUR—Are you so frightened of me? (RONNIE *does not reply.* ARTHUR *gazes at him for a moment, then holds up the letter.*) In this letter it says you stole a postal order. (RONNIE *opens his mouth to speak.* ARTHUR *stops him.*) Now I don't want you to say a word until you've heard what *I've* got to say. If you did it, you must tell me. I shan't be angry with you, Ronnie—provided you tell me the truth. But if you tell me a lie, I shall know it, because a lie between you and me can't be hidden. I shall know it, Ronnie—so remember that before you speak. (*Pause.*) Did you steal this postal order?

RONNIE (*with hesitation*)—No, Father. I didn't. (ARTHUR *takes him by the arm and pulls him violently toward him.*)

ARTHUR (*staring into his eyes*)—Did you steal this postal order?

RONNIE—No, Father. I didn't. (ARTHUR *continues to stare into his eyes for a second, then relaxes and pushes him gently away.*)

ARTHUR—Go on back to bed. (RONNIE *goes gratefully to the door.*) And in future I trust that a son of mine will at least show enough sense to come in out of the rain.

RONNIE—Yes, Father. (*He disappears.* ARTHUR *gets up quite briskly and goes to the telephone in the corner of the room.*)

ARTHUR (*at telephone*)—Hullo. Are you there? (*Speaking very distinctly.*) I want to put a trunk call through, please. A trunk call. . . . Yes. . . . The Royal Naval College, Osborne. . . . That's right. . . . Replace receiver? Certainly. (*He replaces receiver and then, after a moment's meditation, turns and walks briskly into dining room. The curtain falls.*)

SCENE II

In the drawing room on a Spring evening nine months later Dickie is listening alone to some jazz on his gramophone, which has been muffled by a sweater stuffed down its horn. When Catherine appears, in evening dress, Dickie asks if she thinks the old man can hear the music upstairs. She doesn't think so.

"What's the verdict?" queries Dickie.

"I heard him say Father needed a complete rest. . . . He said he ought to go to the country and forget all his worries."

When Violet brings in an evening paper, brother and sister

grab for it and Catherine wins. " 'The Osborne Cadet.' There are two more letters." Ronnie's case is becoming a *cause célèbre* in the letters-to-the-editor departments. This evening, a correspondent signing himself Liberatis Amator is outraged at the high-handed treatment, soulless oligarchy, arbitrary condemnation without trial and the passing of the Englishman's home as the Englishman's castle.

A correspondent named Perplexed, on the other hand, says that with the present troubles in the Balkans and a certain major European power outbuilding our Navy, he thinks the Admiralty has more urgent affairs than Master Ronnie Winslow's little troubles. There has been a review of the case by the judge advocate of the Fleet confirming the original findings, and it has wasted valuable time and taxpayers' money.

Dickie is almost on Perplexed's side. "It does seem rather a much ado about damn all. I mean to say—a mere matter of pinching. And it's all so beastly expensive. . . . Let's cheer ourselves up with some music."

They dance in the manner of the period, arms outstretched and working up and down like pump handles. "When's the happy date now?" asks Dickie.

"Postponed again. His father's gone abroad for six months."

"Why pay any attention to that old—gentleman?"

"I wouldn't—but John does, so I have to."

Dickie knows something has gone wrong with his sister's engagement. He offers her some manly advice: "Suppress your opinions. Men don't like 'em in their lady friends. . . ."

When Dickie said, "It's all so beastly expensive," he was right; it is expensive to Arthur, as well as absorbing. When Arthur comes downstairs it can be noticed that he is walking with more difficulty. His eagerness for the evening paper is at least equal to that of his children's—but, once he has read the letters of Liberatis Amator and Perplexed, he turns to another affair which is on his mind—Dickie.

"What," he asks his son, "do you suppose one of your bookmaker friends would lay in the way of odds on your getting a degree?"

Dickie thinks it might be seven to four against. And the odds against his eventually becoming a civil servant might be steeper. "You don't want me to have a bet, do you?" asks Dickie.

"No, Dickie. I'm not a gambler. And that's exactly the trouble. Unhappily I'm no longer in a position to gamble 200 pounds a year on what you yourself admit is an outside chance."

Slowly the young man realizes what his father means—that he must leave Oxford. Arthur breaks it as gently as possible. He may finish his second year, and after that Arthur will get him a job in the bank. Quite a good job, he says apologetically.

After he is over the shock of realizing his father means what he says, Dickie takes the blow sportingly enough. "I've been rather expecting it—especially since I heard you'd briefed Sir Robert Morton."

The Ronnie Winslow case is one for reporters as well as writers-to-the-editor, and a female journalist—an untidy woman of 40, named Barnes—comes to the house for the British equivalent of the American sob-sister story. "What I'd really like to do," she informs Arthur, "is to get a nice picture of you and your little boy together."

Ronnie should be home from school soon, Miss Barnes is informed. "He is coming to London to be examined by Sir Robert Morton, whom we are hoping to brief."

Miss Barnes is impressed, but wonders if Sir Robert will really take a little case like this. To pass the time before Ronnie's arrival, she goes through the motions of an interview but isn't really interested as Arthur details the history of the case to date.

By now, the history is considerable. Nine months ago the expulsion came. Ronnie's father phoned Osborne to protest and was referred to the Lords of the Admiralty. He hired lawyers to demand the fullest possible inquiry of the Admiralty. For weeks they were ignored, then finally got reluctant consent to a review of the evidence.

But the lawyers thought the evidence was unsatisfactory and wanted the proceedings reopened. They asked the Admiralty for a court-martial and were ignored. They asked for a civil trial and were ignored. Finally, after many letters to editors and questions in the House of Commons, the Admiralty agreed to what it called an independent inquiry.

It was no good, this inquiry. The judge advocate of the Fleet found Ronnie guilty again. But Arthur will not let the case rest there. He has a plan—

Miss Barnes isn't interested in the plan. She likes the curtains in the room and wants to know what they are made of. When Ronnie arrives home, a boy with normal enthusiasms who doesn't seem to realize he is becoming a national figure, Miss Barnes calls in her photographer, gets her father-and-son picture, and is off.

The woman's visit profoundly depresses Arthur. When Catherine comes in to show a made-over frock to her mother he says,

"I suddenly feel suicidally inclined. 'A father's fight for his little boy's honor,' " he bitterly mimics the lady journalist. "Photo insert of Mrs. Winslow's pink curtains. Is there any hope for the world?"

"I think so," Catherine reassures him.

"You realize that if we go on, your marriage settlement must go?"

Lightly and bravely Catherine acknowledges, "Oh, yes. I gave that up for lost weeks ago."

"Very well, then. Let us pin our faith on Sir Robert Morton."

Mention of Sir Robert very definitely does not set well with Arthur's daughter. He may be the best advocate for a monopoly attacking a trade union or a Tory paper libeling a labor leader— but for this case, now. He wouldn't have even a tenth of his heart in it. And if he did accept the case, it would only be if he could advance his own interests.

Arthur doggedly clings to his hope in Sir Robert—but when that great gentleman arrives in a few moments, Catherine grows even surer of her opinion. Morton is tall, thin, cadaverous, elegant almost to the point of foppishness, and in his early forties. With him is Desmond, who explains, "Sir Robert has a most important dinner engagement, so we came a little early." Morton won't even doff his overcoat as he sits in a hard chair.

When Desmond goes to fetch Arthur, Catherine tries to play the hostess with little success. Coldly he declines a drink or a cigarette; his replies to her questions and hostessy comments are blunt and brief. He seems inordinately conceited and the young woman's anger rises.

Arthur comes down with his wife and informs Sir Robert that Ronnie will be down in a moment. "I expect you will wish to examine him."

Indifferently, the barrister replies, "Just a few questions. I fear that is all I will have time for this evening."

"Desmond has been telling me," continues Arthur, "you think it might be possible to proceed by Petition of Right." Catherine wants to know what that is.

Desmond explains that it is a granting of redress as a matter of grace. On behalf of the King, the Attorney General may endorse the petition and allow a case to come to court. "It is interesting to note," interjects Sir Robert, "that the exact words he uses on such occasions are, 'Let Right be done.' "

When Ronald comes down his father instructs him to answer all questions truthfully, and Sir Robert begins an interrogation which seems more like a prosecution. Ronnie goes back to the fateful day—July 12 last year. He went to the Chief Petty Officer to get 16 shillings out of what he had in the school bank to buy an air pistol. He had two pounds, three shillings in his balance. He put the sixteen bob in his locker, got permission to go to the post office to buy a money order for the pistol, took his money from the locker and went to the post office.

Back at college, Ronnie had run into a schoolmate who informed him that somebody had pinched a postal order from his locker, and that he had reported it to the post office. After a while, Ronnie was called to the Commander's office, where a woman from the post office said he might be the boy.

He quotes her as saying, "I only know that the boy who bought a postal order for fifteen and six was the same boy who cashed one for five shillings." Then, he continues, he was made to sign his schoolmate's name on an envelope—and ten days later was sacked.

As Sir Robert relentlessly pursues his interrogation, Ronnie becomes more deeply involved. He admits he had practiced writing his schoolmate's signature—Charles K. Elliott—but only for a joke. It wasn't forging, it was "writing." A most damaging detail of Ronnie's case is that a noted handwriting expert has testified that Ronnie's sample signature of Elliott's name and the one on the stolen money order are the same.

Sir Robert is pointedly curious as to why Ronnie should put his sixteen shillings in his locker for a while, instead of keeping it in his pocket. Ronnie is becoming rattled. He gets confused as to the time he went back to the locker room and how much time he spent there. He can't account for a half hour—cannot, for a while, think of anybody whom he saw during this time. Then he does remember seeing a chap called Casey outside the Commanding Officer's office.

"What did you say?"

"I said, 'Come down to the post office with me. I'm going to cash a postal order.'"

Triumphantly Sir Robert pounces on the word "cash."

RONNIE—I mean get.

SIR ROBERT—You said cash. Why did you say cash if you meant get?

RONNIE—I don't know. I didn't mean it.

SIR ROBERT—I suggest cash was the truth.

RONNIE—No, no. It wasn't. It wasn't really. You're muddling me.

SIR ROBERT—You seem easily muddled. Why did you lie about the time you went to the post office?

RONNIE—I didn't.

SIR ROBERT—You told the Commander 2:30. You told me 3:15.

RONNIE—I was muddled, with the Commander.

SIR ROBERT—Muddled again? How many other lies have you told?

RONNIE—None. Really I haven't.

SIR ROBERT (*bending forward malevolently*)—I suggest your whole testimony is a lie.

RONNIE—No! It's the truth.

SIR ROBERT—I suggest there is barely one single word of truth in anything you have said either to me or to the judge advocate or to the Commander. I suggest that you did break into Elliott's locker, that you did steal the postal order, that you did cash it and forge his name.

RONNIE (*wailing*)—I didn't. I didn't.

SIR ROBERT—I suggest that you did it for a joke, meaning to give Elliott the five shillings back, but that when you met him and he said he had reported the matter that you got frightened and decided to keep quiet.

RONNIE—No, no, no. It isn't true.

SIR ROBERT—I suggest that by continuing to deny your guilt you are causing great hardship to your own family and considerable annoyance to high and important persons in this country—

CATHERINE (*on her feet*)—That's a disgraceful thing to say!

ARTHUR—I agree.

SIR ROBERT (*leaning forward and glaring at* RONNIE *with the utmost venom*)—I suggest, boy, that the time has at last come for you to undo some of the misery you have caused by confessing to us all now that you are a forger, a liar and a thief.

RONNIE (*in tears*)—I'm not! I'm not! I'm not! I didn't do it.

GRACE (*who has flown to his side and enveloped him*)—There, darling! Never mind, now! Never mind—

ARTHUR—This is outrageous, sir.

JOHN (*appearing at the door, dressed in evening clothes*)— Kate, dear, I'm most terribly sorry— (*He stops short as he takes in the scene, with* RONNIE *sobbing hysterically on his mother's*

breast, and ARTHUR *and* CATHERINE *glaring indignantly at* SIR
ROBERT, *who is engaged in putting his papers together.*)

SIR ROBERT (*to* DESMOND)—Can I drop you anywhere? My
car is at the door.

DESMOND—Er—no— I thank you.

SIR ROBERT (*carelessly*)—Well, send all this stuff round to my
chambers tomorrow morning, will you?

DESMOND—But—but will you need it now?

SIR ROBERT—Oh, yes. The boy is plainly innocent. I accept
the brief. (*He bows to* ARTHUR *and* CATHERINE *and walks languidly to the door past the bewildered* JOHN, *to whom he gives a
polite nod as he goes out.* RONNIE *continues to sob hysterically.*)

The curtain falls.

ACT II

SCENE I

Nine months have passed since Sir Robert's abrupt decision to
take Ronnie's case, and there has been much about it in the
papers—all of which Arthur has read. He is reading, now, aloud
to his wife and his son—but it is 10:30 P.M. and Ronnie is nodding.

The Winslow case is being debated in the House of Commons,
and according to the account in the paper, the First Lord of the
Admiralty is defending the original official action.

"My poor sleepy little lamb!" exclaims Grace as her son dozes
off. "It's long past his bedtime, Arthur."

"Grace, dear," says Arthur firmly, "at this very moment your
poor sleepy little lamb is the subject of a very violent and heated
debate in the House of Commons." He rouses Ronnie and continues reading the account. Sir Robert has advanced his Petition
of Right and the Admiralty is opposing it. Ronnie, said the First
Lord in the day's debate, was a servant of the Crown and had
no right to sue the Crown in open court.

Ronnie can't stay awake. When the reading is finished, Arthur takes up another topic. "I fancy," he suggests to his wife,
"this might be a good opportunity of talking to Violet."

GRACE (*quite firmly*)—No, dear.

ARTHUR—Meaning that it isn't a good opportunity? Or meaning that you have no intention at all of ever talking to Violet?

GRACE—I'll do it one day, Arthur. Tomorrow, perhaps. Not
now.

ARTHUR—I believe you'd do better to grasp the nettle. Delay only adds to your worries. . . .

GRACE (*bitterly*)—My worries? What do you know about my worries?

ARTHUR—A good deal, Grace. But I feel they would be a lot lessened if you faced the situation squarely.

GRACE—It's easy for you to talk, Arthur. You don't have to do it.

ARTHUR—I will, if you like.

GRACE—No, dear.

ARTHUR—If you explain the dilemma to her carefully—if you even show her the figures I jotted down for you yesterday—I venture to think you won't find her unreasonable.

GRACE—It won't be easy for her to find another place.

ARTHUR—We'll give her an excellent reference.

GRACE—That won't alter the fact that she's never been properly trained as a parlormaid and—well—you know yourself how we're always having to explain her to people. No, Arthur, I don't mind how many figures she's shown, it's a brutal thing to do.

ARTHUR—Facts are brutal things.

GRACE (*a shade hysterically*)—Facts? I don't think I know what the facts are any more—

ARTHUR—The facts at this moment are that we have half of the income we had a year ago and we're living at nearly the same rate. However you look at it, that's bad economics—

GRACE—I'm not talking about economics, Arthur. I know about those facts as well as you—probably better, as I have to deal with them. I'm talking about ordinary, common or garden facts—things we took for granted a year ago and which now don't seem to matter any more.

ARTHUR—Such as?

GRACE (*with rising voice*)—Such as a happy home and peace and quiet and an ordinary respectable life, and some sort of future for us and our children. In the last year you've thrown all that overboard, Arthur. There's your return for it, I suppose— (*She indicates the headline in the paper.*)—and it's all very exciting and important, I'm sure, but it doesn't bring back any of the things that we've lost. I can only pray to God that you know what you're doing. (RONNIE *stirs in his sleep.* GRACE *lowers her voice at the end of her speech. There is a pause.*)

ARTHUR (*quietly*)—I do know what I'm doing, Grace.

GRACE—Do you? I'm not so sure. I sometimes think you're

just marching blindly ahead without knowing where you're going.

ARTHUR—I know exactly where I'm going, Grace. I'm going to publish my son's innocence before the world, and for that end I am not prepared to weigh the cost.

GRACE—But the cost may be out of all proportion—

ARTHUR—It may be. That doesn't concern me. I hate heroics, Grace, but you force me to say this. An injustice has been done. I am going to set it right, and there is no sacrifice in the world I am not prepared to make in order to do so.

GRACE (*with sudden violence*)—Oh, I wish I could see the sense of it all! (*Pointing to* RONNIE.) He's perfectly happy, at a good school, doing very well. No one need ever have known about Osborne if you hadn't gone and shouted it out to the whole world. As it is, whatever happens now, he'll go through the rest of his life as the boy in that Winslow case—the boy who stole that postal order—

ARTHUR (*grimly*)—The boy that didn't steal that postal order.

GRACE (*wearily*)—What's the difference? When millions are talking and gossiping about him a did or a didn't hardly matters. The Winslow boy is bad enough. You talk about sacrificing everything for him, but when he's grown up he won't thank you for it, Arthur—even though you've given your life to—publish his innocence as you call it. (ARTHUR *makes an impatient gesture*.) Yes, Arthur—your life. You talk gaily about arthritis and a touch of gout and old age and the rest of it, but you know as well as any of the doctors what really is the matter with you and how vital it is for you to have some rest and quiet. (*Nearly in tears*.) You're destroying yourself, Arthur, and me and your family besides—and for what? For what, I'd like to know? I've asked you and Kate to tell me a hundred times—but you can't. You never can— For what, Arthur? For what?

ARTHUR (*who has struggled painfully out of his seat and approaches her, speaking quietly*)—For Justice, Grace.

GRACE—Justice? That sounds very noble. Are you sure it's true? Are you sure it isn't just plain pride and self-importance and sheer brute stubbornness? You and Kate can't bear the thought of anyone ever getting the better of you. Isn't it just plain selfishness in you both that stops you saying "All right. I'll give up. They've won"?

ARTHUR (*putting a hand out*)—No, Grace. I don't think it is. I really don't think it is—

GRACE (*shaking off his hand*)—No. This time I'm not going

to cry and say I'm sorry and make it all up again. It's past that now, Arthur. I can't stand it any more. If there was a reason at all, it's unfair to ask so much of me. It's unfair— (*She breaks down. As* ARTHUR *puts a comforting arm around her she pushes him off and goes out of the door.*)

The debate has continued into the evening and Catherine has been there. When she gets back home her father inquires if it is over. "As good as," she replied. "The First Lord gave an assurance that in future there would be no inquiry at Osborne or Dartmouth without informing the parents first."

"But what about our case? Is he going to allow us a fair trial?"

"Apparently not." Catherine samples the sandwiches which Violet has brought in for her.

"But didn't Sir Robert make any protest?"

"Not a verbal protest—something far more spectacular and dramatic. He uncoiled those long legs of his—he'd had his feet on the Treasury table and his hat over his eyes during most of the First Lord's speech—and suddenly got up very deliberately, glared at the First Lord, threw a whole bundle of notes on the floor, and stalked out of the House. It made a magnificent effect."

But Catherine believes it was sham and show business, all for the benefit of Sir Robert Morton. He is, she is more than ever convinced, a hard, cold-blooded, supercilious, sneering fish. She is just saying so when Sir Robert himself is announced by Violet, causing Catherine to choke over a sandwich. Sir Robert calmly pats her on the back, then compliments her on the hat she wore during the day's proceedings. "Ah," he says, observing the sleeping Ronnie, "the *casus belli*—dormant." Arthur goes to wake his son up.

SIR ROBERT—No, no. I beg of you. Please do not disturb his innocent slumbers.

CATHERINE—*Innocent* slumbers?

SIR ROBERT—Exactly. Besides, I fear since our first encounter he is, rather pardonably, a trifle nervous of me.

CATHERINE—Will you betray a technical secret, Sir Robert? What happened in that first examination to make you so sure of his innocence?

SIR ROBERT—Three things. First of all, he made far too many damaging admissions. A guilty boy would have made many fewer; he would have been alert and on guard. Then I laid him a trap and left him a loophole. A guilty boy would have fallen into the one and darted through the other. Ronnie did neither.

CATHERINE—The trap was to ask him suddenly what time Elliott put the postal order in his locker. Wasn't it?

SIR ROBERT—That was one of them—yes.

CATHERINE—And the loophole?

SIR ROBERT—I reduced him to a state of some hysteria. I then suggested to him that he had stolen the postal order for a joke—which, had he been guilty, he would surely have admitted—as by far—considering my apparent certainty of his guilt—the lesser of two evils.

CATHERINE—I see. It was very cleverly thought out.

SIR ROBERT (*with a little bow*)—Thank you, Miss Winslow.

ARTHUR—Could we offer you some refreshment, Sir Robert? A whiskey and soda?

SIR ROBERT—No, thank you. Nothing at all.

ARTHUR—My daughter has told me of your demonstration during the First Lord's speech. She described it as—magnificent.

SIR ROBERT (*with a glance at* CATHERINE)—Did she? That was good of her. It's a very old trick, you know. I've done it many times in the courts. It's nearly always surprisingly effective. (CATHERINE *catches her father's eye and nods triumphantly.*) Was the First Lord at all put out by it—did you notice?

CATHERINE—How could he have failed to be? (*To* ARTHUR, *approaching his chair.*) I wish you could have seen it, Father—it was— (*She notices a letter on the table beside* ARTHUR *and snatches it up with a sudden gesture. She examines the envelope.*) When did this come?

ARTHUR—A few minutes ago. Do you know the writing?

CATHERINE—Yes. (*She puts the letter back on the table.*)

ARTHUR—Whose is it?

CATHERINE—I shouldn't bother to read it if I were you. (ARTHUR *looks at her, puzzled, then takes up the letter.*)

ARTHUR (*to* SIR ROBERT)—Will you forgive me?

SIR ROBERT—Of course. (ARTHUR *opens the letter and begins to read.* CATHERINE *watches him for a moment, and then turns to* SIR ROBERT *with a certain forced liveliness.*)

CATHERINE—Well, what do you think the next step should be?

SIR ROBERT—I have already been considering that, Miss Winslow—I believe that perhaps the best plan would be to renew our efforts to get the Director of Public Prosecutions to act.

CATHERINE (*with one eye on her father*)—But do you think there's any chance of that?

SIR ROBERT—Oh, yes. In the main it will chiefly be a question of making ourselves a confounded nuisance—

CATHERINE—We've certainly done that quite successfully so far, thanks to you.

SIR ROBERT (*suavely*)—Ah. That is perhaps the only quality I was born with—the ability to make myself a confounded nuisance. (*He too has his eyes on* ARTHUR, *sensing something amiss.* ARTHUR *finishes reading the letter and lays it slowly on the table.*)

CATHERINE (*with false vivacity*)—Father—Sir Robert thinks we might get the Director of Public Prosecutions to act.

ARTHUR—What?

SIR ROBERT—We were discussing how to proceed with the case—

ARTHUR—The case? (*He stares a little blankly from one to the other.*) Yes. We must think of that, mustn't we? (*Pause.*) How to proceed with the case? (*To* SIR ROBERT, *abruptly.*) I'm afraid I don't think, all things considered, that much purpose would be served by going on. (SIR ROBERT *and* CATHERINE *stare at him blankly.* CATHERINE *goes quickly to him and snatches the letter. She begins to read.*)

SIR ROBERT (*with a sudden change of tone*)—Of course we must go on.

ARTHUR (*in a low voice*)—It is not for you to choose, sir. The choice is mine.

SIR ROBERT (*harshly*)—Then you must reconsider it. To give up now would be insane.

ARTHUR—Insane? My sanity has already been called in question tonight—for carrying the case as far as I have.

SIR ROBERT—Whatever the contents of that letter—or whatever has happened to make you lose heart, I insist that we continue the fight.

ARTHUR—Insist? We? It is my fight—my fight alone—and it is for me alone to judge when the time has come to give up.

SIR ROBERT (*violently*)—But why give up? Why? In Heaven's name, man, why give up?

ARTHUR (*slowly*)—I have made many sacrifices for this case. Some of them I had no right to make, but I made them none the less. But there is a limit, and I have reached it. I am sorry, Sir Robert—more sorry, perhaps, than you are, but the Winslow case is now closed.

SIR ROBERT—Balderdash! (ARTHUR *looks surprised at this unparliamentary expression.* CATHERINE *has read and reread the letter, and now breaks the silence in a calm, methodical voice.*)

CATHERINE—My father doesn't mean what he says, Sir Robert.

SIR ROBERT—I'm glad to hear it.

CATHERINE—Perhaps I should explain that this letter—

ARTHUR—No, Kate.

CATHERINE—Sir Robert knows so much about our family affairs, Father, I don't see it will matter much if he learns a little more. (*To* SIR ROBERT.) This letter is from a certain Colonel Wetherstone who is the father of the man I'm engaged to. We've always known he was opposed to the case, so it really comes as no surprise. In it he says that our efforts to discredit the Admiralty in the House of Commons today have resulted merely in our making the name of Winslow a nationwide laughing-stock. I think that's his phrase. (*She consults the letter.*) Yes. That's right—a nationwide laughing-stock.

SIR ROBERT—I don't care for his English.

CATHERINE—It's not very good, is it? He goes on to say that unless my father will give him a firm undertaking to drop this—this—(*She consults the letter again.*)—whining and reckless agitation—I suppose he means the case—he will exert every bit of influence he has over his son to prevent his marrying me.

Catherine, with a not quite successful air of bravado, insists that this will make no difference—that John is his own master and they can live perfectly well without the allowance. Sir Robert advances more compliments on Miss Winslow's hat, then questions her about her political activities, which seem so unbecoming to such a hat.

She is, she tells him, an organizing secretary of the Woman's Suffrage Association—voluntary and unpaid.

Violet announces an unexpected visit of John Wetherstone. He wants a private word with Catherine, so Sir Robert and Arthur withdraw to the usual retiring-place—the dining room. John looks depressed and anxious. When he has made sure that Ronnie is really asleep on the sofa and not shamming, he says, "My father's written your father a letter."

"I know. I've read it."

"Well, what's his answer?"

"My father? I don't suppose he'll send one."

John is afraid that, if the Winslow case isn't dropped, his father will forbid the match as he has threatened. "Isn't that rather an empty threat, John?" asks Catherine.

"Well, there's always the allowance."

"Yes, I see," says Catherine dully. "There's always the allowance."

It is a big thing with John, for he fancies he has a practical mind—and he thinks that two inquiries, a Petition of Right and an appeal, should have been enough for the Winslow boy.

"And now, good Heavens, you've had the whole damned House of Commons getting themselves worked up into a frenzy about it. Surely, darling, that's enough for you? . . . *He* won't mind" —and he points to Ronnie.

Very quietly and earnestly Catherine explains that Ronnie's innocence or guilt is not important to her—she thinks Ronnie may have pinched the postal order—but it is to her father. "All that I care about is that people should know that a government department has ignored a fundamental human right and that it should be forced to acknowledge it."

John cannot see the point. To him, the case is out of proportion, with a European war blowing up, a civil war looming in Ireland and a coal strike on.

Spiritedly Catherine retorts, "All I know is that if ever the time comes when the House of Commons has so much on its mind that it can't find time to discuss a Ronnie Winslow and his bally postal order, this country will be a far poorer place than it is now."

Catherine wearily realizes what her situation is with John. He still stoutly insists that he wants to marry her—but there is the allowance. He is expressing the confidence that nothing so stupid and trivial as the Winslow case could come between them when a telephone call comes for Sir Robert. Catherine calls him out of the dining room.

It is quite a long phone call, with Sir Robert mostly listening. At its end he tells Arthur, who has followed him out, that there has been a most interesting development. Shortly after 9:30 this evening a barrister friend of Sir Robert's delivered in the House a scathing denunciation of the Admiralty and this revived the debate.

"My secretary tells me," he announces, "that rather than risk a division the First Lord has this moment given an undertaking that he will instruct the Attorney General to endorse our Petition of Right. The case of Winslow versus Rex can now therefore come to court."

Arthur and Catherine stare at him unbelievingly.

"Well, sir, what are my instructions?"

Slowly Arthur says, "The decision is no longer mine. You must ask my daughter."

Catherine is ready with her answer. In a flat voice she says, "Do you need my instructions, Sir Robert? Aren't they already on the Petition? Doesn't it say, 'Let right be done'?"

John turns abruptly toward the door, furiously bids Kate good night. Sir Robert, languidly munching one of Kate's sandwiches, declares, "Well, then—we must endeavor to see that it is."

The curtain falls.

SCENE II

It is two years less than one month since Ronnie got sacked— a hot June day. By the open garden door is a wheel chair. Dickie carries in a suitcase, mops his face, finds no one in the room, and answers the ringing telephone. Four more months have gone by, and it's still the Winslow case, and the *Daily Mail* is calling about it.

No, Dickie says, it isn't Senior, it's Junior. Elder brother. In the banking business. No, no opinion, except that he hopes we win, of course. Verdict is expected tomorrow, isn't it?

No sooner has he hung up than the phone rings again, but this time his mother comes in and takes it. "Everyone out," she says, and hangs up. She greets her son, and in return he queries, "How's it all going?"

"I don't know," his mother confesses. "I've been there all four days now and I've hardly understood a word that's going on. Kate says the judge is against us, but he seems a charming old gentleman to me. Sir Robert's so rude to him—"

Kate, she explains, takes the morning session in court, then comes home to relieve her mother in caring for Arthur. Right now it's lunch time, and Grace calls to Arthur in the garden. She resumes her description of the trial—the crowds, the cheers and applause, the battles between the Attorney General and Sir Robert. Ronnie has done very well in two days of cross-examination. As for Kate's broken engagement, "You never can tell with Kate. She never lets you know what she's feeling."

Arthur walks groggily through the garden door and Grace helps him into the wheel chair—a ludicrous form of propulsion, he ruefully admits to Dickie. Dickie, he thinks, looks well, but a trifle thinner, and he has had a good report of Dickie's work from the Reading branch of the bank.

A further report, too: "Mr. Lamb says you've joined the Territorials. Why have you done that?"

"Well," answers his son, "from all accounts there is a fair chance of a bit of a scrap soon. If there is I don't want it to be all over before I can get in on it."

Arthur notes that Catherine is late getting back from the trial, and further that he does not approve of his wife's pretty dress. "Your son," he admonishes, "is facing a charge of theft and forgery."

"I'll tell you what," she offers. "I'll wear my black coat and skirt tomorrow—for the verdict." She urges him to take the cold lunch she has readied for him because Violet and the cook are at the trial.

"Is Violet still with you?" asks Dickie. "She was under sentence the last time I saw you."

Violet is, indeed, still with them—for nobody has had the courage to tell her she is under sentence. Arthur wheels into the dining room and Dickie inquires of his mother, "How *is* he?" She shakes her head—but at any rate, Arthur has promised to go into a nursing home after the trial.

And from the trial comes Catherine. The judge, she believes, is antagonistic, and Sir Robert is worried because the Attorney General's speech made a great impression on the jury. "To listen to him yesterday you would have thought that a verdict for Ronnie would simultaneously cause a mutiny in the Royal Navy and triumphant jubilation in Berlin."

Appearing in the dining room door, Arthur asks his daughter, "How did it go this morning?" and she reports:

"Sir Robert finished his cross-examination of the postmistress. I thought he'd demolish her completely. She admitted she couldn't identify Ronnie in the Commander's office. She admitted she couldn't be sure of the time he came in. She admitted that she was called away to the telephone while he was buying his fifteen and six postal order, and that all Osborne cadets looked alike to her in their uniforms, so that it might quite easily have been another cadet who cashed the five shillings. It was a brilliant cross-examination—so gentle and quiet. He didn't bully her or frighten her—he just coaxed her into tying herself into knots. Then when he'd finished, the Attorney General asked her again whether she was absolutely positive that the same boy that bought the fifteen and six postal order also cashed the five shilling one. She said yes. She was quite, quite sure because Ronald was such a good-looking little boy that she had specially noticed him. She hadn't said that in her examination-in-chief. I could see those twelve good men and true nodding away to each other. I believe it undid the whole of that magnificent cross-examination."

Another item of news is that John Wetherstone was in court to wish the family luck—an impertinence, thinks Grace.

"Grace, you will be late," Arthur warns her—and indeed she will, for already it is twenty minutes past the afternoon starting time. She and Dickie hasten out. "When you get to the front door," she instructs him, "put your head down like me and just charge through them all"—for there is a crowd at the house as well as the trial.

When Catherine tells her father Sir Robert is worried, he wonders if they could have got a better man. There couldn't be one, she replies. "He's the best advocate in England and for some reason—prestige, I suppose—he seems genuinely anxious to win this case. I don't go back on anything else I've ever said about him." And today Sir Robert has pulled another brilliant trick, telling the judge he felt ill and getting the sympathy of the court and, possibly, providing himself with an excuse if he is beaten.

Desmond appears at the garden door, knocks diffidently. He has come in this way to escape the crowd at the door; he has a taxi waiting and wants to see Catherine alone—so Arthur wheels back to finish his lunch. Catherine smilingly comments that keeping a taxi waiting is quite extravagant.

DESMOND (*also smiling*)—Yes. But it shows you how rushed this visit must necessarily be. The fact of the matter is—it suddenly occurred to me during the lunch adjournment that I had better see you today.

CATHERINE (*her thoughts far distant*)—Why?

DESMOND—I have a question to put to you, Kate, which, if I had postponed putting until after the verdict, you might—who knows?—have thought had been prompted by pity—if we had lost. Or—if we had won, your reply might—again who knows?—have been influenced by gratitude. Do you follow me, Kate?

CATHERINE—Yes, Desmond. I think I do.

DESMOND—Ah. Then possibly you have some inkling of what the question is I have to put to you?

CATHERINE—Yes, I think I have.

DESMOND (*a trifle disconcerted*)—Oh.

CATHERINE—I'm sorry, Desmond. I ought, I know, to have followed the usual practice in such cases and told you I had no inkling whatever.

DESMOND—No, no. Your directness and honesty are two of

the qualities I so admire in you. I am glad you have guessed. It makes my task the easier—

CATHERINE (*in a matter-of-fact voice*)—Will you give me a few days to think it over?

DESMOND—Of course. Of course.

CATHERINE—I need hardly tell you how grateful I am, Desmond.

DESMOND (*a trifle bewildered*)—There is no need, Kate, no need at all—

CATHERINE—You mustn't keep your taxi waiting.

DESMOND (*fiercely*)—Oh, bother my taxi. (*Recovering himself.*) Forgive me, Kate, but you see I know very well what your feelings for me really are.

CATHERINE (*gently*)—You do, Desmond?

DESMOND—Yes, Kate. I know quite well they have never amounted to much more than a sort of—well—shall we say friendliness? A warm friendliness, I hope. Yes, I think perhaps we can definitely say warm. But no more than that. That's true, isn't it?

CATHERINE (*quietly*)—Yes, Desmond.

DESMOND—I know, I know. Of course, the thing is that even if I proved the most devoted and adoring husband that ever lived—which, I may say, if you give me the chance, I intend to be—your feelings for me would never—could never—amount to more than that. When I was younger, it might, perhaps, have been a different story. When I played cricket for England— (*He notices the faintest expression of pity that has crossed* CATHERINE's *face. Then apologetically:*) And, of course, perhaps even that would not have made so much difference. Perhaps you feel I cling too much to my past athletic prowess. I feel it myself, sometimes—but the truth is I have not much else to cling to save that and my love for you. The athletic prowess is fading, I'm afraid, with the years and the stiffening of the muscles—but my love for you will never fade.

CATHERINE (*smiling*)—That's very charmingly said, Desmond.

DESMOND—Don't make fun of me, Kate, please. I meant it, every word. (*Clearing his throat.*) However, let us take a more mundane approach and examine the facts. Fact 1. You don't love me and never can. Fact 2. I love you, always have and always will. That is the situation—and it is a situation which, after most careful consideration, I am fully prepared to accept. I reached this decision some months ago, but thought at first it would be better to wait until this case, which is so much on all

our minds, should be over. Then at lunch today I determined
to anticipate the verdict tomorrow and let you know what was
in my mind at once. No matter what you feel or don't feel for
me—no matter what you feel for anyone else—I want you to
be my wife. (*Pause.*)

CATHERINE (*at length*)—I see. Thank you, Desmond. That
makes everything much clearer.

They talk of Sir Robert and agree that he is cold and fishlike,
yet Desmond happens to know he has made a great personal
sacrifice to bring the case to court.

"Sacrifice? What? Of another brief?"

"No, no. That would be no sacrifice to him. No, he was
offered—you really promise to keep this to yourself?"

"Of course. What was he offered, Desmond?"

"The appointment of Lord Chief Justice. He turned it down
simply in order to be able to carry on with the case of Winslow
versus Rex."

Desmond goes for his taxi and Catherine stands deep in thought.
When Arthur wheels in, she says slowly, "I've been a fool,
Father." But she can't tell more, she explains, because she is
under a pledge of secrecy.

"I trust," Arthur says dryly, "the folly wasn't your acceptance
of Desmond?"

"No, Father. Would it be such a folly, though?"

Desmond, she points out, is nice and is doing very well—and
she is nearly 30. She has got a salary out of the Suffrage Association—but it is a small two pounds a week. "The choice," she
reasons, "is quite simple. Either I marry Desmond and settle
down into quite a comfortable and not really useless existence—
or I go on for the rest of my life earning two pounds a week in
the service of a hopeless cause."

Arthur has never before heard her talk of her cause as hopeless. One of the elements of this hopelessness is the news that
John is getting married—rather gracelessly soon after jilting Catherine, but he thinks there is going to be a war soon and his
regiment will be one of the first overseas.

"Poor Kate," sympathizes Arthur, taking her hand. "How I've
messed up your life, haven't I?"

"No, Father. Any messing-up that's been done has been done
by me."

A newsboy can be heard dimly shouting in the street. Probably "Winslow Case—latest." But no, it doesn't sound like

"latest." It isn't. Heard more clearly now, it is "Result!"
Catherine and Arthur are puzzling over this when Violet bursts
in, excited and smiling.

"Oh, Miss Kate," she exclaims, "what a shame you missed it!
Just after they came back from lunch—and Mrs. Winslow, she
wasn't there neither, nor Master Ronnie. The cheering and the
shouting and the carrying-on—you never heard anything like it
in all your life—and Sir Robert standing there at the table with
his wig on crooked and the tears running down his face—running
down his face they were and not able to speak because of the
noise. Cook and me, we did a bit of crying too; we just couldn't
help it—you couldn't, you know. Oh, it was lovely. We did enjoy
ourselves. And then Cook had her hat knocked over her eyes by
the man behind who was cheering and waving his arms about
something chronic and shouting about liberty—you would have
laughed, Miss, to see her, she was that cross—but she didn't mind,
really, she was only pretending and we kept on cheering and the
judge kept on shouting but it wasn't any good because even the
jury joined in, and some of them climbed out of the box to
shake hands with Sir Robert. And then outside in the street it
was just the same—you couldn't move for the crowd and you'd
think they'd all gone mad the way they were carrying on. Some
of them were shouting 'Good old Winslow' and singing 'For he's
a jolly good fellow,' and Cook had her hat knocked off again.
Oh, it was lovely! (*To* ARTHUR.) Well, sir, you must be feeling nice and pleased, now it's all over."

When Violet goes to her household duties, Arthur remarks, "It
would appear, then, that we've won." Catherine, sobbing on
her father's lap, says, "Yes, Father, it would appear that we've
won."

Suddenly Violet announces Sir Robert. Her description of him
in court does not tally now with his composed features as he
walks calmly toward Arthur. "I thought you might like to hear
the actual terms of the Attorney General's statement, so I jotted
it down for you." From a scrap of paper he reads a formally
couched exoneration of Ronnie, "without any reservation of any
description, intending it to be a complete acceptance of the boy's
statements."

Arthur gropes for words of gratitude, but Sir Robert begs him
not to search for them. "Now, on the question of damages and
costs. I fear we shall find the Admiralty rather niggardly. You
are likely still to be left considerably out of pocket. However,
doubtless we can apply a slight spur to the First Lord's posterior

in the House of Commons."

"Please, sir—no more trouble—I beg," says Arthur. "Let the matter rest here." Showing the scrap of paper, he declares, "This is all I have ever asked for."

Catherine wonders why the Admiralty threw up the case. Sir Robert carelessly comments that it was a foregone conclusion. Did he seem distressed this morning? It was the heat in the courtroom, and fatigue.

Violet informs Arthur that newspapermen at the front door want a statement—and this time he will make one. But what shall he say?

"I hardly think it matters," says Sir Robert indifferently. "Whatever you say will have little bearing on what they write."

Over his daughter's protest, Arthur gets out of his chair and walks to greet the press. "Perhaps," he concludes, "I had better say what I really feel, which is merely, Thank God, we beat 'em."

Abruptly Sir Robert asks Catherine for some whiskey and droops in a chair. "I have not been feeling myself all day. I told the judge so this morning, if you remember, but I doubt if he believed me. He thought it was a trick. What suspicious minds people have, have they not?"

Catherine—Yes.

Sir Robert (*handing her back the glass*)—Thank you.

Catherine (*puts the glass down, then turns slowly back to face him as if nerving herself for an ordeal*)—Sir Robert, I'm afraid I have a confession and an apology to make to you.

Sir Robert (*sensing what is coming*)—Dear lady—I am sure the one is rash and the other superfluous. I would far rather hear neither—

Catherine (*with a smile*)—I am afraid you must. This is probably the last time I shall see you, and it is a better penance for me to say this than to write it. I have entirely misjudged your attitude to this case, and if in doing so I have ever seemed to you either rude or ungrateful, I am sincerely and humbly sorry.

Sir Robert (*indifferently*)—My dear Miss Winslow, you have never seemed to me either rude or ungrateful. And my attitude to this case has been the same as yours—to win it at all costs. Only—when you talk of gratitude—you must remember that those costs were not mine but yours.

Catherine—Weren't they yours also, Sir Robert?

Sir Robert—I beg your pardon?

CATHERINE—Haven't you too made a very special sacrifice for the case? (*Pause.*)

SIR ROBERT—The robes of that office would not have suited me.

CATHERINE—Wouldn't they?

SIR ROBERT (*with venom*)—And what is more, I fully intend to report Curry to the Law Society.

CATHERINE—Please don't. He did me a great service by telling me.

SIR ROBERT—Well, I must ask you never to divulge it to another living soul and even to forget it yourself.

CATHERINE—I shall never divulge it. I'm afraid I can't promise to forget it myself.

SIR ROBERT—Very well! If you choose to give an unimportant incident a romantic significance, you are perfectly at liberty to do so. I must go. (*He gets up.*)

CATHERINE—Why are you always at such pains to prevent people from knowing the truth about you, Sir Robert?

SIR ROBERT—Am I indeed?

CATHERINE—You know you are. Why?

SIR ROBERT—Perhaps because *I* do not know the truth about myself.

CATHERINE—That is no answer.

SIR ROBERT—My dear Miss Winslow, are you cross-questioning me?

CATHERINE—On this point, yes. Why are you so ashamed of your emotions?

SIR ROBERT—Because, as a lawyer, I must necessarily distrust them.

CATHERINE—Why?

SIR ROBERT—To fight a case on emotional grounds is the surest way of losing it. Emotions muddy the issue. Cold, clear logic—and buckets of it—should be the lawyer's only equipment.

CATHERINE—Was it cold, clear logic that made you weep today at the verdict? (*Pause.*)

SIR ROBERT—Your maid, I suppose, told you that? It doesn't matter. It will be in the papers tomorrow, anyway. (*Fiercely.*) Very well, then, young lady, if you must have it, here it is in all its highfalutin repulsiveness. I wept today because right had been done.

CATHERINE—Not justice?

SIR ROBERT—No. Not justice—right. It is not hard to do justice—very hard to do right. Unfortunately, while the appeal of justice is intellectual, the appeal of right appears, for some odd reason, to induce tears in court.   That is my answer and my excuse.   And now, may I leave the witness box?

It was, he allows, a good experience to get a little of his own medicine.   Catherine would make a good advocate; indeed, why doesn't she canalize her feminine impulses toward the law courts, and abandon the lost cause of woman's suffrage?

But Catherine has regained heart.   "Because I don't believe it *is* a lost cause."

Sir Robert offers her good-by.   "In the House of Commons in days to come I shall make a point of looking up at the gallery in the hope of catching a glimpse of you in that provocative hat."

In comes Ronnie, quite a man about town in a lounge suit and Homburg hat—but an apologetic one.   "I didn't know anything was going to happen," he explains to Sir Robert.

"Where were you?"

"At the movies."

There was a cinematograph show near the court and Ronnie, after sitting in court four days, went and had a squint at it.   "I say—we won, didn't we?"

"Yes," says Sir Robert, "we won.   Now that it's all over, tell me something, Ronald.   What were you really doing in the locker room all that time?"

"I was smoking, sir."

"That's just what I thought."   And calmly but sharply, Sir Robert brings his stick down on Ronnie's backside.

"Good-by, Miss Winslow.   Shall I see you in the House, then, one day?"

"Yes, Sir Robert," smiles Catherine.   "One day.   But not in the gallery.   Across the floor."

With a faint smile and a "Perhaps" he turns to go.

THE CURTAIN FALLS

THE HEIRESS

A Play in Three Acts

By Ruth and Augustus Goetz

IN the season of 1944-45 Ruth Goodman and her husband, Augustus Goetz, were represented by a play, "One Man Show," which ran for only 36 performances. It was, thus, a commercial failure; but it impressed some people, including the editor of this volume, with the good quality of its writing and its human observations.

"One Man Show" was set in the esoteric world of art dealers and it concerned itself with an unusually but not unnaturally profound attachment between a father and his daughter. Although it was a failure, it had in it the key to a subsequent success—"The Heiress."

"We were mighty unhappy about the failure of 'One Man Show,'" write the Goetzes. "We thought it was a very good play. We had said our good-bys to the stage hands and our thank-yous to the cast and started back to the farm in Pennsylvania where we live. One of us said to the other, 'Well, we're better off than Henry James.'

"Mr. James had the experience to stop all experiences. He came out on the stage the opening night of 'Guy Domville' to calls of 'Author, Author,' and then was hooted.

"Thinking about James, one day we picked up an early novel of his, 'Washington Square.' This exquisitely written and delicate story was forgotten and out of print. But as dramatists we saw in it a number of things: first, it was about the father-daughter relationship of which we still had much to say; second, it was told in terms of characters who did what people always do—the worst things for the best reasons; third, there was the real challenge of turning poor, dull Catherine Sloper into a true heroine. One night in front of our fireplace we got a vision of her the night Morris jilted her in front of hers—and then we had our second act."

Their play from the James novel, "The Heiress," had the rare boon of a second chance. When it went the rounds of producers' offices it aroused enthusiasm—except for its "unhappy" ending.

Five managers said they would produce the play if the adapters would change the last act; and the Goetzes succumbed to the fifth manager.

"We opened in New Haven," they recall. "Well, we had friends in New Haven and, as always, your friends make excuses. They tell you to recast—that the weather is tough—that you've got Rodzinski against you—and that New Haven is a comedy town. But in Boston a few nights later, we had no friends. We had only an audience of forty-three people on the second night—and they told us the truth. They liked the first act, were attentive and respectful through the second, then they got that false ending and in three minutes we destroyed the two previous hours of participation and identification. At the final curtain we heard the echoes of the hoots and jeers that Henry James had heard."

The production was closed in Boston—but other managers still were interested. Ultimately, with Fred F. Finklehoffe as producer and Jed Harris as director, "The Heiress" was recast and brought to Broadway—with the Jamesian ending the Goetzes had written in the first place. "It is extremely difficult," they declare, "to tell what turned us from such a flop into such a success. All we know is that we owe that Boston audience for a tremendous lesson in playwriting."

They also owe, and acknowledge, their debt to Henry James, Jr.—which is the way he signed himself when he wrote "Washington Square." The people in the play, their motivations, the progression of the story, and much of the dialogue are as they were in the novel. The major change is the introduction of the scene in which Catherine and Morris prepare to elope and she is jilted.

The play takes place in the front parlor of Dr. Sloper's house in Washington Square in 1850. It is a spacious, handsome room in a spacious, handsome house in a neighborhood of high fashion. Two windows at the front of the room look out on the Square; behind the room are the foyer and the front door. In the wall opposite the windows is a fireplace, and next to it a door leading to the doctor's study. The foyer is divided from the drawing room by an archway, outlined by pillars of the period, and through them is seen the staircase leading to the second floor.

Dr. Sloper set up housekeeping here with his young bride in 1820, and he and she were in a position to buy Duncan Phyfe's furniture and to combine it with some English heirlooms; the room, therefore, does not have the gaudy look of the Victorian period. . . . It is an evening in October, and Dr. Sloper comes home from his visits carrying his medical bag. He is a distinguished, middle-aged man, pleasant in manner and impeccably dressed. Maria, a parlormaid, offers him some supper.

Surprised, he inquires if Miss Catherine and her aunt have not waited for him; then he remembers—company. Maria explains that the women ate early, wanting time to dress. The doctor declines food; he had a little something at the Garrisons', where Mrs. Garrison is the mother of the new citizen. Sipping a glass of sherry, he muses about babies.

"Such beautiful little creatures. . . . Why don't they grow up that way? . . . Maria, when you are married you must have a lot of children. That way you won't put all your hopes on one. Give yourself more than a single chance."

Catherine's aunt, Lavinia Penniman, comes down the stair and greets her brother. "How nice that you are home! I was afraid the baby might take all evening, and then our little party would be spoiled." Mrs. Penniman, who may be described as fluttery and unsure of her status in the household, being a homeless widow, asks Maria to serve the collation late. "I would like a long visit with Sister Elizabeth," she explains to her brother, "and I'm anxious to get to know the engaged couple."

The doctor asks Lavinia if she likes it here well enough to stay on; he is going to a medical congress in Paris in December and would like her to remain. "Of course," he says, "Catherine is of an age where she can perfectly well stay alone with the servants, but I think if you lived here with her while I am away, you might help her."

Lavinia can't understand what help she can be; Catherine goes out so little she needs no chaperone, and she runs the house most competently. "What am I to help her to?"

"Well, for instance, this evening while our company is here—perhaps you could persuade Catherine to stay quietly in the room with us and join in the conversation. . . . Help her to be clever, Lavinia. I should like her to be a clever woman."

"But she is so gentle and good!"

"You are," pronounces the doctor as he starts for his study, "good for nothing unless you are clever!"

Catherine, clad in an overelaborate red satin gown with gold trimmings which makes her look opulent and matronly, comes down and joins her aunt. She is a healthy, quiet girl in her late twenties. When she expresses the hope that her father will like her dress, Lavinia assures her he is bound to. "You know, one

of the last times I ever saw your poor mother, Catherine, she had
the most delicious little bows of that color in her hair. It was
only a week before you were born. . . ."

While they are waiting for the guests, the girl tells her aunt
of her afternoon's shopping and a hospital committee meeting.
The committee want Catherine to do the marketing, because the
others can't contrive a decent menu for twenty-five sick children.
The girl is about to go to her father's door when Lavinia halts
her, embarrassed, and suggests, "Er . . . since you are so hand-
somely dressed you will let Maria attend to all the details of the
collation this evening? . . . I mean, you won't have any reason
to go into the pantry—will you?"

"You," says Catherine after a pause, "have been talking to
Father." She knows. Father would like her to be composed and
direct the conversation. "I can't, Aunt Lavinia. That is why I
go into the pantry." She would do anything to please her father,
she continues—anything. She has even sat upstairs and made
notes of things to say—and loses them all in company.

Her aunt assures her it isn't necessary to make all conversation important. "If you will observe your cousin Marian this
evening, you will see that what she says is never of any great
consequence."

Marian, Catherine observes, might recite the alphabet and Arthur Townsend would still think her the cleverest girl in New
York.

"Are you envious of Marian?"

"Why, I have never even met Mr. Townsend!"

Mrs. Penniman tries to make her meaning clear. It was her
way of wondering if Catherine shouldn't like to be an engaged
girl too.

Catherine has thought about it, yes. "It is the *person* I think
of. It is to find someone to love."

"And someone who loves you."

"It is all the same," declares Catherine simply, and she taps
at her father's door.

"Do I disturb you, Father?"

He emerges from his study smiling. "You are not a disturbing
woman, Catherine." Eyeing her dress, he asks, "Is it possible
that this magnificent person is my daughter? You are sumptuous,
opulent. You look as if you had eighty thousand a year."

Catherine murmurs that she thought he would like the color—
cherry red, the color her mother used to wear.

"But, Catherine," interposes Dr. Sloper, "your mother was

dark. *She* dominated the color."

With a meek "Yes, Father," Catherine goes to her embroidery frame. "Are you starting another one of those samplers?" he inquires.

"Why, yes, Father. I find it a most agreeable pastime."

"Don't let it turn into a life work, Catherine," he warns.

Maria answers the front doorbell, admitting the guests. The first is Mrs. Almond, a handsome woman in her forties, who is the doctor's other sister. With her is her pretty, vivacious daughter, Marian. Following is Marian's fiancé, Arthur Townsend. Various greetings and introductions over with, as each of the guests comes in, another figure appears. "I have taken the liberty of bringing my cousin," Arthur Townsend explains to the doctor. "I thought that since you were meeting me, you wouldn't mind meeting him."

Arthur presents Morris Townsend, who smoothly apologizes for his intrusion. "I am newly returned from Europe and feel somewhat lost," he explains. He is introduced to Catherine, who, holding onto her father's arm with both hands, gives him a "How do you do, sir."

The conversation of the group is mostly about the coming wedding. Morris, sitting near Catherine, offers an opening gambit: "I hear that you are to be a bridesmaid, Miss Sloper."

Twisting her handkerchief in an agony of shyness, Catherine manages a "Yes . . . I think so." Marian expostulates that Catherine is to be her maid of honor.

The doctor has been watching his daughter sharply. Firmly he removes the twisted handkerchief from her hand, suggests a cue for more conversation. "Mr. Townsend has just come from Europe, Catherine."

"Have you been away long, sir?" she asks Morris.

"Yes, I have, to my disadvantage as I now see. . . . I find that I have missed some lovely things at home."

Catherine emits an "Oh."

Uneasily, she rises, and the young men rise with her; she is going to her embroidery, but subsides at a word from her father. The doctor diverts his attention to Morris, asking about his European travels and saying that he, too, will soon be in Paris.

Marian chimes in, "We have been having a wonderful time listening to all the new French songs. We kept Morris playing for hours last evening." She suggests that Morris play some now on the spinet in the study, and he agrees.

"But that's Mother's!" cries the appalled Catherine. And the doctor adds that it is out of tune and can't be played on.

"Let them try it, Austin," urges Mrs. Almond. "I haven't heard music here in a long time." The doctor gives in, and as the party moves toward the study Catherine picks up a small kerosene lamp to put on the spinet. Morris moves to take the lamp from her, but Catherine clings to it with a breathless "Oh, no!"

As this little struggle goes on Dr. Sloper commands, with controlled irritation, "Let the young man carry it for you!" When all the others have gone into the study he declares to Mrs. Almond, "I will never understand it. Her mother was witty and quick and talented. She was beautiful. . . . And *that* is our child."

Lavinia comes back in; the spinet is locked. It is always locked. Her brother gives her the key. "Isn't he charming?" asks Lavinia as she returns to the study.

"She does *not* mean Arthur, Elizabeth," observes Dr. Sloper. "What about this cousin? Who is he?"

It seems that Morris is a distant cousin. Mrs. Almond doesn't really know what he does. He had a very small inheritance, she believes, and he lives up on the Second Avenue with his sister—a Mrs. Montgomery, a nice little widow with five children.

"A widow with five children? Do you mean he lives *on* her?"

As to Marian's fiancé, Arthur, Dr. Sloper thinks he is nice enough but not very lively; he'll probably be president of a small bank at 50. "Do you suppose there is another Arthur somewhere in this great city of ours?"

"Oh, Catherine will find a husband," assures Mrs. Almond.

"You think so?"

"You must remember that she has the prospect of thirty thousand a year."

Smilingly he comments, "I see that you appreciate her."

"Austin," his sister asks, "are you really as detached about Catherine as you seem?"

DR. SLOPER—Detached? Why, that's the last thing I am? I am deeply interested in every phase of her life. Everything she does or says concerns me! Detached! Hah, I wish I were!

MRS. ALMOND—Why?

DR. SLOPER—Because I wish I could have confidence in her ability to manage herself, and her future, with some wisdom or even some intelligence. I have none.

MRS. ALMOND—I see that you haven't. I imagine that Catherine sees it too.

DR. SLOPER—If you are reproaching me, Liz, you must be

more specific. What would you like me to do for her that I have not done? Is there something that I have missed? She has gone to the best schools in the city. She has had the finest training I could get her in music and dancing. She has sat here with me evenings on end, and I have tried to make conversation with her and give her some social adeptness. She has never been constrained in the spending of money or in the directing of this household. I have given her freedom wherever I could. The result is what you see—an entirely mediocre and defenseless creature with not a shred of poise. What did I do wrong, my dear sister? If you know, I wish you would tell me, for *I* do not.

MRS. ALMOND—I do not mean that you haven't done your duty as a father. I know that you have.

DR. SLOPER—I have been as good a father as it was possible for me to be with the material Providence gave me. (*The music starts in the study. They listen for a moment.*)

MRS. ALMOND (*surprised*)—Why, it *is* in tune, Austin!

DR. SLOPER—Yes.

MRS. ALMOND—That's quite remarkable after all these years.

DR. SLOPER—I keep it tuned. I have a man who comes in four or five times a year.

MRS. ALMOND—Does Catherine play?

DR. SLOPER (*sharply*)—You know she doesn't!

MRS. ALMOND—How can she, if you keep it locked?

DR. SLOPER (*bitterly*)—Catherine cannot read a note.

MRS. ALMOND (*defensively*)—She has other accomplishments—

DR. SLOPER—Yes—her eternal cross-stitch!

MRS. ALMOND—Austin, you are so intolerant! And you *expect* so much!

DR. SLOPER (*suddenly angry*)—Yes, I expect everything! Do you remember her mother? *Do you,* Liz? Her mother who had so much grace and gaiety! Her mother who was a pleasure to look at and be with! This is her child. I was entitled to expect that someday she would make it up to me, wasn't I?

MRS. ALMOND—Make up what?

DR. SLOPER—Her mother's death! She killed her mother in getting born. And I was not a good enough doctor to stop it!

MRS. ALMOND (*pityingly*)—Oh, Austin!

DR. SLOPER—I have lived these years in loneliness, waiting for Catherine to be all the lovely things her mother was. I let nothing interfere with it. I did not marry. I did not do anything to endanger the process. I concentrated my life on seeing her approach the perfection of her mother!

MRS. ALMOND (*severely*)—No child could compete with this image you have of her mother. You have idealized that poor dead woman beyond all human recognition.

DR. SLOPER (*outraged*)—You are not entitled to say that. Only *I* know what I lost when she died. . . .

MRS. ALMOND—You got her child in her place! You should have thanked God for your luck and taken joy in her very being!

DR. SLOPER—Perhaps I would have if she had only grown into the girl I wanted her to be.

MRS. ALMOND—She couldn't be that girl, Austin. Because that girl never existed!

DR. SLOPER—Then we are both cheated! (*The music swells. They listen.* MRS. ALMOND *watches the* DOCTOR.) When I hear that spinet played I remember the day she got it. . . . We were in Paris and she bought it at Pleyel's. She wouldn't sail for home until she found a captain who was willing to let her take it on board ship with her. Six months later she was dead.

MRS. ALMOND (*gently*)—That was a long time ago, Austin.

DR. SLOPER—That is no consolation. (*As they listen to the music, the lights dim and the curtain falls.*)

SCENE II

The room is brilliant with the sunlight of an afternoon two weeks later. Mrs. Penniman and Morris Townsend are chatting on the settee. "Did you tell her that I would call today?" he asks.

"I must confess, Morris, that I did not. She is so gentle, so timid, I was afraid she would take flight at your third visit within the week."

"Does Catherine—I mean Miss Sloper—"

"Dear boy," smiles Aunt Lavinia, "you may let yourself go when you are with me."

"Does Catherine see many young men, Mrs. Penniman?"

"Er—well, she receives many invitations. And she always attends the cotillions."

Morris can't believe that Catherine is so reserved with everybody; he is afraid she disapproves of him. "Oh, no, Morris!" cries Mrs. Penniman in alarm. She can assure him that, in the privacy of her room, Catherine has a wealth of feeling.

"It's odd," he muses. "In Europe, a girl like that would have been married long since. Why, in Paris, with her income, she might have got a count!"

He switches to Dr. Sloper—does he have any interests like art, or a hobby? Nothing but medicine, he is informed. "It's a devil of a difficult thing for a man like me to talk about."

"Once he knows what is going on in your heart," Mrs. Penniman comforts him, "you will have plenty to talk about between you!"

When Catherine comes home her aunt contrives to inform her, privately, that Morris "has come a-courting."

"Yes, Aunt, I know," is the placid reply.

Morris does a very good job of courting. He talks of a poem which he copied for Catherine last night when he couldn't sleep. He thinks of her constantly, and regards himself modestly. "I am not a glib man, Miss Sloper. Oh, when I'm with Mrs. Penniman, or in my room at home, I can think of the most delightful things to say. . . . But here with you I sound like a fool."

"I don't think so," she smiles.

Having warmed the girl to the proper degree, Morris gets on with it: "Miss Sloper, I have fallen in love with you."

Catherine gasps—but the pursuit of whatever advantage Morris has had is interrupted by the arrival of Dr. Sloper. "I wanted to thank Miss Sloper and yourself for having received me the first time," Morris explains.

After ordering sherry and biscuits, the doctor settles down and addresses Catherine. "Did you decide anything further about the music lessons?"

"Yes," she replies, "I went to see Mr. Rougini after lunch. . . . He said the harp was a very difficult instrument. . . . He did not think I was exactly suited to it."

"Why not?"

"You need a true ear for the harp. It seems that I have not a very true ear."

Her father thinks this is nonsense—impossible. Her mother could even tune her own piano. Tactfully, Morris suggests, "Miss Sloper has a great appreciation for music. That is a sufficient talent in itself."

"Do you find it so?" chillingly inquires the doctor. Then, sipping the sherry Maria has brought him, he asks, "How do you keep busy since your return to New York, Mr. Townsend? Are you looking for a position?"

MORRIS—Oh, a position is more than I should presume to call it! That sounds so fine. I should like some quiet work—something to turn an honest penny.

DR. SLOPER—What sort of thing should you prefer?

MORRIS—Do you mean what am I fit for? Very little, I'm afraid. I have nothing but my good right arm, as they say in the melodramas.

DR. SLOPER—You are too modest. In addition to your good right arm you have your subtle brain. I know nothing of you but what I see, but I see that you are extremely intelligent.

CATHERINE—Oh, yes. (*Murmuring.*)

MORRIS—I don't know what to answer when you say that. (*Looking right at the doctor.*) You advise me, then, not to despair?

DR. SLOPER (*after a second*)—I should be very sorry to admit that a robust and well-disposed young man need ever despair. If he doesn't succeed in one thing, he can try another. Only, he should choose his line with *discretion.*

MORRIS—Ah, yes, discretion. Well, I have been indiscreet formerly, but I think I have got over it. I am very steady now. (*Now he smiles.*) Were you kindly intending to propose something for my advantage?

DR. SLOPER—I have no particular proposal. But sometimes one hears of opportunities. I hear, for instance, that the West is opening up. Many young men are turning their eyes in that direction.

MORRIS—I'm afraid I shouldn't be able to manage that. I must seek my fortune here or nowhere. You see, I have ties here. (*He turns to* CATHERINE.) I have a sister, a widow from whom I have been separated a long time and to whom I am everything.

CATHERINE—Naturally.

MORRIS (*smiling*)—I shouldn't know how to tell her that I must leave her. She depends on me so much.

DR. SLOPER—That's very proper; family feeling is very proper. There isn't enough of it in our city. I think I have heard of your sister.

MORRIS—It is possible, but I rather doubt it; she lives so very quietly.

DR. SLOPER—As quietly, you mean, as a lady may who has several young children.

MORRIS—Yes, my nephews and nieces—that's the very point. I am helping to bring them up. I'm a kind of tutor; I give them lessons.

DR. SLOPER—That's very proper, but it's hardly a career.

MORRIS—No, it won't make my fortune.

DR. SLOPER (*incisively*)—You must not be too much bent on

a fortune. (*He stands up.*) But I assure you I will keep you in mind; I won't lose sight of you. (*He turns to* CATHERINE.) I am going downstairs, Catherine.

"He doesn't like me—he doesn't like me at all," says Morris. Catherine thinks he may be mistaken.

MORRIS—Ah, well, you ask him and you will see.

CATHERINE (*slowly*)—I would rather not ask him, if there is any danger of his saying what you think.

MORRIS—It wouldn't give you any pleasure to contradict him?

CATHERINE—I never contradict him.

MORRIS—Would you hear me abused without opening your lips in my defense? (*He goes closer to her.*)

CATHERINE—My father won't abuse you. He doesn't know you enough. (MORRIS *laughs.*) I shall not mention you.

MORRIS—That is not what I should have liked you to say. I should have liked you to say, "If my father doesn't think well of you, what does it matter?"

CATHERINE—But it would matter. I could never say that.

MORRIS—Do you know, I think you could? I think you could do anything for one whom you loved.

CATHERINE (*rising*)—Mr. Townsend, I mustn't listen to this. . . . You shouldn't . . . talk that way.

MORRIS (*comes close to her and pleads passionately*)—I adore you! It is two weeks since first I saw you and I have not had an easy moment since that night! I think of nothing else. . . . I am possessed by you!

CATHERINE (*with a desperate sincerity*)—How could you be? How could you? . . .

MORRIS—My dearest girl, my life depends on your believing me, believing how much I care for you! You are everything I have ever yearned for in a woman! (*He takes her hand, puts it to his breast, then kisses it.*)

CATHERINE—But I am so . . . (*Before she can finish, he draws her to him and kisses her. She responds to the kiss completely. When it is over, she is silent. He watches her.*)

MORRIS—Will you marry me, Catherine?

CATHERINE (*looking at him fully for the first time*)—Yes.

MORRIS—You make me very happy. . . . Do you love me?

CATHERINE—Yes.

MORRIS (*kissing her again*)—Dear Catherine.

CATHERINE—I love you.

MORRIS—I will cherish you forever.

CATHERINE (*detaching herself*)—We must do our duty. We must speak to my father. I will do it tonight. You must do it tomorrow.

Morris thinks it is sweet of Catherine to do it first. He promises to be very gentle and respectful to Dr. Sloper; he would rather have her easily than have to fight for her.

"Don't talk about fighting."

"We must be prepared. After all, it's a natural thing for your father to want a brilliant marriage for you; you have everything —position, wealth, and your own sweetness. And I am a poor man, Catherine. . . . He might fear that I am mercenary."

"It will be easy to answer that," she stoutly declares. "I should simply say that he is mistaken."

Kissing her lightly on the cheek, Morris asks her to tell him one thing—that if her father *is* against him, if he forbids their marriage, she will still be faithful, no matter what comes.

"Yes, Morris. . . . No matter what comes." He leaves, promising to be back at 11 sharp tomorrow morning.

The minute he has left Aunt Lavinia flutters down the stair. She senses what has happened and wants to hear it—but Catherine won't talk until she has spoken with her father. When Dr. Sloper returns to the room Catherine asks if she may see him privately in ten minutes, and he humorously agrees upon such an engagement.

Catherine goes to her room, and the doctor observes that they have had a caller.

"Isn't it wonderful?" exclaims Mrs. Penniman.

"What's wonderful about it?"

The woman positively bubbles with romantic excitement. Such a charming young man . . . she never dreamed . . . he is devoted to her . . . she is so lucky.

The doctor is dubious—dubious of Morris's sincerity; but Lavinia assures him she knows all about Morris, who has bared his very soul to her. And he is looking for a position most earnestly.

"Do you suppose," asks the doctor, "he is looking for it here, Lavinia, in this front parlor? Wouldn't the position of husband to a defenseless young woman with a large fortune suit him to perfection?"

Lavinia is shocked at the suggestion. Her brother should be delighted with this courtship.

Catherine comes down for her appointment and her aunt withdraws. There is an uneasy pause while her father waits to hear what she has to say; then she blurts out, "I am engaged to be married!"

"You do right to tell me. And whom have you honored with your choice?"

It is Morris Townsend, of course. It happened here this afternoon. Yes, she likes him very much.

"Mr. Townsend ought to have waited and told me."

"He means to tell you tomorrow morning."

"It is not quite the same thing, my dear. You should not be pleading for him. He should plead for you."

The girl explains that Morris is afraid—afraid the doctor doesn't like him—afraid he will be thought mercenary. "He is poor, Father, and I think it has made him sensitive."

DR. SLOPER—Yes, I understand that. But there are many poor men and they do not go through the streets proclaiming that they are not thieves—especially when no one has accused them.

CATHERINE—Father, you must try to understand him. He loves me, and I love him. What has happened is very important to me.

DR. SLOPER—It is important to both of us.

CATHERINE (*gently*)—Yes, Father, but not equally— My whole happiness is at stake.

DR. SLOPER—I think you exaggerate.

CATHERINE—No, I do not. It is a great wonder to me that Morris has come into my life. I never expected that I would meet a man who would understand me as he has.

DR. SLOPER—You underestimate your many qualities, my dear. I have always hoped that some day you would meet a solid young man who would match your goodness with his own.

CATHERINE (*smiling*)—And here I have found the goodness, and with it everything else! Oh, Father, don't you think he is the handsomest man you have ever seen?

DR. SLOPER—He is very good-looking, my dear. Of course, you would not let a consideration like that sway you unduly. . . .

CATHERINE—Oh, no! But that's what is so wonderful to me, that he should have everything else, everything in the world that a woman could want—and he wants me!

DR. SLOPER (*disturbed*)—Well . . . I will see him tomorrow.

CATHERINE (*happily*)—I knew you would. And you are so good that you will be fair and honest with him.

DR. SLOPER (*slowly*)—I shall be as fair and honest with him as he is with you.

With a "Thank you, Father," Catherine goes to her room. He stares after her for a second, then, moving deliberately, goes over and pulls the bell cord. When Maria answers he informs her he is going out—but she reminds him he has a patient waiting in his study.

"Well, then you must deliver a note for me." He sits at the desk and writes. "It is . . . for . . . a Mrs. Montgomery who lives in the Second Avenue. See that it is delivered directly into her hand. . . . You had better take a hack both ways."

Maria takes the note and he moves toward his study.

The curtain falls.

ACT II

It is an hour before Morris has promised to call—10 o'clock, the following morning. Dr. Sloper is in the drawing room finishing a cup of coffee and reading his newspaper. Mrs. Penniman, a little late getting started on her marketing, still is in the kitchen making out the list. The doctor urges Maria to hurry Mrs. Penniman along "before our callers arrive." Maria says she will do her best.

There is a ring at the door and the parlormaid admits Mrs. Almond and Morris's sister, Mrs. Montgomery, who has been good enough to leave a busy household and come in answer to the doctor's note. After making an introduction, Mrs. Almond joins Mrs. Penniman in the kitchen.

"You will have gathered from my note," the doctor tells Mrs. Montgomery, "that I wish to ask you a few questions. . . . They are about your brother." She understands this.

"Your brother wishes to marry my daughter, so I must find out what sort of young man he is. . . . If my girl should marry your brother her whole happiness will depend on his being a good fellow. I want you to tell me something about his character. What sort of gentleman is he?"

Morris is, Mrs. Montgomery allows, intelligent, charming and a wonderful companion. Dr. Sloper impatiently acknowledges these facts. "But is he reliable? Is he trustworthy? Is he—responsible?"

Morris is not financially secure, she explains—which Dr. Sloper already knows from the young man himself; but he is honest.

Yes, he is selfish—but Mrs. Montgomery thinks we all are rather selfish.

"He told me," pursues the doctor, "that he used up a small inheritance. Did he handle it well?"

"Probably you would not think so, Doctor, but from his own point of view he did a great deal with it. He saw Europe, he met many interesting people, he enlarged his capacities."

"Did he help you, ma'am?"

"No." She has not expected it; she has brought him up as if he were her child and has accepted the good and bad in him just as she accepts them in her children. As for the rapidity with which Catherine and Morris have become engaged, Mrs. Montgomery believes in love at first sight. "They are listening only to the promptings of their own two hearts. They have not taken time to consider the consequences or weigh the difficulties."

The doctor would like her to meet his daughter, and calls Catherine down from upstairs. Mrs. Montgomery is rather struck by the girl's plainness, but recovers and holds out her hand.

Catherine, whose mind manifestly is on the pending arrival of Morris, manages a snatch or two of small talk, then goes to fetch some cookies for the guest.

"She is very shy," observes Mrs. Montgomery. But, more cheerfully, "Perhaps she is less shy with Morris."

Dr. Sloper continues his probing. "Has your brother listened *only* to the promptings of his heart?" She wouldn't know, but can only suppose that Morris is more mature in his feelings than she had thought, and this time has not sought out superficial charms, but has considered the gentle character underneath.

The doctor bluntly expresses his own opinion—that Catherine's money is the prime attraction.

"What money?"

"She is an heiress! Didn't your brother tell you that?"

"No . . . he did not."

"She has ten thousand a year from her mother, and on my death she will have twice as much more."

"She will be immensely rich!" marvels Mrs. Montgomery.

"Yes, she will. Of course, if she marries a man I don't approve, I shall leave my part to the clinic."

Slowly the visitor absorbs this. "But," she says, "she has ten now. . . . That is still a great deal of money, Doctor."

Sloper drives on. He doubts if Morris would help his sister with this fortune he hopes to marry. He begs assurance that his

daughter is not a victim of Morris's avariciousness—which is a
little too much for Mrs. Montgomery. "I must go now," she
announces.

"He is in love with her money," the doctor insists.

"You want me to tell her *that?*"

"Yes."

"I won't!"

"You see, you still protect him!"

"No, it is the girl I protect!   Am I to tell her that she is undesirable—that she is unloved?   Why, it would break her heart!
. . . If you are so opposed to this marriage, then as a father you
must find a kinder way of stopping it.   Good day, Doctor."   The
lady makes a most dignified departure.

Mrs. Almond and Mrs. Penniman—the latter now dressed for
shopping—come through, learn that Mrs. Montgomery has left.
Mrs. Penniman has other news—Catherine has just asked Mrs.
Almond if Marian may be her maid of honor.

"She must get over it," snaps the doctor.   "He is worthless."

Profoundly shocked, Lavinia protests that it will kill Catherine
if he denies her this marriage.

"Nonsense!   My dear, people don't die of one dreadful night
or even of a dozen.   Remember, I am a physician."

The doctor's other sister also pleads for compassion on Catherine, but his mind is made up.   "She must not love people who
don't deserve to be loved.   I don't."

"But," argues Mrs. Almond, "you have said yourself that she
is not a girl likely to attract many men.   And if this man likes
her, wants to marry her, and will take good care of her, and
her money, what is lost?"   The reasoning falls on deaf ears.

Catherine appears with a small silver tray of cookies, only to
learn that the guest has already taken her departure.   "Did Mrs.
Montgomery tell you something bad, Father?"

"She told me what I must tell you, my dear"—but before he
does attempt to tell her anything the bell sounds.   It is Morris.
Dr. Sloper sends his daughter to her room.   With great effort she
begs him, "Tell him, Father . . . tell him about me.   You know
me so well. . . . It will not be immodest in you to . . . to
praise me a little."

Mmes. Almond and Penniman depart for marketing, but as she
leaves Mrs. Almond drops a suggestion: her brother could take
Catherine to Europe with him and it might be just the thing
for the girl.

The doctor wastes no time with the newly arrived Morris.

"You must allow me to say," he declares, "that it would have been becoming of you to give me notice of your intentions before they had gone so far."

Smoothly the young man replies, "I should have done so, Doctor, if you had not left your daughter so much liberty. She seems to me quite her own mistress."

"She is. But I trust that she isn't quite so emancipated as to choose a husband without consulting me."

Morris defends his regard for Catherine, whom he considers "charming"—an odd word to use on her, her father thinks. "Did you," asks the doctor, "really expect that I would throw my daughter into your arms?"

"No, I had an idea you didn't like me."

"What gave you that idea?"

"The fact that I am poor."

"That has a harsh sound," the doctor crisply states, "but it's about the truth."

Morris protests that he is offering the most tender affection and lifelong devotion—but Dr. Sloper thinks he might also offer a few securities besides a handsome face and figure and a very good manner. As another security Morris pledges the word of a gentleman that he is not mercenary. "I care no more for her fortune than for the ashes in that grate!"

As the debate continues Morris takes a pleading note—that the doctor think of his daughter's feelings if he forbids the marriage. "She may as well be miserable that way as with you," is the brutal reply. Morris's anger begins to rise as he reiterates that he loves Catherine. "I believe if I say the word she will walk out of this house and follow me," he exclaims. "And may I add, Dr. Sloper, if I did not love your daughter as much as I do, I should not have put up with the indignities you have offered me today."

The elder man coolly suggests that all Morris has to do to escape the indignities is to leave the house; the young man puts on his hat and turns to the door—but is halted by a call from Catherine, who runs down the stairs.

"You promised me, Morris, you promised you would be respectful when you saw my father!" she expostulates, and, taking him by the arm, leads him back to the drawing room. "What is the matter, Father?" she demands.

The matter is, he explains rather gently, that Catherine must give Morris up—that Morris is a selfish idler, who loves no one. "You must simply take my word for it," he declares.

"Father," she cries, "I can't! I can't! I love him! . . . I have promised to marry him, to stay by him, no matter what comes."

"You," snarls the doctor to Morris, "are beneath contempt!"

Stolidly Catherine insists, "Don't abuse him, Father! . . . I think we shall marry quite soon."

"Then," coldly declares her parent, turning away, "it is no further concern of mine."

But Morris puts in a word: much as he is in love, they cannot marry without his approval, for it would bring unhappiness to all.

"Then will you put it off, Mr. Townsend? . . . For six months. I would like Catherine to go to Europe with me."

Catherine is dismayed at this suggestion, and Morris counsels, "He thinks you will forget me." The doctor challenges, "Are you afraid, Catherine? Are you afraid of a six months' separation?"

Stoutly she declares she will still love Morris when she comes back. "You are romantic, my dear, and very inexperienced. . . . And at the moment you are exalted with the feeling of undying devotion to a lover. You are very sure of *your* love . . . but, Catherine, do you dare test *him?*"

The challenge, although it is directed at the girl, is met by the young man. Taking her hand, Morris advises, "Catherine, go to Europe with your father."

The curtain falls.

SCENE II

The six months have passed and it is an April night, with Mrs. Penniman and Morris cozily playing backgammon in the drawing room. He is sipping a glass of claret as he watches Mrs. Penniman's play—and as the game continues he refills his glass more than once. "By the way," he inquires, "what will you say when the doctor asks where his claret has gone to?"

Laughingly she answers, "I'll tell him it was a cold Winter and *I* drank it." It *was* a cold Winter, he agrees—and if it weren't for her kindness it would have been lonely and unbearable. He talks of the absent father and daughter, and wonders if the doctor's consent is still being withheld. In her last letter, written six weeks ago, Catherine told Morris she didn't dare mention his name to her father, who has not been well, for fear of angering him.

The backgammon game ends about 9:30—the latest they've played all Winter, and Morris rises to go. Selecting a cigar from the doctor's humidor, he removes the band, which he puts in an ash tray, clips the end of the cigar, lights it and advises, "Mrs. Penniman, you will have to tell Catherine all the details tomorrow . . . as soon after the boat docks as possible. And it would be well if she did not unpack."

Mrs. Penniman promises to be at the slip at 10 o'clock—no, at 7, should the ship dock earlier.

"Planning an elopement by messenger . . . it's . . . it's rather cold," he grimaces.

"Leave it to me, Morris. I wish I could go with you both tomorrow night. . . ."

"You must stay behind to pacify the doctor." This, of course, she admits—but she would so enjoy it! A private marriage in the dead of night. Catherine is a lucky girl.

An unpleasant reminder comes to Morris. "He told my sister he'd disinherit her. "Do you think that's possible?"

Just a threat, opines Mrs. Penniman. "He can't take away the ten thousand a year she already has."

"That would be small comfort," muses Morris, and she bridles at the word "small." "On ten, Ma'am," he continues, "you live like your neighbor. . . . But thirty is something to look forward to. On thirty you live"—his hand takes in the room—"like this." Very frankly Morris admits he likes this house—admires it and all the things in it. It's strange that he and the doctor should like the same things.

Mrs. Penniman cheerily hopes this fondness for nice things will be a bond between the two men, once her brother has forgiven Morris.

The young man suddenly becomes alert to a noise outside—a coach. It is Dr. Sloper and Catherine, Mrs. Penniman discovers by looking out the window. Morris snatches his hat and his cigar butt and retreats to the kitchen. "Tell her everything! Tell her I love her!" he reminds Mrs. Penniman.

The doctor has been knocking at the door and Maria opens it. Father and daughter look somewhat the worse for wear—she anxious and he with a shawl over his overcoat. Obviously, their boat has come in early. There are effusive but slightly uneasy greetings from Mrs. Penniman, and her unease increases when she sees her brother going toward the hall to the kitchen. "Where are you going, Austin?"

"I have a beastly cold, Lavinia, and I want some hot water."

Blocking him, she volunteers, "I'll get it." He wants some

brandy too. "Er . . . there's some here . . . here in the decanter."

Rather surprised, Dr. Sloper inquires if his sister has taken to
drink. Lamely she explains she thought it would help her heart,
and goes to tell Maria about the hot water. The doctor, part
Sherlock Holmes and part bird dog, goes to the brandy decanter,
then sees the claret bottle, sniffs into the air, pours a bit of the
wine into a glass and savors it for vintage, then notes the backgammon board—saying nothing to his daughter the while.

"You have not addressed a word to me all day," she pleads.
"What have I done?"

Mrs. Penniman, back from her errand, begins with "Now,
where did you go, and what did you like most?"

Catherine informs her they saw a great deal, but the doctor
is more interested in the hot water. Maria is bringing it right
away, says his sister. He takes a cigar from the humidor, sniffs
the air again, deposits the band in the ash tray—and notices the
other band there.

"Tell me, Lavinia, how do you like smoking cigars?" he inquires. She can't think of an answer for that one, but the arrival of Maria with the hot water gets her off the spot—for the
moment. Then he resumes: "Do you prefer my Massachusetts
Home Grown or my Sumatras?"

"I don't know what you're talking about."

"When I detect the delicious aroma of bay rum and find a loose
cigar band and my brandy decanter half empty, I can only think
of one person. What happened to Mr. Townsend—has he jumped
out of the window?"

Mrs. Penniman falters that Morris merely stopped by to inquire about him. He happened to be in the neighborhood. Nervously she turns to Catherine and asks if her niece has brought
her anything.

"Yes, Aunt. I have a Cashmere shawl for you. . . . It is in
my dressing case. Maria will open it for you." Lavinia escapes.

DR. SLOPER—What a ridiculous position to be in. Well, it's
a fitting end to the most futile six months of my life.

CATHERINE—They were not futile to me. I thought they
were wonderful.

DR. SLOPER—Wonderful! Yes, that's the very word you used,
Catherine. Tintoretto is a wonderful painter; the ices at the
Café Riche are wonderful; Talma has wonderful lace gloves;
almost as wonderful as Michelangelo's David.

CATHERINE—If you mean I did not appreciate it, you are wrong. I appreciated everything.

DR. SLOPER—You saw nothing, Catherine! What was Rome to you? Just a place where you might receive a letter from him.

CATHERINE—This is why you have not spoken to me since yesterday; because I told you I still loved him. . . .

DR. SLOPER—You carried the image of that wastrel with you every place we went. He blotted out any pleasure we might have had. . . . I waited a long time for my trip to Paris. I never thought I should have to see it all arm in arm with him. (*Disgusted*.) There are some things one cannot do for people, even one's own daughter—one cannot give her eyes or understanding if she has none.

CATHERINE—I have eyes, and I have understanding, Father. You were not thinking of me in Paris—you were with my mother.

DR. SLOPER—I wish I had been! (*There is a pause*.)

CATHERINE—Our trip has not changed you.

DR. SLOPER—Nor you . . . nor Townsend. Well, I suppose you'll be going off with him any time now?

CATHERINE—If he will have me.

This strikes the doctor as funny—if he will have her! Why, her value has doubled, with all the knowledge and taste she has acquired. "Your gaiety and brilliance will have to make up the difference between the ten thousand a year you have and the thirty thousand he expects."

Serenely Catherine maintains Morris does not love her for her money; he finds her—pleasing.

"Yes, I'm sure he does," he continues contemptuously. "A thousand women are prettier, and a million are cleverer, but you have one virtue that outshines them all!" Fearfully she inquires what it is. "Your money."

She slumps into a chair, puts her face in her hands. "Oh, Father," she cries, "what a monstrous thing to say to me!"

Picking up his glass and bowing ironically, the doctor declares, "Well, since I shan't be at the wedding, I'll drink your health up in my bed. Good night, daughter mine!"

Mrs. Penniman comes furtively in, makes sure her brother has gone, and whispers to Catherine, "I have a surprise for you. . . . Now you just stand there a moment. You close your eyes and count ten." She hurries into the hall.

In a moment Morris appears, calling softly, "My darling."

The girl runs to his arms, almost sobbing his name. "We didn't expect you till tomorrow," he explains. "I was in your father's chair when he knocked on the front door," he laughs. "Has your aunt told you about my plan?"

"What plan?"

"For our marriage . . . our elopement? It is for tomorrow night! In a country parsonage up on Murray's Hill. There is a Reverend Lispenard there who knows our story and is prepared to help us."

Catherine is transfixed, speechless. He goes on with the details—a closed carriage at the corner of the Square at 5 in the afternoon, before the doctor has come home from his calls, but when it already is dark. They'll load her trunks, and after the marriage spend the night at an inn up the river. Then, next day, they will go to Albany on their honeymoon.

Catherine is in heaven. "Oh, Morris, my husband!" She has brought him a beautiful silk waistcoat he can wear at the wedding, and a set of buttons—rubies and pearls, and quite nice. He is delighted.

A disturbing thought comes to Catherine—her father has caught cold, and what if he should not go out on his calls tomorrow? "Well, then," decides Morris, "we must wait until the day after."

Catherine becomes excited and alarmed. She cannot, she insists, she cannot stay here any longer. She could not bear it. "Morris, take me tonight!"

"How can we?"

They must, she insists. Her cases and bags are all downstairs. In another hour everybody will be asleep, and they can get away quietly. "I implore you! If you love me, take me away tonight. . . ." They can stay at his sister's or at the Reverend Lispenard's.

Morris, who has been offering objections, at last agrees. They'll do it. It is almost 10:30 now; he can find a carriage and be back with his own things packed in two hours. She must be ready at 12:30 on the dot. And now another thing.

"We must think carefully of how we shall word your letter."

CATHERINE—What letter?

MORRIS—The letter you leave for your father. Shall I write it for you?

CATHERINE—No.

MORRIS—You must be very clever in it. You must melt his heart.

CATHERINE—I do not want to leave him a letter.

Morris—But you must! You must make him feel your love and affection!

Catherine—I will not write him.

Morris—Why, of course, we will write him! We want him to forgive us!

Catherine—Please don't, Morris; please don't. (*Backing away from him.*) We must ask no favors of him—we must ask nothing more. He won't relent, ever. I know it now. I have good reason to.

Morris (*startled*)—What reason?

Catherine—My father doesn't—like me.

Morris—Why, what an unhappy thing to say! You must not think such things!

Catherine—It is true.

Morris—No, Catherine, your father is disappointed that his plans for you have not turned out as he wanted. He is perhaps hurt, and angry at us both. But that will pass.

Catherine—It won't pass.

Morris—My dear, if I am to be your husband you must begin to trust my judgment, to rely on me.

Catherine—I do, Morris.

Morris—That's right. How many times do you think fathers have spoken angrily to the daughters they love, particularly when marriage is the question?

Catherine—He does not love me.

Morris—Of course he does! Indeed he must love you very much, or he would not be trying so hard to protect you. It is only your future happiness he is thinking of.

Catherine—No, Morris. In this one thing I know I am right. I could not say it unless I were sure. I understood it tonight for the first time in my life. You can tell when a person speaks to you as if—as if—

Morris—As if what?

Catherine—As if they despised you!

Morris—*Despised!*

Catherine—We must be very happy together . . . and you must never despise me, Morris.

Morris—Oh, Catherine, of course not!

Catherine—I will never ask him for anything again or expect anything from him. We must be very happy and we must depend on him for nothing!

Morris—No . . . no . . .

Catherine—I will try to be the best wife in the world.

Morris—I know you will. (*He is restless.*) Was that a noise?

Catherine—Perhaps it was my aunt.

Morris—I think I'd better go.

Catherine—I will get ready immediately.

Morris—Yes, you had better.

Catherine—I'll try to be punctual, Morris. I know you like that.

Morris—Till twelve-thirty, then . . .

Catherine—Aren't you going to embrace me?

Morris—Yes. (*He kisses her on the brow. He puts on his hat and hesitates.*) He can't dislike you that much! He's bound to come round.

Catherine—Morris, dear, even if he would, *I* would not.

Morris—I see. (*He prepares to leave.*) Until later, dear. (*He exits quickly to the back of the house.* Catherine *is in a state of exaltation. Her arms reach out to him after he has left, then she recovers herself. She goes to the mirror over the mantel and is pleased and even a little vain at what she sees. Then re-membering all she has to do, she picks up her skirts and runs upstairs as—the curtain falls. It remains down briefly to indi-cate the passage of two hours.*)

And now, at 12:30, only a flicker from the fireplace illumines the room as a dark figure rustles down the stairs carrying some-thing. It is Catherine, in a bonnet and traveling coat. She puts down a little bag next to her luggage in the hall. She has brought a candle, which she lights; now she goes back to the stairs, gets another small bag, brings it to a chair in the drawing room and puts it in her lap when she sits down.

Mrs. Penniman, in a dressing gown and sleeping cap, and also holding a candle, comes down the stair. "Catherine!" she ex-claims.

"Hush!"

Catherine tries to shoo her aunt back to bed, but Lavinia wants to know what is up and is informed of the elopement. Mrs. Penniman can't understand the advancement of the plan. A clock strikes the one note of 12:30 and Catherine, taking her bag in hand, runs to the window. Lavinia expostulates that Catherine has misunderstood—that Morris is coming tomorrow afternoon.

Smiling, then laughing exultantly, Catherine corrects her. "No, Aunt, he will be here in the next fifty seconds." They are going directly to the Reverend Lispenard's, and if he will marry them they may stay with him—otherwise they will drive all night;

she doesn't care which.

Catherine thinks she hears a carriage, but it is only imagination. Mrs. Penniman volunteers to dress and come along as chaperone, but the offer is declined. "You must have a chaperone," she insists. "Your father would be shocked—"

"It serves him right," laughs Catherine. Mrs. Penniman can hardly believe her ears as the girl continues, "He finds me so dull. It will surprise him to have such a dull girl disgrace his name."

There is another sound—not wheels, though; a box blowing in the wind. "Think of it," Catherine exults. "I may never stand in this window again." This sounds like nonsense to Lavinia. "You will be reconciled with Austin within the year. I guarantee it," she assures her niece.

"You had better not do that. I will never see him again in my life." Five minutes have passed and Catherine nervously checks the clock. "I am leaving tonight instead of tomorrow," she goes on, "because it is one time less that I will ever have to lay eyes on him. Or him on me."

"But, good God, child, you're disinheriting yourself!"

"Yes . . . completely."

Mrs. Penniman wants to know if Morris knows of this, and is assured that he does—which is distressing to her. Catherine should have waited until she was married.

Now there *is* a carriage in the street. Feverishly gathering up her two bags, shawl and gloves, Catherine cries, "Good-by, Aunt!" and runs to the door. As she gets there the sound of the carriage recedes; she stands for a moment as she realizes this, then comes back to the drawing room. "It went by. . . ."

Now it is 22 minutes to 1. "Aunt, why shouldn't I have told Morris?"

"Oh, dear girl, why were you not a little more clever?" remonstrates Mrs. Penniman. "Clever about your father's money— about Morris. Oh, Catherine, if you have spoiled this opportunity . . ."

Catherine can see no spoiled opportunities. In about an hour, she and Morris will be married. After all, he is only eleven and a half minutes late now; her aunt is just being ridiculous.

"No, I am not, Catherine. I know him so well. . . ." Morris, she tries to explain, would not want to be the cause of Catherine's losing her natural inheritance. He could not see her impoverished. . . . Yes, for some people ten thousand a year would be a great comedown—if one had expected thirty.

"He has expected nothing!" expostulates Catherine. Desperately she tries to explain, "He loves me! He wants me for his wife!" As if quoting, she declares, "I am everything he ever yearned for in a woman."

Mrs. Penniman—Oh, Catherine . . .

Catherine—I am! I am! He has told me so! *He* thinks I am pretty! *He* wants me. He could not wait for tomorrow night! He said we must go tonight! . . . (*She remembers the truth with anguish.*) No—I said that, didn't I? I said we must go tonight— (*With sudden hope.*) But he agreed! He was willing! You can see that for yourself. He was very willing. . . .

Mrs. Penniman (*hopefully*)—Perhaps he will come.

Catherine—Oh, my God! *Perhaps!*—Don't say that to me!

Mrs. Penniman—What am I to say?

Catherine—I cannot stand it! I cannot stand one more minute of it! (*Wildly.*) He *must* come! He must take me away! He must love me!

Mrs. Penniman—Catherine, you are hysterical.

Catherine—No one can live without that! You can't bear it in the end. . . . Someone must love me; someone must tell me he wants me. I have never had anyone!

Mrs. Penniman—You must control yourself!

Catherine—Morris is the only one! I have never heard tenderness in anyone's voice but his!

Mrs. Penniman—I don't think you should say that.

Catherine—Why not? Am I not supposed to know it? Am I too dull? That's what my father thinks. He thinks that when you are stupid you do not feel! That is not true, Aunt. I am very stupid, but I have felt everything. . . . I used to think my misfortune was that Mother died. But I don't think so any more. She was so clever that if she had lived, she too could not have loved me! (*She puts her head down now and weeps.*)

Mrs. Penniman—Catherine, you must take hold of yourself!

Catherine—No, no, Morris must take hold of me! (*Moaning.*) Morris must make it up to me. Morris will love me for all those who didn't— (*She weeps again.*)

Mrs. Penniman—Catherine dear, I have explained it to you. I have told you why he might not come.

Catherine—You have not told me how I will go on living if he doesn't.

Mrs. Penniman—You have your father and me, my dear.

Catherine—I have nothing! I have always had nothing!

And if Morris tricked me, then I know that no one has ever loved me in my life. And no one ever will! (*As she says this, the clock strikes a quarter to one. She listens and then she breaks down completely.*) Oh, my God! My God! (*She bends over, racked with pain.*)

MRS. PENNIMAN (*softly*)—Catherine . . .

CATHERINE—Leave me alone, Aunt. Please leave me alone. . . .

MRS. PENNIMAN—There will be other young men, Catherine. (*Trying to quiet her.*)

CATHERINE—They would only want what he wanted. And I won't want them. I will love him all my life. . . .

MRS. PENNIMAN (*wearying of her task*)—You will not let yourself be consoled!

CATHERINE (*rocking dully*)—No, not consoled—loved, Aunt, but not consoled. (*Again she puts her face in her hands.* MRS. PENNIMAN *can find nothing more to say. She looks at the girl, shakes her head, then picks up her candle and goes upstairs.*)

The curtain falls.

ACT III

It is three days later and a rainy morning, when a caller comes to the door and tells Maria that a Mrs. de Rham across the Square is ill and wants Dr. Sloper. "Dr. Sloper is ill. He isn't making any calls," Maria informs him. Remaining firm against his importunities, she advises him to try Dr. Isaacs in Great Jones Street.

Catherine, coming in from above, is not much interested in Maria's information about Mrs. de Rham; what she wants is mail, and seems disappointed at what Maria gives her. Her interest revives, however, with the arrival of her aunt from outside. "Aunt," she demands excitedly, "what did he say?"

"I didn't see him, Catherine."

"Oh, my God! Why not?"

"He wasn't there." Nobody, in fact, was there at Mrs. Montgomery's house. The children were in school, according to a neighbor, and the house was closed. "Here," says Mrs. Penniman, "is your note."

Beside herself, Catherine chides, "You mean you didn't leave it! Oh, Aunt, you have done everything wrong! Give it to me. I will take it back there right away!"

This, the shocked Mrs. Penniman forbids. The girl cannot go to a man's residence. "I must tell him," insists Catherine, "that I will do anything he wants me to!"

Dr. Sloper, fully dressed but with a quilted dressing gown over his suit, comes downstairs with the fluttering maid behind him. She has told him about Mrs. de Rham and he is determined to attend to her. "I want my bag," he tells Maria, "and in the top of that medical box in my study you'll find a black instrument. Bring that with my bag."

When Mrs. Penniman goes to change to dry clothing the doctor observes to his daughter, "I have not seen you for three days. You have obviously avoided me and also your normal household and social duties. I understand by that that your departure must be imminent. In fact, though you are still here in body, you are already absent in spirit."

CATHERINE—I am not absent.

DR. SLOPER—Your mind has taken up lodgings with your prospective husband, and you might quite as well be under the conjugal roof for all the benefit I'm going to get from your society.

CATHERINE—I don't think that my society means much to you.

DR. SLOPER—Nevertheless, it would be a convenience to me to know when I may expect to have an empty house. When you go, your aunt marches. Is it tomorrow?

CATHERINE—No.

DR. SLOPER—Is it next week?

CATHERINE—No.

DR. SLOPER—The week after?

CATHERINE—No, it is not the week after.

DR. SLOPER—I see. Well, he has not been to the house. Maria would have told me. I assume you are meeting him outside on street corners. Has he asked you to keep your plans secret from me?

CATHERINE—No. . . . Will you excuse me now? (*She starts to leave.*)

DR. SLOPER—Come here a moment, Catherine; over here in the light. (CATHERINE *reluctantly does so. The* DOCTOR *looks at her closely.*) You are flushed. Have you a little fever?

CATHERINE—No.

DR. SLOPER—Your eyes look sick. You have been weeping! (*She does not answer.*) Why, Catherine? (*Still no answer.*) Oh . . . (*A pause.*) Have you . . . have you broken your engagement? (CATHERINE *bows her head.*) If you have, I must tell you, Catherine, that I admire you greatly for it. (*She does not answer.*) It is a most courageous thing to do. (*He takes her by the shoulders.*) I understand your feelings. I know the effort you must have made.

CATHERINE (*barely audibly*)—Do you?

DR. SLOPER—I see that it is painful still for you to talk about it. I will not insist. In time the pain will pass and then you will see better how wise and strong you have been. (MARIA *returns with bag and instrument*. DR. SLOPER *takes them*. *To* MARIA.) Ah, thanks, Maria.

CATHERINE (*almost blindly*)—Excuse me, Father, I have some letters to write. . . . (*She exits into the study.*)

Maria is curious about the instrument she has brought; is it a flute? "It's a stethoscope," explains the doctor. "I got it in Paris. It's for listening to people's hearts. . . . I wish I had had it years ago."

When he goes to make his call Catherine opens the study door and asks Maria to do an errand for her—to take a note to an address in the Second Avenue, as soon as she has added a line to it. Catherine returns to the study as the front bell rings, and Maria admits Marian. When the maid announces that it is Miss Townsend, Catherine, misunderstanding the "Miss" for "Mr.," flings open the door calling, "Morris!"

Then, recovering, she makes an effort to converse with her cousin, asking abstractedly about the wedding and the honeymoon. "If it hadn't been for Morris," Marian explains, "we would never have known you were home."

"Morris?"

"He came by last night—to see Arthur," she informs Catherine confidentially. "He wanted money for his ticket. . . ."

"His ticket?"

"To New Orleans. . . . His ship sails at midnight—and from New Orleans he goes to California. He's convinced he'll find gold in California."

Bitterly, Catherine comments, "He will go to great lengths to find it."

Arthur doesn't care much for Morris, Marian confides. "But I thought he was gay. You know, Cathie, he admired you—"

Catherine laughs hysterically, and Marian grows embarrassed. "Did you—did you like him, Cathie?"

"I loved him!"

Maria returns to tell her mistress she is ready to go on her errand—and is informed that it is no longer urgent; she needn't go. Marian, whom Catherine's passionate declaration has unsettled somewhat, tries other conversational tacks: one, that she is going to have a baby; two, that she'd like to come back tomorrow and see the things her cousin must have brought from Paris.

"I am completely outfitted," says Catherine. "Gowns, and cloaks, and street dresses, and I have six dozen of each kind of underthing."

"It's a trousseau for a princess!"

"Yes. And, Marian, there is a shop in Paris that makes only baby things. I bought a great deal there too. I got different sizes and both pink and blue trimmings. I would like you to have everything."

The embarrassed Marian is grateful and promises to take care of everything because someday Catherine will want the things back.

"I shall never want them," declares her cousin firmly.

The two young women prepare to go have a look at the layettes when Dr. Sloper returns; the doctor greets Marian, then sits wearily in a chair. When the maid takes his things and asks about Mrs. de Rham he confesses he never got that far. He was a little dizzy and lurched against the railing outside. Puzzled at himself, he says, "I had a little difficulty getting back up our steps."

As Maria starts to take his things to the study he asks for the stethoscope and, left alone, puts it to his chest and listens methodically and carefully. When Marian comes down from above with her cousin and leaves, he bids Catherine to come into the room. The maid returns from the study.

"I think that both of you should know this," he announces. "I am ill. It's not just a simple congestion. There are already rales in the lungs. I'll need very good nursing. It will make no difference, for I shall not recover, but I wish everything to be done as if I should. I hate an ill-conducted sickroom, and you will be so good as to nurse me on the hypothesis that I will get well."

Without particular enthusiasm Catherine says maybe he will get well—but the doctor is sure of his own diagnosis. He continues with instructions: when need arises, get Dr. Isaacs; give him light food—and do not permit Aunt Lavinia in his room at all, unless he should go into a coma. Maria can go fix his bed for him now—and she does, on the verge of tears.

Dr. Sloper doesn't like this display of emotion; he prefers his daughter's obvious emotional discipline. Catherine, he says, is the brave one. "I told you that I was proud of you, my dear," he says. "Today I see that you have sound judgment and the courage to follow it. . . . I cannot begin to tell you how deeply proud of you I am."

This does not impress Catherine, for he does not know the truth. So she tells him the truth. "He jilted me!" she informs her father. "*Now* do you admire me?"

Dr. Sloper feels, as much as he can feel, a little sorry for himself and for Catherine. He is ill, and he wants his daughter's natural affection at this time.

"I have no affection for you, Father," she declares.

For once it is he who is shocked. He tries to find out why; was it because he tried to protect her from Morris? She tells him it is because he has cheated her; if he could not love her, he should have allowed someone else to try. It took her twenty years to discover that her father did not love her, and perhaps Morris would not have starved her for affection so much.

DR. SLOPER—Catherine, Catherine. Should I have let him ruin your life? I think you are fortunate. You will meet some honest, decent man someday, and you will make him very happy. You have many fine qualities. . . .

CATHERINE (*interrupting*)—And I will have thirty thousand a year.

DR. SLOPER—That should make it possible for you to choose with discretion.

CATHERINE—If I am to *buy* a man—I would prefer buying Morris!

DR. SLOPER—Don't say such things!

CATHERINE—Does it humiliate you?

DR. SLOPER (*violently*)—Catherine, promise me that you are done with him!

CATHERINE—No.

DR. SLOPER—Why not? You know him to be a scoundrel!

CATHERINE—I won't promise.

DR. SLOPER—Please explain, then!

CATHERINE—I can't explain, and I won't promise.

DR. SLOPER—Then I must alter my will! (*Angrily.*)

CATHERINE—You should. You should do it immediately.

DR. SLOPER—I will do it when I please!

CATHERINE—That is very wrong of you. You should do it now, while you can. (*She rises and goes to the small desk.*)

DR. SLOPER—I will attend to it tomorrow.

CATHERINE—You may not be well enough tomorrow.

DR. SLOPER—I—I spoke hastily. I want to consider more carefully.

CATHERINE (*coming back to him, she holds out the pen and tablet of paper*)—There is nothing to consider. Since I am unwilling to promise, I should not enjoy your fortune.

DR. SLOPER (*desperately*)—But I don't want to disinherit my only child!

CATHERINE—You want your money used for purposes you approve, don't you? *I* certainly should! If you leave it to the Clinic it will do what you wish it to do. If you leave it to me, you know in whose pocket it may end— (*She almost smiles.*)

DR. SLOPER—I do not feel well, and you are chivvying me!

CATHERINE (*sitting down and preparing to write it herself*)— You had better tell me how you wish it worded.

DR. SLOPER—No!

CATHERINE (*writing and speaking the words*)—I, Austin Sloper, surgeon, of 16 Washington Square, do hereby make my last will and . . .

DR. SLOPER—Catherine, this is an absurdity! You can't want me to do it, and I don't want to do it!

CATHERINE—I know that you don't. You want to think of me sitting in dignity in this handsome house rich, respected, and unloved forever. That is what you think I deserve. But I may fool you, Father. I may take your money and chase after Morris, and squander it all on him! . . . Which do you think I will do?

DR. SLOPER—I don't know.

CATHERINE—Well, you must decide and act accordingly.

DR. SLOPER—I can't. I don't know!

CATHERINE—Perhaps you will in time.

DR. SLOPER—But I shan't, for I shall be dead.

CATHERINE (*her head rises proudly*)—That's right, Father. You'll never know, will you?

The curtain falls.

SCENE II

Two years have passed and it is a Summer evening. (In the Henry James novel, twenty years had passed.—Ed.) The only change in the drawing room is that now there are two embroidery frames near the windows—one for Catherine and one for her aunt. Mrs. Penniman is working at hers, and the faithful Maria has brought in a pitcher of lemonade, when Catherine descends the stair.

Catherine, in her large, placid way, is becoming a dignified and almost attractive woman; but, although she is dressed almost fussily, she still is intent upon female handiwork and is carrying a work bag full of wool yarns and needles. Maria notes that Catherine has changed into one of her Paris gowns. She sits at her embroidery frame and attacks her sampler with enjoyment.

Mrs. Penniman, who is aware of the Summer heat, hints that Catherine might like to go somewhere by the sea; but Catherine is firmly set in her groove here on the Square and will not budge. After the preliminary talk about the weather and going away, Aunt Lavinia carefully advances an item of news—she has seen Morris—by accident, at Marian's house. He is handsome, but looks older and less animated, and seems to be sad. Probably he wasn't very successful in California.

"He asked ever so many questions about you, Catherine. He had heard that you hadn't married. He seemed very interested in that. He hasn't married either."

"Please," says Catherine, apparently unmoved, "say no more."

But there is more. Mrs. Penniman brings a message—that Morris wants to see Catherine. Catherine wants no message from a man who has deserted her. She will *not* see Morris.

There is someone at the front door now—Morris, obviously, according to the way Aunt Lavinia acts. She implores her niece, "I want your happiness so. It must be right that you see him. . . ."

"Go to the door, Aunt, and tell Mr. Townsend that I am not at home."

Wiltingly, Mrs. Penniman does so—but suddenly Catherine calls out, "Come in, Morris."

He tells Catherine he has been sitting in the Square for half an hour watching the windows, and he knew she was home. He has never ceased to think of her. "Can we not be friends again?"

"We are not enemies."

He could not, he explains, break up her life with her father, and rob her of her due.

"Morris," she informs him, "my father did not disinherit me. He threatened it, to test *you*."

"But I could not be sure of that the night I went away."

Smilingly she agrees. "No, you could not."

Morris hopes that, therefore, Catherine understands what his intention was that night, and she declares that she does understand it after two years of thinking about it. "We have nothing further to discuss," she announces. "I will bid you good night."

When he begins to protest she says it is too late, but he pleads for a hearing. He would have been back sooner, had he had the money. He even worked as a common seaman to get here. He insists that she hear him out, and she relents and allows him to take a chair. Breathing a sigh of relief, he presses his case.

He has very little to offer her, except his tenderest affection. . . . It was *because* he loved her that he disappeared. It looked as if he behaved abominably, but he had to be strong for both of them. "It was an expression of a husband's love protecting a wife's future. Can you think of it that way?"

The agreeable Catherine thinks she can, to Morris's delight. Pleasantly she forgives him the pain he has caused her. Then, he exults, nothing stands between them now.

"Do you mean you love me?" she asks.

"I did not dare say it."

"I believed you once, didn't I?"

"Perhaps," pursues Morris, "I sound fatuous, but I believe that your nature is such that you will always care for me a little."

"Yes, Morris, that is true."

Then that is all there is to it. They can pick up where they left off—marry, elope even, to Dr. Lispenard's. "You are as persuasive as ever, Morris," she submits. They talk of the inn up the river they had planned to stay at, and the exultant Morris is ready to go. He will go to his sister's and pack right away.

And Catherine will give Morris the ruby buttons she bought in Paris for their wedding. She will get them now. On the way she calls her aunt down, and Mrs. Penniman, vastly surprised, is embraced by Morris. "I am home, really truly home!" he exclaims.

Mrs. Penniman's joy is immeasurable as Morris recounts his own—he has found Catherine superb, magnificent, an admirable woman, and the elopement is to take place almost immediately. Aunt Lavinia permits herself a sniffle and a "You will be good to her!"

When Catherine comes back down Aunt Lavinia tries to embrace her, but Catherine kindly and smilingly keeps her distance. She gives Morris his wedding present—the buttons. Murmuring that he will cherish them all his life, he opens his arms—but Catherine avoids them and urges him to hurry about his packing. Before his departure he does manage one kiss.

When he has gone Mrs. Penniman is in a romantic dither. She *knew* it would turn out this way. She has faith in love. She has always been romantic. . . .

As she prattles on, Catherine closes the window facing the
street and lowers the Venetian blind. Her aunt says she needn't
bother with things like that now.

"There is no hurry," says Catherine.

Mrs. Penniman would like to pack the Paris lingerie and sprin-
kle it with fresh lavender.

"Not yet, Aunt." Catherine goes to her embroidery frame,
picks up her needle and begins work. To her aunt's protests she
replies, "I must finish it now, for I shall never do another."

Mrs. Penniman—That's right! You have better things to do.

Catherine—I have indeed! I can do anything now!

Mrs. Penniman (*coaxing*)—Come upstairs with me now, dear.
You must look your prettiest.

Catherine—Sit down, Aunt.

Mrs. Penniman—Oh, no. . . .

Catherine—*Sit down!*

Mrs. Penniman—But, Catherine, Morris will be here. . . .

Catherine—Morris will have to wait.

Mrs. Penniman—What!

Catherine—He came back with the same lies, the same silly
phrases. . . . He thought I was so stupid that I would not detect his falseness. That means that it is *he* who is stupid, not *I!*

Mrs. Penniman (*horrified*)—No, no, Catherine! That is not
true!

Catherine—He has grown greedier with the years. The first
time he only wanted my money; now he wants my love too. Well,
he came to the wrong house, and he came twice. I shall see that
he never comes a third time.

Mrs. Penniman (*stricken*)—Catherine, do you know what
you're doing?

Catherine—Yes.

Mrs. Penniman—Poor Morris, poor Morris. . . . (*Moaning.*)

Catherine—If I ever hear you mention his name again, Aunt
Penniman, should you even whisper it, I will understand that
you wish to live alone.

Mrs. Penniman—Catherine!

Catherine—It will be a sign to me that you are leaving Washington Square forever.

Mrs. Penniman (*frightened*)—Can you be this cruel?

Catherine—Yes, I can be very cruel. I have been taught by
masters!

MRS. PENNIMAN (*after a pause; she goes to the stairs*)—Good night, Catherine.

CATHERINE—Good night. (MRS. PENNIMAN *exits.* CATHERINE *sits at the frame and embroiders. We hear a carriage in the distance.* CATHERINE *listens to it. It grows louder and louder. In front of the house it stops. There is a pause and then the front doorbell rings.* CATHERINE *does not move. It rings again and* MARIA *comes from the back of the house. As* MARIA *passes the drawing room door,* CATHERINE *calls to her.*) I will attend to that. It's for me.

MARIA—Yes, Miss. (*She stops. The bell rings again.* CATHERINE *does not move.* MARIA, *puzzled, watches her a moment.*) Miss Catherine . . . ?

CATHERINE—Bolt it, Maria.

MARIA—Bolt it . . . ?

CATHERINE—Yes. (MARIA *goes to the door and slides the bolt. She waits a moment—a loud knock is heard.*) Good night, Maria.

MARIA—Good night, Miss. (*She exits.* CATHERINE *takes a final stitch and then breaks off the wool thread. Now she rises and extinguishes the lamp that has lighted her sampler.* MORRIS *knocks again.* CATHERINE *goes into the hall and picks up the small lamp at the newel post. There is another knock. As she starts up the stairs,* MORRIS *calls: "Catherine!" There are frantic knockings now, and under them we hear* MORRIS *again call: "Catherine!"* CATHERINE *continues up the stairs, the light dims.*

THE CURTAIN FALLS

ALLEGRO *

A Musical Play in Two Acts

BY RICHARD RODGERS AND OSCAR HAMMERSTEIN II

EARLY in the morning of April Fools' Day, 1948, Richard
Rodgers and Oscar Hammerstein II, the most successful music-
show team since Gilbert and Sullivan, helped the Theatre Guild
celebrate the fifth Broadway birthday of their "Oklahoma!" There
was an elaborate after-theatre party in a hotel ballroom at which
the "Oklahoma!" company presented a number of specially written songs and sketches. Among these was a burlesque of
"Allegro," the newest Rodgers-Hammerstein work.

Hammerstein, librettist and/or lyrist of so many of the New
York theatre's musical hits, keeps his head down to size by buying an advertisement in each anniversary number of *Variety,* list-
ing the many failures he also has written and boasting, "If I did
it once, I can do it again." A good many wise people thought
that he and his melody-writing partner, Rodgers, had "done it
again" with "Allegro." These wise people were wrong, for their
new musical play captured the fancy of the public—or a sufficient part of the public—and it became another in their string of
hits.

Their "Carousel," based on Molnar's "Liliom," had been an
unusual production; abandoning the happy-go-lucky formula of
the usual musical comedy, it had some of the qualities of grand
opera in its musical treatment and its rather sadly sentimental
theme. "Allegro" was an even greater departure. Hammerstein
had written a play—a serious play with a point and a moral, and
Rodgers had striven to equip it with music which also would have
dramatic outline and texture, rather than being the usual collection of song numbers which might become radio and juke-box
hits. Some of the Rodgers songs, like "A Fellow Needs a Girl,"
did become such hits—but they were in "Allegro" for the chief
purpose of carrying the play forward.

The story concerns the life of Joseph Taylor, Jr., from his
birth to maturity—mental maturity, that is; and when Joe reaches
this point he turns his back on the easy and hollow success he
has had and aims for a life of more solid satisfaction. In de-

* Lyrics reproduced by permission of Williamson Music, Inc., publishers.

scribing the work in a foreword to the published version (Knopf), Mr. Hammerstein states, "Setting out to tell so simple a tale carries with it an indigenous risk. There is no high drama or broad comedy to lean on. Complete dependence must be placed on one's efforts to interest an audience in a group of characters. . . . In the case of 'Allegro' Mr. Rodgers and I succeeded in this ambition with some critics and failed with others."

One criticism leveled at the play was that it sounded like a soap opera radio script. "This," says Mr. Hammerstein, "is entirely true. A story like this must, of its very nature, be built of familiar material. There is no novelty in 'Allegro' except its style of presentation.

"When an old problem is discussed, it is an easy thing to say, 'We've heard all that before.' But hearing it all before has done no good if one hasn't learned anything from what he has heard. If men are continuing to squander their time and usefulness for the wrong things, it would seem important to point this out to them. That is the simple reason why 'Allegro' was written. If you don't like that reason, you won't like 'Allegro.' "

The mounting of the play and the manner of presenting it are deliberately simple. Settings and properties are few, changes of scene often being merely hinted at by symbolic designs being projected against a backdrop. A chorus functions frequently in the Greek fashion, admonishing its characters, making its own editorial comments and, sometimes, speaking the private thoughts of an individual.

The story begins shortly after the birth of a son to Marjorie Taylor, wife of a small-town doctor. The chorus, standing by and looking upon a bed, starts it:

> "The lady in bed is Marjorie Taylor,
> Doctor Joseph Taylor's wife.
> Except for the day when she married Joe,
> This is the happiest day of her life."

Joe, who has been out making his rounds, asks how Marjorie is feeling. "Like jumping out of bed and dancing." And the baby? He's asleep. Softly the chorus chants,

> "His hair is fuzzy,
> His eyes are blue.
> His eyes may change—
> They often do.

He weighs eight pounds
And an ounce or two—
Joseph Taylor, Junior!"

"Do many people know yet?" Marjorie asks her husband.

Chaffingly he replies, "Why, the whole town's in an uproar!
Women are rushing to church!   Men are pouring into the sa-
loons!   Early this morning the townspeople gathered in front of
Elks Hall!   His Honor the Mayor addressed them!"

The chorus elaborates upon this exaggeration, offering a cross-
section of a town in happy celebration while Dr. Taylor takes
his wife's temperature.   "You fool," she laughs, when the ther-
mometer comes out of her mouth.

Grandma breaks in to tell her son that there's more work to
be done—another baby to be delivered, and he'd better go right
over.   "This town," testily observes Joe, "needs about ten more
doctors.   I wish old Skeezicks would hurry and grow up so's he
could help me."

"What makes you think he's going to be a doctor?" queries
Marjorie.

"I dunno—he *looks* like a doctor."

Marjorie isn't so confident of her son's looks at the moment.
"Do you think he'll ever get to look any better?" she asks
Grandma.

"Sure he will," replies Grandma.   "He'll look younger when
he's older!"

Grandma croons to the baby and individuals of the chorus
offer the lines infants usually have to listen to—"Say goo goo,"
"Papa's boy," "Mama's precious" . . .

Speaking for the baby, the chorus announces that it's a funny
place to be coming to life in, and those things with the big heads
don't help to clear things up.   You have to puzzle it out for yourself.

And the infant does puzzle it out.   He gets to know that voice
and face as his mother's.   There's another face with a loud, rough
voice, and when this one says "Got to go out and kill a few more
patients" his mother waves to him.

"Look!
She's waving at the big one.
Why does she do that? . . .
Why isn't she looking at *you* instead of him?
Make her look at you.

> (*A loud wail.* MARJORIE *turns.*)
> That's getting her!
> (*A louder wail.* MARJORIE *comes forward anxiously.*)
> You've got her!"

Time continues to pass and the baby to grow. Grandma and Marjorie see with astonishment that Joseph, Jr. is standing up— and falling down. "Come on, Joey. Try again," urges his mother.

CHORUS—
> Wonder if she knows how dangerous it is!
> You're sorry you started now.
> What got into you today, anyway?
> All of a sudden crawling wasn't good enough!
> Well, there they are watching you.
> Go to it!

GRANDMA—
> That's Grandma's good boy!

CHORUS—
> Grandma's good boy!
> But what do you do now that you're up?
> As usual nobody helps.
> You've got to puzzle everything out for yourself. . . .
> Whoops!
> Almost fell again.
> Hey! Wait!
> Do you realize what happened just then?
>> (*The voices of the* CHORUS *are charged with the excitement of discovery.*)
> You felt yourself falling
> And you put one foot out to save yourself,
> And you didn't fall! . . .
> Say! Maybe if you keep taking steps,
> One after the other—
> One after the other . . .
> Maybe going forward is easier than standing still!
>> (*Slowly and significantly.*)
> *Maybe going forward is easier than standing still!*
> Come on!
> Step out!
>> (MARJORIE *and* GRANDMA *in unison with the* CHORUS *plead and exhort while projections on the drop convey the thrills of* JOE's *hazardous trip.*)

One foot, other foot,
One foot, other foot,
One foot, other foot,
Faster,
Faster,
Faster,
Faster.
Ah-h-h-h-h-h-h-h!
> (*The lights go out on* MARJORIE *and* GRANDMA *as*
> *they open their arms to catch* JOE. *The* CHORUS
> *spreads out across the stage and sings, to express*
> JOE'S *first big conquest.*)

CHORUS—
One foot, other foot,
One foot, other foot,
One foot, other foot,
One foot, other foot,

Now you can go
Wherever you want,
Wherever you want to go,
One foot out
And the other foot out—
That's all you need to know!

Now you can do
Whatever you want,
Whatever you want to do,
Here you are
In a wonderful world
Especially made for you,
Especially made for you!

> Now you can march around the yard,
> Shout to all the neighborhood,
> Tell the folks you're feeling good.
> (Folks ought to know when boys feel good.)

> Now you can imitate a dog,
> Chase a bird around a tree,
> You can chase a bumblebee.
> (Once is enough to chase a bee.)

> Now you can play among the flow'rs,
> Grab yourself a hunk o' dirt,

Smudge it on your mother's skirt.
(That little dirt won't hurt a skirt.)

One foot, other foot,
One foot, other foot,
 (*From here they sing with mounting triumph.*)
Now you can do
Whatever you want,
Whatever you want to do.
Here you are
In a wonderful world,
Especially made for you,
Especially made for you!
Especially made for you
To walk in, to run in,
To play in the sun in,
Especially made for you!
For now you can walk,
You taught yourself to walk!
You puzzled it out yourself
And now you can walk!

One foot, other foot,
One foot, other foot,
One foot, other foot,
One foot, other foot,
Now you can go
Wherever you want,
Wherever you want to go!
One foot out
And the other foot out,
One foot out
And the other foot out
One foot out
And the other foot out
And the world belongs to Joe!
And the world belongs to Joe!

Dancers, representing Joe's playmates, scamper on—including one Jenny Brinker, who is already known as Joey Taylor's girl. She tries to act the tomboy but can't; she's a girly girl and always will be. At the end of the ballet the children drift away and the lights dim, and Grandma, although she is trying to smile, is troubled. She sings,

> "The Winters go by,
> The Summers fly,
> And all of a sudden . . .
> > (*A cloud crosses her face.*)
> All of a sudden . . ."

The lights change and two boys come hollering for Joey to come out and play—but the chorus admonishes Joey that he can't go this time. "Gee! That's right. I forgot—his grandma," says one of the boys.

Joey stays home while his father and mother go to Grandma's funeral—but Grandma's ghost comes to visit Joey, for the boy is thinking of her. "Death is a sad thing," she tells him. "People cry and sob. Grown people. You haven't seen your father cry. He just looks kind of angry." And, when Jenny comes to tell Joey how sorry she is and his eyes begin to water, Grandma urges him to smile.

The chorus announces a further passage of time:

> "The Winters go by,
> The Summers fly,
> And soon you're a student in 'High!'
> And now your clothes are spotlessly clean,
> Your head is anointed with brilliantine!
> You're brimming with hope
> But can't quite cope
> With problems that vex and perplex,
> For you don't quite know how to treat
> The bewilderingly opposite sex!"

Jenny, now sixteen and wearing a party dress, invitingly bids Joe good night. A more sophisticated escort would know she wants to be kissed—but not Joe. The lights fade out on a girl with a frustrated heart and a disgusted face, while the chorus speaks for Joe: "It would have been nice. . . . Gee, wouldn't it be wonderful if girls liked it too!"

Now Joe is seventeen and is up in his room packing to go to college.

"Don't look so mopey," Dr. Taylor counsels Marjorie. "The boy isn't going away forever."

"I'm losing him," mourns Marjorie. "When he comes back from college he'll be a different boy. I won't know him."

They talk of their son, unaware that he can hear them through his open window—nor can they hear him as he talks to himself.

Dr. Taylor looks a little mopey himself; Mrs. Mason is worse since yesterday, and it's a baffling case. "You'll pull her through. I have a feeling," Marjorie reassures him.

The audience can hear Joe in his room. "I've been hearing this kind of talk ever since I can remember. Dad always has one case that stumps him, and Mother always has a 'feeling' he'll beat it."

"Do you think Joe takes to medicine?" Marjorie asks her husband.

"He's a born doctor! Could tell when he made rounds with me this Summer."

"He was telling me how he helped you with the Jacobs boy."

"Yep," agrees Dr. Taylor. "That was a quick one."

"Boy, was I scared!" says Joe in his room. "Nothing in the world mattered except saving a ten-year-old boy I'd never seen before. Gosh! Who would want to be anything else but a doctor!"

For a moment the parents' talk drifts from their son to the hospital Dr. Taylor hopes to have one day. The fund is coming slowly, for people can't give much—some only 50 cents. But again Marjorie has a feeling—that the hospital will come.

"I hope Joe marries a girl who gets 'feelings' about things."

"I hope," counters Marjorie, "he gets a girl with good sense."

Joe's father wonders if he'll marry Jenny Brinker, and Marjorie points out that he'll be meeting a lot of new girls at college.

"But not like Jenny," says Joe. "No other girl could ever be like her."

It's only dumb luck, opines Dr. Taylor, when a boy picks the right girl—the way he did. He sings:

> "A fellow needs a girl
> To sit by his side
> At the end of a weary day,
> To sit by his side
> And listen to him talk
> And agree with the things he'll say.

> "A fellow needs a girl
> To hold in his arms
> When the rest of his world goes wrong,
> To hold in his arms
> And know that she believes
> That her fellow is wise and strong.

"When things go right
And his job's well done,
He wants to share
The prize he's won.
If no one shares,
And no one cares,
Where's the fun
Of a job well done—
Or a prize you've won?

"A fellow needs a home
(His own kind of home),
But to make this dream come true,
A fellow needs a girl,
His own kind of girl . . .
My kind of girl is you."

(The music continues. The light remains on MARJORIE *and* TAYLOR *as they sit contentedly together.)*

JOE'S VOICE—They're funny when they're by themselves—not like a mother and a father. A fellow and a girl—like Jenny and me—almost.

MARJORIE *(singing)*—

My fellow needs a girl
To sit by his side
At the end of a weary day,
So I sit by his side
And I listen to him talk
And agree with the things he'll say.

My fellow needs a girl
To hold in his arms
When the rest of his world goes wrong,
To hold in his arms
And know that she believes
That her fellow is wise and strong.

When things go right
And his job's well done,
He wants to share
The prize he's won,
If no one shares,
And no one cares,
Where's the fun
Of a job well done?

TAYLOR—
> Or a prize you've won?

MARJORIE—
> My fellow needs a home
> (His own kind of home),
> But to make his dreams come true,

TAYLOR—
> A fellow needs to love

MARJORIE—
> His one only love,

BOTH—
> My only love is you.

(*The lights fade.*)

There is a freshman dance at the college gym, with a tacky crowd of boys and girls, gauche but gay, giving some painful illustrations of what were considered snappy dance steps in 1921. Suddenly they stand in a frozen picture and the chorus explains that, although this is the way they look when they are dancing, they feel different. They feel they are floating, flying. . . . Another ballet, beautifully garbed, dances the way the youngsters feel—gracefully and dreamily, and the little jazz band becomes a symphony orchestra. There is another transition back to reality, and a spotlight tries to find Joe Taylor on the floor. After a couple of false tries it locates him: he's the boy stepping on that girl's toe. He apologizes.

"I never had any dancing lessons until six months ago."

"You mean to say," says the girl crushingly, "this is not the first time you've ever danced?"

Joe assures her he's better if he counts while he's dancing—a way he figured out. It goes, "one foot, other foot . . ."

As the lights change Joe is, suddenly, alone on the campus. A darn nice campus—but he wishes he were home. A classmate, Charlie Townsend, passes and flings him a greeting. Two girls look admiringly at Charlie. "Only freshman to make the varsity," says one of them—the one who was Joe's partner at the dance. She gives Joe a chilly hello, and after the girls pass him they giggle.

Poor Joe. It's a darn nice campus—and he's lonely as hell. And he doesn't seem to get the hang of college life either. Now, for instance, he is on the football field, where the freshmen are being taught the college cheer by the coach. "The Wildcats are on the rampage! Hear those Wildcats yell!—Yow!" Unpre-

pared for the shout, Joe gives a start. The "yows" and "wows"
continue and Joe begins to get the spirit of things—the spirit
but not the hang, for he puts in an extra wow all by himself and
goes off the field in disgrace.

On the campus he encounters Charlie again, who is boasting to
three gaping girls about his football prowess. When he sees Joe
he orders the girls to beat it. "We seem to be taking the same
courses. Premedical?" he asks Joe.

If Joe were a dog he'd wag his tail at being thus addressed by
the freshman football star. "Yes," he says. "Are you?"

Charlie is, because he has a pill-juggling uncle in Chicago who
will take him in with him if he's any good. Charlie gets to his
point: he wants to borrow Joe's notebook, because during the lectures he has been reading a magazine, *Snappy Stories*.

Joe willingly hands over the notebook and Charlie magnani-
mously asks Joe to lunch at "the house"—a fraternity house!
Joe accepts with awe, and the lights fade once more.

Now it is the garden at Jenny's house and Jenny is reading a
letter to her friend Hazel. She sings:

> "It's a darn nice campus,
> With ivy on the walls,
> Friendly maples
> Outside the lecture halls.
> I like my roommate
> And you would like him too—
> It's a darn nice campus,
> But I'm lonely for you."

Jenny's father, Ned Brinker, strolls into the garden and guesses
that his daughter has another letter from Romeo. "Let's see,"
says Ned. "Only two and a half more years in college—then four
years in medical school—then two years as in intern—then God
knows how long before he can get enough paying patients to support a wife! You're making a brilliant match, my girl. Brilliant!" He leaves, chuckling.

Hazel herself wonders if Jenny doesn't worry about having to
wait so long. Hazel doesn't see why Joe *has* to be a doctor.

"Because his *mother* wants him to be," explains Jenny. "Her
father was a doctor and her husband is a doctor, and if her darling
son Joey isn't a doctor this whole town will get sick and die!"

"Gosh, I don't envy *you!* With his mother against you there
isn't much you can do."

Wisely Jenny replies, "Oh, I wouldn't say that, Hazel. There might be a lot I can do. Might take a little time. But I think there's a *lot* I can do." She is smiling smugly as the scene changes to Joe's study, where Joe is reading a letter from Jenny. As he reads it is Jenny's voice he is hearing:

Does he remember Hazel Skinner? Hazel is going to marry a man only a year older than Joe who is making lots of money selling automobiles. His family wants him to be a lawyer, but he says if you study a profession you are an old man before you make any money. . . .

Joe swallows hard, puts down the letter and goes to work on his Latin as Charlie breezes in, late for a date.

CHARLIE—'Lo, Joe.

JOE—'Lo. What's your hurry?

CHARLIE—Late for a date. Wanta come along? I think she's got an older sister. I dunno how *much* older.

JOE—No, thanks, Charlie. I got a lot of Latin to translate.

CHARLIE—Okay, boy. You take the dead language. I'll take my live woman.

JOE—Only one I care about is back home. Just got a letter from her.

CHARLIE—Got a clean shirt?

JOE—Y-yes. But I've only got one.

CHARLIE—Swell! (*Fishing it out of a bureau drawer.*) That the dame you want to marry?

JOE (*looking down at* JENNY's *letter*)—If she'll wait for me. . . . I don't know if I ever told you this, Charlie, but she's the only girl I ever had a date with. . . . I suppose you think I'm crazy.

CHARLIE—Well-ll, you're something like a guy who goes fishing for the first time in his life and decides to quit after he's caught his first fish. For all you know the waters might be filled with gorgeous and tasty tuna, and you may be settling for a sardine.— I'm taking your tie. You don't mind, do you?

JOE (*sore*)—I'm not settling for any sardine. (*He goes back to his Latin.*)

CHARLIE—'Course you're not. She's probably a wonderful girl. Only thing I say is— (*Pointing to a dollar bill on the bureau.*) Is that dollar bill yours or mine?

JOE (*snappily*)—Mine!

CHARLIE (*taking it*)—I'll pay you tomorrow when I get my

check. Only thing I say is it's all right to get married eventually, but I want to have plenty of fun first.

JOE—People can have fun after they're married.

CHARLIE—What people?

JOE—My father and mother. They have lots of fun. Don't yours?

CHARLIE—I guess so. But not with each other, I don't think. (*Putting on his coat, starting to go.*) Sure you don't want to come? Relax?

JOE—Uh-uh.

CHARLIE—Leave that translation out so I can copy it when I get back.

JOE (*not looking up*)—Okay.

CHARLIE—Thanks. S'long.

When the lights dim and come up again, Joe is in a classroom—a composite of all the classrooms. Five professors are giving lectures on five subjects, but instead of listening or reciting Joe is mostly dreaming of Jenny—and seeing her, even, as the chorus sings seductively,

> "She is never away
> From her home in your heart,
> In your heart, every day,
> She is playing her part."

Joe's mind is on a new letter. Hazel is going to have a baby and how Jenny envies her! And now another letter! Jenny dashes on to impart the news, "Popper is taking me to Europe. He wants me to meet new friends."

"Some lousy nobleman, perhaps," muses the chorus for Joe . . . and the professors go on talking. Jenny and a boy appear dancing a passionate tango. While dancing, Jenny reports to Joe, "I met a charming boy named Bertram Woolhaven." And the chorus warns, "She wants to get married. She's tired of waiting for you."

"Bertram's father," continues Jenny, "is in the coal and lumber business too." This, advises the chorus, is the handwriting on the wall—an alliance between two big lumber families.

Charlie, too, has been having some dreams in the classroom, particularly when an English prof gets to reading a particularly fruity passage from Keats—dreams of girls disrobing before him as they do in "The Eve of St. Agnes." Jenny's letters continue to torture Joe—Bertram, pretending to teach her to swim, picking her up and carrying her off in a bathing suit.

For Joe the breaking point has come. "Did you say that girl friend of yours had a friend?" he asks Charlie.

"I'll say she has!"

"Then get her! I'm on the loose!"

Charlie and a girl named Molly are in a woodland—Charlie sitting on an auto seat with the girl's head on his lap. He looks bored, for the romance of the evening obviously has gone beyond its climax. Charlie, looking at his wrist watch, wonders what happened to the other two—but Molly wants to talk of her own romance.

"You aren't just kidding around with me, are you?" she asks.

"Absolutely not. What gives you ideas like that?"

"Oh, I don't know. Sometimes I think this is just a college romance. And when you graduate you'll go away and forget all about me—just like all the other boys."

"Like all what other boys?" sharply queries Charlie.

Molly takes a moment to recover her wits, then explains, "I mean like all the other boys with all the other girls."

They start to look for Joe and Molly's girl friend. In another part of the woodland Joe is lying on his back and Beulah is regarding him ruefully. "Do you," she queries, "go out with girls much?"

"What makes you ask?"

"I was just thinking. You meet all kinds of fellows, don't you —I mean, don't I?"

"Let's pep up the party," suggests Joe, which is O.K. with Beulah. He offers her a flask. When she has had a drink she passes it back and he finishes it. The bootleg liquor thaws Joe out, and he wonders what Beulah would do if he kissed her.

"You're not that type," observes Beulah.

"And you're not that type of girl. You're romantic—like me."

This is a new one on Beulah, but she plays along with the idea, fluffing her hair, talking about the starlight and singing, "So far your heart has never fluttered so near, so near, that my own heart alone could hear it. . . ."

Joe has just about made up his mind to kiss her, and when Jenny and Bertram appear in his thoughts that does it—he kisses Beulah. This forthright young woman throws her arms around him and kisses him with such verve that he falls flat on his back. Fondly she sings to him some more: "And now at last we've met,

and now we can look forward to the things we'll never forget. . . ."

Joe lies with his head on his arm. Beulah finishes her song
and calls seductively to him. There is no answer. She leans
over, looks at him tenderly, and cries, "The little louse is asleep!"

Snatching a blanket from beneath Joe, she stalks off through
the wood, and the lights go down.

On the campus a student gives Joe a letter that had got mixed
up in his mail—a letter from Jenny. As he opens it, Joe mutters
bitterly, "Probably announcing her engagement to Bertram! As
if I cared!"

Charlie, followed by a pair of girls, comes up. "Hey, Joe! I
fixed up another date tonight!"

But Joe is reading. "She's coming home!" he shouts. "She's
through with Bertram! Says she can't stand the sight of him!
She gets home in July! Oh, how can I wait?"

Charlie disgustedly remarks that he thought Joe was on the
loose. "I'm through with that—philandering," says Joe, and
Charlie and the girls drift on.

As the scene begins to change Joe plans what he will do and
say when he sees Jenny. . . .

And now it is July and he is with her in the moonlight in her
garden—but instead of saying something wonderful to her, as
the chorus has suggested, he observes, "I noticed your house has
a new coat of paint."

With the chorus urging him on, Joe gets the conversation
around to Jenny—and him—but awkwardly. The chorus suggests something nice like, "You are never away from your home
in my heart," but the best he can do is, "I always think of you—
quite a lot."

CHORUS (*prompting*)—There is never a day—
JOE—There is never a day when you— (*Emotion comes into
his voice.*) Jenny, I think about you all the time.
JENNY—Do you, Joe?
JOE—Every minute! (*She nestles close to him. Timidly, he
steals his arm around her. The* CHORUS *hums softly. Then* JOE
starts to sing:)

> You are never away
> From your home in my heart;

There is never a day
When you don't play a part
In a word that I say
Or a sight that I see—
　　You are never away
　　And I'll never be free.

You're the smile on my face,
Or a song that I sing!
You're a rainbow I chase
On a morning in Spring;
You're a star in the lace
Of a wild, willow tree—
　　In the green, leafy lace
　　Of a wild, willow tree.

But tonight you're no star,
Nor a song that I sing;
In my arms, where you are,
You are sweeter than Spring;
In my arms, where you are,
Clinging closely to me,
　　You are lovelier, by far,
　　Than I dreamed you could be—
　　　　You are lovelier, my darling,
　　　　Than I dreamed you could be! . . .

(*He can only manage to whisper it.*)   I love you.

JENNY—I love you. (*A pause. Then* JENNY *opens up reality.*)   Going to medical school next year?

JOE—Yep. I've been working a lot with Dad this Summer. Gosh, it's exciting watching sick people get better!

JENNY (*flatly*)—Is it?

JOE—You know, a doctor doesn't always know what to do at first. He tries this or that, and it doesn't do any good. Then he hits it. And you see the patient get better every day. Well, then you know it's about the best thing a man can be—is a doctor. (JENNY *sits on the bench.* JOE, *sensing her disappointment, goes to her.*)   I'm not going to wait till I get out of medical school. We've got to get married sooner than that. I'm going to speak to my dad about it—I guess I better speak to your father too. Do you know if he likes me?

JENNY—He likes you a lot. Only he's going to ask you about how you're going to support me.

JOE—He is?

JENNY—The other night on the boat he was saying how he needs a young man to help him in his coal and lumber business. It's getting awful big. And now he wants to go in for farm machinery too. He might say something to you about whether you'd like to—to go in with him.

JOE—You mean instead of being a doctor?

JENNY—Well, he'll tell you how. rich we could— (*Afraid she has started this line too quickly.*) But whatever happens, Joey, it's got to be you who decides. I'd never influence one way or the other— (*She slides down onto* JOE's *lap and nestles in his arms.*) You have to make up your own mind—my darling.

On another Summer evening Jenny and her father are having lemonade with Dr. Taylor and Marjorie on the Taylors' porch. Ned is giving Taylor a piece of his wisdom. The reason the doctor is having trouble raising money for his hospital is that he isn't asking enough. "People don't want a little hospital. They'd rather put money in a skyscraper hospital in the nearest big town."

Dr. Taylor can't see it that way. People need small hospitals. For a modest start the Taylors have put an ell on their house and have three beds there—and when Joe is ready to help there will be more.

"A young fellow like him," says Ned, "might be too ambitious to be a small-town doctor. What do you say, Jenny?"

Jenny warns her father off the subject by reminding him he has a date for an Elks meeting. As he departs Ned taunts Taylor, "Say, Joe, I got one on you. That stock I told you about has gone up twenty-two points. You were a sucker not to buy."

Taylor is ready for him. A smart man once said, he replies, that if you get ten per cent on your money you can eat better— and if you get two per cent you can sleep better.

"Whoever said that didn't know much about business," laughs Ned. "Who was he?"

"J. P. Morgan."

With a quiet "Oh" Ned goes to his meeting and Dr. Taylor goes upstairs. "Oh, Marge," he asks as he leaves, "feeling better, darling?" Marjorie reassures him with a "Yes, dear."

Marjorie has been watching Jenny closely and now she demands to know what her father meant by Joe being too ambitious to be a small-town doctor. Has Joe said anything about that?

"No. It's just that Pop thinks—well, he thinks it's awful for us to have to struggle along for years like—like you and Dr. Taylor."

"And do you agree with him?"

"Well, it seems a shame with a wonderful business like Pop's— he has no son—and he says he could teach it to Joe in a couple of years. Pop thinks Joe is smart."

Jenny is beginning to show her fangs, but sweetly. When Marjorie opines that Joe wouldn't be happy selling coal and lumber, Jenny replies that she wouldn't be happy as the wife of a starving doctor.

"Jenny," demands Marjorie, "what would you do if Joe refused to give up medicine?"

"What would I do? I'd see that he became a real doctor, a rich one. We'd go to some big city. I'd help him get to be the most successful doctor in town. I guess I'm more ambitious than you."

The enmity between the two becomes more open. Marjorie does not deny it when Jenny cries, "You don't like me and you never did." She starts for home, then comes back and says, "You know, I feel better now that war's declared."

"So do I, Jenny," replies Marjorie coolly.

"Try and get him away from me! You just try!"

When Jenny has gone, Marjorie loses the outward strength she has been assuming. She walks to a chair . . . suddenly clutches it for support, her other hand going to her chest. Weakly she calls for her husband and tries to get to the door. "Hurry— sweetheart—" The lights fade.

There is a glimpse of Joe's study at college, with Charlie handing him a telegram and putting an arm around him.

Joe comes home. His father is on the porch sitting beside Marjorie's chair, and the melody of "A Fellow Needs a Girl" is softly heard. Joe sits in his mother's chair and timidly puts his hand on his father's hand. Neither says anything.

Now it is the wedding day, and the guests, as they go into the church, sing, "What a lovely day for a wedding!" Jenny's father sings that it may be a lovely day, but not for the father of the bride:

> "What I'm about to get
> I don't exactly need—
> A doctor for a son-in-law,
> Another mouth to feed!"

As the friends of the Taylors go in they ask each other, "What can he see in her?" As the Brinker group enter they query, "What can she see in him?"

Charlie, who is best man, agrees with the bridesmaids that it's a lovely day for a wedding—as long as the bridegroom isn't himself. He sings:

> "It may be a good idea for Joe,
>   But it wouldn't be good for me
> To sit in a mortgaged bungalow
>   With my little ones on my knee.
> I'd much rather go and blow my dough
>   On a casual chickadee.
> I don't want a mark that I'll have to toe;
>   My toe can go where it wants to go;
> It wants to go where the wild girls grow
>   In extravagant quantity!
> To bask in the warm and peaceful glow
>   Of connubial constancy
> May be awfully good for good old Joe,
>   But it wouldn't be good for me!"

Inside the church are all the appurtenances and people involved in a wedding—and more: present also at this important moment are two others who have loved Joe very much—his grandmother and his mother . . . for they, too, are much in his mind.

JOE—I hope I'll make Jenny a good husband.

GRANDMA—You were always a good boy.

JOE—Funny—I've been thinking a lot about Grandma lately.

MINISTER—Dearly beloved, we are gathered together here in the sight of God, and in the face of this company, to join together this man and this woman in holy matrimony. (*His lips continue to move as the* CHORUS *speak their thoughts.*)

CHORUS (*speaking softly, earnestly*)—
>   A change has come over us.
>   The simple words,
>   The commonplace words,
>   And the two serious children listening—
>   A change has come over us!
>   The whispered jokes,
>   The "cracks" that seemed funny
>   A few moments ago,

> Aren't funny any more!
> This is no time for the humorous skeptic
> Or the gloomy prophet.
> This is a time for hope.
> These children desperately
> Need our hope!

MINISTER—If any man can show just cause why they may not be lawfully joined together, let him now speak, or else hereafter forever hold his peace. (*His lips continue to move as* CHARLIE, HAZEL *and* NED *speak their thoughts.*)

CHARLIE—I hardly know the girl. She may turn out swell.

HAZEL—

> I know she loves him.
> She fought his mother,
> She fought her own father.
> She loves him, all right!

NED—The boy has a right to try medicine if he wants. He could always come in with me later, as Jenny says.

MINISTER—Joseph, wilt thou have this woman to thy wedded wife, to live together— (*His lips continue to move as* GRANDMA *sings.*)

GRANDMA (*looking at* JOE)—

> Starting out so foolishly small,
> It's hard to believe they will grow at all,
> But Winters go by and Summers fly,
> And all of a sudden they're men! . . .

JOE (*answering the* MINISTER)—I will.

MINISTER—Janet—

MARJORIE—Jenny! Listen!

MINISTER—Janet, wilt thou have this man to thy wedded husband, to live together after God's ordinance in the holy estate of matrimony? (*His lips continue to move, but it is* MARJORIE'S *insistent voice that* JENNY *hears.*)

MARJORIE—Wilt thou love him, comfort him, honor, and keep him in sickness and in health; and forsaking all others, keep thee only unto him, so long as ye both shall live?—Jenny?

JENNY (*deeply affected*)—I will.

MINISTER—Who giveth this woman to be married to this man?

NED—I do.

MINISTER—I, Joseph, take thee, Janet, to my wedded wife—

JOE—I, Joseph, take thee, Janet, to my wedded wife—

MINISTER—To have and to hold from this day forward—

CHORUS (*singing*)—
>   To have and to hold
>   From this day forward
>   For better, for worse,
>   For richer, for poorer,
>   In sickness and in health,
>   To love and to cherish,
>   'Til death do us part,
>   'Til death do us part.

(*As they sing,* MARJORIE *walks slowly over to* TAYLOR *and stands before him as if she longed to touch him, to be alive with him for a moment.* TAYLOR *puts his hand to his forehead, hurt by a sudden memory.* CHARLIE *steps forward and hands the ring to the* MINISTER.)

MINISTER (*placing the ring on* JENNY's *finger*)—With this ring I thee wed.

JOE—With this ring, I thee wed. (*The* MINISTER's *lips continue to move, delivering the balance of the service as the* CHORUS *sings.*)

>   Two more lovers
>   Were married today.
>   Wish them well!
>   Wish them well!
>   Wish them well!
>   Brave and happy,
>   They start on their way,
>   Wish them well!
>   Wish them well!
>   Wish them well!
>   (JOE *raises* JENNY's *veil and kisses her.*)
>   They have faith in the future
>   And joy in their hearts,
>   If you look in their eyes
>   You can tell
>   How brave and happy
>   And hopeful are they.
>   Wish them well, wish them well,
>   Wish them well, wish them well, wish them well.

(JENNY *and* JOE, *married, walk up the aisle together as the* CHORUS *sings exultantly.* MARJORIE *covers her eyes with her hands, afraid of what she can foresee.*)

The curtain falls.

ACT II

Indeed, times have changed. In the back yard of the Taylor home Jenny, in a very plain housedress, stands between a clothesline and a washbasket. Her father, looking tired and spiritless, carries a garden hose and a newspaper as he asks if Joe is out making calls.

"No, he went up to State College for a fraternity reunion." There is something subtly disrespectful in Jenny's voice as she talks with her shabby father. Ned has been caught in the crash. The Brinker's Coal and Lumber Yard has been taken over by a man named Ramazotti—and so has the Brinker house. Ned opens his paper to read and complains, "If this government would only do something a man'd have a chance to get back on his feet."

"What could the government do?" queries the wash-hanging Jenny.

"Well, it could do something! That's what a government is for. . . . That Hoover!"

From across the yard Millie, Addie, Hazel and Dot come, no better clad than Jenny, to show her a chinchilla coat—a picture of one in *Vogue*. They all admire it and marvel that, somewhere, some girls are getting such things. Suddenly Millie laughs. "Look," she says. "On the opposite page is an article, 'Money Isn't Everything.' "

"Well, fine! I don't want everything," declares Jenny. "I'll just take money." The girls sing, satirically, about the worthlessness of things money can buy, like automobiles, champagne and yachts. Queries Dot: "Can money make your hands get rough, as washing dishes does?" Just before the lights fade they chorus, "Money isn't everything as long . . . as . . . you . . . have . . . dough!"

In the bedroom Jenny is sitting up in bed glaring at her husband, back from the reunion. She won't believe what he has been saying; he's just trying to be funny.

"No, I'm not," insists Joe. "Charlie's uncle came to the reunion especially to talk to me."

"And you were offered a chance to be his partner? A partner of Dr. Denby?"

Jenny can't believe all this, but Joe explains that he was a kind of a white-haired boy when he was an intern at Dr. Denby's hospital.

"And you have the nerve," rails Jenny, "to stand there and tell me you turned him down!"

"I've got to think of my father," explains Joe. "I'm just beginning to be of some help to him."

Jenny pulls the old one about Joe caring more about his father than he does about her, and Joe slams out of the bedroom.

"Go easy, Jenny," cautions a chorus of women. "Use your head! This is the biggest chance you'll ever have. . . . Be clever!"

Jenny gets clever. When Joe comes back from the bathroom, his coat off and his tie loosened, she loosens a few sobs, then slips down to his lap, buries her head on his chest and sobs some more. "I'm a mean, selfish girl!" she confesses. "I was only thinking of myself and how wonderful it would be to have a beautiful house in Chicago, and servants, and lovely dresses to wear so I could look pretty for you when you came home at night."

This, decides the chorus, is just right. "Good!"

Jenny pursues her advantage and Joe is a gone goose. She envisions Joe as being so rich he can give his father the money to complete the hospital, and hints not too delicately that now they might be able to have a baby. Joe kisses his wife, picks her up and starts to carry her back to bed.

"That's all, brother!" concludes a chorus of men.

In his office, Joe's father stands looking at two diplomas that hang side by side—his and his son's. Hearing Joe coming, Dr. Taylor slips back to his desk and begins looking at papers. "Just looking over your parting instructions," he tells Joe.

"Not instructions, Dad. Just a few—er—suggestions about the people I've been taking care of." He tells about the Reilly kid, who works on a farm all day and studies all night, and wants to be a priest. He has tuberculosis. "We've got to—you've got to see that he doesn't lose hope."

TAYLOR (*looking at* JOE *with an understanding smile*)—Well, I'll do what I can, Joe. (*He picks up another paper.*) Jan Malinowski—the old Polish fellow with a chronic catarrh?

JOE—Well, the only note I made about him is that I haven't been charging him anything—

TAYLOR—We'll continue that policy.

JOE—He's out of work now.

TAYLOR (*studying* JOE)—Get kind of wrapped up in these people, don't you?

JOE (*self-consciously*)—Yes—you do—don't you?

TAYLOR—One night—I was about fourteen, I guess—I was out in the barn hitching the mare to your grandfather's sleigh. He had a bad chest cold—probably running a fever—but he was going to drive twelve miles through a blizzard on a call. I asked him why—asked him if it was because he loved people so much. He said, "Hell, no!" Didn't give a hoot about them—didn't really like anybody till after he had done something for them. After that he figured he had a stake in them.

JOE—I see what he meant. (MARJORIE *enters.*)

MARJORIE—Of course you do. They're your people after you've helped them. . . . (*Coming up close behind* JOE.)

> Why does your heart feel so heavy?
> If it is so fine to go to Chicago
> To be rich and successful and famous—
> Why does your heart feel heavy?
> You could still change your mind!
> Let the train go without you!
> (*Sound of an auto horn.*)

TAYLOR—I guess that's Jenny in the car.

MARJORIE—Lean out the window and tell her it's all off. (JOE *starts for window.* CHARLIE'S *face appears before him, dimly lit.*)

CHARLIE—You going nuts? People will think you are crazy. Not just Jenny. Me. Everybody. (CHARLIE *disappears.* JOE *turns back from the window.*)

TAYLOR (*holding out his hand*)—Well— Good luck, son.

JOE (*blurting it all out*)—I'm doing this for Jenny, Father. It'll be easier for her, and it's a wonderful practice—wonderful people. I even figured in a few years I might be able to give you the ten grand you need to finish the hospital.

TAYLOR—Fine, Joe! Just fine!

JOE—And another thing. Now Jenny and I can afford to have a baby.

MARJORIE—Your father and I didn't know whether we could afford you or not. We just wanted you. (*Automobile horn off.*)

JOE—Well—so long, Dad. (*He turns to go, then suddenly stops and wheels around.* MARJORIE *and* TAYLOR *stand transfixed with wild hope.*) I forgot my diploma. (JOE *crosses and takes down his diploma.* MARJORIE *goes to* TAYLOR, *throws her arms around him from behind, and holds both hands on his heart.*)

MARJORIE—You're hurt!

JOE—Guess I can get this in the big suitcase.

MARJORIE—

> I'm here with you, darling,
> I love you.
> Don't let him hurt you.

TAYLOR (*his voice hoarse as he attempts to throw the thing off lightly*)—Lucky you remembered that. A doc isn't much good without his shingle. They'd think you were a horse doctor or something. No room for horse doctors in a fancy office like that. (JOE *and* TAYLOR *force a laugh.* JOE *gulps and, fearing to trust his voice further, waves at his father as he starts out.* TAYLOR *calls to him, a tired smile on his face.*) Don't take any wooden nickels. (JOE *is gone.* TAYLOR *sinks down at his desk.* MARJORIE *sings part of "A Fellow Needs a Girl."* TAYLOR'S *head falls to his arms. The lights fade.*)

In Chicago, Joe Taylor has become a success, and to prove it Jenny is having a cocktail party in her salon. A mass of chattering people is packed close together; a butler and a maid hold trays of drinks aloft, and Jenny glides from one guest to another with the manner of an assured hostess.

There is a confusion of sound in the room, as though all were chanting, "Yatata yatata yatata yatata." Occasionally a snatch of conversation can be distinguished: "Balderdash!" . . . "Broccoli!" . . . "Hogwash!" . . . "Phoney baloney!" "I'm as busy as a bee," sings a girl to two others. "I start the day at half-past one! When I am finished phoning its time to dress for tea."

Among those present is Charlie Townsend who, reflective for once, sings:

> "The deep-thinking gentlemen and ladies
> Who keep a metropolis alive
> Drink cocktails
> And knock tails
>   (*Which they all do in two beats.*)
> Ev'ry afternoon at five."

Dr. Denby, Joe's patron, circulates, the cynosure of all eyes.

A GROUP OF LADIES (*surrounding* DENBY)—

> Doctor!
> Doctor!
> I need another shot!

A SECOND GROUP (*explaining to a third group*)—
   The shots he gives are too divine!
   He fills a little needle and he gives you all it's got!
   Your fanny hurts but you feel fine!

ALL—
   Yatata yatata yatata yatata
   Yatata yatata yatata yatata
   Yatata yatata yatata yatata
   Yatata yatata yatata yatata

ALL—
   Broccoli Hogwash Balderdash
   Phoney Baloney Tripe and Trash!
   Goodness knows where the day has gone!
   The days come fast and are quickly gone,
   But the talk talk talk goes on and on
   And on and on and on!

MEN (*indicating* LANSDALE, *who is telling a story to a sycophantic group that includes* JENNY)—
   Lansdale!
   Lansdale!
   The multimillionaire!
   He manufactures Lansdale soap!

CHARLIE—
   So when he tells a story
   His listeners declare
   He's twice as comical as Bob Hope!
    (LANSDALE's *listeners smack their thighs and bend over as they laugh.*)

ALL—
   Yatata yatata yatata yatata
   Yatata yatata yatata yatata
    (*The following speeches are not in meter but the "yatata yatata yatata" continues softly underneath.*)

MRS. LANSDALE (*shouting right in the face of a friend*)—I can't sleep at night!

MAN (*to a sympathetic young woman*)—When I was four years old I tried to murder my nurse. My psychiatrist says my wife is taking her place.

DENBY (*to an extremely* HEALTHY-LOOKING WOMAN)—What you need, little lady, is a good rest! One month at Hot Springs for you! Golf, dancing!

HEALTHY ONE—Oh, thank you, Doctor!

DENBY—And when you come back I'll give you some shots. (*He gives her an assuring pat on the shoulder and a pinch on the cheek.*)

MRS. LANSDALE (*telling it to someone else*)—Not one wink!

CHARLIE (*to a* FAIR PATIENT)—Hot Springs for you, little lady.

FAIR PATIENT—I just came from Hot Springs.

CHARLIE—All right, then. Palm Springs! (*He gives her the same pat and pinch that his uncle gave his patient.* NED *appears in the crowd, well dressed and with his old assurance returned.*)

Joe appears, bringing a tray of cocktails and looking just as silly as he feels—but he does manage the fashionable-doctor manner. To a female insomniac he recommends Lake Louise, Canada. The party goes on, yatata yatata yatata, and the scene fades out.

Out in the foyer Emily, a neatly dressed young woman, is seated at a table with a brief case in her lap. She has been announced, and Joe, carrying a highball, leaves the party to ask her what is on her mind.

"X-ray films. Gilbert Martin's."

In a mildly rebuking tone Joe reminds Emily that he has already looked at them and has said there is nothing to worry about, but Emily won't be put off. Showing Joe the films, she says, "You were in such a hurry to leave this afternoon! Don't blame you, of course, with fifty guests here—all high-bracket patients and hospital trustees. . . . See what I mean, Doctor? Couldn't that be an ulcer crater?

Jenny comes ahunting for her husband. Mrs. Lansdale is leaving and she wants to talk to Joe. "Mrs. Brook Lansdale," she explains impressively to Emily.

"I know," says the young woman. "Twenty million dollars and she can't sleep."

Jenny bridles. "She wants to talk to my husband about donating three hundred thousand dollars toward our new private pavilion. . . . I guess that's about as important to you as anything else can be right now, isn't it, Joe?" Joe is still looking at the X-rays, but he now puts them aside for Mrs. Lansdale.

"Shall I phone Mr. Martin and tell him his stomach is fine and dandy?" asks Emily.

Joe is pretty sure he was wrong about his original diagnosis but isn't quite ready to admit it. He makes an excuse about the light in the foyer and says he wants to take another look in his office later. Jenny shoos him off to Mrs. Lansdale. "Forgive me," she says to Emily, "for taking him away from you. Social contacts play such an important part in a practice like ours."

Dryly, Emily agrees and leaves. At the street entrance of the apartment building she discovers it is raining. The doorman is whistling for a cab, but two couples are already waiting; putting up her coat collar, Emily sets out to get a cab of her own. . . .

"Taxi—taxi— (*Mumbling to herself.*) This is what I get for being a Girl Scout. Save the doc, save the patient, and get pneumonia myself— Way I feel now, I wouldn't care much. That wife of his leads him around by the nose— Well, if a man lets himself be led by the nose, that's all he rates! (*Continuing her mumbling but now to music.*)

> "The boss gets on my nerves.
> I've got a good mind to quit.
> I've taken all I can,
> It's time to get up and git,
> And move to another job—
> Or maybe another town!
> The gentleman burns me up!
> The gentleman gets me down. . . .

> "The gentleman is a dope,
> A man of many faults,
> A clumsy Joe
> Who wouldn't know
> A rhumba from a waltz.
> The gentleman is a dope,
> And not my cup of tea—
>   (Why do I get in a dither?
>   He doesn't belong to me!)"

Emily continues singing as she fruitlessly hails passing cabs.

In his private office, Dr. Bigby Denby has called Joe for an interview. "I am very pleased with you, Joseph," he begins. "Not only because of your work here at the office, but at the hospital—you—well, you have won the regard of Brook Lansdale, and the approval of our—ha! ha!—biggest trustee is even more important than *my* approval, hmm?"

Suddenly Denby switches subjects: "Charlie, my nephew—in this recent—ah—rebellion at the hospital—the nurses demanding eight-hour duty—he actually took their side! You don't think he's been drinking too much, do you?"

Joe starts to say, "As a matter of fact, Dr. Denby . . ." when
Charlie comes in and promptly pours himself a drink of his
uncle's brandy. A moment later Brook Lansdale pushes in and
Dr. Denby all but clicks his heels at attention. Gruffly and in a
hurry, Lansdale explains his visit:

"It's about the trouble we've been having with the nurses."

"But I squelched that, old boy," protests Denby. "They're
continuing on the old basis of twelve-hour duty."

Impatiently, Lansdale snaps, "I know that, but I've got the
name of the agitator who started the whole thing. . . . I want
to get rid of this woman."

"Well, naturally!" agrees the doctor. "We'll have to make
an example of her."

"Name of the woman," says Lansdale, "is Carrie Middleton."

This is a shock to Joe, Charlie—and even Dr. Denby—for
Carrie has been with the hospital for thirty years. But Denby,
the dutiful stooge, buzzes for Emily and orders her to call Nurses'
Registry and strike off the name of Carrie Middleton. He
brushes aside Emily's protest as he follows Lansdale out of the
office.

"He's only my uncle by marriage," apologizes Charlie.

JOE—I wonder if Carrie would go down and help my father
out. He's up to his neck in a flu epidemic.

CHARLIE—Good idea! But don't tell Lansdale. Mustn't be
friendly with anybody he doesn't like. My uncle *never* is. That's
why he's Physician-in-Chief at the hospital.

JOE—Well, to hell with Lansdale!

CHARLIE (*imitating his uncle's voice and manner*)—Tut, tut,
my boy! There are many things that one would like to do that
one does not. Duty— (*He strikes a chord on the piano.*)

EMILY—You must be good soldiers. (CHARLIE *strikes another chord.*)

CHARLIE—This is a big-time medical practice, Joe.

JOE (*bitterly*)—Sure! Through the portals of this office pass
the biggest screwballs in town.

CHARLIE—*And* the most repulsive. (CHARLIE, *playing his own
accompaniment, starts singing ironically.*)

> Our world is for the forceful,
> And not for sentimental folk,
> But brilliant and resourceful
> And paranoiac gentle folk!

JOE (*to* EMILY)—

> Not soft and sentimental folk!

CHARLIE—

> "Allegro," a musician
> Would so describe the speed of it,
> The clash and competition
> Of counterpoint—

EMILY—

> The need of it?

CHARLIE—

> We cannot prove the need of it!
> (*Faster and crisper.*)
> We know no other way
> Of living out a day.
> Our music must be galloping and gay!

JOE—

> We muffle all the undertones,
> The minor blood-and-thunder tones,
> The overtones are all we care to play!

ALL THREE—

> Hysterically frantic,
> We are stubbornly romantic
> And doggedly determined to be gay!

EMILY—

> Brisk, lively,
> Merry and bright!
> Allegro!
> Same tempo
> Morning and night!
> Allegro!
> Don't stop, whatever you do,
> Do something dizzy and new,
> Keep up the hullabaloo!

CHORUS (*off, alternates with* EMILY)—

> Allegro!   Allegro!
> Allegro!   Allegro!
> Allegro!   Allegro!

(*Now the singing* CHORUS *is faintly seen through a gauze curtain.* DANCERS *are also seen spinning across the stage.*)

The ironic "Allegro" chorus and dance continue with increasing tempo and sound until, as the stage direction puts it, "the stage is now left to the dancers, who in their own medium depict

the confusion and the futility that pervade the society in which
Joe practices medicine."

The next day, perhaps, Joe is in his office when Emily appears
to report on the list of waiting patients. She notices that he is
looking kind of low, and he explains:

"I just had a letter from a boy who used to be a patient of
mine. He was going to study for the priesthood at one time. It
was a sad, hopeless little letter."

"The T.B. case," Emily remembers—for Joe has told her about
most of his life.

"I guess I feel guilty about him," he explains. "I can't get
rid of the feeling that if I'd spent the last five years on one boy
like Vincent, I'd have done the world more good than I could do
in a lifetime here."

"Getting sour on rich city people?" queries Emily.

"No. . . . There's nothing wrong with people just because they
have money or live in the city—nothing wrong with being a city
doctor—but this crowd that we get!"

Joe gets back to the business in hand—patients. Emily reports that Harry Buckley is outside, on his way through from
California, and so is Mrs. Lansdale. She came in last but wants
to get in first—and she does get in first by walking in. She wants
to report on her insomnia.

"I was just dozing off about two in the morning when the
phone rang. It was my husband to say that he'd be home late.
It then occurred to me that most nights I lie awake wondering
when and if he is coming home."

Joe has begun to murmur about Lansdale working too hard
when she continues: "So I put a detective on him! It seems my
husband has got himself a girl. Here's a carbon copy of the report"—and she throws a paper on Joe's desk. "Read that little
blue paper when you get time," she advises as she leaves. "It'll
give you quite a kick."

Emily brings in the next patient, Harry Buckley. He is a
movie producer who fancies he has a low metabolism and wants
some thyroid pills. When Joe gets rid of Buckley Emily comes
in again.

JOE—Emily! Is there anyone out there with a broken arm
or a gallstone? Is there anybody out there worth a doctor's time
and knowledge? Can't you scare us up a ruptured appendix or a
pair of infected tonsils. . . . What the hell kind of a practice is
this anyhow? (*He picks up the detective's report again.*) All

we seem to attract is . . . (*His voice drops off as he becomes interested in what he's reading.* EMILY, *looking worried, speaks to him.*)

EMILY—Dr. Denby wants me to remind you that you all have to leave the office in a few minutes and go over to the dedication of the new private pavilion. They're going to unveil the bronze plaque. (JOE *frowns at what he is reading and doesn't seem to have heard her.*) Mr. Lansdale will come in his car and pick you up at—

JOE—Mr. Lansdale, you say? Why, he's the very man I'm reading about! This paper tells all about how he meets his girl and where he takes her— (*Looking up.*) And, Emily, do you know who Mr. Lansdale's girl is? (*Pause. She lowers her eyes.*)

EMILY—Yes. I do.

JOE—Does everybody know?

EMILY—They seem to.

JOE—Well, that's the way it is, I guess— (*Rising from his desk and walking away.*) Do you know what is very sad about this? The heartbreaking part of it is that I don't give a damn! (*Thoughtfully.*) I must have stopped loving her some time ago and I didn't know it—not until this minute! Somewhere in this rat race, somewhere along the line, we lost each other. But I don't know when it happened. (EMILY *sits very still and listens.*) What became of her? The dream girl of my college days! There was a time when if she danced with another boy and he held her close, there would be murder in my heart. . . . Now she's Lansdale's girl, and it means no more to me than just another cheap little setup, like so many that pass through this office every day. . . . These benzedrine romances! They have no faint resemblance to love. There's nothing real about any of it—nothing real about the whole damn place. What the hell am I doing here! What the hell am I doing!

Joe drops his head on his arms, thinking of home. He envisions his friends, his father, even his dead mother, urging him to come. Marjorie sings pleadingly,

> "Come home, come home,
> Where the brown birds fly
> Through a pale, blue sky
> To a tall green tree. . . ."

As the images pass from his mind Joe lifts his head, just as Denby and Lansdale come to pick him up. "Shall we tell him now?" asks Denby, beaming.

"Might as well," grins Lansdale. "Give him time to compose a speech on the way over."

An acceptance speech, Lansdale explains to the dazed Joe. "You're about to be made Physician-in-Chief to the hospital. You'll be the head man. We're making Bigby president of the Medical Board."

Joe is bowled over, but Emily merely utters a dry "Well, gee whillikers." Charlie has come in, and when the other three men leave he asks Emily what she's thinking about.

EMILY—Just thinking how hard it is for a man to get off a merry-go-round after it gets going fast.

CHARLIE—You couldn't expect him to turn down a plum like this. Being head man at our hospital makes a fellow one of the biggest men in medicine.

EMILY—Big politician, big social lion and banquet man—not much of a doctor. He could've been, though. When he first came here, I thought—I hoped— (*She swallows hard.*) He could've been a hell of a doctor!

CHARLIE—There's something about Joe—something so *good* about him that you want him to be even better. I can understand a girl getting stuck on a fellow like that. Wouldn't blame her.

EMILY—Thanks, pal. (*Pause.*)

CHARLIE—Want to take the day off and go to a burlesque show?

EMILY—I don't know. I think the dedication ceremony will be funnier.

CHARLIE—Okay. We'll go there.

EMILY—Can we stop on the way and have a drink?

CHARLIE—A drink? We'll get cockeyed! How else can you go to such things? (*Exeunt.*)

The ceremony is under way in the lobby of the new hospital pavilion. Lansdale, standing before a bronze plaque dedicated to Denby, is addressing a group of trustees and guests. Behind him stands a chorus of simply dressed people "representing Joe's memories, the principles he has forgotten, his roots."

Lansdale's oratorical platitudes in praise of Denby are drowned out by the chorus singing, "Broccoli Hogwash Balderdash . . . yatata yatata yatata yatata," and they continue, but softly, as

Denby begins his own speech; then they drown him out, too, with

> "The prattle and the tattle,
> The gab and the gush,
> The chatter and the patter,
> And the twaddle and the tush
> Go on and on and on and on and on!"

". . . My co-worker, my young but very talented friend," Denby is heard saying, "Joseph Taylor, Junior—the youngest man ever to receive this appointment."

Charlie and Emily come in from some fast, hard drinking in time to pretend they are clapping hands with the rest—but they aren't. The chorus warns: "Look out, Joe! Once you cross this threshold the door will close behind you."

"Don't be a fool!" counter the trustees and guests. They remind him of the fame and success that will be his.

Joe begins his speech. A complete surprise . . . Deep humility . . . So illustrious a predecessor. "He has been an ornament to medicine, an ornament to his city, an ornament—"

Joe and the entire company freeze in a still picture as the chorus speaks:

> " 'Ornament'—
> A man's brain is sometimes cleared
> By the sudden light of one word.
> In the flash of a split second
> He sees a signpost, pointing down a new road,
> And he may take a new turning
> That will affect the rest of his life.
>   (*Pause. They speak in a hushed tone.*)
> The split second is over."
>   (*The company relaxes from its frozen tableau.*)

JOE (*a different note in his voice*)—It takes a special talent to be an ornament. . . . I am not blessed with this talent!

GRANDMA (*entering and seeing* JOE, *then calling off to his mother just as she did the day he learned to walk*)—Marjorie! (MARJORIE *rushes on, stands with* GRANDMA *and listens to* JOE *"learn to walk" again.*)

CHORUS (*starting quietly but with exhortation in their voices*)—
> One foot, other foot,
> One foot, other foot—

(*They keep this up under* JOE's *speech.*)

JOE—I must therefore . . . (*With a sudden burst of courage.*)
I decline the appointment!   As a matter of fact, I have another
offer, in a smaller hospital, where my father is Physician-in-Chief.
I'll be his assistant.   I want to practice medicine again among
people I understand. . . . I'm going home.
   CHORUS (*singing to him happily*)—
              Come home, come home
              Where the brown birds fly,
              Through a pale blue sky
              To a tall green tree.
(*The* TRUSTEES, GUESTS, LANSDALE, *et al. laugh in derision at*
JOE.)
   JOE (*shouting them down*)—
              There's no finer sight
              For a man to see!
(JENNY *glares at* JOE *and goes to the shelter of* LANSDALE'S *consoling arms.*)
   CHORUS—Come home, Joe, come home!
   DENBY—You can't do this!   What'll I tell the papers?
   LANSDALE—Tell the papers he's sick!
   JOE—Tell them I'm just getting well!   (*He starts to go.*)
   CHORUS (*singing ecstatically, triumphantly*)—
              Now you can do whatever you want,
              Whatever you want to do—
   EMILY (*shouting to* JOE)—Dr. Taylor!   Can you use a nurse
back there?   (JOE *turns and holds out his hand to welcome her.
She joins him.*)
   CHORUS—
              Here you are in a wonderful world
              Especially made for you!
   CHARLIE—Hey!   What about me?
   DENBY—Charlie!
   JOE (*to* CHARLIE)—Come on!   (CHARLIE *staggers forward.*)
   EMILY (*as she supports* CHARLIE *and helps him walk steadily*)—
              One foot, other foot,
              One foot, other foot—
   ALL (*with increasing volume and spirit*)—
              One foot, other foot,
              One foot, other foot,
              Now you can do whatever you want,
              Whatever you want to do—

One foot out and the other foot out,
One foot out and the other foot out,
One foot out and the other foot out—
And the world belongs to you!

(JOE *walks away, out into the sunlight.* EMILY *and* CHARLIE *follow.*)

THE CURTAIN FALLS

EASTWARD IN EDEN

A Play in Three Acts

By Dorothy Gardner

BEING a woman, and yet an impassioned singer of love songs, the poet Emily Dickinson has long had some of her greatest champions among women readers. And, as an odd figure about whom not too much is known, Miss Dickinson has been a challenge to the researcher and the speculative romanticist alike.

In the script of "Eastward in Eden," Mrs. Gardner states the case for her drama as follows:

"There have been two plays on Emily Dickinson's love story, one which concerned itself with the problem of giving her poems to the world after her death, in which she never appeared; the other based on the assumption that Helen Jackson's husband was the lover to whom she wrote. Later evidence has revealed the identity of the man she loved as a minister, Dr. Charles Wadsworth of Philadelphia, whom she met while visiting friends.

"The known facts involved are few and yet in themselves highly dramatic, consisting of the meeting in Philadelphia, two calls at her home in Amherst, frequent letters and, after a parting in 1861, a last call twenty years later, which Dr. Wadsworth made a short time before his death.

"The internal evidence of the love poems gives many clues. Most of them were written during the twenty years she did not see Wadsworth, when she became a recluse. Prof. George Frisbie Whicher of Amherst says, in 'This Was a Poet': 'Emily Dickinson was the only American poet of her century who treated the great lyric theme of love with entire candor and sincerity. . . . [These poems] record with minute veracity the subtle changes in a woman's nature as she becomes conscious of her heart's unalterable commitment, passes through self-sustained illusion and painful disillusion to an agony of frustration, and emerges . . . on a new plane of being. . . .'

"The love story itself has seemed to me the strongest and most dramatic one I know of. I have used the known facts imaginatively, combined with revelation in the poems themselves, employing fantasy for Act II, Scene III, which is based on internal evidence of the love poetry.

"In the dialogue, Emily speaks for herself in paraphrasings of her poems and letters. I have tried to make it a portrait of her vivid and fascinating personality, which was original, dynamic, rebellious and truth-seeking."

It is 9:30 in an evening of September, 1852, in the parlor of Edward Dickinson's home in Amherst, Massachusetts. The room indicates Whig elegance in white woodwork and paneling that comes halfway up the wall; the furnishings are mahogany heirlooms. In the middle of the rear wall are double doors revealing a dim hall and a mahogany-railed white stair leading to rooms above. In the left corner of the room, near the rear, is a square piano with candelabra at each end. In the middle of the left wall is a window. On this side of the window is a white marble fireplace, with a chair, small table and stool near it. The right wall is broken by a shallow bay window, curtained full length with shadow lace against the glass. The window can be closed off by golden brown drapes. On either side of the window are a small table and a small secretary. Armchairs, straight chairs, a small pendulum clock and prism candelabra further decorate the room.

Now the parlor is lighted by candles, and from somewhere else in the house comes the sound of somebody giving a stilted rendition of a piano recital piece. Austin Dickinson, slim, tall, dark-haired and 23, has been lighting the candles. One of his sisters, Lavinia, a dignified girl of 19, comes in and urges him to hurry. She is wearing a tight-bodiced, full-skirted, pale blue party dress.

"What's the hurry?" asks Austin.

"When Eliza stops playing the next piece it's the signal!"

"For dancing?"

"No, for refreshments."

The girl supervises the illumination and her brother amusedly mocks her: "Light the ones on the mantel, Austin. Then light the ones in the summerhouse, Austin." Lavinia informs him that Ben and Emily are taking care of the summerhouse lights. Looking out the bay window, she exclaims: "She planned it for the full harvest moon—and look! Not a cloud in the sky!"

Austin has another viewpoint. "She planned it for Mother's and Father's being away," he declares.

Lavinia takes a hooked rug off the hearth, hides it in a corner. "Do *you* dance at the parties in Cambridge?" she asks Austin. He won't tell. Again she urges him to hurry, and he assures her,

"Everything's all right, Vinnie. With you for a chaperone, everything's all right."

The girl bridles at the word "chaperone" and her brother continues, "You act like an old maid of 25."

Maggie, the Dickinsons' fortyish maid, comes in to inform Lavinia that the ice cream is out of the freezer. She has been told by Emily to wait for the signal for refreshments, but she can't remember what the signal is to be. Lavinia reminds her that it is when the music stops.

"Signals and lanterns in the yard and young people running around in the dark with no chaperone!" snorts Maggie. But she admits it is the most fun she ever had, or, at least, the worst thing she ever did. She decides she will put the ice cream back in the freezer and await the signal.

Lavinia speculates on how her father would act if he should walk in on *this*. "Emily says Father's heart is pure and terrible. I suppose you'll settle down to a law office and be just like him."

This, her brother denies. "No Amherst for me. I'm tired of this old-fogy town run by the college, with no theatres, no card playing, no dancing." Austin is not going to marry, he announces, or build a house next door and be treasurer of the college when his father retires, as Emily has planned. And Emily has even planned the wife for him—Sue Gilbert, who has been purposefully invited tonight. No, indeed; Austin is going West.

As for matchmaking, Austin has tried a bit of his own. He has invited Gerry Hood, so his sisters won't be old maids, and Lavinia thinks Gerry likes Emily.

"They all do," agrees Austin. "Why doesn't she like one of them? What's the matter with this Ben Newton?"

Nothing, apparently. Ben brings Emily books, which he hides in the bushes so Mr. Dickinson won't see them, and he and Emily talk for hours. . . .

The music stops, and with Austin in tow, Lavinia goes to announce to the guests that refreshments are being served in the garden and the parlor. Laughing and chattering young pepole flock into the parlor, dressed in colorful party clothes—poised and beautiful young girls and gallant young men. Among them are Susan Gilbert, Lucy Plum, Helen Fiske, Gerald Hood and Ben Newton. Ben is a tall, smart-looking man of 30.

Helen Fiske is saying that she is going to Europe—to spend the Winter in Rome and write a novel. Austin and Lavinia begin passing trays of ice cream and cake. Helen says Gerry was wonderful at charades; Lucy expresses pleasure at seeing Mr. Newton at a social, and hints that she is just longing to go to the Fair.

"I plan to go to the Fair," says Ben deliberately. . . . "I plan to take Miss Dickinson."

"That's what you get for joining the church!" mourns Gerry. "Emily didn't and she gets the eligible bachelors." But in Lucy's eyes Emily is a heathen. "She was the only girl at Mt. Holyoke who didn't even *want* to become a Christian." Lucy begins playing "If a Body Meet a Body" on the parlor piano softly. Susan allows that it is a nice party, and Gerry agrees it is nice enough— for a party without dancing. "Don't they *ever* dance in Amherst?" he asks the room.

"Certainly not," says Lucy. "Dancing is immoral, a sin."

"Even the minuet," says Susan. "That does seem a harmless dance, doesn't it? I can see why they might think a waltz is immoral, it's so delightful." Susan can waltz, because she lives in Baltimore.

As Lucy begins to play her song more loudly, and the company sings it, Emily enters, followed by Ben, who has seen her coming through the window and has gone to accompany her. Emily is a small young woman in a pale, corn-color dress, with auburn hair parted in the middle and curled up in a round effect all over her head. Over one ear she has pinned scarlet berries.

Emily listens to the music a moment, then suddenly supplants Lucy at the piano and begins a rapid, rhythmic improvisation on "If a Body," to the surprise and pleasure of everybody. "And now," she cries, flinging up her arms, "there will be . . . dancing!" She bids the astonished Lucy to play a minuet or a waltz, and Ben, bowing, inquires, "May I have the pleasure?" The pair make a few turns, with Emily humming Lucy's song in waltz time.

"Don't ever let Father see you doing that!" warns Austin.

The ebullient Emily has still another announcement: This is a meeting of the P O M—Poetry of Motion, Amherst's secret dancing society. "We're all members except you and you and you," she says, pointing to Lucy, Austin and Gerry. "Good for Amherst!" cheers Gerry.

"Right this way, everybody!" calls Lavinia. "The rugs are up now." The company flocks back to the other room eagerly. Last to go are Austin and Susan. Susan surprises Austin by saying that she likes Amherst and would like being a leader in a small college town; of course, she would want a husband who is a leader in the community—something like Austin's father, for instance.

Music for the lancers is heard, and Emily, on the hunt for more music, shoos Susan and Austin into the other room. Ben follows her in as she goes to the parlor piano.

BEN—I know all the steps to the lancers, don't you? (*He goes to the bay window.* EMILY *crosses to window and holds back the curtain.*)

EMILY—Look at the moon with everything quiet. When people go you can hear all the important sounds— (*Listens.*) Crickets, frogs, and night moths!

BEN—You can't *hear* night moths!

EMILY (*still listening*)—I can. You can't. They don't speak to lawyers.

BEN—As a matter of fact, they do and a lot more than you think. Lawyers are not made of flint.

EMILY—They are by thirty. (*She leans against window frame and inhales deeply.* BEN *looks down at her.*) Doesn't the garden smell—exciting!

BEN (*intensely*)—*You* are exciting, Emily.

EMILY—Listen to the frogs! Doesn't that sound go straight to your heart—and take your breath?

BEN (*tenderly*)—*You* take my breath and you went straight to my heart the first time I saw you.

EMILY (*playfully*)—Tell me! (*Drifts downstage right.*)

BEN (*remaining at window*)—The first day I worked in your father's law office, you came in to see him. . . .

EMILY—To see the new law clerk from Worcester, you mean!

BEN—You were wearing the most bewitching brown bonnet.

EMILY—New! I *had* to wear it. I think I went to the office just to wear that bonnet.

BEN—When I saw you under that new bonnet, something went straight to my heart, and it wasn't frogs! You were beautiful!

EMILY—Oh, Ben, you are very sweet, but . . . (*Looks in mirror.*) I'm not . . . (*Reaches for word.*) regulation! (*Turns to* BEN.) I have a gypsy face!

BEN—You have a poet's face. (*Goes to her. Takes a small volume from his coat pocket.*) Emily, I've brought you another book. (*Gives it to her.*)

EMILY—Emerson's "Poems"— Oh, Ben!

BEN—Don't let your father see them. They're hardly what you call "lonely and rigorous literature."

EMILY (*sitting in chair downstage right*)—I can't go on reading the Bible, the Almanac and the newspaper forever. (*Turns pages.*) Are these as good as the "Essays"?

BEN—They're better. He has radical ideas about poetry, too, you know.

EMILY—Does he? What does he say?

BEN—He says, "To make a poem requires a thought so passionate and alive it has an architecture all its own." (*Slight pause.*) Your thoughts are like that—if you could capture them in your poems—

EMILY—But he's a man of affairs. All I have is Amherst—this house—and garden . . .

BEN (*taking the book from her and finding a place*)—Now, you listen to this. Mr. Emerson says, "The poorest experience is rich enough to express thought . . . a house . . . a garden, a few actions, can be used with terrible simplicity. . . ."

EMILY (*taking book*)—I like that! (*Turns pages, reading.*) "Give All to Love."

BEN—He has an intuition that goes beyond logic and finds man one with God.

This launches Emily into speculating whether or not she is a heathen because she hasn't joined the church. " 'In the name of the Father and the Son and the Holy Ghost,' " she quotes. "It means more to me to say, 'In the name of the breeze, the butterfly and the bee.' I believe in them!"

Ben himself believes in immortality—believes in it because he is not well, and when one comes close to "it" one thinks about it differently. And, to him, Emily's gift of poetry is evidence of immortality. Suddenly Ben asks Emily to marry him, points out that they are always happy together.

"Ben," says Emily, "I love you as my playmate. You've taught me so much about books and poetry. I love you as my dear friend. . . ."

They are interrupted by the sound of a voice outside—Mr. Dickinson's. He is demanding, "What's *this!* What is going on? Where is Emily?"

He strides into the room, sternly inquires of his daughter what she means by giving a dance during his absence.

"It was only a lesson in the lancers," she replies.

Her father's anger increases. Dancing is forbidden—and, furthermore, certain forbidden books have been coming into the house and he suspects Ben. "Did you bring 'Mrs. Child's Letters' from New York?" he asks. Emily explains that she had asked Ben to bring the book. "I'll speak to you later," he declares. In a rage he attacks Ben for his radical ideas and for the fact that he is a unitarian. "I can no longer welcome you to my home—or my office," he thunders.

Ben accepts the dictum quietly. He is sorry if he has offended but, anyhow, the doctor has advised a long rest, and he will return to Worcester tomorrow.

Emily pleads with him to stay in Amherst, then, to her father, declares, "I wanted to read books you forbade. I won't live locked up in this little country town. Ben is my best friend. You have been rude to him. You are unjust."

All the same, Ben leaves. "If you loved him," Dickinson asks his daughter, "why didn't you marry him and go with him?"

"I don't want to marry him."

Dickinson says he tries to be just—but what Emily needs is the grace of God. She is such a rebel. This tonight, and last week she raced the horses home from a funeral.

"Only last year," she points out, "you rang the fire alarm to get the whole town out to look at a red sunset."

He calms down. When Lavinia appears in the doorway Emily pleads with her father to allow the party to go on—to punish her and not the guests. Reluctantly he gives in. "But just games and music! No dancing!" he warns.

But this isn't enough for Emily. She wants dancing, too, and informs him that they've been meeting at the Fowlers' secretly, and dancing. She doubts if it is a sin.

"It is a trivial joy," pronounces her father. Timidly Lavinia asks if she should tell the guests to go home. "No!" explodes Dickinson. "I said you could go on—but no dancing!" Lavinia withdraws.

Gerry appears in the hall an instant, then withdraws out of sight and eavesdrops as Emily and her father continue their argument—which becomes gentler now. Girls of Emily's age, he points out, are marrying now.

She urges him to be patient, for marriage is so holy it frightens her. "Oh, Father, I've been so happy here." She puts her head on his arm and he regards her affectionately. "Join your guests," he suggests, and goes out.

Gerry steps from the shadow of the hall. "Just how do you expect to feel when you're in love?"

All Emily wants is to be struck by lightning. She wants to pour out her love to someone who is beautiful, tall, "just a little sinister, with a wild dark beauty that a superior pirate might have, the kind that would sweep you off your feet and carry you away and you couldn't resist. . . ."

Amusedly, Gerry urges her on. "And you would write poems for him."

Yes, crazy poems every day, and he would think her the only sane person living.

"You want the Garden of Eden," Gerry observes.

"Eden is here and now."

"And you're Eve?"

"I'm Eve."

"And Adam?"

As the music swells to a classical waltz, Emily begins swaying to its rhythm and murmurs, "Adam is due home.' . . ."

"To Adam!" offers Gerry, bowing, and she echoes "To Adam!" The curtain falls.

Scene II

Miss Simpson, a plain, slender woman in her thirties, is discovered in a pastor's church study in Philadelphia. The time is more than a year later—May, 1854. The study is paneled with brown wood, and its furnishings include high-backed church armchairs upholstered in red velvet. There is a flat-topped desk, and on a wall are pictures of the pastor's wife, mother and children. Miss Simpson is listening to an argument outside the door.

"Dr. Wadsworth," she hears a man saying, "the Citizens' Committee of Philadelphia does not approve of your attitude on abolition."

"You cannot expect me to change my opinion," firmly replies Dr. Wadsworth.

"The church is not the place for politics," the man counters. Vehemently, Dr. Wadsworth asserts that the church is a vital part of society and must function vitally. "Good day, gentleman!"

Miss Simpson retreats as Wadsworth enters and slams the door. He is angry at the "blind and stupid fools." He believes that if the church is not to enter into political controversies, then it has no position in society. And abolition must come, for "no man is free until *all* men are free."

Miss Simpson dutifully agrees as the pastor, pacing, continues his statement of his own position. Suddenly he sits at his desk and begins to write. Timidly Miss Simpson seeks to interrupt. "There is—"

"Not now, Miss Simpson. . . . In the future please keep to the usual number of visitors."

Miss Simpson takes another tack, observing that yesterday's sermon had made a great stir. "There was a strange young woman came to see me after the sermon and asked how she could see you. . . . I told her she would have to make an appointment —and so—she *did!*"

An appointment for this afternoon, in fact—a strange young woman with big eyes, who is visiting the Colemans.

Wadsworth informs Miss Simpson that he has a sermon to prepare and must work now without interruption. The strange young woman can come back Thursday. He resumes his work as Miss Simpson makes a nervous exit.

Dusk comes on. The Doctor ponders, motionless, then looks at a book and puts it down, walks about the room looking at the family pictures, and finally stands at the window as the church bell rings 5 o'clock. The door opens very slowly and Emily, clad in a dark green cape coat and bonnet, cautiously lets herself in. She has the look of one on holy ground. In a moment the Doctor returns to his desk and sees Emily as he is about to take his chair. She regards him with such a look of joy and wonder that he is compelled to silence.

"I heard your sermon," she says softly. "I *had* to see you!" When Miss Simpson told her to go away she did go away—but came back.

"Are you in trouble?" asks Wadsworth.

"No . . . I am in great joy."

"How may I help you?"

"I am not sure you can."

Wadsworth takes Emily's coat and suggests that at least he can try to help her. She tells him she is from Amherst; tells him of the sunsets there, which are beautiful and a little sad—sometimes they hurt.

This sunset this afternoon was hurting him, Wadsworth admits. He had a sermon to write and it wouldn't come. Quietly and skillfully, Emily gets him to talking about himself, his work and his philosophy. He does not believe in the "divine calling" of the ministry, but rather in the divine fulfillment of a man's purpose—and every man has a purpose.

"What is a minister's purpose?" she asks.

"A little like a surgeon's. To probe the body of mankind and discover where it hurts and why. . . ." To him, happiness is the best religion; to the Puritan-bred Emily this sounds wicked. "Where I come from," she explains, "they believe that denial is essential to salvation by way of discipline. If you haven't a cross to bear you must go out and find one as Jesus did."

"Jesus didn't seek a cross," observes the Doctor. "It was thrust upon Him." Emily listens with wonder as he explains that it is easy enough to join a church, but a hard thing to become a devoted child of God. "It is a race—a battle—a taking of heaven by violence!"

Now Emily wants to know of immortality. She had a dear friend, Ben Newton, who died. He had brought her books opening new worlds to her. He was interested in her poetry. Ben did not condemn her for her unwillingness to renounce the world or for her belief that the world is beautiful. Ben had faith in a life after death, and now he is dead. "Where is he? I am quite lost. Can you help me?"

In reply to questions, Emily admits she does not believe in God—or at least can't bring herself to merge with anything, even God. She doesn't pray in the ordinary sense, for she thinks people on their knees, with their eyes rolled to heaven, asking for something, must look ridiculous to God.

"I keep the Sabbath in my own way," she continues in an outpouring of self. "At home, in the orchard, with God for a preacher"—and she looks at him impishly. "You wear a surplice but I wear wings, and my creed is that instead of getting to heaven *at last,* I'm going all along! Am I wicked?"

He studies her intently, then answers, "No, that is part of my creed too."

Now he is intensely curious about this strange young woman. Dickinson—Emily Dickinson, she gives her name. About Ben, he asks, did he want to marry her, and did she him?

EMILY—Yes.

WADSWORTH—And you refused him?

EMILY—Yes.

WADSWORTH—And your conscience troubles you?

EMILY—In a way . . . but it's more that I feel he . . . is lost.

WADSWORTH—Have you ever loved—another—enough to marry him?

EMILY—No.

WADSWORTH—But many love you?

EMILY—Yes.

WADSWORTH—What has kept you from loving them—one of them—?

EMILY—Ben used to say that I want too much, that the man I want does not exist.

WADSWORTH—What kind of man do you want?

EMILY (*looks at him helplessly for a moment, turns away as though searching for expression of something difficult to say, then suddenly speaks to him very directly and deliberately as though it were safe to reveal her inmost soul*)—Sometimes, when I am working in my garden, when the day is hot and still, I am transported to another world. The hum of bees seems like singing wires from Eternity. It is as though a message were trying to come through and I know what it means but I can't hear the words. . . . Always I have listened for something to come out of the void . . . like thunder! I want the gates to roll back and show me all *meaning*. . . . It isn't so much a person that I want as . . . a . . . state of *Being* . . . the ecstasy of being understood. . . . I like to think my garden is Eden, but I know it is only *evidence* of Eden. It is as though my garden said: Here it is, now go and find out. . . . Well, at least I learned how love should feel. . . . Love should be—(*Rapturously and passionately*)—Love should be all Being, every flower, all color, all sound, all earth and sky, all life (*Pause*), and Death. When I give myself, it will be like that, all of me . . . forever.

WADSWORTH (*rising and going to her, leans down and takes her hand, covering it with one of his with a paternal gesture, but obviously impressed*)—Such love makes the average idea of religion seem a little small. I wouldn't worry about your Ben. You say he desired immortality. Then he *is* immortal. The fact is father to the wish, and is a magnet.

EMILY (*slowly analyzing his meaning*)—You mean the thing we wish for already exists and is drawing us toward it by our own longing?

WADSWORTH—Always. You have described perfectly the hunger of the soul imprisoned in this world. (*He looks at her understandingly and drops her hand.*) I understand how you feel. It is the not finding that makes great loneliness.

Wadsworth rises, studies the pictures of his family, and explains who they are to Emily. His life, she thinks, must be very rich—yet he can understand the loneliness of another. "You do in a sermon what I would like to do in a poem. You . . . you fumble at the spirit like a musician! Then you rap with faint hammer blows, and then . . . then after the breath has time to straighten, you deal a thunderbolt that scalps the naked soul!" Again her face is radiant, as it was when she came in.

Softly Wadsworth says, "I used to write poetry when I was a boy."

"Did you? I might have known." She smiles.

He asks her to send him some of her verse. "I would love to," she agrees. "May I write to you?"

"Please do, and I will always answer."

She wrenches herself away and he helps her into her coat. "Miss Dickinson," he suggests, "I have a friend in Northampton. I have been intending to visit him for a long time. Amherst isn't far from Northampton, is it?"

"An hour's ride by stage."

"May I call on you?"

"I will show you my garden. Let me know—so I may antici- pate!"

As she bids him a soft good-by at the door,
The curtain falls.

ACT II

It is a Summer afternoon several years later. Sunlight floods the bay window of the Dickinson parlor. Emily, wearing a simple orchid dimity, surveys the room happily, dashes to the hall for a basket of flowers, starts to put the flowers on a table, and pauses to regard herself in a mirror. She seems not exactly pleased with herself as she arranges a curl for better effect. Then she resumes her flower arranging, studies the room once more, ad- justs a chair or moves a vase here and there. Finally, going to the chair by the hearth, she makes a "be seated" gesture toward it and studies the imagined occupant with adoration.

Maggie interrupts her dream by bringing in a pitcher of lemon- ade and two glasses. "When shall I bring in the sandwiches and cookies?" she asks.

"Soon after he arrives. He'll be hungry from the ride."

Gerry Hood appears in formal Summer afternoon attire. "You can't come in!" objects Emily. "I'm expecting a caller."

But Gerry has come to take her to the Faculty tea; her family all are there now. "I'm not going," she announces, "and you must leave . . . at once!"

To Emily's distress, Gerry tantalizingly occupies the hearth chair and inquires if he has a rival. If he does, he is going to stay right here. The rival couldn't live in Amherst, or he'd be at the tea. Unless it is a professor playing hooky. Or a lawyer. Or Judge Simms. Emily divulges no information.

"A doctor?" he queries, and notes Emily's start. He must

be getting warm. "It's a minister!" he guesses. "What a minister's wife you'd be," he laughs.

Ignoring her repeated pleas for him to leave, he asks, "When are you going to marry me, Emily? I can have my own office in Boston. I'm only teaching to be near you. I'll give you a lovely home where you can meet famous poets and write all day. When . . . Emily?" As she bows her head he says, tenderly teasing, "You're an old maid, you know."

He continues, "Your father doesn't want you to be an old maid. If you marry, then Vinnie may marry too." He pictures a marriageless future—Emily and Vinnie two doddering little ghosts living alone in this big house.

"When . . . Emily?" he repeats.

"Never!" She stands as tall as she can.

When the doorbell rings Emily tries to rush past Gerry, but he blocks her, and Maggie answers it. "Is it a minister sitting in that chair?" he asks, indicating the one he was in. She nods.

"Well, if that's all, I'll go." Gerry passes Dr. Wadsworth in the doorway with an "Excuse me, sir."

Wadsworth is wearing a black suit and carrying a brief case, a rolled package and a light Summer hat. With a cry of "Welcome to Amherst" Emily greets him. He takes her hands, regarding her intently and remarking, "I haven't seen you with your bonnet off."

Emily has looked forward so long to this call, and he has planned it so many times, and now finally he is here. He had rather imagined that Emily's home would be a cottage and not a mansion like this. And he likes this part of the country too; the years rolled away from him as he came into Amherst, as though he were coming home.

"It's rather strange seeing you again," he tells her. "Your letters have created their own image. I feel as though I know you better than I do." He looks about the room—at the portrait of Emily's grandfather, Samuel Dickinson, who was a deacon in the First Church; at the portrait of her father. "Isn't he terrifying?" she asks. "I adore him and he never really scolds me, but when I displease him he takes his hat and cane and leaves the house. Then I am terrified."

Laughingly, she relates, "When he proposed to Mother, he said, 'Will you join me in a life of rational happiness rather than a life of pleasure?'"

He is all questions about her home and her life in it. Touching the blotter on the desk he asks, "Is this where you write your letters to me?"

"Yes—when they have all gone to bed."

There have been many, many letters. And, by way of reply from him, many, many sermons he has written. His sermons, he thinks, seem to be very long letters to Emily. In fact, he has brought her the last page of a new one now to see if she approves of it.

"I have never read so many sermons!" exclaims the happy Emily.

"I've never had so much criticism!"

"I was afraid you might be angry," she apologizes.

"For giving me in a few words," he asks, "what I had been striving through a whole sermon to say?"

Often, he tells her, she has said what he has been trying to say in a single sentence, and then he has had to expand it a little "just to make it suitable." She cannot understand why brevity shouldn't be suitable in church; this is, in fact, why she doesn't go to church.

Emily runs to the desk cupboard and brings out a paper. "You read mine while I read yours," she proposes. Hers is a poem. They read quietly, undisturbed by Maggie's bringing in a couple of plates to put by the lemonade tray.

Suddenly breaking into laughter, Emily exclaims, "Isn't that ridiculous!"

What is "ridiculous" is a mystifying coincidence. She reads from his sermon: "The value of a gem is not in its composition but in its crystallization. Even the diamond is composed mainly of carbon and differs from the black coal of our furnaces only in this mysterious transfiguration."

And he, in turn, reads her poem:

"As carbon in the coal
And carbon in the gem
Are one and yet the former
Were dull for diadem."

They look wonderingly at each other.

"I didn't get it from you this time!" he marvels.

"And I didn't get it from you—"

Emily pours more lemonade and brings Wadsworth a glass and a sandwich plate. She still is impressed by the same idea having reached out to both of them at the same time—but now it is wonderful to be talking to him, for presence is a miracle. She wishes she had a picture of him.

He has brought her one in his paper package. She leaps to get it from where he has laid it on a chair and, when it is unwrapped, studies it, enraptured. "Doctor—Charles—Wadsworth," she muses.

"I'm just Charles Wadsworth and you must stop calling me 'Doctor,'" he objects. "You are my dear friend Emily and I feel as though I had known you always."

In reply she says, almost in a whisper, "You are my dearest friend." Rising and drawing him up by the hand, she announces, "And now—I'm going to show you my garden. Get your hat."

She puts on her own broad leghorn hat, tying the ribbons under her chin. Then she dashes to the cookie plate, wrapping some in a napkin and giving them to him for his pocket; finally she takes a slim volume from the bookcase.

"Shakespeare's sonnets," she informs him. "You must read to me." He holds open his other pocket and she slips the book in. Looking down at her, he quotes, " 'Shall I compare thee to a Summer's day—? Thou art more lovely—' "

There is an instant's flash between them. "I have my own first line for a poem," she says, taking his arm and looking up with rapture. " 'There came a day at Summer's full—entirely for me—' "

They depart for the garden, laughing happily.

The curtain falls.

Scene II

It is another afternoon in the Dickinson parlor—the following year, in December. The decorations now are small vases of evergreen and Winter berries and flowers. The fire is lighted, and so is the lamp on the desk. Mr. Dickinson, wearing an overcoat, is in an armchair reading a newspaper. When the clock strikes 5 he compares its time with his watch, then sets the clock ahead five minutes. He calls out, "Emily! Lavinia!"

From upstairs they call that they are coming. When Emily appears her father urges her to put on her coat. They are late.

"I'm not going," she says quietly. Lavinia comes downstairs, already clad in a fur-caped coat and fur-trimmed bonnet.

Dickinson urges Lavinia to talk to Emily, and he strides angrily out ahead of his daughters.

"Why aren't you going?" Lavinia asks her sister. "What explanation shall I give Sue?"

"The truth. Tell them that I have an unexpected caller. . . .

He says he has something important to tell me—something he doesn't want to write."

Lavinia has observed that Emily has a bag packed in her room. Emily has thought she might take a trip; December is depressing and she is restless.

"You wouldn't run away with him, would you?" asks Lavinia.

"I might."

"And disgrace us— You don't love us any more."

Flinging her arms wide, Emily exclaims, "I love you all! Can't you see I'm full of love? That's all I do—love everything until I'm ready to burst!"

Lavinia believes that Emily is stark, raving mad, for she knows that Emily knows "he" is a married man. "Has he asked you to go away with him?" she inquires.

"No."

Lavinia is bursting with woeful speculation about how they would live and the possibility of his work being destroyed, but Emily hasn't the patience to listen. Emily wearily gets rid of Lavinia by assuring her that Charles has never said he loves her— and that she will never let him know how she feels unless he does.

Soon after Lavinia's departure, Dr. Wadsworth arrives wearing a dark overcoat with a fur collar and carrying a large black hat. She takes his things, invites him to sit in "his" chair by the fire.

"You look like an angel. Your hair is a halo," he admires.

"I'm a very earthly creature, *but* I'm happy enough at this moment to *be* an angel." She holds out her hands and he takes them.

Her happiness is not to last long. Most obviously Charles has something on his mind. He cannot stay for dinner, for the driver is returning for him shortly. Now he begins, leaning back in his chair and looking at her searchingly:

"Emily, I think about you a great deal. You should have a home of your own."

EMILY—I have this house.

WADSWORTH—A home of your own—and children.

EMILY—Austin will have children.

WADSWORTH—I should like to think you were protected.

EMILY—Charles—you frighten me!

WADSWORTH—I am only concerned about your life.

EMILY—In a way, I have no life. I keep waiting—as though I hadn't been really born.

WADSWORTH—You have your poetry. . . .

EMILY—Living is the first art!   Poets only light the lamps.   If the light is vital—it goes on burning—like the sun's.

WADSWORTH (*taking her hands*)—You give a light so vital that it draws one toward it.

EMILY—I only reflect the sun.   (*Regards him adoringly.*)

WADSWORTH (*rising and going to desk*)—I am no sun, dear child.   (*Sighs.*)

EMILY (*low-voiced*)—Every night I light that lamp.   I think of the lamp in your study.   I see you working on a sermon.   I light your lamp.   (WADSWORTH *goes to bay window and looks out.*)   Every night I look up at the stars and think you can see the same stars.

WADSWORTH (*half turning, speaking with difficult directness*) —Emily, I am going away.

EMILY (*stunned*)—Away?

WADSWORTH—To California.

EMILY—A church?   (WADSWORTH *nods.   A long pause.*)   Is that why you came to see me—to say that you are going away?

WADSWORTH—Yes . . .

EMILY—This is good-by?

WADSWORTH—Yes.

EMILY (*increasing desperation*)—Well, I can write you—

WADSWORTH (*sternly*)—Don't look like that!   (*Takes a few steps away from her, turns and lashes out.*)   I must put distance between us—and time—and silence—I must!   (*They stare at each other.*)   I have no right.   I am a minister—and a father. Religion—isn't a sentiment.   It is a life.   Salvation is a battle. I must fight—struggle—agonize!   You can't know the pain.

EMILY (*tightly*)—You are bigger than I.   Perhaps I can't hurt as much as you.

WADSWORTH—We must have faith.

EMILY—You serve God!   I can't!

WADSWORTH (*turning to her*)—You must be free to fulfill your own life.   There is power in you.   Power and flame.

EMILY—I'm nobody!

WADSWORTH—There isn't anything you can't do—if you try. There isn't anything you can't have if you want it enough.

EMILY (*with quiet deliberation*)—You are all I ever wanted, Charles.   I wanted you before I met you.   I will always want you.   There will never be anyone but you.

WADSWORTH (*stepping toward her*)—There is a fire in me almost beyond control.   (*The clock strikes once for the half hour. They exchange looks of pained rapture.   Sleigh bells fade in to loud.* EMILY *slowly walks left past* WADSWORTH *to chair and takes his wraps.*)

EMILY (*in a dead voice*)—They've come to take you away. (*She stands facing door.* WADSWORTH *remains center a moment —struggling—goes to her and takes wraps, looks at her. She does not look at him. After a pause—he goes slowly to the door —opens it suddenly—exits—closes door.* EMILY *goes to door, presses against it—turns—dazed—goes downstage left—as though lost—sees hearth chair—goes toward it slowly—and sinks into it—prostrated.*)

The curtain falls.

SCENE III

Outside the house the sound of sleigh bells fades into distance. It is 11 o'clock at night, three days after Charles's departure. The window curtains are tightly drawn, and Emily is writing at her desk. She wears a simple dress. In a moment she moves lifelessly to the bookcase, runs her fingers along the titles, drops her arm listlessly, goes to the piano and strikes a chord, then puts a shawl over her shoulders and holds her hands over a small chunk stove which is burning before the fireplace.

Lavinia, coming in, is surprised to see her sister, inquires how she feels.

"Oh, I don't know," Emily answers.

It is nearly zero outside. Mr. Dickinson, who has been working late, should be coming home from the office about now. Hasn't Emily anything to say to Lavinia? After all, she hasn't been near anybody for three days.

"I tried to write," falters Emily.

Dickinson comes home, stamping his feet outside first. Lavinia takes his wraps. Taking a wrapped book from the bookcase, he gives it to Emily, saying, "I—I got you this book for your birthday. I heard you say you wanted it. I can't recommend this George Sand. I advise you not to read it. It'll joggle your mind. . . ."

He is desperately trying to help Emily. He suggests that, perhaps, she would like to take a trip to Cambridge—but Emily merely shakes her head.

There is the sound of a sleigh approaching and stopping. Sue, Austin and Gerry come in, and all stop at the sight of Emily. After a pause, Sue offers, "Happy birthday, Emily! I'm so glad you're downstairs again. We missed you."

Nothing can arouse Emily—not even the discussion of a reception to Mr. Emerson at which Sue was a hostess, nor a spirited argument between Austin and his father over morality and the way to prepare a law case.

To Dickinson, undeviating concentration is the way to succeed; to his son, it is something more—the principle of justice behind it. Austin quotes Emerson: " 'Pretense may sit still—but cannot act. Pretense never wrote an Iliad—nor Christianized the world—nor abolished slavery—' "

The word "slavery" prompts Dickinson to the dark prediction that the country will be at war, with guns dividing it from New England to California. Angrily, Austin counters, "If there were more Emersons and more men to listen we could free ourselves as well as slaves—and avoid wars!" Snapping a "Come on, Sue," to his wife, he departs angrily.

Emily and Gerry also leave the room and, alone with Lavinia, Dickinson voices his concern over his other daughter and his puzzlement at what has been going on. But Lavinia knows no more than he does; Emily avoids everyone, never going out except for a walk around the grounds at sunset.

"Well," explodes Dickinson, "I won't have it! I won't have her wasting away! Going around like a ghost! The light burns till dawn in her room. I've been watching it. Why?"

"Father, I don't know any more about it than you do! Maybe she's writing."

"People will think she's mad," continues Dickinson. "Watch her tonight. If there's a light in her room, let me know."

Agreeing to do so, Lavinia says good night. Dickinson puts a chunk of wood in the stove, adjusts the draft, puts out the desk lamp, chains the front door and goes upstairs. The upper hall light goes out. After a moment of darkness Emily comes down in a flowing white gown carrying a candle. She is quickly followed by her sister.

"That's the party dress you never wore!" exclaims Lavinia.

"It's my birthday."

"Is this your idea of a birthday party?"

Emily pleads with her sister not to scold. "I'm trying to reach a place of safety," she explains. She doesn't want to see people because they interfere. She begs for Lavinia's patience, but her sister announces she is going to get their father.

"Don't go, Vinnie," pleads Emily. "I've been struck by lightning—struck dumb—and I am hiding. I'm afraid of midnight—

of the dark—" She breaks into sobs and embraces her sister. "Oh, Vinnie, if only he were coming—next month—next year— ten years—!"

Lavinia is profoundly affected. "Vinnie understands," she assures Emily, "and will never leave you. . . . If you want to stay down here and write, no one can see a light with the curtains tightly drawn."

"It helps the pain to tell it," says Emily.

Lavinia quietly leaves her sister. Emily writes a moment, takes up a candle and reads what she has written; then, with the candle, she goes to the mirror and looks at herself. She lifts her arms as though to someone, stops at the chair before the fireplace, sits on the stool before it and then falls prostrate on the chair as the lights fade and the diminishing sound of sleigh bells is heard.

The lights come up—blue lights—in a cottage in Eternity. It is, somehow, like the Dickinson parlor, but sheer white drapes have replaced the brown ones and there is a flood of white light in the bay window. Emily lifts her head, looking toward the bay window, and Charles Wadsworth, looking younger and handsomer in a gray suit, comes through the window. He is reading a book—an invisible book, for the scene is played with invisible props—and Emily watches him radiantly.

Wadsworth begins to write at the desk and Emily begins the pantomime of housewifery—tying on an apron, shaking a rug out the door, brushing the walls with a broom, filling a teakettle and putting it on a stove.

It is an idyllic time, this time with Charles and Emily—a time of writing, and reading, and happiness, and the ordinary affairs of having tea and doing the dishes. Wadsworth reads something he has been writing, and Emily, kneeling by the table, listens.

"In the beginning God created the heaven and the earth. . . . And darkness was upon the face of the deep. And the Spirit of God moved upon the face of the waters. And God said, Let there be light: and there was light."

"How do you know?" asks Emily.

"Because now I am free!" exclaims Charles. He goes on. . . .

"So God created man in his own image . . . male and female created he them. . . ."

She regards him with awe.

"And God planted a garden eastward in Eden, and there he

put the man and caused a deep sleep to fall upon him, and he took one of his ribs and made a woman and brought her to the man. . . ."

"Where are we, Charles?" asks Emily. "Is it a dream?"

"No, it's very real."

"It was snowing in Amherst last night and here there are whole continents of Summer, strange bright flowers and birds. . . ."

He holds her face and kisses her very tenderly; and now it becomes night, with stars shining.

"Charles," she asks, "what month is it? And what time is it? We have no clocks."

"It's now," he replies simply.

After they have had their supper and done the dishes they waltz for a moment as Emily sings "If a Body." Happily she exclaims, "I always knew dancing was no sin!"

"You are beautiful in that white dress," declares Charles.

"I shall always wear white—because I am a wife now!" she answers. "Oh, Charles, I love our house. It's *my* house and I want to live here forever!"

And now, she announces, she will sew and he will read aloud. He looks over some books—Shakespeare—and Browning—and Keats. And here is one he never heard of. There is no author's name, but it is called "My Letters to the World." He will read from this one.

> " 'Forever is composed of nows. . . .
>   'Tis not a different time. . . .'

"Strange," he muses, "I wonder who wrote that?" Leafing through, he observes, "They seem to be love poems."

> " 'Forever at his side to walk
>   The smaller of the two,
>   Brain of his brain, blood of his blood,
>   Two lives, one Being, now.'

"Do you like that?"

Emily nods.

And another one:

> " 'And then he bore me high
>   Before this mortal noise,
>   With swiftness as of chariots
>   And distance as of wheels.' "

For a moment he looks at her intently, then resumes:

> " 'Wild nights!   Wild nights!
> Were I with thee,
> Wild nights should be
> Our luxury!' "

Without looking up from her sewing Emily continues the poem:

> " 'Rowing in Eden!
> Ah! the sea!
> Might I but moor
> Tonight in thee!' "

She flings herself against his breast. "You wrote—this—Letter to the World," he realizes, and softly she replies, "You are my world!"

Again she declares she likes their house.

WADSWORTH—It isn't our house—yet. The price is high.

EMILY—Haven't you paid for it?

WADSWORTH—The price is high. . . .

EMILY—Can't you afford it?

WADSWORTH—How much is it worth to you?

EMILY—My life!

WADSWORTH—Is it worth waiting for?

EMILY—Must we wait?   How long?

WADSWORTH—Until we can pay the price . . . which is two lives . . . yours and mine. (EMILY *rises and looks at him, goes to windows and looks out.* WADSWORTH *follows her.*)

EMILY (*alarmed*)—Where are we, Charles?

WADSWORTH—In Eternity.

EMILY (*desperately*)—But *where* is Eternity?

WADSWORTH (*exaltedly*)—Where the Word is God—

EMILY—Is God!

WADSWORTH—Where everything exists and is good. Where Man was created in the image of God. . . .

EMILY (*with awe*)—The image of God!

WADSWORTH (*going to her*)—Male and female created he them. Two halves of one whole. That is why you searched for me. That is why you found me. That is why we can never lose each other.

EMILY (*leaning against his breast*)—But I am only a rib taken from your side.

WADSWORTH (*placing his arms around her*)—Woman taken out of man. One flesh.

EMILY—Where you are, that is home. (*The light fades out. In blackout,* LAVINIA's *voice immediately calls, "Emily! Emily!" Sound of door closing. Dim spot comes up on door left, showing* LAVINIA *in dressing gown.*)

LAVINIA—Emily! (*She moves right out of spot into darkness.*) It's nearly dawn! You must come to bed. Father will be down soon to fix the fire! (EMILY *moves into light area, looks around, bewildered, turns suddenly and flings herself against the doors.*)

EMILY—Let me out of here!

LAVINIA (*from darkness*)—Where would you go?

EMILY—Home! I want my home! (*She slips to floor against the doors.*)

The curtain falls.

ACT III

Twenty years have passed, and it is another Summer day— Sunday afternoon, about 5:30. The Dickinson parlor, with shades half drawn, has a dark, cool quality. The curtains and upholstery have been changed now. Lavinia is eating an apple and reading a paper; Martha Dickinson, a pretty girl of sixteen, is playing Chopin on the square piano. Others present are Austin, Helen Hunt Jackson, now a popular novelist, and Thomas Wentworth Higginson, a publisher.

The elders applaud Martha for her playing, and Mr. Higginson suggests that if she keeps it up she can come to Boston and give a concert. "And," says Helen Hunt Jackson, "I'll come all the way from Colorado to hear you." Which reminds Higginson that he has come all the way from Boston to Amherst to beg a poem or a story from Mrs. Jackson, only to find her about to rush out West with nothing to give him. "How," he inquires, "is the *Atlantic Monthly* going to survive?"

Martha asks Helen to sign the name of her favorite author in Martha's autograph book; Helen acquiesces, and her publisher naturally surmises it will be her own name. But it isn't. It is Emily Dickinson's.

Martha asks Higginson, "Are you going to publish Aunt Emily's poems? I know she sent you some."

"She sends them to Mr. Higginson," Lavinia explains, "only for criticism."

"To which," adds the publisher, "she pays not the slightest attention." The Dickinson poems fascinate him, he admits, but he is afraid the public wouldn't accept them.

Helen Hunt Jackson insists that the poems are very important and should be published; she has just seen many of them and they kept her awake all last night. Emily could be famous. . . .

"I wouldn't know about such things," announces the apple-eating Lavinia. "She never shows them to me."

"Miss Lavinia," says Higginson, "I am disappointed not to see your sister." He is preparing to leave. "For eighteen years I've been urging her to come to Boston. I wish I could take her by the hand and feel she is real."

"She never leaves the grounds," Lavinia informs him.

"The gathering is breaking up. As he goes with the others, Higginson observes to Lavinia that Emily's grammar is a stumbling block. "Now, what does 'I wish I were a hay' mean?"

When all have gone except Austin, Austin calls upstairs to Emily: "Are you coming down? No one is here." While he is waiting he unconsciously repeats an earlier performance of his father's, checking the clock with his watch and setting the clock ahead five minutes. Emily catches him at it and observes, "You look the way Father did when he was going to scold me."

Austin is indeed going to scold her. She frightened him last night, looking like a ghost out there in the dark long past midnight. "Walking around the grounds—around and around for years—as though you were a prisoner—I shrink from some of the gossip your way of living has brought down on you."

Emily is unperturbed. The facts of her life are quite simple, and she always wears white because she likes white, and that's that. And as for Helen thinking she should be famous for her poems, well— "If fame belonged to me I couldn't escape her. If not, I couldn't catch her by running after her."

And another thing, pursues Austin: why doesn't she mind the doctor?

"Oh, I'm all right. It's just that my strength gathers until I could move mountains, and then it explodes."

"One day," he warns, "*you* will explode and there'll be no more *Emily*."

Martha comes back in to urge her father to come along, but hangs back when he leaves in order to have a private word with Emily. She is proud of her aunt, and tomorrow is going to walk her new friend past the house. "Will you be watching?" Emily will.

At last only the two sisters are left; the room is flooding with late sun. Eagerly Emily faces the bay window and announces, "We're going to have a red sunset—a blood-red sun poured over the hills—and then—stars—for a diadem! The first one is going to show right over there," and she points. "When they come out, one by one, I think God is lighting all the lamps in heaven."

"That's a lot of lamps," observes the practical Lavinia.

EMILY—The unknown is the largest need of the intellect—but no one thinks to thank God for it. There's no end to voyage in the mind. It's exciting—just as that sunset is going to be exciting with its burst of glory one moment and sudden plunge the next. There's more drama in a setting sun than in a rising one. You can see more clearly by a light that goes. (*Goes behind hearth chair, leans on it, looking at the sunset.*)

LAVINIA (*turning to* EMILY)—How can you feel that way? I wish I could.

EMILY (*facing front*)—Water is taught by thirst—transport by pain. Unless we know despair, how can we rise above it? We learn valor in the dark. Anguish makes us know death a little ahead of time, so we can tell others not to be afraid. I had one taste of life and it cost me exactly—an existence—but it taught me Eternity. Love is before life and after life, and when we love, earth is a part of heaven. That is what I believe—*but* without the loved one Eternity's wide pocket will be picked! I have faith but I want *proof*.

LAVINIA—How can you *prove* it?

EMILY (*going swiftly to* LAVINIA)—Sometimes I would like to toss this life away just to find out. Even to know the worst would be sweet. I have a dream and I have reality. The dream is more real. That is home and this is not. Home is where the heart is—only to get home again—no matter how late. (*Goes to window and looks up at the sky.*) The lamp is lighted. God is very punctual!

LAVINIA (*rising*)—It's nearly six o'clock and I've got things to do. (*She exits.* EMILY *turns from the window, places letter on desk. The room has darkened a little.* EMILY *lights desk lamp, adjusts the wick, studies the lamp, opens the upper cupboard of the desk and removes a sheaf of poems tied together. She studies them in the lamplight a moment, then goes to the hearth chair with them; she stands back of the chair and runs her hand along the back of it, sits in the chair and leans her cheek against the back. Then she lights the candle on the table by the chair and sits down to read. Sunset colors are beginning to flood the bay window.*)

Emily reads a moment, then, taking her shawl, goes for the garden—so that, when the bell rings, it is a greatly aged Maggie who answers the door. It is Wadsworth—gray-haired now, wearing his black minister's suit and carrying his black hat. He stands surveying the parlor as if refreshing his memory, when Emily enters slowly, staring as though at an apparition. "Are you real?" she asks in almost a whisper.

He is indeed. And he has come from Philadelphia. He returned there several years ago. He spent sixteen years in California, he explains, and then took another church in Philadelphia.

Now, he goes on, he has come directly to Amherst by train just to see Emily.

"What about your poetry?" he asks. "I've looked for it—"

"It wasn't for publication.—Have you been well, Charles?"

"No—not well."

"You always worked too hard. . . . The trip must have tired you. How long did it take you to make the journey?"

Wadsworth rises and goes to her, leaning down and taking her hand. "Twenty years!" he says.

He has come, he explains, straight from the pulpit. "Today I was preaching on immortality and faith. It flashed on me that of all the congregation, this was most pertinent to me. I stood facing death. I was alone. Suddenly I saw you in my study. I could hear you saying, 'I am lost. Can you help me?' Do you remember?"

Emily nods.

He knew that when the service was over he had to see her— for when he first met her he came alive. "And now I'm going to die. Who am I? Where am I going? To a heaven I have described a thousand times for other men? I don't know—I'm not sure."

He sits in "his" hearth chair and Emily, leaning over him, tenderly says, "Death is a gentle miracle. It's revelation!" She is smiling radiantly now. "Love is Eternity." And then, more practically, "Maggie will have supper ready."

With a gay housewifely manner, she sets about lighting candles and placing a low tray table before him, while he picks up a manuscript and begins reading—first to himself, then aloud:

" 'Forever is composed of nows:
'Tis not a different time. . . .'
Title divine is mine
The wife without the sign. . . .
Born—bridalled—shrouded
In a day. . . .
'My husband,' women say
Stroking the melody.
'Is this the way? . . .' "

Charles, turning pages, reads to himself a moment, then aloud again:

" 'Given in marriage unto Thee,
O Thou Celestial Host,
Bride of the Father and the Son,
Bride of the Holy Ghost!' "

From the kitchen, Emily returns with a tray, which she puts on the table before the staring Wadsworth. Gaily she pours the tea and exclaims, "I have so many things to tell you I don't know where to begin!"

"Begin," he urges tenderly, "at the beginning."

She smiles at him with increasing radiance, and

THE CURTAIN FALLS

SKIPPER NEXT TO GOD

A Play in Three Acts

By Jan de Hartog

BY the time the Germans invaded Holland, Jan de Hartog was known in this country as a novelist, playwright and actor. In April, 1940, there was shown a film he had made, in which he played the lead, titled "Somewhere in the Netherlands." It glorified the Dutch Navy. It was well received, and it was scheduled for an opening on May 10 in Brussels, with Leopold of the Belgians among the invited guests.

"But," recalled de Hartog a few years later in England, "there was another premiere the night of May 10 which was so upsetting that the Brussels showing had to be suspended indefinitely." Five days later the Germans were in possession of the Low Countries, and one of their little measures was to ban "Somewhere in the Netherlands" on the ground that it overexcited Netherlands nationalists' feelings.

De Hartog became general producer of all the United Netherlands film companies, but he could not produce much because the two main studios were seized by the Germans and handed over to UFA.

In the Fall of 1940 de Hartog had published a book, "Holland's Glory," a saga of Dutch ocean-going tugboats. It became a best-seller among patriots, and cigars, candies, writing paper, toothpaste and lipstick began to appear under the name of Holland's Glory. At first even the Nazis praised the work as representative of "a truly Germanic talent, hammering into the Jewish-idea-ridden minds of his compatriots the immortal message of race."

By the beginning of 1942, however, the Nazis were beginning to tire of de Hartog, who had insisted on clarifying his own position by making a lecture tour. They froze his royalties on "Holland's Glory," then ordered his family to leave their home. Tipped off that he would soon be arrested as a hostage, de Hartog went underground. In the Spring of 1943 he escaped to England and was condemned to death *in absentia* by the Germans.

The first play by de Hartog to be seen in New York was "This Time Tomorrow," produced November 3, 1947, by the Theatre

Guild. It was greeted as a confused drama involving medical research, the imminent invasion of Holland and a tubercular girl who, by all the laws of science, should have been dead quite some time. It was a quick failure.

Then, on January 4, 1948, the Experimental Theatre presented "Skipper Next to God," with John Garfield in the title role, at Maxine Elliott's Theatre. It was well received, and subsequently was moved to the Playhouse for a commercial run which was halted only when Garfield had to leave the company because of a Hollywood movie commitment. The plan had first been produced in London in 1945, with its author in the leading role.

It is a warm, bright Summer day on the South American coast in 1938. In the Captain's cabin of *The Young Nelly*, an old tramp steamer, young Dr. Richter is whistling a sailor's song as he potters among his mildewed belongings—shoes, ties, shirts—in his chest. He is taking things out and rearranging them—for he is changing from this cabin into another one. The cabin is as old-fashioned as the ship—a bunk, a settee, a washstand, a medicine cabinet, and on the wall by the door in the rear a framed photo of a woman and two children. When the door is opened, it reveals a lifeboat hanging from its davits beyond.

The Doctor stops whistling as he fishes the remnants of a tropical helmet out of his chest. Once he had been proud of it; now it is battered out of shape. He takes off his straw hat and tries on the helmet, admiring himself in the washstand mirror—but quickly removes it when he hears someone come in. It is Henky, the messroom boy, bringing a jug of hot water.

"This your brush or the Captain's?" asks the boy, holding up a shaving brush.

"Any hairs on it?"

"No."

"The Captain's," says the Doctor.

Henky wants to know whose soap is whose, and is informed that the Doctor and the Captain share the soap—an arrangement which the boy regards with disfavor. They might get beard fever and get pimples all over the face, and the only cure would be to tar their faces.

"That's a good one," laughs the Doctor. "I'll remember that for the *Lancet*."

He offers Henky the helmet and the boy tries it on; it comes down over his ears and he inquires if it isn't a scrap on the large side. The Doctor assures him he looks like a king and will have vast sex appeal when he wears it ashore.

Next the medic fishes out a pair of tropical shoes and asks, "What size are those flat feet?"

Henky steps right into the trap: "I don't know, but they fit me to a tick."

"Now I understand where my brown shoes have gone to! You dirty thief, you!" He orders the boy to bring back the brown ones, but relents enough to give him the mildewed pair he has just offered.

For some time Willemse, a lean, smiling gentleman in tropical dress, has been watching from the doorway and now he steps in to greet the Doctor. "Hullo, lady-killer. Rather unexpected, eh?"

Indeed he is. The Doctor hasn't known that Willemse's tub, the *Amsterdam,* also is lying in the harbor. "Henky," he orders, "scram and get two drinks!" Then he notices a bulge under the boy's shirt and seizes him; the lad yells "Mamma!"

"Dr. Willemse," asks Richter, "what's your diagnosis of the tumor this patient has on his chest?"

Willemse advocates an immediate operation, which Richter performs, bringing forth a bundle of neckties. He boots the protesting messboy out of the cabin with a reminder to get the drinks; then, noting that it is almost noon, returns to a flurry of packing. If he doesn't hurry he will catch hell from the Old Man.

"You weren't so badly off here, I should say," observes Dr. Willemse. "It almost looks like a captain's cabin."

And that's what it is, agrees Richter. He has been camping here for over two months.

"Really?"

"What do you expect, with one hundred and forty-six passengers aboard and only four cabins?"

Willemse can't believe the number.

"Emigrants," explains Richter.

Henky returns with the drinks just as an officer of the Military Police enters, salutes and inquires if the Captain is here. He has a message from the Commander-in-Chief. Richter replies that the Captain has gone ashore, but is due back any minute.

"I'm sorry, I can't wait," says the officer. "Then we'll have to do it without warning." After another impressive salute he disappears.

"Now what does that mean?" wonders Richter. "Could he have come to arrest someone?"

"They don't use soldiers for that over here," informs Willemse. "What's your cargo? Only these emigrants?"

"Yes."

"No contraband?"

"Not our Captain. Didn't I tell you? He's a Christian—some sort of his own. The sort Nero used to throw to the lions, I suppose. But if he had thrown our old man, he would have had the surprise of his life—and so would the lions."

"And these passengers," pursues Willemse, "they haven't got anything on their conscience?"

"Get along! Those miserable Jews?"

The men raise their glasses for a toast as a mingled sound of voices comes nearer. One is Henky's, crying, "Oh, D-Doctor! The passengers!" The other voices are protestations, lamentations and cries of terror. Richter and Willemse spring to the porthole over the bunk, and what they see makes them catch their breath. The Mate, Meyer, a fat man of fifty with a childish drunkard's face, comes looking for the Captain.

"The Captain must come!" cries Meyer. "They won't let them in! They are kicking them back. Soldiers are driving people back aboard ship!"

In the tumult a rifle shot is heard and a piercing cry which brings on a moment's terrified silence, then panic breaks loose and the three officers run out of the cabin while Henky hides behind the door.

As the panic reaches its height the Captain's whistle is heard piercingly, and from outside the Captain is heard to order, with quiet force, "Stop there!" Except for one woman wailing and a child whining the noise subsides, as the Captain continues with orders for everybody to go below down the hatches. "Everybody to his bunk until further orders."

The two doctors return hurriedly to the cabin seeking bandages and splints. "God knows there are broken legs," says Willemse.

They are joined by Captain Kuiper—a fair-haired hothead, about 30, who has the outward composure of authority. He is in his best uniform, but it is rather shabby. Richter introduces Dr. Willemse of the *Amsterdam,* and the Captain, shaking hands, advises, "Take it easy. It looks worse than it is"—and withdraws.

Willemse is amazed at the Captain's youth.

The physicians leave the cabin, and in a moment Henky pokes his head in the door, then opens it for a tiny old gentleman who carries a cane and an attaché case and wears his Panama hat as if it were a bowler. He is the Consul. Henky asks him to wait while he fetches the Captain, and the Consul waits impatiently.

When Kuiper arrives and offers a drink, the Consul begins by observing that it's an unpleasant business. "Jews, eh? How many?"

He is told, and continues, "I don't understand how they managed to get ashore at all. Weren't you informed that they wouldn't be allowed to enter?"

No, the Captain has had no telegram, no hint from the pilot. The Consul can't understand all the excitement simply at the sight of soldiers, but Kuiper dryly informs him, "Those men have memories of soldiers."

"What company do you sail for?" the Consul interrogates.

"Myself."

"You own this ship?"

"Yes."

"Ai . . . that's going to be unpleasant. . . . It's going to cost you money unless you transported these people under security."

Kuiper knows nothing about any security, and the Consul tells him he should have arranged for it for the return voyage when he accepted the passengers. "You knew beforehand that you ran a great risk of being refused entry here in South America."

This the Captain denies. After all, his passengers had their visas and their papers. "Visas in these times," declares the Consul, "are of very doubtful value."

The official chides the Captain for having started the voyage— for having allowed himself to get mixed up in this sort of slave trade, "to drag men, crazy with fear, overseas at exorbitant prices and with accommodation that doesn't meet even the most primitive needs. . . ."

Kuiper is proud and indignant. "For five years I have carried on a decent trade with this ship, and so did my father for thirty years before me. When I got the offer of one hundred and forty-six passengers for South America, I didn't ask if they were Christians or heathens." Furthermore, the accommodations aren't bad, with the forward hold for the men and the aft hold for women and children . . . and, as to prices, the Captain has charged only $94 a head, which is lower than the Royal Dutch would have charged.

After knocking at the door, a rabbi and two Jews, confused and frightened, come in, wearing clothing quite unsuitable to the climate. Kuiper tells them he is busy and to come back in half an hour. They withdraw, protesting, and one of them asks, "But,

Captain, what are we to say to them?"

When the two men are alone again, the Consul asks if the ship has been ordered to sail already.

"Not yet, no," says Kuiper.

"The military themselves must be a bit taken aback by the results of their action, so I'll try to take advantage of that to get some respite for you—but it won't be more than twenty-four hours in any case. . . . Then you'll have to sail off with your passengers at your own cost."

"All right," accepts Kuiper. "I'll sail to another port where they will be taken in."

The Captain, says the Consul, is indeed innocent. Hasn't he learned that this country was the last one on the American continent to accept refugees? Argentina, Brazil, Chile are closed; so are even the Galápagos Islands. There is nowhere to land, and the only one solution is to take them back to the country they came from.

Kuiper's gorge rises. "These men are men; that's enough for me. . . . I've got a heart that feels, and a conscience that must answer to God, and a soul that's immortal. And so have they, even if their faith is not the true one, and so have you, even if you don't trouble yourself about it."

In a burst of self-revelation the Captain tells the shore official about his own life—how for ten of his thirty years he lived without God, drinking and lying and going with women, being "such a swine that my father cursed me, until God himself gripped me by the scruff of the neck and flung me to my knees!"

"That has nothing to do with this matter, Captain."

"It has everything, sir! For five years now, by the grace of God, I have lived in peace with my conscience and the laws of the world, growing in the Faith like a tree. What good would these five years have been if I let myself be felled by the first gale. He blows at me to try my roots? I'll bend, sir, if God wills it; I'll let myself be split and splintered if God wills it; I'll have the branches ripped off my body if God wills it; but I will not take these people back."

The Consul refuses to believe that the Captain can't take the people back just because of his conscience. He is full of false notions. "You don't really believe that these men, as the sensational papers write, will be slaughtered the moment they set foot in their home country?"

The Captain doesn't know about the papers; all he knows is what he has seen and heard.

"I saw, eight weeks ago, one hundred and forty-six men come aboard my ship. Jews, driven away, that was all I knew. I had never gone in for politics, never wanted to, but I saw over my own gangway one hundred and forty-six times God's son come aboard my ship, flogged, beggared, cast out, with the crown of thorns on his head and the cross on his back. Men like you and me struck them, kicked them, flung them down—children, like the two of my own who at Christmas sing 'Silent Night, Holy Night' with tiny voices so high that the tears come pouring down your face, now sang 'Perish Judah!' And then: the eyes of those Jews, sir. . . . A man who has looked in those eyes once knows more than after reading the papers for five years. And then, as we sailed, as the Doctor dealt with the miscarriages below, as the pilot on the bridge said to me: 'Nice weather, eh?' then I knew: Never. Never, till Judgment Day, will Christendom be able to wash this crime off its hands. The Jews crucified Jesus once, but the Christians? Seven hundred thousand times over. And now you come and ask me to deny the gospel of my Saviour and to deliver these hundred and forty-six into the hands of their murderers? No, Consul. The cock will not crow for me!"

Still the Consul persists in attempting to reason with Kuiper. Suppose the passengers *were* smuggled ashore somewhere; they would just be arrested and sent back, for governments, even Christian governments, have been forced to take harsh measures.

"But public opinion?" asks the desperate skipper. "What do the people of these countries say?"

"The only people who might be interested in your unhappy cargo, Captain, and the only country in this hemisphere where public opinion might prove stronger than the law, is the United States. But unfortunately . . ."

Kuiper won't hear of any "unfortunatelys." He will take his passengers to the United States. If the coastal guard is difficult to get through, he will find some unpatrolled stretch of barren coast.

Even so, persists the Consul, eventually they'd be picked up and sent back. The only way would be to smuggle one hundred and forty-six people ashore in the full light of public opinion—not secretly—and that would be impossible.

"It's going to make no difference," declares Kuiper.

Clearly defeated, the Consul goes ashore, wishing the Captain good luck. And in the doorway he almost bumps into Chief Davelaar, who obviously has been listening. An old, short-sighted, bony man in greasy overalls, Davelaar announces to Kuiper, "I want a word with you, youngster. For thirty years I sailed with your father. I knew him as if he had been my own brother, and let me tell you this: if he were still alive now he would put you over his knee and spank you till you screamed. That's not religion, what you have been talking to that man, that's boys' rubbish."

"I thank you," says Kuiper curtly. But old Davelaar won't be brushed off. Kuiper is not going to put the ship in danger.

The Captain inquires how much coal is left and is told sixty tons—ten days' supply. "Then we take on five hundred tons today."

The chief engineer protests that this is impossible, that the ship will be lying over the mark.

"Just pump out the tanks till we have risen high enough."

DAVELAAR—All right, all right! But now listen: for all I care you may be as religious as—as the devil. But the moment you put the ship in danger, you'll have to reckon with me. Do you hear that? Then I won't rest until I've knocked you flat, my friend. Your money you can gamble away for those Jews, as far as I'm concerned, and your eternal soul and your feeling heart into the bargain, but hands off *The Young Nelly*. Your father—

KUIPER—And now that's enough! You know as much about my father as you know about the Ten Commandments, and that's mighty little. But for all your big talk, you're an old man, so I'll let you read what my father wrote in the Bible he gave me when I took over this ship. Then you'll know better.

DAVELAAR—Wrote? Don't make me laugh. He couldn't even write. First he broke three pens and then he wrote "faithful" with one "l."

KUIPER (*who has taken a Bible out of the bunk and opened it*)—Here, read this.

DAVELAAR—I can't. I haven't got my glasses with me.

KUIPER (*reading aloud*)—"For my son, Joris, as he'll be skipper next to God of *The Young Nelly*. Let nobody pull your leg, child; in this book you'll find your true course. When I'll be up yonder, I'll go on keeping guard over you. If you get the devil aboard, hoist the flag of the cross that you'll find in the drawer with the papers, and I'll be standing by your side. Never despair, even if you are black with sin, for one thing I know now: Our God is a God of mercy. Father."

DAVELAAR—Does he write God with "d"?

KUIPER—You are an old stinker. Get out!

DAVELAAR—And you are a good skipper. Stick to that! Better a good skipper than a rotten missionary. That flag of the cross . . . ha! Laugh meself sick, I could. If you knew . . ." (*There is a knock on the door.*)

Henky announces a visitor—an admiral, he thinks. Behind him appears a short, sturdy captain, named Bruinsma, in dazzling white and gold stripes. He carries his 60 years with boyish carelessness. He is the skipper of the *Amsterdam* and, having heard from Willemse of the trouble aboard *The Young Nelly*, he has come to offer help.

Kuiper is grateful, but he fears there isn't much Bruinsma can do. The *Nelly* will have to sail in twenty-four hours, with all souls.

"No greater pest than refugees," observes Bruinsma. "No need to tell me. Only three weeks ago, a shipful of these poor blighters was lying off Alexandria. The same old story. Offered themselves for sale, one dollar a head for lifelong service, only to get to shore. But buyers? They would sooner buy a leper. You're going to take them back, I reckon."

"No."

"H'm. Smuggle them ashore?"

That is Kuiper's plan. Long Island, perhaps.

"You're crazy. . . . Brazil, man, somewhere in the pampas. Nobody'll notice and you'll be rid of the mess."

"No," insists Kuiper, "I want to set these people free, not leave the murder to someone else."

Bruinsma notices the framed photo on the wall and guesses correctly that it is of Kuiper's wife and children. "If I were you, my friend," he advises, "I should have a good look at that picture before sailing off to Long Island."

Nevertheless Bruinsma offers the information that, two months hence, he will be in the neighborhood of Long Island and will look for Kuiper then.

KUIPER—I hope to be finished with it by then.

BRUINSMA—Make no mistake, you'll be just beginning. If two months from now you're still a Christian, then I, a confirmed unbeliever, would be ready to take that as proof of the existence of God.

KUIPER—You gave that proof yourself a moment ago.

BRUINSMA—I?

KUIPER—Your story about the Jews lying off Alexandria who tried to sell themselves at a dollar a head, but they would sooner buy a leper.

BRUINSMA—What has that got to do with the existence of God?

KUIPER (*looking it up in the Bible that still lies open before him*)—Deuteronomy 28, I think it's verse 68 . . . Yes, here it is. What God will do to the Jews if they don't remain true to their vow. "And the Lord shall bring thee into Egypt again with ships . . . and there ye shall be sold unto your enemies for bondmen and bondwomen, and no man shall buy you." A promise made five thousand years back, fulfilled three weeks ago. (BRUINSMA *stands a moment taken aback, then takes his glasses out of his breast pocket and reads the text over again. After there has been a knock at the door twice without either of them noticing it, the door is opened hesitatingly and* KUIPER *explodes.*) Now what's this? I told you I didn't want to be dis— (*It is the* RABBI, *small and helpless, hat in hand.*)

RABBI—The half hour is over. . . . Am I too early still . . . ?

KUIPER—It is too early in any case to say anything positive, Rabbi. The Consul has not informed me yet of the final decision of the authorities.

RABBI—But my people, Captain. What am I to tell my people? Three have tried already to take their lives. Is there then no possibility, however small, that we might be accepted?

KUIPER—No.

RABBI—Ach!

KUIPER—But you may tell your people, in my name, that I will do whatever is in my power to give them back their freedom.

RABBI—You . . . you won't take us back?

KUIPER—No. I'll sail. And God help me.

RABBI—Captain! (*Grasps his hand.*) Thank you! Thank you! Thank you! All the children of Israel . . .

KUIPER—Come, Rabbi. . . . Our God is the same. (*He goes out with* BRUINSMA.)

The curtain falls.

ACT II

Six weeks later, and *The Young Nelly* is off the American coast near Sandy Hook. The cabin is almost dark, for the portholes have been blacked out; there is the steady, soft sound of rain, and the voice of a man taking soundings, "Five small . . . five

. . . five big . . ." An oil lamp throws light on a table, and over it Kuiper and three Jews stand looking at a map.

Pointing out spots on the map with a compass, Kuiper says, "So you understand? Here we'll put you ashore, the starboard boat first, carrying the men under the command of Mate Meyer; then the port boat with the women under Mr. Fruithof, then the dinghy with the sick under the command of the bo'sun."

"So it's the same as the other times," wearily observes one Jew.

So far, yes, admits Kuiper. But it will be different as soon as they are ashore. This time, the whole group will be guided at daybreak to this spot on the map—a crowded seaside resort. "Once you manage to reach it and to alarm the whole village so that everybody runs out of his house, you are safe."

At the sound of a knock on the door Kuiper covers the lamp with his cap and the Doctor and Henky slip in and pick up some medical supplies. Kuiper now makes sure that his instructions to the Jews are clearly understood, and he bucks them up. "It's a perfect night. Black with rain. The chances of their catching us this time are one in a thousand. But everything, gentlemen, depends on your raising hell in that village the moment you get there. Shout, smash windowpanes . . ."

Mate Meyer, in dripping oilskins, hurriedly slips in. "Four fathoms at the lead, Captain. It is high time." Kuiper orders the engine stopped.

"Now, gentlemen, here we go. Rabbi . . . your papers. Let's say, third time lucky. Henky, cover the lamp."

In the dark four men leave the cabin and close the door behind them; when they have gone Henky, badly frightened, uncovers the lamp and quavers to the Doctor, "I'm scared."

"You're crazy. You haven't got to go ashore, have you?"

"No—but I have to go in that boat, and suppose they start shooting like they did the other nights?"

Outside, the Captain orders the starboard boat to let go and the port boat to stand by. Henky douses the cabin lamp and follows the Doctor out. As he stands in the doorway a siren shrieks and a dazzling white light flashes on the ship; then a gunshot cracks out. Henky takes his old refuge behind the cabin door and again cries, "Mamma!"

Outside, the wailing of many voices begins, and at three blasts on the ship's siren the engines begin to pound astern. "Up with your boat!" shouts Kuiper. "Bo'sun, rope ladder to starboard!"

Henky, fearful of dying, babbles a complete confession to the

Lord—the mate's knife, the cook's cigarette holder, Mr. Fruit-hof's hair lotion . . . a list longer than a magpie's collection all will be returned if he is spared. His fears and protestations finally are silenced after the Doctor, Mate Meyer and Davelaar, the chief engineer, hurry into the cabin and the lights are switched on.

Meyer wants to hide the map marking the landing places for the Jews before the Yankees board the ship; the Doctor takes it, crumples it and shoves it into his clothing chest. Suddenly the Doctor asks Meyer, "Give me a straight answer. Have you been beating those Jews?" The mate ignores the query by specu-lating, "If they had meant to take us into the harbor, they would have brought a pilot. . . ."

Kuiper is followed into the cabin by an American and a Dutch naval officer—the American breezy and good-natured, the Dutch-man wooden and unmoved. They are soaked with rain, and they carry brief cases.

"Hiya, gentlemen," the American greets the others in the cabin. "Everything okay since last time? . . . It's your own damn choice. I'm doing my duty, and the only part of it I like is your gin." At the hint, Kuiper orders the mate to pour a drink. Nobody else wants one.

The Dutch officer is all for getting down to business, but Kuiper wants to know what he is to do—sail or stay put. He is informed that the orders are for the visiting officers to stay aboard until daylight, so Kuiper may as well order the ship anchored. He does and orders Davelaar to cover his fires.

"Are you still hoping to put it over on us?" demands the Amer-ican.

Kuiper counters, "What about taking us into the harbor this time?"

The American makes no answer to this query, but instead amiably explains that, while there is a sympathetic attitude on the part of the U.S. authorities toward the Captain and his "unlucky bunch of Hebes," rules are rules and duty is duty. He turns the floor over to the Dutch officer, who opens his brief case and introduces himself as the representative of Her Majesty's Ambassador at Washington. "Anything you say in my presence may be used against you."

The Dutchman's language is formal and expansive—but what he means to convey is that the next shot won't be dropped short of the *Nelly*, but on it, and he is here to "neutralize the conse-quences to the Royal Netherlands Government of an eventual sinking."

Kuiper thinks this sounds like a joke, but it isn't. "Tell the United States Coast Guard, sir, in my name, that they couldn't do me a greater favor." Kuiper advises the American to go back to his commander and tell him that tomorrow Kuiper will make a fresh try. "And ask him to shoot. But ask him to do me the favor of hitting me aft, for then he'll do the least damage and she'll sink in the nicest way."

"Didn't I tell you?" exclaims the American to his companion. "He's nuts."

But Kuiper knows what he is saying; if the *Nelly* were sunk, the Coast Guard would have to pick up his Jews and take them to an internment camp.

This, interjects the Dutchman, would make little difference. The Jews would ultimately be sent back to their country.

Not so, argues Kuiper. This could have been done if public opinion were kept out of the situation; but now every holiday maker from Cape Hatteras to Sandy Hook knows that a shipful of famished Jews is trying to sneak ashore, and the newspapers are following the story.

The Dutch officer doggedly sticks to his purpose. "In case you should go on trying to force these undesirable aliens on the United States, I'm afraid I shall have to ask you to sign the declaration I will now read to you—a declaration that the Royal Netherlands Government declines all further political responsibility for your acts."

In other words, the American explains, the *Nelly* will no longer be regarded as Dutch territory.

Kuiper's attempts to land his cargo, and his avowed Christian reasons for doing so, have inspired the Dutch Naval Attaché in Washington to suggest a visit from a Reformed Church pastor in New York, and that gentleman has come along in the boarding party to reason with Kuiper.

The Captain objects, "I don't need any catechism from a clergyman who is in league with murderers!"

Nevertheless the minister is summoned, and the officers withdraw. The reverend offers a "Good evening, brother," which Kuiper ignores. He pursues, "Are you a Christian?"

When the Captain answers in the affirmative, the minister hauls off and gives him a mighty wallop on the ear. Kuiper cocks a fist, but the reverend makes no defensive move. Instead, he quotes the "other cheek" passage from the Sermon on the Mount. "So you are not a Christian," he observes. "You are trying to become one, just like me." This pacifies Kuiper.

The Captain wants to know if he is doing anything wrong in trying to save his Jews; the clergyman can't see where they are going to be saved. There are scores of destroyers, planes, shadowing the *Nelly*. . . .

"Answer me," begs Kuiper, "not as a representative of the government, but as a man of God. Do you think it could be God's will that I should take these people back?"

"I think it is God's will," says the clergyman, "that you should try to become a Christian. You won't by torturing one hundred and forty-six people for the sake of your own salvation." He suggests a way out: Kuiper should resign—hand over command to his mate and leave the sea. Thus he would be making a sacrifice for his faith.

The master of the *Nelly* argues that this doesn't settle the fate of the passengers. The churchman admits, "If I could believe, only for one second, that you really would be able to save these people, I would say you were right." Kuiper has faith that God will show him the way. Unconvinced, the pastor formally advises the Captain to quit trying and leave the Jews to God. "All real Christians," he says, "are troubling their heads over the Jewish problem."

"For a real Christian there is no Jewish problem, only a Christian problem," counters the skipper.

"I'll pray for mercy for you," offers the pastor.

"And the rabbi and I will pray for you and for the Reformed Church of the Netherlands."

The minister departs—and the rabbi enters, bringing back his box of papers. He begs for some slight hope, but Kuiper can see none. The best he can offer for the rabbi to tell his people is that he has informed a committee ashore that they have passed the exhaustion point and an answering radiogram may come any minute.

The rabbi starts to go to convey this information when the Doctor braces the Captain. "The crew is mishandling the Jew—the passengers." The officers, he relates, were kicking and beating them as they were loaded into boats, and had struck them with belts to drive them back into the holds.

"Is this true?" Kuiper asks the rabbi. At first the rabbi denies it, then admits it, but says it is of no importance at all. The Captain sends him on his way, and the Doctor continues with what he has learned from the messboy. The cook, the ringleader, has been setting the whole ship against the Jews, and the

Doctor has had to treat many injuries which at first were passed off as accidental.

The physician too seems to be against the skipper. The people are half crazy with claustrophobia. They all have some kind of poison, and one of them is dying now from what appears to be laudanum. "If you don't free these people within a week the ship will be a blazing madhouse," he declares. "And if that is to be the result of your practical Christianity . . ."

Kuiper orders the Doctor below to his patients. Alone, he goes to the picture of his family, covers his face with his hands.

Chief Davelaar interrupts, to report that a mutiny is brewing, and the two naval officers have come back for the Captain's decision—which, they hope, has been reached after the talk with the minister. The Dutch officer presents a declaration for Kuiper to sign, wordy and formal, but meaning that if Kuiper tries again to unload his cargo he will be doing it in the admitted knowledge that it is against the wish of his government.

Time is short for the two official visitors, but the Captain temporizes: "If I sign this," he asks, "I'll become a pirate, won't I?"

The question, says the Dutchman, is this: Is Kuiper willing to become stateless just for the sake of those Jews? "If you are not, give me back that paper and get the hell out of here." Kuiper signs the document. "And now," he is instructed, "get ready for sailing as soon as possible, for we are going to take you outside the three-mile limit. And after that you'll have to get yourself out of this region altogether because of the regatta."

What regatta? Kuiper wants to know. He is told it is the biggest stunt of the year—the annual race for the Hatteras cup, with the most expensive yachts of all states taking part.

Something begins to cook in the Captain's mind. He wants to know if the waters will be closed to ordinary navigation, and what time the races start, and how long they last. The races begin at noon and last four days.

"One question. This ship. This ship is Netherlands territory?"

The Dutch officer assures him it is, and Kuiper begins to laugh —and keeps on laughing more and more heartily. He orders a drink for everybody. "My God! I was ready for everything but for this. . . ."

Opening the cabin door and giving a toot on his whistle, Kuiper yells for the mate, Meyer. Yanking open the drawer of his table, he takes out a piece of paper; then his eyes fall on something else in the drawer and he takes it out too—a folded flag. On the paper he begins to write hastily as Meyer arrives, followed by the chief engineer.

"Take this message to Sparks, urgent," Kuiper orders his mate. "Get ready to sail and hoist this flag in the foretop." In the red glow of the dawn the Captain ushers his visitors outside.

Davelaar wants to know what the urgent message is, and Meyer reads it: "To Anna Kuiper, Helder, Holland. Dear wife: I have got to choose. Deny my faith and keep everything, or keep my faith and lose everything. Answer for you and the children, what am I to do? JORIS."

While the chief engineer is puzzling over the meaning of this, Meyer lets fall open the dirty white flag the Captain has given him to hoist.

"The old man's flag of the cross!" Meyer exclaims.

The curtain falls.

ACT III

It is sunset, four days later . . . the end of the regatta. The *Nelly* is silent, in a calm sea with engine dead; but within her noises can be heard—the intonation of a cantor, the monotonous tolling of a bell. Henky, the messboy, seems to be waiting for somebody in the cabin, and while he is waiting he is trying to memorize something from a crumpled paper he holds. Then, from outside, Henky hears the Captain speaking clearly and quietly, "One. Two. Three, in God's name." There is a rasping noise, a splash and the noise of Jewish laments. A burial at sea.

When it is over Chief Davelaar, Kuiper and the Doctor come into the cabin. Kuiper orders Davelaar to the engine room to prepare for sailing as soon as the *Amsterdam's* boat comes alongside—for Captain Bruinsma's vessel is now in these waters, as he had said it would be.

The Doctor, who looks odd and strained, asks Kuiper some strangely leading questions about dizziness or possible falls on his head. Finally he comes out with it: "I have been asked to certify you are insane."

"If you think I'm insane, go ahead."

"I'll go ahead, Skipper," agrees the Doctor, "even if I don't think so. I can't watch this torture any longer. So I must make use of the chance I've been given of eliminating you without bloodshed."

The plan is nicely arranged. Dr. Willemse of the *Amsterdam*

will also sign the doctor's certificate of insanity. Bruinsma doubtless will take Kuiper aboard the *Amsterdam* for transfer to a
hospital. Then Mate Meyer will assume command of the *Nelly*
and take the Jews back home.

The only way out for Kuiper, the Doctor suggests, is for him
to take the Jews back of his own free will. Dr. Richter has a
ship's committee in back of him.

"Call them," suggests the Captain.

"This will mean a mutiny."

"Let's have it!"

The Doctor opens the door after a moment's hesitation, revealing Meyer and Davelaar, who obviously have been listening.

"Pack your things and get ready to leave. You're under arrest, both of you," Kuiper orders the two men. "And you"—to
the Doctor—"start rolling pills mighty quick, before I have you
arrested with the rest."

Bruinsma, skipper of the *Amsterdam,* knocks on the doorpost
and comes in as the Doctor, the mate and the engineer are ordered out. He takes Kuiper by the shoulders and gives him a
careful look. "How's the holy fire? . . . Dying out a bit, eh?"

It isn't dying out. The Captain begins to unfold his hopes.
Nine miles away the regatta is in progress. "If I send out an
S O S those yachts will be obliged to come and pick up my boats,
won't they?"

Bruinsma agrees.

"If I scuttle my ship and those yachts pick up my boats, then
the Jews will be on American territory, with the full knowledge
of public opinion.

Correct so far, surmises Bruinsma—but if Kuiper scuttles his
ship he will get three years and never be allowed to command
another ship for the rest of his life.

Kuiper doesn't intend to do any more commanding; he will go
down with his ship. "My children," he declares, "will have a
richer inheritance in an unbroken faith than in a ship and a bag
of money."

Bruinsma doubts that Kuiper's wife will agree, and is told that
a message has already been sent her, but no reply has come yet.

Bruinsma still thinks his friend is foolish—but admits that, had
he been in Kuiper's place in South America two months ago, he
would have done the same thing—not in the name of Christianity, but as a plain, decent man. He asks how far away the regatta is, and is told nine miles; and the speed of the *Nelly* is

eight knots. "Then," he says, "reckon that it'll take me half an
hour to get far enough away for you to give your S O S. Otherwise I might be compelled to pick up your Jews myself, and
that's not the idea. Anything else I can do?"

KUIPER—Thank you, too late now. Only, I've got two pris-
oners, mutineers. What am I to do with them?

BRUINSMA—Set them free before you go down. Anything
more?

KUIPER—Yes. A declaration I drew up to save my officers
from prosecution. Would you mind having a look at it and tell
me if it's in order? (BRUINSMA *takes out his spectacles.* KUIPER
gives him a paper and he reads. Then he hands the paper back.)
All right?

BRUINSMA—I wish I were your father.

KUIPER—My father would have done exactly the same thing.
Of that I am certain.

BRUINSMA—But why? You're not a family of lunatics, are
you? What's the point of this act of madness?

KUIPER—That God, if He troubles to make His will known to
us, will provide the means to fulfill it. That much I have proved.

BRUINSMA—Not yet, young man, not yet! Your ship is still
afloat and within half an hour the world can come to an end.
(*At the door.*) I'll stand by my wireless. If I don't hear your
S O S I'll give my whole crew a double ration out of pure satisfaction. If I do hear it, then I hope that God of yours, if He
exists, will one day save my soul too, if I've got such a thing.
Good-by. (*Exits. The moment he has gone,* CHIEF DAVELAAR
stalks in, very worked up.)

DAVELAAR—So! Now the moment has come!

KUIPER—Hey, what's this? Who is at the engine?

DAVELAAR—Your father would have done exactly the same
thing, eh? He stands by your side, does he? That's why you
hoisted that flag of the cross, because of what he wrote into that
damned Bible!

KUIPER—Go back to your post!

DAVELAAR—If he is standing by your side now, he can whisper
into your ear that I am telling you the truth! Do you know what
that flag is that flies from your foretop now? The dirty shirt of
the devil! . . . No, no, let me go. . . . The truth! If the memory of your father is holy to you, then listen to the truth! Listen
to the story of the flag of the cross! You don't know it!   .

KUIPER (*who has dragged him to the door, lets him go*)—If you say one word against my father . . .

DAVELAAR—If I say one word that isn't true, may I fall dead on the spot, so help me God!

KUIPER—Put that hand down!

DAVELAAR—New Guinea, twenty years ago. In debt to every shopkeeper in the East. Three more days and the ship would have been put on a chain by the bailiff, and no cargo, nowhere. Then two missionaries came aboard, out of a jungle port, fifty miles over East. Your father asked them in order to talk about the Bible. But those missionaries told him that they had a nice little deal for him. For over two years they'd raised heaven all over the jungle and what did they teach those poor niggers? "Out of every two cocoanuts you cut down you have to put one aside for Jesus." The missionaries would see to the delivery to heaven. Now there they sat, their rat's eyes glittering in the candlelight, and offered your father Christ's cocoanuts at half price because he was a brother. One moment I thought your father would kill them, for he turned as white as a sheet, but he kept hold of himself. But after they had gone he weighed anchor and out we sailed to that jungle port fifty miles over east.

KUIPER—What for?

DAVELAAR—I'll tell you. He got the bo'sun to make a flag, a white flag with a black cross, the thing you are flying now. He got the third officer to put on a nightshirt, and a beard of twine, gave him a piece of copper steam pipe bent like a shepherd's crook. When the boy was put on top of the railing, he made him sing "Abide with Me." Then your father went ashore with the boat to tell the niggers Jesus had come to take his cocoanuts away. (MEYER *enters with a telegram, but stops short, frightened, and stays to listen, unobserved.*) The niggers seemed to be going mad. They leapt and yelped and flung their children up in the air and set all the sleeping monkeys jabbering. Then the first canoe came out, bursting with cocoanuts. And as we weighed anchor at sunset we were lying over the mark with the nuts of Jesus, for nothing. . . . No, don't touch me! The truth, I swear! I— (*Sees* MEYER, *who has tried to hide in vain.*) There! There he is! There is the proof! It was him! He was Jesus!

MEYER (*after a terrified silence during which* KUIPER *stares at him, motionless*)—Telegram, Captain.

DAVELAAR (*whispering hotly*)—Tell him! Tell him it was you

that played Jesus in the old man's nightshirt. Tell him, man!
Open your trap, damn you!

MEYER—Yes, Captain, that's right. But— (KUIPER *sits
down heavily at the table and covers his face with his hands.*)

Davelaar takes the message from the abashed Meyer, puts it on
the table and whispers to his captain words of advice not to sink
his ship but to take the Jews back. Kuiper does not react and
the engineer leaves him alone in the gathering darkness. Henky
slips in nervously. "Captain, Captain, write it down. Write it
down before I forget. . . ." The boy is beckoned out of the
room by the engineer, and in a moment the rabbi, after knocking, comes hesitantly in. He has heard that a message has come
and wants to relay its contents to his people below decks.

Kuiper brings his mind back into focus, takes the message
from the table and reports its contents. It is from the committee
ashore, advising that a decision must be postponed for eight weeks
because of a recess of the U.S. Senate. "And within half an
hour," comments the Captain, "the world can come to an end."

The rabbi is giving in; he feels that all Kuiper is doing is putting himself between the Jews and God. He quotes the awful
anathema pronounced upon his people in the Pentateuch beginning, "Cursed shalt thou be in the city and cursed shalt thou be
in the field. . . ."

In the hold, the rabbi says, his people have lost their fear and
their despair; now they are standing on the threshold of eternity.
"Only a short pain and we shall be free. . . . Don't let us yearn
any longer after the Promised Land. . . . Take us back."

The rabbi disappears in the darkness like a shadow. Henky
reappears, again with his plea to "write it down." It is, he thinks,
Matthias 10, 37 and 38. "The telegram," he explains—a telegram from Kuiper's wife that the mate and the engineer held
back from him and the boy saw. The more the boy tries to remember details, the more he becomes confused; it might have
been Matthias 7 and 8, 10, or 37, 8, 3 . . ."

The Captain seizes upon the boy's first recollection. It would
be Matthew, not Matthias, 10, 37 and 38. He brings a Bible
from his bunk and the boy holds a match while he reads: "He
that loveth father or mother more than me is not worthy of me.
He that loveth son or daughter more than me is not worthy of
me, and he that taketh not his cross and followeth after me is
not worthy of me."

This message, Kuiper feels, is not from his wife; it's from

Jesus. "Call the rabbi," he orders the boy. "And Mr. Meyer and Chief Davelaar and the Doctor. . . ."

When the men arrive, Kuiper is writing. "Rabbi," he says, "we were wrong. It is not God's will that you go back. Tonight you will be on American territory and tomorrow you will be free."

To the whole group, when they have arrived, the Captain makes an official statement. Having failed to land his passengers on three attempts, he has decided on emergency measures. Two miles away the regatta is on. Everybody will take to the boats, and when they have done so, he will send out an S O S. Once he has made sure that the regatta yachts have sighted the life-boats, he will scuttle *The Young Nelly* by an explosion in the propeller shaft. "It is," he says, "the only means left to me to get my passengers taken on to American territory with the full knowledge of public opinion."

The chief engineer objects, but Kuiper declares that, as the owner of the ship, he can do whatever he wants. Furthermore, he has written a formal declaration that he alone is responsible. He wants witnesses to his declaration.

Meyer protests a bit, then signs. Davelaar flatly refuses, but gives in and signs when Kuiper threatens him with prosecution for mutiny and sabotage. The Captain orders Davelaar to go below and put three ice-bombs in the propeller shaft, with five-minute fuses.

Davelaar shies from the duty, protesting that he will not send to hell with his own bloody hands the ship he has sailed on for thirty years; but when Kuiper offers to plant the bombs himself, the chief engineer accepts the order.

The Doctor signs the Captain's statement of responsibility too, and is told to get his papers together and arrange for everything for his sick boat. Then the rabbi signs, and after him, two Jews.

Left alone with the rabbi, Kuiper hands him his box of documents and says, "Pray for me." The rabbi will, always.

Outside, the Captain whistles and begins ordering the lowering of the first boat. Inside, the Doctor empties the medicine cupboard into a bag. The messboy is wondering whether they all will go aboard the windjammers or yachts. Henky suddenly has become conscious of religion and wonders if he could become a Christian and follow the Captain, whom he now regards as a saint. In the hurry of packing, the boy declines to take along the tropical helmet the Doctor gave him. "The Captain is scuttling his ship. I scuttle my hat," says the boy.

The hooter of *The Young Nelly* starts roaring—a long-drawn, continuous cry of despair.

DOCTOR—Hurry, there they go! (*They stuff the rest into the bag like mad.* KUIPER *hurries in.*)

KUIPER—What's the matter with you? Do you want to drown?

DOCTOR—Are they coming?

KUIPER—The whole skyline is full of them! Get into the boat, quick! (*They hurry off; he calls after them.*) Keep room for me; I'm coming, straight away! (*He collects, in a great hurry, papers, Bible, and portrait. The moment he has taken the picture off the wall two, three muffled explosions from below make everything clatter and shudder in the cabin. The lights go out. The hooter is silent. The stage becomes dark. But out of the silence comes a new sound: the* JEWS *start cheering in the distance, singing a faraway chant of rejoicing. Then a swinging light draws rapidly near offstage.* DAVELAAR *appears in the doorway with a lantern in his hand.*)

DAVELAAR—Joris, we are sinking! Joris! (*Then he discovers* KUIPER, *who is kneeling on the floor. He goes to his side.*) Look at him! Look at him, the skipper next to God! His country gone, his church gone, his father gone, his ship gone, and what does he say now?

KUIPER (*getting up*)—The Lord gave, the Lord has taken away, blessed be the Lord. (*He hurries out.*)

THE CURTAIN FALLS

AN INSPECTOR CALLS

A Play in Three Acts

By J. B. Priestley

THE first score of years of the Twentieth Century seemed to be favored ones among the season's theatre writers. Shaw's "Man and Superman," Van Druten's "The Druid Circle," Longstreet's "High Button Shoes," Rattigan's "The Winslow Boy," Berg's "Me and Molly," and other offerings were set in this time—a time in which, it seems, the costumes were more quaint than beautiful. For the first of his two plays of the season, "An Inspector Calls," Priestley chose 1912—more, one would guess, because British labor was beginning to awaken to a new sense of power than because the world was on the eve of a war.

Mr. Priestley's people, the Birlings, live in a fairly large suburban house. Birling, a prosperous manufacturer, is now dominating a family party—the end of a dinner—in the big, square dining room. There is only one door to the room, on the right, and on the left wall is a curtained window; the fireplace would be on the "fourth wall"—something of an innovation among British dramatists, who love their fireplaces and mantelpieces. The furnishings are substantial and old-fashioned without being cozy or comfortable; on the walls are imposing but tasteless pictures and engravings; and there is a telephone on a small table. As if at each side of the invisible fireplace are two leather armchairs.

There are four Birlings at the dining table. At one end is Arthur, a rather portentous man in his middle fifties who has fairly easy manners but is rather provincial in his speech. At the other end is his wife, Sybil, a little younger than her husband and socially superior. Elsewhere at table are their son and daughter, Eric and Sheila. Eric, in his middle twenties, seems never quite at ease; Sheila, in her early twenties, is a pretty girl who is very pleased with life.

All the men are in tails and white ties—and the third is Gerald Croft, an easy, well-bred man about town about 30 years old. He is to become a member of the family, and the dinner has been in celebration of this prospect.

When the maid, Edna, brings the port, Birling urges it on Gerald, informing him, "Finchley assures me it's exactly the same port your father gets from him." To his wife's embarrassment, Birling is expansive about the dinner too, and bids Sybil to congratulate the cook. "Arthur, you're not supposed to say such things," she reproaches him—but Birling dismisses the correction in manners by saying he is treating Gerald like a member of the family.

Affably, Gerald reminds the group that he has been trying to become a member of the family for some time. "Except," Sheila reminds him, "for all last Summer, when you never came near me, and I wondered what happened to you."

Gerald points out that he has told her before: "I was awfully busy at the works all that time." The girl, half serious, half playful, comments, "Yes, that's what *you* say."

Young Eric suddenly begins to laugh, for no reason that he can explain; he just felt he had to, he says. His sister accuses him of being "squiffy," which he denies. Mrs. Birling forestalls any further bickering by suggesting that now is the time for Arthur's toast. Clearing his throat, Arthur begins by addressing himself to Gerald: "It's a pity that Sir George and—er—Lady Croft can't be with us. . . ." But they are abroad and have sent a very nice cable. Speechmaking at a quiet celebration like this is difficult, Birling proceeds—and is only momentarily halted by his son's suggestion that he not make any speech.

"Oh, yes, I will. It's one of the happiest nights of my life. And one day, I hope, Eric, when you've a daughter of your own, you'll understand why. Gerald, I'm going to tell you frankly, without any pretenses, that your engagement to Sheila means a tremendous lot to me. She'll make you happy. I'm sure you'll make her happy. You're just the kind of son-in-law I've always wanted. Your father and I have been friendly rivals in business for some time now—though Crofts Limited are both older and bigger than Birling and Company—and now you've brought us together, and perhaps we may look forward to the time when Crofts and Birlings are no longer competing but are working together—for lower costs and higher prices."

Pleasantly Gerald allows that his father would agree to that, and Arthur gets on with his toast to the happiness of Gerald and Sheila, and the fiancé brings forth a ring for the girl—a lovely one, naturally, which delights her. Mrs. Birling thinks it is time now for her and her daughter to repair to the drawing room, leaving the men alone, but her husband has more to say.

BIRLING (*rather heavily*)—I just want to say this. I'm delighted about this— (*Noticing that* SHEILA *is still admiring her ring.*) Are you listening, Sheila? This concerns you too.

SHEILA—I'm sorry, Daddy. Actually, I was listening. (*She looks attentive, as they all do.*)

BIRLING—I'm delighted about this— (SHEILA *crosses to him and shows the ring.*) Yes, dear, very pretty. (*Holding them for a moment before continuing.*) I'm delighted about this engagement and I hope it won't be too long before you're married. And I want to say this. There's a good deal of silly talk about these days—*but*—and I speak as a hardheaded businessman, who has to take risks and know what he's about—I say, you can ignore all this silly pessimistic talk. When you marry, you'll be marrying at a very good time. Yes, a very good time—and soon it'll be an even better time. We're in for a time of steadily increasing prosperity.

GERALD—I believe you're right, sir.

ERIC—What about war?

BIRLING—What?

ERIC—What about war?

BIRLING—Don't interrupt, Eric. Oh, war? I was just coming to that. Glad you mentioned it, Eric. Just because the Kaiser makes a speech or two, or a few German officers have too much to drink and begin talking nonsense, you'll hear some people say that war's inevitable. And to that I say—fiddlesticks! The Germans don't want war. Nobody wants war, except some half-civilized folks in the Balkans. And why? There's too much at stake these days. Everything to lose and nothing to gain by war.

ERIC—Yes, I know—but still—

BIRLING—Just let me finish, Eric. You've a lot to learn yet. And I'm talking as a hardheaded, practical man of business. And I say there isn't a chance of war. The world's developing so fast that it'll make war impossible. Look at the progress we're making. In a year or two we'll have aeroplanes that will be able to go anywhere. And look at the way the automobile's making headway—bigger and faster all the time. And then ships. Why, a friend of mine went over this new liner last week—the *Titanic*—forty-six thousand eight hundred tons—forty-six thousand eight hundred tons—New York in five days—and every luxury—and unsinkable, absolutely unsinkable. That's what you've got to keep your eye on, facts like that, progress like that—and not a few German officers talking nonsense and a few scaremongers here making a fuss about nothing. Now you three young people, listen to this—and remember what I'm telling you now. In twenty or thirty years' time—let's say, somewhere in the 'forties—you may be giving a little party like this—your son or daughter might be getting engaged—and I tell you, by that time you'll be living in a world that'll have forgotten all these Capital versus Labor agitations and all these silly little war scares. There'll be peace and prosperity and rapid progress everywhere—except, of course, in Russia, which will always be behindhand naturally. (*As* MRS. BIRLING *shows signs of interrupting.*) Yes, my dear, I know— I'm talking too much.

MRS. BIRLING—Of course, dear—

BIRLING—But we can't let these Bernard Shaws and H. G. Wellses do all the talking. We hardheaded, practical business-men must say something sometime. And we don't guess—we've had experience—and we *know.*

MRS. BIRLING (*rising; the others rise*)—Yes, of course, dear. Well—don't keep Gerald in here too long. Eric—I want you a minute. (*She and* SHEILA *and* ERIC *go out,* ERIC *whistling "Rule Britannia."*)

With a cigar and some more port, Birling expands further in the presence of his son-in-law-to-be. He suggests, to Gerald's embarrassment, that Lady Croft may think that her son could do better socially—but there is a fair chance that Birling might get a knighthood on the next Honors List. He's been a sound, useful party man and was Lord Mayor two years ago. . . . There should be a very good chance so long as the Birlings behave themselves. Gerald laughingly comments that the family seems very well behaved.

Eric comes back for a drink of port and to join in the talk. What talk there is continues to be mostly his father's. The ring of the front doorbell finally interrupts quite a speech about conditions today, and "the way some of these cranks write and talk now, you'd think everybody has to look after everybody else, as if we were all mixed up together like bees in a hive. . . ." This does not sit well with the self-made Birling.

The doorbell, they soon learn from Edna, was rung by a police inspector—name of Goole—who wants to see Birling on something important. Gerald lightly suggests that Eric may have been up to something and Eric uneasily resents the humor.

Inspector Goole proves to be a solid, purposeful man in his fifties, dressed in a plain, darkish suit. He speaks carefully and weightily and has a disconcerting habit of looking hard at the person he addresses before beginning to speak. He introduces himself to Birling and that gentleman correctly observes that the Inspector is new; he would know, having been an alderman and Lord Mayor and still being on the Bench.

BIRLING—Well, what can I do for you? Some trouble about a warrant?

INSPECTOR—No, Mr. Birling.

BIRLING (*after a pause, with a touch of impatience*)—Well, what is it then?

INSPECTOR—I'd like some information, if you don't mind, Mr. Birling. Two hours ago a young woman died in the Infirmary. She'd been taken there this afternoon because she'd swallowed a lot of strong disinfectant. Burnt her inside out, of course.

ERIC (*involuntarily*)—My God!

INSPECTOR—Yes, she was in great agony. They did everything they could for her at the Infirmary, but she died. Suicide, of course.

BIRLING (*rather impatiently*)—Yes, yes. Horrible business. But I don't understand why you should come here, Inspector—

INSPECTOR (*cutting through, massively*)—I've been round to the room she had, and she'd left a letter there and a sort of diary. Like a lot of these young women who get into various kinds of trouble, she'd used more than one name. But her original name—her real name—was Eva Smith.

BIRLING (*thoughtfully*)—Eva Smith?

INSPECTOR—Do you remember her, Mr. Birling?

BIRLING (*slowly*)—No—I seem to remember hearing that name—Eva Smith—somewhere. But it doesn't convey anything to me. And I don't see where I come into this.

INSPECTOR—She was employed in your works at one time.

BIRLING—Oh—that's it, is it? Well, we've several hundred young women there, y' know, and they keep changing.

INSPECTOR—This young woman, Eva Smith, was a bit out of the ordinary. I found a photograph of her in her lodgings. (*Rises.*) Perhaps you'd remember her from that. (*The IN-SPECTOR takes a photograph, about postcard size, out of his pocket and goes to BIRLING, who is now standing. Both GERALD and* ERIC *rise to have a look at the photograph, but the* INSPECTOR *interposes himself between them and the photographs. They are surprised and rather annoyed.* BIRLING *stares hard and with recognition at the photograph, which the* INSPECTOR *then replaces in his pocket.*)

GERALD (*showing annoyance*)—Any particular reason why I shouldn't see this girl's photograph, Inspector?

INSPECTOR (*coolly, looking hard at him*)—There might be.

ERIC—And the same applies to me, I suppose?

INSPECTOR—Yes.

GERALD—I can't imagine what it could be.

ERIC—Neither can I.

BIRLING—And I must say I agree with them, Inspector.

INSPECTOR—It's the way I like to go to work. One person and one line of inquiry at a time. Otherwise, there's a muddle.

Birling remembers the girl right enough; she had been one of his employees and he had discharged her nearly two years ago. Certainly this dismissal couldn't be the cause of the suicide after all this time.

Gerald suggests that perhaps he should bow out, but Birling does not mind his presence. Gerald is introduced to the Inspector as the son of Sir George Croft of Crofts Limited. When the Inspector learns that Gerald is going to marry Sheila he announces, "Then I'd prefer you to stay."

Birling is getting impatient with the inquiry, but Goole doggedly continues. He reasons that what happened to the girl two years ago may have determined what happened to her afterward, until the chain of events drove her to suicide.

Birling remembers this girl, Eva Smith, as lively and good-looking, and a good worker in one of the machine shops. She was about to be promoted to charge of a small group of girls, but when the girls came back from their holidays they were "restless" and asked for more money—a raise from 22 to 25 shillings a week. "I refused, of course."

"Why?" asks the Inspector, to Birling's great surprise. Certainly it is no concern of the Inspector's how a man chooses to run his business. Goole quietly insists that it is his duty to ask questions and Birling less quietly insists that it his duty to keep labor costs down. He recalls that he told the girls if they didn't like the rates they could work somewhere else—and that the resulting lockout didn't last long. The girls all came back and were forgiven, except for four or five ringleaders, including Eva Smith.

GERALD—You couldn't have done anything else.

ERIC—He could. He could have kept her on instead of throwing her out. I call it tough luck.

BIRLING—Rubbish! If you don't come down sharply on some of these people, they'd soon be asking for the earth.

GERALD—I should say so!

INSPECTOR—They might. But after all it's better to ask for the earth than to take it.

BIRLING (*rises, crossing to the* INSPECTOR)—What did you say your name was, Inspector?

INSPECTOR—Goole.

BIRLING—Goole. Tell me, Inspector Goole, how do you get on with our Chief Constable? Colonel Roberts?

INSPECTOR—I don't see much of him.

BIRLING—Perhaps I ought to warn you that he's an old friend of mine, and that I see him fairly frequently. We play golf together sometimes up at the West Brumley.

INSPECTOR (*dryly*)—I don't play golf.

BIRLING—I didn't suppose you did.

ERIC (*bursting out*)—Well, I think it's a damn shame.

INSPECTOR—No, I've never wanted to play.

ERIC—No, I mean about this girl—Eva Smith. Why shouldn't they try for higher wages? We try for the highest possible prices. And I don't see why she should have been sacked just because she'd a bit more spirit than the others. You said yourself she was a good worker. I'd have let her stay.

BIRLING (*steps toward* ERIC *rather angrily*)—Unless you brighten your ideas, you'll never be in a position to let anybody stay or tell anybody to go. It's about time you learnt to face a few responsibilities. That's something this public school and varsity life you've had doesn't seem to have taught you.

ERIC (*sulkily*)—Well, we don't need to tell the Inspector all about that, do we?

BIRLING—I don't see we need to tell this inspector anything more. In fact, there's nothing I can tell him. I told the girl to clear out, and she went. That's the last I heard of her. Have you any idea what happened to her after that? Get into trouble? Go on the streets?

INSPECTOR (*rather slowly*)—No, she didn't exactly go on the streets. (SHEILA *has now entered.*)

SHEILA (*gaily*)—What's this about the streets? (*Noticing the* INSPECTOR.) Oh—sorry. I didn't know. Mummy sent me in to ask you why you didn't come along to the drawing room.

BIRLING—We shall be along in a minute now. Just finishing.

INSPECTOR—I'm afraid not.

BIRLING (*abruptly*)—There's nothing else, y' know. I've just told you that.

SHEILA—What's this all about?

BIRLING—Nothing to do with you, Sheila. Run along.

INSPECTOR—No, wait a minute, Miss Birling.

BIRLING (*angrily*)—Look here, Inspector, I consider this un-called-for and officious. I've half a mind to report you. I've told you all I know—and it doesn't seem to me very important—and now there isn't the slightest reason why my daughter should be dragged into this unpleasant business.

SHEILA (*coming further in*)—What business? What's happening?

INSPECTOR (*impressively*)—I'm a police inspector, Miss Birling. This afternoon a young woman drank some disinfectant and died, after several hours of agony, tonight in the Infirmary.

SHEILA—Oh—how horrible! Was it an accident?

INSPECTOR—No. She wanted to end her life. She felt she couldn't go on any longer.

BIRLING—Well, don't tell me that's because I discharged her from my employment nearly two years ago.

ERIC—That might have started it.

SHEILA—Did you, Dad?

BIRLING—Yes. The girl had been causing trouble in the works. I was quite justified.

GERALD—Yes, I think you were. I know we'd have done the same thing. Don't look like that, Sheila.

SHEILA (*rather distressed*)—Sorry! It's just that I can't help thinking about this girl—destroying herself so horribly—and I've been so happy tonight. Oh, I wish you hadn't told me. What was she like? Quite young?

INSPECTOR—Yes. Twenty-four.

SHEILA—Pretty?

INSPECTOR—She wasn't pretty when I saw her today, but she had been pretty—very pretty.

BIRLING—That's enough of that.

GERALD—And I don't really see that this inquiry gets you any-where, Inspector. It's what happened to her since she left Mr. Birling's works that is important.

BIRLING—Obviously. I suggested that some time ago.

GERALD—And we can't help you there because we don't know.

INSPECTOR (*slowly*)—Are you sure you don't know? (*He looks at* GERALD, *then at* ERIC, *then at* SHEILA.)

BIRLING—Are you suggesting now that one of them knows something about this girl?

INSPECTOR—Yes.

Birling suffers a marked change of tone and is almost apologetic now. Gerald declares he is out of it because he has never known an Eva Smith. Eric and Sheila both declare the same. "So where are you now, Inspector?" asks Gerald.

Goole explains that after the sacking the girl changed her name. She was out of work two months, and she had no family and little savings. She was feeling desperate, but she had a stroke of luck and was taken into a good shop—Milward's. Sheila knows Milward's well; has been there, in fact, today.

The girl was happy among the pretty clothes, the Inspector continues, but after a couple of months, just when she was settling down nicely, she was told she would have to go. "All she knew was that a customer complained about her—and so she had to go."

Sheila stares agitatedly at Goole. "When was this?"

"At the end of January, last year."

"What—what did this girl look like?"

The Inspector produces the photograph. Sheila looks closely at it, recognizes it with a little cry, gives a half-stifled sob and runs from the room. The Inspector puts the picture back in his pocket as the other three men stare in amazement.

Birling becomes indignant at the way his daughter has been upset. "We were having a nice little family celebration tonight," he says angrily, "and a nasty mess you've made of it now, haven't you?"

Goole counters by saying he was thinking more or less the same thing earlier—"When I was in the Infirmary looking at what was left of Eva Smith. A nice little promising life there, I thought, and a nasty mess somebody's made of it."

Gerald would like to have a look at the picture now, but the Inspector very firmly puts him off with "One line of inquiry at a time." Eric uneasily says he has a headache and thinks he had better turn in—but the Inspector thinks he had better stay here. Gerald is waxing indignant at Goole's treatment of respectable citizens.

Sheila, having got over crying, comes back in. She knows the Inspector knew it was she all the time; she felt badly about the girl at the time and now she feels a lot worse. "Did it make much difference to her?" she asks, hopeful of a denial.

"I'm afraid it did," says Goole. "It was the last real steady job she had. When she lost it—for no reason that she could discover—she decided she might as well try another kind of life." Sheila is partly to blame, just as her father is. The girl explains to her brother just what happened:

Sheila was in Milward's trying on a dress. Her mother, who was with her, had advised against the dress, and so had the sales-girl, but Sheila strongheadedly thought the dress would be becoming and she tried it on. As soon as she saw herself in the mirror she knew she was wrong. But it had been right for the pretty girl who had brought it up from the workroom and who had held it up to herself for a moment. The pretty girl was Eva Smith. When Sheila tried on the dress she caught sight of this pretty girl smiling at the salesgirl as if to say, "Doesn't she look awful." So Sheila became furious, told the manager that the girl had been impertinent, and as the daughter of a good customer had thus caused the young woman to be sacked.

Sheila has hidden nothing from the Inspector, and her contrition is immense. If only she could help that girl now. . . .

The Inspector now has shown that two members of the household, Sheila and her father, have had something to do with Eva Smith's last years. Continuing the girl's history, he says, "Now she had to try something else. . . . First she changed her name to Daisy Renton—"

Gerald, pulling himself together, pours himself a drink at this point.

The Inspector decides he wants to see Birling again and Eric takes him to the drawing room. When the affianced pair are alone, Sheila knowingly queries, "Well, Gerald?" She brushes off his half-hearted denials that he ever knew an Eva Smith or a Daisy Renton.

"All right," admits Gerald, "I knew her. Let's leave it at that."

But his fiancée won't leave it at that. She guesses that he was seeing Daisy Renton last Spring and Summer when he said he was so busy. His failure to reply convinces her she is right, and in the end he admits it. "But it was all over and done with last Summer. I don't come into this suicide business."

"I thought I didn't half an hour ago," she reminds him.

"You don't. Neither of us does. So—for God's sake—don't say anything to the Inspector."

"About you and this girl?"

"Yes. We can keep it from him."

Sheila laughs, almost hysterically. "Why, you fool, *he knows!* . . . And I hate to think how much he knows that we don't know yet. . . ."

The curtain falls.

ACT II

The action is continuous: Sheila and Gerald are just as they were when the Inspector returns, leaving the door open behind him. "Well?" he says to Gerald.

"You see?" Sheila laughs again. "What did I tell you?"

Gerald suggests that Sheila be allowed to go, and the Inspector acquiesces—but the girl wants to stay.

The Inspector knows why she wants to stay, and tries to tell Gerald. Sheila has just been made to understand what she did to this girl, and now if she doesn't hear any more she will feel she's entirely to blame. She wants, if possible, to share her guilt.

Sheila is a forthright young woman and she admits the Inspector is right. She stares wonderingly at him because he is so right.

Her mother, brisk and self-confident, comes through the open door and gives the Inspector a smiling and social "Good evening." She has heard why he has come, and will be glad to tell anything she knows. Sheila tries to warn her mother to stop. She has a hunch—a silly feeling—that her mother will say something or do something she will be sorry for afterward. Mrs. Birling thinks this is nonsense and tries to shoo Sheila off to bed.

"I'm staying here," insists the girl, "until I know why that girl killed herself."

Mrs. Birling has no sympathy with such curiosity. After all, the things that happen to girls of that class . . .

Slowly and carefully, Sheila tells her mother, "You mustn't try to build up a kind of wall between us and that girl. If you do, then the Inspector will just break it down. . . ."

Mrs. Birling turns on the Inspector rather grandly. His inquiry is being conducted in a rather peculiar and offensive manner, she believes, and she would like to remind him that her husband was Lord Mayor and still is a magistrate. Goole is imperturbable and not to be moved from his inquiry. He would like now to know where Mr. Birling is, and Mrs. Birling explains that he is talking to his son, who may have had rather too much to drink.

"Isn't he used to drinking?"

"No, he's only a boy."

But Sheila knows different. Eric has been drinking too much for the last two years, and this isn't the time to pretend. Her mother is genuinely staggered by this statement, and asks Gerald for support. Gerald, however, is constrained to admit that, although he hasn't seen much of Eric, he has heard that he drinks pretty hard. Revelations just seem to come out in the presence of the Inspector and, Sheila warns her mother, "He hasn't started on you yet."

Mrs. Birling recovers and says she will be glad to answer the Inspector, though naturally she doesn't know anything about this girl. Gravely, Goole says, "We'll see, Mrs. Birling."

Birling comes in, hot and bothered—and annoyed with the Inspector for having told Eric to stay up when he should be in bed. "I don't propose to give you much more rope," Birling informs the visitor. Sheila laughs rather wildly that it's the Inspector who is giving *them* rope—to hang themselves.

"Well, come along—what's it you want to know?" Mrs. Birling demands angrily. Quietly the Inspector continues the girl's story: When Eva Smith had to leave Milward's because of Sheila's complaint, she became Daisy Renton, "with other ideas." He asks Gerald directly when he first got to know Daisy Renton— and Mr. and Mrs. Birling exclaim in surprise. Gerald would like to deny the implication, but realizes it is useless and tells his story:

He met the girl some time in March last year in the bar at the Palace Music Hall here in Brumley. He had gone for a drink during a dull spot in the show. The bar is a favorite haunt of what Gerald calls women of the town and the Inspector labels prostitutes.

Mrs. Birling suggests it would be better if her daughter didn't hear any more of the story. Sheila replies, "But you forget I'm supposed to be engaged to the hero of it." She declines to leave and Gerald goes on:

All Gerald wanted was the drink; he hated those hard-eyed, dough-faced women. But he noticed one who was different— pretty, with soft brown hair and big dark eyes. Nicely dressed too. Obviously out of place, and old Joe Meggarty, half drunk, had wedged her into a corner. . . .

"Surely you don't mean Alderman Meggarty?" interposes Mrs. Birling.

"Of course I do. He is one of the worst sots and rogues in Brumley"—more staggering information for Mrs. B. to ponder.

Well, the girl saw Gerald and appealed with her eyes for help, so Gerald got rid of Meggarty by telling him the manager had a message for him, and then offered to take the girl out of there. He took her to a quiet hotel for a drink or two and she talked about herself. She told about losing jobs in a works and in a shop, and she let it slip that she now was actually hungry. So Gerald ordered food.

"And then you decided to keep her—as your mistress?" asks the Inspector.

Another shock for Mrs. Birling, but Sheila suspected it all along.

Not just then, Gerald replies to the Inspector. A couple of nights later he met the girl again—not accidentally this time—and learned she was about to be turned out of her room. A friend of Gerald's had gone to Canada for six months and had left him a key to his nice little apartment. So Gerald moved Daisy Renton there and gave her some money to keep her going. He had done all this out of sympathy, wanting nothing in return; the idea of making love came later.

Sheila's bitterness and sarcasm increase as Gerald gets along with his tale. Daisy Renton did become his mistress—inevitably, he supposes. She was young and pretty and warm-hearted and intensely grateful.

"Were you in love with her?" asks the Inspector.

"Just what I was going to ask," chimes in Sheila.

It's hard for Gerald to say, except that he didn't feel about her as she obviously felt about him.

The affair ended in the first week of September. Gerald had to go away for several weeks on business, and Daisy knew the break was coming—so he broke it off. She took it gallantly, and she told Gerald she'd been happier than she had ever been before. She knew the end had to come and she didn't blame him. "I wish to God she had now. Perhaps I'd feel better about it."

Of course, Daisy had to move out of the rooms. She had saved some out of the allowance he'd been giving her, and he gave her enough more to see her through to the end of the year. She would not say what she intended to do, but Gerald thinks she went to some seaside place.

That is right, the Inspector confirms. The girl had kept a

rough diary and in it she said she had to go away and be quiet, alone, and remember—"just to make it last longer."

"Well," Gerald concludes, "I never saw her again and that's all I can tell you." He asks if he can go out for a walk now. "I'll come back." Goole acquiesces.

"But just in case you forget—or decide not to come back, Gerald, I think you'd better take this with you," says Sheila—and she gives him the engagement ring.

"Well, I was expecting this," says Gerald.

But Sheila isn't playing the outraged maiden. She explains, "I don't dislike you as I did half an hour ago, Gerald. In fact, in some odd way, I rather respect you more than I've ever done before. I knew anyhow you were lying about those months last year when you hardly came near me. I knew there was something fishy about that time. And now at least you've been honest. And I believe what you told us about the way you helped her at first. Just out of pity. And it was my fault really that she was so desperate when you first met her. But this has made a difference. You and I aren't the same people who sat down to dinner here. We'd have to start all over again, getting to know each other—"

Mrs. Birling now announces that she thinks they finally have come to an end of this wretched business—but they haven't. The Inspector wants to show Mrs. Birling the photograph of the girl. She looks at it and says she does not recognize it.

"You're not telling me the truth," the Inspector calmly accuses—and Sheila, who is plainly fascinated by his perspicacity, feels he must be right. She tells her mother, "You're just pretending you don't recognize her."

The front door slams and Birling goes out to see whether it was Gerald coming back or, perhaps, Eric going out. The Inspector turns to Mrs. Birling. "You're a member—a prominent member—of the Brumley Women's Charity Organization?" She is.

An organization for helping women in various forms of distress? Yes, for deserving cases.

There was a meeting of the interviewing committee two weeks ago and Mrs. Birling was in the chair? Yes, if it's any of the Inspector's business.

Birling returns, agitated. Apparently Eric has gone out, and he has been in one of his excitable, queer moods. . . .

The Inspector returns to his examination of Mrs. Birling, and

Birling indignantly demands if there is any reason why his wife should answer his questions.

INSPECTOR—Yes, a very good reason. You'll remember that Mr. Croft told us—quite truthfully, I believe—that he hadn't spoken to or seen Eva Smith since last September. But Mrs. Birling spoke to and saw her only two weeks ago.

SHEILA (*astonished*)—Mother!

BIRLING—Is this true?

MRS. BIRLING (*after a pause*)—Yes, quite true.

INSPECTOR—She appealed to your organization for help?

MRS. BIRLING—Yes.

INSPECTOR—Not as Eva Smith?

MRS. BIRLING—No. Nor as Daisy Renton.

INSPECTOR—First she called herself Mrs. Birling. . . .

BIRLING (*astounded*)—*Mrs. Birling!*

MRS. BIRLING—Yes. I think it was simply a piece of gross impertinence—quite deliberate—and naturally that was one of the things that prejudiced me against her case.

BIRLING—And I should think so! Damned impudence!

INSPECTOR—You admit being prejudiced against her case?

MRS. BIRLING—Yes.

SHEILA—Mother, she's just died a horrible death—don't forget.

MRS. BIRLING—I'm very sorry. But I think she had only herself to blame.

INSPECTOR—Was it owing to your influence as the most prominent member of the committee that help was refused the girl?

MRS. BIRLING—Possibly.

INSPECTOR—Was it or was it not your influence?

MRS. BIRLING (*stung*)—Yes, it was. I didn't like her manner. She'd impertinently made use of our name, though she pretended afterwards it just happened to be the first she thought of. She had to admit, after I began questioning her, that she had no claim to the name, that she wasn't married, and that the story she told at first—about a husband who'd deserted her—was quite false. It didn't take me long to get the truth—or some of the truth—out of her.

INSPECTOR—Why did she want help?

MRS. BIRLING—You know very well why she wanted help.

INSPECTOR—No, I don't. I know why she *needed* help. But as I wasn't there, I don't know what she asked from your committee.

MRS. BIRLING—I don't think we need discuss it.

INSPECTOR—You have no hope of *not* discussing it, Mrs. Birling.

MRS. BIRLING—If you think you can bring any pressure to bear on me, Inspector, you're quite mistaken. Unlike the other three, I did nothing I'm ashamed of or that won't bear investigation. The girl asked for assistance. We are asked to look carefully into the claims made upon us. I wasn't satisfied with this girl's claim—she seemed to me to be not a good case—and so I used my influence to have it refused. And in spite of what's happened to the girl since, I consider I did my duty. So if I prefer not to discuss it any further, you have no power to make me change my mind, because I've done nothing wrong—and you know it.

INSPECTOR (*very deliberately*)—I think you did something terribly wrong—and that you're going to spend the rest of your life regretting it. I wish you'd been with me tonight at the Infirmary. You'd have seen—

SHEILA (*bursting in*)—No, no, please. Not that again. I've imagined it enough already.

INSPECTOR (*very deliberately*)—Then the next time you imagine it, just remember that this girl was going to have a child.

SHEILA (*horrified*)—No! Oh—horrible—horrible! How could she have wanted to kill herself?

INSPECTOR—Because she'd been turned out and turned down too many times. This was the end.

SHEILA—Mother, you must have known.

INSPECTOR—It was because she was going to have a child that she went for assistance to your mother's committee.

BIRLING—Look here, this wasn't Gerald Croft—

INSPECTOR (*cutting in sharply*)—No, no. Nothing to do with him.

SHEILA—Thank goodness for that!

INSPECTOR (*to* MRS. BIRLING)—And you've nothing further to tell me, eh?

MRS. BIRLING—I'll tell you what I told her. Go and look for the father of the child. It's his responsibility.

INSPECTOR—That doesn't make it any the less yours. She came to you for help, at a time when no woman could have needed it more. And you not only refused it yourself, but saw to it that the others refused it too. She was here alone, friendless, almost penniless, desperate. She needed not only money, but advice, sympathy and friendliness. You've had children. You must have known what she was feeling. And you slammed the door in her face.

Sheila thinks this was cruel and vile, and her father doesn't think it will look good in the press when it comes out in the inquest. Mrs. Birling is now on the defensive, and she defends herself strongly. She got the truth out of the girl finally, she relates, and found that the girl knew who the father was—so it was up to the girl to make him responsible by marrying her or at least supporting her.

And the girl replied to this with a lot of silly nonsense, giving herself ridiculous airs and claiming elaborate fine feelings. "She said the father was only a youngster—silly, wild, and drinking too much. . . . She didn't want to take any more money from him for some fancy reason."

The Inspector insists on knowing the reason and finally gets it —the girl had learned that it was stolen money. Mrs. Birling feels she was entirely justified in advising her committee not to allow the girl's claim for assistance. She is sorry about the horrible end, but accepts no blame for it at all.

"Who is to blame then?" asks the Inspector.

"First, the girl herself. Secondly, I blame the young man who was the father of the child she was going to have. If, as she said, he didn't belong to her class, and was some drunken young idler, then that's all the more reason why he shouldn't escape." And if he also had stolen money, he should be dealt with severely.

Sheila, suddenly alarmed, implores her mother to stop. Mrs. Birling goes on, to the Inspector: "And if you'd take some steps to find this young man and then make sure that he's compelled to confess in public his responsibility . . ."

Sheila has begun crying quietly. The Inspector assures Mrs. Birling that he will do his duty. "And now," she says, "no doubt you'd like to say good night."

"Not yet. I'm waiting."

"Waiting for what?"

"To do my duty."

The distressed Sheila pleads, "Now, Mother, don't you see?"— and understanding finally comes upon Mrs. Birling. She is frightened, and so is her husband. "Look, Inspector," says Birling, "you're not trying to tell us that—that my boy—is mixed up in this—?"

Sternly Goole answers: "If he is, then we know what to do, don't we? Mrs. Birling has just told us."

The group stands thunderstruck. They hear the front door, and in a moment Eric comes in, looking pale and distressed. With a little cry his mother collapses into a chair.

The curtain falls slowly.

ACT III

"I had to come back and have it out," Eric declares. "You know, don't you?"

They know—but Mrs. Birling still can't believe it.

"Could I have a drink first?" the young man asks.

"No!" explodes his father.

"Yes," says the Inspector. And Eric takes one with the practiced hand and gullet of an accomplished quick drinker. He begins his story:

One night last November he met Daisy Renton in the Palace bar. He was a bit squiffy and he bought her a few drinks. He found out that she hadn't had much to eat that day. He insisted on taking her to her lodgings and going in with her— threatened to make a row if she didn't let him in. He can't remember too clearly, though, but recalls enough to exclaim, "And that's when it happened. And I didn't even remember—that's the hellish thing."

Birling orders Sheila to take Mrs. Birling from the room and the Inspector gets on with quizzing Eric. About two weeks later Eric met the girl again—not by appointment, for he couldn't remember her name or where she lived; it was at the Palace bar again and he took her home again.

This time they talked—told their names and something about themselves; and they made love again. And there was a third time, and now the girl thought she was going to have a baby.

"Did she suggest that you ought to marry her?"

"No. She didn't want me to marry her. Said I didn't love her—and all that."

"So, what did you propose to do?"

"Well, she hadn't a job—and didn't feel like trying again for one—so I insisted on giving her enough money to keep her going —until she refused to take any more."

"How much did you give her?"

"I suppose about fifty pounds all told."

This sum arouses Eric's father. Where could his son get it?

"I got it—from the office—" Eric maintains he didn't really steal the money by taking cash that had been paid him for accounts; he meant to pay it back. His father is outraged, but another family squabble is quelled firmly by the Inspector asking: "Just one last question. The girl discovered that this money you were giving her was stolen, didn't she?"

Eric admits it—and is startled. How could the Inspector have known it? Sheila explains that the girl told Mother and Mother told the Inspector. Eric vents his rage upon his mother, almost threatening bodily violence. "You killed her! She came to you to protect me—and you turned her away— My child—your own grandchild—you killed them both—damn you, damn you!"

A masterful "Stop!" from the Inspector quiets the family again. He has finished his work. The girl killed herself, and each of them has had something to do with it. "Never forget it." Birling had fired her, Sheila had caused her to be fired, Eric had used her for the end of a stupid, drunken evening. . . . Gerald, at least, had some affection for her and made her happy for a time.

"Well," the Inspector sums up, "Eva Smith's gone. You can't do her any more harm. . . . One Eva Smith has gone—but there are millions and millions and millions of Eva Smiths and John Smiths still left with us, with their lives all intertwined with our lives. We don't live alone. We are members of one body. We are responsible for each other. Good night."

The Inspector walks straight out of the house, leaving them staring, subdued and wondering. . . .

In a moment, violent recriminations begin. Birling blames his son for all this, and sees his knighthood gone for good. Mrs. Birling is ashamed of her son. And Eric is ashamed of both his parents.

Sheila is suddenly scornful of her family. She admits she behaved badly too, and is ashamed of it—but they—the rest of them—don't seem to have learned anything. Her father says he has learned much since the five of them sat down so happily at dinner. Eric remembers that it was just when his father was making a speech about how everybody must look after himself and not listen to the cranks, when one of those cranks—the Inspector—walked in.

Sheila has become sharply attentive and is thinking carefully. Something is very queer. *Was* the man really a police inspector? They all are sure he was, of course. Sheila continues thinking aloud: It doesn't much matter who it was who made them confess—it was the truth and not whether the man was an inspector or not that was important. But there *was* something curious about the man. Had they noticed that they hardly ever told him anything he didn't already know?

The maid, Edna, answers a ring at the front door. It is Gerald, who hopes they don't mind his returning, but he has a special reason. Obviously, he has learned something, and the Birlings are eager to hear it.

"That man wasn't a police officer."

They are astounded. Is Gerald absolutely certain? Almost; he has talked with a police sergeant friend, has described Inspector Goole, and has been flatly informed there is no such man on the force.

Birling's good feeling begins to return. A fake! He will make certain now by calling up his friend the Chief Constable and asking him. He makes the call and listens carefully, as do the others. The Chief Constable confirms Gerald's information—no such man on the force.

The relief is immense, except in Sheila's case. The girl says, bitterly, that she supposes this makes them all nice people again.

Birling thinks the whole affair may have been a plot—that there are, believe it or not, enough people in town who dislike him enough to put somebody up to such a hoax. "I'll admit that that fellow's antics rattled us a bit," he says, "but we've found him out—and all we have to do is to keep our heads."

Eric interposes that this doesn't change the fact that the girl is still dead, and this is what Sheila feels too. Eric still has stolen money on his conscience, but the important thing is what they all did to the girl.

"Eric's absolutely right," says Sheila. "And it's the best thing any one of us has said tonight, and it makes me feel a bit less ashamed of us. You were just beginning to pretend all over again."

Eric agrees, "It doesn't alter the fact that we all helped kill her."

"But is it a fact?" asks Gerald.

This simple question is astonishing and provocative, and Gerald elaborates on it. Certainly, he kept a girl last Summer—but did they all drive her to suicide? A man pretending to be an inspector comes to the house and, artfully working on bits of information he has picked up here and there, bluffs them all into confessions.

The confessions are true, Eric points out. "But," Gerald counters impressively, *"how do you know it's the same girl?"*

In amazement they discover that they don't know. The Inspector always showed the photograph to one person at a time, and not one of them ever saw the picture together with another of them. "How do you know it's the same photograph?" Gerald demands. And he himself never saw a picture; he confessed after hearing the name of Daisy Renton.

Birling eagerly brings up the point that there wasn't the slightest proof that Daisy Renton was really the Eva Smith whom he had sacked. Mrs. Birling recalls that the girl didn't call herself Eva Smith when she came asking for help, or even Daisy Renton.

"Gerald's dead right," says Birling. "He could have used a different photograph each time and we'd be none the wiser. We may all have been recognizing different girls." And even the interview with Mrs. Birling may have been a put-up job—part of the hoax. "The whole damned thing can have been a piece of bluff."

"How can it? The girl's dead, isn't she?" his son reminds him.

Gerald asks, "What girl? There were probably four or five different girls."

Eric answers that this doesn't matter to him, for the one he knew is dead.

"Is she?" asks his father. *"How do we know she is?"* His question is triumphant. "He took us, all right. He had the laugh on us."

Eric would laugh too, if he knew it was all a hoax.

The logical Gerald knows how to settle it at once, very simply: just call the Infirmary, and either there is a dead girl there or there isn't. And even if there is, they don't know if it's the one who has been talked about tonight.

He makes the call while the others wait tensely. When he gets the Infirmary on the wire he explains that he is Gerald Croft of Crofts Limited, and they are rather worried about one of their girl employees who may have committed suicide by drinking disinfectant. He has to hold the wire while the Infirmary makes a check, and the tension in the Birling home is acute.

GERALD—Yes? . . . You're certain of that? . . . I see. Well, thank you very much. . . . Good night. (*He puts down the receiver and looks at them.*) No girl has died in there today. Nobody's been brought in after drinking disinfectant. They haven't had a suicide for months.

BIRLING (*triumphantly*)—There you are! Proof positive. The whole story's just a lot of moonshine. Nothing but an elaborate sell! (*Produces a high sigh of relief.*) Nobody likes to be sold

as badly as that—but—for all that— (*Smiles at them all.*)
What a relief! Gerald, have a drink.

GERALD (*smiling*)—Thanks, I think I could just do with one
now.

BIRLING (*going to sideboard*)—So could I.

MRS. BIRLING (*smiling*)—And I must say, Gerald, you've
argued this very cleverly, and I'm most grateful.

GERALD (*going for his drink*)—Well, you see, while I was out
of the house I'd time to cool off and think things out a little.

BIRLING—Yes, he didn't keep you on the run as he did the rest
of us. I'll admit now he gave me a bit of a scare at the time.
But I'd a special reason for not wanting any public scandal just
now. (*Raises his glass.*) Well, here's to us. Come on, Sheila,
don't look like that. All over now.

SHEILA—The worst part is. But you're forgetting one thing I
still can't forget. Everything we said had happened really had
happened. If it didn't end tragically, then that's lucky for us.
But it might have done.

BIRLING (*jovially*)—But the whole thing's different now.
Come, come, you can see that, can't you? (*Imitating* INSPECTOR
in his final speech.) *You all helped to kill her.* (*He points to*
SHEILA *and* ERIC *and laughs.*) And I wish you could have seen
the look on your faces when he said that. And the artful devil
knew all the time nobody had died and the whole story was
bunkum. Oh, he was clever. But he who laughs last—whatever it is. (SHEILA *moves towards the door.*)

BIRLING—Going to bed, young woman?

SHEILA (*tensely*)—I want to get out of this. It frightens me,
the way you talk.

BIRLING (*heartily*)—Nonsense! You'll have a good laugh
over it yet. Fellow comes here and starts inventing—

SHEILA—He didn't invent what each of us admitted to doing—
did he?

BIRLING—What if he didn't? Look, you'd better ask Gerald
for that ring you gave back to him, hadn't you? Then you'll
feel better.

SHEILA (*passionately*)—You're pretending everything's just as
it was before.

ERIC—I'm not!

SHEILA—No, but these others are.

BIRLING—Well, isn't it? We've been had, that's all.

SHEILA—So nothing really happened. So there's nothing to

be sorry for, nothing to learn. We can all go on behaving just as we did.

MRS. BIRLING—Well, why shouldn't we?

SHEILA—I tell you—whoever that Inspector was, it was anything but a joke. You knew it then. You began to learn something. And now you've stopped. You're ready to go on in the same old way.

BIRLING (*amused*)—And you're not, eh?

SHEILA—No, because I remember what he said, how he looked, and what he made me feel. And it frightens me the way you talk, and I can't listen to any more of it.

BIRLING—Well, go to bed then, and don't stand there being hysterical.

MRS. BIRLING—She's overtired. In the morning she'll be as amused as we are.

GERALD—Everything's all right now, Sheila. (*Holds up the ring.*) What about this ring?

SHEILA—No, not yet. It's too soon. I must think.

BIRLING (*pointing to* ERIC *and* SHEILA)—Now look at the pair of them—the famous younger generation who know it all. And they can't even take a joke— (*The telephone rings sharply. There is a moment's complete silence.* BIRLING *goes to answer it.*) Yes? . . . Mr. Birling speaking. . . . *What?*—Here— (*But obviously the other person has rung off.* BIRLING *puts the telephone down slowly and looks in a panic-stricken fashion at the others.*) (That was the police. A girl has just died—on her way to the Infirmary—after swallowing some disinfectant. And a police inspector is on his way here—to ask some—questions— (*They stare guiltily and dumbfounded.*)

THE CURTAIN FALLS

ME AND MOLLY

A Comedy in Three Acts

By Gertrude Berg

IN November, 1929, *Variety,* the theatrical weekly, was too absorbed in larger matters ("Wall St. Lays an Egg," it head-lined) to pay much attention to a new radio program on WJZ. In it a woman named Molly had a husband named Jake who dreamed of setting himself up in the garment business. The author was Gertrude (Mrs. Lewis) Berg. For sixteen years she wrote about the rise of Molly and Jake Goldberg for the radio, reading the part of Molly herself.

For a long time Mrs. Berg wanted to make a play for her characters, but didn't get around to starting it until two years ago. Then she wrote enough for two plays. Her friend, John Golden, had many conferences with her suggesting changes and cuts. "At last," says the author, "I seemed to lose all my feel-ing for the thing, and I asked Mr. Golden to let me return the option money he had paid."

Another manager, Oliver Smith, heard about the play and asked to see it. He was given the original version—too long, he knew, but he felt it had spontaneity, and he urged Mrs. Berg to go to work on it again. "This time it went better," she says. And it got to the Belasco Theatre with Philip Loeb playing Jake and Mrs. Berg playing Molly. It was her stage debut—but not, she says, her acting debut, for everybody always acted on the radio shows. The only difference now was that she had to remem-ber everything and couldn't carry a script in her hands.

We discover the Goldbergs moving into their new apartment in the East Bronx in February of 1919. We can see the whole place, except the entrance hall, which is in back of the dining room, and a bedroom. When it is all fixed up there will be a double brass bed in the bedroom to the right of the stage; in the main view is a combination dining-living room. At the left of the stage the kitchen is reached through a swinging door. The dining room will have a day bed, an oak sideboard, a round table, chairs, a sewing machine and other equipment. In the kitchen are the usual accouterments, including a dumbwaiter and a real-ice icebox.

But right now the place is just being moved into. In the dining room are a barrel stuffed to overflowing and a wicker basket, also stuffed. Elsewhere is a rolled-up rug. The bed hasn't been set up yet in the main bedroom, which is Molly's, but it is stacked there, and the furniture includes a brass clothes tree. Joe and Max, the moving men, are wrestling with a china closet in the dining room, while a neighbor, Mrs. 2C, looks things over, investigates the icebox and sets up a watch at the window. Her son, Hymie, comes hollering for her, followed by her sons Benjy and Milty. The kids swarm over the apartment, investigating too, noisily.

Molly Goldberg arrives, carrying a coat, a clock, and a shopping bag. She stops short at seeing Mrs. 2C, and Mrs. 2C says, "I wish you all the best of luck. . . . It's a beautiful flat. If you'll leave the window open in this bedroom and the window in the kitchen you'll never be hot. . . . I'm in 2C. It's a back flat."

A baby is heard crying and Mrs. 2C goes to minister to it. "I have four," she informs Mrs. Goldberg.

"I have two," says Molly.

Crying baby or not, Mrs. 2C seems loath to go, and while Molly unpacks and unwraps this and that she sounds out the newcomer about her husband and confirms what she has heard—that Mr. Goldberg is the head sample maker for S & J. Her own husband, Mrs. 2C confides, was all right until he got heart murmurs.

Molly's Uncle David has come along to help, and he does water a plant. The children haven't come up yet. "They're standing yet on the stoops they're standing," David tells their mother.

Molly stops to admire her apartment. "The bedroom has one window with cross ventilation," she points out. Then, "David, you're sure you don't want to move in with us?"

David is sure. "You know why not, Molly. When you needed me to live with you, when the few extra dollars I paid was something that helped, it was all right for me to be a boarder. Now, Molly, it's a new beginning." But, he assures her, every Friday he will be a guest.

The dumbwaiter buzzes. When Molly has located it she calls down, "Twice a week iceman, you can deliver me."

Sammy Goldberg comes in just in time to help with the ice, and tells his mother his sister "Rosiely" is on the stoop yet talking to a girl. "You hear, David? Rosiely has a friend already," says Molly. The moving men keep working and furniture is settling into place. Sammy thinks that the couch would look better along another wall.

"If I put the couch there, where will the piano go?" Molly asks. "Ai, David, when my curtains are up and my rugs are down, it'll be a palace. And when we buy the piano, I'll be happy beyond my vocabulary."

David is willing to keep on helping, but Molly tells him to sit in a chair and read his paper and tell her what is revolving in the world. Obediently, David sits, gives a look at a newspaper and comments, "I wouldn't be surprised, Molly, if by the next presidential election, women will be able to vote."

Sammy lugs in a package of old pictures and begins going through them, laughing at an old family picture. He doesn't recognize his mother, or his aunt, or Cousin Simon. David dryly observes, "Rich relatives are always strangers. It makes them feel richer."

Sammy wants to know how old his mother was in this picture. "If we live here as long as we lived downtown, you'll be as old as I was on this picture," she tells her son—which is something for him to ponder a bit.

Molly prevents the moving men from depositing an ottoman chair and a garbage pail along that certain wall, which is reserved for the piano. Sammy wonders if they really are going to have one. "Molly," says David, "if you take my advice, you would buy the piano before Jake begins to talk about going into business again, like you took the apartment. You took it, you got it! Otherwise you'd still be downtown and without a park."

Sammy voices disgust. "What does he want to go into business for? Gee!"

Sammy's mother cautions him about saying "Gee" and then tells him: Papa remembers his own home, when Thursday came and there was nothing in the house for Friday. He remembers the look on his mother's face, and his father always reading a book. Papa has always worried about the future, and always will —but for Sammy and Rosie it's going to be different.

"How much does it take to go into business?" asks Uncle David.

"More than we have," replies Molly.

David starts figuring on who might supply the rest, but Molly isn't hopeful. Jake's friend Mendel, a single man, should have saved enough—but Mendel buys books. Cousin Simon? No;

Jake might ask Simon for advice, but not for money. David figures Simon wouldn't even be good for advice, for he isn't so smart; he didn't make his money by being smart, but by running a sweat shop. . . . David goes back to his paper, and news of the high cost of living, Mayor "Hyland," President Wilson and the impending visit of the Prince of Wales.

Rosie, a pert little pig-tailed girl, comes bouncing in excitedly. "Ma! Ma! There's a piano teacher in the house!" She has found out from Jessie Siegel, who lives in 3H, and Jessie can play two pieces without looking at the music and she's only taking lessons four weeks! Mrs. Siegel is on her way, indeed, to tell Mrs. Goldberg about the teacher. Molly hastily unearths a clean apron.

"Mrs. Siegel? She's American-born?"

"No, she talks worse than you do," replies her daughter matter-of-factly.

At the entrance archway, Mrs. Siegel asks if it is all right for her to come in, and it is, of course. She tells about the teacher— Miss Wertheimer, a next-door neighbor. Molly introduces her to Uncle David and Sammy. "In six months three days Sammy'll be bar-mitzvahed," she declares proudly.

Mrs. Siegel's Jessie will be confirmed, for they go to the re-formed temple. Mrs. Siegel helps herself to a nut from a bowl on the dining table. "After four weeks' lessons," she continues, "my Jessie's playing 'Poet and Peasant' with two hands."

Mrs. 2C breezes back in with a pot of hot coffee; she didn't know if the Goldbergs' gas was on yet. And, she volunteers, she will send over her seltzer man, and Hazelcorn is the only butcher in the neighborhood who doesn't put his hand on the scale.

With a "Drink it first and thank me after," Mrs. 2C leaves the coffee and departs. Mrs. Siegel really ought to be going, but first she wants to know if the Goldbergs are going to pay for their piano on time or cash. "Cash," says Molly.

"It's a good investment," says Mrs. S. "What you put in a child you always take out." Finally, several nuts later, she goes.

Rosie is dreaming about her piano and wondering if the stool will go up and down; Sammy is hunting for a crystal for the radio set he has unpacked. The moving men have finished at last, and one of them presents a receipt for Molly to sign. Molly, embarrassed, wipes her hands on her apron. "If you can't write your name, make a mark and I'll write your name under it," says the mover, to whom this is nothing unusual. But Molly summons her son to sign for her. When the men have gone she announces, "I must find out where I can find a school for big people. If this is uptown and a new beginning there must be a real new beginning for me too."

Molly thrusts open a window and calls, "Yoo-hoo, Mrs. Bloom! I'm all moved in. If I live, I'll see you tonight. If not, I'll see you tomorrow." At this kitchen window she notices that, by leaning far out, she can see a tree. She calls David and her children to share in this rare sight. "Oh, how I love nature!" she exults.

"Is this the Goldberg residence?" The question is humorously formal, and the questioner, at the archway, is Jake, home at last. He has brought a special treat for a special occasion—a box of charlotte russes, into which everybody dives. And, for Molly, he has brought a dress. "And don't tell me it don't fit," he warns.

Life is indeed full for Jake. A new home, with a tree—and a future too. He brings forth, for David's admiration, five swatches of cloth—samples of a job lot of crepe de Chine which he can buy for a ridiculous price if he has the capital.

David is not enthusiastic. He reminds Jake that he has a good job now and what more does he want?

Jake, the dreamer, considers a good job a trap. "No, David! I wouldn't rest in my grave if I didn't die a businessman!" All he wants now is for his friend Mendel to go into business with him, and if he has to he'll even go to Molly's Cousin Simon for a loan.

Molly is admiring her dress, which is to be for Sammy's bar mitzvah—but she has discovered the usual flaw. "I'd like once to have a dress without alterations," she sighs.

"Maybe your waistline ain't in the right place," suggests her husband. And Molly counters meaningfully with, "How many waistlines *are* in the right place?" Here the dress is tight and there it is loose; if just once Jake would bring her some material. . . .

"How many women are perfect measurements, Jake?" she demands.

"Dresses are made on models, Molly."

"Models? How many people are models? . . . Look around, Jake. Wherever there are people, are they beautiful or are they like me?"

Jake explains impatiently, "Everybody knows a dress has to be altered."

Molly won't accept this, any more than Columbus accepted the belief that the world is flat. "I'm not flat, I'm also round," she insists. "And there are many million others like me. I'm only saying, why shouldn't someone like me be able to go into a store and come out without being altered?"

From across the way there is music from a piano, and Rosie exclaims, "That's my piano teacher."

The curtain falls.

Scene II

It is late evening three weeks later. Cousin Simon is here, and so is Jake's friend Mendel, and, of course, the Goldbergs are hosting. Jake is buttering Cousin Simón up; Simon, however, is skittish. He'd like to be going. "You never saw my house, did you?" he asks. "It's the show place of Borough Park."

Molly thinks it would be nice if Simon and his wife, Sophie, would come for supper some time, but her cousin observes that Sophie is so busy, what with her societies and charities. . . .

Simon is indeed a smug and lordly man. Molly's plan for Sammy to go to college and be an engineer does not impress him; Simon has a shop full of educated people and they are working for him, not he for them. His car is downstairs waiting to take him home.

"Mendel," Jake nervously pleads with his friend. "Say the word and before Simon leaves I'll ask him." But Mendel stalls; he is a cautious young man. Klein or Weinstein might be better partners for Jake than Mendel . . . and, besides, Mendel is satisfied.

Well, almost satisfied. If he had a drugstore, now, it would be near enough to being a doctor, and a doctor is what he wanted to be. Mendel takes his departure, and when he has gone Jake begins praising him to Cousin Simon as one of the best men in the dress business—a perfect cutter . . . and the perfect partner for Jake. All Jake needs is Mendel, and a little capital. . . .

"Good-by, Jake!" says Simon. But, before leaving, he donates some advice: Jake should just live simply, holding on to the little, sweet things of life and not, like Simon, become disillusioned by success, money and everything. Jake is the lucky man, now, whereas life to Simon is all an illusion, a fake, a cheat. The cousin escapes and Jake is balked.

Rosie calls across the areaway from the kitchen window to Miss Wertheimer, announcing, "Our company left." Miss Wertheimer answers that she will be right over. Jake may have his plans for a dress business, but Molly and her little daughter have more important plans for piano lessons. Molly hopes that Miss Wertheimer and Jake will be able to go with her and Rosie on Saturday to look at a piano.

But Jake's head is not for pianos now, or Saturday, or Sunday. He is concerned with other things. Abstractedly he takes a bottle of seltzer from the icebox, fills a glass and sips.

MOLLY—I'm only asking because the piano teacher is coming in and—

ROSIE (*subdued*)—She was going to go with us, Pa.

JAKE (*at doorway*)—And if a piano is purchased a year later? . . .

ROSIE (*on the verge of tears, to back of upstage table chair*)—A year?

MOLLY—Only . . .

JAKE—Yes, only! There's only one only, Molly; there's only one thing, only one, and until that time everything else waits; everything! (*Sits.*)

MOLLY—But . . .

JAKE (*with finality*)—No buts, Molly!

MOLLY (*after a pause*)—I was only going to say the piano money was money that we put aside . . .

ROSIE (*kneeling on chair, still on verge of tears*)—Mama saved it, Pa. That's why she didn't buy the sealskin coat, Pa.

MOLLY—Rosiely. (ROSIE *cries, exits to bedroom.* JAKE *follows her with his eyes, turns and looks at* MOLLY.)

JAKE—One thing I want to ask, one question.

MOLLY—Jake.

JAKE—Is a man alone? For years what has been my hope, my dream, my desire—what? To be a man in business; to build something for myself that was mine—the fruit of my labor. To who was I telling my dreams to who? The four walls or to my own flesh and blood? I'm asking questions; where are the answers?

MOLLY—But the money for the piano . . .

JAKE—Every penny we have and every penny we can scrape together goes for one thing. Until that time everything else waits, everything! You can't take piano lessons without a piano? Abraham Lincoln walked ten miles for a book when he wanted to read; the book didn't walk ten miles to Abraham Lincoln. I thought if we were climbing, we would climb together, not separate, not apart. What I want is for you; I thought what you wanted was for me, so we could all enjoy a future with a foundation. But, whether you would or not, I'm not letting a future slip out of my fingers, that not! That not.

MOLLY—Jake!

JAKE—So . . . would it have meant so much to him if he had said yes instead of no?

MOLLY—Who said what?

JAKE—Who do you think?

MOLLY—Not Simon!

JAKE—And why not Simon?

MOLLY—You asked Simon, Jake? You always said . . .

JAKE—So I asked! Why shouldn't I ask? Would he have to eat less? Would his children go without shoes? Nothing for him would change, nothing! But for me a Yes instead of a No would mean the difference between being a slave or a free man . . . a piano or not a piano.

MOLLY—Jake, please! Don't worry about a piano. It's not so important.

JAKE—What? A piano for Rosie is not important?

MOLLY—You're important, Jake. Rosiely will learn to play on someone else's piano.

JAKE—Simon's No I won't forget, Molly! Of that you can be sure. (*He walks out.*)

MOLLY—So where are you going, Jake? . . . Not without your coat!

JAKE—I got my coat. (*Out.*)

MOLLY (*at archway; looks from sofa to wall*)—Sammyle, help me. (*They move sofa to space reserved for piano.*) The stores will have pianos next year also, Rosie.

ROSIE—I know . . . I'm sorry.

MOLLY—Papa knows what's good for his family, Rosiely. Lincoln did walk ten miles to read a book; the book didn't come to him; he went to the book.

The arrival of Miss Wertheimer is not the happy occasion it should have been, but Molly and Rosie make the best of it. They are—er—postponing the piano, but of course the lessons don't have to be postponed.

Miss Wertheimer, whose first name is Vera, pleasantly agrees. Rosie can use her piano. Molly explains that Mr. Goldberg has decided to go into business for himself and every penny counts; however . . .

Molly goes to the kitchen and takes a wad of money from a

cereal bowl. "Miss Wertheimer, I want to pay for Rosiely's lessons in advance for one year."

"That isn't necessary."

"Yes, it is very necessary. Every penny we have is going to go into the business, and—who knows?—maybe it'll all be lost; and if yes, then whatever will be, at least one year's lesson Rosiely will be sure of getting."

When the outer door slams Molly thinks it is her husband—but it is Mendel, who becomes very shy when he sees Vera and is introduced to her. The piano teacher leaves and Mendel, having learned that Jake has gone out, also departs—but not before making sure he has the piano teacher's first and last names right. Jake comes back just as Mendel goes, and the family gets ready for bed.

Jake empties the icebox pan, and Molly, in the bedroom, takes down her hair and removes her dress. Sammy emerges from the bathroom in pajamas, carrying bedding for the day bed in the dining room. He makes up his couch, takes a magazine from beneath a cushion, lies on his stomach and begins reading—but hides the magazine when his mother, in a kimono, comes to tuck him in. Jake leaves his shoes by the ottoman, puts his shirt on the buffet and heads for the bath; his wife picks up after him. In the other bedroom, Rosie calls good night.

When Jake too has gone to bed, Molly turns out the lights and crawls into the brass bed with her husband. "Jake, you sleeping?" she inquires.

"I'm sleeping," he says.

But he isn't; he is burning. Burning about Cousin Simon and his advice. "How long can a man live like a worm in an apple?" he demands. "I'll find a way, Molly; with Simon or without Simon I'll find a way. I won't be a slave to a crust of bread for the rest of my life—not me!"

His wife manages to soothe him and to kiss him good night. "Tomorrow is another day," she comforts him.

The curtain falls.

Scene III

Several days later the piano is definitely out of the picture, with the sofa along the wall where it was to have been, and with a sewing machine where the sofa used to be. There is a dressmaker's dummy in the room too, and a bowl of fruit on the table. Uncle David is at the machine while Molly is pinning a dress on the dummy. It is the dress Jake gave her for Sammy's bar mitzvah, and she is hoping to get it altered in time.

Sammy comes home from school—and, since he is home so early, it is obvious that he didn't go on to the Hebrew school to work on his bar mitzvah speech. His mother orders, "This minute go into Rosiely's room and sit and study and put away the baseball pictures. If not I'll tell Papa to stop smoking Sweet Caporals." Sammy announces that he isn't interested in the pictures now; he has a new cat's whisker for his radio which will get him more than Station KDKA. He wonders if the janitor will let him and his friends have part of the basement for a sort of radio club.

Molly says she will see about asking the janitor after Sammy's next report card comes in—and it must be A-A-A, not less.

"Do you think Marconi got all A's?" the boy objects.

"I don't care what other boys get, I know what I want from you." Sammy, disgusted at his mother's ignorance, goes into the bedroom to study.

Uncle David, a great one for newspapers, has taken one up again and reads an interesting story about something new—a blood transfusion.

Molly wonders if this would be called a discovery or an invention. "The paper says a discovery," says David.

"I always thought," puzzles Molly, "that a discovery was for a place and an invention for a thing. Like a dumbwaiter or an electric light. Tell me, David—the size of women's dresses, was that a discovery or an invention?"

"Could be . . ." David starts.

"Well," continues Molly, "if it's a discovery like America, it's final. But if it's an invention, then there's room for a new invention. Everybody said No, but Edison said Yes, and there was light."

"But, Molly, dresses are dresses, no?"

"Not if they don't fit, they're not dresses."

They are interrupted by Hymie, one of Mrs. 2C's youngsters, bursting in to borrow a cup of sugar for his mother and to snitch a banana from the fruit bowl. The generous Molly gives him a second banana and with brief thanks he runs out. "Today," Molly continues to her uncle, "in the grocery store, six women were ordering—so, just so, I asked who can go in and walk out with a dress and not be altered. How many do you think, David? . . . Not one! And in the whole house only Miss Wertheimer is normal."

Hymie's brother Benjy comes in—for onions this time, and an apple and a banana.

Mention of Miss Wertheimer has started Uncle David thinking. Miss Wertheimer must be in her late middle twenties . . . and . . .

The third 2C child comes in and announces, "I don't like apples. My mother said I could have a banana better."

Molly has begun setting the table with a fresh tablecloth. She goes to the kitchen now "to throw her eye into her soup" when Rosie comes in from her room to get her music and go take a lesson. David kisses her, tickling her face with his mustache, and inquires about her piano progress. From the kitchen Molly summons Rosie to read the directions on a package of Jello for her. Rosie reads, "Two cups of water to a package," and hurries off to her lesson. At the door she calls out that her report card is in the fruit bowl, and she got A-B-A on it.

"Why didn't you show it to me?" asks her mother.

"Because Papa always signs it." In such little ways Molly Goldberg is frequently reminded of her own illiteracy.

From the bedroom Sammy complains about the long speech the rabbi has given him to learn. "According to my figures," announces his mother, "you get three months in which to learn the speech, so if you only learn one word a day I'm sure you will be able to learn the whole speech."

The hall door slams; it is Jake, home and in a bad temper. He embraces his son, and Molly comes in with a glass of napkins and some silver for the table. "I'll put seltzer and we'll eat. Jake, when you're ready to sit, say."

"I'm saying."

"So go wash yourself."

But there is time, because Molly has more things to put on the table; and Jake is low. Cousin Simon is out of the picture, and Mendel hasn't got ambition, let alone capital. Mendel's whole mind is occupied with social conditions, and he is interested only in masses.

"A new system of sizes would be for the masses," hints Molly —but Jake won't listen. David now comes up with an idea which does interest Mr. Goldberg—Miss Wertheimer. If Mendel needs somebody and something to be ambitious for, why . . .

Molly has been setting six places, not five, and the extra one is for Mendel, who arrives late because he had a little work to finish. "Go wash, Mendel; we'll sit on the table and eat," says Molly.

Back from her music lesson, Rosie is excited; Miss Wertheimer has given her a ticket for a concert tonight in the high school auditorium, and the teacher is going to go with her.

Molly, a matchmaker like all women, has an immediate idea. She takes Rosie into the kitchen, with David following, and announces her plot: if Rosie couldn't go to the concert tonight, and would give Mendel her ticket, why, then, he'd be accidentally sitting in the next seat to Miss Wertheimer. And then . . ." A word brings a word and a word bring a sentence and—"

"And a sentence brings a question and a question brings an answer—yes or no," finishes David.

Rosie can't see it. She wants to go to the concert.

Molly finishes putting plates of liver on the table and the family fall in. She tells Jake about Rosie's ticket, and Jake too observes that it would be better if Mendel were going. "What the man needs and what I need is to see that man married, to have the responsibilities that a man is entitled to if he is to call himself a man."

Rosie hardly touches her food, and runs to the bedroom to dress for the concert. Mendel, washed up now, takes his place at the table, and while the others begin their great maneuver Rosie can be seen getting into a fresh dress. When food is mentioned, Molly observes that the greatest hunger in the world is for love. Jake agrees that love is everything. David says it is love which puts people in paradise. Two, says Jake, can be as one. . . .

It is all for Mendel's benefit—and Rosie's loss. The little girl realizes the futility of her situation and changes back into her other dress. "Ma, I don't feel well," she declares.

"Oh, my! So what'll be with the ticket?" asks her mother.

Jake says that if he only liked good music, he'd go. So would David, only "When it comes to music, by me good is bad."

It is to be a Chopin concert too.

The meal has not yet been completed, but a concerted operation is begun upon Mendel. David urges him into his suit coat, Jake gives him a last bite to eat and Molly rushes him a cup of tea. "Here, Mendel, swallow and go."

"What's all this about? Where am I going?" demands the bewildered Mendel.

Rosie hands the ticket to her mother; Jake takes it from Molly and thrusts it into Mendel's hand. "To a concert!" says Jake.

The curtain falls.

ACT II

Spring has come—April. The Goldbergs' dining table is festively set and Molly is working at the kitchen table, where there are matzoths and napkins, or at the stove, where there are pots on all four burners. Rosie has just put a clean towel in the bathroom.

It is Spring vacation for Rosie and Sammy—and for Molly too —for Molly has been going to night school. She is the only one who doesn't enjoy the vacation. "I shouldn't only be left back with my head," she tells her daughter. To David she boasts how she can spell her name.

Molly tells Rosie what the seating arrangement will be around the table—with Miss Wertheimer next to Mr. Mendel. Miss Wertheimer will arrive in time for the Seder.

David thinks Rosie looks so pretty Miss Wertheimer should see her right away—come in for a minute now. So Rosie goes to get her. "And don't mention Mendel," warns her mother.

David edges over to the bathroom door, humming, and opens it. When Molly wants to know what he is up to he explains he just wants to look out of the window. When his niece heads for the bedroom to get a handkerchief he neatly blocks her off by offering his. Molly suspects he is hiding presents—presents for Pesach—in the bedroom but he is noncommittal.

Rosie races in. "Ma—Ma—Ma! A piano somebody's getting; a piano!" She doesn't know who might be getting it—but when David begins moving the sofa to the other wall, Molly knows. She embraces her uncle, but David gives her a warning "Sh!" They finish with the sofa, shift the sewing machine and ignore Rosie's questions. The doorbell rings, and David admits Max, the moving man. Max is carrying a piano stool . . . and now Rosie knows who is getting the piano. She is utterly joyful.

"Thank Uncle David," says her mother.

The lass asks him, "Did you buy it for me?"

"Why not? What other pleasures has Uncle David?"

Neighbors begin to stream in, and soon the apartment is a bedlam. Max and his partner hoist the instrument in through the bedroom window and move it into place amid cries of "Wonderful! Beautiful! Gawjiss!"

When the job is done Max demands, "Who signs for this?" The proud Molly replies, "Me—I sign for it." Mrs. Siegel, Mrs. 2C, Mrs. Gross and other neighbors begin a debate about the piano's position—about whether it is too near the heat or too far from the window or what, and whether milk or vinegar is better for washing the keys. Finally David commands, "Sit, Rosiely."

And Rosie plays—scales.

The piano is a major event in the building. The women argue over it, argue over music, argue about their children. Mrs. 2C's obstreperous son, Hymie, leaps in and takes a bang at the new instrument and gets his hand slapped by his mother. The only quiet onlooker is Vera Wertheimer, who will not be drawn into debate as to whether the piano is too near the window or if it should be kept closed or open when it is not being played. Rosie's beautiful present is more than beginning to look like the cue for a female free-for-all, with sundry children adding to the racket, when Uncle David pleads for peace.

"Go home," he urges. "Go home. Tonight is not a night to be mad. Tonight is a holiday. Go home to your Seders." He and Molly herd the mob out, and David returns with the just-arrived Mendel in tow. Vera, too, has done her part to quiet the arguments by beginning to play the piano. When quiet falls, Rosie inquires if it is Beethoven she is playing.

"No, it isn't," Mendel announces. Then, "Hello, Vera."

Vera stops playing and returns the greeting. Rosie still wants to know what the piece was. "Mozart," says Mendel—and he urges Vera to keep on playing. To him it is a great accomplishment that anybody can play an entire Chopin prelude from memory. It looks like the beginning of a good twosome, so Molly lures Rosie into the kitchen and David sneaks out into the foyer.

"It must be wonderful to do the things you like best," sighs Mendel.

"Don't you like your work?" inquires Vera.

"No. It's a good job, but what's there to dresses? Once I wanted to be a doctor. For years now I've been planning to study pharmacy. Even that takes three years. A man could get married and raise a family in that time."

The sympathetic Vera allows that three years isn't so long, if one is patient.

"You must have a lot of friends," Mendel observes.

"I don't," Vera declares—and with that she gets up from the piano and goes home. The watchful Molly and Rosie pop in from the kitchen and Rosie is quickly planted at the piano. "Sit and play," her mother urges. "Ai, will Papa love it!" Sammy arrives with the information that Papa, indeed, will be up as soon as he gets through talking with 4C on the stoop.

By the time Jake does get upstairs the stage is set. Sammy is quiet, Molly is quiet and so is David, as Rosie runs through her scales.

"So you did buy it!" exclaims Jake. "You couldn't wait, huh? That was more important, huh?"

Gently Uncle David explains that he is the one who bought the piano, not Molly; but Jake will not cool off. "It could have waited and it should have waited," he objects, "until the time when *I* could have bought it." He goes into the bedroom, and Uncle David gets on with still more important business of the day, bringing four yamilkes, four books and a pillow to the table, while Molly and Sammy bring chairs from the kitchen.

From elsewhere in the building comes the sound of a chant. Sammy says it is 3D, who have started their Seder. "And 4A too," says Rosie.

Jake comes from the bedroom, sits at his place at the table, and starts the chant.

The curtain falls.

Scene II

It is a night several weeks later. In the bedroom, Molly is getting ready to go someplace, and around the dining table are Uncle David, Mendel and Jake playing pinochle. Rosie is working on a map at the kitchen table, and Sammy is in the kitchen, too, trying to tattoo himself with a strip of decalcomania.

Molly comes into the front room, gets some books off the buffet and calls to her daughter, "Rosiely, look out of the window and see if the streets are sliding." Mendel looks up from the pinochle game long enough to inform Mrs. Goldberg that it is very wet and slippery out; Rosie, after a look out the kitchen window, confirms the information. Her ma had better put on her rubbers.

Ma is going out, obviously—out to night school. Equally obviously, the pinochle players are staying in, except, perhaps, Mendel. Rosie is staying in too to have a piano lesson. "Ma," Rosie asks, "can I go to the movies with Miss Wertheimer and Mr. Mendel if it's not too late?" Molly has made up her mind in advance that it will be too late, and she tells Rosie so. From his game Jake chips in the observation that two's company and three's a crowd.

Before going, Molly asks Sammy to check her on her homework. Jake jeers at his wife's going to school; to him, getting into business with just ten machines to start is more important.

Molly has an idea about this too, but Jake won't listen—it's the old one about sizes. "Sizes are sizes." Jake seeks to dismiss the subject.

Moreover, Jake thinks another important subject is Mendel's possible marriage. "Mendel is more than thirty and he's not even a husband." His wife's school question about the qualifications of a Senator and how she answers it in a practice quiz with Sammy seem trivial, when he wants to know how far is the romance progressing and at what speed.

David interjects, "How can Molly ask Miss Wertheimer such a personal question?" "If she don't, I will," Jake threatens.

The doorbell rings and to the usual cry of "Come, whomever you are," Mrs. Gross appears. She asks Molly, "Do you want to take my measurements now?" Molly takes them, and Mrs. Gross promises her sis-in-law's measurements tomorrow.

Jake snorts at these goings-on, and Mrs. Gross reminds him of one J. P. Marmelstein, whose wife suggested that he sew a waist and a skirt together, thus inventing the first machine-made dress. "Today," Mrs. Gross reminds Goldberg, "in her memory she has a blue glass window with her name on it in the West Side Synagogue. I wish you the same, Mr. Goldberg."

Mrs. Siegel comes in for a measurement and to report she has bought 3½ yards of material. Finally Molly and her two friends are ready to start for school, when Miss Wertheimer arrives to give Rosie her music lesson.

"Hello, Vera," says Mendel.

"Hello, Mendel," says Vera.

The three big schoolgirls depart at last and the pinochle game continues, with side comments from Jake, and the piano lesson begins.

Jake keeps talking about love and marriage, very pointedly. He more than hints that Mendel had better make up his mind quickly. He poses a hypothetical question: if a man can offer a woman love, should his financial status be an obstruction? Furthermore, if the woman has a little saved, shouldn't she share what she has? Particularly if it would put a man in business?

From the piano Vera seems to agree. "If the financial help can help them build a life together, I don't see why . . ."

Mendel, who has begun to catch on, flatly disagrees. Moreover he is angry at Jake and embarrassed before Vera. "I'm sorry," he says to her. And to Jake: "I'm not an animal and I can't be led, and you can't push me. I don't want the same things you want. Don't ask me to your house again, Jake, and if you see me in the street, don't say hello—I won't answer you. We're not friends any more." Mendel leaves in a dudgeon.

David thinks it is about time for some tea, and he fixes it in the kitchen. Vera leaves and Rosie heads for bed. Jake can't understand why everybody is so upset just because he wanted to help a friend. David brings in two glasses of tea, but when he hears the door slam and hears Molly call he escapes into the bedroom.

Molly is back so soon because the teacher was sick. She notices the extra glass of tea and wonders whose it is. Hers if she wants it, Jake sourly informs her. It isn't David's because David has gone to bed.

Molly observes that the tea is hot yet.

"So it's hot."

"Why didn't whoever drink it?"

"Because whoever didn't want it."

"Who was the whoever? Rosie don't drink tea, and Sammy isn't home, and if the tea is still hot and Mendel is not here, then David can't be sleeping yet." She calls to her uncle.

"I'm sleeping," replies David. So Molly, accepting the tea, turns to her husband and says gently, "If you don't want to tell me, don't tell me." Jake won't talk, no matter how many direct questions Molly asks about the obvious early departure of Mendel.

David finally comes from the bedroom to explain, "Jake only asked a question, Molly. . . ."

Jake is contrite to a point; if Molly had been here it wouldn't have happened. And he wonders now if Mendel don't say hello to him should he say hello to Mendel? No, he decides angrily.

The curtain falls.

SCENE III

Outside a hurdy-gurdy is playing; it is a Midsummer evening. Inside are Rosie, drying silver at the sink; Sammy, on the sofa with his radio and earphones, and David, sewing a button on a vest. From below Molly calls to Rosie to save Papa's plate even though he is so late he has missed supper, and she wants Sammy to get together all the measurements.

"I'm nearly finished measuring all the ladies on this floor."

Pretty soon she comes in with a handful of paper bags. Out the window she calls, "Yoo-hoo, Mrs. Bloom—you're not a forty-four any more; you're a twenty-two and a half. So come up and take a fit." Molly rummages around saying, "I put the grocery lady's hips some place and I don't remember." Rosie locates the measurements on the buffet.

The little girl should practice, for tomorrow is her lesson day. Molly wishes Miss Wertheimer would at least put her head in the door, and wonders how long the young woman is going to stay mad. David wonders the same about Mendel.

Mrs. Goldberg does some measuring on herself, with Sammy making the notes. She is pleased to discover she is two inches less than the grocery lady. This is news to Rosie, who hadn't noticed this, and it doesn't impress David, who pooh-poohs, "What's two inches!"

"Two inches is a full size. . . . Sometimes, Rosiely, you're not so absorbent."

Sammy corrects her. "Observant, Ma."

"Absorbent is cotton in a blue box," says David.

"Thank you," says Molly.

Sammy counts up twenty-eight sets of measurements, and Rosie and her friend Jessie have canvassed the whole block for a lot more.

Rosie is shooed to her piano and Sammy is ordered to write some more invitations to his bar mitzvah, which is only six weeks away.

"Is Papa really going into business?" the boy inquires. Indeed Jake is. He's got a loft already, and partners. The only partner Molly knows is Mr. 2C.

Some man rings the bell and leaves a letter for Jake with Sammy; he won't come in and Sammy didn't ask his name. Next the boy—who is getting tired of being told to do things—is urged to go down for a pitcher of soda for Papa, taking money from the blue bowl on a kitchen shelf. The money in a cup is for rent, and in two other cups are funds for Rosie's birthday and Sammy's bar mitzvah.

Rosie quits practicing and begins on Sammy's invitations. No, Cousin Simon is not to be invited, her mother says; on this occasion Molly wants Papa to be happy. The Siegels are all right, and Jessie can have a separate invitation.

At the door, with fire in her eye, appears Mrs. Ellenbogen. "I want to see Mr. Goldberg. I just want to tell him face to face what I think of him."

Molly hurries Sammy on his errand and sends Rosie to her room. Mrs. Ellenbogen is a stranger and Molly and David haven't heard the name before. The irate woman exclaims, "You mean to tell me that your husband didn't mention Mr. Ellenbogen? He didn't tell you he bamboozled Louis Ellenbogen into business? My husband is an operator on corset covers. What does he know about dresses that he should take his last penny out of the bank and gamble?" She begins to weep, even though Molly assures her that Jake is no bamboozler.

Mrs. Ellenbogen won't believe Jake is not home. She thinks he is hiding in the bedroom; so, as she leaves, she calls loudly, "Mr. Ellenbogen changed his mind!"

David has an uncomfortable hunch about the letter the man left; he thinks Molly should open it—but the doorbell interrupts. It is Hymie, Benjy and Milty, returning things their mother has borrowed from time to time. Solemnly they decline Molly's offer of bananas. Says Hymie, "My mother said now she knows why you were so good to us"—and the brothers depart.

David opens the letter and Rosie reads it. It begins, "Dear Mr. Goldberg: I'm very sorry but I have changed my mind about going into the contracting business. . . ." Molly takes the letter away from Rosie and moans, "How will I tell Papa; how?"

When Sammy returns with the soda pitcher his sister informs him, "Papa hasn't any more partners."

When Jake gets home he is cheerful. "I'm on the first rung of my ladder," he exclaims, and begins singing. He has put a deposit on the loft and has paid spot cash for the material.

Finally he notices Molly's glum look. He decides, "You're worried already I won't be able to make a bar mitzvah if I go into business? In six weeks, Molly, you'll hear my machines humming!" Uncle David turns away, and Molly brings Jake some soup. Jake fishes a card out of his pocket and tells Sammy to go where it says and tell Mr. Ellenbogen he'll be calling within an hour. Molly shakes her head No at Sammy and gives Jake the letter.

"So I won't have three partners," he shrugs. "Ellenbogen is a better man."

"Not Ellenbogen either, Jake," his unhappy wife informs him. "And not 2C also not. They sent messages, Jake."

Goldberg's happiness is shattered. He querulously scolds Sammy for having drunk the last little bit of seltzer in the siphon, lectures the family in general and voices his sorrow for himself. "What am I killing myself for? Why am I eating my heart out?" Sadly he goes to the bedroom, takes off his coat and shoes, and lies on the bed. He makes no reply to Rosie's offer to get his slippers, and no answer to David's suggestion of a pinochle game; Sammy's offer to buy some ice cream is ignored. But Molly thinks ice cream is a good idea.

Jake becomes penitent. "Why are you all so good to me?" he asks his wife.

"Because YOU are good."

Jake won't accept this statement. "I'm only half a man, Molly. And don't say NO!" Suppose she does think he is brave, and kind—he hollered loud at Sammy, didn't he?

"Jake," Molly asks, "when can you give back the money you took from Mr. Ellenbogen?"

"It's not money any more," he informs her. "Its crepe de Chine in five colors. It's three months' rent on a loft; it's ten machines and equipment. It's not only Ellenbogen, Molly; it's 2C and it's Mr. Klein and it's every penny we had in the bank!"

Molly suggests that maybe his boss will help out.

"If I had a boss I'd ask him. There's no boss and there's no job, Molly—there's not even a future."

The curtain falls.

ACT III

It is in September. Molly is dressing in her room. Sammy is looking at his bar mitzvah presents on the buffet. Rosie is dressing, and Jake and David are in the kitchen. David mixes a Seidlitz powder and suggests that Jake drink it before going to the synagogue.

"How many disappointments can a man take? I'm a sick man, David," Jake moans. Maybe he is having a thrombosis.

Molly calls to ask if she should call Mendel or Simon. "Absolutely not! Mendel spoiled and your Cousin Simon spoiled. My machines could be humming now." Instead of machines, all Jake has is a loan on his insurance policy, so now when he dies the lodge will have to bury him.

Molly and David strive fruitlessly to cheer Jake up. Molly comes in, dressed now, to be admired. "That's the way I want to remember you," is Jake's dejected compliment.

Sammy has his new suit on and he thinks it's "schnazzy." His mother suggests that he rehearse his synagogue speech, and after much urging the boy steps up on the ottoman and begins, rapidly, "This day marks unto me the beginning of a dutiful life."

MOLLY—Slower! And with expression.

SAMMY (*starts slower, accelerates*)—I know that many dangers and temptations will beset my path.

JAKE—That's better.

SAMMY—I am at present like a young plant that is exposed to the storms and the inclemencies of the weather. . . . To you, my dear parents: I know how great and difficult has been your effort to raise me from the day of my birth to the present day. I know how you cared for me every day and every hour. Can more words express the gratitude which I bear in my heart for you? Can I in any way repay you for all you have done for me? No. Because what parents do for their children is . . .

MOLLY—Infinitely.

SAMMY—. . . infinitely more important and valuable than all things else. I think, however, that the most fitting reward and token of gratitude I can offer you is to fulfill the commandment: Honor thy Father and thy Mother—and to live up to all the other commandments which it is my duty to observe both as a Jew and a man. And to you, loving sister, may God bless you for your unselfishness. May Providence keep away from our family all sorrows; may the chain of love that holds us together forever remain unsevered; and may happiness, joy and peace be our share of life. God grant my earnest petition. (MOLLY *crosses behind* JAKE, *puts arms around him.*)

SAMMY—That's why I didn't want to say it!

MOLLY—You made four mistakes.

ROSIE—I counted six.

SAMMY—Where?

ROSIE—You said blessing and you left out guidance.

MOLLY—You left out affection and you didn't say love.

SAMMY—That's only two.

Somebody rings and Sammy opens the door.

It's Mendel!

He gives Sammy a present. "It's from Vera and me," he explains.

Mendel's arrival and his mention of Vera are immensely cheering to Jake, and he burbles enthusiastically. "Molly, you're silent," he observes.

"I'm besides myself, Jake; and when I'm besides myself I get silent."

Mendel, Jake continues, is a new man. And now Jake even wishes that Cousin Simon would come. "Before you came in, Mendel—now I can tell you, Molly—you were on the brink of being a widow." He urges Mendel to go get Vera, so they all can drink a toast. David starts getting out glasses, Mendel goes for Miss Wertheimer and Jake philosophizes that while there's life there's hope, and vice versa.

The bell again—and this time it is Simon. He isn't bringing a present for Sammy because it has been sent already—one of the six fountain pens the boy has got already. "I hope someday you'll be able to write your name to a million-dollar check," says Simon.

"Maybe he won't be a capitalist of such altitudes," says Jake, "but it's all right—it won't be long before his papa will be a man in business."

Molly puts on her hat, urges the others to get ready. Jake expands about the business: it will be Mendel and Goldberg, or Goldberg and Mendel. "What we're going to do—" he begins, and Molly interrupts with, "New sizes, Simon."

"New sizes, Jake?" Simon queries. "Did you discover new people? Giants and midgets?"

Molly keeps Jake from talking by talking herself. No, not giants and midgets, but real people—the people in between sizes, which is where most of them are.

Mendel and Vera arrive and Jake performs the introductions.

MENDEL—Here's the pattern, Mrs. Goldberg.

JAKE—What pattern, Mendel?

MENDEL—Mrs. Goldberg asked me to make a pattern for a half size, Jake.

JAKE—The partnership hasn't even started and you're mixing already, Molly?

MENDEL—Partnership?

JAKE—Goldberg and Mendel, or Mendel and Goldberg! Take your choice. (MOLLY *is at bedroom door*.)

MENDEL—I made my choice.

VERA—In three years Mendel will be a pharmacist.

JAKE—But, Mendel . . . you said the world wasn't big enough. . . .

MENDEL—It's not, but the world isn't the dress business, Jake. I'm sorry, Jake. You have your dreams and I have mine. (*Turns to* DAVID.) Maybe our son will be a doctor like your son, David. For me, that's too late, but a pharmacist I can be in three years if I study nights. I'll buy a little store. I'll be able to read prescriptions. I mean— That's what I want, that's what I always wanted. I don't want to exploit and I don't want to be exploited. (SIMON *laughs*.) If I hire a clerk, I'll make him a partner. And maybe someday somebody will call me Doctor Mendel by mistake.

MOLLY—Jake . . .

JAKE—Jake! (*Goes into bedroom for hat and coat;* MOLLY *follows him.*)

MENDEL—Maybe we better go ahead to the synagogue, David.

DAVID—Maybe.

MENDEL—Come, Vera. Why does it always have to be this way?

DAVID (*rising*)—Because you're you and Jake's Jake. So don't worry. (DAVID *takes them out.* MOLLY *returns, puts on hat.*)

SIMON (*in chair, laughing*)—A drugstore! Stamps, change he'll give for telephones, and a prescription he'll fill once a week! Molly, this dress was cut on the new pattern. (*She starts to bedroom, is stopped by* SIMON.)

This half-size business is beginning to interest Simon—and his interest increases during the next few moments, when various of Molly's friends come in, bringing gifts for Sammy. They'll all be going to the synagogue—and they all are dressed in Molly's creation. The garments vary in color, but not in pattern. Mrs. Siegel, Mrs. Gross, Mrs. 2C . . .

They are proud of their dresses. "Fits like a glove," says one; another: "Just like I was spilled into it."

When they troop off to the synagogue Simon confides in Jake that he likes the half-size idea—liked it the first time he heard about it. He pretends that word has got around in the trade about what Jake Goldberg is up to.

Jake stammers, "Well—just an idea that—"

"—just an idea that Jake had," finishes Molly.

Simon would like to help. He could use a man like Jake.

"You mean," asks the unbelieving Jake, "that I would be your partner in this?"

Not exactly, apparently. Simon would give him a corner of his loft and let him experiment.

Jake protests that there's no need for experimenting. They have the pattern, and Molly has been canvassing the neighborhood for weeks getting sizes. "Look around you, Simon," he urges enthusiastically. "How many women are exact dimensions? With the proper garment, we can make the average American woman look more average!"

"I'll make this the biggest thing that ever hit the dress industry," Simon predicts—but Molly catches him up short with,

"What do you mean *you* are going to make?"

Jake tries to shush his wife, but she won't be quieted. This is going to be Jake's business. Simon dangles a rosy future before Jake, hinting that he'll be Simon's right hand before long. It sounds good to Goldberg, but Molly is firm—and aroused.

"You have enough hands, Simon. Everybody that works for you are hands. Only hands—hands without heads, without hearts —only hands to make your dresses. . . . Jake wants to be a man, not only two hands."

Jake would still like her to be quiet, but Molly keeps on: "Simon—the wool over my eyes you can't pull. Months ago you had your chance to say Yes, but you said No. Now, when you see something for yourself, you want it."

Simon begins to protest, and she tells him, "You're mean because you're selfish. . . ."

Jake pleads, "Molly!"

"Don't Molly me!" she shouts. She gets Sammy's pen from the buffet and makes Simon take it back. Sammy won't be needing it.

Simon starts to go, and Molly advises him, "Get yourself the Book of Knowledge, Simon, and learn life like I'm learning. Man is not meant to be a money bag."

To Jake she says, "Once before you found partners without an idea. Now you'll find them again with your new idea!"

"My idea?" asks Jake.

"What then, my idea?" says his wife. "If it's good enough for Simon it's good enough for you."

"You're not afraid? We'll have less than we ever had before."

"You'll have what you want, Jake."

Molly gathers her family. "Come, Jake! Rosiely, Sammy! It's time to go—to the temple with a free and happy heart."

THE CURTAIN FALLS

THE PLAYS AND THEIR AUTHORS

"A Streetcar Named Desire," a drama in three acts by Tennessee
Williams. Copyright, 1947, by the author. Revised version
copyright, 1948, by the author. Published by New Directions, New York.

This is the second appearance of Tennessee Williams in the
Best Plays series, his first having been for "The Glass Menagerie"
in the 1944-45 season. Mr. Williams was born in Columbus,
Mississippi, and his parents named him Thomas Lanier Williams.
When he was asked how come the Tennessee, he answered that
he did not like the Thomas Lanier. Young Mr. Williams took
naturally to writing and has done a lot of it, in college and out.
But there were years after he graduated from Iowa State when
he made his living in a variety of other pursuits. He has been
a clerk for a shoe company, an elevator pilot, a bellhop, a movie
usher, a waiter and a teletyper. There also is a story that for a
time he read verse in a Greenwich Village night club. He has
written more than a dozen plays, short and long, but mostly
short. He was well known to Little Theatre groups before he
hit the big time. His first long play to reach production was
"Battle of the Angels," which the Theatre Guild offered to Boston audiences in 1943 and withdrew after the tryout there. At
least one new Williams drama is promised to Broadway for the
1948-49 season.

"Mister Roberts," play by Thomas Heggen and Joshua Logan.
Copyright, 1947, by the authors. Published, 1948, by Ran-
dom House, New York. Based on a novel by Thomas
Heggen, published 1946 by Houghton Mifflin Co., Boston.

Thomas Heggen was born in 1919 in Fort Dodge, Iowa, of
Norwegian parentage and was graduated from the University of
Minnesota in 1941. "Mister Roberts" is his first novel and his
first play, but students will remember him for his humor columns in the Minnesota *Daily*. Mr. Heggen has been a member
of the editorial staff of the *Reader's Digest* since his release in
the Fall of 1945 from the Navy, where he attained the rank of

lieutenant. He spent three years on sea duty and saw active service in the Guam, Pelelieu, Iwo Jima and Okinawa campaigns.

"Mister Roberts" also is Mr. Logan's first play, although Mr. Logan has long been favorably known in the theatre as a director. He was born in Texas and attended Princeton, where he was involved in Triangle Club theatricals. After college he helped found the University Players, along with Charles Leatherbee and Bretaigne Windust, and this company set up its first shop on Cape Cod. Its players included Henry Fonda (who played the lead in "Mister Roberts"), Margaret Sullavan, James Stewart, Myron McCormick, Kent Smith and Mildred Natwick. One result of the University Players was that it gave Mr. Logan a fellowship to study with Stanislavsky in Moscow. The offerings which he has most recently directed include "Mister Roberts," "Annie, Get Your Gun," "Happy Birthday" and "John Loves Mary." During the war he served as a captain in Air Forces Combat Intelligence, overseas.

"Command Decision," drama by William Wister Haines. Copyright, 1946, 1947 and 1948, by the author; copyright in Canada, 1948, by the author. Novel of the same title published by Little, Brown & Co., Boston. Play published and copyright, 1947, by Random House, Inc., New York.

William Wister Haines was born September 17, 1908, in Des Moines, Iowa, where he lived for eighteen years except for Summers spent in Minnesota, Colorado and New Mexico. He attended Culver Military Academy and graduated from the University of Pennsylvania in 1931. During Summer vacations he did power and light company line work, and other "high tension" tasks for the Pennsylvania Railroad. He also worked as a surveyor's helper, a road construction foreman, an automobile mechanic and a tram line rigger.

Mr. Haines always wanted to write and always wrote; since 1934 he has done nothing but write, turning out magazine short stories and novels, the first of the latter, based on his power-line work, having been "Slim" and "High Tension." In college he was editor of the U of P *Red and Blue*. In March, 1942, Mr. Haines was made a lieutenant in Army Air Forces Intelligence. He spent nearly three years overseas with the Eighth Air Force Composite Command, Eighth Fighter Command, Eighth Air Force and U. S. Strategic Air Forces. In 1934 he married Frances Tuckerman. They have a boy and a girl and live in Laguna Beach, California.

"The Winslow Boy," drama by Terence Rattigan. Copyright, 1946, by Terence Rattigan.

This drama marks the second appearance of Terence Rattigan in the Best Plays series—and a switch in technique, for up to now Mr. Rattigan has devoted himself to comedy. His first Best Play was "O Mistress Mine," which was presented in New York in January, 1946, with Alfred Lunt and Lynn Fontanne playing a gay pair of lovers. Previously he had had some Broadway success—in 1937—with a comedy, "French Without Tears." Another comedy, "While the Sun Shines," was a hit in London but a failure in New York in 1944. Mr. Rattigan was born in London in 1912. He attended Harrow and Oxford and was headed for the diplomatic service when he wrote a play called "First Episode," afterward renamed "College Sinners." During the war Mr. Rattigan spent nearly five years on North Sea air patrol with the RAF. He is well known in England as a screenwriter as well as a dramatist.

"The Heiress," by Ruth and Augustus Goetz. Adapted from "Washington Square," a novel by Henry James, Jr. Copyright, 1947, by the authors.

Augustus Goetz, whose father was in the insurance business, was born in Buffalo and was a Navy flier in World War I. He attended a number of Catholic schools, the last two being Fordham and Georgetown Universities. Out of college, he went into Wall Street, which bored him; so he went abroad to study life. Abroad he met and married Ruth Goodman and they lived for several years in Paris, Vienna, the Midi and other retreats. Returning to the U. S., they holed up in Bucks County, a Pennsylvania farming district with a literary overcast. With Arthur Sheekman, Goetz dramatized a book by Philip Goodman, "Franklin Street," and the ensuing theatrical production was withdrawn after a tryout. Next, with his wife, Goetz wrote "One-Man Show." "The Heiress" is their second dramatic collaboration.

Ruth Goodman is the daughter of the late Philip Goodman, a producer of some notable musicals and plays, including W. C. Fields' "Poppy," Clark & McCullough's "The Ramblers," "Another Language," "Rainbow," and, with Arthur Hopkins, "The Old Soak." Mr. Goodman's memoirs, "Franklin Street," were published after his death in 1940. Thus, Ruth Goodman was born and brought up in show business, and when she was barely in her teens she sat in on rehearsals of her father's productions and gave sound advice on them. Later she read scripts for Samuel Goldwyn. She had considerable schooling abroad, and in New York attended P.S. 93, another alumna of which is the playwright, Lillian Hellman. The Goetzes live in Pennsylvania and have a small daughter.

"Allegro," a musical play by Richard Rodgers and Oscar Hammerstein II. Copyright, 1947, by the authors. Published by Alfred A. Knopf, New York. Lyrics reproduced by permission of Williamson Music Inc., publisher, New York.

Richard Rodgers and Oscar Hammerstein, who have been as successful as producers as they have been as writers, first were represented together in these volumes in the 1942-43 book, which included their fabulous "Oklahoma!" Before it ended its run last May, this offering had set the world's long-run record for musicals. "Allegro" represents a more serious approach to the musical stage.

Both Hammerstein and Rodgers are native New Yorkers. Both attended Columbia University—but Rodgers withdrew because there was no school of music and attended the Juilliard School after he and the late Lorenz Hart had written one Columbia Varsity show. Rodgers and Hart had their first Broadway success in "The Garrick Gaieties." Rodgers maintains homes in New York and Fairfield County, Connecticut; Hammerstein has abodes in New York and Bucks County, Pennsylvania.

Oscar Hammerstein II was named for his first grandfather, the famous Oscar, who made several fortunes in the cigar business and lost just as many in the opera business. The first Oscar's Manhattan Opera House was the great and enlivening competitor of the Metropolitan, until the "Met" bought old Oscar out. Oscar II went to Columbia to be a lawyer, but found that his ambition was toward show business. This was easy to get into, for his uncle, Arthur Hammerstein, was the noted showman. Uncle Arthur started Oscar out as an assistant stage manager. Oscar II's hits include librettos or lyrics, or both, for "Rose Marie," "Show Boat," "New Moon," "The Desert Song," "Oklahoma!" and "Carousel."

"Eastward in Eden," play by Dorothy Gardner. Copyright, 1947, by the author. Published and copyright, 1948, by Longmans, Green & Co., New York. Revised and copyright, 1948, by the author.

Dorothy Gardner (nee Dorothy Worthington Butts) was born in San Francisco forty-seven years ago, with a New England heritage. She was educated in New York and New England, and was Class of '21 at Smith. There she studied play production and writing with Samuel Eliot. She acted in amateur productions and published poetry under her maiden name. She lives in New York with her husband and a son.

"Eastward in Eden" is her first play. The Theatre Guild and Theatre, Inc., had options on it at various times, but Nancy Stern was the ultimate producer. Mrs. Gardner was living in the village of Newfane, Vt., when, in 1936, she first read Emily Dickinson's collected poems. In 1939 she read Prof. George Whicher's Dickinson biography, "This Was a Poet," and determined that a play could be made about the poet's life.

"Skipper Next to God," drama by Jan de Hartog. Copyright, 1945, by the author.

Jan de Hartog was born in Haarlem, Holland, in 1914, the son of a professor of theology. By the time of the German invasion of the Lowlands, he had already made a name for himself as a novelist, playwright, screenwriter and actor. In 1940 he produced and appeared in a film, "Somewhere in the Netherlands," about the Dutch Navy. This picture soon was banned by the Germans. De Hartog wrote a book, "Holland's Glory," about seagoing tugboats, which became a best-seller among patriots. The Nazis sought to win the author over by "every form of cajolery," but failed. De Hartog was driven underground, finally escaped to England. In 1945, in England, he wrote "Skipper Next to God" and appeared in the leading role in the successful London production.

"An Inspector Calls," drama by J. B. Priestley. Copyright, 1945, by J. B. Priestley.

It is about time for John Boynton Priestley to be represented in the American Best Plays series, for this highly productive British dramatist has often had his works presented in New York. Last season there were two Priestley plays, "An Inspector Calls" and "The Linden Tree." The latter, a drama about a professor who feels that a 65-year-old man has no right to retire in the time of Britain's crisis, won the 1947-48 Ellen Terry Award in London— an honor which previously had gone to "The Winslow Boy."

But New York audiences found "The Linden Tree" too talkative for their tastes and it closed abruptly; "An Inspector Calls," which was in the Priestley vein of plot-twisting, had a fairly satisfying Broadway run and considerable success on tour.

J. B. Priestley was born in Bradford, England, in 1894 and was educated at Cambridge. He was the son of a schoolmaster and was a schoolmaster himself for a short time. He served five years in World War I in the Duke of Wellington's and Devon Regiments. His first venture as a writer was a volume of verse; his first play, in collaboration with Edward Knoblock, was "The Good Companions." American playgoers are familiar with his "Dangerous Corner," "Laburnum Grove" and "Eden End." Also well known are his novels, "The Good Companions" and "Angel Pavement." As a political pamphleteer, Priestley is an outspoken spokesman for British Socialists.

"Me and Molly," comedy by Gertrude Berg. Copyright, 1948, by the author.

It isn't often that a brand-new playwright and a brand-new actress make a hit the first time at bat on Broadway—but Gertrude Berg did it when she wrote "Me and Molly" and played the role of Molly. Mrs. Berg's Goldberg family, whom the play concerns, had long been familiar to her and to the radio listeners who heard her in this pioneer radio serial. Mrs. Berg, the wife of Lewis Berg, a chemical engineer, was born in New York. Her father owned a vacation resort in Delaware County, N. Y., and there the pig-tailed Gertrude wrote and acted in plays for the guests. She made further studies of writing and acting at Columbia University. When, married and the mother of two children, she began looking for more things to do, she began appearing in Sunday night charity benefits, doing a monologue sketch. She also earned an occasional $5 reading recipes and other oddments on the wireless. Eager to get on in radio, she offered a story about a Bronx husband and wife and their attempts to improve the lot of the family. This was "The Rise of the Goldbergs," which made its air debut November 20, 1929. The program ran five nights a week for sixteen years. "Me and Molly" represents a long-held ambition of Mrs. Berg's to put the Goldbergs into a play.

PLAYS PRODUCED IN NEW YORK

June 1, 1947—June 1, 1948

(Plays marked "continued" were still playing June 1, 1948)

LOUISIANA LADY

(4 performances)

A musical comedy in two acts by Isaac Green, Jr., and Eugene Berton; lyrics and music by Monte Carlo and Alma Sanders; orchestrations by Hans Spialek and Robert Russel Bennett; based on "Creoles" by Samuel Shipman and Kenneth Perkins. Produced by Hal Shelton at the Century Theatre, June 2, 1947.

Cast of characters—

El Gato...Ray Jacquemot
Joe..Lou Wills, Jr.
Michel...Val Buttignol
Sarah..Tina Prescott
Corrine...Ann Lay
Germaine.......................................Patti Hall
Annette.....................................Angela Carabella
Suzanne.......................................Patti Kingsley
Yvonne...Ann Viola
Marie-Louise..................................Edith Fellows
Charley......................................Howard Blaine
Christophe.....................................Bert Wilcox
Hugo...Lee Kerry
Genevieve...................................Isabella Wilson
Madame Corday...............................Monica Moore
Pierre..Gil Cass
Marquet....................................Robert Kimberly
Merluche.....................................George Baxter
Alphonse.....................................Charles Judels
Celeste......................................Bertha Powell
A Drunk.....................................George Roberts
Hoskins.......................................Berton Davis
Janet..Frances Keyes
Colondrina..................................Victoria Cordova
Lieutenant Mason.............................Patrick Meany
Judge Morgan...................................Bert Wilcox

Act I.—Scene 1—Levee in New Orleans, 1830. 2—Study in Miss Browne's Finishing School. 3 and 5—Parlor of the Casino De Luxe of Mme. Corday. 4—A Garden. Act II.—Scene 1—Canal Street. 2—The Cucacheena Café. 3—Street. 4—Garden.

Staged by Edgar MacGregor; dances by Felicia Sorel; music directed by Hilding Anderson; settings by Watson Barratt; lighting by Leo Kerz.

Marie-Louise was a lady, but her mamma wasn't. Her mamma, in fact, was the keeper of a bordello in New Orleans owned by her patron. When Marie-Louise comes, straight from a convent,

339

to visit mamma, everybody in the cast is at great pains to make her believe that nothing is at all what it plainly seems to be. She is saved from harm late that same evening.

Musical numbers—Act I.—"Gold, Women and Laughter," "That's Why I Want to Go Home," "Men About Town," "Just a Bit Naive," "The Cockoo-Cheena," "I Want to Live—I Want to Love," "The Night Was All to Blame," "Beware of Lips That Say 'Cherie,' " "Louisiana's Holiday." Act II.—"It's Mardi Gras," "No, No, Mam'selle," "When You Are Close to Me," "No One Cares for Dreams," "Mammy's Little Baby."

(Closed June 4, 1947)

OPEN HOUSE

(7 performances)

A comedy in three acts by Harry Young. Produced by Rex Carlton at the Cort Theatre, June 3, 1947.

Cast of characters—

Mrs. Barrett	Mary Boland
Glenn Stewart	John Harvey
Lee Elkins	Don Gibson
Olivia Corey	Augusta Roeland
Expressman	Sammy Schwartz
Mrs. Corey	Ann Dere
Flo Elkins	Joyce Mathews
Mike	Dave Tyrrell
Joe	Steven Gethers
Bob	Del Hughes
Jennie	Dulcie Cooper
Letter Carrier	Harold Grau
Uncle Watterson	Curtis Cooksey
Chicf	Ben Loughlin
Policeman	Dennis Bohan
Mr. Westcott	William David
Photographer	Forrest Taylor, Jr.
Mr. Pilsudski	Will Kuluva

Acts I, II and III.—Living Room of Mrs. Barrett's Home in Small Industrial City in the East.

Staged by Coby Ruskin; setting and costumes by Leo Kerz.

Mrs. Barrett, open-hearted but shallow-minded, decides to do her bit in relieving the housing shortage by taking in roomers, two young men and a girl. The Barrett home is in a highly restricted residential section, and certain of Mrs. B.'s neighbors frown on both her kindness and her enterprise, contending that they represent a violation of the zoning law.

(Closed June 7, 1947)

LAURA

(44 performances)

A drama in three acts by Vera Caspary and George Sklar, based on a book by Vera Caspary. Produced by H. Clay Blaney in association with S. P. and Roy P. Steckler, by special arrangement with Hunt Stromberg, Jr., at the Cort Theatre, June 26, 1947.

Cast of characters—

Mark McPherson	Hugh Marlowe
Danny Dorgan	Tom Walsh
Waldo Lydecker	Otto Kruger
Shelby Carpenter	Tom Rutherfurd
Bessie Clary	Grania O'Malley
Mrs. Dorgan	Kay MacDonald
A Girl	K. T. Stevens
Olsen	Walter Riemer

Acts I, II and III.—Living Room of Laura Hunt's Apartment in New York City.

Staged by Clarence Derwent; setting by Stewart Chaney; costumes by Robert Lanza.

The story of a beautiful corpse whose face was shot away, permitting the substitution of a heroine who was her best friend. Practically everyone is convinced that the dead woman is Laura Hunt, but she isn't, as Detective Mark McPherson goes to some trouble to prove before he marries Laura himself. The motion picture bearing the same time title, and taken from the same source, was much the better entertainment of the two, according to accredited movie critics.

(Closed August 2, 1947)

NEW YORK CITY CENTER OF MUSIC AND DRAMA

The first in a Summer series of plays produced by New York City Theatre Company at New York City Center opened July 15, 1947.

RIP VAN WINKLE

(15 performances)

A play in two acts adapted by Herbert Berghof from the Jefferson version of Dion Boucicault's adaptation of the folk legend in Washington Irving's "Sketch Book." Revived by New York City Theatre Company at New York City Center, July 15, 1947.

Cast of characters—

Gretchen	Grace Coppin
Minnie	Jimsey Somers

Nick Vedder....................................Martin Wolfson
Derrick Van Beekman............................Byron McGrath
Peter..Edwin Bruce
Cockles..Jack Manning
Rip Van Winkle.................................Philip Bourneuf
Jacob Stein....................................Jack Bittner
Town Crier.....................................Del Hughes
Seth...Jack Bittner
Katie..Haila Stoddard
Minnie...Frances Reid
Peter..Arthur Franz
    Village children: Patti Foster, Mary Pope, Betty Lou Keim, Alan Shay, Dickie Orlan, Bobby Nick. Villagers: William Bales, Del Hughes, Colin Craig, Gerald Prosk, Fred Wayne, Lili Mann, Carol Harriton, Anne Feris, Mary Anthony, Florence Aquito. Hendrik Hudson's Crew: Hendrik Hudson, Jack Bittner; Dwarf, Martin Wolfson and others.
    Act I.—Scene 1—Village of Falling Waters. 2—Inside Rip's House. 3—Path in Catskills. 4—High Up in Catskills. Act II.—Scene 1—High Up in Catskills, twenty years later. 2—Path in Catskills. 3—Village of Falling Waters.
    Staged by Herbert Berghof; settings and lighting by Carl Kent; masks by Remo Bufano; music by Andre Singer.

Joseph Jefferson opened the 1866-67 season at the Olympic Theatre, New York, September 3, 1866, with "Rip Van Winkle" and thereafter played the part for half a century. He had previously played the part in London and other cities. James Henry Hackett played "Rip" in 1830 at the Park Theatre, New York, and McKee Rankin in 1869 played the part in Brooklyn. The comedy was last presented in New York at Wallack's Theatre in 1905 with Joseph Jefferson's son, Thomas, in the title role, when it ran for 16 performances.

(Closed July 26, 1947)

The Ballet Russe de Monte Carlo opened its Fall season at City Center September 7 and lasted through September 21, 1947. The details may be found in the chapter "Dance Drama."

The New York Symphony season opened at City Center under the direction of Leonard Bernstein, September 22, 1947, with "Symphonia Amamith," a Palestinian Folk Symphony by Manuel Mahler-Kalkstein, its first performance in America. The choral parts were sung by the Schola Cantorum. Symphony No. 2, in C Minor (The "Resurrection") by Gustav Mahler with Ellabelle Davis (soprano), Nan Merriman (mezzo-soprano) and the chorus of the Schola Cantorum providing the singing, Hugh Ross directing the chorus. The program was dedicated to the Resurrection of Palestine. An All-Mozart program, September 29 and 30, 1947, included the overture to "The Magic Flute," Symphony No. 25 in G Minor and Piano Concerto in B-flat Major with Leonard Bernstein at the piano. Jennie Tourel, mezzo-soprano, sang. An All-Stravinsky program was presented October 6 and 7,

with "Scenes de Ballet," Concerto for Violin and "Petrouchka."
Tossy Spivakovsky was the violin soloist. The program October
13 and 14 consisted of Bach's "Brandenburg Concerto No. 3,"
Debussy's "Clarinet Rhapsody," Piston's "Violin Concerto" and
"Symphony No. 1" (Spring) by Schumann. October 20 and 21 a
Mendelssohn Anniversary program consisting of Symphony No. 5
("Reformation") and Violin Concerto were presented with Arnold
Eidus as soloist and also Copland's "Statements for Orchestra"
and Gershwin's "American in Paris." November 3 and 4 Beetho-
ven's Symphony No. 2, Prokofieff's Fifth Concerto (first perform-
ance in New York), Liszt's Concerto No. 1 and Ravel's "La
Valse" with Samson François as pianist were presented. Haieff's
"Divertimento," Haydn's Concerto in C Major, Szymanowski's
Second Concerto, Strauss' "Thus Spake Zarathustra" were played
November 10 and 11 with Isaac Stern as violinist and November 17 and 18 the program consisted of Suzanne Bloch's "Elegy
for War Children," Rachmaninoff's Third Concerto for Piano and
R. Vaughan Williams' Symphony in F Minor with Miss Gold-
stein at the piano.

"The Cradle Will Rock" by Marc Blitzstein was revived by the
New York City Symphony in a complete concert performance
November 24 and 25 and dedicated to the League of Composers.
Leonard Bernstein directed the music and it was staged by Howard
Da Silva. Michael Myerberg revived it December 26, 1947, at
the Mansfield Theatre with practically the same cast and it ran for
21 performances. The cast may be found in that production.

The Ballet Theatre at City Center for the season 1947-48 may
be found under "Dance Drama."

The New York City Opera Company launched the 1947-48
season with "Salome" by Richard Strauss based on the poem by
Oscar Wilde, September 25, 1947. Laszlo Halasz directed the
music, Leopold Sachse was stage director and H. A. Condell designed the scenery. Brenda Lewis sang Salome, Frederick Jagel
(Herodes), William Horna (Narraboth) Terese Gerson (Herodias)
and Ralph Herbert (Jochanaan). There were 5 performances.

The operas presented during the Fall season were Richard
Strauss' "Salome" with 5 performances, Puccini's "La Bohème"
(4), Bizet's "Carmen" (4), Verdi's "Rigoletto" (3), Tchaikovsky's "Eugene Onegin" (3), Massenet's "Werther" (2), Verdi's
"La Traviata" (4), Puccini's "Madame Butterfly" (4), Rossini's
"Barber of Seville" (3) Richard Strauss' "Ariadne auf Noxos"
(2), Mascagni's "Cavalleria Rusticana" and Leoncavallo's "Pagliacci" (3) and Mozart's "Don Giovanni" (4), a total of 41.

The New York City Opera Company included in its casts in the Fall season Dalisay Aldaba, Ann Ayars, Margit Bokor, Ellen Faull, Marie-José Forgues, Panna Genia, Virginia Haskins, Evelyn Keller, Brenda Lewis, Virginia MacWatters, Brenda Miller, Suzy Morris, Lenore Portnoy, Gertrude Ribla, Dorothy Sarnoff, Wilma Spence, Camilla Williams, Lydia Edwards, Terese Gerson, Winifred Heidt, Mary Kreste, Rosalind Nadell, Vasso Argyris, Eugene Conley, Irwin Dillon, Guilio Gari, William Horne, Luigi Infantino, Frederic Jagel, Frank Murray, Edward Molitore, Nathaniel Sprinzena, Ilya Tamarin, George Vincent, Norman Cordon, Paul Dennis, Edwin Dunning, Gean Greenwell, Frank Guarrera, Ralph Herbert, Enzo Mascherini, Arthur Newman, James Pease, Michael Rhodes, Donald Richards, Norman Scott, Giuseppe Valdengo, Richard Wentworth and Norman Young.

Music conductors included Laszlo Halasz, Jean Morel, Thomas P. Martin, Julius Rudel, Frederic Kurzweil, and Lee Shaynen. The stage directors were Theodore Komisarjevsky, Elemer Nagy, Leopold Sache, John S. White and Hans Sondheimer. Scenic designers were H. A. Condell and Richard Rychtarik. Ballet director was William Dollar.

The Hasty Pudding Club of Harvard University in December presented its one hundredth annual production, "Here's the Pitch," an original musical comedy by Craig P. Gilbert, music by Courtney Crandall, lyrics by William Scudder, staged by John F. Baird, dances directed by John Pierce, settings by Lawrence Goldwasser, costumes by Pat Havens. The musical comedy was in three acts and the musical numbers were "Believe," "Baseball," "When We Were Young," "Great Guy," "So Well So Soon," "Baby Ain't a Baby Anymore," "In a Town," "Little Ladybird," "Never Trust a Man," "Rally Chant," "All's Right with the World," "Extra Currickeler Girl," "Just as Long as I Have You" and "In the Lobby of the Ritz."

Paul Draper and Larry Adler with Josh White started their season at City Center December 25, 1947. They presented a variety program especially designed for children which included the Salici Puppets, supervised by Noel Wesley, Paul Winchell with Jerry Mahoney and the magician, Prince Mendes. Ray Gorobetz was at the piano. The performances lasted through January 4, 1948. The evening programs of dance and harmonica music included "Spanish Dance No. 6" by E. Granados, "Meine Stadtele Belz" a Yiddish folk song, "Gavotte" and "Praetudium" by J. S. Bach, "Dip Your Fingers in the Water," a South Carolina spiritual, "The Lass with the Delicate Air," "Hard Time Blues," "Evil Hearted Man" and others.

The New York Theatre Company opened a repertoire with "Volpone."

VOLPONE

(14 performances)

A play in two parts by Ben Jonson, adapted by José Ferrer, Richard Whorf and Richard Barr. Revived by New York Theatre Company with the co-operation of Theatre Incorporated (Richard Aldrich, managing director) at City Center, January 8, 1948.

Cast of characters—

Volpone (The Fox)	José Ferrer
Mosca (The Fly)	Richard Whorf
Nano (The Dwarf)	Leonardo Cimino
Androgyno (The Hermaphrodite)	Richard McMurray
Castrone (The Eunuch)	Charles Mendick
Concubina	Susan Center
Voltore (The Vulture)	John Carradine
Corbaccio (The Crow)	Fred Stewart
Corvino (The Raven)	Le Roi Operti
1st Gentleman	Victor Thorley
2nd Gentleman	Bobby Busch
Celia (Corvino's wife)	Phyllis Hill
Bonario (Corbaccio's son)	Walter Coy
Lady Politic Wouldbe	Paula Laurence
Notario (The Court Clerk)	Lou Gilbert
Commendatori (The Court Officers)	Earl Jones / Frank Campanella
Avocatori (The Judges)	Sidney Bassler / Bob Harrison / Leigh Whipper
Cittadina	Marjorie Byers

Parts I and II.—Sixteenth Century Venice.

Staged by Richard Barr; settings and lighting by Herbert Brodkin; costumes by Emeline C. Roche.

"Volpone" was first produced in London in 1665. In New York the Stefan Zweig version was translated by Ruth Langner and produced by The Theatre Guild at the Guild Theatre for 46 performances starting April 9, 1928. Dudley Digges was Volpone, Margalo Gillmore (Columba), Alfred Lunt (Mosca), Henry Travers (Corbaccio) and Helen Westley (Canina). The play was revived by The Theatre Guild with Sidney Greenstreet, Earle Larrimore and Sylvia Field March 10, 1390. The Donald Wolfit Repertory Company revived the play February 24, 1947.

(Closed January 18, 1948)

ANGEL STREET

(14 performances)

A play in three acts by Patrick Hamilton. Revived by the New York City Theatre Company at City Center, January 22, 1948. ·

Cast of characters—

Mrs. Manningham...................................Uta Hagen
Mr. Manningham....................................José Ferrer
Nancy...Phyllis Hill
Elizabeth...............................   ....Nan McFarland
Rough...Richard Whorf
Two Policemen....................Victor Thorley, Ralph Roberts
    Acts I, II and III.—Angel Street, Pimlico District, London.
    Staged by Richard Barr; settings and lighting by Herbert Brodkin; costumes by Emeline Roche.

"Angel Street" was produced by Shepard Traube at the Golden Theatre December 5, 1941, and closed December 30, 1944, after 1,295 performances.

(Closed February 1, 1948)

A TRAGEDIAN IN SPITE OF HIMSELF

THE BEAR

ON THE HARMFULNESS OF TOBACCO

THE WEDDING

(14 performances)

Four comedies by Anton Chekhov. Revived by New York City Theatre Company at City Center, February 5, 1948.

A TRAGEDIAN IN SPITE OF HIMSELF
Ivan Ivanovitch Topkachov........................Richard Whorf
Alex Alexeyevitch Murashkin......................Robert Carroll
                (Directed by José Ferrer)

THE BEAR
Elena Ivanova Popova..............................Frances Reid
Luka..Francis Letton
Grigory Stephanovitch Smirov......................José Ferrer
                (Directed by Richard Barr)

ON THE HARMFULNESS OF TOBACCO
Ivan Ivanovitch Nyukhin...........................José Ferrer

THE WEDDING
Anna Martynova Zmeyukin.........................Paula Laurence
Ivan Mihailovitch Yat.............................Francis Letton

```
The Best Man.................................Leonardo Cimino
Nastaya Timofeyevna..............................Grace Coppin
Epaminond Maximovitch Aplombov.................Robert Carroll
Yevdokim Zaharovitch Zhigalov....................Victor Thorley
Harlampy Spiridonovitch Dymba......................Will Kuluva
Dashenka..........................................Phyllis Hill
Dmitry Stepanovitch Mozgovoy.....................Ralph Roberts
Andrey Andreyvitch Nyunin.......................John Carradine
Fyodor Yakovlevitch Revunov-Karaulov.............Richard Whorf
First Waiter.......................................Bobby Busch
S cond Waiter...............................Richard McMurray
Third Waiter...............................Frank Campanella
```
(Directed by José Ferrer)
Staged by José Ferrer and Richard Barr; sets and lighting by Herbert Brodkin; costumes by Emeline Roche.

Final offering of the New York City Theatre Company's first season. A sketch about a package-laden commuter, two playlets about a man with a bad temper and about a wedding supper, and a monologue by a henpecked lecturer.

(Closed February 14, 1948)

The New York City Opera Company opened its Spring season March 19, 1948, with "Don Giovanni," a drama in two acts with music by W. A. Mozart and book by L. da Ponte. The stage director was Theodore Komisarjevsky; conductor Laszlo Halasz; designer H. A. Condell; ballet choreographer Arthur Mahoney. "Don Giovanni" was presented 4 times during the season, "La Traviata" (3), "Carmen" (3), "La Bohème" (3), "Pelleas and Melisande" (5), "Madame Butterfly" (3), "Cavalleria Rusticana" and "Pagliacci" (3), "Rigoletto" (2), "Tosca" (3), "The Old Maid and the Thief" and "Amelia Goes to the Ball" (3), 32 performances in all. "The Old Maid and the Thief" and "Amelia Goes to the Ball" were presented for the first time at the City Center. They were written by Gian-Carlo Menotti and also directed by him. The music conductor was Thomas P. Martin. The singers were Virginia MacWatters, Marie Powers, Ellen Faull, Norman Young, Frances Yeend, Walter Cassel, William Horne, Gean Greenwell, Bette Dubro, Lenore Portnoy and Ruth Shor. Singers not listed in the company in the Fall season of 1947 were Mario Binci, Adelaide Bishop, Robert Weede, Rudolph Petrak, Rosa Canario, Mack Harrell, Arlene Carmen, Cesare Bardelli, Antonia Annalora and Oscar Natzka. The season closed April 25, 1948.

The Spring season of the New York City Center Theatre Company opened with "The Alchemist," a Ben Jonson comedy first produced in London in 1610 at the Globe Theatre.

THE ALCHEMIST

(14 performances)

A comedy by Ben Jonson; original music by Deems Taylor. Revived by the New York City Theatre Company (José Ferrer, general director), at New York City Center, May 6, 1948.

Cast of characters—

PROLOGUE

Lovewit	Bert Thorn
Jeremy	José Ferrer
Cook	Stanley Carlson
Maid	Tyler Winn
Subtle	George Coulouris
Doll Common	Nan McFarland

THE PLAY

Face	José Ferrer
Subtle	George Coulouris
Doll Common	Nan McFarland
Dapper	William Nichols
Drugger	Ray Walston
Sir Epicure Mammon	Ezra Stone
Pertinax Surly	Robert Carroll
Ananias	Robinson Stone
Kastril	Hiram Sherman
Dame Pliant	Phyllis Hill
Parson	Will Kuluva
Lovewit	Bert Thorn
1st Officer	Stanley Carlson
2d Officer	Leonardo Cimino

Neighbors: Bobby Busch, Jacqueline Soans, Winston Ross, Mack Busch, Richard McMurray, Anne Terris, Margaret Suttle.

Action takes place in Seventeenth Century London.

Staged by Morton Da Costa; settings and lighting by Herbert Brodkin; costumes by Emeline Roche.

(Closed May 16, 1948)

S.S. GLENCAIRN

(14 performances)

Four one-act plays by Eugene O'Neill. Revived by the New York City Theatre Company at New York City Center, May 20, 1948.

THE MOON OF THE CARIBBEES

Cast of characters—

Yank	Richard Coogan
Driscoll	George Mathews
Olson	Ralph Roberts
Davis	Ray Walston
Cocky	Kenneth Treseder
Smitty	Robert Carroll
Paul	Leonardo Cimino
Ivan	Harold J. Stone
Scotty	Winston Ross

The Donkey Man.............................George Coulouris
Big Frank................................Stanley Carlson
Dick...Bobby Busch
Max...Mack Busch
Paddy.......................................Harry Kadison
Bella..Juanita Hall
Pearl.................................Mildred Joanne Smith
Violet......................................Rena Mitchell
Susie.......................................Catherine Ayers
The First Mate.............................Charles Summers
    Scene: A Forward Section of the Main Deck of the British Tramp
Steamer *Glencairn* at Anchor off an Island in the West Indies.

IN THE ZONE

Cast of characters—

Smitty......................................Robert Carroll
Davis..Ray Walston
Olson.......................................Ralph Roberts
Scotty......................................Winston Ross
Ivan.......................................Harold J. Stone
Yank..Richard Coogan
Driscoll...................................George Mathews
Cocky.....................................Kenneth Treseder
    Scene: The Seamen's Forecastle.
    Time: Ten minutes of twelve, on a night in the Fall of the year
1915.

BOUND EAST FOR CARDIFF

Cast of characters—

Yank..Richard Coogan
Driscoll...................................George Mathews
Cocky.....................................Kenneth Treseder
Davis..Ray Walston
Scotty......................................Winston Ross
Olson.......................................Ralph Roberts
Paul.......................................Leonardo Cimino
Smitty......................................Robert Carroll
Ivan.......................................Harold J. Stone
The Captain................................Ralph Sumpter
The First Mate.............................Charles Summers
    Scene: The Seamen's Forecastle.

THE LONG VOYAGE HOME

Cast of characters—

Fat Joe, Proprietor of a Dive.....................José Ferrer
Nick, a Crimp..............................Victor Beecroft
Mag, a Barmaid...............................Phyllis Hill
Olson.......................................Ralph Roberts
Driscoll...................................George Mathews
Cocky.....................................Kenneth Treseder
Ivan.......................................Harold J. Stone
Kate......................................Phillippa Bevans
Freda......................................Nan McFarland
Two Roughs.....................Robinson Stone, Bobby Busch
    Scene: The Bar of a Low Dive on the London Water Front.
    Time: Nine o'clock in the evening.
    Staged by José Ferrer; settings and lighting, Herbert Brodkin; cos-
tumes, Emeline Roche.

Eugene O'Neill had written a number of one-act plays in the
Gaylord Farms Sanatorium when he was 27. Later in Green-

wich Village in collaboration with George Cram Cook, Susan Glaspell, Mary Heaton Vorse, Frank Shay, Hutchins Hapgood and Harry Kemp (The Provincetown Players) these short plays were first produced. "Bound East for Cardiff" (1916). "The Long Voyage Home," and "The Moon of the Caribbees" had their first showing at the Provincetown Theatre in the 1917-18 season. "In the Zone" was done by the Washington Square Players in 1917. All four were presented at the Providence Theatre, November 3, 1924. The principal role of Driscoll was acted by Lawrence Cecil and Walter Abel played Olson. The plays were last done for 90 performances at Provincetown Playhouse, beginning January 9, 1929. Byron Russell was the Driscoll, Lionel Stander (Yank), Walter Abel (Olson) and Mary Johns (Bella).

(Closed May 30, 1948)

THE MAGIC TOUCH

(12 performances)

A comedy in three acts by Charles Raddock and Charles Sherman. Produced by John Morris Chanin at the International Theatre, September 3, 1947.

Cast of characters—

Cathy Turner	Sara Anderson
Jeff Turner	William Terry
Eddie Mitchell	Sid Melton
J. L. Thompson	Howard Smith
Amy Thompson	Frances Comstock
Baker	Le Roi Operti
Flossie Claypool	Hope Emerson
Larry Masters	Carleton Carpenter
Wilbur Grigsby	Norman Tokar
Ken White	Burke McHugh

Acts I, II and III.—Modest Little New York Apartment of the Turners.

Staged by Herman Rotsten; settings by Louis Kennell.

Cathy and Jeff Turner, a young couple, are trying to live on Jeff's wage of $28.50 a week. Cathy, an inspired housewife, manages to get by with her own money-saving recipes. Jeff's employer, a hit-hunting publisher, sees publicity in Cathy's efforts and a best-seller in a book of her recipes. The Turners survive the hardships of the $28.50 salary and the buccaneering ministrations of the publisher and finally wind up with fame and fortune.

(Closed September 13, 1947)

ANNA LUCASTA

(32 performances)

A play in three acts by Philip Yordan. Revived by John Wildberg at the National Theatre, September 22, 1947.

Cast of characters—

Katie	Wesleen Foster
Stella	Rosetta Le Noire
Theresa	Laura Bowman
Stanley	Roy Allen
Frank	Warren Coleman
Joe	Frank Wilson
Eddie	Ralf Coleman
Noah	Slim Thompson
Blanche	Claire Jay
Officer	Maxwell Glanville
Anna	Isabelle Cooley
Danny	Lance Taylor
Lester	Sidney Poitier
Rudolf	Duke Williams

Act I.—Scene 1—Lucasta Living Room, Pennsylvania, 1941. 2—Noah's Bar, Brooklyn. Act II.—Lucasta Living Room. Act III.—Scene 1—Living Room. 2—Bar.

Staged by Harry Wagstaff Gribble; settings by Frederick Fox; costumes by Paul Dupont.

"Anna Lucasta" was presented by John Wildberg at the Mansfield Theatre, New York, August 30, 1944, and continued through 957 performances until November 30, 1946.

(Closed October 18, 1947)

I GOTTA GET OUT

(4 performances)

A comedy in three acts by Joseph Fields and Ben Sher. Produced by Herbert H. Harris and Lester Meyer at the Cort Theatre, September 25, 1947.

Cast of characters—

Swifty	Reed Brown, Jr.
Bernie	David Burns
Radtke	Hal Neiman
Jake	Don Grusso
Angie	Kenneth Forbes
Steve	Griff Evans
Timmie	John H. Conway
Mary	Peggy Van Vleet
Frances	Eileen Larson
Gussie	Peggy Maley
Mrs. Clark	Edith Meiser
A Taxicab Driver	Ralph Smiley
Larry	Ted Erwin
Dr. Flugelman	E. A. Krumschmidt
Dr. Perrin	Edwin Whitner
Constantin	Richard Shankland
Stoddard	Charles Rondeau

Hogan..Mickey Cochran
A Woman Player................................Ruth Saville
Broderick.....................................Dan Evans
A Ticket Seller...........................Charles F. O'Connor
Jerry...Ralph Simone
A Player......................................Robert Gallagher
A Second Woman Player.........................Vici Raaf
A Third Woman Player..........................Barbara Thorson
Tom Hill......................................Donald Foster
A Waiter......................................William Ayers
   Act I.—Scene 1—Bookmaker's Poolroom Above a Stable. 2—
Kitchen of Mrs. Clark's Home in Nassau, L. I. Act II.—Belmont
Park. Act III.—Kitchen of Mrs. Clark's Home.
   Staged by Joseph Fields; settings by Raymond Sovey.

A group of bookmakers, driven by the police from their hideout
in New York, establish their telephones in the Long Island kitchen
of Mrs. Clark, who is innocent of all forms of gambling. At the
Belmont track the bookies lose and Mrs. Clark blunders into
several winners. She is arrested by detectives as a tipster, but her
innocence is proved—and a boy-girl affair is solved happily.

(Closed September 27, 1947)

OUR LAN'

(41 performances)

A play in two acts by Theodore Ward. Produced by Eddie
Dowling and Louis J. Singer at the Royale Theatre, September 27, 1947.

Cast of characters—

Edgar Price..................................Irving Barnes
Gabe Peltier.................................Ferman Phillips
Emanuel Price................................Louis Peterson
Patsy Ross...................................Theresa Merritte
Joe Ross.....................................Augustus Smith, Sr.
Charlie Setlow...............................Emory Richardson
Ellen..Valerie Black
James..Harold Conklin
Daddy Sykes..................................Service Bell
Roxanna......................................Margo Washington
Delphine.....................................Muriel Smith
Beulah.......................................Dolores Woodward
Ruth...Martha Evans
Martha.......................................Paula Oliver
Alice..Mary Lucille McBride
Fred Douglas.................................Augustus Smith, Jr.
Tom Taggart..................................Jay Brooks
Minnie.......................................Blanche Christopher
Sarah..Estelle Rolle Evans
Joshua Tain..................................William Veasey
Georgana.....................................Virginia Chapman
Dosia..Edith Atuka Reid
Ollie Webster................................Richard Angarola
Lem..Chauncey Reynolds
Chester......................................Edmund Cambridge
Hank Saunders................................Charles Lillienthal
Captain Bryant...............................Jack Becker
Libeth Arbarbanel............................Julie Haydon
Oliver Webster...............................James Harwood

Yank Sergeant.....................................Stuart Hoover
Captain Stewart...................................Gene O'Donnell
John Burkhardt...................................Frank Tweddell
Cotton Broker....................................Graham Velsey
1st Rebel Soldier.................................Nathan Adler
2nd Rebel Soldier................................Michael Higgins
    Act I.—Scene 1—Cave on Road to Savannah, Georgia, January, 1865. 2—Forge on Island off Coast of Georgia. Act II.—Scenes 1, 2, 3 and 4—Forge on Island off Coast of Georgia.
    Staged by Eddie Dowling and Edward R. Mitchell; choral arrangements and direction by Joshua Lee; settings and lighting by Ralph Alswang.

A group of freed Negroes has taken possession of and is cultivating a small island off the Georgia Coast in 1865. They have taken the counsel of General Sherman and the liberating Union Army. As freed men and women they have a right to property. But the Union Army reverses itself and returns to the island to restore it, by force, to the Southern white planter who has claimed ownership.

"Our Lan' " was produced by Associated Playwrights at the Grand Street Playhouse, New York, April 18, 1947, and closed April 27 after 12 performances. (See "Best Plays 1946-47.")

(Closed November 1, 1947)

THE HEIRESS

(280 performances)

(Continued)

A play in two acts by Ruth and Augustus Goetz; suggested by Henry James' novel "Washington Square." Produced by Fred F. Finklehoffe at the Biltmore Theatre, September 29, 1947.

Cast of characters—

Maria...Fiona O'Shiel
Dr. Austin Sloper..................................Basil Rathbone
Lavinia Penniman.................................Patricia Collinge
Catherine Sloper..................................Wendy Hiller
Elizabeth Almond................................Katharine Raht
Arthur Townsend...................................Craig Kelly
Marian Almond...................................Augusta Roeland
Morris Townsend..................................Peter Cookson
Mrs. Montgomery..................................Betty Linley
    Acts I and II.—Front Parlor of Dr. Sloper's Home in Washington Square, New York, 1850.
    Staged by Jed Harris; setting by Raymond Sovey.

See page 165.

HOW I WONDER

(63 performances)

A play in three acts by Donald Ogden Stewart. Produced by Ruth Gordon and Garson Kanin in association with Victor Samrock and William Fields at the Hudson Theatre, September 30, 1947.

Cast of characters—

Professor Lemuel Stevenson	Raymond Massey
An Unusual Character	Everett Sloane
Walter Smith	Henry Jones
Cliff Saunders	John Marriott
Margaret Stevenson	Carol Goodner
Christina Stevenson	Bethel Leslie
George Drummond	Byron McGrath
Dr. Hiller	John Sweet
Lisa	Meg Mundy
Henry Harkrider	Wyrley Birch

Acts I, II and III.—Roof-top of Home of Professor Lemuel Stevenson.

Staged by Garson Kanin and George Greenberg; setting and lighting by Donald Oenslager; costumes by Helene Pons.

Prof. Lemuel Stevenson, an astronomer and college professor, undertakes a mystic brooding about the future of the world in the age of the atom bomb. His cogitations are made clear, the author thinks, by the presence in person of his Mind, with whom the amiable professor has several losing arguments. The message of the drama is that, unless the selfish warmakers are halted in the work, the Earth may be subjected to complete nuclear fission and become just another flaming star for another astronomer on another planet to discover.

(Closed November 22, 1947)

COMMAND DECISION

(278 performances)
(Continued)

A play in three acts by William Wister Haines. Produced by Kermit Bloomgarden at the Fulton Theatre, October 1, 1947.

Cast of characters—

Tech. Sergeant Harold Evans	James Whitmore
War Correspondent Elmer Brockhurst	Edmon Ryan
Brigadier General K. C. Dennis	Paul Kelly
Colonel Ernest Haley	Neill O'Malley
Major Belding Davis	Robert Pike
Enlisted Armed Guard	West Hooker
Captain Lucius Jenks	Arthur Franz
Major General Roland Goodlow Kane	Jay Fassett

Brigadier General Clifton C. Garnett.................Paul McGrath
Major Homer Prescott...........................William Layton
Colonel Edward Martin...........................Stephen Elliott
Lt. Jake Goldberg.................................John Randolph
Major Desmond Lansing............................Lewis Martin
Major Rufus Dayhuff.............................Walter Black
Mr. Arthur Malcolm...............................Paul Ford
Mr. Oliver Stone...............................Frank McNellis
N.C.O. Photographer...............................Ed Binns
Captain G. W. C. Lee..............................James Holden
    Acts I, II and III.—Office of Brigadier General K. C. Dennis at
Headquarters of 5th American Bombardment Division, Heavy, in
England.
    Staged by John O'Shaughnessy; setting and lighting by Jo Miel-
ziner; costumes by Julia Sze.

See page 94.

MUSIC IN MY HEART

(125 performances)

A romantic musical play with melodies of Tchaikovsky in two
acts by Patsy Ruth Miller; lyrics by Forman Brown; music
adapted by Franz Steininger. Produced by Henry Duffy at the
Adelphi Theatre, October 2, 1947.

Cast of characters—

Tatiana Kerskaya...............................Vivienne Segal
Mischa...George Lambrose
Peter Ilych Tchaikovsky...........................Robert Carroll
Desirée Artot....................................Martha Wright
Maurice Cabanne....................................Jan Murray
Capt. Nicholas Gregorovitch....................Charles Fredericks
Ivan Petrofski....................................James Starbuck
Natuscha.......................................Dorothy Etheridge
Gypsy...Jean Handzlik
Joseph..Robert Hayden
Princess Katherine Dolgoruki....................Della Lind
Olga..Pauline Goddard
Messenger of the Tsar............................Edward White
Sonya..Jeanne Shelby
Vera Remisova....................................Olga Suarez
Lord Chamberlain.................................Ralph Glover
Prima Ballerina..................................Olga Suarez
Premier Danseur...............................Nicholas Magallanes
    Act I.—Scene 1—Ballet "The Storm." 1A—Stage of Odeon Thea-
tre, St. Petersburg. 2—Café Samovar. Act II.—Scene 1—Nikki's
Country House. 2—Road to St. Petersburg. 3—Foyer of Imperial
Opera House. 4—Stage of Imperial Opera House. 5—Backstage of
Imperial Opera House.
    Staged by Hassard Short; music directed by Franz Steininger; cho-
reography by Ruth Page; settings and costumes by Alvin Colt.

A slightly biographical moment in the life of Peter Ilych Tchai-
kovsky, in which he writes some music out of admiration for the
French singer, Desirée Artot.
    Musical numbers—Act I.—"Unrequited Love," "Flower
Waltz," "Natuscha," "Love Is a Game for Soldiers," "Stolen
Kisses," "No! No! No!", "While There's a Song to Sing,"
"The Belaika Serenade," "Trepak," "Am I Enchanted." Act

II.—"Gossip," "Once upon a Time," "Three's a Crowd," "Song of the Troika," "The Ballerina's Story," "Song of the Claque," "Beauty and the Beast," "Love Song," "Love Is the Sovereign of My Heart."

(Closed January 24, 1948)

UNDER THE COUNTER

(27 performances)

A comedy with music in two acts by Arthur Macrae; music by Manning Sherwin, lyrics by Harold Purcell. Produced by Lee Ephraim in association with Messrs. Shubert, at the Shubert Theatre, October 3, 1947.

Cast of characters—

Eva	Winifred Hindle
Detective Inspector Baxter	Francis Roberts
Mike Kenderdine	Ballard Berkley
Tim Garret	Thorley Walters
Jo Fox	Cicely Courtneidge
Mr. Burroughs	George Street
Zoe Tritton	Glen Alyn
Kitty	Ingrid Forrest
Sir Alec Dunne	Wilfrid Hyde-White
Lt. Cmdr. Hugo Conway, RNVR	John Gregory
Mr. Appleyard	Frederick Farley

Acts I, II and III.—Jo Fox's House in London.

Staged by Jack Hulbert; dances arranged and directed by Jack Hulbert and John Gregory; décor by Clifford Pember.

Jo Fox, a popular British actress, is in temporary retirement from the stage in London. She occupies her time by staging charity shows, conniving to buy everything she wants on the black market and interfering with the lives of her friends. She is not happy unless she is working an angle or pulling a wire.

Principal musical numbers: "Everywhere," "No-one's Tried to Kiss Me," "The Moment I Saw You," "Let's Get Back to Glamour," "Ai Yi Yi."

(Closed October 25, 1947)

DEAR JUDAS

(17 performances)

A drama in two acts adapted by Michael Myerberg from the original work of Robinson Jeffers; Johann Sebastian Bach music selected and arranged by Lehmann Engle. Produced by Michael Myerberg at the Mansfield Theatre, October 5, 1947.

Cast of characters—

```
The Carpenter...................................Ferdi Hoffman
Judas........... ...............................Roy Hargrave
The Woman...................... ..........Margaret Wycherly
Lazarus.......... ... ........................Harry Irvine
The Mutes:
    Peter............................. ...............Tony Charmoli
    Simon.............................................Richard Astor
    John................................................Betts Lee
Alter Ego.........................................Alfred Rogers
    Dancers: Clara Cordery, Eva Desca, Annie Ferris, Beatrice Seckler,
Emy St. Just, Anne Widman.
    Priests: David Fulford, Joseph Mego.
    Roman Guards: Larry Buchanan, Douglas Haden.
    Torchbearers: Jean Pugsley, Jacqueline Soans, Hope Zee.
    Singers: Karl Brock, Jane Davis, Robert Davis, Warren Galjour,
Louise Gerard, Morris Gedzel, Arlene Hershey, Kaye Janice, Angela
Lappart, Dorothy Page, Helen Rice, Walter Rinner, Cecile Sherman,
Vicki Starr, Peter Sozio.
    Acts I and II.—The Garden.
    Staged by Michael Myerberg; music conducted by Morris Gedzel;
dances and mimes by Esther Junger; setting and lighting by Albert
Johnson; costumes and masks by Mary Percy Schenck.
```

The events in the Garden of Gethsemane just before and just after the Crucifixion, as examined by Poet Robinson Jeffers. An attempt is made to rationalize Judas' act of betraying Jesus to His executioners. The Biblical narrative is closely followed.

(Closed October 17, 1947)

DUET FOR TWO HANDS

(7 performances)

A drama in two acts by Mary Hayley Bell. Produced by Robert Reud at the Booth Theatre, October 7, 1947.

Cast of characters—

```
Abigail Sarclet...................................Joyce Redman
Herda Sarclet.....................................Wynne Clark
Fletty................. ..........................Ruth Vivian
Edward Sarclet..............................Francis L. Sullivan
Stephen Cass...................................Hugh Marlowe
    Acts I and II.—Forsinard Castle, The Orkneys, 1904.
    Staged by Reginald Denham; setting by Charles Elson; costumes
by Helene Pons.
```

Edward Sarclet, a surgeon of twisted genius, grafts upon the mangled wrists of poet Stephen Cass the hands of a man who was unjustly executed for murder. The hands communicate to Stephen some of the personality and memories of the dead man. He falls in love, as the previous owner of the hands had done, with Dr. Sarclet's daughter, Abigail. And the hands he has inherited wreak final vengeance upon the sinister surgeon.

(Closed October 11, 1947)

MAN AND SUPERMAN

(271 performances)
(Continued)

A comedy in three acts by George Bernard Shaw. Revived by Maurice Evans at the Alvin Theatre, October 8, 1947.

Cast of characters—

Roebuck Ramsden	Malcolm Keen
Maid	Miriam Stovall
Octavius Robinson	Chester Stratton
John Tanner	Maurice Evans
Ann Whitefield	Frances Rowe
Mrs. Whitefield	Josephine Brown
Miss Ramsden	Phoebe Mackay
Violet Robinson	Carmen Mathews
Henry Straker	Jack Manning
Hector Malone, Jr.	Tony Bickley
Hector Malone, Sr.	Victor Sutherland

Act I.—Roebuck Ramsden's Study, Portland Place, London, 1905. Act II.—Coachyard of the Whitefield Residence, Near Richmond. Act III.—Patio of a Villa in Granada, Spain.

Staged by Maurice Evans and George Shaefer; settings by Frederick Stover; lighting by George Shaefer; costumes by David Ffolkes.

The first professional Broadway production of G. B. Shaw's comedy about the ascendancy of Woman since 1912. The first New York production was in 1905, when Charles Dillingham produced it at the Hudson Theatre where it opened September 5 and continued for 192 performances with Robert Lorraine (John Tanner), Clara Bloodgood (Violet Robinson) and Richard Bennett (Hector Malone, Jr.). The revival September, 1912, was produced by Liebler and Co. at the Hudson and ran for 32 performances with Robert Lorraine again as John Tanner.

HIGH BUTTON SHOES

(271 performances)
(Continued)

A musical comedy in two acts by Stephen Longstreet; music and lyrics by Jule Styne and Sammy Cahn; orchestrations by Philip Lang; vocal arrangements by Bob Martin. Produced by Monte Proser and Joseph Kipness at the Century Theatre, October 9, 1947.

Cast of characters—

Harrison Floy	Phil Silvers
Mr. Pontdue	Joey Faye
Uncle Willie	Paul Godkin
Henry Longstreet	Jack McCauley
General Longstreet	Clay Clement

Stevie Longstreet...................................Johnny Stewart
Fran...Lois Lee
Sara Longstreet...................................Nanette Fabray
Nancy...Helen Gallagher
Hubert Ogglethorpe (Oggle)........................Mark Dawson
Shirley Simpkins..................................Carole Coleman
Elmer Simpkins....................................Nathaniel Frey
Elmer Simpkins, Jr................................Donald Harris
Coach...Tom Glennon
Mr. Anderson......................................William David
A Boy at the Picnic...............................Arthur Partington
His Playmate......................................Sondra Lee
A Popular Girl....................................Jacqueline Dodge
A Betting Man.....................................George Spelvin
Another Betting Man...............................Howard Lenters
    Corps De Ballet: Jean Marie Caples, Jacqueline Dodge, Virginia
Gorski, June Graham, Betty Hyatt, Elena Lane, Sondra Lee, Audrey
Peters, Gloria Smith, Toni Stuart, Eleonore Treiber, Vincent Carbone,
Raul Celada, Lenny Claret, Evans Davis, Fred Hearn, Ray Kirchner,
Tommy Morton, Arthur Partington, William Pierson, William Sum-
ner, Don Weissmuller.
    Act I.—New Brunswick, New Jersey. Act II.—Atlantic City.
    Staged by George Abbott; music directed by Milton Rosenstock;
dances and staging by Jerome Robbins; settings by Oliver Smith; light-
ing by Peggy Clark; costumes by Miles White.

Based on a semi-autobiographical novel by Stephen Longstreet, the musical tells of life in New Brunswick, N. J. (the
college town of Dear Old Rutgers), in the year 1913. A ballet
devised by Jerome Robbins, depicting a typical "chase" in a
Mack Sennett Keystone Comedy of the period, was the highlight
of the show.

Principal musical numbers: "He Tried to Make a Dollar,"
"Can't You Just See Yourself in Love with Me?", "There's Noth-
ing Like a Model T," "Next to Texas, I Love You," "Security,"
"Bird Watcher's Song," "Get Away for a Day in the Country,"
"Papa, Won't You Dance with Me?", "On a Sunday by the
Sea," "You're My Girl," "I Still Get Jealous," "Nobody Ever
Died for Dear Old Rutgers."

ALLEGRO

(268 performances)
(Continued)

A musical play in two acts by Oscar Hammerstein II; music
by Richard Rodgers; orchestrations by Russell Bennett. Produced by The Theatre Guild at the Majestic Theatre, October 10,
1947.

Cast of characters—

Marjorie Taylor...................................Annamary Dickey
Dr. Joseph Taylor.................................William Ching
Mayor...Edward Platt
Grandma Taylor....................................Muriel O'Malley
Friends of Joey...................Ray Harrison, Frank Westbrook

```
Jennie Brinker.....................................Roberta Jonay
Principal..........................................Robert Byrn
Mabel..............................................Evelyn Taylor
Georgie............................................Harrison Muller
Hazel..............................................Kathryn Lee
Charlie Townsend...................................John Conte
Joseph Taylor, Jr..................................John Battles
Miss Lipscomb......................................Susan Svetlik
Cheer Leaders...........................Charles Tate, Sam Steen
Coach..............................................Wilson Smith
Ned Brinker........................................Paul Parks
English Professor..................................David Collyer
Chemistry Professor................................William McCully
Greek Professor....................................Raymond Keast
Biology Professor..................................Robert Byrn
Philosophy Professor...............................Blake Ritter
Shakespeare Student................................Susan Svetlik
Bertram Woolhaven..................................Ray Harrison
Molly..............................................Katrina Van Oss
Beulah.............................................Gloria Wills
Minister...........................................Edward Platt
Millie.............................................Julie Humphries
Dot................................................Sylvia Karlton
Addie..............................................Patricia Bybell
Dr. Bigby Denby....................................Lawrence Fletcher
Mrs. Mulhouse......................................Frances Rainer
Mrs. Lansdale......................................Lily Paget
Jarman.............................................Bill Bradley
Maid...............................................Jean Houloose
Emily..............................................Lisa Kirk
Doorman............................................Tom Perkins
Brook Lansdale.....................................Stephen Chase
Buckley............................................Wilson Smith
```

Act I.—The Home Town and the College Town of Joseph Taylor, Jr.   Act II.—A Large City. 1905 on the Day Joseph is Born Until His Thirty-fifth Year.

Stage production supervised by Lawrence Langner and Theresa Helburn; music directed by Salvatore Dell'Isola; choreography by Agnes de Mille; settings and lighting by Jo Mielziner; costumes by Lucinda Ballard.

See page 201.

MEDEA

(214 performances)

A tragedy freely adapted by Robinson Jeffers from the "Medea" of Euripides; music by Tibor Serly. Revived by Robert Whitehead and Oliver Rea at the National Theatre, October 20, 1947.

Cast of characters—

```
The Nurse..........................................Florence Reed
The Tutor..........................................Don McHenry
The Children............................Bobby Nick, Peter Moss
First Woman of Corinth.............................Grace Mills
Second Woman of Corinth............................Kathryn Grill
Third Woman of Corinth.............................Leone Wilson
Medea..............................................Judith Anderson
Creon..............................................Albert Hecht
Jason..............................................John Gielgud
Aegeus.............................................Hugh Franklin
Jason's Slave......................................Richard Hylton
Attendants to Medea................Martha Downes, Marian Seldes
```
Soldiers: Ben Morse, Jon Dawson, Richard Boone, Dennis McCarthy.

One intermission. Entire action takes place before Medea's House in Corinth.
Staged by John Gielgud; setting by Ben Edwards; costumes by Castillo; lighting by Peggy Clark.

Played in New York by Matilda Heron at the New Bowery Theatre, 1866, Mrs. J. H. Hackett at Wood's Museum in 1876, Januschek at Booth's in 1881, Margaret Anglin in 1918 at Carnegie Hall and by many others.

(Closed May 15, 1948)

AN INSPECTOR CALLS

(95 performances)

A play in three acts by J. B. Priestley. Produced by Courtney Burr and Lassor H. Grosberg at the Booth Theatre, October 21, 1947.

Cast of characters—

Arthur Birling	Melville Cooper
Gerald Croft	John Buckmaster
Sheila Birling	Rene Ray
Sybil Birling	Doris Lloyd
Edna	Patricia Marmont
Eric Birling	John Merivale
Inspector Goole	Thomas Mitchell

Acts I, II and III.—Dining Room of the Birlings' House in Brumley, an Industrial City in the North Midlands. Spring of 1912.
Staged by Cedric Hardwicke; setting, costumes and lighting by Stewart Chaney.

See page 286.

(Closed January 10, 1948)

THE DRUID CIRCLE

(70 performances)

A play in three acts by John Van Druten. Produced by Alfred de Liagre, Jr., at the Morosco Theatre, October 22, 1947.

Cast of characters—

Miss Dagnall	Lillian Bronson
Professor White	Leo G. Carroll
Professor Parry Phillips	Noel Leslie
Maddox	Boyd Crawford
Tobin	Aiden Turner
Tom Lloyd-Ellis	Walter Starkey
Megan Lewis	Susan Douglas
Brenda Maddox	Neva Patterson
Mrs. White	Ethel Griffies
Miss Trevelyan	Merle Maddern
Blodwen	Cherry Hardy

Act I.—Scene 1—Senior Common Room, Small University Town Near Borders of England and Wales, Before the War. 2—The Mad-

doxes' Flat. Act II.—Professor White's Flat. Act III.—Scene 1—
Senior Common Room. 2—The Maddoxes' Flat.
  Staged by John Van Druten; settings and lighting by Stewart
Chaney.

John Van Druten goes back to the period and mood of his early
hit, "Young Woodley," to tell of the dull, narrow life of an impoverished college on the Welsh border in the early 1920's. Instructors and students alike suffer from repressions and complexes. Most complex and repressed is the headmaster, who hates youth simply because it is young. He almost wrecks the love idyll of two students.

(Closed December 20, 1947)

THE WINSLOW BOY

(215 performances)

A play in two acts by Terence Rattigan. Produced by Atlantis Productions, The Theatre Guild, H. M. Tennent, Ltd., and John C. Wilson at the Empire Theatre, October 29, 1947.

Cast of characters—

Ronnie Winslow	Michael Newell
Violet	Betty Sinclair
Grace Winslow	Madge Compton
Arthur Winslow	Alan Webb
Catherine Winslow	Valerie White
Dickie Winslow	Owen Holder
John Wetherstone	Michael Kingsley
Desmond Curry	George Benson
Miss Barnes	Dorothy Hamilton
Fred	Leonard Michell
Sir Robert Morton	Frank Allenby

Acts I and II.—Arthur Winslow's House in Kensington, London.
Staged by Glen Byam Shaw; setting by Michael Weight.

See page 134.

(Closed May 1, 1948)

EDITH PIAF

(44 performances)

A program of French songs and dances in two acts by Edith Piaf and her continental entertainers. Presented by Clifford C. Fischer at The Playhouse, October 30, 1947.

Cast of entertainers—

Edith Piaf, chanteuse	George and Tim Dormonde
Les Compagnons de la Chanson	Les Canova
George Andre Martin, Conferencier	Lyda Alma and Vanni Fleury
Dorrit Merrill, Announcer	Winter Sisters

Act I.—Poetry in Motion, Hellenic Dancers, Scientific Nonsense, Digital Dancing and French Voices in Satiric Ballads. Act II.—Edith Piaf.

Staged by Edward Lewis; music directed by Lou Forman.

(Closed December 6, 1947)

THIS TIME TOMORROW

(32 performances)

A drama in two acts by Jan de Hartog. Produced by The Theatre Guild at the Barrymore Theatre, November 3, 1947.

Cast of characters—

Wilts...John Archer
Karels...Tyler Carpenter
Yolan..Ruth Ford
Wouterson..Sam Jaffe

Act I.—Scene 1—Dissecting Room in Amsterdam Institute of Scientific Research, Prior to Nazi Invasion. 2—Deck of Ferry Boat on Zuyderzee, Prior to Spanish Civil War. 3—Room in Dr. Wouterson's House, Amsterdam. Act II.—Scenes 1 and 4—Dissecting Room. 2 and 3—Dr. Wouterson's House.

Staged by Paul Crabtree under supervision of Theresa Helburn and Lawrence Langner; settings by Herbert Brodkin; costumes by Patricia Montgomery.

A hopelessly tubercular girl and a talented Dutch research physician fall in love. A great scientist, becoming interested in the girl's case, discovers that, by all medical rules, she should have been dead for a fortnight, and that only love is keeping her alive. As soon as this love is expressed, he believes, she will die. His diagnosis proves correct.

(Closed November 29, 1947)

TRIAL HONEYMOON

(8 performances)

A comedy in two acts by Conrad S. Smith. Produced by Harry Rosen at the Royale Theatre, November 3, 1947.

Cast of characters—

Elsie..Mildred Munroe
Linda Melton.......................................Ellen Fenwick
Craig Denning......................................Joel Thomas
George Willoughby..................................Jack Fletcher
Dr. Trumbull.......................................Stapleton Kent
Bill Daniels.......................................Ed Moroncy
Irene Smith..Eileen Heckart
Fanny Willoughby...................................Helen Waters

Acts I and II.—Bungalow No. 9, Hotel Del Rey, Near Los Angeles.

Staged by Edward Ludlum; setting and costumes by Philip Kessler; lighting by Chester Manzer.

A boy and girl get married twenty-four hours earlier than they are supposed to under the law. Because of the housing shortage the honeymoon takes place in a tent. Sample line of snappy dialogue: "Let's go into the dark room and see what develops."

(Closed November 8, 1947)

FOR LOVE OR MONEY

(241 performances)
(Continued)

A comedy in three acts by F. Hugh Herbert. Produced by Barnard Straus at Henry Miller's Theatre, November 4, 1947.

Cast of characters—

Nita Havemeyer	Vicki Cummings
Mrs. Early	Maida Reade
Queenie	Elizabeth Brew
Wilbur	Grover Burgess
Mrs. Tremaine	Paula Trueman
Mr. Tremaine	Kirk Brown
Bill Tremaine	Mark O'Daniels
Preston Mitchell	John Loder
Janet Blake	June Lockhart

Acts I, II and III.—Drawing Room of Preston Mitchell's Home at Port Washington, Long Island, December, 1946.

Staged by Harry Ellerbe; setting by Raymond Sovey; costumes by Anna Hill Johnstone.

Into the home of an aging matinee idol is driven, by an automobile breakdown and a storm, a girl. In all her innocence and enthusiasm, she conquers. "Daddy Long Legs" set on modern Long Island.

THE FIRST MRS. FRASER

(38 performances)

A play in three acts by St. John Ervine. Revived by Gant Gaither at the Shubert Theatre, November 5, 1947.

Cast of characters—

Ninian Fraser	Lex Richards
Mabel	Hazel Jones
James Fraser	Henry Daniell
Philip Logan	Reginald Mason
Alice Fraser	Emily Lawrence
Murdo Fraser	Kendall Clark
Janet Fraser	Jane Cowl
Elsie Fraser	Frances Tannehill

Acts I, II and III.—Janet Fraser's Apartment, Knightsbridge, London.

Staged by Harold Young; setting by Charles Elson; costumes by Natalie Barth.

The original New York production of "The First Mrs. Fraser" opened at the Playhouse, December 28, 1929, and continued for 352 performances. The play was produced by William A. Brady and Grace George was the first Mrs. Fraser.

(Closed December 9, 1947)

EASTWARD IN EDEN

(15 performances)

A play in three acts by Dorothy Gardner; incidental music by Andre Singer. Produced by Nancy Stern at the Royale Theatre, November 18, 1947.

Cast of characters—

```
Austin Dickinson...............................John O'Connor
Lavinia Dickinson..............................Beatrice Manley
Maggie.........................................Kate Tomlinson
Lucy Plum......................................Barbara Ames
Helen Fiske (Hunt Jackson).....................Emma Knox
Susan Gilbert..................................Penelope Sack
Gerry Hood.....................................Don Peters
Ben Newton.....................................Ernest Gaves
Emily Dickinson................................Beatrice Straight
Edward Dickinson...............................Edwin Jerome
Dr. Charles Wadsworth..........................Onslow Stevens
Miss Simpson...................................Mary Jackson
Martha Dickinson...............................Robin Humphrey
Thomas Wentworth Higginson.....................John D. Seymour
```
    Act I.—Scene 1—The Dickinson Parlor, Amherst, Mass., 1852. 2—Pastor's Study, Philadelphia, 1854. Act II.—Scenes 1, 2 and 3—The Dickinson Parlor. 4—A Cottage. Act III.—The Dickinson Parlor.
    Staged by Ellen Van Volkenburg; settings and costumes by Donald Oenslager.

See page 237.

(Closed November 29, 1947)

ANTONY AND CLEOPATRA

(126 performances)

A tragedy by William Shakespeare with music by Paul Nordoff and rearranged in two parts. Produced by Katharine Cornell at the Martin Beck Theatre, November 26, 1947.

Cast of characters—

```
Philo..........................................Alan Shayne
Demetrius......................................Theodore Marcuse
Antony.........................................Godfrey Tearle
Cleopatra, Queen of Egypt......................Katharine Cornell
A Messenger....................................David J. Stewart
Dolabella......................................Robert Duke
Proculeius.....................................Charlton Heston
Iras...........................................Maureen Stapleton
```

```
Charmian...........................................Lenore  Ulric
Alexas.............................................Oliver  Cliff
Diomedes...........................................Eli  Wallach
Enobarbus..........................................Kenth  Smith
Mardian............................................Joseph  Wiseman
Octavius  Caesar...................................Ralph  Clanton
Lepidus............................................Ivan  Simpson
Agrippa............................................David  Orrick
Pompey.............................................Joseph  Holland
Menas..............................................Martin  Kingsley
Varrius............................................Barnet  Biro
Ventidius..........................................Bruce  Gordon
Octavia............................................Betty  Low
Canidius...........................................Dayton  Lummis
Eros...............................................Douglass  Watson
Silius.............................................Charles  Nolte
Thyreus............................................Robert  Carricart
Taurus.............................................Gilbert  Reade
Gallus.............................................Rudulph  Watson
An  Old  Soldier...................................Bruce  Gordon
Scarus.............................................Anthony  Randall
Euphronius.........................................Ernest  Rowan
Dercetas...........................................Martin  Kingsley
A  Clown...........................................Oliver  Cliff
```

Slaves, Guards, Servants, Soldiers: John Russo, Peter Barno, Drummond Erskine, Milfred Hull, Orrin Redfield, Charles Holt, James Grudéer, Lawrence Perron.

Part I.—Egypt, Italy and Syria. Part II.—Greece and Egypt.

Staged by Guthrie McClintic; settings by Leo Kerz; costumes by Valentina and John Boyt.

The first production of "Antony and Cleopatra" in New York was at the Park Theatre in 1846. It was the first production at the New Theatre in 1909 with E. H. Sothern, Julia Marlowe, Beatrice Forbes-Robinson and Jessie Busley in the cast. Jane Cowl and Rollo Peters played the leading parts in 1924 and Laurence Rivers, Inc., revived the play with Tallulah Bankhead and Conway Tearle at the Mansfield Theatre, November 10, 1937.

(Closed March 13, 1948)

A STREETCAR NAMED DESIRE

(207 performances)
(Continued)

A play in three acts by Tennessee Williams. Presented by Irene M. Selznick at the Barrymore Theatre, December 3, 1947.

Cast of characters—

```
Negro  Woman....................................Gee  Gee  James
Eunice  Hubbel..................................Peg  Hillias
Stanley  Kowalski...............................Marlon  Brando
Harold  Mitchell  (Mitch).......................Karl  Malden
Stella  Kowalski ...............................Kim  Hunter
Steve  Hubbel...................................Rudy  Bond
Blanche  DuBois.................................Jessica  Tandy
Pablo  Gonzales.................................Nick  Dennis
A  Young  Collector.............................Vito  Christi
Mexican  Woman..................................Edna  Thomas
```

A Strange Woman.....................................Ann Dere
A Strange Man.....................................Richard Garrick
    Acts I, II and III.—Spring, Summer and Early Fall in New Orleans.
    Staged by Elia Kazan; settings and lighting by Jo Mielziner; costumes by Lucinda Ballard.

See page 32.

CARIBBEAN CARNIVAL

(11 performances)

A musical revue in two acts; lyrics and music by Samuel L. Manning and Adolph Thenstead; drum rhythms by Mario Costillo; orchestrations by Ken Macomber. Presented by Adolph Thenstead at the International Theatre, December 5, 1947.

Principals engaged—

Pearl Primus	Claude Marchant
Josephine Premice	Sam Manning
Pamela Ward	Billie Allen
Eloise Hill	Alex Young
Smith Kids	Trio Cubana
Peggy Watson	Duke of Iron
Padjet Fredericks	Curtis James
Dorothy Graham	Fred Thomas

    Others prominent in the cast: Eddie Talifferro, Gem Bolling, Charles Queenan, Alphonse Cimber, Bernard Taylor, Andrew King, Clifton Gray, Louis Sterling, Donald Curtis, James Brown, William Johnson, Jerry Meeres, Helen Carr, Lillie Peace, Mildred Thomas, Clara Hubbard, Wahnetta San, Fannie Turner, Jacqueline Hairston, Marjorie James, Dorothy Macdavid and Helen Tinsley.
    Acts I nd II.—Caribbean Islands.
    Staged by Samuel L. Manning and John Hirshman; choreography by Pearl Primus and Claude Marchant; orchestra directed by Ken Macomber; costumes by Lou Eisele.

(Closed December 13, 1947)

THE GENTLEMAN FROM ATHENS

(7 performances)

A comedy in three acts by Emmet Lavery. Produced by Martin Gosch in association with Eunice Healy, at the Mansfield Theatre, December 9, 1947.

Cast of characters—

Cousin Vincent Kilpatrick.........................Watson White
Miss Mary Kilpatrick..............................Ethel Browning
Morgan Kilpatrick.................................Alan Hewitt
Lee Kilpatrick....................................Edith Atwater
Daniel.......................................Creighton Thompson
Big Ed Lawrence...................................Gavin Gordon
Hon. Stephen Socrates Christopher.................Anthony Quinn
Igor Stepenov....................................Feodor Chaliapin
News Reel Director................................Lorance Kerr
Mike Rykowski.....................................Lou Polan
Congressman Andrews...............................Leopold Badia

Congressman Borgsen..............................Ed Latimer
Congressman Harnell...........................Arthur Jarrett
Congressman (Mrs.) Stringley.................Elsie May Gordon
    Radio and Newsreel Crews: Frank Rowan, Oliver Crawford, Leonard
Auerbach.
    Acts I, II and III.—Drawing Room of Kilpatrick Hall, One of the
Great Old Halls of Virginia.
    Staged by Sam Wanamaker; setting by Ralph Alswang.

Stephen S. Christopher, a Greek-American from the California
vineyard country, buys his way into Congress. His home town
is named Athens and his middle name is Socrates. Becoming acquainted with the Socratic ideal of democracy, he attempts some
national reforms and wins a high-born Washington girl.

(Closed December 13, 1947)

ANGEL IN THE WINGS

(197 performances)

(Continued)

A musical revue in two acts; music and words by Bob Hilliard
and Carl Sigman; musical arrangements by David Mann; sketches
by Ted Luce, Hank Ladd and Grace and Paul Hartman. Presented by Marjorie and Sherman Ewing at the Coronet Theatre,
December 11, 1947.

Principals engaged—

Grace Hartman	Paul Hartman
Elaine Stritch	Robert Stanton
Nadine Gae	Peter Hamilton
Eileen Barton	Johnny Barnes
Viola Roache	Hank Ladd
Eugenie Baird	Bill McGraw

    Staged by John Kennedy; choreography by Edward Noll; settings
and lighting by Donald Oenslager; costumes by Julia Sze; music directed by Phil Ingalls.

Paul and Grace Hartman, veteran vaudeville and night club
entertainers, headed a song and sketch revue whose principals
also included Hank Ladd, a monologist and master of ceremonies,
and Elaine Stritch, who sang "Civilization," a song which already
had become popular via radio.

Principal musical numbers: "Long Green Blues," "Holler Blue
Murder," "Breezy," "Civilization," "Tambourine," "If It Were
Easy to Do," "Thousand Islands Song," and "The Big Brass
Band from Brazil."

CRIME AND PUNISHMENT

(40 performances)

A drama in two acts by Dostoyevsky; dramatized by Rodney Ackland. Revived by Robert Whitehead and Oliver Rea at the National Theatre, December 22, 1947.

Cast of characters—

Lebeziatnikoff	Ben Morse
Sonia	Dolly Haas
Katerina Ivanna	Lillian Gish
Polya	Betty Lou Keim
Leda	Sherry Smith
Ivan	Paton Price
Amalia	Elizabeth Neumann
Street Vendor	Howard Fischer
Anyutka	Wauna Paul
His Assistant	Robert Donley
Ex-Soldier	Michael Arshansky
Nastasia	Galina Talva
Daria	Susan Steell
Lizavieta	Mary James
Rodion Romanitch Raskolnikoff	John Gielgud
Simon Zaharitch Marmeladoff	Sanford Meisner
Dmitri Prokovitch Razoumikhin	Alexander Scourby
Zametoff	Richard Purdy
Casimir Stanislawowitch Looskinsky	E. A. Krumschmidt
Pulcheria Alexandrovna	Alice John
Dounia	Marian Seldes
Porfiri Petrovitch	Vladimir Sokoloff
A Strange Man	Mort Marshall
Priest	Sandy Campbell
Doctor	Patrick McVey
Coachman	William Beal
Government Clerk	David Elliott
His Wife	Cecile Sherman
Widow	Amy Douglass

Acts I and II.—A Lodging House in St. Petersburg in 1860.

Staged by Theodore Komisarievsky; associate director, Bea Lawrence; setting by Paul Sheriff; costumes by Lester Polakow.

Richard Mansfield played Rodion in a dramatization of "Crime and Punishment" by Charles Henry Meltzer called "The Story of Rodion, the Student" at the Garrick Theatre, December 3, 1895. In 1904 Alla Nazimova and Paul Orleneff presented the play in repertory at the old Windsor Theatre in the Bowery, in Russian. In 1907 and 1908 E. H. Sothern played in repertoire a dramatization by Laurence Irving called "The Fool Hath Said in His Heart There Is No God." In January of 1935, Wolfson and Victor Trivas revived "Crime and Punishment" in a dramatization by Victor Trivas and Georg Schdanoff at the Biltmore Theatre for 15 performances with Morgan Farley as Raskolnikoff.

(Closed January 24, 1948)

THE CRADLE WILL ROCK

(21 performances)

A play in music by Marc Blitzstein. Revived by Michael Myerberg at the Mansfield Theatre, December 26, 1947.

Cast of characters—

Moll	Estelle Loring
Gent	Edward S. Bryce
Dick	Jesse White
Cop	Taggart Casey
Reverend Salvation	Harold Patrick
Editor Daily	Brooks Dunbar
Yasha	Jack Albertson
Dauber	Chandler Cowles
President Prexy	Howard Blaine
Professor Trixie	Leslie Litomy
Professor Mamie	Edmund Hewitt
Professor Scoot	Ray Fry
Doctor Specialist	Robert Pierson
Harry Druggist	David Thomas
Mr. Mister	Will Geer
Mrs. Mister	Vivian Vance
Junior Mister	Dennis King, Jr.
Sister Mister	Jo Hurt
Steve	Stephen West Downer
Sadie Polock	Marie Leidal
Gus Polock	Walter Scheff
Bugs	Edward S. Bryce
Larry Foreman	Alfred Drake
Ella Hammer	Muriel Smith
Attendant's Voice	Hazel Shermet
First Reporter	Rex Coston
Second Reporter	Gil Houston
Clerk	Howard Shanet

Chorus: Lucretia Anderson, Robert Burr, John Fleming, Michael Pollock, Germaine Poulin, Napoleon Reed, Gwen Ward.

Staged by Howard Da Silva; music directed by Howard Shanet.

The first production of "The Cradle Will Rock" was planned with elaborate scenery, costumes and orchestra, but it was banned by the Federal Theatre officials of WPA after one dress rehearsal, June 15, 1937. Orson Welles and John Houseman then took it to the Venice Theatre (now the Century) where Union actors bought admission tickets and spoke their roles from the auditorium. The producer was announced as Helen Deutsch. Marc Blitzstein provided the music, playing on a tinny piano. Before the closing date, July 1, 1937, nineteen performances had been given. John Houseman and Orson Welles gave the play in music its first official showing in a series of Sunday night performances at the Mercury lasting from December 5, 1937, until after Christmas. Sam H. Grisman sponsored a regular Broadway engagement at the Windsor Theatre beginning January 3, 1938, and lasting for 108 performances. It was one of the plays included in the voting in 1938 when the Drama Critics' Circle gave their award to John

Steinbeck's "Of Mice and Men." The play was presented in orchestral form at City Center, November 24, 1947.

(Closed January 11, 1948)

TOPAZE

(1 performance)

A comedy in three acts by Marcel Pagnol; adapted by Benn W. Levy. Revived by Yolanda Mero Irion at the Morosco Theatre, December 27, 1947.

Cast of characters—

Topaze	Oscar Karlweis
Jacques Blondet	Alan Shay
Muche	Robert Chisholm
Ernestine	Carol Gustafson
Tamise	Joe E. Marks
Suzanne Courtoise	Tilly Losch
Monsieur Cordier	Kevin Matthews
Monsieur Jesserand	Clifford Sales
Monsieur Pitart-Verginolies	Edward Benjamin
Monsieur de Victor	Roy Rogers
Monsieur Tronche-Bobine	Preston Zukor
Monsieur Durand	Sonny Cavell
Monsieur Ramon	David Burke
Monsieur Gaston	Jimmie Dutton
Monsieur Perron	Harold Calvin
Baroness Pitart-Verginolies	Helen Bonfils
Regis Castel-Benac	Clarence Derwent
Butler	David Jones
Roger de Berville	Philip Robinson
Odette	Lucille Patton
Policeman	Jean Saks
Germaine	Ethel Madsen
A Venerable Old Man	G. Swayne Gordon

Act I.—Classroom in Pension Muche. Act II.—Small Salon in Home of Suzanne Courtoise. Act III.—Office of the Topaze Company.

Lee Shubert produced "Topaze" at the Music Box, February 12, 1930, and the play ran for 150 performances. In February, 1931, J. A. Gauvin revived it at the Forty-ninth St. Theatre for 8 performances.

(Closed December 27, 1947)

RUTH DRAPER

(27 performances)

A repertory of dramatic sketches. Presented by John C. Wilson at the Empire Theatre, December 28, 1947.

Sketches—

Three Breakfasts
At an Art Exhibition
The Actress
In County Kerry—1919

A Children's Party
A Scotch Immigrant at Ellis Island
A Southern Girl
Doctors and Diets
Three Women and Mr. Clifford
The Return
Viva la France
Opening of a Bazaar
A Dalmatian Peasant in Hall of New York Hospital
On a Porch in a Maine Coast Village
Debutant at a Dance
At Court of Philip IV of Spain
Three Generations in the Court of Domestic Relations
Class in Greek Poise
A Church in Italy

(Closed February 1, 1948)

D'OYLY CARTE OPERA COMPANY

(136 performances)

A repertory of seven Gilbert and Sullivan operettas was presented by the D'oyly Carte Opera Company of London at the Century Theatre starting December 29, 1947.

THE MIKADO

Cast of characters—

The Mikado of Japan...........................Darrell Fancourt
Nanki-Poo............................ ....Thomas Round
Ko-Ko.................................... ....Martyn Green
Pooh-Bah...................................... ....Richard Watson
Pish-Tush........... ....Charles Dorning
Go-To...Peter   Pratt
Yum-Yum......................................Margaret Mitchell
Pitti-Sing............................. ....Denise Findlay
Peep-Bo......................... ....Joan Gillingham
Katisha.......................... ....Ella Halman

TRIAL BY JURY

January 5

Cast of characters—

The Learned Judge..............................Richard Watson
Counsel for the Plaintiff................ ....Charles Dorning
The Defendant...................................Leonard Osborn
Foreman of the Jury............... ....Radley Flynn
Usher..Richard Walker
Associate.......... ....C. William Morgan
The Plaintiff...................................Gwyneth Cullimore
First Bridesmaid.....................................Enid Walsh

Followed by—

THE PIRATES OF PENZANCE

Cast of characters—

Major-General Stanley..............................Martyn Green
The Pirate King.............................Darrell Fancourt
Samuel..Richard Dunn
Frederic...Thomas Round
Sergeant of Police........................ ....Richard Walker
Mabel...Helen Roberts
Edith..Joyce Wright
Kate.................... ....Joan Gillingham
Isabel...Enid Walsh
Ruth (Pirate Maid-of-All-Work).....................Ella Halman

IOLANTHE

January 12

Cast of characters—

The Lord Chancellor..............................Martyn Green
Earl of Mountararat.................. ....Darrell Fancourt
Earl Tolloller.......................................Thomas Round
Private Willis....................................Richard Walker
Strephon....................... ....Charles Dorning
Queen of the Fairies...............................Ella Halman
Iolanthe..Denise Findlay
Celia..Gwyneth Cullimore
Leila..Joan Gillingham
Fleta...Patricia Hadfield
Phyllis...Margaret Mitchell

COX AND BOX

January 19

Cast of characters—

Cox..Richard Dunn
Box............................ ....Leonard Osborn
Bouncer..Richard Walker

Followed by—

H.M.S. PINAFORE

Cast of characters—

The Rt. Hon. Sir Joseph Porter, K.C.B..............Martyn Green
Captain Corcoran.................................Charles Dorning
Ralph Rackstraw................... ....Thomas Round
Dick Deadeye..................Darrell Fancourt—L. Radley Flynn
Bill Bobstay......................................Richard Walker
Bob Beckett........ ....L. Radley Flynn—Donald Harris
Josephine...Helen Roberts
Hebe..Joan Gillingham
Little Buttercup..Ella Halman

THE GONDOLIERS

January 26

Cast of characters—

The Duke of Plaza-Toro	Martyn Green
Luiz	Thomas Round
Don Alhambra Del Bolero	Richard Watson
Marco Palmieri	Leonard Osborn
Giuseppe Palmieri	Charles Dorning
Antonio	Eric Hutson
Francesco	Thomas Hancock
Giorgio	Radley Flynn
Annibale	Richard Dunn
The Duchess of Plaza-Toro	Ella Halman
Casilda	Margaret Mitchell
Gianetta	Gwyneth Cullimore
Tessa	Denise Findlay
Fiametta	Enid Walsh
Vittoria	Joan Gillingham
Giulia	Laura Crombie
Inez	Caryl Fane

THE YEOMEN OF THE GUARD

February 2

Cast of characters—

Sir Richard Cholmondeley	Richard Watson
Colonel Fairfax	Leonard Osborn
Sergeant Meryll	Darrell Fancourt
Leonard Meryll	Thomas Hancock
Jack Point	Martyn Green
Wilfred Shadbolt	Richard Walker
First Yeoman	Rhys Thomas
Second Yeoman	Richard Dunn
First Citizen	C. William Morgan
Second Citizen	Peter Pratt
Elsie Maynard	Helen Roberts
Phoebe Meryll	Denise Findlay
Dame Carruthers	Ella Halman
Kate	Gwyneth Cullimore

PATIENCE

February 9

Cast of characters—

Colonel Calverley	Darrell Fancourt
Major Murgatroyd	C. William Morgan
Lieut. the Duke of Dunstable	Leonard Osborn
Reginald Bunthorne	Martyn Green
Archibald Grosvenor	Charles Dorning
Mr. Bunthorne's Solicitor	Milton Rees
The Lady Angela	Joan Gillingham
The Lady Saphir	Gwyneth Cullimore
The Lady Ella	Muriel Harding
The Lady Jane	Ella Halman
Patience	Margaret Mitchell

Staged by Ann Bethell; music directed by Isadore Godfrey; settings by Charles Ricketts, Peter Goffin, Joseph and Phil Harker; costumes by Norman Wilkinson, George Sheringham, Peter Goffin and Hugo Rombold.

The repertory was then repeated as follows: THE MIKADO—
February 16, 1948; H.M.S. PINAFORE and COX AND BOX—
February 23; THE GONDOLIERS—March 1; TRIAL BY
JURY and THE PIRATES OF PENZANCE—March 8; PA-
TIENCE—March 15; THE YEOMEN OF THE GUARD—
March 22; IOLANTHE—March 29; THE MIKADO—April 5,
12 and 19.

The D'Oyly Carte Opera Company was last presented in New
York, January 5, 1939, with 77 performances.

(Closed April 24, 1948)

HARVEST OF YEARS

(16 performances)

A play in three acts by DeWitt Bodeen. Produced by Arthur
J. Beckhard at the Hudson Theatre, January 12, 1948.

Cast of characters—

Astrid Bromark	Virginia Robinson
Bertha Bromark	Phillipa Bevans
Jenny Nelson	Lenka Peterson
Chris Bromark	Russell Hardie
Bernhard Jonson	Robert Crawley
Anna Bromark	Esther Dale
Mellie Bromark	Emily Noble
Margareta Bromark	Leona Maricle
Jules Bromark	Philip Abbott

Acts I, II and III.—Bromark Parlor in a Farmhouse in San Joaquin
Valley, California.

Staged by Arthur J. Beckhard; setting by Raymond Sovey; costumes by Peggy Morrison.

In the farmhouse of the Bromarks, in the California vineyard
country, the household is ruled by a rugged-minded Swedish
mother, Anna Bromark. The life which goes on about her is
complex, and "big" to those it touches. One daughter marries
another daughter's beau; the fiancée of a son marries another
man; babies are born, and a woman dies in childbirth. Events
such as these fail to shake the aplomb of Anna. To her, the important things of living are not the big events but the little,
homely affairs of daily routine.

(Closed January 24, 1948)

POWER WITHOUT GLORY

(31 performances)

A play in three acts by Michael Clayton Hutton. Produced by John C. Wilson and the Messrs. Shubert at the Booth Theatre, January 13, 1948.

Cast of characters—

Flo	Joan Newell
Maggie	Marjorie Rhodes
Edith	Helen Misener
Eddie	Lewis Stringer
Anna	Hilary Liddell
Cliff	Peter Murray
John	Trevor Ward

Acts I, II and III.—John Lord's Living Room, London.
Staged by Chloe Gibson; setting by Charles Elson.

A drab, shop-keeping family named Lord, living in London's East End, is variously affected by the murder of a girl on the nearby bank of the Thames. Evidence indicates that a weakling son, Cliff, committed the crime. To the father, this event is the shattering of a lifetime of drab respectability. To the mother, brother and sister, knowledge of Cliff's guilt brings varying reactions of loyalty, disloyalty and sorrow. As in J. B. Priestley's "An Inspector Calls," an offstage crime is used to illumine the characters of those who have knowledge of it.

(Closed February 7, 1948)

STRANGE BEDFELLOWS

(159 performances)
(Continued)

A comedy in three acts by Florence Ryerson and Colin Clements. Produced by Philip A. Waxman at the Morosco Theatre, January 14, 1948.

Cast of characters—

Julia Cromwell	Ruth Amos
Beulah	Leta Bonynge
Ling	Tom Chung Yun
Addie Cromwell Hampton	Nydia Westman
Senator William Cromwell	Carl Benton Reid
Lillian Hampton	Mary Kay Jones
Nickey	Billy Nevard
Mrs. Gimble	Frieda Altman
Mrs. Worley	Marion Weeks
Gifford Hampton	Robin Craven
Vincent Pemberton	Michael Hall
Matthew Cromwell	John Archer
Clarissa Blynn Cromwell	Joan Tetzel

```
Mrs. Tillie Sparker....................................Doris  Rich
Mayor Ambrose Tibbett............................William  Lee
Birdie.................................................Ruth  Miles
Zita.............................................Ann  Thompson
Opal.........................................Stephanie  Foster
```
Acts I, II and III.—Winter Parlor of Senator Cromwell's Mansion on Nob Hill, San Francisco, Fall of 1896.
Staged by Benno Schneider; setting and lighting by Ralph Alswang; costumes by Morton Haack.

The fight for women's rights invades the gaudy home of a buccaneering Nob Hill, San Francisco, millionaire Senator in 1896. Senator Cromwell's son, Matthew, brings a bride, Clarissa. Clarissa is a well-known, militant suffragette. She is opposed by the Senator and his cronies, by the women of the household and even by her husband, but finally she maneuvers everybody over to her side of the political fence.

MAKE MINE MANHATTAN

(158 performances)
(Continued)

A musical revue in two acts by Arnold B. Horwitt; music by Richard Lewine; orchestrations by Ted Royal. Produced by Joseph Hyman at the Broadhurst Theatre, January 15, 1948.

Principals engaged—

Eleanor Bagley	David Burns
Sheila Bond	Sid Caesar
Perry Bruskin	Danny Daniels
Ray Harrison	Jack Kilty
Hal Loman	Kyle MacDonnell
Biff McGuire	Joshua Shelley
Nelle Fisher	Max Showalter

Staged and lighted by Hassard Short; sketches directed by Max Liebman; music directed by Charles Sanford; choreography by Lee Sherman; settings by Frederick Fox; costumes by Morton Haack.

Principal musical numbers: "Phil the Fiddler," "Movie House in Manhattan," "Traftz," "The Good Old Days," "Saturday Night in Central Park," "Ringalevio," "Noises in the Street," "Subway Song," "A Night Out."

THE MEN WE MARRY

(3 performances)

A play in three acts by Elisabeth Cobb and Herschel Williams. Produced by Edgar Luckenbach at the Mansfield Theatre, January 16, 1948.

Cast of characters—

Maggie Welch	Shirley Booth
Phillip	David Anderson
Warren Throckmorton	Robert Willey
Gwennie	Margaret Hamilton
Dr. Alan Lambert	Neil Hamilton
Julie Madison	Marta Linden
Mark Kennicott	John Williams
Leda Mallard	Doris Dalton
Ned Snyder	Joseph Allen, Jr.
Mary	Anne Sargent
Peter Sterling	John Hudson

Acts I, II and III.—In the Home of Maggie Welch, Located in a Fashionable Section of Maryland.

Staged by Martin Manulis; setting and lighting by Donald Oenslager; costumes by Helene Pons.

Three sophisticated matrons try to arrange the marital affairs of a young war widow. They almost wreck her romance and come close to losing their own men. There is, however, a happy ending.

(Closed January 17, 1948)

THE SURVIVORS

(8 performances)

A play in three acts by Peter Viertel and Martin Gabel. Produced by Bernard Hart and Martin Gabel at The Playhouse, January 19, 1948.

Cast of characters—

Rutson Hedge	Marc Lawrence
Roy Clemens	Russell Collins
Alcott	Neil Fitzgerald
Finlay Decker	E. G. Marshall
Vincent Keyes	Louis Calhern
Tom Cameron	Anthony Ross
Steve Decker	Richard Basehart
Morgan Decker	Kevin McCarthy
Jane Decker	Jane Seymour
Lucy Dunne	Marianne Stewart
Jodine Decker	Hume Cronyn
Marcus Hedge	Edwin M. Bruce
Leonard Hawkes	Kenneth Tobey
Reverend Hoyt	Guy Arbury
Sheriff Bagley	Tom Hoier

Townspeople: Edith Rand, Ray Walston, Edgar Small, Eugene Steiner.

Acts I and III.—Court Hotel, Decker City, Missouri. Act II.—Veranda of the Decker Ranch.

Staged by Martin Gabel; settings and lighting by Boris Aronson; costumes by Rose Bogdanoff.

Steve and Morgan Decker, brothers, return to their Missouri ranch home after having spent most of the Civil War in a Confederate prison camp. Their one idea is to kill Tom Cameron, their former officer, for abandoning them to capture. Besides, there is a ranch feud between the Deckers and Cameron. Morgan

Decker dies from prison injuries, leaving Steve to finish the vendetta—but Steve half believes that talking things out with Cameron may bring a peaceable settlement. This belief is nurtured by Vincent Keyes, a fatherly lawyer. But others drive Morgan Decker and Cameron to a duel in which both are killed. The drama carries the modern political connotation that nothing is settled by war.

(Closed January 24, 1948)

THE LAST DANCE

(7 performances)

A play in three acts adapted from August Strindberg's "Dodsdancen" by Peter Goldbaum and Robin Short. Produced by James Russo and Michael Ellis in association with Theatre Associates, Inc., at the Belasco Theatre, January 27, 1948.

Cast of characters—

Edgar..Oscar Homolka
Alice.......................................Jessie Royce Landis
Curtis..Philip Bourneuf
Judith..Anne Jackson
Alan..Richard Hylton

Act I.—The Major's Living Quarters in an Old Fortress on a Semi-tropical Island. 1910. Acts II and III.—Villa Belle Vue, Residence of Health Supervisor.

Staged by John O'Shaughnessy; settings and costumes by Ralph Alswang.

This new version of Strindberg's "Dance of Death" combines the two sections of the original, eliminates some of the characters, changes the locale from Scandinavia to a tropical island and adds a new ending in which the Major dies from a stroke, but even in death maintains his maleficent hold upon his wife, who had thought that widowhood would free her from his influence.

(Closed January 27, 1948)

LOOK, MA, I'M DANCIN'

(142 performances)
(Continued)

A musical conceived by Jerome Robbins; music and lyrics by Hugh Martin; book by Jerome Lawrence and Robert E. Lee; orchestrations by Don Walker. Produced by George Abbott at the Adelphi, January 29, 1948.

Cast of characters—

```
Wotan.............................................Don  Liberto
Larry.............................................Loren  Welch
Dusty Lee.........................................Alice  Pearce
Ann Bruce.........................................Janet  Reed
Snow White........................................Virginia  Gorski
Eddie Winkler.....................................Harold  Lang
Tommy.............................................Tommy  Rall
F. Plancek........................................Robert  Harris
Tanya Drinskaya...................................Katharine  Sergava
Vladimir Luboff...................................Alexander  March
Lily Malloy.......................................Nancy  Walker
Mr. Gleeb.........................................James  Lane
Mr. Ferbish.......................................Eddie  Hodge
Tanya's Partner...................................Raul  Celada
Bell Boy..........................................Dean  Campbell
Stage Manager.....................................Dan  Sattler
Suzy..............................................Sandra  Deel
```

Act I.—Scene 1—Pennsylvania Station, New York City. 2 and 4—
On Tour. 3—Rehearsal Hall, Joplin, Mo. 5—Hotel Room, Amarillo,
Texas. 6—Outside Theatre, Phoenix, Arizona. 7—Stage Door of
Philharmonic Auditorium, Los Angeles. 8—Back Stage, Philharmonic.
9—Stage, Philharmonic. Act II.—Railroad Platform, Glendale, Cali-
fornia. 2—A Pullman Car. 3—On Tour. 4—Theatre Basement, Des
Moines, Iowa.

Staged by George Abbott and Jerome Robbins; music directed by
Pembroke Davenport; ballet arrangements by Trude Rittman; settings
by Oliver Smith; costumes by John Pratt.

Lily Malloy, a brewery heiress, becomes the angel of a traveling ballet company and finally takes it over from its conservative
Russian impresario. Both the company and the repertoire
liven up.

Principal musical numbers: "Gotta Dance," "I'm the First
Girl," "I'm Not So Bright," "I'm Tired of Texas," "Tiny Room,"
"The Little Boy Blues," "Jazz," "The New Look," "If You'll be
Mine," "Shauny O'Shay," "The Two of Us."

KATHLEEN

(7 performances)

A romantic comedy in three acts by Michael Sayers. Produced
by Bea Lawrence at the Mansfield Theatre, February 3, 1948.

Cast of characters—

```
The Housekeeper: Lily.............................Anita  Bolster
The Priest: Father Keogh..........................Whitford  Kane
The Poor Man's Son: Christy Hanafey...............James  McCallion
The Doctor: Dr. Horatio Houlihan..................Frank  Merlin
The Father: Professor Jasper Fogarty..............Jack  Sheehan
The Daughter: Kathleen Fogarty....................Andree  Wallace
The Rich Man's Son: Seamus MacGonigal.............Henry  Jones
The Soldier: Lieutenant Aengus MacOgue............Whitfield  Connor
The Rich Boy's Father: Jamie MacGonigal...........Morton L.  Stevens
```

Acts I, II and III.—Living Room Study in Professor Fogarty's
House Not Far from Dublin.

Staged by Coby Ruskin; setting by Charles Elson; costumes by
Rose Bogdanoff.

Kathleen Fogarty, an Irish girl, is a problem to her father and two uncles when she makes up a story that she is pregnant. Her father is a professor and her uncles are a priest and a doctor —so, to each of them, Kathleen is a different kind of problem. Everything is settled when she falls in love with a nice young soldier.

(Closed February 10, 1948)

DUBLIN GATE THEATRE

(30 performances) .

A festival of Irish comedies presented by Richard Aldrich and Richard Myers in association with Brian Doherty at the Mansfield Theatre, beginning February 10, 1948.

JOHN BULL'S OTHER ISLAND

(8 performances)

A comedy in three acts by Bernard Shaw. Presented February 10, 1948.

Cast of characters—

Hodson	Norman Barrs
Tom Broadbent	Hilton Edwards
Tim Haffigan	Reginald Jarman
Larry Doyle	Micheal Mac Liammoir
Father Keegan	Edward Golden
Patsy Farrel	Roy Irving
Norah Reilly	Meriel Moore
Cornelius Doyle	Dennis Brennan
Father Dempsey	Bryan Herbert
Aunt Judy	Nora O'Mahony
Matthew Haffigan	Liam Gannon
Barney Doran	Patrick Nolan

Act I.—Scene 1—Home and Office of Doyle and Broadbent, Civil Engineers, Great George's Street, Westminster, London. 1904. 2—Hillside Near Roscullen, Ireland. 3—Round Tower. Act II.—Outside Cornelius Doyle's House, Roscullen. Act III.—Parlor in Cornelius Doyle's House.

Staged by Hilton Edwards; settings by Molly MacEwen.

First produced in New York by Liebler & Co. who presented Arnold Daly and his company in a repertory of George Bernard Shaw's plays at the Garrick Theatre in 1905. "John Bull's Other Island" opened October 8, 1905, and continued for 16 performances. Arnold Daly played the Larry Doyle, Dodson Mitchell (Thomas Broadbent), Winchell Smith (Matt Haffigan) and Chrystal Herne (Norah Reilly).

(Closed February 15, 1948)

THE OLD LADY SAYS "NO!"

(8 performances)

A romantic play in two parts with choral interludes, by Denis Johnston. Presented February 17, 1948.

Cast of characters—

The Speaker (Robert Emmet)...............Micheal Mac Liammoir
Sarah Curran.......................................Meriel Moore
Major Sirr....................................Reginald Jarman
First Redcoat.....................................Bryan Herbert
Second Redcoat.....................................Liam Gannon
 The other ones: Roy Irving, Edward Golden, Dennis Brennan, Patrick Nolan, William Dalzell, Nora O'Mahony, Helena Hughes, Betsy Bogues, Patricia Kennedy, Edna O'Rourke.
 The action of the play takes place on stage of Dublin Theatre. Scene 1 represents the garden of "The Priory," the Home of John Philpot Curran, close to Rathfarnham, Dublin, August 25, 1803. The rest of the play takes place in the mind of the Speaker.
 Staged by Hilton Edwards; settings by Micheal Mac Liammoir and Molly MacEwen; costumes by Micheal Mac Liammoir.

An actor, taking part in a costume drama about the Irish hero, Robert Emmet, is struck on the head during a stage battle and is knocked out. While he is unconscious he dreams that he is indeed Robert Emmet, come back to look with a critical and disheartened eye at modern Ireland.

(Closed February 22, 1948)

WHERE STARS WALK

(14 performances)

A comedy in three acts by Micheal Mac Liammoir. Presented February 24, 1948.

Cast of characters—

Sophia Sheridan...................................Meriel Moore
Robert Twomey..................................Dennis Brennan
Rex Dillon..Roy Irving
Tommy Millington...............................Edward Golden
Sheila McCann...............................Patricia Kennedy
Mrs. Dempsey....................................Nora O'Mahony
Eileen...Helena Hughes
Martin....................................Micheal Mac Liammoir
Nigel Brunton....................................Norman Barrs
 Acts I, II and III.—Sophia Sheridan's House in Dublin.
 Staged by Hilton Edwards; setting by Molly MacEwen.

A fantasy, in which a Princess and an ancient King of Ireland return to earth in the guise of servants named Martin and Eileen, and fall in love all over again.

(Closed March 6, 1948)

DOCTOR SOCIAL

(5 performances)

A play in three acts by Joseph L. Estry. Produced by Harold Barnard at the Booth Theatre, February 11, 1948.

Cast of characters—

Dr. Norman Farrar	Dean Jagger
Ann Harris	Eda Heinemann
Dr. Tom Morrisey	Ronald Alexander
Mrs. Hamilton	Nelly Malcolm
Yvonne Tompkins	Mae Questel
Dr. Isaac Gordon	Al Shean
Lee Manning	Haila Stoddard
Dr. Fleming	Donald Foster
Paul Harris	Drake Thorton

Acts I, II and III.—Dr. Farrar's Office, Laboratory and Treatment Room.

Staged by Don Appell; setting and lighting by Stewart Chaney.

Dr. Norman Farrar, a plastic surgeon, falls in love with a patient, Lee Manning, and through her finds a new aim in life. Abandoning the high fees and prestige of being a beauty doctor, he consecrates himself to cancer research.

The medical research in "Doctor Social" stems in part from authentic scientific work reported in *Science* magazine and from technical advice by American Cancer Society.

(Closed February 14, 1948)

MISTER ROBERTS

(118 performances)
(Continued)

A play in two acts by Thomas Heggen and Joshua Logan, based on a novel by Thomas Heggen. Produced by Leland Hayward at the Alvin Theatre, February 18, 1948.

Cast of characters—

Chief Johnson	Rusty Lane
Lieutenant (jg) Roberts	Henry Fonda
Doc	Robert Keith
Dowdy	Joe Marr
The Captain	William Harrigan
Insigna	Harvey Lembeck
Mannion	Ralph Meeker
Lindstrom	Karl Lukas
Stefanowski	Steven Hill
Wiley	Robert Baines
Schlemmer	Lee Krieger
Reber	John Campbell
Ensign Pulver	David Wayne
Dolan	Casey Walters
Gerhart	Fred Barton

Payne..James Sherwood
Lieutenant Ann Girard...........................Jocelyn Brando
Shore Patrolman....................................John Jordan
Military Policeman.............................Marshall Jamison
Shore Patrol Officer............................Murray Hamilton
   Seamen, Firemen and Others: Tiger Andrews, Joe Bernard, Ellis
Eringer, Mikel Kane, Bob Keith, Jr., Walter Mullen, John (Red)
Kullers, Jack Pierce, Len Smith, Jr., Sanders (Sandy) Turner.
   Acts I and II.—Aboard the U. S. Navy Cargo Ship, *AK 601*, Oper-
ating in the Back Areas of the Pacific. Before V-E Day Until a Few
Weeks Before V-J Day.
   Staged by Joshua Logan; setting and lighting by Jo Mielziner.

See page 63.

TONIGHT AT 8:30

(26 performances)

A repertory of one-act comedies by Noel Coward. Revived by
Homer Curran, Russell Lewis and Howard Young at the National Theatre, February 20, 1948.

FIRST GROUP

HANDS ACROSS THE SEA

A Light Comedy in One Scene

Walters...Sarah Burton
Lady Maureen Gilpin (Piggie)..................Gertrude Lawrence
Commander Peter Gilpin, R.N......................Graham Payn
Lieut. Commdr. Alastair Corbett, R.N............William Roerick
Mrs. Wadhurst..................................Valerie Cossart
Mr. Wadhurst......................................Philip Tonge
Mr. Burnham......................................Booth Colman
The Hon. Clare Wedderburn........................Norah Howard
Major Gosling (Bogey).........................Rhoderick Walker
   The Action of the Play Takes Place in the Drawing Room of the
Gilpins' Flat in London.

FUMED OAK

An Unpleasant Comedy in Two Scenes

Doris Gow.....................................Gertrude Lawrence
Mrs. Rockett (Her Mother).......................Norah Howard
Elsie...Valerie Cossart
Henry Gow..Philip Tonge
   The Action of the Play Takes Place in the Sitting Room of the
Gows' House in South London.

SHADOW PLAY

A Fantasy with Music

Lena..Valerie Cossart
Victoria Gayforth.............................Gertrude Lawrence
Martha Cunningham...............................Norah Howard
Simon Gayforth....................................Graham Payn

Hodge (dresser)....................................Booth Colman
Sibyl Heston..Sarah Burton
Michael Doyle.....................................William Roerick
A Young Man.....................................Rhoderick Walker
George Cunningham................................Philip Tonge
    The Action of the Play Begins and Ends in the Gayforth House in
Mayfair

SECOND GROUP

WAYS AND MEANS

A Light Comedy in Three Scenes

Stella Cartwright........................ ....Gertrude Lawrence
Toby Cartwright.....................................Graham Payn
Gaston..Booth Colman
Lord Chapworth (Chaps).........................William Roerick
Olive Lloyd-Ransome................................Sarah Burton
Princess Elena Krassiloff.........................Valerie Cossart
Murdoch..Philip Tonge
Nanny....:...Norah Howard
Stevens..Rhoderick Walker
    The Action of the Play Takes Place in a Bedroom in the Lloyd-
Ransomes' Home, Villa Zephyre, on the Cote d'Azure.

FAMILY ALBUM

A Victorian Comedy with Music

Jasper Featherways..............................Graham Payn
Jane...Gertrude Lawrence
Lavinia..Sarah Burton
Harriet...Norah Howard
Emily..Valerie Cossart
Richard..William Roerick
Charles Winter................................Rhoderick Walker
Edward Valance..................................Booth Colman
Burrows..Philip Tonge
    The Action of the Play Takes Place in the Drawing Room of the
Featherways' House in Kent, Not Far from London.

RED PEPPERS

An Interlude with Music

Lily Pepper...................................Gertrude Lawrence
George Pepper.....................................Graham Payn
Alf...Booth Colman
Bert Bentley..................................Rhoderick Walker
Mr. Edwards......................................Philip Tonge
Mabel Grace......................................Norah Howard
    The Action of the Play Takes Place on the Stage and in a Dressing
Room of the Palace of Varieties in One of the Smaller English Pro-
vincial Towns.
    Staged by Noel Coward; music directed by Frank Tours; dances by
Richard Barstow; settings by George Jenkins.

Revival of Noel Coward's series of playlets. The second series
was presented February 23, and thereafter the performances were
given on a repertory schedule.

These plays were produced by John C. Wilson for Noel Coward

at the National Theatre in November of 1936 and ran for 118 performances. The digests of the plays may be found on page 435 of "The Best Plays of 1936-37."

(Closed March 13, 1948)

The American Repertory Theatre and Louis J. Singer presented Eva Le Gallienne in a repertory of plays beginning February 24, 1948, at the Cort Theatre.

GHOSTS

(10 performances)

A play in three acts by Henrik Ibsen; translated by Eva Le Gallienne. Revived February 24, 1948.

Cast of characters—

```
Regina  Engstrand..................................Jean  Hagen
Jacob  Engstrand................................Robert  Emhardt
Rev.  Mr.  Manders.............................Herbert  Berghof
Mrs.  Helena  Alving...............................Alfred  Ryder
    Acts I, II and III.—Mrs. Alving's Country House Beside One of
the Large Fjords in Western Norway.
    Staged by Margaret Webster; setting by Watson Barratt.
```

"Ghosts" was first produced in New York at the Berkeley Lyceum Theatre in January, 1894, and ran for 16 performances with Ida Jeffreys Goodfriend as Mrs. Alving. At the Carnegie Lyceum, an independent theatre backed by P. Kester, John Blair and Norman Hapgood, the play was produced in 1899 with Mary Shaw as Mrs. Alving. Nazimova and Paul Orleneff played "Ghosts" in 1905 in a small theatre on the lower East Side and Paul Orleneff played Oswald to Ludmiller Liarove's Mrs. Alving for 4 performances in 1912 at the Garrick Theatre. Walter Hampden included the play in his repertory season of 1924. Charles Coburn revived it at the Mansfield January 10, 1927, with Mrs. Fiske as Mrs. Alving. Nazimova played the part at the Empire Theatre, in a production of Luther Greene's. Harry Ellerbe played Oswald and the play ran for 81 performances.

(Closed February 22, 1948)

HEDDA GABLER

(15 performances)

A drama in three acts by Henrik Ibsen; translated by Eva Le Gallienne. Revived February 24, 1948.

```
Miss Juliana Tesman.........................Marion G. Evensen
Berta.......................................Merle  Maddern
George Tesman...............................Robert Emhardt
Hedda Tesman........................ ............Eva Le Gallienne
Mrs. Elvsted................................Emily  McNair
Judge Brack.................................Herbert Berghof
Eilert Lovborg.............................Efrem Zimbalist, Jr.
    Acts I, II and III.—Drawing Room of Tesman's Villa in West End
of Christiania.  Early 1890s.
    Production supervised by Margaret Webster.
```

The first production of Hedda Gabler in New York was at the Fifth Ave. Theatre in March, 1898, with Elizabeth Robins in the name part. Other famous "Hedda" portrayals in America have been by Blanche Bates (1900), Nance O'Neill (1903), Mary Shaw (Chicago, 1904), Mrs. Fiske (Chicago, 1904 and later in New York), Mrs. Pat Campbell in repertoire in the season of 1907-08, Nazimova at the Plymouth Theatre, N. Y., April 8, 1918, Clare Eames (1924), Emily Stevens (1926), Blanche Yurka (1929). The latest revival was Luther Greene's at the Longacre Theatre in 1942 with Katina Paxinou as "Hedda," except for a presentation by the Equity-Library Theatre in 1947.

(Closed March 6, 1948)

ME AND MOLLY

(110 performances)
(Continued)

A comedy in three acts by Gertrude Berg; music arranged by Lehman Engel. Produced by Oliver Smith, Paul Feigay and Herbert Kenwith in association with David Cummings at the Belasco Theatre, February 26, 1948.

Cast of characters—

```
Max..............................................Henry  Lascoe
Joe.............................................Michael  Enserro
Mrs. 2C.........................................Paula Miller
Hymie...........................................Arthur  Cassel
Benjy...................... .....................Charles  Furman
Milty...........................................Herbie  Hahn
Molly Goldberg..................................Gertrude  Berg
Uncle David......................................Eli  Mintz
Sammy  Goldberg.................................Lester  Carr
Rosie Goldberg..................................Joan  Lazer
Mrs. Siegel.....................................Bertha  Walden
Jake  Goldberg..................................Philip  Loeb
Cousin Simon.....................................Louis  Sorin
Mr. Mendel......................................David  Opatoshu
Vera Wertheimer.................................Margaret  Feury
Piano  Man......................................George  Spelvin
Mrs. Gross......................................Sarah  Krohner
Mike...................... .......................David  Burke
Mrs. 3C.........................Bessie  Samose  Blumstein
Jessie..........................................Phyllis  Liverman
Mrs.  Ellenbogen................................Sally  Schorr
```

Acts I, II and III.—Apartment in the Bronx, 1919.
Staged by Ezra Stone; setting by Harry Horner; costumes by Rose Bogdanoff; lighting by Leo Kerz.

See page 309.

MAURICE CHEVALIER

(33 performances)

A program of songs and impressions. Produced by Arthur Lesser at the Golden Theatre, February 29, 1948.

The program included—

J'ai du Ciel Dans mon Chapeau
It's Good to Fall in Love
George Bernard Shaw
Quai de Bercy
Mimi
A Barcelone
Fox a Poil Dur
Weeping Willie
Priere
Place Pigalle
La Symphonie des Smelles de Bois

Another visit from the noted French entertainer. Maurice Chevalier was last on Broadway in March of 1947, when he gave 46 performances.

(Closed March 27, 1948)

THE LINDEN TREE

(7 performances)

A play in two acts by J. B. Priestley. Produced by Maurice Evans Productions, Inc., at the Music Box, March 2, 1948.

Cast of characters—

Mrs. Cotton.....................................Una O'Connor
Alfred Lockhart..................................Noel Leslie
Mrs. Linden...................................Barbara Everest
Rex Linden............................Halliwell Hobbes, Jr.
Jean Linden.......................................Viola Keats
Marion Linden.............................Cathleen Cordell
Edith Westmore.................................Mary Kimber
Dinah Linden................................Marilyn Erskine
Professor Linden................................Boris Karloff
Bernard Fawcett...............................Emmett Rogers
Acts I and II.—Professor Linden's Study in the Provincial City of Brumanley, in Northern England.
Staged by George Schaefer; supervised by Maurice Evans; setting by Peter Wolf; costumes by Frank Thompson.

Professor Linden, history teacher in a small English college, is urged by family and faculty to retire at the age of 65. He refuses to do so at a time when England is in a troubled state. He reasons that too many people of all ages are retiring from the world by hiding from reality, and that the only hope for the future lies with the very old and the very young.

(Closed March 13, 1948)

THE HALLAMS

(12 performances)

A play in three acts by Rose Franken. Produced by William Brown Meloney at the Booth Theatre, March 4, 1948.

Cast of characters—

Mrs. Hallam	Ethel Griffies
Etta Hallam	Mildred Dunnock
Paul Hallam	Royal Beal
Grace Hallam	June Walker
Helen Hallam	Mildred Wall
Victor Hallam	Alan Baxter
Walter Hallam	Matt Briggs
Harry Hallam	Frank M. Thomas
Mr. Hallam	John McKee
Jerry Hallam	Dean Norton
Kendrick Hallam	Katharine Bard

Acts I and III.—Dining Room of the Hallam Residence in the East Seventies, Manhattan. Act II.—Jerry's and Kendrick's Apartment.

Staged by Rose Franken; settings by Raymond Sovey; production associate, Richard E. French; costumes by Bianca Strook.

Another play about the family which was involved in Miss Franken's earlier success, "Another Language." In the new play the family is dominated by Mrs. Hallam. A grandson, Jerry, comes home from a tuberculosis sanitarium, bringing a bride, Kendrick. Over Mrs. Hallam's objections they set up in their own apartment, and Kendrick earns the living. Jerry has a relapse and dies.

(Closed March 13, 1948)

YOU NEVER CAN TELL

(39 performances)

A comedy in four acts by George Bernard Shaw. Revived by The Theatre Guild in association with Alfred Fischer at the Martin Beck Theatre, March 16, 1948.

Cast of characters—

Dolly	Patricia Kirkland
Valentine	Tom Helmore
Maid	Scott Douglas
Philip	Nigel Stock
Mrs. Clandon	Frieda Inescort
Gloria	Faith Brook
Crampton	Ralph Forbes

McComas..Walter Hudd
Waiter..Leo G. Carroll
Bohun..William Devlin
    Act I.—Valentine's Room in a Seaside Resort in Devon, England,
1896. Act II.—The Terrace. Acts III and IV.—Sitting Room in
Hotel.
    Staged by Peter Ashmore; supervised by Theresa Helburn and Law-
rence Langner; settings and costumes by Stewart Chaney.

"You Never Can Tell" was first produced in New York by
Liebler and Company at the Garrick Theatre, January 9, 1905,
and ran for 129 performances with Arnold Daly as Dr. Valentine
and Mabel Taliaferro as Dolly Clandon.

(Closed April 17, 1948)

THE RESPECTFUL PROSTITUTE

(88 performances)

(Continued)

A play in two scenes by Jean-Paul Sartre; adapted from the
French by Eva Wolas. Produced by New Stages, Inc., at the
Cort Theatre, March 16, 1948.

Cast of characters—

Lizzie McKaye....................................Meg Mundy
The Negro..John Marriott
Fred...Karl Weber
John...Willard Swire
James..William Brower
Senator Clarke...................................Wendell Holmes
A Man..Martin Tarby
    Scenes 1 and 2.—Room in Southern Town.
    Staged by Mary Hunter; production supervised by Norman Rose
and David Heilweil; setting by Robert Gundlach.

Lizzie McKay, a New York prostitute, arrives in a Southern
town and becomes innocently involved in the pursuit by aroused
citizens of an alleged Negro rapist. She saves the Negro, whom
she knows to be innocent, but succumbs to the Southern social
order which prescribes unfaltering White supremacy.

THE HAPPY JOURNEY TO TRENTON AND CAMDEN

(As a Curtain Raiser)

A one-act play by Thornton Wilder.

Cast of characters—

The Stage Manager................................William Brower
Ma Kirby...Peggy Allenby
Arthur...Clifford Sales

Caroline...Mari Lynn
Pa (Elmer) Kirby..............................Don MacLaughlin
Beulah...Jean Gillespie
    Staged by Mary Hunter.

The Kirby family takes a trip in their car and observe the roadside. A popular one-acter for amateurs.

JOY TO THE WORLD

(86 performances)

(Continued)

A play in three acts by Allan Scott. Produced by John Houseman and William R. Katzell at the Plymouth Theatre, March 18, 1948.

Cast of characters—

Mary Magille...................................Mary Welch
Floyd.......................................Michael Dreyfuss
Mildred..Lois Hall
Edith Wham...................................Peggy Maley
J. Newton McKeon.........................Myron McCormick
Mortimer Behrman.............................Leslie Litomy
Richard Stanton................................Hugh Rennie
Edward F. Gannon................................Bert Freed
Alexander Soren...............................Alfred Drake
Tilworthy.....................................Harris Brown
Ann Wood.....................................Marsha Hunt
Steve Walton..................................Herb Ratner
John V. Hopper................................Clay Clement
Dmitri Oumansky.............................Kurt Kasznar
Barbara Benton..............................Lucille Patton
Henry Saintsbury...........................Walter F. Appler
Sampson...Hal Gerson
Mr. Wilcox...............................Theodore Newton
Harry...Sam Bonnell
Sam Blumenfeld...........................Morris Carnovsky
    Messengers: Beverly Thawl, Blanche Zohar, Jeanne Jorden, Vicki Carlson.
    Acts I, II and III.—Offices of Alexander Soren, Vice President in Charge of Production of Atlas-Continental Pictures.
    Staged by Jules Dassin; setting by Harry Horner; costumes by Beverly Woodner; lighting by Jean Rosenthal.

Alexander Soren, executive producer of a large Hollywood film studio, finds himself in the political doghouse for having broadcast a liberal speech prepared for him by a pretty young woman in the research department named Ann. Studio bosses do not agree with his notion that movies should be about important matters. He is squeezed out—but wins a better job with a veteran independent producer, and wins Ann too.

MACBETH

(29 performances)

A Shakespearean tragedy in two parts and twenty-one scenes; music by Alan Bush. Revived by Theatre Incorporated in association with Brian Doherty at the National Theatre, March 31, 1948.

Cast of characters—

Duncan, King of Scotland	Stephen Courtleigh
His Sons:	
Malcolm	Elliott Reid
Donalbain	Michael Reilly
Macbeth	Michael Redgrave
Banquo	Geoffrey Toone
Macduff	Whitfield Connor
Lennox	John Cromwell
Ross	Hector MacGregor
Angus	John Straub
Menteith	Paul Mann
Caithness	Thomas Palmer
Fleance	Ken Raymond
Siward	John McQuade
Young Siward	Arthur Keegan
Lady Macbeth	Flora Robson
Lady Macduff	Beatrice Straight
Son to Macduff	Judson Rees
Wounded Sergeant	John McQuade
Messenger at Inverness	Robinson Stone
Porter at Inverness	Russell Collins
Old Man	Blair Cutting
Seyton	Harry Hess
A Murderer	Paul Mann
His Younger Accomplice	Thomas Palmer
A Lord	Lamont Johnson
A Murderer at Fife	Martin Balsam
A Doctor	Russell Collins
A Gentlewoman	Penelope Potter
2 Watchmen at Dunsinane	{ Michael Reilly / John Straub
A Singer	Arthur Keegan
A Page	Sonny Curven
The Three	{ Robinson Stone / Martin Balsam / Harry Hess
The Weird Sisters	{ Gillian Webb / Julie Harris / Ann Hegira
An Armed Head	Whitfield Connor
A Bleeding Child	Ken Raymond
A Child Crowned	Marcia Marcus

Gentlewomen, Servants, Soldiers, etc.: Alan McKirdy, Whit Vernon, Marcia Marcus, Sonny Curven, Ken Sutton, Dan Barton, William Skelton.

Parts I and II.—Scotland, and in One Scene, England.

Staged by Norris Houghton; settings and costumes by Paul Sheriff; music directed by Lehman Engel.

The above production of "Macbeth" closed in London, February 21, 1948, and toured Canada before coming to New York. The tragedy was first produced in New York, May 3, 1768, at

John Street Theatre, by The American Theatre, Lewis Hallam playing Macbeth. Famous American portrayals were those of Charlotte Cushman, Sothern and Marlowe, Edwin Booth, Robert Mantell, James K. Hackett with Viola Allen, Walter Hampden with Gilda Varesi, Lionel Barrymore and Julia Arthur, Philip Merivale and Gladys Cooper, Margaret Wycherly and John Cromwell, Maurice Evans and Judith Anderson and others. In England Peg Woffington, Mrs. Siddons, J. P. Kemble, Edmund Kean, Edwin Forrest, Henry Irving, John Gielgud, Laurence Olivier, Charles Laughton, Margaret Webster and Flora Robson are remembered. November 11, 1941, at the National Theatre, Maurice Evans produced the tragedy with Judith Anderson as Lady Macbeth, playing the part of Macbeth himself for 131 performances.

(Closed April 29, 1948)

THE EXPERIMENTAL THEATRE, INC.

The Experimental Theatre, Inc., under the sponsorship of The American National Theatre and Academy, presented six productions at Maxine Elliott's Theatre, beginning December 7, 1947.

(36 performances)

GALILEO

(6 performances)

A drama in two acts by Bertold Brecht, translated by Charles Laughton; music by Hanns Eisler; lyrics by Albert Brush. Presented by T. Edward Hambleton, December 7, 1947.

Cast of characters—

Singers	Richard Leone, Michael Citro, Albert Ares
Curtain Boy	Allen Martin
Galileo	Charles Laughton
Andrea	Michael Citro
Sarti	Hester Sondergaard
Ludovico	Philip Swander
Priuli	Fred Stewart
Sagredo	John Straub
Virginia	Joan McCracken
Federzoni	Dwight Marfield
Senator I	Sidney Bassler
Senator II	Frank Campanella
Prince	Larry Rosen
Philosopher	Thomas Palmer
Lord Chamberlain	Harry Hess
Elderly Lady	Mary Grace Canfield
A Scholar	Frank Campanella
A Monk	Leonard Bell

Infuriated Monk...............................Werner Klemperer
Old Cardinal.......................................Wesley Addy
Supporting Monk..................................Pitt Herbert
Little Monk......................................Don Hanmer
Clavius..Taylor Graves
Bellarmin.......................................Lawrence Ryle
Barbarini..Rusty Lane
Inquisitor.......................................John Carradine
Andrea...Nehemiah Persoff
Giuseppi.......................................Donald Symington
Ballade Singer..................................Harris Brown
Ballade Singer's Wife..........................Elizabeth Moore
Ballade Singer's Daughter...........................Iris Mann
A Monk...Sidney Bassler
Duke of Florence...........................Earl Montgomery, Jr.
Informer.......................................Warren Stevens
Matti...Philip Robinson

Act I.—Scenes 1 and 3—Galileo's Study, 1609. 2—The Great Arsenal of Venice. 4—Galileo's New House, Florence. 5—Collegium Romanum, Rome. 6—Cardinal Bellarmin's Palace, Rome. 7—Garden of Florentine Ambassador, Rome. Act II.—Scene 1—Galileo's House, Florence, 1623. 2—Market Place of Small Town in Italy. All Fools' Day, 1632. 3—Medicean Palace, Florence. 4—The Vatican. 5—Florentine Ambassador's Garden, Rome. 6—Country House Near Florence, 1637.

Staged by Joseph Losey; original choreography by Lotte Gosler, executed by Joan McCracken; music conducted by Josef Schmid; settings and costumes by Robert Davison.

(Closed December 14, 1947)

SKIPPER NEXT TO GOD

(6 performances)

A play in three acts by Jan de Hartog. Produced by The Experimental Theatre, Inc., at the Maxine Elliott Theatre, January 4, 1948.

Cast of characters—

Richters.......................................Joseph Anthony
Henky...Robert White
Willemse..Si Oakland
Officer of South American Military Police.............Carmen Costi
Meyer...John Becher
Joris Kuiper, Captain..............................John Garfield
South American Consul...........................Wallace Acton
Rabbi..Wolfe Barzell
First Jew......................................Michael Lewin
Second Jew.......................................Peter Kass
"Chief" Davelaar................................John Shellie
Bruinsma, Captain of the Amsterdam................Jabez Gray
American Naval Officer..........................Richard Coogan
Dutch Naval Officer...........................Eugene Stuckmann
The Clergyman...................................Harry Irvine

Passengers: Florence Aquino, Joe Bernard, Nola Chilton, Allan Frank, Frances Gaar, Ruth K. Hill, Bill Lazarus, John Marley, Edwin Ross, Paul Wilson.

Act I.—Captain's Cabin in Steamship The Young Nelly Lying in a South American Port. Acts II and III.—Just Off the United States Coast.

Staged by Lee Strasberg; production supervised by Cheryl Crawford; setting by Boris Aronson.

"Skipper Next to God" moved to The Playhouse for a commercial run, January 29, 1948, where it ran until March 27, 1948, with a total of 93 performances.

See page 264.

(Closed March 27, 1948)

A LONG WAY FROM HOME

(6 performances)

A play in two acts by Randolph Goodman and Walter Carroll, based on Maxim Gorki's "The Lower Depths." Produced by Nat Karson at the Maxine Elliott Theatre, February 8, 1948.

Cast of characters—

Duke	Henry Scott
Bessie	Edna May Harris
Dee	Harry Bolden
Lily	Mildred Smith
Mary	Beatrice Wade
Four-Eyes	Catherine Ayers
Silky	Maurice Ellis
Sad-Act	William Marshall
Grady Horn	Augustus Smith
Joebuck	Josh White
Marcy	Ruby Dee
Preacher	Alonzo Bosan
Billy-Boy	James Wright
Celine	Fredi Washington
Cotton	Earl Sydnor
Cyril	Ken Renard
Stud	Joseph James
Bartender	Eric Burroughs

Neighbors: Virginia Givin, Doris Block, Ellsworth Wright, Quentin Foster.

Act I.—Basement of Grady Horn's in a Lodging House Under a Poolhall, Outskirts of Durham, North Carolina. Act II.—Scene 1—The Back Yard. 2—Basement of Grady Horn's.

Staged by Alan Schneider; settings and lighting by Leo Kerz; costumes by Rose Bogdanoff.

A TEMPORARY ISLAND

(6 performances)

A play in three acts by Halsted Welles; original songs by Lorenzo Fuller; calliope music by Lehman Engel. Produced by Cheryl Crawford and T. Edward Hambleton at the Maxine Elliott Theatre, March 14, 1948.

Cast of characters—

Cordelia	Nancy Franklin
Heloise	Karen Lindgren
Bunny	Rita Gam
Miss Evans	Jane Hoffman

```
Miss Rector...................................Hilda Vaughn
Mr. Fisk...................................Philip Bourneuf
Miss Wampsey...............................Philippa Bevans
Mr. Totiningham...............................Blair Davies
Mr. Chanter...............................Harrison Dowd
Mr. Avery...................................Gregory Robins
Junius...........................................Bill Dillard
Ned.............................................Bill Myers
Mr. Prince.....................................Leon Askin
Suzette........................................Vera Zorina
Felicity.......................................Ruth Vaughn
Mr. Boutourlinsky..........................Walter Palance
Mrs. Boutourlinsky...........................Ann Sullivan
Mr. Smith....................................Taylor Graves
Uncle Benny..................................Ernest Truex
Sophomore...................................Shirley Ames
Senior...................................Anne-Marie Gayer
Freshman...................................Elaine Bradford
Farmer..........................................Carl Judd
Farmer's Wife.............................Natalie Benisch
Farmer's Daughter.......................Winnie Mae Martin
Chief of Police................................Gene Galvin
Policeman...................................Geoffrey Lumb
Millhand.......................................Dion Allen
```

Act I.—Scene 1—Office of President of Massachusetts Female Seminary. 1881. 2—Willow Grove Across the Canal. Act II.— Scene 1—Willow Grove. 2—Circus Tent—Main Entrance. Act III.— Willow Grove.

Staged by Halsted Welles; settings and lighting by Lawrence Goldwasser; costumes by Mildred Sutherland.

A professor becomes enchanted by a circus, falls in love with a performer, and almost chucks his job to follow her. But reason prevails and he gives her up.

SIX O'CLOCK THEATRE

(8 performances)

Three one-act plays produced by Fred Stewart and presented by Six O'Clock Theatre at the Maxine Elliott Theatre, April 11, 1948.

HOPE IS THE THING WITH FEATHERS

By Richard Harrity

Cast of characters—

```
Oscar...........................................Philip Robinson
Doc.............................................E. G. Marshall
Steve.........................................George Mathews
Wiler............................................Robert Alvin
Sweeney...........................................Will Geer
Charlie..........................................Lou Gilbert
Old Man Nelson..............................Daniel A. Reed
Joe.............................................Fredric Martin
A Man.............................................Jabez Gray
```
Staged by Joseph Kramm.

CELEBRATION

By Horton Foote

Cast of characters—

Red..Hilda Vaughn
Babe..Perry Wilson
Sonny...Warren Stevens
Ellen Belle.....................................Sally Gracie
Tom...James Karen
    Staged by Joseph Anthony.

AFTERNOON STORM

By E. P. Conkle

Cast of characters—

Mary..Helen Marcy
Lizzie..Eleanora Barrie
Speed...Dan Morgan
Abe...John Morley
Ninian..Stanley Tackney
Ann...Norma Chambers
    Bridesmaids: Lynn Masters, Herta Ware, Mary Patton, Joan De-Weese.
    Wedding Guests: Philippa Bevans, Ellen Herbert, Fred Stewart, Joseph Kramm, Syl Lamont, Clement Brace, Ed Kaufman, Joseph Kapfer, Joseph Anthony.
    Staged by John O'Shaughnessy.

"Hope Is the Thing with Feathers," together with two other playlets by Richard Harrity titled "Gone Tomorrow" and "Home Life of a Buffalo," were presented commercially by Eddie Dowling at the Playhouse, March 11, 1948.

BALLET BALLADS

(24 performances)
(Continued)

Lyrics by John Latouche, music by Jerome Moross; produced by Nat Karson; directed by Mary Hunter; choreography by Katherine Litz, Paul Godkin and Hanya Holm; musical director, Hugh Ross. Presented May 9, 1948, and moved the following week to the Music Box for a commercial run.

SUSANNA AND THE ELDERS

The Parson....................................Richard Harvey
Susanna (The Dancer)..........................Katherine Litz
Susanna (The Singer)..........................Sheila Vogelle
The Cedar from Lebanon........................Sharry Traver
The Little Juniper Tree.......................Ellen R. Albertini
The Handmaidens...............Margaret Cuddy, Barbara Downie
The Elder (Moe)...............................Frank Seabolt

The Elder (Joe).....................................Robert Trout
The Angel...James R. Nygren
   The Scene Is a Revival Meeting. The Parson takes his sermon from
the story of Susanna and the Elders as found in the Apocrypha.

WILLIE THE WEEPER

Choreography by Paul Godkin

Singing Willie.....................................Robert Lenn
Dancing Willie.....................................Paul Godkin
Cocaine Lil...Sono Osato
   The Singing Ensemble.
   Dancers: Cecile Bergman, Nora Bristow, Mary Ann Cousins, Sandra
Lipton, Iona McKenzie, Rosa Rolland, Jack Warren Konzal, James R.
Nygren, William Weaver, Walter Stane, Richard Goltra, Charles
Yongue.
   The Scene: The Action Takes Place in Willie's Untidy Mind. Epi-
sode I—Rich Willie.   Episode II—Lonely Willie.   Episode III—
Famous Willie.   Episode IV—Baffled Willie.   Episode V—Super-
Willie.   Episode VI—Self-sufficient Willie.   Episode VII—Lover
Willie.

THE ECCENTRICITIES OF DAVY CROCKETT

(as told by himself)

Choreography by Hanya Holm

Davy Crockett.....................................Ted Lawrie		
Sally Ann...Barbara Ashley		
Indian Chief.......................................Lorin Barrett		
A Backwoodsman...................................Carl Luman		
The Mermaid.......................................Betty Abbott		
The Comet...Olga Lunick		
Brown Bear.....................................William A. Myers		
Ghost Bear .... Robert Baird		
John Oldham	{ Sung by......................William Ambler { Danced by.......................John Castello	
Ann Hutchinson	{ Sung by.................Gertrude Lockway { Danced by.......................Sharry Traver	
Nathaniel Bacon	{ Sung by........................Eddie Varrato { Danced by.......................Frank Seabolt	
Grace Sherwood	{ Sung by..................Arlouine Goodjohn { Danced by....................Barbara Downie	
Nathaniel Turner	{ Sung by......................Arthur Friedman { Danced by..................Beau Cunningham	
Friends and Neighbors......................The Singing Ensemble		

   Dancers: Ellen R. Albertini, Margaret Cuddy, Barbara Downie,
Sharry Traver, Beau Cunningham, John Castello, Frank Seabolt,
Robert Trout, Spencer Teakle.

   The people assemble to celebrate the memory of Davy Crockett.
In the terms of his own tall tales they recall his exploits; his
youth, courtship, and marriage; how he built a living house in the
wilderness; how he fought the Indian Wars; how he hooked a
Mermaid; how he saved the world from Halley's Comet; how
he went to Congress and left it; how he died at the Alamo and
became a legend.

SAN CARLO OPERA COMPANY

(21 performances)

The eleventh annual New York engagement of the San Carlos Opera Company, under the direction of Fortune Gallo, opened at the Center Theatre, April 14, 1948. The musical director was Carlo Moresco; Anton Coppola was guest conductor and Mario Valle was stage director. The principals in the ballet were Lydia Arlova and Lucien Prideux. The first opera presented was "La Traviata," Lucia Evangelista singing the role of Violetta and Norman Kelly the Alfredo.

Other operas were "Carmen," "Rigoletto," "Madame Butterfly," "Aida," "La Boheme," "La Tosca," "Faust," "Cavalleria Rusticana" and "Pagliacci," "The Barber of Seville" and "Il Trovatore." The singers included: Elizabeth Carron, Mina Cravi, Elizabeth Devlin, Lucia Evangelica, Jane Frazier, Selma Kaye, Hizi Koyke, Marybelle Norton, Graciela Rivera, Tina Savona, Coe Glade, Winifred Heckman, Martha Larrimore, Mary Pasca, Gino Fratesi, Norman Kelly, Adrien La Chance, Mario Palermo, Alfonso Pravadelli, Nino Scattolini, Stefan Ballarini, John Ciavola, Grant Garnell, Carlo Morelli, Fausto Bozza, Lloyd Harris, Ugo Novelli, Victor Tatozzi and William Wilderman.

(Closed May 2, 1948)

THE RATS OF NORWAY

(4 performances)

A play in three acts by Keith Winter. Produced by James S. Elliott at the Booth Theatre, April 15, 1948.

Cast of characters—

Robin Claydon	Colin Keith-Johnston
Jane Claydon	Jeanne Stuart
Stevan Beringer	William Howell
Tilly Shane	Rett Kitson
Mann	Arthur Gould-Porter
Weyland	Victor Wood
Chetwood	Bert Jeter
Hugh Sebastian	John Ireland

Acts I, II and III.—Fallgates, a Preparatory School in Northumberland.

Staged by James Elliott; assistant director, Carl Schreuer; setting by William De Forest.

Hugh Sebastian, an instructor in an English prep school, falls in love with Jane Claydon, wife of the headmaster. Other instructors have other love affairs, one of them homosexual. Hugh's romance is an unhappy one, ending with his death from a heart attack in his mistress's bed.

(Closed April 17, 1948)

THE CUP OF TREMBLING

(31 performances)

A play in two acts by Louis Paul. Produced by Paul Czinner and C. P. Jaeger at the Music Box, April 20, 1948.

Cast of characters—

Mrs. Bosshardt	Beverly Bayne
Ellen Croy	Elisabeth Bergner
Dr. Broen	Philip Tonge
John Croy	Millard Mitchell
Ann	Iris Mann
Gracie	Hope Emerson
Walter Fowler	John Carradine
Jamesson	Louis Hector
Elderly Woman	Amelie Barleon
Nurse	Joan Nordlander
Another Nurse	Gloria Whitney
Sheila Vane	Arlene Francis
A Deliveryman	William Robertson
Dr. Denning	Martin Wolfson
William Lundeman	Anthony Ross
Peewee	Herman Kluse

Act I.—Scenes 1, 2, 3, 5 and 6—Croy's Apartment. 4—Walter Fowler's Home. 7—A Hospital Ward. Act II.—Scenes 1 and 4—Croy's Apartment. 2—Dr. Denning's Office. 3—Lundeman's Office. 5—A Mean Street.

Staged by Paul Czinner; settings by Charles Elson; costumes by Natalie Barth Walker.

Ellen Croy, a newspaper columnist, has become a dipsomaniac. She is about to lose her husband, her home and her career, but finally is cured by the combined efforts of a psychiatrist and two members of Alcoholics Anonymous.

(Closed May 15, 1948)

THE PLAY'S THE THING

(39 performances)
(Continued)

A play in three acts by Ferenc Molnar, adapted from the Hungarian by P. G. Wodehouse. Revived by Gilbert Miller in association with James Russo and Michael Ellis at the Booth Theatre, April 28, 1948.

Cast of characters—

Sandor Turai	Louis Calhern
Mansky	Ernest Cossart

```
Albert Adam.....................................Richard Hylton
Johann Dwornitschek..........................Francis Compton
Ilona Szabo....................................Faye Emerson
Almady........................................Arthur Margetson
Mell..............................................Claude Allister
Lackeys..........................................⎰Ted Paterson
                                                 ⎱Fred Wentler
```

Acts I, II and III.—Room in Castle on Italian Riviera.
Staged by Gilbert Miller; setting by Oliver Messel; lighting by Ralph Alswang; gowns by Castillo.

"The Play's the Thing" was produced by the Charles Frohman Co. at the Henry Miller Theatre, November 3, 1926, and continued for 326 performances. Holbrook Blinn was Sandor Turai and Catherine Dale Owens played Ilona Szabo. Later Gilbert Miller revived the play at the Empire Theatre for 24 performances beginning April 9, 1928, with the same cast with the exception of the Ilona, which was played by Selena Royle.

INSIDE U.S.A.

(36 performances)
(Continued)

A musical revue in two acts suggested by John Gunther's book of the same title; sketches by Arnold Auerbach, Moss Hart and Arnold B. Horwitt; lyrics and music by Howard Dietz and Arthur Schwartz; orchestrations by Robert Russell Bennett; incidental music for dances by Genevieve Pitot. Produced by Arthur Schwartz at the Century Theatre, April 30, 1948.

Principals engaged—

Beatrice Lillie	Jack Haley
Valerie Bettis	John Tyers
Thelma Carpenter	Herb Shriner
Estelle Loring	Eric Victor
Jane Lawrence	Lewis Nye
Joan Mann	Carl Reiner
Beverlee Bozeman	William LeMassene
Holly Harris	Albert Popwell
Hilde Palmer	J. C. McCord
Rod Alexander	Ray Stephens
Jim Hawthorne	Ronald Chetwood
Robert Hamilton	

Act I.—Scene 1—The Jones' Living Room. Any Town. 2—Pittsburgh. 3—Regal-Palace Hotel, Miami Beach. 4—Churchill Downs, Kentucky. 5—In Front of a Movie Theatre, Chillicothe, Ohio. 6—Rhode Island. 7—Waterfront, San Francisco. 8—Fair Grounds, Kenosha County, Wisconsin. Act II.—Scene 1—New Orleans. 2—New York City, Schoolroom for Waiters. 3—Street in Jackson Hole, Wyoming. 4—Miss Shelton's Dressing Room, Just Off Broadway. 5—Chicago. 6—Railroad Station, Albuquerque, New Mexico.

Production associate, Victor Samrock; music directed by Jay Blackton; sketches directed by Robert H. Gordon; dances and musical numbers directed by Helen Tamiris; settings by Lemuel Ayers; costumes by Eleanor Goldsmith and Castillo.

Principal musical numbers: "Inside U.S.A.," "Come, O Come," "Blue Grass," "Rhode Island Is Famous for You," "Haunted Heart," "Wyoming," "We Won't Take It Back."

HOLD IT!

(32 performances)

(Continued)

A musical comedy in two acts by Matt Brooks and Art Arthur; lyrics by Sam Lerner; music by Gerald Marks; orchestrations by Hans Spialek and Ted Royal; vocal arrangements by Clay Warnick. Produced by Sammy Lambert at the National Theatre, May 5, 1948.

Cast of characters—

Rodney Trent	Bob Shawley
Mrs. Simpkins	Ruth Saville
Mr. Simpkins	Douglas Rutherford
Mrs. Blandish	Helen Wenzel
Mr. Blandish	Budd Rogers
"Sarge" Denton	Larry Douglas
Bobby Manville	Johnny Downs
Helen	Helen Wenzel
Jack	Jack Warner
Chuck	Bob Evans
"Judge" Rogers	Kenny Buffett
Sid	Sid Lawson
Jessica Dale	Jet McDonald
Pamela Scott	Patricia Wymore
Millie Henderson	Ada Lynne
Budd	Budd Rogers
Bernie	Bob Bernard
"Dinky" Bennett	"Red" Buttons
Paul	Paul Lyday
George Monopolis	Douglas Chandler
Penny	Penny Carroll
Mr. Jenkins	Paul Reed
Joe	Tom Bowman
Charlie Blake	Pat McVey
Headwaiter	Douglas Rutherford
Mrs. Jollop	Ruth Saville
O'Brien	Scott Landers
Martin	Martin Kraft
Reporters	Budd Rogers, Sid Lawson, Helena Schurgot
Felix Dexter	John Kane

Act I.—Scene 1—Lobby of Lincoln University Auditorium (The Present). 2—Stage of University Auditorium (Immediately Following). 3—The Tasty Toasty (The Following Day). 4—The Campus Walk (Nine Days Later). 5—The Tasty Toasty (The Following Day). 6—The Tasty Toasty (The Following Evening). 7—The Campus Walk (Same Night). 8—Lobby of the Pink Angel Night Club (Later That Night).

Act II.—Scene 1—Outside of Sorority House (Later That Night). 2—The Sorority Dormitory (Immediately Following). 3—The Campus Walk (The Following Afternoon). 4—The Tasty Toasty (Later the Same Day). 5—Outside of Sorority House (A Few Minutes Later). 6—Living Room of Dexter's Hotel Suite (That Night).

Staged by Robert E. Perry; dances and musical numbers staged by Michael Kidd; music directed by Clay Warnick; dances directed by Irma Jurist; settings by Edward Gilbert; costumes by Julia Sze.

Principal musical numbers: "Heaven Sent," "Buck in the Bank," "Always You," "About Face," "Fundamental Character," "Hold It!", "Nevermore," "Roll 'Em," "So Nice Having You," "Down the Well," "You Took Possession of Me," "Friendly Enemy."

SALLY

(29 performances)

(Continued)

A musical comedy in two acts by Guy Bolton; lyrics by P. G. Wodehouse and Clifford Grey; music by Jerome Kern; orchestrations by Robert Russell Bennett. Revived by Hunt Stromberg, Jr., and William Berney at the Martin Beck Theatre, May 6, 1948.

Cast of characters—

Nadina	Gloria Sullivan
The Young Waiter	Charles Wood
The Old Waiter	Holger Sorenson
Otis Hooper	Jack Goode
Rosie	Kay Buckley
Lily Bedlington	Bibi Osterwald
Shendorf	Henry Calvin
Mickey Sinclair	Robert Shackleton
Sally	Bambi Linn
The Grand Duke Constantine	Willie Howard
Mrs. Vischer Van Alstyn	Kathryn Cameron
Toto	Lucy Hillary
Olga	Andrea Mann

Act I.—Scene 1—Shendorf's Café in Greenwich Village. 2—Long Island Garden of Mrs. Van Alstyn, the Early Nineteen Twenties. Act II.—Scenes 1 and 5—The Church Around the Corner. 2—Kitchen of Shendorf's Café. 3—"The Follies." 4—Backstage.

Staged by Billy Gilbert; music directed by David Mordecai; music supervised by Pembroke Davenport; dances and musical numbers by Richard Barstow; production associates, David Lowe—Sue Davidson; settings and lighting by Stewart Chaney; costumes by Henry Mulle.

Principal musical numbers: "Down Here in Greenwich Village," "Bungalow in Quogue," "Look for the Silver Lining," "Looking All Over for You," "Tulip Time in Sing Sing," "The Siren Song," "Cleopatra," "Wild Rose," "The Church Around the Corner," "Dear Little Girl," "Reaching for Stars."

"Sally" was first produced December 21, 1920, by Florenz Ziegfeld. Marilyn Miller was Sally, Leon Errol, "Connie" and Walter Catlett, Otis Hooper. There were 570 performances.

HOPE'S THE THING

(7 performances)

Three one-act plays by Richard Harrity, produced by Eddie Dowling, under the sponsorship of the American National Theatre and Academy, at the Playhouse, May 11, 1948.

GONE TOMORROW

Cast of characters—

Mrs. Muldoon......................................Peg Mayo
Mrs. Lacey..Ruth Vivian
Willie..Ken Terry
Peter Muldoon.....................................Ralph Cullinan
Jerry Canavan.....................................Barry Macollum

At Mrs. Muldoon's house everybody is waiting for an uncle to die upstairs so they can have an excuse for a wake.

HOME LIFE OF A BUFFALO

Cast of characters—

Joey..Kevin Mathews
Josey...Ray Dooley
Eddie...Eddie Dowling
Molly...Leona Powers
Otto..Vaughn Taylor

The vaudevillians and their son refuse to admit that vaudeville is dead, even though their livelihood is pitifully precarious.

HOPE IS THE THING WITH FEATHERS

Cast of characters—

Doc...E. G. Marshall
Steve...George Mathews
Wiler...Robert Alvin
Oscar...Philip Robinson
Sweeney...Will Geer
Charlie...Lou Gilbert
Old Man Nelson....................................Dan Reed
Joe...Fredric Martin
A Man...Jabez Gray

A group of homeless men sleeping in Central Park become excited by the plan of one of them to capture a duck off the Park lake, and the plan of another to cook the bird. The hunter fails, but does steal a monkey from the zoo, which is rejected as fodder.

(Closed May 15, 1948)

THE VIGIL

(11 performances)

A play in three acts by Ladislas Fodor. Produced by Alexander Markey by arrangement with George Jessel, at the Royale Theatre, May 21, 1948.

Cast of characters—

```
Violet...............................................Louise Jones
Mr. Woods...........................................John Seymour
Judge..........................................Edward Van Sloan
Court Clerk..........................................Tony Dowling
Court Stenographer..................................Lee Baxter
Courtroom Guard....................................Rand Elliot
Prosecutor......................................Henry Wilcoxon
Counsel for Defense............................Ian MacDonald
The Gardener........................................Tom Fadden
Assistant to the Prosecutor.....................Andrew George
Assistant to the Defense...........................Tom Donovan
Esther............................................Mary James
Lucius..........................................Dennis King, Jr.
Mr. Pinchas........................................Joe E. Marks
Joseph of Arimathea............................Lauren Gilbert
Lady Procula...................................Muriel Hutchison
Pontius Pilate.......................................Guy Spaull
Saul of Tarsus..................................Milton Parsons
Beulah.........................................Helen Seamon
Sadoc............................................King Donovan
Susanna...........................................Ann Pearce
Prof. Thaddeus......................................Dan Reed
Mary Magdalene.................................Maria Palmer
Simon............................................Walter Palance
```
    Acts I, II and III.—Courtroom in Any Small Town in the United
States. Between Good Friday and Easter Sunday.
    Staged by Alexander Markey; setting and lighting by Yellenti.

An examination, in modern American courtroom style, of the occurrences between the death of Jesus Christ and His resurrection. On trial is a gardener, accused of removing a body from a tomb and concealing it in order to make credible the rumor of a resurrection. The audience is the jury, and after all the testimony is in the judge leaves the case up to the jury to decide.

(Closed May 29, 1948)

SEEDS IN THE WIND

(7 performances)

A play in two acts by Arthur Goodman. Produced by Eunice Healey and Harald Bromley at the Empire Theatre, May 25, 1948.

Cast of characters—

```
Stefan Jakubec....................................Tonio Selwart
Tonya.............................................Sidney Lumet
```

Marta..Abby Bonime
Josef...Jerry   Stone
Poldi...Teddy Rose
Grischa...Richard Kenny
Vladi..Donald Rose
Eric...Kenneth Terry
Jani...Jimmy Dutton
Carl...David Burke
Franz...Micha 1 Citro
Nikos...Bobby   Nick
Boris..Stanley Martin
Katerin...Mimi   Strongin
Liza...Eeta Linden
Phillipa.......................................Winnie-Mae   Martin
Maminkoo.......................................Lee Graham
    Act I.—Inside the House the Children Built. Act II.—Scene 1—
Outside the House.   2 and 3—Inside the House.
    Staged by Paul Tripp; settings by Ralph Alswang.

A group of children, survivors of Lidice and other massacres,
have lasted out the war in a hideout in the Carpathian Mountains.
Their plan is to seize government of the world, on the grounds
that grown-ups have managed the world badly and have cared
nothing for children. They capture one grown-up and at a trial
convict him of being an adult.

(Closed May 29, 1948)

EQUITY-LIBRARY THEATRE

By George Freedley

The Equity Library Theatre underwent considerable revisions during the season 1947-48—in fact its very name became a misnomer, as the New York Public Library no longer participated in the project. The reason for this lay in the fact that most of the branch libraries containing theatres utilized in the project had to be redecorated, repainted or rebuilt.

Whether the library will participate in a future season will depend on negotiations between Actors' Equity Association and the Library, the original sponsors of the project. John Golden, who has given—along with others—financial support to the project, carried it alone in the past season and under his active directorship. Sam Jaffe remained as nominal chairman, George Freedley having resigned as co-chairman. A supervising committee was set up to examine the choice of plays and casts with a sponsor from the committee to be assigned to guide each production. In practice this did not work out too well as approximately half the productions were unsponsored.

Twenty-four standard and classical plays were performed at the Guild for the Blind, the Greenwich Mews Playhouse, the Madison Square Boys' Club, the Society of Illustrators, the Lighthouse for the Blind, the Lenox Hill Playhouse, the Joan of Arc High School and the Central High School of Needle Trades.

THE EXPERIMENTAL THEATRE

By Theron Bamberger

The Experimental Theatre was conceived in 1940 and incorporated in the State of New York in 1941, with the late Antoinette Perry as president. Three plays were presented the first year; then, due to lack of organizational strength and the onset of the war, it ceased functioning.

After the war, late in 1946, when the American National Theatre and Academy was being reactivated, one of the first projects was the revival of the Experimental Theatre. With the joint blessing of the Dramatists' Guild and Actors' Equity Association, five plays were presented at the Princess Theatre between February and April, 1947, each for a total of five performances; the audiences were limited to workers in the theatrical field; admission was by subscription only, the total for the series coming to $15.

Last season, 1947-48, the Experimental Theatre may be said to have reached man's estate.

Instead of operating in the 300-seat Princess, Maxine Elliott's Theatre, also on Thirty-ninth Street, was leased. This property, owned by the Shuberts, had been rented to the Columbia Broadcasting Company, which, having come upon a period where it had no use for the playhouse, was willing to sublet it. The Experimental Theatre, with the necessary approval of Lee Shubert, took it over from CBS for a six months' period, from November 15 to May 15, for the sum of $15,000. Whereas five plays had been presented the previous season, six were scheduled for the '47-'48 season. The rental of $15,000 presented a considerable obligation, as opposed to $3,000 the season before, but Maxine Elliott's had a capacity of 900 seats. Whereas the total possible income from memberships the year before had been $15,000, it was now possible to realize in excess of $70,000. Instead of 1,500 memberships being available there were now 5,400. A membership campaign was launched, with subscriptions open to the general public for the first time. Performances were scheduled monthly; each play was to open on a Sunday night, with performances on the following Monday, Wednesday and Friday evenings, Sunday afternoon and Sunday night. Memberships for the six plays were priced at $18 in the orchestra, $14 in the balcony and $7 in the second balcony.

The first play announced was Bertold Brecht's "Galileo," in which Charles Laughton was to be starred. The second was to be "Skipper Next to God," by Jan de Hartog, with John Garfield as the star.

The announcement of these two plays stirred a storm of controversy. For quite a few weeks pro and con letters appeared in the drama section of the New York *Times* and other newspapers. One of the complaints was that both plays had been written by foreigners. Another was that if the Experimental Theatre was to justify its name, it should experiment with actors. It was contended that there was nothing venturesome about Laughton or Garfield; the Experimental Theatre was accused of selling out, of having gone commercial by using big names to snare the public's money. Various officials of the organization, however, supported by several drama columnists, pointed out that Experimental Theatre did not mean amateur theatre, and that furthermore there was nothing wrong in using the best actors available.

The fact is that the organization had undertaken a heavy risk in leasing Maxine Elliott's, and in order for the venture to succeed it was necessary to sell virtually all of its available memberships. There is no doubt that the names of Laughton and Garfield accomplished a good deal in this respect, for the membership campaign was highly successful. All seats were subscribed for the two Sunday evening performances and the Sunday matinee and all but a few for the Monday, Wednesday and Friday evenings. The total memberships exceeded 5,200, only 200 short of capacity.

Two plays about Galileo had been on the market, the Brecht piece and "Lamp at Midnight," by Barry Stavis; the latter, having been turned down by the Experimental Theatre, was announced as the first production of New Stages. Some of the letter writers who attacked the Experimental Theatre did so on the ground that it had chosen the lesser of the two Galileo plays in order to enlist the services of Mr. Laughton, a compromise which was frowned on in the letters to the editors. But when the votes were counted neither "Galileo" nor "Lamp at Midnight" evoked overwhelming enthusiasm in the press. The production of "Galileo," which opened December 7, 1947, marked however a considerable advance physically over offerings of the previous season. Actually, the play had been tried out in California during the Summer of 1947, and the scenery, which was first class in every respect, had been transported to New York.

The second production, "Skipper Next to God," opening January 4, 1948, was also a first-class production, designed by Boris Aronson and built and painted under first-class auspices in a union shop. The critical reaction was mixed, although praise for John Garfield's dynamic performance was universal, and there was no doubting the fact that many persons were deeply stirred by the theme.

Unquestionably there was a public for the play, and it was decided to continue the run. Instead of closing at the end of the scheduled six performances, the play continued at the Elliott for two weeks and three days and then was moved to the Playhouse on Forty-eighth Street, where business was excellent. How long it might have stayed is, of course, problematical, but it closed March 27 when it was averaging a profitable $15,000 weekly, due to the fact that Mr. Garfield had a film commitment and it was thought unsound to continue without a name in the leading part.

The extension of the "Skipper" run was accompanied by a controversy over the scenery. Since it was not contemplated in the original set-up of the Experimental Theatre that the organization would operate a play on a commercial basis, "Skipper Next to God" was taken over by Blevins Davis, wealthy and public spirited producer, who announced he would turn all the profits over to the American National Theatre and Academy, which sponsored the ET. The stagehands' union, one of several unions which had made concessions to make it possible for the ET to operate, notified the producer that he would not be permitted to move the scenery to another theatre; he would have to rebuild it. After some stormy discussions, the stagehands agreed to allow the production to be moved, but insisted on new scenery if the play caught on at the Playhouse and the run was extended. The play did catch on, but the stagehands modified their demand. It was finally agreed that for each of six weeks the sum of $500 be taken from the profits and distributed to various charities, three to beneficiaries designated by the stagehands, three to choices of Mr. Davis.

The third play of the Experimental Theatre was "A Long Way from Home," which was adapted from Gorki's "The Lower Depths," by Randolph Goodman and Walter Carroll. This was a foreign play again, although the adaptation was the work of two Americans who had conceived the idea of placing the locale in the South, and having all the parts played by Negroes. Incidentally, due to the criticism against foreign plays, the Experimental Theatre abandoned one of the plays announced originally because it was written by a Frenchman. This was "The Respectful Prostitute," by Jean-Paul Sartre. It was acquired by New Stages and turned out to be a thundering success, meriting transfer to Broadway.

Despite a handsome production, "A Long Way from Home" failed to register. Nor did the succeeding play, "A Temporary Island" by Halsted Welles, the first completely American play of the series, win general approval.

By this time, the Experimental Theatre began to recognize that it was in financial difficulty. Each production had gone over the amount allotted to it and a sizable deficit was in prospect. The 1947 season, in a theatre with a limited capacity, had gone into the red, due to the small income. But rigid economy had been practiced; difficult though it may be to believe, the actual scenic productions had cost an average of a little over $300. But now the same economy was no longer being followed. Simple imaginative scenery had been replaced by first-class realistic sets which vied with the commercial theatre. While less expensive than the Broadway theatre, due to co-operation by the unions and the theatre tradespeople, it was far beyond the pocketbook of the ET.

Retrenchment was necessary. It was decided to put on as the fifth offering three one-act plays under the auspices of the Six O'Clock Theatre, a group of actors, sponsored by ANTA, who had been rehearsing steadily more or less for their own amusement. They were produced on a bare stage, without scenery, and while only one of them, "Hope Is the Thing with Feathers," by Richard Harrity, was completely successful, the attempt to do plays without scenery was accepted. As an outgrowth of this offering, Eddie Dowling decided to take three one-act plays by Mr. Harrity, including "Hope Is the Thing with Feathers," and also "Gone Tomorrow" and "Home Life of a Buffalo," to the Playhouse. The venture was a quick failure, lasting only seven performances.

Incidentally, the annual Clarence Derwent awards went to Experimental Theatre performers—Lou Gilbert, who was in "Hope Is the Thing with Feathers," and Catherine Ayers, who was in "A Long Way from Home."

The last production of the season was "Ballet Ballads," by John Latouche and Jerome Moross. This consisted of three one-act pieces, "Susanna and the Elders," "Willie the Weeper," and "The Eccentricities of Davy Crockett," in a novel art form which combined music, dancing and drama. This was an ambitious undertaking, requiring the services of seventy people, and despite simple scenery was quite costly. Nevertheless, in the opinion of many observers, it was the most successful undertaking of the Experimental Theatre's season. Robert Sylvester in the *Daily News* called it "the best song and dance show of the season." Brooks Atkinson in the *Times* confessed to having been "thoroughly delighted."

A run at a Broadway theatre seemed indicated; "Ballet Ballads" was taken over by T. Edward Hambleton and Alfred R. Stern and moved to the Music Box under a philanthropic deal similar to the "Skipper Next to God" arrangement, namely, that profits were to go to ANTA.

Another activity of the Experimental Theatre, at the close of its regular season, was the Invitational Series. This consisted of the presentation of five plays by young American writers in simplified studio style. The budget for each play was $150 and the emphasis was on the play and the acting. The productions were off Broadway, at the Lenox Hill Settlement House, 531 East 70th Street, and the Educational Alliance on East Broadway. Each play was given four performances, to which producers, agents, etc., were invited, and also subscribers to the Experimental Theatre who desired to attend.

The five plays presented were: "Seeds in the Wind," by Arthur Goodman; "Danny Larkin," by James McGee; "Battle for Heaven," by John Carter; "These Tender Mercies," by Barton Yarborough; and "E Equals m.c. Squared," a living newspaper organized and compiled by Hallie Flanagan Davis. "Seeds in the Wind" was taken over by Harald Bromley and Eunice Healey and transferred late in May to the Empire Theatre, where it failed.

As to the intent of the Experimental Theatre, a report made to the Council of Actors' Equity Association in October, 1947, states that it was instituted "as a showcase for actors and playwrights— in the interest of stimulating more theatre." Its purpose has been further described to present plays with "a new and fresh spirit either in writing, content, concept, direction or acting." The ET is proud of the fact that at the end of its first season it received the Sidney Howard award as "the most important development in the theatre this year."

The Experimental Theatre is run by a board consisting of five members of Actors' Equity Association and five members of the Dramatists' Guild, headed by Clarence Derwent as Chairman, who is also President of Equity and a member of the ANTA Board of Directors.

The Executive Committee of the Board consists of one member from Equity and one from the Dramatists' Guild, last season under the chairmanship of Cheryl Crawford. The actual production of each play is supervised by a production committee consisting of two members of the ET Board and one or two theatre people who have shown special interest in the particular script. Robert Breen, executive secretary of ANTA, is an important factor in all ET operations and last season gave of his energies without stint.

All the actors participating in Experimental Theatre productions must be members of Equity and all playwrights members of the Dramatists' Guild. The actors' scale of pay in the ET is on a per performance basis according to the number of people in the cast. For instance, with a cast of under 10, the pay is $12 per performance, between 10 and 20 actors, $10 per performance, and above 20, $8 per performance. Charles Laughton received $8 per performance and John Garfield $10. Both these stars were sufficiently interested in the work of the ET not to consider financial return, and when "Skipper Next to God," moved uptown, Garfield insisted that he would not accept more than the salary of the highest priced actor in the company.

As to the future of the Experimental Theatre, the first problem is to obtain its own home, since there is no guarantee that a theatre of the necessary size will be available each season. There is a strong likelihood, if negotiations now in progress materialize, that Daly's Theatre in 63d Street will be acquired by Blevins Davis for the use of ANTA and the ET.

A second step will be financial reorganization which will enable the ET to live within its budget. During the past season the ET had an overall income from subscriptions, of nearly $70,000, plus $4,000 contributed in equal amounts by Equity and the Dramatists' Guild. Yet this sum, augmented by the proceeds of "Skipper Next to God," did not suffice to pay expenses. It is the opinion of many persons connected with ET that certain extravagances during the '47-'48 season were the result of faulty organization and too elaborate scenery, and that this can be corrected to the essential end that it live within its means—a requisite for its permanent life.

DANCE DRAMA

Peter Hamilton and his company opened the season at Studio Theatre, June 8, 1947. The assisting artists were Linda Laun, Felicia Conde, Betts Lee, Joan Roessle, dancers; Jack Ferris and Robert Herget, narrators and Ada Reif, pianist. The dances were "Dance for Five," "Joe Kitchener," "Boy Criminal," "Beau Soir" (Debussy), "Box Plastique" (Shostakovitch), "Gigue" (Bach), "Silent Snow, Secret Snow" (text from Conrad Aiken; music Schoeberg-Reif), "Jesse James" (based on a poem by W. R. Benét).

Paul Swan at Carnegie Hall on the same date started his season with "Glimpse of the Chinese Theatre," "Medieval Pantomime," "The Temptation," "Pierrot, the Gossip." Eric Coates "London Suite," "Juggler at the Circus," "At a French Country Dance," "Spider Web," "Legend of Narcissus," "Nostalgic Oriental" and "Desert Dance." June 15, he added "Fourteen Quatrains of Omar Khayyam," and other dance dramas. Evelyn Hansen was pianist.

Le Meri appeared June 19th at Ethnologic Dance Center in "Hindu Ballet," Gauba's "Journey to Paradise," and "The Spanish Cuadro Flamengo." She also presented in July Josefina Garcia in a Mexican dance and Cebyn Dwajtu Maufaunawy, an Oklahoma Indian dancer in "Footbeats of India, Spain and the Americas." October 4, Le Meri made her formal Exotic Ballet Fall seasonal debut with a repertoire including dance dramas from India, Spain, Java, Hawaii, the Americas and elsewhere. The dancers included Lilian Rollo, Edna Dieman, Rebecca Harris, Eleanor Oliver, Patricia Penn, Richard Cressy, Peter di Falco and others.

The Summer's first ballet performance of the 1946-47 season at the Lewisohn Stadium took place in early August when Alicia Markova and Anton Dolin with their ensemble presented "Nutcracker Suite," "Chopiniana," "Hymn to the Sun," "Black Swan," "Waltz from 'Eugene Onegin,' " "Don Quixote," etc. Robert conducted the music (Tchaikovsky, Rimsky-Korsakoff, Saint-Saëns and others). In the company were Bettina Rosay, Roszika Sabo, Albia Kavan, Carol Melson, Wallace Seibert, Rex Cooper, Royes Fernandez, David Tihman and George Reich.

The first of Paul Swan's weekly programs for the Fall season started September 7, 1947, at Carnegie Hall. The program included "The Devise," "Musical Lines," "House That Jack Built," "Triumph of Spirit over Matter," "The Elements," and "Oriental Fantasy." Robert Zeller conducted.

"Around the World in Dance and Song," sponsored by the American Museum of Natural History and directed by Hazel Lockwood Muller, began a series of dance dramas with dances of Indonesia with Devi Dja and her ensemble, October 16. Other engagements included Spain and Mexico with Aldo Cadena, Teresa Zayas, Josefina Garcia, and Gustavo Sosa; Old Cathay, with Averil Tam and members of the Chinese Cultural Group; "Dance Ways from Spain to the Philippines" with Juanam Salvacion, Leonore Oroso and Matilda Rivera; dances of Norway and Sweden; dances of American Indian with Reginald and Gladys Laubin; dances of India with Wasantha Wanasingh and his group and Gina; folk dances of Switzerland and other countries.

Iris Mabry made her season's debut at the International Theatre, with Ralph Gilbert as pianist-composer, November 2. Her dances were "Allemande," "Doomsday," "Rhapsody," "Scherzo," "Bird Spell," "Cycle," "Dreams," "Litany" and "Witch."

Harald Kreutzberg, in his first dance program in New York since before the war, made his appearance at the Ziegfeld Theatre, November 9. The series ended December 7. Among his dance dramas were "Evocation of the Evil One," "From an Old Calendar" (Mozart), "Lament," "Night Terror," "Hungarian Dance" (Brahms), "Selige Walzer" (Strauss), "Vagabond's Dance" (Smetana), "The Gardener in Love" (Mozart), and "Four Little Etudes" (Czerny).

Anita Zahn and a group of Duncan Dancers enacted "The Story of the Nativity" December 20 at Carnegie Hall in the Christmas Celebration of the National Orchestral Association.

Fern Helscher's Holiday Dance Series opened at Times Hall December 27 and ended December 31. The series included Valerie Bettis with Duncan Noble and company who staged a program which included "Yerma," "Status Quo," "Rondel for a Young Girl," "Toccata for Three," "In Transit" and "Figure 47." Other groups on succeeding nights were Reginald and Gladys Laubin in dances of the American Indian: "Invocation," "Ceremonial Buffalo Dance," "Battle of the Washita," "Hoop Dance" and others; Le Meri and her Exotic Ballet presenting the Hindu version of "Swan Lake," "Devi Murti," etc.

José Limon presented "Lament for Ignacio Sanchez Mejias"

(choreography by Doris Humphrey) with Letitia Ide and Meg Mundy at the Mansfield Theatre, January 4, 1948.

Iva Kitchell gave her annual New York recital at the Ziegfeld Theatre, January 11. Her program included "The Tale of the Bird," "The Hunted," "The Hunter," "The Hunt," "Mort Oiseau," "Portrait of a Hostess" and "Bacchanal—as seen at the Opera."

At Radio City Music Hall January 18, 1948, Margaret Sande and George Tatar headed a company of 86 presenting Maurice Ravel's "Bolero," choreographed by Florence Rogge.

The annual dance festival for the benefit of the Spanish Refugee Appeal took place at the Ziegfeld Theatre January 25, 1948. Among the famous dance groups were Martha Graham's, Charles Weidman's and Peter Hamilton's. The Weidman group presented a preview of his new choreographed "Fables for Our Times" by James Thurber, with music by Freda Miller and Jack Ferris as narrator. The sections presented were "The Unicorn in the Garden," "The Shrike and the Chipmunks" and "The Owl Who Was God"; Antonia Cobos, "Padedu," "Cuatro Muleros" and "Bolero Classique"; Jane Dudley, Sophie Maslow and William Bales in "Field Hand," "Dust Bowl Ballads," "Harmonica Breakdown" and "Partisan Journey." Martha Graham made a solo appearance in "Salem Shore" and José Limon assisted by Miriam Pandor and Betty Jones presented the Vivalda-Bach "Concerto in D Minor." Nadine Gae and Peter Hamilton danced their torch-song number "If It Were Easy to Do" from "Angel in the Wings" with Faye Elizabeth Smith from "Brigadoon" singing it for them. From Billy Rose's Diamond Horseshoe, Ruth Mata and Eugene Hari danced their "Pas de Deux." Rosario and Antonia and their company including Pastora and Maclovia Ruiz and Roberto Iglesias danced native Spanish dances.

Martha Graham with Erick Hawkins, May O'Donnell, Pearl Lang and Dance Company, Louis Horst directing the music, began her 1947-48 season at Maxine Elliott's Theatre February 17 and closed the season February 29. The dance-drama program was sponsored by the American National Theatre and Academy. The first dance drama of the series was the New York première of "Night Journey" (music by William Schuman and décor by Isamu Noguchi). Other premières were "Letter to the World," with a new score by Hunter Johnson, and "Tale of Seizure," danced by Yuriko. Other dances were "Appalachian Spring," "Every Soul Is a Circus," "Herodiade" (score by Paul Hindemith), "Cave of the Heart," "Dark Meadow," "Stephan Acrobat," "El Penitente," "Punch and Judy," "Salem Shore," "Deaths and Entrances," "John Brown," "Errand into the Maze," "Tale of Shadows," etc. Other principals who danced were Mark Ryder, May O'Donnell, Ethel Winter and Yuriko.

Haydee Morini made her New York debut at the Barbizon-Plaza March 9. Artur Kleiner was the assisting pianist and the dances were "Music Box" (Liadoro), "Neapolitan Flower" (Rossina), "Longing" (Debussy), "After the Ball" (Lehar), "Rag Doll" (Debussy), "Nightmare" (Barwinsky), "Blue Danube" (Strauss), "Jungle" (Scott), "Impressions of Paris" (Strauss).

Charles Weidman and his dance company including several guest artists, under the management of Eunice Healey and Ernest D. Glucksman, opened an engagement at the Mansfield Theatre, April 18, 1948. Music collaborators were Freda Miller, Lionel Nowak and Lehman Engel. The feature of the first program was "Fables for Our Time," for which a Guggenheim Fellowship had been awarded Mr. Weidman. The "Fables" were based on James Thurber's stories and set to music by Freda Miller. Jack Ferris acted as narrator. The four episodes were "The Unicorn," "The Shrike and the Chipmunks," "The Owl Who Was God" and "The Courtship of Al and Arthur." Other dance dramas in the repertory were "Lynch Town," "Jesse James" (based on William Rose Benét's poem), with choreography by Peter Hamilton and read by Robert Herget, "A House Divided," a study of Abraham Lincoln and the problems of reconstruction, with Spencer Teakle reading the lines of the alter ego, Peter Hamilton's "None Seeth Me," based on Biblical quotations, with music by Ada Reif, "And Daddy Was a Fireman," "Silent Snow, Secret Snow," by Hamilton, "Ringside," based on a short story by Conrad Aiken with music by Schoenberg and Jack Ferris as an off-stage speaker, "The Unconquered," a solo danced by Beatrice Seckler, "On My Mother's Side" and "Flickers." The principals included Nadine Gae and Peter Hamilton (borrowed from "Angel in the Wings"), Betty Osgood, Saida Gerrard, Marc Breaux, Beatrice Seckler, Sherry Parker, Felicia Conde, Spencer Teakle, Betts Lee, Emily Frankel, Carl Morris, Nicholas Vaneff, Jack Ferris and Sharry Traver.

Marie Marchowsky and her group of six dancers appeared at the Cort Theatre, April 26, 1948. The program consisted of five dance dramas, "Antigone," "Odyssey" and "Ebb Tide" with music by Nemiroff, "Seed in the Wind" (Chavez), "Image of Obsession" (Haufrecht). John Boyt designed the costumes, Martin Craig and Ibrim Iassow décor and David Shapiro was the pianist.

Rosario and Antonio with their company gave two performances at the Adelphi Theatre, May 9.

AT THE METROPOLITAN

Alicia Markova and Anton Dolin and their company were presented in a series of dance dramas at the Metropolitan Opera House by S. Hurok, October 17, 18 and 19, 1947. The series opened with "Fantasia," a New York première with music by Schubert-Liszt, choreography by Bronislava Nijinska and costumes by Rose Schogel. The dancers were Bettina Rosay, Rozsika Sabo, Albia Kavan, Oleg Tupine, Wallace Siebert and Rex Cooper, with Richard Gregor at the piano. Markova, Dolin and Andre Eglevsky danced "Pas de Trois" by Hector Berlioz music in "Damnation of Faust." Costumes were by John Pratt and Edith Lutyens. Divertissement by Jerome Robbins. Bettina Rosay and Wallace Siebert danced "The Black Swan" (from Act III of "Swan Lake"), choreographed by Anton Dolin after Petipa, music by Tchaikovsky and costumes by Karinska. "The Dying Swan" (music by Saint-Saëns) was danced by Markova.

The world première of "Henry VIII (and His Wives)" was presented on October 17 and 19, 1947, with music of Rossini adapted and arranged by Robert Zeller, choreography by Rosella Hightower, and costumes by Russell Hartley and Rose Schogel. James Starbuck staged the production. The dancers were: Anton Dolin, Natalie Conlon, Alicia Markova, Rozsika Sabo, Bettina Rosay, Kirsten Valbor, Royes Fernandez, George Reich, Wallace Siebert, Oleg Tupine.

The New York première of "Lady of the Camellias," a romantic ballet in three acts based on "Camille" by Dumas, fils, was presented October 18 and 19, 1947. Music of Giuseppe Verdi was adapted and arranged by Robert Zeller. Choreographic pantomime was by Anton Dolin. Costumes and decorations: Antonio Ruiz, Hazel Hilliard, and Henri de Chatillon. The dancers were: Alicia Markova, Anton Dolin, Rex Cooper, George Reich, Bettina Rosay, Royes Fernandez, Albia Kavan, Roszika Sabo and Wallace Siebert.

"The Bluebird" from "Princess Aurora" (music by Tchaikovsky) was danced by Bettina Rosay and Andre Eglevsky; "Pas de Trois" by Kirsten Valbor, Natalie Conlon and Royes Fernandez; "Grand Pas de Deux" from "Don Quixote" (music by

Leon Minkus) by Alicia Markova and Anton Dolin with choreography by Anatole Oboukhoff after Petipa and costumes by
Karinska.

The Ballet Theatre under the sponsorship of Lucia Chase and
Oliver Smith by arrangement with S. Hurok opened its Spring
season at the Metropolitan Opera House, April 3, presenting
dance dramas until May 8, 1948. World premières were Antony
Tudor's "Shadow of the Wind" and "Fall River Legend" by
Agnes de Mille. "Shadow of the Wind" (April 14) was based
on Gustav Mahler's musical work, "Das Lied von der Erde," and
the Mahler songs were sung by Louise Bernhardt and Robert
Bernauer. Scenery was designed by Jo Mielziner and costumes
by Karinska and Yuji Ito. Max Goberman directed the orchestra.
"Fall River Legend," whose première was April 22, was choreographed by Agnes de Mille on a theme suggested by the Lizzie
Borden case. Scenery was by Oliver Smith, costumes by Miles
White and Morton Gould, composer of the music, conducted the
orchestra.

Included in the revivals were "Theme and Variations," "Jardin
Aux Lilas," "Tally-Ho," "Gala Performance," "Princess Aurora,"
"Billy the Kid," "Helen of Troy," "Giselle," "Fancy Free,"
"Aleko," "Les Patineurs," "Swan Lake," "Romeo and Juliet,"
"Peter the Wolf," "Pillar of Fire," "Pas de Quatre," "Les
Sylphides," "Interplay," "Petrouchka," "On Stage," "Six
Waltzes," "Pas de Deux" ("The Nutcracker"), "Pas de Deux"
("The Black Swan"), "Apollo," "Undertow," "Dialogue," "Fall
River Legend," "Facsimile," "Shadow of the Wind," "Orpheus,"
"Punch and the Child," and others.

Antony Tudor acted as artistic administrator and the symphony orchestra was directed by Max Oberman and Ben Steinberg. Morton Gould directed the music for "Fall River Legend," Igor Stravinsky for "Apollo," Aaron Copland for "Billy
the Kid," and the settings were by Oliver Smith. "Billy the
Kid" was designed by Jared French.

A company of 100 included the principal dancers, Alicia
Alonso, John Kriza, Antony Tudor, Igor Youstevitch, Zachary
Solov, Eugene Loring, Peter Gladke, Nora Kaye, Hugh Laing,
Lucia Chase, Dimitri Romanoff, Muriel Bentley, Norma Vance,
Melissa Hayden, Mary Burr, Diana Adams, Shellie Farrell, Nana
Gollner, Jean Sullivan, Michael Maule, Ruth Ann Koesun, Cyn-
thia Riseley, Barbara Fallis, Anna Cheselka, Crandall Diehl and
Eric Braun. Dania Krupska, guest artist, danced the leading
role in "Fall River Legend."

AT THE CITY CENTER

The Ballet Russe de Monte Carlo, presented by Ballet Foundation and directed by Sergei J. Denham, opened the New York 1947-48 season at the City Center, September 7, 1947, with George Balanchine's "Ballet Imperial." The first première of the season was "Cirque de Deux" September 10. Choreography was by Ruthanna Boris, music by Charles Gounod and costumes by Robert Davison. The conductor was Ivan Boutnikoff and the principal dancers were Ruthanna Boris, Leon Danielian, Patricia Wilde and Frank Hobi. There was one other première, "Lola Montez," a ballet in one act with story by Dr. N. Wolf, choreography by Edward Caton, music by Fred Witt, orchestrated by Ivan Boutnikoff who also directed the music. Costumes and scenery were by Raoul Pene du Bois and Paolo D'Anna. The cast was as follows: Alexandra Danilova, Frederic Franklin, Joy Williams, Nikita Talin, Michel Katcharoff, George Verdak, Ruthanna Boris, the Misses Garfield, Lanova, Seaver, Toby, Tweedie, Tyven, Peter Deign, Bernice Rehner, the Misses Haynes, Taanila, Weaver, White, Patricia Wilde, Messrs. Hobi, Lindgren, Zompakos, Dorn, Glenn, Herrera, Kelly, Thomas, Trapaga, Myrna Galle, Jeanette Tannan.

The scene takes place in a Mid-Western town in the period of the Gold Rush.

Other dance dramas were "Madronos," a ballet in one act by Antonia Cobos, "Le Baiser de la Fee," a ballet-allegory in four scenes by Igor Stravinsky based on a tale, "The Virgin of the Lake," by Hans Christian Andersen, inspired by music of Tchaikowsky, with choreography by George Balanchine and scenery and costumes by Alice Halicka, "The Bluebird," "Le Beau Danube," "The Swan Lake," "The Nutcracker," "The Night Shadow," "Scheherazade," "Concerto Barocco," "Pas de Deux Classique," "Gaite Parisienne," "Les Sylphides," "Raymonda," "Serenade," "Frankie and Johnny" and "Rodeo."

Principals engaged included Alicia Alonso, Gregory Alexandroff, Ruthanna Boris, Vida Brown, Yvonne Chouteau, Antonia Cobos, Leon Danielian, Alexandra Danilova, Peter Deign, Harding Dorn, Frederic Franklin, Myrna Galle, Constance Garfield, Tatiana Grantzeva, Frank Hobi, Michael Katcharoff, Nora Kaye, Nathalie Krassovska, John Krisa, Hugh Laing, Merriam Lanova, Robert Lindgren, Nicolas Magallanes, Mary Ellen Moylan, Bernice Rehner, Edwina Seaver, Nikita Talin, Jeanette Tannan, Harriet Toby, Louis Trapaga, Gertrude Tyven, George Verdak, Shirley Weaver, Nora White, Joy Williams, Patricia Wilde, Igor Youskevitch and Stanley Zompakos.

The two-week Fall program closed September 21.

Lucia Chase and Oliver Smith presented Ballet Theatre at City Center November 19, 1947, with Antony Tudor as artistic administrator, Max Goberman and Ben Steinberg director of music, and Dimitri Romanoff as manager. The season opened with "Les Sylphides." The series ended December 17. Ballets not included in the September season were "Pillar of Fire," "Interplay," "Giselle," "Fancy Free," "Peter the Wolf," "Romeo and Juliet," "Les Patineurs," "Princess Aurora," "Tally-Ho," "Helen of Troy," "Theme and Variations," "Jardin Aux Lilas," "Dark Elegies," "Pas de Quatre," "Apollo," "Summer Day," "Gala Performance" and "Facsimile." Many of the principals in the September season were the same. Those not included as principals then were Norma Vance, Zachary Solov, Melissa Hayden, Dimitri Romanoff, Crandall Diehl, Jean Sullivan, Diana Adams, Marvin Krauter, Harry Asmus, Fernando Alonso, Michael Maule, Eric Braun, Barbara Fallis, Anna Cheselka, Lucia Chase, Mary Burr, Fernald Nault, Paula Lloyd, Cynthia Riseley, Ruth Ann Koesun, Peter Rudley, Jerome Robbins, Shellie Farrell, Antony Tudor, Marc West and Doreen Oswald.

The Spring season of Ballet Russe de Monte Carlo started February 15, 1948, and closed after a four-week run. There was one première, "Billy Sunday," a sermon in four episodes by Ruth Page and Remi Gassman based on the evangelist's dramatic sermon on "Temptation," danced first on March 2. Dialogue was written by J. Ray Hunt, music by Remi Gassman, choreography by Ruth Page, décor by Herbert Andrews, costumes by Paul du Pont and Helene Pons. Alexandra Danilova and Frederic Franklin danced the principal parts.

The Ballet Society with George Balanchine as director, Leon Barzin as musical director and lighting by Jean Rosenthal started a program of five performances featuring six ballets new to the general public April 29. "Orpheus" with choreography by Balanchine and music by Igor Strawinsky was a world première. Book and music were by Strawinsky, lighting by Jean Rosenthal, settings and costumes by Isamu Noguchi. Nicholas Magallanes, Francisco Moncion, Maria Tallchief, Herbert Bliss, Edward Bigelow and Job Sanders were the principals. Other ballets were "Elegie," "Renard," "Symphonie Concertante," "Punch and the Child," a character ballet in three scenes with music by

Richard Arnell, choreography by Fred Danieli and scenery and costumes by Horace Armistead. Leon Barzin conducted and the principal dancers included those named above in the cast of "Orpheus," and Tanaquil LeClercq, Beatrice Tompkins, Elise Reiman, Todd Bolender, John Taras and Lew Christensen.

BALLETS IN MUSICAL DRAMA

The New Dance Group Festival, a series of variety dance programs, was presented at the Mansfield Theatre, May 23 through 27, 1948. The principal dancers were Jean Erdman, Jane Dudley, Hadassah, Sophie Maslow, William Bales, Pearl Primus, Duncan Noble, Joseph Gifford, Eve Gentry, Lily Peace, Padjet Fredericks, Nina Caiserman, Lili Mann, Mary Anthony, Elizabeth Sherbon, and Mark Rider. The dance dramas were "Dawn Song," "Transformation of Medusa," "Kebyar Legong," "Shuvi Nafshi" (with cantorial singing by Cantor Leibel Waldman), "Leela," "Dust Bowl," "Folksay," "Harmonica Breakdown," "Peon Portraits," "Champion," "The Lonely Ones," "Sea Deep," "Soliloquy," "Fable," "Hamadryad." "Broadway Hindu," "Santo," and others.

During the season in New York, the plays which presented dance drama were "Louisiana Lady" (Felicia Sorel), "Music in My Heart" (Ruth Page), "Under the Counter" (dances arranged and directed by Jack Hulbert and John Gregory), "Dear Judas" (dances and mimes by Esther Junger), "High Button Shoes" (Jerome Robbins), "Allegro" (Agnes de Mille), "Caribbean Carnival" (Pearl Primus and Claude Marchant), "Make Mine Manhattan" (Lee Sherman), "Look, Ma, I'm Dancin'!" (Trude Rittman), "Angel in the Wings" (Edward Noll), "Inside U.S.A." (Helen Tameris).

OFF BROADWAY

At the Lewisohn Stadium July 15, 1947, Puccini's "Madame Butterfly" was presented by the Philharmonic-Symphony Orchestra. In the cast were Eleanor Steber, Felix Knight, Thelma Altman and John Brownlee. Dimitri Mitropoulos was the conductor. July 19, Paul Robeson sang Beethoven's "Creation Hymn," "O Isis and Osiris," from Mozart's "Magic Flute," and "Lord God of Abraham" from Mendelssohn's "Elijah." Alexander Smallens was the conductor. Robeson also sang a group of Negro folk songs and spirituals with Lawrence Brown at the piano. Among the songs were "Water Boy," a special version of "Ol' Man River," "On My Journey," "Swing Low, Sweet Chariot," "The House I Live In" and "Ezekiel Saw de Wheel." In early August, Arthur Whittemore and Jack Lowe, duo-pianists, played a group of popular works for two hands with Richard Korn as director. August 6, Alicia Markova and Anton Dolin with their ballet company danced excerpts from "Don Quixote" and "Eugene Onegin," "The Nutcracker" and seven numbers to Chopin music under the direction of Robert Zeller. The outdoor concerts at the Stadium closed August 10, when Eugene Istomin, pianist, and Joseph Fuchs, violinist, were the soloists with the Philharmonic-Symphony Orchestra with Alexander Smallens conducting.

"Jeanne d'Arc au Boucher," a dramatic oratorio in prologue and seven scenes by Arthur Honegger, was performed January 2, 1948, for the first time in this country at Carnegie Hall by the Philharmonic-Symphony and the Westminster choir. Vera Zorina appeared in the title role and Raymond Gerome as Frere Dominique. Charles Munch conducted and the text was sung and spoken by Paul Claudel in the original French. Nadine Conner, Jarmila Novotna, Enid Szantho, Joseph Laderoute and Lorenzo Alvary were in the cast.

The Snark production of "The Turn of the Screw" and "The Aspern Papers," dramatizations of two Henry James stories, was presented at the Amateur Comedy Club, March 3, 4 and 5.

The Masque and Lyre Company produced a Gilbert and Sullivan season at the Heckscher Theatre.

ICE SHOWS

The "Ice Follies of 1948" opened November 18, 1947, at Madison Square Garden and continued through November 30. The principal skaters were Roy Shipstad, Evelyn Chandler, Mae Ross, Frick and Frack, Hazel Franklin, Norris and Roman, and Phyllis and Harris Legg.

Sonja Henie with a company of 200 appeared at Madison Square Garden in "Hollywood Ice Revue," January 22 through February 10.

IN GREENWICH VILLAGE

PROVINCETOWN THEATRE

The Actors Theatre produced a series of revivals at the Provincetown Theatre starting with Lynn Riggs' "Roadside," June 3, 1947. The Actors Theatre was under the management of Paul L. Miner. The play was directed by Joe O'Brien and Ernst Ehrman designed the scenery. Woody Parker played the role of Texas and Marilyn Stuart Miner, Hannie. Others in the cast were Oren Redfield, Matthew Dolkey, Jerome Leonard, Leo Daviou, Bernard Barrow, Bradley Bransford, Kenneth Schwartz and Michelle Cousins. The play closed June 12 and Elmer Rice's "The Adding Machine" was presented June 13. June 24, the troupe played Irwin Shaw's "The Gentle People" and "Helena's Room" by John Lynn, Jr., opened July 5 and closed July 14. The fifth and last opening was "Hi Ho Figaro," which had its premiere July 22. This comedy was the work of William Whiting, who also served as director. The principal roles were enacted by James Noble and Bernard Barrow. The play continued through July 27.

The Light Opera Company opened its 12th season of Gilbert and Sullivan repertory at the Provincetown Playhouse October 16, 1947. They played until New Year's Eve. The revivals were staged by John F. Graham.

CHERRY LANE THEATRE

On Stage, a dramatic group "seeking to bridge the gap between the University theatre and Broadway," presented a series of plays at Cherry Lane Theatre beginning June 9, 1947, with "No Exit," by Jean-Paul Sartre. "Juno and the Paycock" was produced June 23 and continued through July 5. Other plays were "Ethan

Frome," by Owen Davis (July 7 through 19), "The Dog Beneath the Skin," by W. H. Auden and Christopher Isherwood (July 21 through August 16), "Gas," by Georg Kaiser, directed by Irv Striber with Jean Saks and Marvin Shilbersher in the cast (August 18 through August 30), "Life Sentence" by Philip van Dyke, directed by Marjorie Hildreth (October 7 through 26), "The Watched Pot," a comedy by Saki, nom de plume for H. H. Munro, staged by Walter Mullen, settings by Bob Ramsey, October 28. Jean Saks and Kchast Sayers were the principal players. On stage actors included Alex Solomis, Sarah Sigler, Brenda Ericson, Glenn Alvery, Arthur Koulias, Lola Ross and Dennis Ellsworth. Robert Ramsey was general manager, Walter Mullen, director, and Alan Harper was in charge of lighting. "Henry IV" by Pirandello, directed by Alexis Solomis, opened December 19, and "The Family Reunion" by T. S. Eliot was also produced in December.

Paul and Virginia Gilmore revived four plays during the season at the Cherry Lane Theatre. The first was "Baby Mine," which opened January 11. The other three were "This Thing Called Love," "The Bishop Misbehaves" and "Angel Street." The closing date was May 22.

GREENWICH MEWS PLAYHOUSE

At the Greenwich Mews Playhouse the Greenwich Mews Players started a series of plays in early December. "A Christmas Carol," adapted from the Dickens story by Ray B. Yates, was produced under the direction of Roland von Weber and Robert Stapleton, December 16 to 20. "Night Must Fall" was revived March 18 for four performances. "Come Back Laughter," an Irish play in three acts by Mary Coburn opened at the Greenwich Mews Playhouse May 5, 1948. The Village House Drama Association, Phillip Schrager, president, presented the Greenwich Mews Players in this play which was staged by Bob Arden; designed by Larry Klein and the costumes were by May Werbin. Connected with the management were Al Fiering, Pauline Sharpe, Edwin F. Strome, R. M. West, Vicki Bregman, Sara Katchen, Zee Warner, and Ray Yates. The play closed May 12 with 7 performances.

The Lemonade Opera Company presented a number of operas at the Greenwich Mews Playhouse beginning with Mozart's "Don Giovanni," presented in English, June 21, 1947. The second production was a double bill, Humperdinck's "Hansel and Gretel" and Pergolesi's "La Serva Padrona," June 27. Nancy Kendall sang the soprano role in "La Serva Padrona" and in "Hansel and Gretel" the principal roles were sung by Maurice Falkow, Sylvia Meredith and Edward S. Bryce. During the Christmas holidays "Hansel and Gretel" had a week's run with Carol Leonard and Robert Davis in the name parts. Harry Wayne was the father and Dean Mundy the mother, Ruth Kobart sang the Witch, and Nancy Kendal the Sandman. Sam Morgenstern was conductor and Joan Slessinger and Bertha Melnik were the pianists. The opera was repeated in April, 1948, when William Diehl sang Hansel and Carol Donn, Gretel.

NEW STAGES PLAYHOUSE

"Lamp at Midnight," a play about Galileo by Barrie Stavis, with incidental music by Andre Singer, was produced by New Stages, Inc., at the New Stages Theatre on Bleecker Street from December 21 until February 1. Norman Rose and David Heilweil were managing directors of this group of 75 actors, who also were stockholders in enterprise. The play was directed by Boris Tumarin; settings by Robert Gundlach. In the cast were Peter Capell, Kathryn Eames, Leon Janney, Paul Mann, Kermit Murdock, Ralph Camargo, Karl Weber and Eugene Paul. There were 48 performances.

New Stages presented "An Evening of Two Plays" at its Playhouse commencing February 9. There were two weeks each of "Church Street" by Lennox Robinson and "The Respectful Prostitute" by Jean-Paul Sartre, and "The Respectful Prostitute" with "Happy Journey" by Thornton Wilder. The productions were staged by John O'Shaughnessy and supervised by Norman Rose and David Heilweil; settings were by Robert Gundlach; costumes by Dorothy Croissant. "The Respectful Prostitute," with Thornton Wilder's "The Happy Journey" as a curtain raiser, were later presented at the Cort Theatre on Broadway.

"To Tell You the Truth," by Eva Wolas, was presented by New Stages April 18, 1948. Music was composed and arranged by George Karlin. The cast included Anthony Randall, Raymond Edward Johnson, Judy Somerside and Jean Gillespie. The comedy, in three acts, was staged by Ezra Stone, the setting was designed by Ralph Alswang and the production was supervised by Norman Rose and David Heilweil. There were 15 performances.

"A House Possessed," a psychological drama in three acts by William and Karlton Kelm, staged by Edward R. Mitchell, opened the 1947-48 season at the Henry Street Settlement Playhouse and played from November 21 through November 30. In the cast were Patricia Beaudry, Ruth Lilienthal, Lucia Baker, Iris March, Edwin Rawce, Keene Curtis, Norma Sverd, Richard Hawkins and Betty Morrissey. The second production was a revival of "Wings over Europe," by Robert Nichols and Maurice Browne. It had seven performances between January 29 and February 8, 1948. "The Third Floor Back," by Jerome K. Jerome, with Margaret Perry directing, was played from February 26 to March 8 (8 performances). The Associated Playwrights, Inc., opened their Spring season under the management of Edward R. Mitchell March 25 with "The Golden Falcon," by Daniel Rudsten. The play continued until April 4. "My Sister Eileen," by Joseph Fields and Jerome Chodorov, was revived April 26 and played through May 2. "g-II" by Edmund B. Hennefeld opened May 27. The play was staged and settings were designed by Edward R. Mitchell; costumes by Charles Queenan; choreography by Pearl Primus. The cast included Ruth Lilienthal, Jeanette Cliff, Herman Freedman, Jennie Breines, Ken Sutton and Henry Hart. Scheduled for eight performances, it was given discouraging notices by the few uptown reviewers who ventured to see it.

The Blackfriars' Guild staged three plays at Blackfriars' Theatre, during the 1947-48 season, with 87 performances in all. "Hoboes in Heaven," a drama in three acts by G. M. Martens and Andre Obey, with music by Claude Arrieu, opened October 23 and ran for 26 performances. "Trial by Fire," a play (with no intermission) by George H. Dunne, S.J., was presented December 4, 1947 and ran until December 21 with 20 performances. It was staged by Albert McCleery; settings by William Riva and lighting by Rebecca Jennings. This was a social problem play in documentary dramatization of a famous case in California, when race discrimination resulted in an explosion in a house and the burning of four members of a family. "Lady of Fatima," a play in two acts by Urban Nagle, O.P., was staged by Dennis Gurney with setting and lighting by David Reppa and costumes by Irene Griffin. It was presented February 12, 1948, and closed April 25 after 41 performances.

AMERICAN NEGRO THEATRE

The American Negro Theatre, Inc., presented "Rain" a drama in three acts by John Colton and Clemence Randolph, based on a novelette by Somerset Maugham, in a revival which opened its 1947-48 season December 26, 1947, at the A.N.T. Playhouse in Harlem. The revival was staged by Ted Post and continued for 28 performances. "Sojourner Truth," a play in three acts by Katherine Garrison Chapin, opened April 23. Muriel Smith played the leading role. The play was directed by Osceola Archer; settings by Richard Bernstein; lighting by George Lewis; costumes by Willanna Cephas; choreography by Gertrude Shurr; choral arrangements and direction by Joshua Lee; technical direction by Richard Brown.

COLLEGES

The Fordham University Drama Festival opened August 1, 1947, with "Aaron Slick from Punkin Crick" and was followed August 8 with "The Devil to Pay," by Dorothy L. Sayers; directed by Albert McCleery; settings by William Riva. Among the players were Charles Mattingly as Faustus, Charles Metten as Mephistopheles and Paul Friedman as Wagner. Eugene O'Neill's "Lazarus Laughed" was produced April 8, 1948. The play was directed by Albert McCleery, with settings by William Riva, costumes and masks by Florence Lamont, choral direction by Edgar Kloten, choreography by Jean Sullivan and supervising by Frank Ford. The musical score was by Chris Kiernan. John Dugan took the part of Lazarus.

The Hasty Pudding Club of Harvard University presented its 100th annual production, "Here's the Pitch," at the City Center December 19 and 20. (See City Center elsewhere in this book.) Princeton University Triangle Club gave one performance of "All Rights Reserved" December 18, 1947. This musical comedy in two acts was written by Clifford W. Hankin, Edward H. Tuck, Thomas J. King and E. E. Norris, Jr. Music and lyrics were by John C. Leonard, Alexander L. Taggart, 3rd. Edward H. Tuck, W. Hamlin Neely, Jr., Eugene L. Goldberg, M. Donald MacInnis, John B. Lovelace, Jr., Harold C. Buckminster, Walter Clemons, Thomas J. King, Robert M. Barron,

Charles Sack and the orchestrations were by Sanders Maxwell. Robert H. Chapman was director, Patricia Norris dance director, Arthur Dorfner music director and the settings were by Maxwell G. Mayo. This was the 56th annual offering of the Triangle Club.

Columbia University's 54th annual varsity show was presented at McMillin Academic Theatre April 27, 1948. The play was "The Streets of New York." "Evangeline," an opera in three acts based on Longfellow's poem with text and music by Otto Luening, was given its first public performance May 5, 1948, by the Columbia Theatre Association in co-operation with the Columbia Department of Music at Brander Matthews Hall. "Murder in the Cathedral," by T. S. Eliot, was presented by Columbia University Players February 26, 27 and 28 at St. Paul Chapel.

Christopher Marlowe's "Edward II" was given by the Theatre Workshop of the New York City College at the Pauline Edward Theatre, April 30 and May 1. "Saint Joan" by Bernard Shaw was presented by Wigs and Cues, dramatic society of Barnard College in Brinckerhoff Theatre, December 5 and 6, 1947. The play was directed by Donald Richardson. The principals in the cast include Margaret McCay, Patricia Cowan, Sara Sue Lewis, Carol Reynolds, Victoria Thomson and Lynn Bellamy. Ann Ford was stage manager.

SOLO SHOWS

Helen Waren gave a one-woman show at the Plymouth Theatre November 2, 1947, which consisted of a series of monologues based on biblical legends. Called "Immortal Seed," it was presented under the auspices of Zionist Organization of America. Music was by Caesar Finn, lighting by Ralph Alswang and costumes by Eleanor Goldschmidt. The monologues were presented at the Barbizon Playhouse February 24, 25 and 26.

Francis Renault, female impersonator, gave programs Saturday and Sunday evenings in November at the Carnegie Chamber Music Hall, assisted by Sheila Barrett, Fred Keating, the Watson Sisters and Evelyn Nesbit.

Raymond Duncan presented a three-act solo drama, "My Life Is Yours," at Town Hall, February 17.

Eva Lorraine and Ted Montague appeared in a program of famous scenes from famous plays February 18 at Carnegie Recital Hall. There were excerpts from "Waterloo Bridge,"

"The White Steed," "Honeymoon," "Camille," etc., with improvisations.

Del Monte, magician and hypnotist, presented "Magic and Hypnotism" at Barbizon-Plaza Concert Hall, April 16.

Deborah Bertonoff, mime and comedy dancer, made her debut May 23 at the Cort Theatre in a recital with Carl Mosbacher as pianist. Her solo program consisted of dance mimes and pantomimes. Costumes were designed by Sebba of Tel Aviv.

CHILDREN'S THEATRE

The Children's World Theatre, Inc., consisting of Bette Butterworth, Jo Ann Sayers, Julie Thompson, Sheldon Thompson, Monte Meacham and Charlotte B. Chorpenning, produced a series of plays for children at the Barbizon-Plaza Theatre during the season of 1947-48. "Jack and the Beanstalk" opened November 8 and closed December 7. The play was directed by Monte Meacham, with Julie Thompson as associate director and Sheldon Thompson designed the sets. It was Charlotte Chorpenning's adaptation, was in three acts, ran for an hour and a half and had fourteen roles. The second production was "Many Moons," dramatized from James Thurber's fairy story by Charlotte Chorpenning, and was presented from December 13 to January 4. "Little Red Riding Hood," a play in three acts with settings by Herald Perry, opened January 12 and closed March 7, with week-end schedules. "Rumpelstiltskin," in three acts, was played from March 14 until April 25. Adaptations from the originals were all made by Charlotte Chorpenning.

"Robin Hood of Sherwood Forest" was produced at the Pauline Edwards Theatre by the Children's Drama Guild, November 28 and 29.

"This Is Our Play," a modern version of "Hansel and Gretel" with a cast of children, was presented at the Master Institute Theatre, April 30.

"Tom Sawyer-Ballad of Mississippi" was played at the Engineering Societies Theatre on Christmas. The performance was sponsored by the Walt Whitman School's Theatre Arts program. The entertainment was based on Paul Kester's stage version. The lyrics were by Alfred Kreymborg and the music by Sam Morgenstern. The entertainment was supervised by Maria Ley-Piscator.

"The Rose and the Ring" was presented by King-Coit Children's Theatre for six performances at the Cosmopolitan Club from May 12 to May 15.

Suzari's Marionette troupe gave "Aladdin and His Wonderful Lamp" in Carnegie Hall Chamber Theatre, March 25.

The Yiddish Theatre

By Jeannette Wilken

The 1947-48 Yiddish season opened at the Downtown National Theatre on August 29, 1947, with the condensation of Ben Hecht's "A Flag Is Born," starring Celia Adler. Another highlight of the year at the National was the return of Jennie Goldstein, after a retirement of five years, to play in "Grandma's Sweetheart," "Tseril Mirel from Galicia," "Schwartze Mama" and "Her Great Secret." Such players as Moishe Oysher, Lillian Lux, Paul Burstein, Irving Jacobson, Mae Schoenfeld, Mollie Picon, Herman Yablokoff, Leo Fuchs, Edmund Zayenda, Sylvia Grayson and Dina Halpern appeared in a varied series of musicals, dramas, operettas and comedies, including "Moishe's Wedding," "Tzipke Fire," "Shepsel Schlemiel," "Yankele," "Street Singer," "Molly Dolly," "The Galician Wedding," "Schmendrick," "The Lucky Fool," "The Yeshiva Bucher," "Children Without a Home," "Stronger Than Love," "Children Come Home," "David and Esther," "A Wedding in Town," "The Cantor's Melody," and "The Golden Bride."

Maurice Schwartz' Yiddish Art Theatre presented just one new play during the season, but that was the memorable "Shylock's Daughter," adapted from the novel by Ari Ibn-Zahav. Schwartz, who staged the drama, acted the leading role and was supported by a company which included Isidore Casher, Dina Halpern, Charlotte Goldstein, Edmund Zayenda, Muni Serebrov and Gustave Berger. The musical director was Joseph Rumshinsky. The play ran 147 performances before going off on an extended road tour.

The Second Avenue Theatre had two new shows, both starring Menasha Skulnik. "Just My Luck," by Abe Ellstein, opened September 24 and ran 114 performances, and "The Big Shot" by William Siegel started January 16 and had a run of 67 performances. In both musical comedies Skulnik was surrounded by his usual company, which includes Yetta Zwerling, Lilly Lilliana, Leon Liebgold, Anne Winters and Moses Feder.

The Parkway Theatre started its season September 24th in customary fashion with a musical comedy. Louis Frieman's

"A Little Mazel" starring Leo Fuchs, with music by Yasha Kreitzberg and Jacob Jacobs, and staging by Nathan Goldberg. The cast included Betty and Jacob Jacobs, Nathan adn Rose Goldberg, Hannah Hollander, Leon Seidenberg, Rebecca Richman and a teenage chorus. On December 12, "When Hearts Are Young," a new play by Rose Shoshona, started its run. The stars were Miriam Kressyn and Gregor Shelkan, and the music was by Sholem Secunda. The third play at this theatre was a Yiddish translation by Isidore Lash of Philip Yordan's "Anna Lucasta," starring Miriam Kressyn and Ben Zion Wittler.

The Downtown Clinton had a variety of shows during the season, many of them with music and most of them starring Vera Rosanko. Some of the plays presented here were: "The Wedding Gown," "The Matinee Wife," "The Jewess," "Love Only Me," "The Golem," "The Sacrifice of Isaac," "The Soul of My People," "The Cantor's Wife" and "Bar Kochba." Other players featured during the season were Aaron Lebedeff, Menachem Rubin, Israel Rosenberg, Michel Michelesko and Perele Feig.

A couple of off-the-beaten-track plays presented during the past season were "Judith" by Friederich Hebbel, adapted and directed by David Licht and presented by the "Folksbihne" at the Stanton Street Settlement, and "Sword by His Side," a play by Max Zweig, shown at Carnegie Hall, starring Miriam Goldina and Jonathan Harris.

Hebrew Theatre

Theatre, Incorporated and the American Fund for Palestinian Institutions sponsored the appearance in New York of Habimah, a Hebrew-speaking troupe from Palestine, which presented six weeks of repertory. The group arrived on May 1 after an adventurous journey and appeared first in S. Ansky's "The Dybbuk." On successive Saturdays at the Broadway Theatre, they introduced their productions of "David's Crown" by Calderon de la Barca, H. Levik's "The Golem," and "Oedipus Rex," Sophocles by way of Saul Chernikhovsky.

The group runs on a co-operative basis, but despite its claim that there are no stars in the outfit, it became increasingly evident that the chief roles invariably fell to Aaron Meskin, Hanna Rovina and Shimon Finkel. Habimah reserved the final two weeks of its run for its two most popular plays. These turned out to be "The Dybbuk," and "The Golem."

STATISTICAL SUMMARY

Plays	Number Performances	
A Young Man's Fancy..	335	(Closed February 14, 1948)
Alice in Wonderland...	100	(Closed June 28, 1947)
All My Sons..........	328	(Closed November 8, 1947)
Barefoot Boy with Cheek	108	(Closed July 5, 1947)
Burlesque	439	(Closed January 10, 1948)
Call Me Mister........	734	(Closed January 10, 1948)
Happy Birthday.......	564	(Closed March 13, 1948)
Icetime of 1948.......	422	(Closed April 3, 1948)
John Loves Mary......	423	(Closed February 7, 1948)
Life with Father.......	3,216	(Closed July 12, 1947)
Love for Love........	48	(Closed July 5, 1947)
Oklahoma!	2,248	(Closed May 29, 1948)
Portrait in Black......	62	(Closed July 5, 1947)
State of the Union.....	765	(Closed September 13, 1947)
Sweethearts	288	(Closed September 27, 1947)
The Telephone and the Medium	212	(Closed November 1, 1947)
The Voice of the Turtle	1,557	(Closed January 3, 1948)
The Whole World Over	100	(Closed June 21, 1947)

LONG RUNS ON BROADWAY

To June 1, 1948

(Plays marked with asterisk were still playing June 1, 1948)

Plays	Number Performances	Plays	Number Performances
Life with Father	3,216	Call Me Mister	734
Tobacco Road	3,182	Claudia	722
Abie's Irish Rose	2,327	I Remember Mama	714
Oklahoma!	2,248	Junior Miss	710
The Voice of the Turtle	1,557	Seventh Heaven	704
*Harvey	1,517	Peg o' My Heart	692
Arsenic and Old Lace	1,444	The Children's Hour	691
Hellzapoppin	1,404	Dead End	687
Angel Street	1,295	Dear Ruth	683
Lightnin'	1,291	East Is West	680
Pins and Needles	1,108	Chauve Souris	673
*Born Yesterday	979	The Doughgirls	671
Anna Lucasta	957	Irene	670
Kiss and Tell	956	Boy Meets Girl	669
Carousel	890	Blithe Spirit	657
Hats Off to Ice	889	The Women	657
Follow the Girls	882	A Trip to Chinatown	657
The Bat	867	Bloomer Girl	654
My Sister Eileen	865	Rain	648
White Cargo	864	Janie	642
Song of Norway	860	The Green Pastures	640
*Annie Get Your Gun	855	Is Zat So?	618
You Can't Take It with You	837	Separate Rooms	613
Three Men on a Horse	835	Star and Garter	609
Stars on Ice	830	Student Prince	608
The Ladder	789	Broadway	603
State of the Union	765	Adonis	603
The First Year	760	Street Scene	601
Sons o' Fun	742	Kiki	600
The Man Who Came to Dinner	739	Blossom Time	592
		The Two Mrs. Carrolls	585
		*Finian's Rainbow	582

434

Plays	Number Performances	Plays	Number Performances
Brother Rat	577	Rosalinda	521
Show Boat	572	Blackbirds	518
The Show-Off	571	Sunny	517
Sally	570	Victoria Regina	517
One Touch of Venus	567	The Vagabond King	511
Happy Birthday	564	*Brigadoon	509
Rose Marie	557	The New Moon	509
Strictly Dishonorable	557	Shuffle Along	504
Ziegfeld Follies	553	Up in Central Park	504
Good News	551	Carmen Jones	503
Let's Face It	547	Personal Appearance	501
Within the Law	541	Panama Hattie	501
The Music Master	540	Bird in Hand	500
What a Life	538	Sailor, Beware!	500
The Red Mill	531	Room Service	500
The Boomerang	522	Tomorrow the World	500

NEW YORK DRAMA CRITICS' CIRCLE AWARD

Each year the members of the New York Drama Critics' Circle have sought to simplify the voting on their Best Play citation, until, last season, they reached the ultimate in efficiency. At their Spring meeting the members sat down and, without discussion or ado, signed individual ballots. This was all there was to it, for the play with the most votes would get the prize (which was an invitation to a cocktail party). In case of a tie, there would have been two citations.

But there was no tie. Tennessee Williams' "A Streetcar Named Desire" was an overwhelming victor with seventeen votes. Reviewers who cast their ballots for other attractions did so as follows: "Command Decision," by William Wister Haines, got one vote; "Mister Roberts," by Thomas Heggen and Joshua Logan, got two; Robinson Jeffers' treatment of "Medea" got one vote.

At the beginning of last season Brooks Atkinson and George Jean Nathan sparked a resolution to amend the Critics' Circle rules so that the award might be given to any drama the majority considered best, either foreign or American. After long deliberation the aisle-sitting first-nighters voted the resolution down. I felt, and still do, that this insistence on giving the prize to an American play should be abandoned. I argued (a) that the Pulitzer Prize rightly was confined to native drama, but that (b) drama is drama, no matter where it is found, and if a superior foreign play should appear, its superiority should be recognized. Certainly, the reviewers make no nationalistic distinctions when they write their criticisms and articles. I was, furthermore, smugly confident that it was unlikely that any foreign drama would appear to overmatch American contenders. At the end of the season I was convinced I had been right all down the line.

The Critics' Circle therefore voted a citation as best foreign play to Terence Rattigan's "The Winslow Boy." Other contenders which received votes were "The Respectful Prostitute," by Jean-Paul Sartre; Denis Johnston's "The Old Lady Says 'No!' "; Micheal Mac Liammoir's "Where Stars Walk" and Bertold Brecht's "Galileo."

No citation was given to a "best" musical.

Previous Circle awards have been—

1935-36—Winterset, by Maxwell Anderson
1936-37—High Tor, by Maxwell Anderson
1937-38—Of Mice and Men, by John Steinbeck
1938-39—No award.
1939-40—The Time of Your Life, by William Saroyan
1940-41—Watch on the Rhine, by Lillian Hellman
1941-42—No award.
1942-43—The Patriots, by Sidney Kingsley
1943-44—No award.
1944-45—The Glass Menagerie, by Tennessee Williams
1945-46—No award.
1946-47—All My Sons, by Arthur Miller
1947-48—A Streetcar Named Desire, by Tennessee Williams

PULITZER PRIZE WINNERS

For the second time since the formation of the New York Drama Critics' Circle, the play committee in charge of the Pulitzer Prize agreed with the Critics in naming Tennessee Williams' "A Streetcar Named Desire." Many of those who indulged in the pastime of mind-betting after the Critics' award was announced felt that this would be the case, as it had been in 1939-40 with William Saroyan's "The Time of Your Life." Others were willing to guess that the Pulitzer citation and $500 would go to William Wister Haines for "Command Decision," and still others felt that the enormously successful "Mister Roberts" would bring 250 scarcely needed dollars each to Thomas Heggen and Joshua Logan.

The Critics' Circle was, I believe, pleased if not flattered that once more the Pulitzer Prize committee had concurred in the reviewers' judgment.

Pulitzer Prize selections to date have been—

1917-18—Why Marry?, by Jesse Lynch Williams
1918-19—No award.
1919-20—Beyond the Horizon, by Eugene O'Neill
1920-21—Miss Lulu Bett, by Zona Gale
1921-22—Anna Christie, by Eugene O'Neill
1922-23—Icebound, by Owen Davis
1923-24—Hell-bent fer Heaven, by Hatcher Hughes
1924-25—They Knew What They Wanted, by Sidney Howard
1925-26—Craig's Wife, by George Kelly
1926-27—In Abraham's Bosom, by Paul Green
1927-28—Strange Interlude, by Eugene O'Neill
1928-29—Street Scene, by Elmer Rice
1929-30—The Green Pastures, by Marc Connelly
1930-31—Alison's House, by Susan Glaspell
1931-32—Of Thee I Sing, by George S. Kaufman, Morrie Ryskind, Ira and George Gershwin
1932-33—Both Your Houses, by Maxwell Anderson
1933-34—Men in White, by Sidney Kingsley
1934-35—The Old Maid, by Zoe Akins
1935-36—Idiot's Delight, by Robert E. Sherwood

1936-37—You Can't Take It with You, by Moss Hart and
          George S. Kaufman
1937-38—Our Town, by Thornton Wilder
1938-39—Abe Lincoln in Illinois, by Robert E. Sherwood
1939-40—The Time of Your Life, by William Saroyan
1940-41—There Shall Be No Night, by Robert E. Sherwood
1941-42—No award.
1942-43—The Skin of Our Teeth, by Thornton Wilder
1943-44—No award.
1944-45—Harvey, by Mary Coyle Chase
1945-46—State of the Union, by Howard Lindsay and Russel
          Crouse
1946-47—No award.
1947-48—A Streetcar Named Desire, by Tennessee Williams

PREVIOUS VOLUMES OF BEST PLAYS

Plays chosen to represent the theatre seasons from 1899 to 1947 are as follows:

1899-1909

"Barbara Frietchie," by Clyde Fitch. Published by Life Publishing Company, New York.

"The Climbers," by Clyde Fitch. Published by the Macmillan Co., New York.

"If I Were King," by Justin Huntly McCarthy. Published by Samuel French, New York and London.

"The Darling of the Gods," by David Belasco. Published by Little, Brown & Co., Boston, Mass.

"The County Chairman," by George Ade. Published by Samuel French, New York and London.

"Leah Kleschna," by C. M. S. McLellan. Published by Samuel French, New York.

"The Squaw Man," by Edwin Milton Royle.

"The Great Divide," by William Vaughn Moody. Published by Samuel French, New York, London and Canada.

"The Witching Hour," by Augustus Thomas. Published by Samuel French, New York and London.

"The Man from Home," by Booth Tarkington and Harry Leon Wilson. Published by Samuel French, New York, London and Canada.

1909-1919

"The Easiest Way," by Eugene Walter. Published by G. W. Dillingham, New York; Houghton Mifflin Co., Boston.

"Mrs. Bumpstead-Leigh," by Harry James Smith. Published by Samuel French, New York.

"Disraeli," by Louis N. Parker. Published by Dodd, Mead and Co., New York.

"Romance," by Edward Sheldon. Published by the Macmillan Co., New York.

"Seven Keys to Baldpate," by George M. Cohan. Published by Bobbs-Merrill Co., Indianapolis, as a novel by Earl Derr Biggers; as a play by Samuel French, New York.

"On Trial," by Elmer Reizenstein. Published by Samuel French, New York.

"The Unchastened Woman," by Louis Kaufman Anspacher. Published by Harcourt, Brace and Howe, Inc., New York.

"Good Gracious Annabelle," by Clare Kummer. Published by Samuel French, New York.

"Why Marry?" by Jesse Lynch Williams. Published by Charles Scribner's Sons, New York.

"John Ferguson," by St. John Ervine. Published by the Macmillan Co., New York.

1919-1920

"Abraham Lincoln," by John Drinkwater. Published by Houghton Mifflin Co., Boston.

"Clarence," by Booth Tarkington. Published by Samuel French, New York.

"Beyond the Horizon," by Eugene G. O'Neill. Published by Boni & Liveright, Inc., New York.

"Déclassée," by Zoe Akins. Published by Liveright, Inc., New York.

"The Famous Mrs. Fair," by James Forbes. Published by Samuel French, New York.

"The Jest," by Sem Benelli. (American adaptation by Edward Sheldon.)

"Jane Clegg," by St. John Ervine. Published by Henry Holt & Co., New York.

"Mamma's Affair," by Rachel Barton Butler. Published by Samuel French, New York.

"Wedding Bells," by Salisbury Field. Published by Samuel French, New York.

"Adam and Eva," by George Middleton and Guy Bolton. Published by Samuel French, New York.

1920-1921

"Deburau," adapted from the French of Sacha Guitry by H. Granville Barker. Published by G. P. Putnam's Sons, New York.

"The First Year," by Frank Craven. Published by Samuel French, New York.

"Enter Madame," by Gilda Varesi and Dolly Byrne. Published by G. P. Putnam's Sons, New York.

"The Green Goddess," by William Archer. Published by Alfred A. Knopf, New York.

"Liliom," by Ferenc Molnar. Published by Boni & Liveright, New York.

"Mary Rose," by James M. Barrie. Published by Charles Scribner's Sons, New York.

"Nice People," by Rachel Crothers. Published by Charles Scribner's Sons, New York.

"The Bad Man," by Porter Emerson Browne. Published by G. P. Putnam's Sons, New York.

"The Emperor Jones," by Eugene G. O'Neill. Published by Boni & Liveright, New York.

"The Skin Game," by John Galsworthy. Published by Charles Scribner's Sons, New York.

1921-1922

"Anna Christie," by Eugene G. O'Neill. Published by Boni & Liveright, New York.

"A Bill of Divorcement," by Clemence Dane. Published by the Macmillan Company, New York.

"Dulcy," by George S. Kaufman and Marc Connelly. Published by G. P. Putnam's Sons, New York.

"He Who Gets Slapped," adapted from the Russian of Leonid Andreyev by Gregory Zilboorg. Published by Brentano's, New York.

"Six Cylinder Love," by William Anthony McGuire.

"The Hero," by Gilbert Emery.

"The Dover Road," by Alan Alexander Milne. Published by Samuel French, New York.

"Ambush," by Arthur Richman.

"The Circle," by William Somerset Maugham.

"The Nest," by Paul Geraldy and Grace George.

1922-1923

"Rain," by John Colton and Clemence Randolph. Published by Liveright, Inc., New York.

"Loyalties," by John Galsworthy. Published by Charles Scribner's Sons, New York.

"Icebound," by Owen Davis. Published by Little, Brown & Company, Boston.

"You and I," by Philip Barry. Published by Brentano's, New York.

"The Fool," by Channing Pollock. Published by Brentano's, New York.

"Merton of the Movies," by George Kaufman and Marc Connelly, based on the novel of the same name by Harry Leon Wilson.

"Why Not?" by Jesse Lynch Williams. Published by Walter H. Baker Co., Boston.

"The Old Soak," by Don Marquis. Published by Doubleday, Page & Company, New York.

"R.U.R.," by Karel Capek. Translated by Paul Selver. Published by Doubleday, Page & Company.

"Mary the 3d," by Rachel Crothers. Published by Brentano's, New York.

1923-1924

"The Swan," translated from the Hungarian of Ferenc Molnar by Melville Baker. Published by Boni & Liveright, New York.

"Outward Bound," by Sutton Vane. Published by Boni & Liveright, New York.

"The Show-Off," by George Kelly. Published by Little, Brown & Company, Boston.

"The Changelings," by Lee Wilson Dodd. Published by E. P. Dutton & Company, New York.

"Chicken Feed," by Guy Bolton. Published by Samuel French, New York and London.

"Sun-Up," by Lula Vollmer. Published by Brentano's, New York.

"Beggar on Horseback," by George Kaufman and Marc Connelly. Published by Boni & Liveright, New York.

"Tarnish," by Gilbert Emery. Published by Brentano's, New York.

"The Goose Hangs High," by Lewis Beach. Published by Little, Brown & Company, Boston.

"Hell-bent fer Heaven," by Hatcher Hughes. Published by Harper Bros., New York.

1924-1925

"What Price Glory?" by Laurence Stallings and Maxwell Anderson. Published by Harcourt, Brace & Co., New York.

"They Knew What They Wanted," by Sidney Howard. Published by Doubleday, Page & Company, New York.

"Desire Under the Elms," by Eugene G. O'Neill. Published by Boni & Liveright, New York.

"The Firebrand," by Edwin Justus Mayer. Published by Boni & Liveright, New York.

"Dancing Mothers," by Edgar Selwyn and Edmund Goulding.

"Mrs. Partridge Presents," by Mary Kennedy and Ruth Warren. Published by Samuel French, New York.

"The Fall Guy," by James Gleason and George Abbott. Published by Samuel French, New York.

"The Youngest," by Philip Barry. Published by Samuel French, New York.

"Minick," by Edna Ferber and George S. Kaufman. Published by Doubleday, Page & Company, New York.

"Wild Birds," by Dan Totheroh. Published by Doubleday, Page & Company, New York.

1925-1926

"Craig's Wife," by George Kelly. Published by Little, Brown & Company, Boston.

"The Great God Brown," by Eugene G. O'Neill. Published by Boni & Liveright, New York.

"The Green Hat," by Michael Arlen.

"The Dybbuk," by S. Ansky, Henry G. Alsberg-Winifred Katzin translation. Published by Boni & Liveright, New York.

"The Enemy," by Channing Pollock. Published by Brentano's, New York.

"The Last of Mrs. Cheyney," by Frederick Lonsdale. Published by Samuel French, New York.

"Bride of the Lamb," by William Hurlbut. Published by Boni & Liveright, New York.

"The Wisdom Tooth," by Marc Connelly. Published by George H. Doran & Company, New York.

"The Butter and Egg Man," by George Kaufman. Published by Boni & Liveright, New York.

"Young Woodley," by John Van Druten. Published by Simon and Schuster, New York.

1926-1927

"Broadway," by Philip Dunning and George Abbott. Published by George H. Doran Company, New York.

"Saturday's Children," by Maxwell Anderson. Published by Longmans, Green & Company, New York.

"Chicago," by Maurine Watkins. Published by Alfred A. Knopf, Inc., New York.

"The Constant Wife," by William Somerset Maugham. Published by George H. Doran Company, New York.

"The Play's the Thing," by Ferenc Molnar and P. G. Wodehouse. Published by Brentano's, New York.

"The Road to Rome," by Robert Emmet Sherwood. Published by Charles Scribner's Sons, New York.

"The Silver Cord," by Sidney Howard. Published by Charles Scribner's Sons, New York.

"The Cradle Song," translated from the Spanish of G. Martinez Sierra by John Garrett Underhill. Published by E. P. Dutton & Company, New York.

"Daisy Mayme," by George Kelly. Published by Little, Brown & Company, Boston.

"In Abraham's Bosom," by Paul Green. Published by Robert M. McBride & Company, New York.

1927-1928

"Strange Interlude," by Eugene G. O'Neill. Published by Boni & Liveright, New York.

"The Royal Family," by Edna Ferber and George Kaufman. Published by Doubleday, Doran & Company, New York.

"Burlesque," by George Manker Watters and Arthur Hopkins. Published by Doubleday, Doran & Company, New York.

"Coquette," by George Abbott and Ann Bridgers. Published by Longmans, Green & Company, New York, London, Toronto.

"Behold the Bridegroom," by George Kelly. Published by Little, Brown & Company, Boston.

"Porgy," by DuBose Heyward. Published by Doubleday, Doran & Company, New York.

"Paris Bound," by Philip Barry. Published by Samuel French, New York.

"Escape," by John Galsworthy. Published by Charles Scribner's Sons, New York.

"The Racket," by Bartlett Cormack. Published by Samuel French, New York.

"The Plough and the Stars," by Sean O'Casey. Published by the Macmillan Company, New York.

1928-1929

"Street Scene," by Elmer Rice. Published by Samuel French, New York.

"Journey's End," by R. C. Sherriff. Published by Brentano's, New York.

"Wings Over Europe," by Robert Nichols and Maurice Browne. Published by Covici-Friede, New York.

"Holiday," by Philip Barry. Published by Samuel French, New York.

"The Front Page," by Ben Hecht and Charles MacArthur. Published by Covici-Friede, New York.

"Let Us Be Gay," by Rachel Crothers. Published by Samuel French, New York.

"Machinal," by Sophie Treadwell.

"Little Accident," by Floyd Dell and Thomas Mitchell.

"Gypsy," by Maxwell Anderson.

"The Kingdom of God," by G. Martinez Sierra; English version by Helen and Harley Granville-Barker. Published by E. P. Dutton & Company, New York.

1929-1930

"The Green Pastures," by Marc Connelly (adapted from "Ol' Man Adam and His Chillun," by Roark Bradford). Published by Farrar & Rinehart, Inc., New York.

"The Criminal Code," by Martin Flavin. Published by Horace Liveright, New York.

"Berkeley Square," by John Balderston. Published by the Macmillan Company, New York.

"Strictly Dishonorable," by Preston Sturges. Published by Horace Liveright, New York.

"The First Mrs. Fraser," by St. John Ervine. Published by the Macmillan Company, New York.

"The Last Mile," by John Wexley. Published by Samuel French, New York.

"June Moon," by Ring W. Lardner and George S. Kaufman. Published by Charles Scribner's Sons, New York.

"Michael and Mary," by A. A. Milne. Published by Chatto & Windus, London.

"Death Takes a Holiday," by Walter Ferris (adapted from the Italian of Alberto Casella). Published by Samuel French, New York.

"Rebound," by Donald Ogden Stewart. Published by Samuel French, New York.

1930-1931

"Elizabeth the Queen," by Maxwell Anderson. Published by Longmans, Green & Co., New York.

"Tomorrow and Tomorrow," by Philip Barry. Published by Samuel French, New York.

"Once in a Lifetime," by George S. Kaufman and Moss Hart. Published by Farrar and Rinehart, New York.

"Green Grow the Lilacs," by Lynn Riggs. Published by Samuel French, New York and London.

"As Husbands Go," by Rachel Crothers. Published by Samuel French, New York.

"Alison's House," by Susan Glaspell. Published by Samuel French, New York.

"Five-Star Final," by Louis Weitzenkorn. Published by Samuel French, New York.

"Overture," by William Bolitho. Published by Simon & Schuster, New York.

"The Barretts of Wimpole Street," by Rudolf Besier. Published by Little, Brown & Company, Boston.

"Grand Hotel," adapted from the German of Vicki Baum by W. A. Drake.

1931-1932

"Of Thee I Sing," by George S. Kaufman and Morrie Ryskind; music and lyrics by George and Ira Gershwin. Published by Alfred Knopf, New York.

"Mourning Becomes Electra," by Eugene G. O'Neill. Published by Horace Liveright, Inc., New York.

"Reunion in Vienna," by Robert Emmet Sherwood. Published by Charles Scribner's Sons, New York.

"The House of Connelly," by Paul Green. Published by Samuel French, New York.

"The Animal Kingdom," by Philip Barry. Published by Samuel French, New York.

"The Left Bank," by Elmer Rice. Published by Samuel French, New York.

"Another Language," by Rose Franken. Published by Samuel French, New York.

"Brief Moment," by S. N. Behrman. Published by Farrar & Rinehart, New York.

"The Devil Passes," by Benn W. Levy. Published by Martin Secker, London.

"Cynara," by H. M. Harwood and R. F. Gore-Browne. Published by Samuel French, New York.

1932-1933

"Both Your Houses," by Maxwell Anderson. Published by Samuel French, New York.

"Dinner at Eight," by George S. Kaufman and Edna Ferber. Published by Doubleday, Doran & Co., Inc., Garden City, New York.

"When Ladies Meet," by Rachel Crothers. Published by Samuel French, New York.

"Design for Living," by Noel Coward. Published by Doubleday, Doran & Co., Inc., Garden City, New York.

"Biography," by S. N. Behrman. Published by Farrar & Rinehart, Inc., New York.

"Alien Corn," by Sidney Howard. Published by Charles Scribner's Sons, New York.

"The Late Christopher Bean," adapted from the French of René Fauchois by Sidney Howard. Published by Samuel French, New York.

"We, the People," by Elmer Rice. Published by Coward-McCann, Inc., New York.

"Pigeons and People," by George M. Cohan.

"One Sunday Afternoon," by James Hagan. Published by Samuel French, New York.

1933-1934

"Mary of Scotland," by Maxwell Anderson. Published by Doubleday, Doran & Co., Inc., Garden City, N. Y.

"Men in White," by Sidney Kingsley. Published by Covici, Friede, Inc., New York.

"Dodsworth," by Sinclair Lewis and Sidney Howard. Published by Harcourt, Brace & Co., New York.

"Ah, Wilderness," by Eugene O'Neill. Published by Random House, New York.

"They Shall Not Die," by John Wexley. Published by Alfred A. Knopf, New York.

"Her Master's Voice," by Clare Kummer. Published by Samuel French, New York.

"No More Ladies," by A. E. Thomas.

"Wednesday's Child," by Leopold Atlas. Published by Samuel French, New York.

"The Shining Hour," by Keith Winter. Published by Double-day, Doran & Co., Inc., Garden City, New York.

"The Green Bay Tree," by Mordaunt Shairp. Published by Baker International Play Bureau, Boston, Mass.

1934-1935

"The Children's Hour," by Lillian Hellman. Published by Alfred Knopf, New York.

"Valley Forge," by Maxwell Anderson. Published by Anderson House, Washington, D. C. Distributed by Dodd, Mead & Co., New York.

"The Petrified Forest," by Robert Sherwood. Published by Charles Scribner's Sons, New York.

"The Old Maid," by Zoe Akins. Published by D. Appleton-Century Co., New York.

"Accent on Youth," by Samson Raphaelson. Published by Samuel French, New York.

"Merrily We Roll Along," by George S. Kaufman and Moss Hart. Published by Random House, New York.

"Awake and Sing," by Clifford Odets. Published by Random House, New York.

"The Farmer Takes a Wife," by Frank B. Elser and Marc Connelly.

"Lost Horizons," by John Hayden.

"The Distaff Side," by John Van Druten. Published by Alfred Knopf, New York.

1935-1936

"Winterset," by Maxwell Anderson. Published by Anderson House, Washington, D. C.

"Idiot's Delight," by Robert Emmet Sherwood. Published by Charles Scribner's Sons, New York.

"End of Summer," by S. N. Behrman. Published by Random House, New York.

"First Lady," by Katharine Dayton and George S. Kaufman. Published by Random House, New York.

"Victoria Regina," by Laurence Housman. Published by Samuel French, Inc., New York and London.

"Boy Meets Girl," by Bella and Samuel Spewack. Published by Random House, New York.

"Dead End," by Sidney Kingsley. Published by Random House, New York.

"Call It a Day," by Dodie Smith. Published by Samuel French, Inc., New York and London.

"Ethan Frome," by Owen Davis and Donald Davis. Published by Charles Scribner's Sons, New York.

"Pride and Prejudice," by Helen Jerome. Published by Doubleday, Doran & Co., Garden City, New York.

1936-1937

"High Tor," by Maxwell Anderson. Published by Anderson House, Washington, D. C.

"You Can't Take It with You," by Moss Hart and George S. Kaufman. Published by Farrar & Rinehart, Inc., New York.

"Johnny Johnson," by Paul Green. Published by Samuel French, Inc., New York.

"Daughters of Atreus," by Robert Turney. Published by Alfred A. Knopf, New York.

"Stage Door," by Edna Ferber and George S. Kaufman. Published by Doubleday, Doran & Co., Garden City, New York.

"The Women," by Clare Boothe. Published by Random House, Inc., New York.

"St. Helena," by R. C. Sherriff and Jeanne de Casalis. Published by Samuel French, Inc., New York and London.

"Yes, My Darling Daughter," by Mark Reed. Published by Samuel French, Inc., New York.

"Excursion," by Victor Wolfson. Published by Random House, New York.

"Tovarich," by Jacques Deval and Robert E. Sherwood. Published by Random House, New York.

1937-1938

"Of Mice and Men," by John Steinbeck. Published by Covici-Friede, New York.

"Our Town," by Thornton Wilder. Published by Coward-McCann, Inc., New York.

"Shadow and Substance," by Paul Vincent Carroll. Published by Random House, Inc., New York.

"On Borrowed Time," by Paul Osborn. Published by Alfred A. Knopf, New York.

"The Star-Wagon," by Maxwell Anderson. Published by Anderson House, Washington, D. C. Distributed by Dodd, Mead & Co., New York.

"Susan and God," by Rachel Crothers. Published by Random House, Inc., New York.

"Prologue to Glory," by E. P. Conkle. Published by Random House, Inc., New York.

"Amphitryon 38," by S. N. Behrman. Published by Random House, Inc., New York.

"Golden Boy," by Clifford Odets. Published by Random House, Inc., New York.

"What a Life," by Clifford Goldsmith. Published by Dramatists' Play Service, Inc., New York.

1938-1939

"Abe Lincoln in Illinois," by Robert E. Sherwood. Published by Charles Scribner's Sons, New York and Charles Scribner's Sons, Ltd., London.

"The Little Foxes," by Lillian Hellman. Published by Random House, Inc., New York.

"Rocket to the Moon," by Clifford Odets. Published by Random House, Inc., New York.

"The American Way," by George S. Kaufman and Moss Hart. Published by Random House, Inc., New York.

"No Time for Comedy," by S. N. Behrman. Published by Random House, Inc., New York.

"The Philadelphia Story," by Philip Barry. Published by Coward-McCann, Inc., New York.

"The White Steed," by Paul Vincent Carroll. Published by Random House, Inc., New York.

"Here Come the Clowns," by Philip Barry. Published by Coward-McCann, Inc., New York.

"Family Portrait," by Lenore Coffee and William Joyce Cowen. Published by Random House, Inc., New York.

"Kiss the Boys Good-bye," by Clare Boothe. Published by Random House, Inc., New York.

1939-1940

"There Shall Be No Night," by Robert E. Sherwood. Published by Charles Scribner's Sons, New York.

"Key Largo," by Maxwell Anderson. Published by Anderson House, Washington, D. C.

"The World We Make," by Sidney Kingsley.

"Life with Father," by Howard Lindsay and Russel Crouse. Published by Alfred A. Knopf, New York.

"The Man Who Came to Dinner," by George S. Kaufman and Moss Hart. Published by Random House, Inc., New York.

"The Male Animal," by James Thurber and Elliott Nugent. Published by Random House, Inc., New York, and MacMillan Co., Canada.

"The Time of Your Life," by William Saroyan. Published by Harcourt, Brace and Company, Inc., New York.

"Skylark," by Samson Raphaelson. Published by Random House, Inc., New York.

"Margin for Error," by Clare Boothe. Published by Random House, Inc., New York.

"Morning's at Seven," by Paul Osborn. Published by Samuel French, New York.

1940-1941

"Native Son," by Paul Green and Richard Wright. Published by Harper & Bros., New York.

"Watch on the Rhine," by Lillian Hellman. Published by Random House, Inc., New York.

"The Corn Is Green," by Emlyn Williams. Published by Random House, Inc., New York.

"Lady in the Dark," by Moss Hart. Published by Random House, Inc., New York.

"Arsenic and Old Lace," by Joseph Kesselring. Published by Random House, Inc., New York.

"My Sister Eileen," by Joseph Fields and Jerome Chodorov. Published by Random House, Inc., New York.

"Flight to the West," by Elmer Rice. Published by Coward, McCann, Inc., New York.

"Claudia," by Rose Franken Meloney. Published by Farrar & Rinehart, Inc., New York and Toronto.

"Mr. and Mrs. North," by Owen Davis. Published by Samuel French, New York.

"George Washington Slept Here," by George S. Kaufman and Moss Hart. Published by Random House, Inc., New York.

1941-1942

"In Time to Come," by Howard Koch. Published by Dramatists' Play Service, Inc., New York.

"The Moon Is Down," by John Steinbeck. Published by The Viking Press, New York.

"Blithe Spirit," by Noel Coward. Published by Doubleday, Doran & Co., Garden City, New York.

"Junior Miss," by Jerome Chodorov and Joseph Fields. Published by Random House, Inc., New York.

"Candle in the Wind," by Maxwell Anderson. Published by Anderson House, Washington, D. C.

"Letters to Lucerne," by Fritz Rotter and Allen Vincent. Published by Samuel French, Inc., New York.

"Jason," by Samson Raphaelson. Published by Random House, Inc., New York.

"Angel Street," by Patrick Hamilton. Published by Constable & Co., Ltd., London, under the title "Gaslight."

"Uncle Harry," by Thomas Job. Published by Samuel French, Inc., New York.

"Hope for a Harvest," by Sophie Treadwell. Published by Samuel French, Inc., New York.

1942-1943

"The Patriots," by Sidney Kingsley. Published by Random House, Inc., New York.

"The Eve of St. Mark," by Maxwell Anderson. Published by Anderson House, Washington, D. C.

"The Skin of Our Teeth," by Thornton Wilder. Published by Harper & Brothers, New York and London.

"Winter Soldiers," by Dan James.

"Tomorrow the World," by James Gow and Arnaud d'Usseau. Published by Charles Scribner's Sons, New York.

"Harriet," by Florence Ryerson and Colin Clements. Published by Charles Scribner's Sons, New York.

"The Doughgirls," by Joseph Fields. Published by Random House, Inc., New York.

"The Damask Cheek," by John Van Druten and Lloyd Morris. Published by Random House, Inc., New York.

"Kiss and Tell," by F. Hugh Herbert. Published by Coward-McCann, Inc., New York.

"Oklahoma!", by Oscar Hammerstein 2nd and Richard Rodgers. Published by Random House, Inc., New York.

1943-1944

"Winged Victory," by Moss Hart. Published by Random House, Inc., New York.

"The Searching Wind," by Lillian Hellman. Published by Viking Press, Inc., New York.

"The Voice of the Turtle," by John Van Druten. Published by Random House, Inc., New York.

"Decision," by Edward Chodorov.

"Over 21," by Ruth Gordon. Published by Random House, Inc., New York.

"Outrageous Fortune," by Rose Franken. Published by Samuel French, New York.

"Jacobowsky and the Colonel," by S. N. Behrman. Published by Random House, Inc., New York.

"Storm Operation," by Maxwell Anderson. Published by Anderson House, Washington, D. C.

"Pick-up Girl," by Elsa Shelley.

"The Innocent Voyage," by Paul Osborn.

1944-1945

"A Bell for Adano," by Paul Osborn. Published by Alfred A. Knopf, New York.

"I Remember Mama," by John Van Druten. Published by Harcourt, Brace and Co., Inc., New York.

"The Hasty Heart," by John Patrick. Published by Random House, Inc., New York.

"The Glass Menagerie," by Tennessee Williams. Published by Random House, Inc., New York.

"Harvey," by Mary Chase.

"The Late George Apley," by John P. Marquand and George S. Kaufman.

"Soldier's Wife," by Rose Franken. Published by Samuel French.

"Anna Lucasta," by Philip Yordan. Published by Random House, Inc., New York.

"Foolish Notion," by Philip Barry.

"Dear Ruth," by Norman Krasna. Published by Random House, Inc., New York.

1945-1946

"State of the Union," by Howard Lindsay and Russel Crouse. Published by Random House, Inc., New York.

"Home of the Brave," by Arthur Laurents. Published by Random House, Inc., New York.

"Deep Are the Roots," by Arnaud d'Usseau and James Gow. Published by Charles Scribner's Sons, New York.

"The Magnificent Yankee," by Emmet Lavery. Published by Samuel French, Inc., New York.

"Antigone," by Lewis Galantiere (from the French of Jean Anouilh). Published by Random House, Inc., New York.

"O Mistress Mine," by Terence Rattigan. Published and revised by the author.

"Born Yesterday," by Garson Kanin. Published by Viking Press, Inc., New York.

"Dream Girl," by Elmer Rice. Published by Coward-McCann, Inc., New York.

"The Rugged Path," by Robert E. Sherwood. Published by Charles Scribner's Sons, New York.

"Lute Song," by Will Irwin and Sidney Howard. Published version by Will Irwin and Leopoldine Howard.

1946-1947

"All My Sons," by Arthur Miller. Published by Reynal & Hitchcock, New York.

"The Iceman Cometh," by Eugene G. O'Neill. Published by Random House, Inc., New York.

"Joan of Lorraine," by Maxwell Anderson. Published by Maxwell Anderson; distributed by Dodd, Mead & Co., New York.

"Another Part of the Forest," by Lillian Hellman. Published by Viking Press, Inc., New York.

"Years Ago," by Ruth Gordon. Published by Viking Press, Inc., New York.

"John Loves Mary," by Norman Krasna. Copyright by Norman Krasna.

"The Fatal Weakness," by George Kelly. Published by Samuel French, Inc., New York and London.

"The Story of Mary Surratt," by John Patrick. Published by Dramatists' Play Service, Inc., New York.

"Christopher Blake," by Moss Hart. Published by Random House, Inc., New York.

"Brigadoon," by Alan Jay Lerner and Frederick Loewe. Published by Coward-McCann, Inc., New York.

WHERE AND WHEN THEY WERE BORN

(Compiled from the most authentic records available.)

Abbott, George	Hamburg, N. Y.	1895
Abel, Walter	St. Paul, Minn.	1898
Adams, Maude	Salt Lake City, Utah	1872
Addy, Wesley	Omaha, Neb.	1912
Adler, Luther	New York City	1903
Adler, Stella	New York City	1904
Aherne, Brian	King's Norton, England	1902
Anders, Glenn	Los Angeles, Cal.	1890
Anderson, Judith	Australia	1898
Anderson, Maxwell	Atlantic City, Pa.	1888
Andrews, A. G.	Buffalo, N. Y.	1861
Andrews, Ann	Los Angeles, Cal.	1895
Arden, Eve	San Francisco, Cal.	1912
Arling, Joyce	Memphis, Tenn.	1911
Arliss, George	London, England	1868
Astaire, Fred	Omaha, Neb.	1899
Bainter, Fay	Los Angeles, Cal.	1892
Bankhead, Tallulah	Huntsville, Ala.	1902
Barbee, Richard	Lafayette, Ind.	1887
Barry, Philip	Rochester, N. Y.	1896
Barrymore, Diana	New York City	1921
Barrymore, Ethel	Philadelphia, Pa.	1879
Barrymore, John	Philadelphia, Pa.	1882
Barrymore, Lionel	Philadelphia, Pa.	1878
Barton, James	Gloucester, N. J.	1890
Beecher, Janet	Jefferson City, Mo.	1887
Behrman, S. N.	Worcester, Mass.	1893
Bell, James	Suffolk, Va.	1891
Bellamy, Ralph	Chicago, Ill.	1905
Berghof, Herbert	Vienna, Austria	1909
Bergman, Ingrid	Stockholm	1917
Bergner, Elisabeth	Vienna	1901
Berlin, Irving	Russia	1888
Blackmer, Sydney	Salisbury, N. C.	1898
Bolger, Ray	Dorchester, Mass.	1906

456

Colt, John Drew ....New York 1914
Conroy, Frank ....London, England 1885
Cook, Donald ....Portland, Ore. 1902
Cooper, Gladys ....Lewisham, England 1888
Cooper, Melville ....Birmingham, England 1896
Cooper, Violet Kemble ....London, England 1890
Corbett, Leonora ....London, England 1908
Corey, Wendell ....Dracut, Mass. 1907
Cornell, Katharine ....Berlin, Germany 1898
Cossart, Ernest ....Cheltenham, England 1876
Coulouris, George ....Manchester, England 1906
Coward, Noel ....Teddington, England 1899
Cowl, Jane ....Boston, Mass. 1887
Crothers, Rachel ....Bloomington, Ill. 1878
Cummings, Constance ....Seattle, Wash. 1911

Dale, Margaret ....Philadelphia, Pa. 1880
Davis, Owen ....Portland, Me. 1874
Davis, Owen, Jr. ....New York 1910
Digges, Dudley ....Dublin, Ireland 1880
Douglas, Susan ....Prague, Czechoslovakia ...1925
Dowling, Eddie ....Woonsocket, R. I. 1895
Drake, Alfred ....New York City 1914
Dressler, Eric ....Brooklyn, N. Y. 1900
Duncan, Augustin ....San Francisco 1873
Dunning, Philip ....Meriden, Conn. 1890

Edney, Florence ....London, England 1879
Eggerth, Marta ....Budapest, Hungary 1915
Eldridge, Florence ....Brooklyn, N. Y. 1901
Evans, Edith ....London, England 1888
Evans, Maurice ....Dorchester, England 1901
Evans, Wilbur ....Philadelphia, Pa. 1908
Ewell, Tom ....Owensboro, Ky. 1912

Fabray, Nanette ....New Orleans, La. 1921
Fay, Frank ....San Francisco 1897
Ferber, Edna ....Kalamazoo, Mich. 1887
Ferrer, Jose ....Puerto Rico 1912
Field, Sylvia ....Allston, Mass. 1902
Fields, W. C. ....Philadelphia, Pa. 1883
Fitzgerald, Barry ....Dublin, Ireland 1888
Fitzgerald, Geraldine ....Dublin, Ireland 1914

Fletcher, Bramwell .... Bradford, Yorkshire, Eng. .1904
Fontanne, Lynn .... London, England 1887
Forbes, Brenda .... London, England 1909
Forbes, Ralph .... London, England 1905
Foy, Eddie, Jr. .... New Rochelle, N. Y. 1907
Francis, Arlene .... Boston, Mass. 1908
Fraser, Elizabeth .... Brooklyn, N. Y. 1920

Garrett, Betty .... St. Louis, Mo. 1919
Gaxton, William .... San Francisco, Cal. 1893
Geddes, Barbara Bel .... New York 1922
Geddes, Norman Bel .... Adrian, Mich. 1893
Gershwin, Ira .... New York 1896
Gielgud, John .... London, England 1904
Gillmore, Margalo .... England 1901
Gilmore, Virginia .... El Monte, Cal. 1919
Gish, Dorothy .... Dayton, Ohio 1898
Gish, Lillian .... Springfield, Ohio 1896
Gleason, James .... New York 1885
Golden, John .... New York 1874
Goodner, Carol .... New York City 1904
Gordon, Ruth .... Wollaston, Mass. 1896
Gough, Lloyd .... New York City 1906
Grant, Sydney .... Boston, Mass. 1873
Greaza, Walter .... St. Paul, Minn. 1900
Green, Mitzi .... New York City 1920
Greenstreet, Sydney .... England 1880
Groody, Louise .... Waco, Texas 1897
Gwenn, Edmund .... Glamorgan, Wales 1875

Hampden, Walter .... Brooklyn, N. Y. 1879
Hannen, Nicholas .... London, England 1881
Hardie, Russell .... Griffin Mills, N. Y. 1906
Hardwicke, Sir Cedric .... Lye, Stourbridge, England .1893
Hart, Richard .... Providence, R. I. 1915
Havoc, June .... Seattle, Wash. 1916
Haydon, Julie .... Oak Park, Ill. 1910
Hayes, Helen .... Washington, D. C. 1900
Heflin, Frances .... Oklahoma City, Okla. 1924
Heflin, Van .... Walters, Okla. 1909
Heineman, Eda .... Japan 1891
Heming, Violet .... Leeds, England 1893
Henie, Sonja .... Oslo, Norway 1912

Leighton, Margaret ....Barnt Green, England 1922
Lillie, Beatrice ....Toronto, Canada 1898
Linn, Bambi ....Brooklyn, N. Y. 1926
Loeb, Philip ....Philadelphia, Pa. 1892
Lonergan, Lenore ....Toledo, Ohio 1928
Lord, Pauline ....Hanford, Cal. 1890
Lukas, Paul ....Budapest, Hungary 1895
Lund, John ....Rochester, N. Y. 1916
Lunt, Alfred ....Milwaukee, Wis. 1893
Lytell, Bert ....New York City 1885

MacMahon, Aline ....McKeesport, Pa. 1899
March, Fredric ....Racine, Wis. 1897
Margetson, Arthur ....London, England 1897
Margo ....Mexico 1918
Marshall, Everett ....Worcester, Mass. 1902
Marshall, Herbert ....London, England 1890
Mason, James ....Huddersfield, England 1909
Massey, Raymond ....Toronto, Canada 1896
Matteson, Ruth ....San Jose, Cal. 1905
McClintic, Guthrie ....Seattle, Wash. 1893
McCormick, Myron ....Albany, Ind. 1907
McCracken, Joan ....Philadelphia, Pa. 1923
McGrath, Paul ....Chicago, Ill. 1900
McGuire, Dorothy ....Omaha, Neb. 1918
Menotti, Gian-Carlo ....Italy 1912
Meredith, Burgess ....Cleveland, Ohio 1908
Merivale, Philip ....Rehutia, India 1886
Merman, Ethel ....Astoria, R. I. 1909
Middleton, Ray ....Chicago, Ill. 1907
Miller, Gilbert ....New York 1884
Miranda, Carmen ....Portugal 1912
Mitchell, Grant ....Columbus, Ohio 1874
Mitchell, Thomas ....Elizabeth, N. J. 1892
Moore, Grace ....Del Rio, Tenn. 1901
Moore, Victor ....Hammondton, N. J. 1876
Morgan, Claudia ....New York 1912
Morgan, Ralph ....New York City 1889
Morris, Mary ....Boston 1894
Morris, McKay ....San Antonio, Texas 1890
Moss, Arnold ....Brooklyn, N. Y. 1910
Muni, Paul ....Lemberg, Austria 1895
Myrtil, Odette ....Paris, France 1898

Nagel, Conrad .... Keokuk, Iowa 1897
Natwick, Mildred .... Baltimore, Md. 1908
Nolan, Lloyd .... San Francisco, Cal. 1903
Nugent, Elliott .... Dover, Ohio 1900

O'Brien-Moore, Erin .... Los Angeles, Cal. 1908
Odets, Clifford .... Philadelphia 1906
Olivier, Laurence .... Dorking, Surrey, England . 1907
Olsen, John Siguard (Ole) .... Perų, Ind. 1892
O'Malley, Rex .... London, England 1906
O'Neal, Frederick .... Brookville, Miss. 1905
O'Neill, Eugene Gladstone .... New York 1888
Ouspenskaya, Maria .... Tula, Russia 1876

Patterson, Elizabeth .... Savannah, Tenn. 1898
Pemberton, Brock .... Leavenworth, Kansas 1885
Petina, Irra .... Leningrad, Russia 1900
Pickford, Mary .... Toronto 1893
Picon, Molly .... New York City 1898
Pollock, Channing .... Washington, D. C. 1880
Price, Vincent .... St. Louis, Mo. 1914

Rains, Claude .... London, England 1889
Raitt, John .... Santa Ana, Cal. 1917
Rathbone, Basil .... Johannesburg 1892
Raye, Martha .... Butte, Mont. 1916
Redman, Joyce .... Newcastle, Ireland 1918
Reed, Florence .... Philadelphia, Pa. 1883
Rennie, James .... Toronto, Canada 1890
Richardson, Ralph .... Cheltenham, England 1902
Roberts, Joan .... New York City 1918
Robinson, Bill .... Richmond, Va. 1878
Robinson, Edward G. .... Bucharest, Roumania 1893
Ross, Anthony .... New York 1906
Royle, Selena .... New York 1905
Ruben, José .... Belgium 1886

Sands, Dorothy .... Cambridge, Mass. 1900
Sarnoff, Dorothy .... Brooklyn, N. Y. 1919
Scheff, Fritzi .... Vienna, Austria 1879
Scott, Martha .... Jamesport, Mo. 1914
Segal, Vivienne .... Philadelphia, Pa. 1897
Shannon, Effie .... Cambridge, Mass. 1867

Sherwood, Robert Emmet ..... New Rochelle, N. Y. 1896
Sidney, Sylvia .... New York 1910
Simms, Hilda .... Minneapolis, Minn. 1920
Skinner, Cornelia Otis .... Chicago 1902
Smith, Kent .... Smithfield, Me. 1910
Stickney, Dorothy .... Dickinson, N. D. 1903
Stoddard, Haila .... Great Falls, Mont. 1914
Stone, Carol .... New York 1917
Stone, Dorothy .... New York 1905
Stone, Ezra .... New Bedford, Mass. 1918
Stone, Fred .... Denver, Colo. 1873
Sullavan, Margaret .... Norfolk, Va. 1910

Taliaferro, Mabel .... New York 1887
Tauber, Richard .... Linz, Austria 1890
Taylor, Laurette .... New York 1884
Tetzel, Joan .... New York 1923
Thomas, John Charles .... Baltimore, Md. 1887
Tone, Franchot .... Niagara Falls, N. Y. 1907
Tozere, Frederick .... Brookline, Mass. 1901
Tracy, Spencer .... Milwaukee, Wis. 1900
Travers, Henry .... Berwick, England 1874
Truex, Ernest .... Red Hill, Mo. 1890

Van Patten, Dickie .... New York 1929
Van Patten, Joyce .... New York City 1934
Varden, Evelyn .... Venita, Okla. 1893
Venuta, Benay .... San Francisco, Cal. 1912

Walker, Nancy .... Philadelphia, Pa. 1922
Walker, June .... New York 1904
Wanamaker, Sam .... Chicago, Ill. 1919
Ward, Penelope .... London, England 1914
Warfield, David .... San Francisco, Cal. 1866
Waring, Richard .... Buckinghamshire, England. 1912
Waters, Ethel .... Chester, Pa. 1900
Watson, Lucile .... Quebec, Canada 1879
Watson, Minor .... Marianna, Ark. 1889
Webb, Clifton .... Indiana 1891
Webster, Margaret .... New York City 1905
Welles, Orson .... Kenosha, Wis. 1915
West, Mae .... Brooklyn, N. Y. 1892
Weston, Ruth .... Boston, Mass. 1911

NECROLOGY

June 1, 1947—June 1, 1948

Beaudet, Louise, singer and actress, 87. Appeared in plays and musical productions for more than fifty years; debut London (1882); with McCaull Company (1883); headed Louise Beaudet Opera Company; appeared with James O'Neill, Clara Morris and other stars of earlier generation; played in "Jim the Penman," "Flo-Flo," "My Maryland," "White Lilacs," "The Man from Home," "The Lady of Lyons," etc.; last appeared on Broadway in "Hay Fever" (1932). Born St. Emilie, Quebec; died New York City, December 31, 1948.

Blair, Mary (Mary Blair Eakin), actress, 52. Won fame in Eugene O'Neill plays; played opposite Paul Robeson in "All God's Chillun Got Wings"; appeared in "Desire Under the Elms," "The Hairy Ape," "Before Breakfast," "The Crime in the Whistler Room," and a revival of O'Neill's "Diff'r'nt." Born Pittsburgh, Pa.; died Pittsburgh, Pa., September 17, 1947.

Braham, Lionel, actor, 68. First appearance on stage in London in "A Persian Princess" (1909); first in America in "Androcles and the Lion" (1915); others in New York, "The Man Who Married a Dumb Wife," "The Wanderer," "Chu-Chin-Chow," "Mecca," "Jewel Robbery," "The Miracle," "The Vagabond King," etc.; on the screen in many plays, the last being "Macbeth." Born Yorkshire, England; died Hollywood, Calif., October 6, 1947.

Brennan, J. Keirn (Jack), composer, 74. Songwriter known particularly for Irish ballads; among best known songs written in collaboration with Ernest Ball are "A Little Bit of Heaven," "Boy of Mine," "Let the Rest of the World Go By" and "Empty Saddles"; with Rudolf Friml wrote songs for numerous Broadway musicals and special material for stars; one of the founders of ASCAP. Died Hollywood, Calif., February 4, 1948.

Brockbank, Harrison, actor and singer, 80. Baritone of musical comedy; first roles in London at Drury Lane and Covent Garden; came to America in 1909; appeared in New York in

465

"Apple Blossoms," "The Last Waltz," "Melody," "The Three Musketeers" and others. Born Liverpool, England; died New York City, November 30, 1947.

Carey, Harry, actor, 69. Film and stage actor and playwright; entered show business in 1906 as author of "Montana," a melodrama; started film career in 1908 and eventually appeared in nearly 400 pictures; made Broadway debut as actor in "Heavenly Express" (1940); played lead in revival of "Ah, Wilderness" and in "—But Not Goodbye" (1944). Born New York City; died Brentwood, Calif., September 21, 1947.

Clements, Colin, playwright and author, 53. Started theatrical career as student at 47 Workshop, Harvard; with Stuart Walker's Cincinnati stock company as actor, playreader and director until World War I in which he served; director of Lobero Theatre, Santa Barbara, California; since 1927 collaborated with his wife (Florence Ryerson) in writing 21 plays; notable among these "Harriet," "June Mad," "Through the Night," "Glamour Preferred," and "Strange Bedfellows," which is one of this season's plays on Broadway. Born Omaha, Nebraska; died Philadelphia, Pa., January 29, 1948.

Clements, Dudley, actor, 58. Became actor after 11 years as boxoffice treasurer for the Percy Williams vaudeville theatres; last appeared in Broadway production of "Song of Norway" (1944). Died November 4, 1947.

Digges, Dudley, actor and producer, 68. Stage and film star; appeared on New York stage for 43 years, giving more than 3,500 performances for the Theatre Guild alone; appeared in over 50 pictures and directed many stage productions; started career in New York with Minnie Maddern Fiske (1904); member of original Abbey Players; stage manager for George Arliss for seven years; notable performances in "John Ferguson" (1919), "Mr. Pim Passes By," "On Borrowed Time," "The Searching Wind," "The Brothers Karamazov," "The Iceman Cometh," etc.; staged "Heartbreak House," "The Doctor's Dilemma," "Pygmalion" and "Man's Estate" for Theatre Guild; vice president of Actors' Equity Association. Born Dublin, Ireland; died New York City, October 24, 1947.

Fischer, Alice (Harcourt), actress, 78. Founder of Twelfth Night Club for actresses, New York; widow of late Shakespearean actor, William King Harcourt; debut in "Uncle Tom's Cabin" when 4 years old; New York debut with Frank Mayo in "Nordeck" (1887); toured with Joseph Jefferson in "Rip Van Winkle"; starred in "Mrs. Jack" (1903); last appearance on Broadway in "Symphony" (1935). Born Terre Haute, Ind.; died New York, June 23, 1947.

Fyffe, Will, actor, 62.   Many years a favorite comedian in London and Continental halls; headlined vaudeville (1927) touring U. S.; starring role in Earl Carroll's "Vanities"; well known as film actor, usually in Scottish roles; during World War II entertained troops in camp shows. Died St. Andrews, Scotland, December 14, 1947.

Hagan, James B., actor, playwright, manager, 65.   Reporter on St. Louis *Post-Dispatch* and New York *World;* started theatrical career with medicine show; followed with vaudeville and stock companies as comedian; stage manager for Henry Miller and Arthur Hopkins; played Shakespeare with Sothern and Marlowe two seasons; first play "Guns," a forerunner of gangster plays (1928); most successful play "One Sunday Afternoon" (1933); other plays: "Trimmed," "Midwest," etc.   Born San Diego, Calif.; died Cincinnati, Ohio, September 1, 1947.

Halliday, John, actor, 67.   Screen and stage actor for nearly forty years; trained as an engineer and fought in Boer War with British Army 1901-2; first stage appearance with Nat Goodwin's company in Sacramento; with Daniel Frawley's company touring Far East; appeared New York as Earl of Brancaster in "The Whip" (1912); among many other plays were "The Tally Method," "Stolen Orders," "The Woman in Bronze," "The Ware Case," "East of Suez," "Dancing Mothers," "Jealousy," "The Dark Angel," "Tovarich" and "Rain from Heaven"; film debut in 1912 in "New Beginnings"; spent last years of life in Honolulu.   Born Brooklyn, New York; died Honolulu, October 17, 1947.

Hellinger, Mark, newspaper columnist, author and film producer, 44.   Started in advertising business; writer for New York *Daily News* and Chicago Tribune Syndicate (1923-30); daily columnist for New York *Daily Mirror* and King Features Syndicate (1930-38); author "Moon over Broadway," "I Meet a Lot of People," etc.; wrote last "Ziegfeld Follies" and many motion pictures.   Born New York City; died Hollywood, Calif., December 21, 1947.

Hinshaw, William W., actor, singer and producer, 80.   Veteran concert singer, opera producer and Grand Opera singer; made more than 5,000 concert appearances in U. S. and abroad prior to retirement (1931); first Grand Opera appearance St. Louis, Mo., 1899, as Mephisto in "Faust"; baritone with Metropolitan Opera, 1910-13. Born Union, Iowa; died Washington, D. C., November 27, 1947.

Huff, Forrest, actor and opera singer, 71. Started career with Castle Square Opera Co. in Boston, 1900; appeared with Al Jolson in "Sinbad" (1918); others, "The Serenade," "Dolly Varden," "The Ham Tree," "The Rose of Panama," "The Merry Countess," "The Chocolate Soldier," etc.; directed for W.P.A. Federal Music Project (1936). Died August 21, 1947.

Humphreys, Cecil, actor, 64. Stage and film player for nearly fifty years; remembered as Prince Mikail in "Tovarich" (1936); London debut in "Madame Butterfly" (1910); toured United States in "Fanny's First Play" in 1915; other plays, "Milestones," "Romance," "Heads Up," "Gentlemen in Waiting," "Nina Rosa," "The Lady of the Camellias," "The Doctor's Dilemma," "Angel Street," "Pygmalion" and many others; appeared in many films. Born Cheltenham, England; died New York City, November 6, 1947.

Hurst, Brandon, actor, 81. Character actor on stage and screen for many years; played Charley in original production of "Charley's Aunt" in London (1892); appeared in many films including "Seventh Heaven." Born London, England; died Hollywood, Calif., July 23, 1947.

Job, Thomas, author and playwright, 46. Associate professor of dramatic literature at Yale University and Carnegie Tech.; wrote "Giants in the Earth"; plays included "Barchester Towers," "Rue with a Difference," "Dawn in Lyonnesse," "Uncle Harry," etc. Adapted "The Two Mrs. Carrolls" for the screen. Born Carmarthen, South Wales; died Santa Monica, Calif., July 31, 1947.

Kalmar, Bert, composer and author, 63. A leading songwriter; started career in tent show; followed with vaudeville as comedian teaming with his wife, Jessie Brown; on the road with "Wine, Women and Song"; wrote "Oh What a Pal Was Mary," "My Sunny Tennessee," "Who's Sorry Now" and many other songs with Harry Ruby; also words and music for "Animal Crackers," Earl Carroll's "Vanities," "Five O'Clock Girl," "Top Speed" and other musical comedies; long Hollywood career. Born New York; died Hollywood, Calif., September 17, 1947.

Kirk, John, actor, producer and director, 86. Veteran actor who operated stock companies in Kansas City, Albany, Minneapolis, Washington, D. C., and many other cities; teamed with Fay Baker in vaudeville many years; on Broadway played in "Sweet Charity," "Run, Sheep, Run," "Lend Me Your Ears," etc.; created role of Judge Omar Gaffney in "Harvey" in 1944 and played the part until his death. Born Wilmington, Delaware; died New York City, May 23, 1948.

Kolker, Henry, actor, 73. Stage and screen actor; brought from Berlin, Germany, to Springfield, Illinois, when very young; first appearance on stage in German Stock Company, Milwaukee, Wisc. (1894); first English-speaking role with Robert Downing in "The Gladiator"; toured with James O'Neill, Ada Rehan, Bertha Kalich, Margaret Anglin, Alla Nazimova, etc.; first Broadway appearance at Wallack's in "Cymbeline" (1898); remembered in "What Happened to Jones," "The Little Minister," "The Great Name," etc.; acting in films since 1925. Born Berlin, Germany; died Los Angeles, Calif., July 15, 1947.

Le Guere, George, actor, 76. Well known in stock and repertory in the South and Midwest; later appearing on Broadway in "Palmy Days," "Just Suppose," "The Old Soak," etc. Died New York City, November 21, 1947.

Larimore, Earle, actor, 48. First appeared in New York in "Made in America" (1925); other appearances in "Juarez and Maximilian," "The Second Man," "Marco Millions," "The Silver Cord," "Strange Interlude," "Mourning Becomes Electra," "Days Without End," etc.; toured with Eva Le Gallienne in repertory; appeared on the screen; in radio had leading role in serial, "This Life Is Mine"; served in First World War; recently conducted course in acting at New York University. Born Portland, Oregon; died New York City, October 22, 1947.

Mantle, Robert Burns, drama critic and author, 74. Dean of dramatic critics until retirement (1943); reporter and theatre reviewer Denver *Times,* Denver *Republican,* Chicago *Interocean, Chicago Tribune,* New York *Mail,* and New York *Daily News;* compiled annual volumes of "Best Plays" of Broadway since 1919-20 and (with Garrison Sherwood) two books of ten years each dating back to 1899; wrote "American Playwrights of Today" (1929) and "Contemporary American Playwrights" (1938); editor with others of "A Treasury of the Theatre"; known on radio and as speaker on theatrical subjects; member The Players, Dutch Treat Club and Drama Critics' Circle, of which he was president in 1940. Born Watertown, New York; died Forest Hills, New York, February 9, 1948.

Mason, Ann, actress, 50. Well known for leading parts in Broadway plays; played in "The Last Warning," "The Acquittal," "Fly Away Home," "First Lady," "Liliom" (Burgess Meredith-Ingrid Bergman revival) and many others; toured Southwest Pacific and European theatres in USO units during Second World War; regular worker at Stage Door Canteen, New York. Died New York City, February 6, 1948.

May, Edna (Pettie), actress and singer, 69. Remembered for her appearance in "The Belle of New York" as the Salvation Army lassie; first seen in New York in 1896 at Hammerstein's Theatre in "Santa Maria"; followed with musical comedies in London and New York—"An American Beauty," "The Girl from Up There," "Three Little Maids," "The School Girl," "The Catch of the Season," "Kitty Grey," and many others; married to Oscar Lewisohn. Born Syracuse, New York; died Lausanne, Switzerland, January 2, 1948.

Norcross, Hale, actor, 70. Stage debut in George Ade's "The College Widow" after graduation from Harvard; appeared in vaudeville and had supporting roles in "Road to Rome," "Is Zat So?", "Caesar and Cleopatra" (with Helen Hayes), "Ah, Wilderness," "Abie's Irish Rose," "Life with Father" and many others; last Broadway appearance as Robert in "Dunnigan's Daughter" (1945). Born San Francisco; died New York City, October 15, 1947.

Painter, Eleanor (Mrs. Charles H. Strong), singer and actress, 57. Star of drama, opera and musical comedy; first stage appearance in "Oberon" at Deutsches Opera House, Germany; sang leading part in "Der Rosenkavalier" when first produced in New York; appeared in operettas and straight dramas from 1914 to 1924, including "Princess Pat" (written for her by Victor Herbert); "The Lilac Domino," "Glorianna," "Florodora," "The Last Waltz," "The Climax," "The Chiffon Girl," etc.; prima donna of San Francisco and Philadelphia Opera companies; retired in 1931. Born Walkerville, Iowa; died Cleveland, Ohio, November 4, 1947.

Sierra, Gregorio Martinez, playwright and author, 66. Spanish writer of books and plays; best known plays in America, "Cradle Song," which Eva Le Gallienne produced in season of 1926-27, and "Kingdom of God," in which Ethel Barrymore starred in 1928; other well-known plays "Holy Night," "Love Magic," "The Romantic Young Lady" and "Two for One"; lived in U. S. and Argentina for sixteen years, a voluntary exile from Spain. Born Madrid, Spain; died Madrid, Spain, October 1, 1947.

Tauber, Richard, 57.   Actor, singer, composer and conductor. Was known for successes on concert stage and opera; became conductor of an orchestra at the age of 18; first appearance on stage in 1912 at Dresden State Opera House; 1920-23 was engaged at State Opera House, Berlin, and State Opera House, Vienna; first appeared in operetta in "Frasquita," followed in "Paganini"; first appearance on London stage in "The Land of Smiles" (1931) and in New York in a concert program the same year; last appearance in New York in "Yours Is My Heart" (September 5, 1946); occasional appearances as symphony orchestra conductor and was well known as a composer.   Born Linz, Austria; died London, England, January 8, 1948.

Thomas, Albert Ellsworth, playwright and author, 74.   Newspaper writer on New York *Tribune, Post, Times* and *Sun* from 1895 to 1909; wrote many plays, including "Her Husband's Wife" (1910), "Come Out of the Kitchen," "Embers" and "No More Ladies"; collaborations: "The Big Idea" and "Thirty Days" (with Clayton Hamilton); "Our Nell" (with Brian Hooker); "The Big Pond" (with George Middleton) and many others.   Born Chester, Mass.; died Wakefield, R. I., June 18, 1947.

Whitty, Dame May (Mrs. Ben Webster), actress, 82.   For more than 62 years on British and American stage; first appearance, Liverpool (1881); first London appearance as Filippa in "Boccaccio" (1882); toured America (1895-6); with Richard Mansfield in "Prince Karl"; with Henry Irving in "Louis XI," and others; toured with Forbes Robertson; on Broadway in "Irene Wycherley," "Trelawney of the Wells," "The Enchanted Cottage," "School for Scandal" and many others; last appearance on Broadway as Madame Raquin in "Therese"; widow of Ben Webster, actor, and mother of Margaret Webster, actress and stage director; created Dame Commander of the Order of the British Empire after World War I.   Born Liverpool, England; died Hollywood, Calif., May 29, 1948.

Withers, Charles, actor, 58.   Character comedian who headlined in vaudeville in own acts for many years; debut with Woodward stock company, Omaha, Neb.; started vaudeville career (1913) with "For Pity's Sake" which ran for 14 years; famous for lovable rube parts; in many musicals including "Hitchy Koo"; four years in "Hellzapoppin"; last appearances with U.S.O. Camp Shows. Born Louisville, Kentucky; died Bayside, Long Island, New York, July 10, 1947.

Ziegler, Edward, music critic and manager, 77. Music critic of New York *Sun* following James Gibbons Huneker; critic for New York *American* and musical columnist for *Town Topics;* music and drama critic for New York *World* and New York *Herald;* assistant general manager of Metropolitan Opera House Association. Born Baltimore, Maryland; died New York City, October 25, 1947.

THE DECADES' TOLL

(Persons of Outstanding Prominence in the Theatre
Who Have Died in Recent Years)

	Born	Died
Baker, George Pierce	1866	1935
Barrymore, John	1882	1942
Belasco, David	1856	1931
Bernhardt, Sarah	1845	1923
Campbell, Mrs. Patrick	1865	1940
Cohan, George Michael	1878	1942
De Koven, Reginald	1861	1920
De Reszke, Jean	1850	1925
Digges, Dudley	1879	1947
Drew, John	1853	1927
Drinkwater, John	1883	1937
Du Maurier, Sir Gerald	1873	1934
Duse, Eleanora	1859	1924
Fiske, Minnie Maddern	1865	1932
Frohman, Daniel	1851	1940
Galsworthy, John	1867	1933
Gorky, Maxim	1868	1936
Greet, Sir Philip (Ben)	1858	1936
Herbert, Victor	1859	1924
Mantle (Robert) Burns	1873	1948
May, Edna	1879	1948
Patti, Adelina	1843	1919
Pinero, Sir Arthur Wing	1855	1934
Russell, Annie	1864	1936
Schumann-Heink, Ernestine	1861	1936
Skinner, Otis	1858	1942
Sothern, Edwin Hugh	1859	1933
Tarkington, Booth	1862	1946
Tauber, Richard	1890	1948
Taylor, Laurette	1884	1946
Terry, Ellen	1848	1928
Thomas, Augustus	1857	1934
Thomas, A. E.	1872	1947
Tyler, George C.	1867	1946
Whitty, Dame May	1865	1948
Yeats, William Butler	1865	1939

INDICES

INDEX OF AUTHORS

INDEX OF PLAYS AND CASTS

483

INDEX OF PRODUCERS, DIRECTORS
AND DESIGNERS

491